Louis Bar   studied at Lancaster
University and, perhaps more fruitfully, Ear Ere Records, the local
independent record shop. He has written for a wide variety of
publications including *Private Eye*, *Publishing News*, *New Statesman*
and *Crescendo and Jazz Music*, the earnings from which he has spent
largely on records. He lives in Suffolk, near a branch of Andy's.

From the reviews:

'An extensive history of the record industry... Barfe's comprehensive
research is peppered with entertaining anecdotes, while his approach
combines a weighty respect for his subject with a healthy dose of
cynicism.' *Metro*

'A riveting book... An exhilarating read that conjures up the world
of those who make recordings, and the commercial realities and
pitfalls facing those who produce them with infectious zeal... A
fascinating exposé on the recording industry in general and the
meteoric rise and slow decline of popular music.' Julian Haycock,
Classic FM magazine Best Buy

'*Where Have All the Good Times Gone?* is an elegant, readable history
of recorded sounds from Edison onwards, alive with fascinating
details... Barfe's fine book covers the imminent fall as well as the
glorious rise of the music biz with a rueful shake of the head...
Magisterial.' Stuart Maconie, *Oldie*

Where have all the good times gone?

The rise and fall of the record industry

Louis Barfe

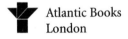 Atlantic Books
London

First published in hardback Great Britain in 2004 by Atlantic Books,
an imprint of Grove Atlantic Ltd

This paperback edition published by Atlantic Books in 2005.

10 9 8 7 6 5 4 3 2 1

A CIP catalogue record for this book is available from the British Library.

ISBN 1 84354 067 3

Printed in Great Britain by Mackays of Chatham

Atlantic Books
An imprint of Grove Atlantic Ltd
Ormond House
26–27 Boswell Street
London WC1N 3JZ

For my late grandmother, Jean Murray, who encouraged me; my late headmistress, Anne Hanlon, who encouraged me to write; and the late Brian Masters, who encouraged me to write this book.

CONTENTS

LIST OF ILLUSTRATIONS   ix
ACKNOWLEDGEMENTS   xi
INTRODUCTION   xiii

1	Buying – and selling – the Edison myth	1
2	Tvinkle, tvinkle, little star	24
3	The Jones boy	42
4	Continental shift	65
5	The Coldstream Guards and all that jazz	86
6	Brother, can you spare 75c for a gramophone record?	109
7	Don't you know there's a war on?	138
8	Picking up the pieces	162
9	Pop goes the weasel	186
10	Paris, Liverpool and British West Hampstead	219
11	The spirit of independence	258
12	You can spread jam on them	293
13	Caught Napstering	324

AFTERWORD   345
NOTES   352
FURTHER READING   368
INDEX   372

LIST OF ILLUSTRATIONS

1　Thomas Alva Edison
2　Diagram of the phonograph, *Illustrated London News*, 1878
3　Advertisement for the phonograph, c.1900
4　'The Song of Mister Phonograph'
5　The Gramophone Company's first studio in Maiden Lane, London, c.1898
6　Fred Gaisberg
7　Emile Berliner and Charles Sumner Tainter
8　Edison 'Gold Moulded' wax cylinder
9　Edison 'Diamond Disc'
10　Edison-Bell advertisement
11　Jack Hylton and his band
12　Edward Elgar opens studio 1 at Abbey Road
13　Ted Heath record sleeve
14　Mike Ross-Trevor in the control room of Levy's Sound Studios, London, 1964
15　Advertisement for the Decca portable gramophone, 1924
16　Sir Edward Lewis
17　Decca calls a halt to its war of advertising with EMI, 1953
18　*Arthur Godfrey's TV Calendar Show*, 1953
19　Goddard Lieberson, Jerry Herman and Clive Davis with Angela Lansbury, 1967
20　Ray Horricks, Arthur Lilley, Johnny Keating, Reg Guest and Tony d'Amato, 1964
21　HMV and Columbia advertisements, 1928
22　HMV French record sleeve, c.1935
23　The *Minneapolis Journal's* interpretation of the HMV logo, 1908
24　Bruce Lundvall
25　Doug Morris
26　Sir Joseph Lockwood with the Beatles
27　1984 trade ad for Dire Straits on CD

The author and publishers are grateful to the following for permission to reproduce images: 1, Getty Images; 2, Bill Kibby-Johnson collection; 5, 6, 12, 26 EMI Records Ltd; 7, Archives Center, National Museum of American History, Smithsonian Institution; 14, Mike Ross-Trevor; 16, Decca Music Group Ltd; 19, Bettmann / Corbis; 20, Michael Ward; 23, Martin Fenton collection; 24, Blue Note Records; 27, Universal Music. All other images are from the author's own collection.

ACKNOWLEDGEMENTS

Thanks to the following, without whom this book would have been a lot shorter.

- Toby Mundy at Atlantic Books for suggesting that there might be a book in my anorakdom, for ongoing encouragement and advice and for his liberal interpretation of the word 'deadline'. Not to mention his colleagues Clara Farmer, Bonnie Chiang and Louisa Joyner for helping shape the whole thing into the form you see here. Thanks also to my copy-editor Rachel Leyshon for telling me when I was turning into Roger Irrelevant.

- Mike Ross-Trevor and the late Brian Masters for motivating me by both saying 'Well, I'd read it'.

- Ruth Edge and Greg Burge, both formerly of the EMI archive at Hayes in Middlesex, without whom the early part of the book would have been very sketchy and their colleague, Chris Jones; John Warren at the Edison National Historic Monument in West Orange, New Jersey, for his time, enthusiasm and letting me make a tinfoil recording; Vince Giordano (ace tuba player) and Mike Panico at the RCA/BMG archive in New York; and to Maureen Fortey, who quite frankly *is* the Decca Record Company archive, for her help. Also, the staff who helped me at the British Library – both at St Pancras and Colindale – as well as their counterparts at the London Library and my local library in Lowestoft.

- The interviewees who, between January 2002 and May 2003, took the time to speak to me. In doing so, they made the story come alive: George Avakian, Jay Berman, Ed Bicknell, Rodney Burbeck (some of the interviewees were easier to locate than others. Rodney was my editor when I worked at *Publishing News*), Richard Elen, Ahmet Ertegun, Derek Everett, David Fine, Tony Hall, Ray Horricks, Alan Kayes, Charles Kennedy, Eddie Levy, Jimmy Lock, Bruce Lundvall, Hugh Mendl, Angela Morley, Mike Ross-Trevor, Tim Satchell, Adele

Siegal, Mike Smith, Coen Solleveld, Clive Stanhope, Seymour Stein, Roger Watson, Diana Weller, Muff Winwood and Walter Woyda. Gratitude also to Tina Taylor for help with transcription as the deadline loomed. There are others who gave me more general pointers and contacts, including Elisabeth Iles and Adrian Strain at the IFPI, Stan Cornyn, Adam White, Irv Lichtman, Norman Lebrecht, Earl Okin, Arthur Zimmermann, Tim Blackmore, Demitri Coryton, Mike Richter, David Sarsner, Brian Southall, Stanley and Edna Black and others who wish to remain anonymous.

- The friends who helped immensely: Mike Brown, Martin Fenton, Nigel Hunter, Gavin Sutherland and John Warburton for reading the manuscript with expert eyes; Bill Kibby-Johnson for historical documents and illustrations; Richard Abram, Bob Flag, Kif Bowden-Smith and Patrick Humphries for clarifying certain details; Bob Baker, Tom Bircher, Mike Hamilton, Anne Hanlon, Beryl Jackson, Howard Turner, Steve Turner, Joost van Loon and Trevor Wallis for laying the foundations, perhaps unwittingly; Nixon Bardsley, Ralph Baxter, Adam Cumiskey, Allen Eyles, Stuart Farnden, Alex George, Geoff Hiscott, Sally Kennedy, Matt Levy, Richard Lewis, Hilary Lowinger, Andrew Malcolm, Steve Mann, James Masterton, Charlie Mounter, Nick Parker, Sue Roccelli, Kerry Swash, Roger Tagholm, Ben Tisdall, David Trevor-Jones, Francis Wheen and Alan Wood for general encouragement; and my childhood partner-in-crime, Stephen Gilchrist, who typed up the Tony Hall interview in exchange for my help with installing a bathroom sink. Who said barter was dead?

- The family: My mother, Maureen Barfe, not only for the obvious biological reasons, but also because she started the whole thing off when I was five, by giving me her Dansette and a bunch of 45s; my grandparents, Bob and Jean Murray, for making me listen to certain things, giving me a vast number of records and the funds to acquire yet more; and finally to my wife, Susannah, who puts up with me, and our own Nipper lookalike dog, Lyttelton, who puts up with us both. Naturally, any errors are my own stupid fault.

Lowestoft and London
November 2003
and October 2004

INTRODUCTION

Hunter S. Thompson once described the television industry as a 'cruel and shallow money trench…a long plastic hallway where thieves and pimps run free and good men die like dogs, for no good reason'. Over the years, Thompson's words have often been adapted and applied to the music industry, for a very good reason. Yet it is a branch of commerce that touches all of our lives, quite often for the better.

Even Warner Bros, for example, which had a reputation in the 1970s for musical enlightenment and attracted artists of the calibre of Paul Simon, Van Morrison, James Taylor, Tower of Power and Little Feat, issued one-sided contracts just like everyone else. After the payment of the initial advance, the act received a percentage so small that they would be in debt to the record company long after it had recouped its investment. The record company also had the absolute right to reject the recordings that their contracted artists had made. If the budget had been spent on the original recordings, the artist had to pay for the remakes. Somehow, though, the glorious end seemed to justify the means. Listen to Lowell George's *Thanks I'll Eat It Here* from beginning to end. Warners, despite the unfair business methods that were the industry standard, were doing something right.

In recent years, however, the industry has gone into freefall. Global music sales fell by 7 per cent in value and by 8 per cent in units in 2002. The pattern had, until the end of the 1990s, been one of growth, but it suddenly slipped into reverse. A business model that had endured untroubled for over a century is now taking a kicking. Some have argued that the problem started when the 'suits' took over – that the music business became everything to do with business and precious little to do with music. It's a romantic idea, but it's a myth. The record business has always been about making money, and from its outset, a few companies have been remarkably successful in doing it and making sure that no one else did without their approval.

That 'no one' includes the artists and producers. Until the 1960s, producers were invariably record company staffers, receiving modest salaries for keeping their bosses in profit. The artists were merely hired hands, with all but the biggest paid on a per session basis. As producers went freelance and artists got better management, royalties for both became the norm, but still the lion's share of the proceeds from any record sale went to the record company.

Now, with the effects of file-sharing, MP3 and CD-R combining with the old problem of industrial-scale piracy allied to organized crime, the business seems to be getting its comeuppance. The old certainties have disappeared from markets all around the world. Record companies can no longer relieve music fans of their cash with the ease that they once did. If you want a particular song and you have an Internet connection, chances are that you can download it from someone, somewhere on the worldwide web. The record company doesn't get paid and neither does the artist.

However, for established artists, there is a silver lining to this particular cloud. They can now abandon their corporate paymasters and start selling direct to their punters, primarily over the Internet. Sales are inevitably lower, but the proportion of cash going straight to the talent is much, much higher. Piracy is all too often presented as a new problem when, in fact, the origins of the current meltdown have been intrinsic to the industry from its start 125 years ago. Piracy has been present from the very beginning.

There have been rises and falls before. From the inception of the industry, in the late nineteenth century, to the outbreak of the First World War, the pattern was one of unchecked growth. The shock of the war grievously depressed sales, but the market recovered. Then came radio, which played the latest records and affected sales in the US (British radio meant the BBC and that august institution shied away from filling its airtime with vulgar, commercial records). Just as the record companies were beginning to reach an accommodation with the broadcasters, the world was affected by the onset of the Great Depression in 1929.

Each time there was a fresh slump, a new development came along that could be brought into play to save the industry. The worst effects of radio were tempered by the advent of electric recording, a vast improvement on the old acoustic system. The massive decline in the industry following the Great Depression was reversed gradually by the application of price reductions. Later on, technical marvels like vinyl microgroove, stereo and, finally, compact disc represented a chance for the industry to revive sales, quite often selling people what they already had in a new, improved format.

Crucially, each of these developments had been created by big business or the record companies themselves. Electric recording was the creation of Western Electric, which made money from its invention by charging record companies that used it a sizeable royalty. The vinyl 33⅓ rpm disc was the creation of the US major Columbia Records, while the 45 was developed by the rival Victor concern. Stereo was a rare case of collaboration and consultation between the majors to avoid conflicting standards. Compact disc was jointly developed by Philips, which controlled the vast PolyGram record combine, and Sony, which owned a Japanese joint venture with Columbia and was shortly to buy the US company.

Now, however, the emergent format is MP3. The record industry did not create the MP3 format and so has no control over it. The free and easy, anarchic nature of non-corporate software developers means that they have no interest in restricting the use of the file-sharing systems that they invent and little interest in licensing the goods to turn a coin. The means of production and replication, for so long the province of big business, have been given to all. Those who stand to lose big call it 'theft'. Informed consumers call it 'democratization'. Less informed consumers look at it as an all-you-can-eat restaurant with no cover charge.

For most of the last century, making a record has been an activity dreamed about by many but only ever enjoyed by a select few. The dominance of a few major companies made sure of that. The closest most people ever got to immortalizing themselves on disc were the 'record your own voice' booths, which used to be found at railway stations or at tiny 'studios' in seaside resorts. The example everybody remembers is the machine that Pinkie uses to inform Rose of the harsh truth of their relationship in *Brighton Rock* by Graham Greene. One summer in the mid-1950s while on a day trip to Southend-on-Sea, two such ordinary people were my grandmother and her youngest brother. Taking advantage of the rudimentary studio facilities at the pierhead, they recorded the 1918 Leo Wood composition 'Somebody Stole My Gal'. It must have been around 1955, because Uncle Terry comes over like a South London version of Johnnie Ray, and that was when Ray's hit version was released. Instead of the Nabob of Sob's backing band, however, Uncle Terry was accompanied by Nan, tickling the ivories of a particularly battered upright piano. This disc acquired a unique position in family mythology, long after all means in our possession of playing it at the right speed (78 rpm, naturally) had spun their last.

The advent of portable tape recorders went some way towards redressing the balance. My mother introduced me to the delights of the reel-to-reel tape deck with an off-air recording that she had made in September 1965 of Kenny Everett on the pirate station Radio London. However, there has always been an extra bit of magic about a proper record – be it vinyl, shellac, acetate or even compact disc. Now, for only a few hundred pounds, we can buy digital multi-track recorders with sound quality that equals professional machinery and computers that will allow us to transfer the results onto compact disc. It's even possible to buy software that allows the DIY remastering expert to reduce the noise. I did exactly this when I was able to present my grandmother and my great-uncle with a CD of their seaside jollity nearly fifty years later.

The anti-globalization protests of recent years might lead one to conclude that consolidation and the creation of conglomerates are recent phenomena. While the pace has certainly increased in recent years, through various mergers and takeovers, the record industry has always been dominated by a few global players. At the start, Edison had a monopoly with his tinfoil cylinder phonograph. When Alexander Graham Bell, his brother Chichester and the English scientist Charles Sumner Tainter improved on Edison's work, a duopoly was created, which briefly became a monopoly again when the two sets of interests joined in a business alliance. Then, when Emile Berliner came to the fore with his disc-based gramophone, a third axis was added.

All of this business activity occurred before 1888, and yet the descendants of two of these groups are still very active. Only Edison, who dropped out of the record game at the time of the Depression, is unrepresented. The corporate history of Columbia, now owned by the monolithic Japanese electronics company Sony, can be traced back directly to the formation, by Tainter and the Bells, of the Volta Graphophone Company in 1886. Meanwhile, the German-owned Bertelsmann Music Group, through its stewardship of the RCA Victor label, is merely carrying on the business that Emile Berliner started in 1888. The UK's EMI group has the distinction of being descended from both lines. It was created in 1931 by the merger of the Gramophone Company – which had been started as Berliner's UK arm – and the British division of the Columbia Graphophone Company.

The fourth major, Universal – now the largest music company in the world – controls the former MCA and PolyGram businesses. MCA was founded in the 1920s, although it didn't enter the record industry until the early 1960s, when it acquired the American Decca company. PolyGram, although dating as an entity only from 1962, encompassed the record business of the Dutch electrical firm Philips, the German label Deutsche Grammophon/Polydor and the British company Decca, all of which also have long histories. Warner Bros, the fifth major and until recently part of the AOL Time-Warner group, is a relative latecomer, the group's record business having started from scratch in the late 1950s, and having added significantly to its reach by the absorption of Elektra and Atlantic in the 1960s to form WEA.

For all of the changes of ownership, the record industry has displayed a staggering degree of continuity over the last 125 years or so, unmatched in almost any other business. In the earliest days, new entrants were kept out of the business by these groups' domination of the various patents pertaining to the mechanical reproduction of music. The mere threat of a lawsuit was usually enough to deter all but the most determined entrepreneur. By the time these patents expired, the Berliner and Bell axes were so entrenched that new companies trying to gain a share of the market had to play by the rules of the established companies or not at all.

Moreover, these concerns – now thought to be bitter, pitched rivals – have, at various times, owned large chunks of each other. Bell begat Columbia. Berliner begat the Gramophone Company, which in turn gave birth to Deutsche Grammophon. Along with Victor, which took over the Berliner business in the US, the Berliner-originated companies had the rights to Francis Barraud's famous painting of his dog Nipper, a canvas better known as *His Master's Voice*. This was all very well when the companies were affiliated, but when the Victor–Gramophone alliance foundered in the 1950s, each side retained Nipper for their home territories. The divide persists to this day, and with global brand image having become seemingly more important than ever, the restrictions mean that one of the most famous trademarks in the world is now largely unused by its owners. In the US, even HMV record stores bear no trace of Barraud's attentive dog.

Thus entrenched, these conglomerates took it upon themselves to record music all around the world. Between 1898 and the start of the Great War, ad hoc tours by 'recording experts' (as sound engineers were then known) and, later, the establishment of permanent subsidiaries in South America, Africa, India, Russia, Asia and Australasia created a repertoire of locally recorded material. Creative considerations were very much secondary: the primary purpose of these tours was to sell gramophones to the natives. Indeed, the whole business model was fundamentally exploitative. As well as selling machines to people who frequently could barely afford them, the companies paid the artists a flat fee. However, the process was paying an artistic dividend, producing a catalogue of recordings that now has vast historical importance. The voice of the last surviving castrato singer, recorded in Rome, was preserved just in time. Japanese folk music was captured in all of its clangour. The Swedish singer Jenny Lind, one of the great stars of the Victorian era, had died before the gramophone took hold, but Enrico Caruso left the world with more than just a second-hand reputation.

This global reach has created a paradox. While the domination of large Anglo-American interests has homogenized the music produced in some fields – all too often, chart pop from Boston or Bangkok can be differentiated only by the language used by the singer – the establishment of semi-autonomous subsidiaries all around the world has helped make international successes of artists and genres who might otherwise have remained local phenomena. Caruso was poached by the Metropolitan Opera in New York on the strength of the early records he made in Milan. The worldwide rise in popularity of the tango in the 1920s can be ascribed directly to the presence in South America of European-owned record companies such as Odeon, a subsidiary of the German Lindström group, who recorded the indigenous music and had the international sales networks needed to take it to a wider public.

Almost every world crisis over the last 100 years has affected the music business. The First World War nearly put the Gramophone Company out of business, as it was hit by the sudden slump in leisure spending and, perhaps more critically, being cut off from its continental subsidiaries. Deutsche Grammophon had been HMV's German subsidiary, but from 1914, it traded in its own right, retaining the Nipper trademark until the Second World War. The Gramophone Company was saved only by turning much of its Hayes, Middlesex, plant over to munitions work for the British war effort and the vigorous promotion of patriotic records as morale-boosters.

The Depression resulted in an extensive consolidation of the industry – most notably the merger of HMV and UK Columbia to form EMI – at about the same time that record sales were being decimated by the growing popularity of radio. Stereo, being developed at this time by Alan Blumlein of EMI and, independently, by Bell Laboratories in the US, was abandoned as a bridge too far. In a global slump, who would be interested in buying a new record player? Victor's early attempt at a long-playing record went much the same way.

The history of recording, from the 1880s onward, has been one of tensions between the businessmen who backed the schemes, the scientists who developed the various advances in recording and playback technology and the artists who created the music. It is easy to slip into thinking of inventors as other-worldly professors, developing ideas for the common good and being recklessly generous with their patents. In the early days of the music industry, however, the inventors were often highly entrepreneurial. Just as the automatic telephone exchange was invented not by an electrical whiz but by an undertaker called Strowger who was tired of telephone operators directing clients to his rivals, the gramophone was developed to generate cash. Thomas Edison – credited with the invention of the cylinder record – retained a strong proprietorial interest in seeing his products earn their keep. Emile Berliner – the progenitor of the flat disc record – was no less business-minded. Meanwhile, Berliner's associate Eldridge R. Johnson was effectively three people in one: a trained mechanical engineer, a businessman and an impresario. The first role saw him pioneering the use of flat discs instead of cylinders and refining the spring-driven motor that powered most gramophones in the pre-electric days. His second self realized the importance of advertising to the record business and negotiated the deal to supply Berliner with the motor. The third Eldridge R. Johnson personally oversaw the building of Victor's roster of artists, which included Caruso. From the start, the record business has been a nexus where commerce has met creativity, where the monetary and the military have joined forces with the musical.

The gramophone turned music into an industry. Previously the only way that music could be enjoyed at home was if one or more members of a household could play an instrument. If the listener's tastes were extremely limited, there were always the tinklings of a music box. Although sales of sheet music acted as a precursor for what became the record market, the interpretation of each piece was very much down to the individual player. Over the century since the gramophone took precedence, the role of the music publishers has changed. As sheet music sales have declined, their purpose has been to administer and collect songwriters' royalties, as opposed to the performer royalties dealt with by the record companies.

Music publishers have also, in many cases, started to play more of a part in developing artists before they sign to a record company. The Beatles joined Parlophone and then found a music publisher, Dick James. In contrast, a modern band writing its own songs might well sign with a music publisher, which pays for the demo recordings that land the group their recording contract. Very often, the publisher will be wholly or part-owned by the record company in question.

The dominance of big business in music has now been challenged, possibly with fatal consequences. This book is an attempt to explain how the global record industry reached its current predicament, and to suggest where, if anywhere, it can go from here. It is also a book about the people who made the industry, with all of its flaws, rather than the artists who made the music. Along the way, these have included more than a few heroes, villains, eccentrics, egocentrics, misers, spendthrifts, thieves and saints. It is fitting that almost all of those appellations can be applied to the first man associated with the industry – Thomas Alva Edison.

1 Buying – and selling – the Edison myth

When history is viewed in Gradgrindian terms as a succession of facts to be learned by rote, it is usually enough to say that Thomas Edison invented the phonograph. Of course, the truth of the phonograph's provenance is less simple. Edison once declared, famously, 'Genius is 1 per cent inspiration and 99 per cent perspiration.' Many before him had given the matter of recorded sound a great deal of very serious thought, followed by a considerable amount of sweat. Unfortunately for them, none had managed to produce a working device that retained sound waves for later playback until Edison produced his first tinfoil cylinder machine in late 1877. Perhaps more importantly, none understood the importance of publicity as well as Edison did.

Some perspired more than others. One of Edison's precursors who got closest was the Frenchman Edouard-Leon Scott de Martinville, who, in 1857, had produced the phonautograph. His invention involved a horn, a stylus – in this case made of bristle – attached to a diaphragm, and a cylinder faced with lampblack-coated paper.[1] This arrangement allowed sound waves to be represented visually. Unfortunately, there was no means of replaying whatever had been etched into the lampblack, so the phonautograph was of limited use. Scott was, however, definitely barking up the right tree.

As was another Frenchman, Charles Cros, a poet, amateur scientist, artist, musician, prodigious absinthe drinker (an enthusiasm that would kill him in 1888 at the age of just forty-six) and friend of the painter Edouard Manet. This appealingly Bohemian polymath deposited a sealed paper at the Academie des Sciences in Paris on 30 April 1877 in which he described, theoretically, a process for recording and reproducing sound. He wrote of 'obtaining traces of the movements to and fro of a vibrating membrane and in using this tracing to reproduce the same vibrations with their intrinsic relations of duration and intensity, either by means of the same membrane or some other one equally adapted to produce the sounds which result from this series of movements'.[2]

The means for achieving this were, he said, 'a delicate stylus' tracing the sound waves on a disc of lampblacked glass. These were then to be transformed, by photoengraving, into indentations 'capable of guiding a moving body, which transmits these movements to the sound membrane'. The whole assembly was to be known as the pareographe. The Cros paper, explaining what it called a 'process of recording and of reproducing audible phenomena', was read out in open session in December 1877. Cros had taken the academic route because he could not afford to apply for a patent, nor could he find any backers willing to meet the cost. He also lacked the resources to turn his theoretical machine into reality, but he had taken theory a step further forward, and an important one at that. He was the first to mention the groove.

Cros, born in 1842, was an almost exact contemporary of Edison's. His theory was lodged with the Academie three months before Edison's first known forays into phonographic development, but not published until the American had already applied for a patent. As a result of this (and of French national pride), Cros is held by his compatriots to be the true inventor of the phonograph, despite having never produced a working model. In the first decent history of the medium to be published, Roland Gelatt formulated a neat compromise: 'Let it be resolved by giving each his due: Charles Cros for being the first to *conceive* the phonograph, Thomas Edison for being the first to *achieve* it.'[3]

During his long life, Edison registered 1,093 United States patents.[4] The first was in June 1869, when he was twenty-two. His last application was made in 1931, the year of his death, when he was working, with limited success, on alternatives to latex that could be grown in the US.

His first phonographic patent – US patent number 200,521 – was applied for in the US on 24 December 1877 and granted on 19 February 1878. Although he was, at this point, only just thirty years old, his achievements and his talent for mythology and self-publicity meant that he was already well on the way to becoming an American folk hero.

Thomas Edison was born on 11 February 1847 in Milan, Ohio. His father had been, at various times of his life, a carpenter, a property speculator and a gentleman farmer, while his mother was a schoolteacher. However, by 1854, the family had moved to Port Huron, Michigan, a lumber town near the Canadian border with a large railroad depot. Much of Edison's education was undertaken at home, which some sources attribute to his weak childhood constitution, while others suggest that it was in order to economize.

He began work at the age of fourteen, selling newspapers on the Grand Trunk Railroad. For most of the details of Edison's early life, we are reliant upon Edison's own version of events. This is problematic, as the inventor was not averse to changing his stories to suit different audiences. According to a set of autobiographical notes that Edison prepared in 1908–9, he claimed to have capitalized on the Civil War battle of Shiloh in 1862 by negotiating credit to buy more newspapers than usual. As he recognized a mounting demand for the news with each station along the line, he upped the price of his stock incrementally. A good story and one pointing to Edison's obvious business acumen, but was it entirely true? In the absence of any other contemporary reports, there is no way of corroborating it or dismissing it, but it is perhaps worthwhile to be a little cynical. Rather better established is the fact that he produced his own news sheet for travellers, called the *Weekly Herald*, using a baggage car as his editorial office and printing works.

At the age of fifteen, Edison began to study telegraphy, and found himself working at various railroad telegraph offices, before eventually taking up a position with the Western Union Telegraph Company. He soon gained a reputation for great speed and accuracy. When he moved to the Boston office in 1868, the incumbents, in order to initiate the new boy, presented him with an impossibly complex 1,500-word special cable from the fastest operator around, a man called Hutchinson.

To everybody's astonishment, Edison sailed through, but he later admitted it was a little daunting. 'After about three-quarters of the special, Hutchinson got nervous and commenced to abbreviate,' Edison remembered. 'As I had to write out in full I knew that soon I would have to break, so to save the day before this took place, I opened the key and said, "You seem to be tired, suppose you send a little with your other foot." This saved me... After this I was all right with the other operators.'[5]

His popularity was also not harmed by his invention of a device to electrocute the cockroaches that infested the office. However, at this time, he was also working his first serious patents, the telegraphic printer and the electric vote counter. Shortly after achieving these, he moved to Newark, New Jersey, and set up in business on his own. Although the vote recorder failed commercially, his telegraphic printer found favour with financial institutions as a 'stock ticker'. His next major breakthrough came in 1873 with his quadruplex telegraph, which could handle four messages at once, two in each direction. The invention was bought for $30,000 by Jay Gould of Western Union's great rival, the Atlantic and Pacific Telegraph Company. Western Union immediately put Edison on a retainer to make sure that it had first dibs on any future inspirations and perspirations.

By 1874, Edison had begun inventing on an industrial scale, with a staff of 120. However, when he established his laboratory at Menlo Park, New Jersey, he took only the twenty most able and trusted of these assistants with him. These were the men that he called his 'muckers', styling himself as the 'chief mucker'. The first project to detain the Menlo Park muckers was the improvement of Alexander Graham Bell's newly unveiled telephone. Working very carefully around the Bell patents, Edison tried to grab a piece of the action, and succeeded with his carbon button transmitter (microphone), which proved to be a vast advance on Bell's own creation.

Having harnessed sound vibrations, Edison wondered whether a point attached to a diaphragm making indentations in a suitable material would capture the sounds for replay. This thought is reputed to have occurred to him after the sharp point on the underside of a moving telephone diaphragm pricked his finger. His phonographic experiments began in the autumn of 1877, although the exact date is uncertain. The job of assembling the prototype phonograph was given to one of the most trusted muckers, machinist John Kruesi. There is, in the archive at the Edison National Historical Site in West Orange, New Jersey, a sketch made by Edison, under which he has written: 'Kreusi [sic], Make This, Edison, Aug 12/77.' However, writing in 1906, another mucker, Charles Batchelor, gave the date of the breakthrough as November 1877. The official version at West Orange nowadays, based on analysis of Edison's writing, is that the inscription on the drawing (which is, in any case, far too vague to have been of any use to Kruesi) and possibly the drawing itself, date from much later, maybe even the 1920s. To confuse matters further, the collection of Edison papers at Rutgers University contains a drawing, also dated 12 August 1877, showing the phonograph as a device that uses reels of paper tape to capture Morse code signals. It is understood that this was the invention which first alerted Edison to the possibilities of sound retention.

Kruesi had made a machined metal cylinder, with a spiral guide groove, around which a sheet of thick tinfoil was wrapped. Thus equipped, Edison shouted, 'Mary had a little lamb' into the mouthpiece attached to the diaphragm and stylus. He then took the stylus back to the start and listened for whatever had been indented in the foil. Batchelor recalled: 'We got, "ary ad ell am," [...] but the shape of it was there and so like the talking that we all let out a yell of satisfaction and a "Golly it's there!" and shook hands all round.'[6]

The contraption needed a name. Among those considered were the polyphone, the autophone and the acoustophone, before Edison settled on phonograph, a name which seems also to have been used to describe Cros's creation by the Abbé Lenoir in the 10 October 1877 issue of *La Semaine du Clerge*. Edison then took the phonograph to the offices of the *Scientific American*. The journal reported in its 22 December 1877 issue that:

> Mr. Thomas A. Edison recently came into this office, placed a little machine on our desk, turned a crank, and the machine inquired as to our health, asked how we liked the phonograph, informed us that *it* was very well, and bid us a cordial good night. These remarks were not only perfectly audible to ourselves, but to a dozen or more persons gathered around.[7]

Two days after the cover date of the journal, Edison applied for a US patent.

Given the sealed nature of Cros's submission to the Academie, it is unlikely that Edison was aware of French developments. Their parity appears, therefore, to be purely coincidental. Some have argued that Cros, had he the proper resources and finance, could have beaten Edison to the punch. Certainly, Edison's progress was aided immeasurably by his 'muckers'. Also, Edison's laboratories, both at Menlo Park and later at West Orange were, for the time, tremendously well equipped. As well as chemical laboratories, the extensive machine rooms and an exhaustive collection of tools, Edison maintained stores that held everything from washers and bolts to samples of elephant hide.[8] He boasted that the laboratory could 'build anything from a lady's watch to a Locomotive'.[9]

Flushed with success, Edison turned to thinking of the possibilities for the phonograph, ten of which he outlined in an article for the *North American Review*. Perhaps surprisingly, the reproduction of music came fifth in Edison's list, behind letter writing, dictation, book readings for the blind and educational purposes (particularly the teaching of elocution), but ahead of recording one's family members, toys,[10] speaking clocks, advertising and recording the speeches of the great and the good. Edison noted:

The phonograph will undoubtedly be liberally devoted to music. A song sung on the phonograph is reproduced with marvelous accuracy and power. Thus a friend may in a morning call sing a song which shall delight an evening company, etc. As a musical teacher it will be used to enable one to master a new air, the child to form its first songs, or to sing him to sleep.

In patenting the phonograph, Edison had tried to cover his back by suggesting future modifications and adaptations. Although the tinfoil recording was, by definition, a one-of-a-kind artifact, Edison suggested that the record 'may be stereotyped by means of the plaster of Paris process, and from the stereotype multiple copies may be made expeditiously and cheaply by casting or by pressing tinfoil or other material upon it'.[11] Here, however, Edison was no better off than Cros. He had the idea that it could be done, and outlined the method, but there is no indication that he ever put the problematic theory into action. Aligning the ends of the tinfoil sheet so that the grooves corresponded was a painstaking job. Also, the very quality that made tinfoil suitable for the initial recording, its malleability, meant that once the sheet was taken off the cylinder, it was prone to further inadvertent indentations and thus became almost useless. Edison knew this, but it didn't deter him from suggesting otherwise. He was reported in the *Illustrated London News* of 3 August 1878 as saying:

This tongueless, toothless instrument, without larynx or pharynx, mimics your tones, speaks with your voice, utters your words; and, centuries after you have crumbled into dust, may repeat every idle thought, every fond fancy, every vain word that you choose to whisper against the thin iron diaphragm... You can have a phonograph in your parlour with an album of selected phonographic matter lying beside it. You can take a sheet from the album, place it on the phonograph, start the clockwork and have a symphony performed; then, by changing the sheet, you can listen to a chapter or two of a favourite novel; this may be followed by a song, a duet, or a quartet; and at the close the young people may indulge in a waltz, all joining in it, for no one need be asked to play the dance music.

These were pretty wild claims on Edison's part. Quite apart from tinfoil being very much a one-shot medium, the fidelity of the recorded sound was not yet good enough for music, and the running time of each cylinder was not long enough to accommodate a symphony or any meaningful part of one.

Contemporary reports display a predisposition to accept unquestioningly whatever line Edison trotted out, however. In the same issue of the *Illustrated London News*, a Dr William F. Channing was quoted:

> We shall have galleries where phonotype sheets will be preserved as photographs and books now are. The utterances of the great speakers will there be kept for a thousand years. In these galleries, spoken languages will be preserved from century to century with all the peculiarities of pronunciation, dialect and brogue ... Certainly, within a dozen years, some of the greatest singers will be induced to sing into the ear of the phonograph ... Nothing will be easier than to catch the sounds of the waves on the beach, the roar of Niagara, the discords of the streets, the noises of animals, the puffing and rush of a railroad train, the rolling of thunder, or even the tumult of a battle.[12]

Actually, at this point, quite a lot would have been easier than attempting to capture any of those sounds, as location recording was all but impossible until the development of electric recording in the 1920s.

Some oddly familiar sentiments can be found in an 1878 book on the inventions of the day, in which author George B. Prescott declared that: 'The phonograph has quite passed the experimental stage and is now practically successful in every respect and must be regarded as instrumental in opening a new field for scientific research, and making one more application of science to industry.'[13]

The phonograph was important, but it was far more of a work in progress than Prescott let on. He admitted that its tone was 'usually rather shrill and piping, but this defect will undoubtedly be corrected by improved instruments' and that 'marvellous as this instrument is, it is still quite new and it is impossible to say to what degree of perfection it may yet be carried'.[14] It is not clear whether Prescott was blinded by the sheer novelty of the machine or whether he simply wished to buy into the Edison myth. The near verbatim repetition of part of Edison's newly issued British patent suggests that he was close enough to the inventor to receive sneak previews of the odd document. In the event, the stereotyping never took place and the malleability of the tinfoil surface proved the enemy of preservation. Prescott's over-enthusiastic claims that 'utterances of the great speakers and singers will there be kept for a thousand years'[15] proved premature, as did Channing's assertion on the acceptance of the phonograph by 'the greatest singers'. It took nearer to twenty years than a dozen.

Thankfully, other observers were not quite so credulous. Reviewing what it called 'Edisoniana' in January 1879, *Punch* attributed to Edison the invention not only of the phonograph, but also of 'the micro-tasimeter, the megaphone and the aeroplane' as well as being responsible at the age of eight for 'considerable improvements in the ordinary pea-shooter' and the addition of 'more than one note to the compass of the Jew's harp'. It was also claimed that Edison, at the age of fourteen, had created both 'an ingenious contrivance to enable persons of an obese habit to pick up things without undergoing the inconvenience of stooping' and the 'instantaneous hat-peg'.[16] Meanwhile, the hokey tendency of yellow-press biographers to see immense significance and destiny in some random childhood occurrence also came under fire with the revelation that, as a baby on a railway journey with his mother, Edison gazed at the lamp in the carriage all the way to the final destination. 'The germ of some great discovery may have been latent in that prolonged stare,' suggested *Punch* improbably.

Edison's commitment to tinfoil is odd, when one considers that he was also looking at more robust materials. In his British patent for the phonograph, numbered 1,644 and dated 24 April 1878, Edison even went as far as to suggest the use of copper recording surfaces and the deployment of electroplating to make a matrix from which further copies could be pressed. He also suggested that, for the finished cylinder, 'Paper or other materials may be used, the same being coated with paratine or other hydrocarbons, waxes, gums, or lacs...'[17]

His laboratory notes show that he did, indeed, experiment with wax as a recording surface. For some reason, however, he decided not to pursue this line of enquiry, preferring instead to see if he could make tinfoil pay.

On 24 April 1878, the Edison Speaking Phonograph Company had been formed by a syndicate of businessmen that included Gardiner G. Hubbard, the father-in-law of Alexander Graham Bell, and Hilbourne L. Roosevelt, a cousin of the politician Theodore Roosevelt. Its purpose was to market and exploit the new invention, paying Edison $10,000 for the rights to market the phonograph and promising him a 20 per cent royalty on any sales. This was another advantage that the American had over Cros. He was an unashamed capitalist, driven to invent things that made money. He grew sentimentally attached to the phonograph, calling it his baby (this in response to press speculation that he and his wife were expecting a third child) and describing it as his favourite of all of his inventions. (*Punch* pooh-poohed this idea, indicating that Edison's 'most cherished invention, and the one on which he rests his surest claim to fame and fortune and the future Presidency of the United States, is his Electric Pen-Wiper.')[18]. However, in Edison's world, even babies had to pay their way.

The topical songwriters were also quick off the mark, if less wounding than *Punch*. 'The Song of Mr Phonograph', allegedly composed by H. A. H. von Ograff, was copyrighted in 1878 and its summary of the invention went:

My name is Mister Phonograph and I'm not so very old,
My father he's called Edison, and I'm worth my weight in gold.
The folks they just yell into my mouth and now I'm saying what's true.
For just speak to me, I'll speak it back and you'll see I can talk like you.[19]

The new company enlisted showmen to undertake demonstrations of the new machine all around the United States. Audiences saw and heard the phonograph repeating speech in all languages, as well as sound effects (coughing was strangely effective) and music, and for a while the enterprise did very well. At the height of the craze, one of the demonstration machines was earning $1,800 a week in hirings. Some declared the phonographic cylinders to be a faithful and perfect representation of the sounds that went into the mouthpiece. This was quite obviously untrue, but these early hi-fi enthusiasts were clearly amazed that such a thing was being done, not just well, but at all.[20]

Not all were as enraptured by the phonograph or its creator, though.

Something ought to be done with Mr Edison, and there is a growing conviction that it had better be done with a hemp rope,' [claimed the *New York Times*]. Mr Edison has invented too many things, and almost without exception they are things of the most deleterious character … Recently he invented the phonograph, a machine that catches the lightest whisper of conversation and stores it up, so that at any future time it can be brought out, to the confusion of the original speaker. This machine will eventually destroy all confidence between man and man, and render more dangerous than ever woman's want of confidence in woman.[21]

This idea was well illustrated in 'Mrs Barstinglow's Phonograph', a short story published in the *Burlington Hawkeye* in early 1878. When Mrs Barstinglow goes away for three days, her husband begs her to stay at home:

'At one time he protested ... he could not endure the lonesome house during her absence. And then again he declared that if she must go, he would neglect his office, and let his business go to the bow-wows, and he would go with her,' but on her return she plays the phonograph and finds that her husband has had his dissolute friends around for drinks and card games, ending with a fight. 'That's right! Believe a senseless diabolical piece of monstrous mechanism rather than your husband,' he beseeches, but to no avail. He took 'the phonograph out into the back yard and smashed it into so many and such small fragments that it couldn't reproduce even a steamboat whistle'.[22]

Although the general public did not agree with this paranoid view of Edison's achievement, it wasn't long before the phonographic bandwagon began to lose momentum. The novelty had worn off. Even Edison was diverted, once the limited commercial potential of his 'baby' became apparent. In any case, he was now preoccupied with the lucre to be gained from being the first to develop a working system of electric light. By November 1878, all development work on the tinfoil phonograph had ceased, and Edison had contracted his services exclusively to the Edison Electric Light Company.

That Edison switched, seemingly so casually, from one epochal invention to another gives a flavour both of the spirit of the era and the degree to which Edison was in tune with it. It was a magnificent time for invention and innovation. The *Illustrated London News* set the context most evocatively in its report of the phonograph's invention:

This is an age of scientific marvels, if not of miracles. To railways and steam-boats, making near neighbours of distant provinces and practically bridging oceans, succeeded the electric telegraph, which turned into a verity Puck's boast of girdling the earth in forty minutes; and now we have that marvellous triad – the telephone, phonograph and microphone.[23]

The Crystal Palace, which figured in Edison's early activities in Britain, had originally been erected in 1851 as part of the Great Exhibition, a chance for Great Britain to show off its 'arts and manufactures'. With James Watt's steam engine having helped mechanize manufacture where it was previously limited by animal or human strength, coal production in the UK had increased by more than twenty times between 1800 and 1900. The Industrial Revolution was well underway and the items on show at the Palace included factory-made fabrics and the powered looms that produced them, metalwork, agricultural machinery, tools, marine engines, hydraulic presses and other steam equipment. Wonder of wonders, Queen Victoria sent a telegraph message from the Exhibition. Armaments figured in the programme, as did products from all parts of the British Empire. There had also been a population explosion. At the time of the 1801 census, only fifteen towns in Britain had more than 20,000 inhabitants. By 1891, the figure was sixty-three. Those that could afford it were being better served by medicine than at any time before. Although Edward Jenner's cowpox vaccine for smallpox had been discovered at the end of the eighteenth century, vaccination was only compulsory in Britain after 1853, beginning the eradication of a disease that at one time killed 10 per cent of the British population.

Socially, too, matters were improving. Just as Abraham Lincoln was bringing an end to slavery in the US in 1865, the UK had witnessed the increasing enfranchisement of the populace, brought about by the Great Reform Acts of 1832 and 1867. The provision of education was being expanded as well, with the 1880 Education Act providing elementary education in Britain for children between the ages of five and ten. America was mired in economic depression for much of the 1870s, and inventors like Edison represented hope for the American people, so there was a captive audience for whatever they produced, and as prosperity returned, the interested populace turned into a large potential market.

Electricity had been a possibility since the Englishman Michael Faraday established the principles of electrical generation in 1831, but the creation of a successful electric lamp had eluded inventors. Edison's work on electric light brought success in late 1879, and for the rest of the early 1880s he was preoccupied with perfecting the system and putting it to commercial use, with financial backing from various sources, including John Pierpont Morgan of the Drexel Morgan banking house. Unfortunately for Edison, his decision to adopt the direct current (DC) system proved to be disastrous, as rival interests made the running with the more powerful and reliable alternating current (AC) system. Even worse for Edison, another inventor, Joseph Swan, who had been working on electric light since 1848, had succeeded at roughly the same time. The result was a long-running patent dispute that ended in a merger of the two inventors' interests. A further merger had great significance for the electric industry. In 1892, J. P. Morgan arranged for the Edison General Electric Company to combine with the Thomson-Houston Electric Company. The result took the name of the

General Electric Company. Towards the end of the 1880s, Edison turned his attention towards moving pictures.

While Edison had been preoccupied with electric light, others had adopted his phonographic offspring, among them the expatriate Scotsman Alexander Graham Bell. Bell's decision to develop Edison's invention came not, it seems, from a desire to 'get even' for the carbon button transmitter, but out of a sense of missed opportunity and not a little self-criticism.

'It is a most astonishing thing to me that I could possibly have let this invention slip through my fingers when I consider how my thoughts have been directed to this subject for so many years past,' Bell wrote to his father-in-law Gardiner G. Hubbard on 18 March 1878. 'So nearly did I come to the idea that I had stated again and again in my public lectures the fundamental principles of the phonograph.'[24] Despite his private displeasure at Edison's head start and the fact that the carbon button device had been sold to the rival Western Union concern, Bell and his associates remained friendly with Edison's camp. Bell's wife had been one of the first to write, congratulating the 'chief mucker' on his achievement, closely followed by a laudatory missive from prospective investor Hubbard.

Within a couple of years of Edison's announcement, Bell also had a well-resourced laboratory in which to undertake his work. He had received the French Academie des Sciences' Alessandro Volta award for inventing the telephone, and had put the $20,000 purse to good use, forming the Volta Laboratory Association in 1880. Devoted to electrical and acoustical research, the VLA established a laboratory in Washington DC, where he was joined by his brother Chichester A. Bell and the English scientist Professor Charles Sumner Tainter. The triumvirate became known as the Volta Laboratory Associates. Initially, the trio worked on improvements to the telephone, gaining eleven patents in this field in 1880 and 1881. Parallel to this, however, they were working all of the time on phonographic modifications and enhancements. As early as February 1880, they had deposited a sealed envelope at the Smithsonian Institution containing some early sketches pertaining to their phonographic work, which eventually became their main project.[25]

For all of Alexander Graham Bell's early interest, it was Tainter who turned out to be the prime mover in the Laboratory's phonographic efforts, aided mainly by Chichester Bell. As eccentric as they come, Tainter's many bursts of creativity were punctuated by a very English ritual. 'Tainter was ...

a confirmed tea-drinker,' remembered Fred Gaisberg – who began his long career in the music business in Tainter's lab at around 1892–3:

> Indeed, he taught me how to brew and enjoy it. The perfume of that special China blend of his haunts me still. Between the cups he would mount the diaphragm and adjust the angle of the cutting stylus. In his clear Yorkshire voice he would test them with, 'Caesar, Caesar, can you hear what I say – this, which, s-ss-sss.' The stress was always laid on the sibilants, these being the most difficult sounds to record. In playing back the test, at the slightest indication of the 's' sound, he would smile with joy and treat himself to another cup.[26]

After countless brew-ups, Tainter and the Bell brothers returned to the Smithsonian on 20 October 1881. This time they brought with them a sealed box containing a device they called a 'graphophone', along with various documents concerning its construction and use, as well as a couple of contemporary newspapers. Most important, however, they included a cylinder upon which Tainter had recorded: 'G-r-r-G-r-r- There are more things in heaven and earth Horatio, than are dreamed of in our philosophy – G-r-r-I am a graphophone and my mother was a phonograph.'[27]

There was indeed a strong family resemblance between the two devices, although the relationship was more one of identical twins than of mother and child. Put bluntly, the crude hand-cranked graphophone deposited in the Smithsonian was almost indistinguishable from the Edison phonograph, in all but one crucial detail. Instead of using tinfoil, Tainter and the Bells had persevered with wax recording surfaces, in which the recording stylus cut the groove rather than indenting it, and produced a cardboard-centred wax cylinder, roughly 2 inches in diameter and 4 inches in length. The result was a recording of much higher quality than could be achieved with foil. This step forward came at the cost of volume: the graphophone was audible only through rubber tubes attached to the listener's ears.

Some work still remained to be done before the graphophone was ready for public consumption. In the event, Chichester Bell and Tainter did not apply for a patent until 27 June 1885. Why it took four years from the Smithsonian submission to the patent application is one of the great mysteries of the record industry's early history, but what is clear from Tainter's notebooks is that these four years were a period of constant development activity. When the Smithsonian deposit was made public in

1937, no one was more surprised than Fred Gaisberg who had assumed that the patent had followed shortly after the beginning of their experimentation. Could the Volta team have been waiting for Edison's patents to expire before making their move? Or could they have simply been unaware that their creation was sufficiently different from the phonograph to be patentable? Whatever their reasoning, the graphophone received US patent number 341,214 on 4 May 1886. As patented, it was, at least, cosmetically different to the phonograph, but it still had a hand-crank (although it was later ditched in favour of a foot-treadle or an electric motor, according to the consumer's choice).

Thus protected, the Volta Associates wasted no time in setting up the Volta Graphophone Company (later the American Graphophone Company) of Alexandria, West Virginia to manufacture and exploit their creation. The machine came to the attention of Andrew Devine, a reporter of the United States Supreme Court, who saw its potential as a dictation and stenographic tool. At Devine's prompting, the Volta team approached Edison with the idea of pooling their patents and going into business together. According to Edison's personal assistant Alfred O. Tate, Tainter and the Bells admitted:

> that their work was merely the projection and refinement of his ideas, and that they now wanted to place the whole matter in his hands and to turn their work over to him without any public announcements that would indicate the creation of conflicting interests...They had named their instrument the graphophone to differentiate it from the phonograph, but if Mr Edison would join them they would drop this name and revert to the original designation.[28]

The approach was rejected. In *From Tinfoil to Stereo*, Oliver Read and Walter L. Welch indicated that this was caused by Edison's loyalty to the stockholders of the dormant Edison Speaking Phonograph Company. In contrast, Roland Gelatt, another historian of the early music industry, has suggested that Edison was more likely piqued, regarding Tainter and the Bells as 'trespassers and usurpers'.[29] There would appear to be more truth in Gelatt's interpretation. After all, one of the Edison's stockholders was Hubbard, who presumably stood to win either way. The Volta developments did, however, have one effect on Edison. They made him return in a great hurry to caring for his 'baby'. On 16 June 1888, after five days and five nights of ceaseless work, Edison had created his 'Improved Phonograph'. Just as the graphophone had closely resembled Edison's original creation, so the 'Improved' resembled the graphophone. Edison had thought better of suing the Tainter and Bell grouping when they appropriated and improved the phonograph, but this generosity was not reciprocated. The graphophone men wanted their day in court. The scene was set for the industry's first patent battle. Lawyers on both sides set about preparing their cases, but following an eleventh-hour intervention from a monied outsider, the legal action was abandoned.

Jesse H. Lippincott was a glass tycoon, the owner of the Rochester Tumbler Company of Pittsburgh. He is reputed to have been fond of the high life, hosting lavish parties, chartering trains and backing Broadway shows. In the late 1880s, he decided to cash in, selling the business for $1m – a lot of money even now, but then a mind-boggling amount. Looking for somewhere to invest his windfall, he was pointed towards this new-fangled phonograph by his friend Thomas Lombard. Investing $200,000 in the American Graphophone Company, Lippincott became its sole sales agent. He then approached Edison, who was, as ever, in need of funds to continue his research in various areas. When Lippincott offered $500,000 for the patent rights to the phonograph – which Edison would continue to manufacture at the vast laboratory and factory complex he had recently established in West Orange, New Jersey – the inventor forgot all about his differences with the American Graphophone Company and took the cash.

So it was that the two warring factions abandoned their feud and became part of the same group – the North American Phonograph Company, which Jesse H. Lippincott had founded on 14 July 1888. Lippincott then set about creating a sales organization for his newly created monopoly, which boasted a market capitalization of $4m and a board of directors that included Thomas Lombard. As Bell had with his telephone business, Lippincott divided the US into territories, each with its own franchised sales operation. In time, there were thirty-three such organizations, all represented on the committee of the specially formed National Phonograph Association. He also decided that selling the machines outright was a short-sighted way of doing business, and opted instead to rent them out for $40 annually, split equally between the local sales company and the North American Phonograph Company.

*

While all of this frenzied competition and consolidation was going on in the United States, both sides were looking to the European market. In 1887, the Bell-Tainter group had established the International Graphophone Company, and in 1889, under Stephen Moriarty and Theodore Seligman, this became the vehicle for the graphophone's entry into Europe. The job of opening up the Continent for Edison fell to his agent in London, Colonel George E. Gouraud, a veteran of the American Civil War and a holder of the Congressional Medal of Honor for his 'valuable assistance in rallying the men ... while under severe fire of the enemy' at Honey Hill, South Carolina, in 1864. Gouraud and Edison had been associates from the inventor's very earliest days in business, and the old soldier had done valuable work on popularizing the telegraph, the telephone and electric light in Britain and the Continent. In 1888, he took offices at 181 Queen Victoria Street (moving later to Northumberland Avenue) and oversaw the establishment of the Edison Phonograph Company.

The arrival of the new toy in the British Isles provoked an uncertain reaction in some quarters. In June 1888, the *Spectator* wondered, 'WHAT WILL COME OF THE PHONOGRAPH?', fearing 'an immense storing up of sounds that it might be better not to store up'. For example:

> It is quite conceivable that in the year 2000 there may be the means not only of hearing figures like Lord Salisbury or Mr Gladstone pour forth in the actual tones of those orators speeches which were made by them in our own day, not only of hearing Lord Tennyson recite 'Maud' in the twentieth or thirtieth century with that rich and peculiar burr ... but of revivifying every little notoriety of our day, from Dr Parker to Dr Tanner – bottling up their voices for the ears of our posterity, as well as making their forms visible to future generations, till 'earth is sick and Heaven is weary.[30]

Asking if we were 'not discovering a great deal too many means of defeating the benefits conferred by oblivion', the *Spectator* also reiterated the *New York Times'* decade-old prediction of dire consequences for human relations, particularly between the different generations of a family:

> Imagine a man in the next century whose great-grandfather was a Gladstonian, whose grandfather was entrusted with a command in the war with Ireland to which Home-rule had led, and whose father had sided with the Irish in resisting the oppressions of the restored government – and

imagine these ancestors addressing their descendant in all the different accents of political passion to which their different situations had given rise, while their portraits look severely down on him, enforcing by their expression the earnestness of their political view – would not such a man carry into life a consciousness even more hesitating and divided than even that which gives birth to our nineteenth-century vacillations?'[31]

Undeterred by such jeremiads, Gouraud went about the business of promoting the phonograph. His devotion to Edison was such that his home at Beulah Hill, Upper Norwood, near Croydon, was called 'Little Menlo' after the inventor's New Jersey laboratory. In addition, the residence was equipped throughout with the very latest Edison technology, including a direct telephone link to the nearby Crystal Palace, over which Gouraud could hear the various concerts and recitals that took place at the venue. Gouraud received one of the very first 'Improved Phonographs' (some have claimed that he got the first) and immediately put it to use. On 26 June 1888, he was at the Crystal Palace, recording an extract of the Handel oratorio *Israel in Egypt*, a cylinder which still survives and which is thought to be the earliest musical recording extant.[32]

Among those in the audience for the Handel concert were William Ewart Gladstone – then between periods of prime ministerial office – and his wife. Shortly after, Gladstone was persuaded to make a recording himself, fulfilling part of the *Spectator*'s prophecy, in which he congratulated Edison on his achievement.[33] As also predicted by the *Spectator*, Alfred, Lord Tennyson took to the phonograph at Gouraud's behest, as did Florence Nightingale, Cardinal Manning and Robert Browning. Gouraud also talked the actor Henry Irving into immortalizing his voice on wax, which he did on 30 August 1888. In time, Irving would become a great enthusiast for the new medium, making several recordings, including one of the soliloquy from Shakespeare's *Richard III*.

The fine words of the great and good brought some welcome respectability to the phonograph in Europe, but little in the way of real business. On 24 February 1890, the Edison United Phonograph Company was founded to look after the inventor's phonographic interests outside of the US and Canada, and Gouraud was joined by Moriarty. In 1892, perhaps unsurprisingly, given Stephen Moriarty's defection from the Bell-Tainter grouping, Edison United was superseded by the Edison-Bell Phonograph Corporation, which represented both sides, mirroring the Lippincott monopoly. Edison United sold the British Edison and Bell-Tainter patents to the new company for £40,000. Although it had the British market almost to itself for several years, Edison-Bell proved as unsuccessful as its predecessor, perhaps due to the prohibitively high price – £60 and upwards – that it placed on the machines.

Edison machines were also coming into the UK by other, unofficial means. Years later, when he was working for the Edison-Bell company in London, salesman Percy Willis recalled how he and a friend, starving in Canada, reckoned that they could make a fortune if they could get a machine and cylinders to the UK and give public demonstrations for which they would charge a fee. Finding a machine and thirty-six cylinders in Boston, they smuggled the gear from the US into Ireland, then onto the mainland. 'Edison United was controlling the earth in the talking machine line,' he recalled. 'They had little or no opposition … My partner agreed with me that there was money in the notion.'[34]

Willis and his partner were proved right. Despite having lost twelve of the cylinders to a handling accident in transit, they managed to take £200 in their first five days. They had with them a cylinder purporting to be by Gladstone, but it was a re-recording of the politician's words by an actor rather than the precious original harvested by Gouraud. Even so, a British member of parliament who attended one of the Willis recitals declared that 'I have sat behind the old man for nearly fifty years and recognize every tone of the voice.'[35] Another smuggling mission to Boston and back ensued, the cylinders carried in apple barrels. Despite the odd run-in with the 'high-handed' Edison United people, nothing was ever proven against Willis, and he continued his business for some time, profiting handsomely.

The arrival of the ruthless Stephen Moriarty had spelled the end for the eccentric showman Gouraud. By the time the Edison-Bell company was formed, he had been forced out of the day-to-day running, although he remained a stockholder. He resurfaced briefly in January 1904 when British trade journal *Talking Machine News* reported that 'the irrepressible Colonel Gouraud' had 'broken out in another place, as Acting Governor to Jacques I, Emperor of the Sahara.' It added, however, that he was 'not entirely off with the old', quoting him as saying:

> Our army, our weapons? We are to have none, sir. Or rather, put it this way –
> our army is the army of industry, our arms the arms of peace. We will charm

them, sir, with the phonograph and gramophone – let them sing their native songs into it and hear their own voices coming out of these wonderful machines. They will be charmed into the ways of peace by the voice of science.[36]

In time, Moriarty moved to gain complete control of the business, to the point of squeezing out even Edison. In December 1896, Moriarty purchased the inventor's shares in Edison United, cutting off the last links with Edison and his British factories.

For all of Lippincott's efforts, the rental plan proved a disaster. Many stenographers had feared the new contraption, and endeavoured to sabotage it at every turn. It seemed that they were prevailing. One of the mistakes Lippincott and Edison had made was to insist that the phonograph was a business tool rather than a mode of entertainment. The local sales companies were soon addressing this short-sightedness by building their own repertoires of original recordings. Within two years of its set-up, the North American Phonograph Company was heading for bankruptcy, and its founder was gravely ill. Edison stepped in to take control, buying back his patent rights for $135,000 – just over a quarter of what he had received for them two years earlier. Lombard took over Lippincott's executive role, and the business model shifted from rental to sales. Suffering from paralysis, Lippincott died in 1891, a broken man.

The venture had proved particularly bad for the graphophone. By the time of the National Phonograph Association's second convention, in New York in June 1891, there were fifty Edison phonographs in use for each graphophone. This led Colonel Payne of the American Graphophone Company to make a speech suggesting that the graphophone had been buried by Lippincott. By 1893, the graphophone enterprise was looking very shaky indeed, its tea-drinking founders having abandoned it some time before. Its salvation, however, was at hand, partly through Edison's desire to shake himself free of the whole sorry affair.

In early 1894, Edison – tired of selling his machines through Lippincott's cumbersome federal structure – threw the North American Phonograph Company into bankruptcy in an effort to regain the right to sell direct from his factory. The judgement went in his favour, but it took nearly two years for the matter to be resolved, in which time Edison was barred from carrying on any phonographic business. However, on 11 January 1896, the courts declared that Edison was allowed to buy his sales rights back from the local agents. The value put on the business was $99,500, a tenth of what the agents had originally paid. Edison paid up without a murmur, and created the National Phonograph Company to handle the affairs of his newly vertical phonograph business. Devoid of merchandise, all but one of the local agents foundered.

The survivor was the Washington-based Columbia Graphophone Company, formed on 22 January 1889 by a group of forward-thinking Congressional stenographers headed by Edward D. Easton. 'When the graphophone came upon the scene, I abandoned shorthand in favour of the talking machine,' Easton told *Talking Machine News* in September 1903. He had been born in Gloucester, Massachusetts, in 1856, the son of a schoolmaster. At fifteen, he moved to New York, becoming a shorthand writer in a newspaper office. Three years later, he was appointed official stenographer to the US Lighthouse Board, moving eventually to his job in Congress, where he gained a reputation for speed and accuracy which earned him a then-record-breaking $6,000 in one year.

Columbia had begun modestly and rather more cautiously than some of its contemporaries. 'The company started in two rooms in a back part of an office building in Washington,' explained Frank Dorian, who joined Columbia in September 1889. 'Well, unlike most of the phonograph companies which were organized about that time, the promoters, instead of going into the business merely with a view to employing their capital at a profit ... had been attracted to the machine ... [as] a great labour saving device, which only needed to be put on a sound commercial basis.' It must be noted here that, although their main focus was on promoting their machine as a business tool, Columbia also built a repertoire of entertainment recordings, just as the other phonograph companies were doing. 'Their success was as pronounced as it was immediate. Within six months they were able to take premises with from fifteen to twenty times the amount of space with which they had started.'[37]

As the AGC's sole agent, Columbia had effective control of the large plant in Bridgeport, Connecticut. Using Bell-Tainter parts, Columbia's chief engineer Thomas Hood Macdonald built a new type of graphophone and brought it to the market. As well as the dictaphone business, Columbia continued to develop the entertainment side of recording, under the direction of a New Englander called Calvin G. Child, who enlisted Tainter's former associate Fred Gaisberg as an accompanist and talent scout. Child set up a studio in New York, while his assistant took up residence in Philadelphia.

The range of fare on offer was rather limited, majoring in honest crowd-pleasing vulgarity, at the expense of the highbrow. The closest they got to the great orchestral works were various Sousa marches played by the US Marine Band. Meanwhile, 'Negro' songs did well, whether sung by a real Negro – as in the case of George W. Johnson – or a white man pretending to be one – as with Billy Golden or Len Spencer.[38] Gaisberg was able to report that George W. Johnson 'achieved fame and riches' with just two recordings – 'The Whistling Coon' and 'The Laughing Song'. Unfortunately, his other main achievement was notoriety. Gaisberg, in his memoirs, held that Johnson was 'hanged for throwing his wife out of a window when in a drunken frenzy'.[39] Gaisberg had been misinformed. George W. Johnson was acquitted of the murder charge and continued to record. He spent his last years working at Len Spencer's Lyceum theatre in New York as a doorman before dying in 1914.

Spencer also played Irish-American characters, as featured on a 1904 recording for Edison called 'Clancy's Prize Waltz Contest'. According to *Edison Phonograph Monthly*:

> 'Clancy's Prize Waltz Contest' is a tale of a Bowery dance hall by Len Spencer. It introduces typical Bowery characters and orchestra music. Clancy offers a De Barrios diamond ring for the best lady dancer and a meerschaum cigarette holder for the best 'gent' dancer, and it is announced that Clancy's only interest in the dance is in the sale of the 'booze'. The dance begins to the music of 'My Little Coney Isle', when word comes up from below that the bar is doing 'nottin'. The orchestra is instructed to play that 't'irsty' music, 'de Wurzburger'. The prizes are awarded to the lady with the red hat, the green veil, and the pink shirtwaist, and to the 'gent' with the derby hat and the linen duster. One of Mr Spencer's best records.[40]

The joke, made more obvious on the record by the punters' howls of disapproval, is that the lady and the gent are both employees of Clancy, the bar owner deciding that no one has bought enough booze to deserve the prizes.

Perhaps the most important of all the early recording artists was Russell Hunting. He was almost certainly the most prolific. 'He was under contract at one time to produce not far short of seven thousand for one phono firm alone, and that is a good while since,' reported *Talking Machine News* in 1903.[41] Born in 1864 at West Roxbury in the United States, he had been an actor since his teens. He began his professional career with the actor Edwin Booth, before moving on to the Boston Theater Company, where he spent nine years, three as stage manager. Through this connection he toured the States with various productions, and also, in one case, Britain. Hunting was best known to the public for the series of humorous records that featured him as an Irishman called Michael Casey, who, on one occasion, went in search of striped paint to decorate a barber's pole. As this was before copyright law applied properly to recordings, each label had its own 'Casey' to cover Hunting's original works and to record items 'inspired' by Hunting's creation.

To the industry cognoscenti, however, he was as well known for his technical prowess with sound effects and voices as he was for his gags. 'As to his mimetic ability, Edison himself declared that the Casey steamboat record was the best that he had ever heard. There were no less than ten different characters and eight mechanical effects, all of them produced by Mr Hunting,' noted *Talking Machine News*, rapt in admiration. The effects included the ship's bell, the chains being rattled, the loading of a cargo of cotton and the sounds of the boat's engine. 'And Mr Hunting would tell you, as he told me – for he makes no secret about it – that all that went to make that record was his own voice, a bell, a couple of bottles and a piece of sandpaper.'[42]

In 1899, Hunting moved to London and began working for Edison-Bell, both as an artist and a recording manager. His most famous production of this era was 'Departure of a Troopship', recorded at the height of the Boer War. 'It is said that during the war time and since, more than one auditor [an interesting usage, suggesting that there was not yet a standard term for record buyers] has been moved to tears on hearing it for the first time,' commented the *Talking Machine News* in 1903, for the record tells the story of the soldier's final 'leave-taking' and evokes 'memories of the hero – husband, lover or brother – now sleeping his last, long sleep under the South African veldt'. Later in his career, Hunting concentrated on his non-performing work, becoming chief of recording for Pathé. He remained a force in the business until retiring in his late sixties.

Those who appeared on records in the early days were some way from being stars in the modern sense. Instead they were journeymen, paid on a piecework basis for each performance. They were selected for the strength of their voice rather than a pleasing tone, as shifting the recording diaphragm took a considerable amount of air.[43] As such, great artistry was neither called for, nor greatly appreciated. However, a popular success could result in many re-recordings of the same piece, all at the agreed rate, which is presumably how George Johnson made his fortune. This was necessary because no satisfactory duplication process existed, so each cylinder was unique. As early as 1891, Edison had indicated that he was thinking about a method of moulding cylinders from a die, and that he would develop it further if sufficient interest was shown. No interest of a financial kind was forthcoming, and Edison left things as they were. The only alternative was to transfer from a master recording to a blank cylinder, using a pantographic device that relayed the vibrations from playback stylus to the attached cutter. This, though, resulted generally in unacceptable losses of quality between the master and the copy.

The recording experts attempted to introduce an element of efficiency to the process by using several horns and machines simultaneously. In this way, an especially strong-voiced performer could create as many as twenty cylinders from one performance,[44] but there were problems with the set-up, not least of which was fraud. Early in his career, one company enlisted Russell Hunting to record one of his Casey skits, ten times at five dollars a go, with four horns capturing each take. After four takes, he was most surprised to spot a boy carrying a tray of twenty-four cylinders across the room, instead of sixteen. Rumbled, the company offered to make good the difference.

This, then, was the state of the record business in the early to mid-1890s. Columbia ruled the roost, while Edison languished in a state of considerable disarray. Gaisberg did not stay with Columbia for long, though. A German émigré elsewhere in Washington was about to make sure that the graphophone would not go short of competition in Edison's absence.

2 Tvinkle, tvinkle, little star

In the late nineteenth century, the American Dream was exemplified by the number of go-getting immigrants who came to the country and worked hard for a better life. Some became household names like the entertainer Al Jolson (born Asa Yoelson in Lithuania), who arrived in 1894, the bodybuilder Charles Atlas (born Angelo Siciliano in Italy), who arrived in 1903, and the songwriter Irving Berlin (born Israel Baline in Siberia), who passed through Ellis Island in 1893. Emile Berliner was another of these. Born in Hanover, Germany, in 1851, he emigrated to the United States of America at the age of nineteen, and took various menial jobs to fund his research. Like Edison, he found himself inspired by the invention of the telephone and strove to make improvements to it, along with Edison, concentrating on the microphone. However, unlike Edison, who handed his modification to Western Union, Berliner sold his development to the Bell Telephone Company, for whom he had worked as an inspector.

Some reports say Berliner's fee was a flat $50,000, others that it was $25,000 and an annual retainer of $5,000 a year. Either way and despite some doubts over technical merits of the Berliner carbon microphone,[1] the Bell subvention allowed the young German to give up his day job.

He began experimenting in recorded sound in 1884 and in 1887 he applied for and received his first patent on his disc machine, which traced sound waves laterally rather than vertically and which he called a 'gramophone'. One of his earliest recording was his rendition of 'Twinkle, twinkle, little star' in his heavy German accent. He gave the instrument its public debut at Philadelphia's Franklin Institute on 16 May of the following year. The first Berliner Gramophone was very crude, consisting of a hand-cranked turntable on a base board, which also supported a sound box and horn, with the workings all on show.

Edison, Bell and Tainter had all experimented with discs, but abandoned the format, largely because by the end of the disc, the surface area tracked by the stylus on each revolution was much less than at the start, with a corresponding drop in quality. The constant speed offered by cylinders was thought to be superior. Berliner got round the problem of side-end distortion simply by ignoring it. It remains a problem to this day.[2]

Having heard of Emile Berliner's experiments with disc records, Fred Gaisberg was 'only too eager to see him at work'. Neither, however, can have realized the importance of their first meeting in 1894 to the eventual history of the device that, in a confusion of proprietary brand names such as phonograph and graphophone, was coming to be known simply as the 'talking machine'. Many of the pivotal developments in the early history of the Berliner disc were Gaisberg-inspired.

At the time, however, Gaisberg's main concern was remaining in work. Columbia had a personal agreement with Lippincott, which had saved them from the Edison axe, but there was uncertainty that this caveat would continue to hold. The introduction to Berliner came from Billy Golden, one of Gaisberg's Negro singers, whose most popular recording had been 'Turkey in de Straw'. '[He] asked me one day … if I would go with him to see a funny German who had started experimenting with a flat-disc talking machine,' recalled Gaisberg in his memoirs.[3] Golden was right enough about Berliner being funny – Gaisberg's chief memories of the inventor were of his 'monkish frock' and his 'guttural, broken English'. His machine, however, was all too serious. Using a muzzle and rubber hose to record Golden's voice onto a zinc disc, the results 'astonished' both Gaisberg and the singer:

> Acquainted as I was with the tinny, unnatural reproduction of the old cylinder-playing phonographs [wrote Gaisberg], I was spell-bound by the beautiful round tone of the flat gramophone disc. Before I departed that day, I exacted a promise from Berliner that he would let me work for him when his machine was ready for development. A few months later, I received a postcard asking me to come and see him.[4]

Even in its earliest, simplest form, however, the gramophone had one advantage over the opposition. It was far louder. Gramophone masters were recorded on zinc discs covered in a thin layer of fat, through which the recording stylus cut a groove. After immersion in chromic acid, a groove of constant depth was left, strong enough to carry the sound box and needle across the record, unlike the cylinder machines.[5] Zinc was a necessity brought about by the fact that Edison and the graphophone controlled all of the wax recording patents, but it proved more robust and capable of handling greater volume.

However, for all of the system's advantages, Berliner still had a lot of work to do. One urgent task was to perfect a means of creating negative impressions of the master disc, so that copies could be pressed. Another was to find a suitable material for the finished product. By 1893, Berliner, assisted by his nephew Joseph Sanders, was getting somewhere. He had formed the US Gramophone Company – based at 1410 Pennsylvania Avenue N.W. in Washington DC – to administer his patents, he had worked out how to make disc stampers from the masters, and he had begun producing discs in vulcanite, a hard rubber. This material, however, proved prone to flat patches in the record surface, and, just as bad, bubbles of trapped air.

One difference between the cylinder machines and the disc alternative offered by the new company was that the gramophone was designed for domestic purposes, as a playback-only medium. The office dictaphone notwithstanding, home phonographs could, with a minimum of adaptation and a suitable wax blank, be used to make private recordings. In contrast, the gramophone could play only pre-recorded discs, and it made a virtue of this in its early publicity literature, asserting that the gramophone would never be tainted by amateur offerings. To this end, Gaisberg set about building a repertoire of recordings. Most of the old Columbia standbys joined Billy Golden in coming over to the new gramophone, including Dan Quinn, Len Spencer and Russell Hunting, who received $25 for five titles.

Artists were therefore released from the old production line methods of the cylinder companies, but there were no lucrative repeat sessions. Only one session was needed to produce as many discs as were necessary, and it was a considerable time before royalties began to enter the equation. Fortunately for them, exclusive artist contracts were a similarly distant prospect, so they generally continued to record for the phonograph as well.

Meanwhile, Berliner himself made the odd contribution to the catalogue, including one disc where he and Gaisberg played an auctioneer and his assistant trying to flog a piano of dubious origin. It wasn't all eccentric improvisation, though. Something resembling high culture made its entry onto the recording scene when Gaisberg discovered a tenor called Ferruccio Giannini working with an Italian touring company and persuaded him to make some records, beginning with a couple of arias from Verdi's *Rigoletto* – 'La donna è mobile' and 'Questa o Quella'. The famous American composer of marches John Philip Sousa also came over to the new machine, being one of the few to sign exclusively with Berliner.

That is not to say that Sousa was a wild enthusiast for the new medium. Roland Gelatt, in his pioneering history of the industry *The Fabulous Phonograph*, quotes an article written by the composer for *Appleton's Magazine*, in which his real feelings become plain. Sousa foresaw: 'a marked deterioration in American music and musical taste ... by virtue – or rather by vice – of the multiplication of the various music-reproducing machines'.[6]

The first list of discs – including Hunting's recording of 'Casey's First Experience as Judge' – was offered in April 1895, pressed initially in the troublesome vulcanite. Fortunately, an alternative came along. Vulcanite was also used in button-making, and it was Gaisberg who noticed that a company in Newark, New Jersey, by the name of Durinoid was having great success with an alternative button material. Their compound was based upon shellac – a resin produced from the secretions of the lac beetle – and after some experimentation, it proved ideal for Berliner's purposes.

Finding the financial backing to bring the gramophone to this point had not been easy. Although they were generally amused and intrigued by the device, speculators and venture capitalists proved unwilling to part with any money. Gaisberg thought he had found the answer in B. F. Karns, a retired Methodist minister of his acquaintance. Karns was trying to gain Congressional approval for a railroad scheme, and his dropping of names like Nelson Rockefeller and the banker J. Pierpont Morgan impressed Gaisberg.

Although Karns was able to extract $100 from Berliner, who could scarcely afford it, on the promise of effecting introductions to these giants of finance, the meetings never materialized. 'At each appointment for a demonstration to Rockefeller or Morgan the most devilish forces seemed to intervene to obstruct their appearance,' noted Gaisberg with the amusement afforded him by hindsight. 'Rockefeller's wife had measles or Morgan's wife was going to have a baby.' Gaisberg and Karns set off on a tour of demonstrations, and it was only on the last stop – Philadelphia – that any interest was shown. A consortium consisting of steel jobbers, a clothing manufacturer and a building contractor came up with $25,000. In late 1895, the Berliner Gramophone Company was established at 1026 Filbert Street, Philadelphia. In nearby Chestnut Street, Berliner opened a retail store, run by a well-born young New Yorker called Alfred Clark – who had begun his career with the North American Phonograph Company, before leaving to join the Edison Kinetoscope film company. A fifteen-year contract was signed with a salesman called Frank Seaman, to run a separate but dedicated sales operation called the National Gramophone Company. The gramophone was in business.

Following the resolution of his battle with the local agents in January 1896, Edison had returned to the fray with his Spring Motor Phonograph, retailing at $40. The absence of any corporate links between the Edison and graphophone interests meant that the fragile truce, which had prevailed since Lippincott's intervention in 1888, was off. The American Graphophone Company responded to the launch of Edison's spring-driven talking machine with a statement that declared every Edison phonograph, 'unless it indents in tinfoil', to be an infringer of its patents.[7] After a very public row, both sides appeared to have reached an accommodation in mid-December 1896, with Edison acknowledging the fundamental nature of the American Graphophone Company's wax recording patents, and the American Graphophone Company acknowledging Edison's many subsequent patented improvements. Unsurprisingly, the peace was shortlived. Columbia, sole agent of the American Gramophone Company, brought out a spring-wind graphophone retailing at a mere $25, and declared its contract with the defunct North American Phonograph Company still to be valid, thus allowing it to sell Edison merchandise as well as its own.

While, in 1897, Columbia was establishing a lavish headquarters in New York, Edison was having to mortgage his phonograph factory for $300,000 to pay off debts incurred in building up his other operations, which included a storage battery business and his film company. It was his 'home phonograph' of 1898 that finally put him back in the ring again, the Edison reputation guaranteeing good business in rural areas, while the more cynical city-dwellers plumped for the graphophone.

Although the Edison-Bell combine had fallen apart in its home country, it remained in operation in the United Kingdom. In 1898, a newly constituted company called the Edison-Bell Consolidated Phonograph Company took over British representation from the old Edison-Bell company. The man in charge was James E. Hough, a Mancunian who had been in the sewing machine business until the early 1890s. He eventually became Stephen Moriarty's sales manager before taking over totally. His early activities did not meet with Edison's approval. The great inventor regarded Hough as an infringer. Indeed, he had been served with a writ by the old company. By the late 1890s, though, he was trusted enough to be sold the UK rights to the Edison and Bell-Tainter patents for £40,000.

The new Edison-Bell company established itself with a large factory at Glengall Road in the south London suburb of Camberwell, and another plant in the centre of the capital at Gower Street, and began to enjoy a measure of success that had eluded its predecessors.

Although gramophones and their flat discs sold from the off, there were many ways in which the product could be improved. For example, while the cylinder machines offered spring-driven motors or even, in a few examples, electric power, Berliner's offering still required hand-cranking. Gaisberg thought he'd found the answer to this problem when he spotted an advertisement in a Philadelphia newspaper, placed by a man who made clockwork motors for sewing machines.[8] When Gaisberg arrived to inspect the merchandise, he found that the motor was too unwieldy for the gramophone. Fortunately, the young machinist who built the motors for the inventor, based over the river in Camden, New Jersey, felt sure he could come up with something more suitable.

Eldridge Reeves Johnson had been born in 1867 in Wilmington, Delaware. In 1886, he took employment at the Standard Machine Shop on North Front Street, Camden, an enterprise run by Captain Andrew Scull for the benefit of his son. The captain and his assistant worked successfully on the development of a book-binding machine, and Johnson became a partner in the business. Eventually, in October 1894, he bought out Scull's holding and became a sole trader.

Johnson encountered talking machines for the first time when a customer brought one to him for alteration. 'It sounded like a partially-educated parrot with a sore throat and a cold in the head, but the little wheezy instrument caught my attention and held it fast and hard,' Johnson later remembered. 'I became interested in it as I had never been interested in anything before.'[9] So, when he was approached by Gaisberg, he was already enthused by the possibilities of the gramophone. The result was the first clockwork-driven disc machine. Joining forces with Alfred Clark, Johnson also developed a pick-up that gave improved sound quality – the Johnson-Clark Improved Soundbox.

As well as being a talented engineer, Johnson was a cosmopolitan and cultured young man. Even before his first contact with the gramophone, he was a music lover, attending concerts and opera performances when time allowed. On 2 January 1895, he wrote to his wife Elsie Fenimore Johnson:

> I went to New York last evening to hear [Dame Nellie] Melba and [Emma] Calve in the double bill of *Lucia di Lammermoor* and *Cavalleria Rusticana*. It was simply glorious. I sat from 8 to 12 in a stupor of delight only interrupted by the impatient periods between the acts. There was a large and handsomely dressed audience and many very beautiful women and they seemed to pay more attention to the music than to each other. This will I think give you an idea of the kind of opera it was.[10]

With such passions, it soon became clear that Gaisberg, Clark, Berliner et al had stumbled upon the right man.

Berliner wasted no time in opening a European front. William Barry Owen (1860–1914) had joined Seaman's National Gramophone Company almost at its inception, but by mid-1897, he was indicating an interest in going overseas, and so Berliner chose to send him to London to look at opportunities there. In July, Owen crossed the Atlantic, took rooms at the Hotel Cecil in the Strand and, with some samples of the merchandise, set about building a business from scratch. The name he chose for his venture was the Gramophone Company.

Although Owen was the Massachusetts-born son of a whaling captain, he had trained as a lawyer. But his main interest was gambling. From the outset, his willingness to take risks was a positive boon. Gaisberg wrote in his memoirs:

> Berliner could have selected no finer agent than Owen to exploit his invention. He was an opportunist of quick decision and a bold gambler. He would always call a *stand pat* in a poker game and his eyes would bulge as he laid a full house on the table. He brought to London an infectious enthusiasm and energetic leadership which I believe was quite new to the conservative English city man of that day.[11]

For all of his eye-bulging, his go-getting and the attention that he was able to draw to the gramophone, Owen found it hard to attract investors. The first to combine interest with cash was Trevor Williams, a London solicitor who had been approached for legal advice, but who decided to invest, offering £5,000 for a stake. Financially fortified, Owen enlisted an English salesman, Theodore B. Birnbaum, who spent much of the autumn of 1897 travelling around the country spreading the Berliner gospel.

The Gramophone Company was, at first, simply a sales agency for the American-made product. Owen purchased machine parts from Johnson, which were then assembled into finished machines in London, under the supervision of Johnson's associate, Belford Royal. In February 1898, Owen and Williams became Berliner's official British licensees. By April, the company had moved to permanent offices at Maiden Lane,[12] just off the Strand, and was ready to begin trading properly, with 3,000 machines for sale and 150,000 records from the American catalogue in stock. The venture was a success from the start, and Johnson struggled to keep up with demand.

In mid-1898, the decision was made to begin recording and manufacturing discs in Europe. Berliner sent Gaisberg and Joseph Sanders over on the Cunard liner *Umbria*, sailing from New York on 23 July. They landed eight days later, and Gaisberg headed straight for Maiden Lane with only a $25 bicycle and his recording gear, which he set up in the 'grimy' basement. Meanwhile, Sanders made for Hanover, where Berliner's brother Joseph was running the Telephon-Fabrik Berliner factory. Improbable as it might seem, Sanders erected a tent in which he set up an impromptu record-pressing factory while more permanent facilities were being built. From these makeshift beginnings grew the European disc business. In November 1898, the Berliners opened a German operation – Deutsche Grammophon Aktiengesellschaft.

Naturally, the catalogue was dominated at the beginning by American recordings, including selections by John Philip Sousa's band and trombone solos by his right-hand man Arthur Pryor. Russell Hunting also featured in the listings, with, among others, 'Casey as Doctor', 'Casey as Book Agent' and 'Casey at Living Pictures'. If the date inscribed on his earliest London recordings is to be believed, Gaisberg was up and running just three days after disembarking from the *Umbria*. The first recording artist was Syria Lamonte, performing 'Star of Twilight'. Lamonte, who went on to make a series of records for the company in its infancy, was discovered next door to the Maiden Lane offices at Rule's restaurant, where she worked as a barmaid. Quite possibly as a result of having called last orders a great many times, Lamonte had a voice robust enough to impress itself on the zinc disc. Then there was Luigi Denza's composition 'Funiculi Funicula', popular enough in its day to be recorded by several gramophone artists.

Another source of recording talent sprung from Gaisberg's passage on *Umbria*. He befriended a fellow passenger called Bert Shepard, who happened to be a music hall entertainer of some note. In return for teaching him some of the latest American songs, Gaisberg was able to extract a promise from Shepard that he would come to Maiden Lane and make some records. This he duly did, as well as enticing fellow turns like Gus Elen ('Half a Pint of Ale' and 'If It Wasn't for the 'Ouses In-Between'), Eugene Stratton (always billed as 'the dandy coloured coon' and best known as the man who popularized 'Lily of Laguna') and Dan Leno. Another artist from the halls was the clown George Mozart, who startled Gaisberg by performing for the recording horn in full make-up.

Recording techniques remained fundamentally as they had since Edison's first breakthrough. A diaphragm, usually made of thin glass, sent vibrations directly through the recording stylus onto the recording surface, in this case a zinc disc. Due to the limited frequency range of the system, some instruments were effectively unrecordable. String basses were replaced by brass instruments such as the tuba, while conventional violins were usually replaced with the Stroh violin – a device that substituted a directional metal horn for the usual soundboard and body. In person, it sounded reedy and thin, but on record it cut through.

Like the Stroh, accordions, melodeons and concertinas, the human voice was in the zone of comfort and singers with sufficient puff and projection recorded well. One such was W. H. Berry, who recorded for the English Columbia company from 1901, and dominated its popular vocal repertoire with selections like 'What I Have I'll Hold', 'Yo Ho! Little Girls! Yo Ho!' and 'That's How I Diddle 'Em'. '[O]ne must employ a loud and penetrating voice, with great smoothness of enunciation, and such things as gestures and facial contortions are of course useless,' he told *Talking Machine News* in May 1903:

> It is a most curious experience for a hardened singer (not sinner) like myself to have to sing the most funny of funny songs without the usual surroundings and embellishments such as stage, lights, audience, applause, laughter and encores. To have to stand with one's face in close proximity to a couple of fierce and greedy-looking horns, and in a most calm and cold-blooded fashion, to shout the most hilarious and mirthful song (or patter) in a voice more in keeping with a gentleman who sells coals, than a highly respectable and harmless humorist, is an experience of a most quaint and unusual nature.[13]

All of this was bearable for sound business reasons. The money from the recordings themselves was not substantial, but 'not only does it keep a singer in constant practice,' added Berry, 'also the wide circulation of his efforts is an excellent advertisement for a professional man'.

Unfortunately, most singers' natural choice of accompaniment would be from a piano, and pianos did not record well unless modified. An upright was preferable to a grand, as the soundboard would be facing the recording horn. The piano was reduced to its basic elements of keyboard, soundboard and frame, and placed on a pedestal, bringing it to the same height as the singer's head and the horn, so that the maximum sound could be captured. Maximum sound, but not maximum tone, for it was common to file the felt hammers down to the bare wood to increase volume. This is why all pictures of Gaisberg's Maiden Lane studio show an elevated piano.

An entertaining account of recording at the turn of the century can be found in the memoirs of Joe Batten, a teenage pianist who would later become a highly respected engineer, producer, conductor and arranger for Edison-Bell and Columbia. His first recording session took place in September 1900 with one of the miniscule cylinder companies in London:

> Musiphone ... was one of innumerable small recording companies scattered about Hatton Garden and the City Road. Knocking on the door and receiving no reply, I turned the handle and walked into the office, which was also the recording room. Here I was met by a verbose and blustering individual who demanded my business. This having been satisfactorily explained, the loquacious one introduced himself as Dan Smoot. He was an American, the first I had met.[14]

Batten 'had to climb four high wooden steps to reach the piano, which brought my head to within a few inches of the ceiling'. [The music was] held up by hand by anybody who had nothing else to do at the time.[14]

Being a cylinder session, countless renditions of the same material were required and Batten laboured for six hours with a baritone called A.H. Gee and a tenor called Montague Borwell, each alternating to provide recordings of 'Come into the Garden, Maud', 'The Diver' and 'The Soldiers of the Queen'. Unfortunately, progress was hampered by the fact that Batten could not see either singer, being obscured first by the piano's bulk and second by the fact that they had almost to stick their head into the horn to make any impression on the wax.

To make matters even more fraught, a battle raged throughout the day between Smoot and the warblers. The record man wanted Batten to hammer the accompaniment out *double forte*, while Gee and Borwell 'whispered appeals to "keep it down"'. Batten found himself agreeing with the singers and moderating his playing accordingly, but 'Smoot would clamber up the rostrum with the agility of a monkey and fiercely command: "Take no notice. Keep it loud. You're doing fine."' Batten admitted that:

> My brain, usually cool, detached and critical of what my hands were doing, was in a state of bewilderment, and I rattled off the accompaniments like an automaton. At the end of the day I was paid fifteen shillings for my six hours' work. I was asked to come again the next day, so the presumption was that I had given satisfaction.[15]

The Gramophone Company was incorporated as the Gramophone Company Ltd, a private limited company, in May 1899. At the same time, Alfred Clark – who had been in Paris for a few months – set up the Compagnie Française du Grammophone as a joint venture with Owen's London organization, to exploit the Berliner machine in France, Belgium, Switzerland, Spain and Portugal. Clark owned 26 per cent of the stock, with the Gramophone Company taking the remaining 74 per cent. By November, the Gramophone Company had taken a 60 per cent stake in Deutsche Grammophon and sent the salesman Birnbaum over to run the show. In addition, an Italian company had been established, run by the fraternal duopoly of Alfred Michaelis in Milan and his brother William in Naples.

To accompany these bureau openings, a roll-out of factories began across the Continent including Spain, France and Russia, which was run as a satellite of Berlin. The continental spread of the gramophone was aided by the first of the famous recording tours to be undertaken by Gaisberg and his fellow recording 'experts' (as sound engineers were then known), in this case, William Sinkier Darby.[16] Setting off in May 1899, they visited Leipzig, Budapest, Vienna, Milan and Dublin, making records as they went, in the hope of impressing the locals enough to make them buy gramophones. India, because of its close links with Britain, also became a very important market for the Gramophone Company. An office was opened in Calcutta in 1901, run by Thomas Addis, to sell discs supplied from Hanover. It might be thought that the main market in India was among the colonials and expats, but in fact the Gramophone Company had identified the potential of a market among the natives and were keen to exploit it. There was already some Indian repertoire in the Company's catalogue, albeit recorded in London, but in September 1902, Gaisberg, assisted this time by George Dillnutt, set off on a year-long expedition across Asia with horn and waxes, which garnered 550 recordings in Calcutta alone.

Although this quantity is impressive, Gaisberg was not struck by the quality. For one thing, the 'accompaniment to most songs was a simple missionary's organ', which 'produced a dull and uninspiring sound, and I soon came to loathe the instrument'. Moreover, the male singers who had been recommended had 'high-pitched effeminate voices', there being 'no admiration or demand for the manly baritone or bass'.[17] However, if Gaisberg thought Indian music was bad, he had not bargained on what he was expected to record in Japan. The work of a group of male singers favoured by the Emperor was described as 'impassioned declaiming' that 'sounded like a donkey braying'.[18]

Back home, Owen had made a non-musical acquisition that was to be of vital importance to the company. One day in 1899, the Gramophone Company was approached by Francis Barraud (1856–1924), an artist who had fallen on hard times after a training at the Royal Academy and a promising early career. He had painted a picture of his late dog, a fox terrier called Nipper, looking quizzically at a black-horned phonograph, which he had submitted for copyright. The painting had been titled *His Master's Voice*. It had already been offered to Edison-Bell, who had shown no interest at all, so Barraud visited Maiden Lane to ask for a fortnight's loan of a brass horn, much brighter than the black phonograph which currently appeared in the picture. He was introduced to Owen, who suggested that the machine should be replaced with a Berliner Gramophone, which Barraud did – to this day, a raised area of paint on the canvas shows where the old machine was painted over.[19]

When he saw the finished picture, Owen immediately offered Barraud £100 to include £50 for reproduction rights and £50 for Barraud's copyright. Perhaps surprisingly, he did not immediately put the picture to use as the Gramophone Company's trademark. After all, they already had one – the Recording Angel, designed at the company's foundation by Birnbaum. Instead, Owen hung the painting in the boardroom at Maiden Lane. Berliner, however, began to use it on records, copyrighting it as a US trademark in 1900.

The purchase of Barraud's painting had been one of Owen's better gambles. Unfortunately, another of his early punts nearly brought the company to its knees. Fearful that the gramophone was a fad, Owen acquired the manufacturing rights for the Lambert typewriter, and in July 1900, changed the company name to the Gramophone & Typewriter Co. Ltd, increasing market capitalization to £600,000. The keys of the Lambert were positioned around a circular dial, and were considerably less easy to operate than the QWERTY typewriter, which had been gaining ground since its invention in the 1860s.

Owen wrote a letter to Johnson on 1 July 1901, in which he said that it was ' written on the "LAMBERT" Typewriter, which we are using regularly in our Typewriting Dept. now, and it is giving very good satisfaction'[20]. Rather tellingly, there is, at that point, a marginal note by an unknown hand, which reads 'No!!!'[21] He believed that it was 'a very fine article to carry along with our other lines' and that 'the combination of the two lines ... will solidify our business very materially.' In 1903, all of the unsold machines were flogged as a job lot for £2,000.

Elsewhere in Europe, others were advancing the cause of recorded sound. In Paris, a pair of brothers installed a phonograph in their bar on the Place Pigalle in the hope of attracting more drinkers. The novelty worked and customers came in their droves. Most of them turned out to be as interested in the curious little machine as they were in their libation. The publicans in question, Charles and Emile Pathé, realized they might be on to something, and found an engineer in Belleville who was willing to manufacture replicas of the Edison machine that had caused the stir. Before long, they had become official Edison licensees for France, effectively taking on the business of the Compagnie Americaine du Phonographe Edison. Thus legitimized, 1894 saw the brothers opening a factory in Chatou, then a village (and now a sprawling Paris suburb). Initially, the plant employed 200 people, mostly concerned with turning out a cheap machine called 'Le Coq'. By 1903, however, the plant had expanded to twenty acres, enough to accommodate between 3,000 and 3,500 workers or, as Pathé Frères' London manager Jellings Blow explained at the time: 'Practically the whole of the inhabitants of Chatou.'[22]

Although it later moved to the factory site, the recording side of the Pathé business was initially based at the company's 98 Rue de Richelieu headquarters. Pathé Frères was an early entrant into the more exalted areas of musical repertoire, drawing on a ready supply of serviceable but far from famous singers from the various Paris opera companies. When it came to bagging bigger names, the company also had a trading alliance with the Anglo-Italian Commerce Company of Milan, an outfit that managed to record most of the top talent in that town. One of their artists was a young tenor called Enrico Caruso, who made a few cylinders for AICC in 1903. This business link meant that Pathé had the right to release AICC material in territories other than Italy. As Caruso became more famous, Pathé retained his AICC recordings in their catalogue, although the Italian company itself had long since folded. At the turn of the century, Pathé Frères began to expand outside France, setting up first in London. The brothers also, like their benefactor Edison, began to take a strong interest in cinematographic developments.

While the Pathé brothers were evidently serious about building a business, other gentleman amateurs played about on the peripheries. Chief among these was an Italian ex-cavalry officer called Lieutenant Gianni Bettini. Born in Novara, he had followed an undistinguished military career by marrying an American socialite, Daisy Abbott, and moving to the US with her. The pair set up home in the Sherwood Studios in New York, an apartment building on 57th Street and 6th Avenue with a large number of professional musicians in residence.

Bettini made up for his lack of forwardness on the battlefield by becoming a pioneer of the phonograph. He bought a machine in 1888 and, despite an almost complete lack of formal scientific training, began to seek ways in which the machine could be improved. The result was his micro-phonograph, and its main advantage over the existing equipment was the use of a much more flexible diaphragm.[23] Bettini also eschewed a single stylus in favour of a 'spider', with several legs connecting the diaphragm to a single needle. He argued that this compensated for any dead spots or uneven resonances on the diaphragm. If nothing else, it improved the bass response.

His social circles and his domestic situation meant that he was in a good position to expose the musical great and good of the era to his device. Yvette Guilbert, Dame Nellie Melba, Sarah Bernhardt, Emma Calve, Adelina Patti, Mark Twain and Lillie Langtry were all reputed to have recorded, privately, for the micro-phonograph. However, in 1891–2, the dilettante went into the record business, opening an office in the Judge Building at 110 5th Avenue. He offered the micro-phonograph attachment as a retrofit for existing machines. Meanwhile, his cylinders retailed at between $2 and $6, when Edison and the graphophone companies were selling their wares at 50c each. Each one sold was duplicated pantographically from one of his master recordings to order. To avoid the ire of his house guests, who had, after all, given their talents for free and for private consumption, his promotional literature boasted that '[w]e have in our collection many records from celebrated artists, not mentioned in this catalog,'[24] seemingly a promise of under-the-counter glories for those with the nous to enquire further.

Bettini applied for a patent on a duplicating system in April 1897, but his enterprise never really took off. He left America for Paris in 1902, selling his US mica diaphragm patent to Edison. Once in France, he established the Societé des Micro-Phonographes Bettini at 23 Boulevard des Capucines. There he continued business in a very small way, despite the coup of recording Pope Leo XIII shortly before his death in 1903. By 1908, he had given up, and by 1917, he was back in the US as an emissary of the Italian government, staying until his death. It is now hard to say exactly what Bettini did record, and how good his micro-phonograph was, as all of his original recordings perished in the Second World War, when the French warehouse they had been stored in since 1914 was bombed. Some copies came to light in Mexico City in 1945, followed by some more in a barn in Syracuse, New York, in 1952. None, however, were by the legends who were believed to have sung for Bettini.

As was the custom, the established companies began looking at Berliner's patents with great interest. Was there some way that an infringement could be established and upheld, to prevent the newcomer from trading or else forcing it to pay a royalty to one of the extant operators for the privilege? The job of catching Berliner out fell to Columbia's legal counsel, Philip Mauro. Mauro was a strange contradiction. On the one hand, he was a ruthless negotiator, who was perfectly willing to lie, steal and buy spurious patents to further the ends of his employers. On the other, he became, following a divine visitation in 1903, a devout and outwardly virtuous Christian. This did not deter him from continuing to pursue much the same path in business as he had in his Godless days. In the case of the gramophone, he seized upon the tone arm, moving freely, driven only by the groove on the disc. Was the 'floating stylus' not a central part of the Bell-Tainter patents? Did the Berliner arm not 'float'? If so, here was an infringement.

In the event, however, Berliner's worst enemy turned out to be within his organization rather than outside. Sales were the province of a separate company, the National Gramophone Company, run by Frank Seaman.

Seaman felt that his cut of the profits was too small, and that Berliner was over-charging for merchandise. Berliner, on the other hand, felt that he and Seaman had a fifteen-year contract, which should be honoured. Mauro must have had intelligence of Seaman's discontent, for he directed his infringement action not at Berliner but at his sales agent. If relations were as sour as they seemed, Seaman would be unlikely to have any loyalty to Berliner and would be quite happy to sell the inventor down the river as long as he could carry on making money.

This was, pretty much, what transpired. By March 1899, with the help of his lieutenant Orville la Dow and an ex-Edison man called Frank Prescott, Seaman had formed a new company, the National Gramophone Corporation, complete with a subsidiary called the Universal Talking Machine Company to run the organization's new factory in Yonkers. In October, Seaman placed his last order for Berliner machines, leaving the inventor with no way of selling his merchandise, due to the exclusivity of his contract with Seaman's old company. By the end of the year, the Yonkers factory was producing the Zon-o-phone, a far more ornate machine than the Berliner Gramophone, but identical in mechanical terms. In May 1900, Seaman caved in, admitting that Berliner's patents infringed Columbia's. Shortly after this, it was announced that Columbia and Seaman had reached an agreement 'for legal protection and commercial advantage'. Columbia, which had previously produced only cylinders, had both formats under its effective control, Seaman had a monopoly of the disc talking machine industry and Berliner had been frozen out of the business he had created.

Berliner, who had, in May 1899, combined his companies into the Consolidated Talking Machine Company of America, prepared to return to trading, Seaman's conduct having rendered the original, exclusive contract invalid. Leon Douglass was to be brought in from the Chicago branch to take over Seaman's sales role, but before Douglass could take up his post, Seaman had slapped an injunction on Berliner on 25 June 1900, preventing him from selling disc machines in the US. Within three months, Berliner had dismissed all of his staff.

Berliner may have had enough, but Eldridge R. Johnson, the engineer who had given the gramophone its motive power, was not willing to give up. For one thing, he had lost his livelihood and gained $50,000 of unsellable merchandise. In addition, he had been working continuously on various improvements to Berliner's invention. The norm had been to inscribe or emboss artist and title details directly into in the unused centre part of the disc. Johnson, however, was looking at more eye-catching alternatives. After some abortive experiments with stencilling, he developed a satisfactory means of fixing paper labels to the discs.

More critical, perhaps, was the development of the 'improved Johnson process of recording'. Berliner had fought shy of using wax for master recordings, believing that it would be an infringement of the Bell-Tainter patents. Johnson, however, believed that the quantum leap in recording quality that it offered over Berliner's zinc discs made it a risk worth taking. He is reputed to have been working on the process as early as September 1896, but it was March 1900 before he felt it was ready.

Johnson, aware that this was a trade secret of the highest magnitude, proposed to leave some of the more arcane elements of the process unpatented. This would leave them without protection, but the opposition would have to spend a very long time figuring out exactly how they worked before trying to come up with a non-infringing alternative. He also said to Owen that he hoped to keep those who had worked with him on the experiments within the fold.[26]

Unfortunately, Seaman had been in the loop at the start of Johnson's experimental programme, and knew full well what the engineer was working on. As late as April 1900, Johnson had suggested that Seaman would want to stay on side with Berliner, believing that he was finding the cost of manufacturing the machines higher than he had anticipated. However, as soon as Seaman's actions made it quite clear that a reconciliation was no longer possible or desirable, Johnson set about making sure that the errant salesman wouldn't have everything his own way. With Berliner on the ropes, Johnson established two new companies – the Johnson Sound Recording Company to take care of the new wax recording process, and, to sell the machines, the Consolidated Talking Machine Company. Two months after breaking out on his own, Johnson found himself in receipt of the inevitable suit from Seaman, who alleged that Johnson was conspiring with Berliner to 'defraud' him. Much was made of the fact that Johnson's new company and Berliner's old company had very similar names.

Johnson denied any ongoing connection with Berliner. He was telling the truth. From contemporary correspondence between the two men, it is obvious that Berliner was now very much on the peripheries and that Johnson was running his own show, with scant regard for anything the inventor said or suggested. Johnson stressed how much of the gramophone and, by definition, the Zon-o-phone was his creation, counter-alleging that Seaman was infringing his patents.

The case dragged on into early 1901, through which Consolidated continued trading and exporting materials to the Gramophone Company. By January, Johnson had, with Owen's approval, adopted the Barraud painting and its title *His Master's Voice* as his trademark, and was using it on his letterhead. Johnson was briefly diverted from his legal travails by a complaint from Owen about consistency of recording quality, to which he responded whimsically:

> My experience has been that the recording machine was a purely mechanical matter, and while it requires care and skill, it certainly cannot be classed with the difficult things, to get one to run accurately. On the other hand I have found that the condition of the recording material, the point and the diaphragm, to be decidedly difficult to handle, so difficult, indeed, that we have grown to avoid looking out for cross-eyed people, making records on Fridays, and walking under ladders. The common tendency to blame our short-comings to bad luck, has made us superstitious.[26]

Eventually, wearying of Owen's complaints, Johnson explained that he could doubtless come to a personally advantageous settlement with Seaman, but that this would leave Berliner's patents and the Gramophone Company's business in jeopardy. He simply wanted to be left alone to fight Seaman on his own mettle, something of which he felt confident. 'I have more suits against me than anyone else in the Eastern District of Pennsylvania,' he observed. 'I have had more litigation in the last five months than any man in that District, but so far I have won nine out of ten points, and believe that I can keep it up ... Seaman I think is practically put to sleep as far as stooping [sic] me is concerned.'[27]

Johnson's self-confidence was justified. In late March, the Philadelphia court found against Seaman. The vanquished salesman headed for Europe, where he could lick his wounds and plan, with Prescott, a concerted assault on the continental market. Johnson, meanwhile, immediately commissioned a new letterhead, advertising him as the 'manufacturer of the Victor Disk Talking Machine'. By November, Johnson was trading as the Victor Talking Machine Company.

Three companies –Victor, Columbia and Edison – now had the record industry to themselves, a set-up that was to remain largely intact until the Depression of the late 1920s.

3 The Jones boy

While all of this was going on, the world was continuing to innovate, not least in transportation. Within a couple of years, powered flight would be achieved by the Wright Brothers, but for the time being, the motor car was startling the public quite enough, the German Karl Benz having produced the first petrol-driven motor car in 1885. Driving (and, in time, flying) became a subject for topical humour, one of the most famous examples being the British comedian Harry Tate's music hall sketch 'Motoring', in which he, as a chauffeur, and his son have trouble starting a car. And, in a neat meeting of the two inventions, Tate recorded his sketch for Columbia, preserving some of the phrases that he gave to the world, including 'Goodbye-e-e-e' and the dismissive 'I don't think'.

Meanwhile, back at Camden, Johnson's victorious euphoria was short-lived. The care that he had taken in selecting and cultivating his research associates had not been enough to prevent a leak. At some point during Johnson's exploratory endeavours, probably around 1896, a young man called Joseph W. Jones had taken a summer job at the Berliner plant. While there, he latched on to Johnson's experiments and the fact that the engineer was keen to ditch the zinc system as soon as possible. It is probable that the seasonal interloper also came to understand that Johnson was not going to patent his system, partly to keep it secret and partly because he had been advised that wax recording was already enshrined in the Bell-Tainter patents.

Armed with this knowledge and the technical expertise that he had picked up from Johnson and his crew, Jones eventually wrote it all down and went for a patent himself – the application going into the US Patent Office on 19 November 1897. It took over four years for the patent authorities to decide whether Jones's claim was valid and original. In the interim, he had already consorted with Johnson's enemies, by working for Zon-o-phone as a recording engineer. In January and February 1900, Jones undertook a recording tour of Britain on Seaman's behalf, making discs with various music hall acts, particularly 'coster singers',[1] but on 10 December 1901, the patent authorities decided that 'his' disc-based wax recording system was sufficiently different to the Bell-Tainter offerings to justify issuing a patent. So it was that US patent number 688,739 was issued to Jones and J. A. Vincent of Philadelphia.

Johnson's demolition of Seaman and, with him, the expedient Graphophone/Zon-o-phone alliance had left the Columbia group without access to products in the disc format, something that troubled them in the face of the gramophone disc's increasing popularity. Johnson knew full well the strength of his hand at this point. In a letter to William Barry Owen, he commented:

> The Graphophone Co's little war on us has been very desastrous [sic] to them. They spoiled their own business and did not get any of ours. They have some rather dangerous fights ahead with the Victor Company, as they have gone a little too far with some of their counterfeiting. We will open the duel in a very few days now. I expect to secure some temporary injunction that will be at least very embarassing [sic] to them. They are in poor condition financially, and we feel almost sure of knocking them out. Their stock is going down in value at a terrible rate, the organization is discouraged and leaving them like rats.[2]

In the same letter, Johnson acknowledges Owen's interest in buying some or all of the Victor company, a topic to which the pair would return regularly over the next couple of years, although the proposal never came to anything. The English company was significantly less at risk from patent troubles, given its dominance in its home market, although the British trade paper *Talking Machine News* felt the need to sound a warning in November 1903:

> The history of the talking machine trade is one of patents and patents – and patents. Moreover, when the trade is not taking out patents, it is litigating ... Whilst we have every respect for the patentee's rights, we cannot but think that there is a little too much litigating amongst the manufacturers. If they spent one-half the money which they spend on the legal profession in improving the record, lovers of the talking machine would be the gainers and, we are equally sure, that the manufacturers themselves would not be the

losers ... There is, of course, no hope of a free board for many years to come, since, though old patents expire, new ones are continually coming into force; still in a few more years there should be a more satisfactory state of things than now, when every man's hand is against every man – and the devil take the hindmost.[3]

The strength of the British Empire also underpinned the Gramophone & Typewriter's early superiority over the American company. Not that they had the territory all to themselves. In India, various competitors had emerged, including Columbia, Edison and Pathé – all imported by the Valabhdas Runchordas wholesaling firm – as well as indigenous operators like Hemendra Bose, who had started in 1900 by making his own cylinders. Nonetheless, the G&T and Victor had, from the start, agreed to carve the world up into territories which one or the other would serve. Records originated by the G&T would be sold through Victor in the Victor-controlled territories and vice versa. So, the G&T took all of Europe and the British Empire, while Victor bagged North and South America, with the exception of Canada, where Berliner had set up the Berliner Gramophone Co. Ltd to make discs and machines. Victor also took the parts of Africa and Asia which weren't British possessions, including the various Dutch, French and German colonies. From a population point of view, Europe – at 447 million in 1902 – was comparable to Victor's holdings in Asia and Oceania – which served a potential audience of 476 million people. In terms of revenue, however, there was no contest. In 1902, total foreign trade in Europe – that is to say imports and exports – was estimated to be worth $16.43bn, while Victor's Asian and Oceanic territories were worth just $762.9m. The G&T's territories contained a total population of 800 million people in countries with an approximate annual foreign trade figure of $18.66bn. The Victor company served only 100 million less, but the countries that they lived in could muster only $4.8bn in foreign trade.

For all of their territorial advantages, the English company soon lost ground to its American partner on one matter – the use of Barraud's *His Master's Voice* painting as a trademark. Johnson had been using the dog and trumpet on his letterhead since January 1901, when he was still trading as the Consolidated Talking Machine Company. In June, he had written to the gentlemen at Maiden Lane, asking whether he could 'secure undisputed title to the use of the picture'[4] in his trading territories. Others had started using the image illicitly to promote their own business and he wanted to put a stop to it.

A transfer of rights duly took place and Johnson began using it on his records almost immediately. With hindsight, it is perhaps surprising to note that the G&T chose to stick with Birnbaum's Recording Angel, but they did, although the original painting remained in London in the Gramophone & Typewriter's board room. Giving the lie to the frequent suggestion that the Gramophone Company never properly recompensed Francis Barraud for his creation, the artist was enlisted to paint a replica of his work for Johnson's use, at a cost of £35.[5] In addition, from 1919, the two companies using the trademark clubbed together to pay the ageing painter an honorarium of £250 a year. This rose to £350 in March 1924, but Barraud enjoyed the increase only partially, as he passed away that August, aged sixty-eight.

Although this meant that everything was in place for Johnson to prosper, he had reckoned neither on the Jones patent application coming to fruition, nor on the opportunism of Columbia's legal counsel Philip Mauro. Mauro, upon hearing of Jones's success, realized that if Columbia could act quickly enough and gain control of the rogue patent, they would not only be able to re-enter the disc business, but also control it.

Columbia were desperate to have a piece of the disc business, so much so that in December 1901, the company's European manager Frank Dorian made overtures to the Gramophone Company about stocking their lines. Happily for Mauro and his employers, Jones proved willing to sell when Columbia offered an enticing $25,000. The possession of the Jones patent allowed Columbia to claim that they were the originators of the wax-recorded master disc. Working with amazing speed, the first Columbia disc graphophones were ready for the market in January 1902, with a range of three models, from $15 to $30. Seven-inch discs retailed at 75c and longer 10-inch recordings retailed for $1.

Gallingly, Johnson and Victor had become infringers, despite having been the true originators of everything included in the Jones patent. As part of the settlement he had been forced to turn over details of all of his methods for the making of disc records. This was a very curious move, as Columbia was claiming to be the inventor of the disc, and thus well aware of all aspects of the methodry.

Unwilling in the short term to risk another tedious and expensive legal battle, Johnson decided to swallow his pride and license his own invention from the usurpers. This was simply a 'matter of insurance', and it allowed him to carry on trading. Victor was already a large business concern. In the year to September 1901, it posted a net profit of $180,000. The following year, this was close to $1m, a huge sum for 1902, when American farm labourers earned less than $200 a year, while their British counterparts got by on £46 per annum. Apart from the domestic business, half of his production was going to Britain. He and Douglass had also pulled off quite a coup by enlisting Cal Child – already as much of an industry veteran as it was possible to be – as their head of recording, an appointment that lasted until his retirement in November 1923.

While Columbia had their victory in the short-term, Johnson's licensing of their system bought him some time to regroup and begin wresting his rightful patents back from the opposition. He began by suing Columbia for aspects of their disc system that infringed Berliner patents, which he had bought from the inventor. It was to be a long struggle, however. Johnson did not regain full control of his inventions until 1911.

Like every other company, Victor's repertoire in its earliest years was provided by largely second-rate performers, whose voices were more cutting than they were subtle, thus being suited to the crude recording system. The company's male vocal recordings emanated mainly from a single young baritone from Brooklyn called Emilio de Gorgoza, although they were issued under various noms-de-disque, such as Signor Carlos Francisco, Herbert Goddard and M. Fernand. Columbia upped the ante with their Grand Opera range of records, which featured the stars of the Metropolitan Opera House in New York, such as Edouard de Reszke and the soprano Marcella Sembrich. Quality came at a price, however. Sembrich's going rate for three discs was $3,000 while de Reszke took a comparatively modest but still far from shabby $1,000 for the same output. As a result, Columbia had to charge a premium price for the finished 10-inch discs, settling on $2 a go, a decision that proved disastrous for sales volume.

Victor responded initially by importing some of the very fine recordings made by Gaisberg and his associates in Europe, the quality of which had been signposted by the use of a red label on each disc. Then, Victor began to enlist better performers for its own sessions and began to develop the red label idea further, creating the Red Seal series. Columbia tried to get in on the red label act as well, but representations from Victor and the G&T soon forced them to retreat and put standard black labels on their higher-class discs. A small, high-ceilinged room in the Carnegie Hall complex was leased as a studio and pressed into service for the first Victor Red Seal session, with Australian contralto Ada Crossley, on 30 April 1903. The room ultimately proved unsatisfactory, and within a couple of months, operations had moved to 234 Fifth Avenue, before shifting to new accommodation at the Camden factory in 1907. As Columbia withdrew hurt from the high-price market, Child was able to scoop up performers like Sembrich and sign them to exclusive contracts, putting the discs out at various prices north of $1.50.[6]

Just as Child and Johnson were getting underway with their campaign to raise Victor's standards and profile, a calamity struck the company. In April 1904 a fire took hold of the Camden plant and caused considerable damage to the record manufacturing areas. In response to obviously concerned communications from London, Johnson cabled back that the fire had not started in the building, that the steam plant was unharmed, that the jigs and most of the tools had been saved and that the machine shop could be 'started as soon as temporary roofing can be erected'.[7] The assembling rooms, the shipping department and the nickel plant were, however, a 'total loss'. Johnson had arranged alternative premises, leasing – aptly enough – a former match factory. Despite the upheaval, Johnson was confident that he could 'make up lost time before next season'. A fortnight later, Child wrote a personal note to William Barry Owen to reassure him that '[t]hings are looking a little brighter every day and although the fire was a terrible blow I think the lost ground will be rapidly made up'.[8]

While Victor was dealing with fires, its UK counterpart was having to cope with increased competition in the form of the Edison-Bell company. By 1903, the company had a staff of 200, a head office in Charing Cross Road and factories at Gower Street and in Peckham, just off the Old Kent Road. At its busiest, the company was turning out 60,000 records a week – all cylinders, until Bell Discs ('Ring out loud and clear' ran the slogan) were introduced to the catalogue in 1908. While a 150 per cent sales increase, from £80,000 to £200,000 in 1901–2 looked impressive, it paled alongside the £1.5m in revenue that the company notched up in the first seven months of 1902–3, partially fuelled by a general growth in the record industry.

All of this was achieved without the help of Stephen Moriarty. James Hough had been in sole charge of the company since the turn of the century, Moriarty having left the organization that he had done so much to shape and make independent. Hough's bluff and bullish Lancastrian management style worked well for the company and, with some prescience, he saw the amazing expansion of 1902–3 as only the start of the industry's growth. The company was expanding its artist roster, with seventy-eight recording personalities on its list by May 1903. However, Hough argued that cheaper merchandise would not be playing any part in this growth, with the company's most affordable machines already producing low margins:

> We list our cheapest machine at ten-and-sixpence. Our cheapest Edison is two pounds fifteen shillings. I think that will prove to be the bed rock in point of price. When you can buy a well-made phonograph, with recorder, in a mahogany case for two pounds fifteen shillings, I do not see how they can go any lower, when you consider the cost of production.[9]

At this stage, although talking machines were big business, it would have been a very bold man who decided to open a shop selling nothing but records. Shops selling musical instruments and sheet music were natural contenders to carry a selection of talking machines and records, and some were quick to see the potential. However, records and machines were also sold by retailers of other, less obviously connected goods as a sideline. As early as 1898, the Columbia Graphophone Company was targeting cycle shop owners:

> We are confident that the sale of graphophones and supplies in connection with your bicycle business will make your establishment profitable every month of the year... The sale of graphophones would involve no additional store expenses ... [and] would be especially brisk and profitable in the months when the bicycle business is dull.[10]

Columbia failed to make clear what evidence it had for this curious synergy. Certainly the shopkeepers themselves took some convincing at the outset. As Columbia salesman Joseph Boam told *Talking Machine News* in October 1903:

> [T]he early work was not without its difficulties. Indeed, it was as a matter of friendship more than as a business transaction that one or two houses consented to take the machine ... I once called upon a music dealer in a large way of business in Nottingham, and asked him if he would kindly allow me to show him a graphophone. 'Talking machines,' he exclaimed, 'I would not stock them if you gave them to me.

Boam's luck seemed to be out, but a customer appeared, asking if the 'conservative British tradesman' in question stocked records. The shopkeeper answered that he didn't, but the Columbia rep asked for and gained permission to demonstrate his wares: 'I took out the machine, a 25/- one, and fixed on a record. When it was through, the dealer opened his eyes; all he said, however, was that he thought the record very good, and this somewhat grudgingly, as though he assented against his will.'

The chance intervention of a record hunter led to a small speculative order from the music shop owner, which proved to be a sound business move. 'No one was more surprised than he was at the result,' noted Baum. As it transpired, 'so great was the demand which followed ... that his subsequent orders ... could not be fulfilled fast enough for him.'

Although it might have impressed that one dealer, Columbia's 25-shilling machine was, in the main, rather looked down upon by prospective talking machine retailers. As wary as the retailers were, though, the reps seemed to have a genuine and almost religious enthusiasm for the wonder of the age. 'From the first I felt absolutely convinced of the future that lay before the machine,' explained Boam. 'This belief strengthened as my experience grew, so that, when I was offered a salary and a commission, I preferred to rely on commission only.' A little preparation, he said, paid dividends: 'Next to having a good article to offer is to know how to handle it'.[11]

In the long term, Columbia (and the faith of men like Boam) was proved quite right. Of the general retailers who began offering records, a disproportionate number were bicycle shops, and many continued with this line of business until the middle of the twentieth century. While the philosophy of most of the companies was that any sales outlet was a good sales outlet, the Gramophone & Typewriter stuck out on this issue, having instead appointed a select band of approved and designated retailers.

Columbia had seen the benefit in being what would now be known as a 'multi-platform' operator. Edison, however, had remained loyal to the cylinder, his fervour increased by the fact that he had at last perfected a method of mass-producing the records without loss of sound quality. This, he thought, would enable him to catch up with the gramophone disc. The idea was, as we have seen, not a new one. His first British patent contained a vague assertion that moulded, mass-produced duplicates of recordings were a future possibility. Then, on 30 June 1888, he applied for a patent on a non-pantographic duplicating method. This involved vaporizing metal in a vacuum as a means of rendering the record surface conductive, which would then be plated and when backed by heavier metal, used as a mold for making duplicates.[12]

Sadly for the progress of the cylinder as a viable format, this and subsequent experiments proved problematic, not least in the matter of shrinkage following the removal of the cylinder from the heated mould. Undeterred, Edison pressed on, as did others. A Frenchman called Lioret developed and patented a celluloid moulding system in 1894, but he had problems with consistency. Meanwhile, in 1899, Thomas A. Lambert of Chicago brought forward a moulding system which involved the application of graphite powder to the wax master to make it conductive enough for electroplating.

Edison had applied for a patent on his own moulding system in 1898, but it was not granted until 1902. Barely three years later, this patent was declared void on the basis that Edison had been using the system for nine years before patenting it. He argued that any moulded cylinders made in this period had been purely experimental and not for commercial use, although given Russell Hunting's experiences with over-production some years earlier, it is possible that a few were issued secretly to test the market. The outcome of this decision was that the Lambert patent prevailed and Edison was barred from producing any celluloid cylinders, a severe setback to his business plans, as the new material was much more robust than the old wax.

It was in wax, or to be more precise, a brittle form of metallic soap, that Edison was forced to produce his first commercial range of moulded cylinders. The records were issued under the brand name 'Edison gold-moulded record', each coming in a stout cardboard tube bearing a picture of the man himself. Reverting to the standard diameter after problems with the larger 'concert' cylinders, the repertoire remained constrained by the two-minute playing time of the format, which ruled most of the classics out. The choice was further hampered by Edison's insistence on retaining complete control of the recording programme – a state made undesirable by his idiosyncratic musical preferences and his partial deafness. As a result, the catalogue was dominated by the usual comedic corn and the martial parpings of Arthur Pryor's band.

One exception came in June 1908, as the United States prepared for a presidential election. The Democratic candidate for the White House, William Jennings Bryan ('the Great Commoner'), was enlisted to make a series of ten records, enshrining his pronouncements on the hot topics of the day. These included 'The Railroad Question' (Edison cylinder number 9,916), 'The Trust Question' (9,917), 'Guaranty of Bank Deposits' (9,921) and 'Immortality' (9,923). The results were described by the *Edison Phonograph Monthly* as 'among the plainest and most natural records we have ever turned out. No one who has ever heard Mr Bryan speak will fail to recognize all of the wonderful charm of voice and manner for which he is famous.'[13]

Edison's decision to record Bryan seems not to have been politically motivated. He and his family were Republicans, with the notable exception of his son Charles, who was the Democrat governor of New Jersey between 1941 and 1944, as well as running the family business. Bryan had tried unsuccessfully for the job twice before, losing to William McKinley in 1896 and 1900, but if he thought that his recording debut would give him the edge over the opposition, he was in for a shock. By September, the Republican candidate for the presidency, William Howard Taft, overcame an initial reluctance to get involved in the recording business and made ten cylinders of his own. Again these were straightforward speeches on matters of policy, except for number 9,997, which concerned the subject of 'Irish Humor'. 'It is of the after-dinner type, at which Mr Taft has no superior, and is delivered in his most affable voice,' crowed the *Edison Phonograph Monthly*. The records certainly made some kind of impact. One American paper saw fit to borrow the Nipper concept for a cartoon showing the Republicans and the Democrats respectively as an elephant and an ass listening to their respective candidates' records. Whether they had any effect on the outcome of the election is unknown, but Bryan lost once again, with this, his last attempt.

Bryan's swansong in public life was his involvement with the Scopes trial of July 1925. Tennessee had, three months earlier, passed the Butler Act, which outlawed the teaching of the theory of evolution in the state's schools. John Scopes, a teacher who flouted the new law, was arrested. The anti-evolutionist Bryan offered himself as State counsel for the ensuing hearings, at which monkeys and human beings with simian tendencies were paraded as evidence, although he did not prepare his own brief. Who did? Step forward, Philip Mauro. After eight days, the Court found in favour of the State and fined Scopes $100. Bryan died of a heart attack five days after the conclusion of the trial.

In November 1908, Edison launched the four-minute Amberol wax cylinder, which used closer-spaced grooves to fit more onto a standard length cylinder. The new product was prompted by the release of the new 6-inch graphophone cylinders, which offered a similar extension in playing time. A problem with the Amberol records soon emerged. The narrower groove pitch resulted in a product that deteriorated after far fewer playings than its predecessor or its celluloid counterparts. The easily damaged records did a lot of harm to Edison's reputation. Mercifully for Edison, celluloid became more freely usable when Thomas Lambert's company went bust, and so he was able to follow up the ill-fated Amberols with a new range – the Blue Amberol record – made of blue celluloid with a plaster of Paris core.

Outside the US, Edison's phonographic business was a little confusing. The Edison-Bell Consolidated Phonograph Company continued to use his name, although his involvement with the company, always limited, was now non-existent. Indeed, in 1904, Edison's National Phonograph Company – under the chairmanship of George Croydon Marks MP – had opened its own factory in the north-west London suburb of Willesden, with additional large premises in the Clerkenwell Road, where the record business was beginning to congregate. In 1905, Edison issued a circular, stating that the name Edison was the exclusive property of the National Phonograph Company. Edison-Bell, now owned and run by James Hough, responded by pointing out that it had purchased all of Edison's patents 'relating to the modern Phonograph' for £40,000 some time before and that 'in the purchase deeds of this transaction it was agreed that the first word of its trading name should be Edison'.[14] The result was that both parties continued to use the Edison name.

The success of the Columbia Indestructible Record – the type of cylinder that had inspired Edison to launch the Amberol – was such that the company found demand for its old products dwindling fast. A clearance of the obsolete stocks at rock-bottom prices was thought necessary. In an April 1909 bulletin to its dealers, Columbia announced that the new product had proved itself:

> We shall quit making XP wax cylinder records. On and after 5 May you may cut the XP cylinder record price (with the exception of vocal records in foreign languages, on which former list and trade prices must be maintained), to any figure you please, from 15c up.
>
> Fill your windows! Advertise! Make it a killing! Clean out your stock and

make it an out-and-out bargain sale – it will bring a stream of people into your store, and that is good business by itself...

If we were in your place, we would make every sale a quick one, and hand the XP cylinder records over in a take-them-or-leave-them way without taking time to play selections for demonstration. But don't lose that splendid opportunity to switch every caller over to a demonstration of the Columbia Indestructible Records.

Such was Columbia's zeal that it even allowed its dealers to utter the previously profane E word:

If you let the Edison users in your town know that Columbia cylinder records will fit their Edison machines, as well as Columbia machines, you will not only move your stock quickly but have a first-class line on a string of good prospects for the Columbia Indestructible Record later on...[15]

Not much later on, however, the Columbia Indestructible Record went the same way as the XP wax cylinder. In June 1912, Columbia abandoned production of cylinder records altogether in favour of discs. Apart from in France, where the early impetus gained by the Pathé brothers had established a healthy market for tubular records, the days of the cylinder were, to all intents and purposes, over. Only Edison continued producing them on a noticeable scale, and would continue to do so until he left the talking machine business altogether a couple of years before his death. However, shortly after Columbia's exit from the cylinder market, even he bowed to the inevitable and launched a range of discs.

Partly because of his ongoing belief that celluloid was the answer, through a desire to avoid infringing the rival patents and, no doubt, through sheer cussedness, Edison came up with discs that were very different to the Berliner, Johnson and Jones type of record. For starters, they were half-an-inch thick, the celluloid playing surfaces being bonded to a stout core made from a wood/flour composite. Then there was the fact that the grooves were, like the cylinders, cut vertically (hill and dale), rather than laterally (zig-zag). Perhaps the most important detail, however, was that instead of using steel needles that needed replacing after each play, the accompanying machine used a permanent jewelled point, which allowed for a higher fidelity of sound. Because of this, the product was branded as the Edison Diamond Disc.

Although Eldridge Johnson was able to dismiss the Edison disc player as 'so clumsy in construction that the advantages ... [of] the fixed, or jewelled, reproducer will not, according to my best judgment, impress the average purchaser as being superior to our system of changeable needles' the Diamond Disc itself was another matter:

> The disturbing factor ... is the unquestionable fact that the Edison disc is infinitely better than any phonographic disc heretofore manufactured; and while I feel that, for general results, our gramophone record is still superior, there is no doubt that they beat us in some things and that, in the hands of more progressive people, a disc similar to the Edison would be formidable competition, and this is exactly what I fear because Edison will demonstrate to other manufacturers the possibilities.[16]

In the event, no licensing of the Edison system took place, and Johnson's hunch that the Diamond Disc would not realize its true potential under its inventor was proved right.

Before it died entirely, however, the cylinder business managed to make the beginnings of a reputation for a young man who would come to be a major record industry figure. Louis Saul Sterling was born in New York in 1879, the son of a not especially prosperous accountant. In 1904, he moved to England, taking up employment with the Gramophone & Typewriter's Zonophone division. He became manager in October 1904, but resigned only a month later. The reason became clear in December when he registered the Sterling Company Ltd to manufacture talking machines. Three months later in February 1905, the Sterling Record Company was established at Bishop Road in east London's Cambridge Heath area. One of the board members of the company was Charles Stroh, the inventor of the horned violin, while Russell Hunting ran the recording department.

Hunting had worked as a recording engineer and as a performer, an odd mixture for this time, nearly seventy years before Todd Rundgren. He had also done a stint as editor of the *Phonoscope*, the talking machine industry's first trade journal. He followed this by becoming recording director for Edison-Bell, before joining Sterling. Having forged a great reputation on both sides of the Atlantic, it soon became obvious that he was a bigger draw than his enterprising young compatriot, and in April, the company was renamed the Russell Hunting Co. Ltd. The records produced by the company, however, were branded as Sterling Moulded Records, a convenient way to namecheck the founder and ape Edison's 'Gold-Moulded' epithet.

Early signs for the company were good. In January 1906, it announced that it had notched up 1m sales in just twenty-two weeks. The year to July 1907 saw 3 million Sterling Moulded Records being sold. In 1908, however, there was a drop, and in May it was announced that Sterling & Hunting Ltd was increasing orders for Fonotipia and Odeon discs, as well as Odeon machines. It was stressed that this company had no connection with the Russell Hunting Co. Ltd, which seems to have fallen into abeyance. Hunting then left to become director of recording for Pathé Frères.[17] What had caused the company's collapse? A general slump in the popularity of cylinders is likely to have had an effect. By November 1908, advertisements were appearing in the trade press offering 500,000 Sterling records – 'the whole of the manufacturer's stock' they claimed – at a rock-bottom $5^1/_2$d each for 'shorts' and $6^1/_2$d each for 'longs'.

Sterling, however, re-emerged in December 1908, this time as a disc magnate, having been appointed managing director of the newly founded Rena Manufacturing Co. Ltd, which had its offices at 27–9 Worship Street in the City of London, near most of the other companies. Rena distinguished itself by issuing a new kind of double-sided disc, retailing at 2/6, sixpence less than Columbia – claiming 'every record' to be 'a picked one', suggesting that it had been hand-selected by experts. From the start, the company had close ties to Columbia's UK arm, the records being pressed by the larger company, which also licensed some of its catalogue to the upstart. In less than a year, Columbia had bought Rena, making Sterling MD of the British company and adopting the Columbia-Rena branding for its main record label.

Throughout the first few years of the new century, the Gramophone & Typewriter expanded rapidly. In late 1901, the company had moved to a large building on London's City Road, having outgrown what William Barry Owen regarded as 'the old rabbit warren' at Maiden Lane. The company's turnover grew from £342,218 in 1901–2 to £685,593 the following year. Net profits jumped by a similar proportion, from £137,268 to £253,285. In 1903–4, however, revenues took a drop to £500,505, although profits did not decline quite so sharply, falling to £211,750. A number of factors had sent the company into reverse, not least the failure of the Lambert typewriter and the resulting financial write-off. The whole debacle put Owen in a difficult position, but he still felt confident enough of his acumen to deserve to be paid a proportion of the company's profits. His fellow directors disagreed, and refused. He then resigned, being replaced as managing director by Theodore Birnbaum.

Another cause for the slide was increased competition in Europe, most notably from the reconstituted Zonophone organization. In March 1901, Frank Seaman and Frederick Prescott had registered the International Zonophone Company in New Jersey, and two months later, Prescott had set sail for Europe to set the company up in the territory it was intended to serve and assume control of it, as managing director. Seaman remained 'a principal stockholder',[18] but remained at home in the United States. Joined by an expatriate recording engineer called John D. Smoot – aka Dan Smoot, who had been resident in Europe for a couple of years in the employ of the Musiphone cylinder operation, and who had made Joe Batten's first recording experience so memorable – Prescott took premises in Berlin at 71 Ritterstrasse and soon built up a network of agencies and licensees across Europe. These included Ch. & J. Ullmann Frères in France and the Pathé-affiliated Anglo-Italian Commerce Company in Italy, both glad to get a piece of the gramophone action to add to their cylinder businesses.

The new continental entrant made a speedy start, issuing its first catalogue in June. It offered the usual burlesque comedy and light musical items, but it soon began recording opera singers, while its AICC connection gave it access to the Italian company's Caruso recordings. By the time Johnson had demolished its parent, the National Gramophone Company, in the courts, Zonophone was importing its wares into Britain through Nicole Frères Ltd of London, and the goods were finding considerable favour with dealers and their customers. The next step was to record and release British repertoire, which the company had in hand by the start of 1902.

Competition from Seaman and Prescott was just what Gramophone & Typewriter had feared, and even their pre-emptive registration of the Zonophone name in the UK was not enough to spike the interlopers' guns. There was only one answer and, on 6 June 1903, it acquired the International Zonophone Company and its sister companies, the Universal Talking Machine Company and the Universal Talking Machine Manufacturing Company, both of which passed into the ownership of Victor. From 1904, ensconced at 81 City Road near the new G&T building, Zonophone was used by its new owners as the brand for a cheaper line of records.

It was a shame that such ructions and upheavals were marring the business side of the company, for on the recording side, Fred Gaisberg and his team were making great strides. Major artists were starting to take the new invention seriously and were coming around to the idea of making recordings. In these non-exclusive days other labels, including AICC, recorded Enrico Caruso, but it was Gaisberg's discs of the Italian tenor that made his recording reputation.

The recording experts were making regular sorties all around the world, recording indigenous repertoire in the hope of opening up new markets for the gramophone. Fred Gaisberg and William Sinkler Darby's first three-month recording tour of Europe, beginning in May 1899, was followed in 1900 by a Russian excursion. Here, overtures were made to the great bass singer Fyodor Chaliapin, but he was 'dizzy with success and would not respond to our humble offers'.[19] Eleven years later, Chaliapin did respond and became one of the great stars of the gramophone's early history. Meanwhile, Gaisberg became acquainted with the rum bunch who were forging the Gramophone Company's destiny in that vast continent. Initially, the responsibility fell to three enterprising retailers – Blumenfeld, Raphoff and Lebel. Almost as soon as he had arrived, the three were trying to take the American into their individual confidences. Lebel was not to be trusted, said Raphoff, because he would 'cheat his own father', while Lebel reciprocated with the intelligence that Raphoff had been transported to Siberia for seducing a schoolgirl, being freed only because of the amnesty on the Romanoff Cemetery. Raphoff was, Gaisberg concluded, 'a brilliant man and a true artist, but a devil for intrigue and foxiness'.[20]

Of all Gaisberg's overseas trips, his 1902 jaunt to Italy is perhaps the most important. Although his main quarry, Pope Leo XIII, eluded him, two other personalities captured by Gaisberg on this trip stand out as significant. One of these was Alessandro Moreschi, the last great *castrato* singer.[21] In recording the voice of Moreschi, Gaisberg was particularly timely. The *castrato* tradition in opera had been effectively dead for a century, the Papal ban on women stage performers having been revoked in 1798. Meanwhile, the practice of castration for non-medical reasons was outlawed in the Papal States in 1870, when they were taken over by Italy. By the turn of the century, the last redoubt of the emasculated soprano men was in the choir of the Sistine Chapel, and it was in 1902, the year of Gaisberg's visit, that Pope Leo XIII finally banned the use of castrati in church music.[22] It has been argued that Moreschi was not a particularly good example of the *castrato* style for Gaisberg to record – Patrick Barbier refers to 'the questionable vocal technique of this ageing singer'.[23] But, by the time Gaisberg got to Rome, he was the best there was, and for history's sake, it is better to have an imperfect example than none.

The other great Italian find of 1902 was Enrico Caruso. Although, as has already been noted, the recordists of the AICC also got to him, Gaisberg's recordings were technically far better. At the time Gaisberg recorded him, Caruso was on the way up, having notched up a couple of successes at La Scala in Milan, but he was not yet fully established. These records – combined with his debut at the Metropolitan Opera House in New York the following year – helped him acquire this status, while achieving something similar for the gramophone.

Born in Naples in 1873, the son of a heavy-drinking mechanic, Caruso became a mechanic's apprentice at the age of ten, and would have followed in his father's footsteps had it not been for the intervention of military service. He had sung in church as a boy, but the talent had lain fallow following an altercation with a jealous rival. The young Neapolitan was no use as a soldier, but his commanding officer realized immediately that his charge had a considerable vocal talent, and suggested that if he could persuade his younger brother Giovanni to join the Army in his stead, Enrico would be allowed to return to civilian life to pursue a singing career.

In 1895, he made his operatic debut in his home city at the Teatro Nuovo in Morelli's *L'amico Francesco*, and his first notable success followed in 1898 at the Teatro Lirico in Milan where he played the tenor lead in Giordano's *Fedora*. The following year he returned to perform in Naples, but vowed never to sing there again after audiences gave him the silent treatment. A similar vow followed in Barcelona in 1904, and in Budapest three years after that, when he was whistled by the punters. Oddly, these hostile responses came at a time when the Met was paying him $1,000 a performance, while an American agricultural worker was lucky to get $191 a year.

Despite his celebrity and riches, Caruso remained relatively free from arrogance. Some of the top-line classical artists who recorded in this era regarded the recording company representatives and the backing musicians as beneath them. Not so Caruso, who happily drew for Fred Gaisberg caricatures of himself singing into the horn, and exchanged banter with the band. 'Once he had to sing "Cujus animam" from Rossini's *Stabat Mater* many times before he was satisfied with the recording,' recalled his wife Dorothy. 'When at last it was finished, he drew a pearl stickpin from his tie and handed it to the exhausted trumpet player. "You merit reward," he said. "In the end I thought you would crack."[24]

According to Gaisberg's memoirs[25], the session, for which a Milan hotel room was turned into a makeshift studio, would not have happened if the gentlemen of the Gramophone & Typewriter back in City Road had their way. Caruso had, through his associate, Maestro Cottone, agreed to record ten songs for a total fee of £100, and Gaisberg claims that head office responded to his request for the money with a telegram instructing 'Fee exorbitant, forbid you to record.', and that he paid for the session himself.

Modern research by Dr Peter Martland has, however, indicated that Gaisberg's recollection is faulty. G&T managing director William Barry Owen had been with Gaisberg and Alfred Michaelis, the company's Milan representative, at La Scala for the performance of Alberto Franchetti's opera *Germania* that convinced the recording men to give Caruso a go. In the meticulously-maintained EMI archive there is no trace of the famous telegram. Instead, there is a paper trail showing that Caruso's fee was sent direct from London without a murmur. Whoever paid got a bargain. Gaisberg recorded ten arias, including 'Questa o quella' from Verdi's *Rigoletto*, without 'one *stecca*, blemish or huskiness…I was stunned with the ease with which a vast sum was earned…[a]ll were issued and I heard the figure of £15,000 net profit mentioned as a result of the venture.'

There was less travel involved in recording Dame Nellie Melba for the gramophone, which came to pass in 1904, but one of Gaisberg's colleagues, the company's sales manager Sydney Dixon, did have to trek to Monte Carlo as part of the wooing process. Meanwhile, several other executives must have felt that they'd been dragged across several continents by the Australian diva. Not least of these poor souls was Landon Ronald, who had been associate conductor at Covent Garden and accompanist to Melba, Adelina Patti, Pol Plancon and many others before joining the Gramophone & Typewriter as musical adviser in 1900. Gaisberg had spotted his talent, conducting a performance of *Florodora* at the Lyric Theatre, and regarded his engagement as 'like finding the Koh-I-Noor diamond … the agent who could bring us those unapproachables'.[26] He began the approach to this most unapproachable of all artistes, but she strung the record men along for several months before Dixon's flying visit clinched a deal. When the salesman eventually reached her, she was dining with the composer Camille Saint-Saëns. Dixon demonstrated a Caruso disc to the pair, and the composer's enthusiasm for the recording finally won Melba over.

Melba, whose real name was Helen Porter Mitchell, was an Australian, born near Melbourne in 1861. Finding Australia unsuited to her ambitions, she moved, in her twenties, to Paris for singing lessons. There she was discovered in 1887 by the operatic agent Maurice Strakosch, who signed her to an exclusive ten-year contract. When she agreed, without Strakosch's blessing, to appear as Gilda in *Rigoletto* at the Monnaie theatre in Brussels, her agent served an injunction preventing her from singing anywhere without his say-so. The headstrong Melba fled to Brussels anyway, where she was met with the news that Strakosch had died. Freed, she quickly became a star, making appearances at La Scala and the Met, before arriving in London in 1888 to make her debut at Covent Garden, where she performed almost every season until 1914. Her fame was such that the great chef Escoffier invented two dishes in her honour – Peach Melba and Melba Toast.

Being so feted, it was unsurprising that she should be a demanding individual. Firstly, she insisted on her first recordings being made in the drawing room of her mansion in London's Great Cumberland Place, the initial session taking place in March with an orchestra far too large to be comfortably accommodated in the room. Then, she held out on signing a contract until May, when the records were due to be released. Having learned their lesson from the near-miss with Caruso, the Gramophone & Typewriter responded to Melba's brinkswomanship with very favourable terms – a £1,000 advance against a royalty of one shilling on each record (price: one guinea) and a personalized lilac-coloured label. Within a month of their release, the discs had sold 2,000 copies and an association began between label and artist that would last until her retirement in 1926, her Covent Garden farewell performance being preserved by her recording company.

Later that year, Gaisberg received the call from Adelina Patti, who was ready – at the age of sixty-two – to record the highlights of her considerable repertoire. In early 1905, he, his brother Will and Landon Ronald set off to Craig-y-Nos,[27] the castle in Wales where Patti lived with her husband, the Baron Cederstrom. The Gaisbergs were to set up their apparatus and wait until Patti declared herself ready to make tracks. This went on for 'two full days', although the ice was broken socially shortly after arrival when Patti's housekeeper told her mistress that the two young men seemed perfectly pleasant and harmless. On this basis, Patti ordered that they be given champagne with their dinner to make up for any disappointment and delay. When Patti finally announced that she was in voice, recording began. On listening back to the first wax, she was quite overcome, as Landon Ronald remembered:

> She threw kisses into the trumpet and kept on saying: 'Ah! Mon Dieu! Maintenant je comprends pourquoi je suis Patti! Oh, oui! Quelle voix! Quelle artiste! Je comprends tout!' Her enthusiasm was so naïve and genuine that the fact that she was praising her own voice seemed to us all to be right and proper.[28]

Thus captivated, she set about leaving her best-loved arias to posterity, which she did in this and another set of sessions the following spring.

Not all of the characters encountered by G&T recordists were as salubrious as Patti. The unholy trinity of gramophone dealers in Russia had been superseded by a full-time manager – Norbert Rodkinson, the Russian-American son of a rabbi. Gaisberg described him as 'handsome and ruthless in business and love, his two absorbing pursuits' while noting, that he 'pretended to speak Russian well, but he stuttered so badly that he was never able to convince me of this claim'.[29] In fact, Rodkinson turned out to be rather more than just ruthless – he was utterly corrupt. Technically, Russia was run as a satellite of Deutsche Grammophon, controlled from Berlin, but distance and poor communications generally meant that the stammering Lothario was left to his own devices, which he exploited to the full. For instance, the printing of the company's Russian catalogues and brochures were contracted to a firm owned by Rodkinson himself, a detail that didn't emerge until after his departure.

Gaisberg got a flavour of Rodkinson's business methods when he visited his apartment, furnished mainly from the largesse of his customers. Surveying the array of gold and silver trinkets, Gaisberg recalled his colleague crowing: 'L-l-look, Fred, at the response to my birthday. Don't they l-l-ove me?' In fact, the presents were given under duress, Rodkinson having hinted to the retailers that their credit would be reduced unless some tribute was paid befitting the occasion. The dealers would usually rush straight to a jeweller and return with such a present. 'The tap of credit would be given one or two more turns according to the purity of the diamond or the weight of the gold watch,' Gaisberg recalled.[30]

In the background of the Gramophone & Typewriter's efforts in Russia was a problem with piracy. Discs were being copied by 'dubbing' onto a new master and re-pressed illegally on a massive scale. If this wasn't the first case of industrialized piracy in the music business, it was certainly the first to be documented in any kind of detail. The leader of the pirates was known to be a dealer called Finkelstein. What was not known for some time was that Rodkinson was Finkelstein's business partner, but by early 1909, the gaff was blown. Not that the knowledge helped matters, as, relieved of any false loyalty, they were now openly infringing. When he worked for the Gramophone & Typewriter, Rodkinson used the fact that he held mortgages on most of the Russian dealers' businesses to force them to buy his illicit merchandise. Now, however, he was just selling them cheaper than the originals and ruining his former employer's trade. Rodkinson's venture was finally thwarted in 1912 when a police raid on his factory, orchestrated with Gaisberg's help, caught him in the act of pressing fake red label discs by Chaliapin and ordered the plant's closure. Destabilized by its own manager's dishonesty, it took some years for the Russian branch to get back on track. A young man called Albert Lack was posted from London to run the show and by the time of the Revolution, he had managed to sort things out admirably. Unfortunately for him and his employers, the Bolsheviks seized the well-maintained, well-run plant and passed it on to a tame local – the dreaded Finkelstein.

Between leaving the G&T's employ and resurfacing in Russia, Rodkinson had spent some time in Britain, including a period working with Sterling at the foundation of Rena. In late 1908, he had decided to go back into business on his own account and was trying to persuade Alfred Clark out of his early retirement in Languedoc to join him. Earlier that year, Clark had left the French company due to a lack of 'complete harmony between Mr Birnbaum and myself'.[31] Johnson advised Clark against taking up with Rodkinson: 'I really believe that his enterprises are apt to take a turn that would be distasteful to you.'[32] It would not be long before something more appetizing and seemly came along for Clark – a return to his old company, but this time at head office as joint managing director with Melba's suitor Sydney Dixon. The company was in deep financial trouble, on top of which Birnbaum had been ill for some time, so it was with some relief that he resigned in 1909. There was also a suggestion in Gaisberg's letter to his brother that 'Rodkinson had some kind of hold on Birnbaum' resulting in the disgraced branch manager receiving an annual £750 honorarium for three years after his exit.

As it transpired, there were no nefarious links between Rodkinson and the blameless Birnbaum, and it must be wondered whether the idea was planted by one of the outgoing MD's enemies. Clark certainly had the motive, and Johnson had been lobbying hard for his deposed friend's reappointment almost from the moment of his exit. The management changes were the final touch in a restructuring that had been happening organically within the company almost since Owen's exit. The company had finally opened an English factory in 1907, in the then semi-rural Middlesex town of Hayes. It began by manufacturing only records, but had added a machine-building capability by 1914. The decision to set up, which Clark promoted enthusiastically prior to his exit, would prove to be a timely one, and the main reason it hadn't happened earlier was fear of the strong British trade unions.

The company had also drawn up a formal agreement with Victor in the United States regarding territorial divisions and the co-operation between the two organizations. The cosy nature of the carve-up is illustrated nicely by Caruso's move to the United States in 1904, to join the company of the Metropolitan Opera. The result was that he transferred from being a Gramophone & Typewriter artist whose records were released on Victor in America to being a Victor artist whose records were picked up by G&T in the UK. He made his first American recordings on 1 February 1904, four days after the start of his first Victor contract. There were no complaints, however, from London that one of their star artists had been snaffled. They still had access to all of his recordings for the British and Empire market. In reality, however, the American company was becoming the senior partner. It was making the running in terms of technology, having launched the Victrola – the first machine issued by the company with an internal horn – in 1906. So many were sold that, for many, the name Victrola became synonymous with the gramophone, as Hoover later did for vacuum cleaners. All talks of Victor being sold to its English partner had died off by the end of the decade. By the time that a partial merger did occur, in 1919, the balance of power had changed utterly and it was Victor that took a 50 per cent stake in the UK company.

The company topped off a busy 1907 by ditching the redundant 'Typewriter' part of its name, reverting to the Gramophone Company. However, the word gramophone was becoming more of a generic term than a trade name, so the legend 'Gramophone Record' at the top of each label was dropped in favour of a new brand name – His Master's Voice. After eight years hanging in the boardroom, Barraud's Nipper went to work in his home country, and the Recording Angel was quietly phased out. But the little terrier – along with the rest of the British record industry – was about to witness a massive increase in competition, and to experience some rather lean times.

4 Continental shift

In the first years of the twentieth century, the power of America and Germany – the latter long regarded as the home of cheap and shoddy merchandise – was markedly on the rise, at Britain's expense. By 1913, the US was producing 31 million tons of steel, while Germany was pumping out 13.5 million tons, comparing favourably with Britain, which was lagging behind at 8 million tons. The shift in power relationships between the nations was played out nowhere more graphically than among the operators in the talking machine business.

Following the Zonophone takeover in 1904, Frederick M. Prescott had one last go at starting a record company. Backed financially by Zonophone's old French agents Ch. & J. Ullmann Frères, the new venture was called the International Talking Machine Company. Although the head office for the new company was in Berlin, at 24 Lehderstrasse, Prescott named the new company's record label after a Parisian theatre, the Odeon, perhaps inspired by his French backers. As the likes of Victor, Columbia and the Gramophone Company had the world sewn up, Prescott needed to offer something new and different to make any sort of impression. That something new was the double-sided record. Previously, all discs sold carried music on one side only. If Prescott was able to achieve this technical feat, it seems likely that the other companies had it worked out as well, but had sat on the innovation to avoid having to give their customers any more value for their money than was strictly necessary.

However, when the double-faced Odeon disc came to the market, the stalwarts had to rethink their plan and respond. Some were quicker off the mark than others. Victor reacted almost immediately by snapping up a double-sided disc patent registered by a man in Whitehorse, Yukon. It took some time before the company began to exploit its acquisition commercially – single-sided discs were still being issued in 1907, and it wasn't until September 1923 that the Red Seal series went double-sided. Up until this point, Victor's double-sided discs had been from the more lowbrow end of its repertoire, and so more popular. The expensive Red Seals were quite often bought by aspirants who wanted to look classier than they really were. Later collectors noted the preponderance of mint single-sided Red Seals and were led to conclude that they were rarely if ever played. Columbia brought out its first duplex discs in 1908, roughly around the same time that Louis Sterling's loosely affiliated Rena Manufacturing Company brought out its doubles. The Gramophone Company finally sprang into action in the same year, but not for its full-price HMV label. Instead, it established a new cheap label, the Twin, offering records that were billed as 'Loudest on Earth' and which retailed at 2/6, the same as a single-sided Zonophone disc. The new venture was placed under the auspices of a wholly owned subsidiary called the Twin Record Co. Ltd, and there was, curiously, no indication in the new company's advertising that it was affiliated in any way to the Gramophone Company.

The Odeon disc would not have caught on if it didn't put something worthwhile on at least one face of the disc. Fortunately, Prescott was quick off the mark in building up a repertoire. By 1905, Odeon was claiming to have 7,000 titles in its catalogue, and a year later this had risen to 11,000. Dan Smoot, Joe Batten's mentor at the Musiphone Company, popped up again to undertake a recording tour of North Africa, a year or so before the Gramophone Company boys made it. It wasn't just a question of quantity, either. The singer Lilli Lehmann was an important addition to the Odeon roster, and a young Irish tenor by the name of John McCormack made his first discs for the new company, much to the chagrin of Fred Gaisberg, who had been interested in signing him.

The International Talking Machine Company seemed intent on living up to its name, going as far as possible for world domination – something that the existing majors had denied themselves with their territorial exclusivity agreements. Rather than opening directly-controlled branches in far-flung outposts, Odeon relied on agents for representation, while maintaining a programme of local recordings. Egypt, India, China, Singapore and the Dutch West Indies soon found themselves in receipt of Odeon's attentions, and the newcomer managed to beat the Gramophone Company into Java. The non-European territory where Odeon made the greatest impact, however, was South America, where the agency was run by one Max Glucksmann, an expatriate German. A factory was set up in Buenos Aires, and Glucksmann set about recording Latin American music. For years after, Odeon and its successors dominated the tango record market.

Another continental company that made its debut in 1904 was the Italian-based Societa Italiana di Fonotipia. This outfit boasted the great and good of the European musical establishment on its board, including Covent Garden opera syndicate director Harry Vincent Higgins and Tito Ricordi, the Italian music publisher. With such a line-up, it is unsurprising that it soon developed a reputation for putting the music and the artists first. While others were recording only the selections that seemed sure to sell, Fonotipia was recording nothing but opera, using the finest performers from the world stage, and encouraging them to record some of the less obviously commercial arias.

Odeon and Fonotipia might not seem like natural partners, but they merged, while retaining their separate identities. Fonotipia took the high-brow, Odeon took the middle-brow, while the Jumbo label – with an elephant's head as a trademark – offered brass bands and variety artists, including George Formby, the father of the gap-toothed Lancashire comedian.

Jumbo advertised their wares as offering 'magnificent recording' and 'skilled musical arrangements' on a 'scratchless surface'. However, at this stage, no one was offering truly scratchless surfaces, and for a very good reason. The points of the disposable steel needles came in all shapes and sizes, as did record grooves, so abrasives were put into the shellac mixture to grind the needle down to the shape of the groove. This ensured a good fit, but the presence of the abrasives was all too audible, being responsible for much of the 'frying bacon' sound of 78s.

Then, in 1911, the Odeon and Fonotipia combine was acquired by Carl Lindström AG, a German manufacturer of talking machines founded by the partially deaf son of a Swedish wagon-axle maker. He emigrated to Germany in 1892, aged twenty-five, and began experimenting with phonographs. His business foundered and was rescued by a pair of sympathetic bankers called Max Straus and Heinrich Zuntz, who soon lost interest in their banking jobs and took over executive control of the company. Lindström stepped aside from the running of the company, becoming technical director and general manager of the factory, positions he held until 1921.

Zuntz died in 1906, and was replaced by his brother-in-law, Otto Heinemann, who would stay with the company until 1914, when he emigrated to America and founded the General Phonograph Corporation. Having conquered its hardware problems, the company began moving into the software business. It established its own Parlophon imprint, the trademark for which was an old German-style letter 'L'. It moved further into the disc-making field by acquisition. In 1910, the Lindström company bought the Beka label, so called because it had been established by a company named Bumb and Konig. A year later, the International Talking Machine Company came into the fold. By 1914, Carl Lindström AG was the largest record organization in Germany.

Away from home, and particularly in the UK, it wasn't doing too badly either. It had factories in Britain, Russia, the Austro-Hungarian Empire, Italy, Spain, Argentina, Brazil and Chile. Discs on Beka's Grand (7-inch, 8-inch and 10-inch double-sided, the last size retailing at 2/6) and Meister (12-inch double-sided retailing at 5 shillings) labels had been available in Britain since 1905, with a London office at 77 City Road, run by Otto Rühl. Beka had also made inroads into the Indian market, undertaking recordings on the subcontinent and selling them through Valabhdas Runchordas. In the British market, one of Beka's most memorable advertising lines of the day was: 'No ear splitters but the smoothest, the most beautiful, the most artistic'. They were even more popular and successful once they had the backing of the mighty Lindström organization, and Beka became one of the most heavily advertised of all the labels in trade press terms. Lindström also added a label called Scala to its UK roster. These discs and the machines that the company was importing were all more keenly priced than the established competition of HMV and Columbia, so it was not too surprising that they began to take a growing share of the British market.

Other German companies also made their mark. The Polyphon Musicwerke of Leipzig retailed their 10-inch double-sided discs in the British market at 2/6, and promised 'good volume' and 'natural tone' on a 'tough-wearing' product. Another factor that made the cheaper discs attractive to purchasers stemmed from the fact that these were, concert stars like Melba and Caruso apart, the days before the exclusive contract. As a result, the recording artists who appeared on the high-price labels were often responsible for the versions of the same selections issued by the cheaper competitors. One of the most prolific of these journeymen was Stanley Kirkby, who recorded for HMV, Edison-Bell's Winner label and Scala, among others.

Kirkby's typical payment for a session was the then-astronomical £90 for six titles in a three-hour session, which the singer could do without breaking sweat. This figure was just slightly less than a skilled printer's annual wage at the time. In his memoirs, recording engineer Joe Batten recalled Kirkby's productivity:

> This was before the days of exclusive contracts and royalty payments. Stanley was a freelance and he was doing similar work at much the same payment with other companies, probably three a week ... Much has been said about the colossal sums paid today by the gramophone companies to artistes, but I am sure that even such outstanding best-sellers as Gracie Fields, Donald Peers or George Formby never approached Kirkby's weekly gramophone earnings of £270 during the peak recording months of September to January. He had the finest recording voice of all the artistes I have heard in recording studios. It was a pure baritone. His diction was perfect, and he had a versatility in interpretation that distinguished him from all others.[1]

The existing players responded with their own cheaper discs, but the damage to their business had been done. In fact, by attempting to come down to Lindström's level, they were probably doing more harm to their existing operations than good. The existence of the cheaper Zonophone operation had expanded HMV's sales, but at a price.

Columbia had been in trouble before the cheap imports, having been brought close to bankruptcy by its American management in 1908. When European manager Frank Dorian spoke to *Talking Machine World* in February 1907, all appeared to be well. He spoke of 'very good business indeed' on the Continent, adding that there had been 'no remarkable falling off after the Christmas season. This I can truthfully apply to England as well, our factories having to run day and night for the last few months'. He also praised the Americans for achieving a year-round business, compared with the UK, which was still beholden to the whims of cycle-shop owners and their willingness to make window space for records.

In the US, greater vigilance on patent matters maintained the status quo to a more marked degree than in Europe. Victor was relatively unaffected by the cheap discs, except where troubles at HMV impacted on it. It was also doing well out of the Caruso transfer. One of his first recordings for the label was 'Vesti la Giubba' from Leoncavallo's *Pagliacci* and, although an expensive Red Seal, it sold in numbers more fitting for a German cheapie. In time, it was reputed to have sold 1 million copies, and if this is true, it would be the earliest recording to achieve such a distinction. In the absence of sales data, however, such anecdotal claims usually have to be taken with a pinch of salt.

There were fears, expressed in the trade press of the time, that the German influx would finish the domestic producers. Then, in 1914, the outbreak of the First World War halted the seemingly irresistible march of Lindström and the other German entrants.

In his autobiography, Fred Gaisberg declared that '[a]fter the First World War several years elapsed before musical activities resumed their stride'.[2] While this may have been true enough when applied to the international concert artists and their recording activities, with many major stars living in enemy countries and thus unable to record for the British and American companies, it gives a false impression of the industry. Although it looked, at the outset, as if the war would claim the Gramophone Company as one of its casualties, the record business managed to keep going by scaling down production and taking war work. By the end of the conflict, though, more records than ever were being sold.

As a bonus, the foreign interlopers had been scuppered, at least for the time being. The Lindström labels remained in business, but moved swiftly to disguise their Teutonic origins. In Beka's August 1914 *Talking Machine News* advertisement, the company's name was given as Carl Lindström (London) of 77 City Road. The following month, however, the company had become plain Beka Records, and the products were being advertised as 'British made throughout in a British factory (Hertford) by British workmen'.[3] By 1917, however, the 19,600 square feet of the all-British Lindström works at Hertford and the company's English matrices were for sale, an opportunity that Columbia picked up gratefully.

At the outbreak of the Great War in August 1914, leisure spending in Britain fell dramatically, and took record sales with it. The populace lived in fear of what the future might hold, and with sons and husbands departing to fight, there seemed to be no room for frivolous expenditure. 'The public, stunned by the unexpected crisis, decided to save rather than spend,' wrote HMV's managing director Alfred Clark in his memoirs.[4] This came as a shock to both Clark and HMV. The first Branch Managers' Convention had just been held at Hayes and the consensus was that business was good, with room for more growth. The company was just about to start making gramophones from scratch at Hayes. Suddenly, war was declared, the bold plans were shelved and HMV went from prosperity to trying to work out how to turn a coin.

The suddenness of the change comes across clearly in a pair of letters sent by Clark to Eldridge Johnson in early August 1914. In the first, sent on 1 August, he recalled:

> I remember we talked about the possibility of the Note that Austria sent to Servia on that Thursday as a source of trouble and it has developed with a rapidity which has been as unexpected as it has been serious ... Our communications with Austria were cut on the Monday and we have been out of touch since then with that country. A cable in from Russia indicates that yesterday most of the factory help has been called to the colours and news from France and Germany are just as bad.[5]

Just nine days later, Clark wrote:

> I little thought when I spoke to you the last time we were together of the possible gravity of the position between Austria and Servia that the storm would be down on us with such terrible quickness. There is, of course, no business, and it would be foolish to attempt to do any; the important part of the Continent today is in a state which cannot be conceived by anyone who has not either seen it himself or had direct accounts of it from eye witnesses as I have. An American lady who escaped from Paris ... told us that there is not a single store or place of business open as far as one can see in the whole of Paris, and nowhere can young men be found. It is a city of women, children and old men, all of them existing on what money they had saved by and can get hold of.[6]

Talking Machine News was quick to pick up on the malaise affecting the business:

> Some of our patriotic British firms are continuing their works, on perhaps not so extensive a basis at present, but with the twin ideas of keeping the trade together and preventing the trouble caused through total lack of employment. It is for our readers to back them up in this laudable work. It may be that they are not in the position to purchase as many records now as in the immediate past, but let them realize that the buying of even a single record is contributing a quota to the alleviation of the unemployment terror. To our readers we earnestly suggest that to the best of their ability they will contribute to this desirable end.[7]

Stirring stuff, which could almost have come direct from the HMV publicity department. As perhaps it did, given that HMV had secretly acquired *Talking Machine News* in 1911.

Over at Columbia, HMV's main rival, the prevailing conditions were not much better, but Louis Sterling – newly promoted to general manager – did not share Clark's view that it would be 'foolish' to try and do business, at least on the home front. His speedy and decisive reaction was recalled by W. S. Meadmore in the *Gramophone* in June 1937, writing on the occasion of Sterling's knighthood:

> Hardly had this [Sterling's promotion] happened when the industry was faced with ruin. War had broken out; wholesalers refused to distribute printed matter, retailers refused to order records. A lot of hard thinking was done in the Clerkenwell Road [where Columbia had settled, at numbers 98–102, after several years in Great Eastern Street] in those days, and it was Louis Sterling who saved the situation. He called all the managers together, told them to rake up all the patriotic records they could find, and to find out if any composers had written new songs. 'Rush them all out as war records,' he said. Within ten days they were issued. The confidence thus expressed reacted on the trade generally, other manufacturers quickly followed this lead, soon records were everywhere expressing the then war-like sentiments of the nation.[8]

HMV was, naturally, one of the 'other manufacturers' referred to by Meadmore, publishing its first 'War Supplement' of patriotic discs in October 1914. Non-martial sentiments got a look-in as well, most notably homesickness. The big hit of the Great War was 'It's a Long Way to Tipperary', which dated from 1913 and had not made much of an impression on its first outing. Once the war was underway, it became popular among the soldiers in the trenches, a phenomenon first noted by a *Daily Mail* reporter. Those who had it in their catalogue reissued it and promoted it vigorously. Those who didn't recorded it pretty sharpish. Another song, this time written in response to the situation, was Ivor Novello's 'Till the Boys Come Home' (now perhaps better known as 'Keep the Home Fires Burning'), which soon featured in every recording label's catalogue. The ever-versatile Stanley Kirkby knocked out versions for several of them, including Scala and Edison-Bell's Winner label.

Although there had been some phonographic activity during the Boer War (most notably Russell Hunting's best-selling cod-documentary recording 'Departure of a Troopship') the First World War was the first war in which the talking machine really played a part. Home sales were important, but many of the subalterns had taken portable gramophones with them into the trenches, and parcels of the latest records were awaited eagerly as morale-boosters. 'Up at the Battery we think that it is only His Master's Voice and the Triumph Motor Cycle that make war humanly bearable,' declared Second Lieutenant S. Humphries at the Stationary Isolation Hospital in Boulogne, in a letter published in the July 1917 issue of HMV's house magazine *The Voice*. One of the most popular portable machines among the soldiers was an instrument made by the Barnett, Samuel musical instrument company, called the Decca.

Shortly after his much-imitated patriotic inspiration, Sterling had another bright idea to help keep Columbia afloat. '[H]e had the imagination to conceive that soldiers in trenches all over the world would delight in records of the revues and musical shows which officers and men on leave flocked to see in the London theatres,' wrote Meadmore. 'He was determined to give them the originals as far as the gramophone could then do so.' Sterling's men set about signing up the casts of the best shows, and the first production to feature in Sterling's plans was E.V. Lucas and Albert de Courville's defiantly jolly show *Business as Usual*, which opened at London's Hippodrome on 16 November 1914. Either shortly before the show's opening or one Sunday early in the run, Violet Loraine and the comedian Harry Tate, two of the show's stars, went to the Columbia studios in Clerkenwell Road to record a sketch called 'Fortifying the Home', while Loraine recorded four musical numbers without Tate – 'We've Been Married Just One Year' and 'When We've Wound Up the Watch on the Rhine' (on both of which she was joined by Ambrose Thorne), then 'Three Cheers for Little Belgium' and 'Come On, You Boys of London Town'.

Perhaps the best-received of all the recorded revues, however, was *The Bing Boys Are Here*, also featuring Violet Loraine, this time with George Robey as the comic element, which opened at the Alhambra, Leicester Square,[9] on 19 April 1916. Among the songs from this show that made it onto disc was 'If You Were the Only Boy in the World', sung by Loraine to Robey. With adjustments as necessary to accommodate the singer's gender, this number became a standard and remains popular nearly ninety years after it was written.

Once again, the other companies followed as best as they could, but they were hampered by the fact that Columbia had managed to sign exclusive contracts with most of the major theatrical producers of the day, including C.B. Cochran. As a result, the other labels, including HMV, were reduced to offering cover versions, of which Columbia made great capital in its advertising. Sometimes, however, HMV could steal a march on its rival by contriving to get their players into the studio before Columbia had a chance to record the real cast. Such a case involved de Courville's 1918 show *Box O' Tricks*. Selections from the show, played by the Mayfair Orchestra[10] under the baton of Arthur Crudge, were recorded by HMV at Hayes on 23 September 1918, six months after the show opened. (Unaccountably, Columbia – which had access to the show's pit band, the London Hippodrome Orchestra under Edwin Sanders – omitted to record its own versions of the same titles until 3 October.)

Following the trends helped HMV keep its corporate head above water in wartime. Indeed, the company's sales across all labels increased from 3.3m discs in 1913 to 5m in 1919. Other measures, however, were necessary to ensure the company's security. The first response to the crisis had been to cut salaries. Clark took a 50 per cent cut, while the factory staff also had to accept reductions. Directors, who in peacetime had been eligible for a total remuneration of £2,500 per annum – £1,000 of which was guaranteed, the rest coming from profit bonuses – agreed to take only the basic pay.

Clark also looked to the government's need for weapons as a potential source of income, and by November 1914, a significant proportion of production capacity at Hayes had been turned over to munitions. By the time of the Armistice, this line had brought £6m of business into the company. In time, the directors thought that they had done so well by the company that they deserved more remuneration than they received in peacetime, and voted themselves a 150 per cent increase in pay. The managing director got his old salary back, with an extra £182 and six shillings on top, while the chairman received an extra £2,000 on top of his increased pay, making a total increase of 650 per cent. Pay restorations on the shop floor were not, unfortunately, of the same order.

One eventuality for which HMV did not have a contingency plan was the loss of its German and Russian factories. The German factories were seized by the government at the commencement of hostilities in 1914, but the Russian factories remained accessible until they were sequestered by the new Bolshevik administration after the Revolution in 1917. Although Clark had originally dismissed any resumption of continental trade as 'foolish', he soon modified this view and the company, for a while, tried desperately to maintain some kind of trade in the territories that were still open to it, albeit with diminishing returns. In a May 1915 letter to Johnson, he observed that:

> On the Continent things are generally speaking about as bad as they could be ... Except where our men have been called up for the war we have kept the organization intact but it is expensive and the result of course is financial loss. So far we have suffered no destruction of assets but we have been greatly worried by the German approach to Riga [where HMV had a factory], and if they should enter this town and cut it off from the rest of Russia our business in Russia would suffer severely.[11]

After the war, Deutsche Grammophon was sold off by the German government and thus became an independent entity, continuing to use the Nipper trademark and the 'Die Stimme seines Herren' brand name. As HMV had suffered grievously from the continental cut-off, Columbia somehow managed to benefit from the same circumstances with the Hertford acquisition. It had added double-sided discs, at 2/6 designed to compete with Zonophone, to its more expensive labels in 1914 with Regal, and Phoenix, also double-sided, which retailed at 1/1 and went head to head with HMV's Cinch. The Lindström matrices provided ideal fodder for these catalogues. Meanwhile, the spare capacity at Hertford proved very useful when in May 1918, a fire took hold of the Columbia plant at Bendon Valley, Wandsworth. 'The only person on the premises was the night watchman, who had made his rounds some half an hour before,' reported *Talking Machine News*. 'He was in his watchman's box when the first intimation of anything wrong was the electric light failing, and a moment later a burst of flame through the door of his box. He had just time to telephone the Fire Brigade and make his escape... [It was] London's most serious fire this year and the first brigade call of 1918... [with] some 160 firemen ... said to have been engaged on it.'[12] The whole factory was affected with two important and very lucky exceptions: the plating department, where wax recordings were electroplated for pressing, and the matrix vault, which contained the master recordings. Amazingly, considering the often bitter battles between the various rival companies, '[g]enerous competitors freely offered their assistance as soon as the news was known, while printers placed their whole resources at the company's disposal for reprinting record labels'.[13]

At around the same time as the Hertford acquisition, the UK branch had reorganized itself as a company in its own right – the Columbia Graphophone Company Ltd. This move was excellently timed. The British company had gone from strength to strength with Sterling left in unfettered charge. The American parent company had, however, suffered a considerable blow when Edward D. Easton, its founder and guiding light, died in 1915. Following Easton's death, financiers moved in and the trouble really started. Unsure of itself, the company was spending far too much money on artists, the result of trying to poach star names from its rivals. Some of the new finance came from members of the DuPont family, and Victor's Artists and Repertoire chief Cal Child observed to Sydney Dixon of HMV that Columbia had been spending the money 'like drunken sailors'. Melba was one of the main targets, and while Child felt that 'she was really pathetic ... considering her former greatness...' and that 'her going to the competition at this late day would mean almost a confession of weakness, and would do us little harm', he believed that her name was 'almost a household word, and she should be kept in line in some way if possible',[14] even if this meant trying to match Columbia's wildest offers.

Child wasted no time renegotiating with his biggest stars, persuading Enrico Caruso, Emma Calve, Geraldine Farrar, Louise Homer, Nellie Melba, Ernestine Schumann-Heink, Antonio Scotti and Marcella Sembrich to sign an agreement permitting Victor to make price cuts in their discs when it was thought to be for both the artist's and the company's good. At the same renegotiation, royalties were taken from a flat fee per disc basis to a percentage. As it transpired, the price reductions were to come into effect almost immediately, and Child said that he believed 'that it will mean a great increase in our Red Seal record orders and sales to bring the records of these big artists down to a popular price'.[15] One point he made quite forcefully was that the 15 per cent offered in the Columbia contracts was not as generous as it first appeared, being 15 per cent of 75 per cent of the total number of records manufactured, which amounted to roughly in monetary terms as Victor's 10 per cent.

Other major artists, however, were considered expendable in the interests of giving Columbia a bloody nose. Titta Ruffo for one, whose grand manner was almost too much for everyone he encountered. The Metropolitan Opera had offered him $1,200 a performance, which was double the sum paid to any baritone before. The arrogant Ruffo would have none of it. He wanted what Caruso was getting. The Met responded by letting him go. As for his recordings, Dixon had, at one point, commented to Child that Ruffo had 'a head too large for any hat that is made'. Now, he was being chased by Columbia and Child knew that they had:

> already made a very extravagant offer. We found him just as you did, a most difficult proposition to handle in the Laboratory, and we were absolutely unable to sell his records in any quantities as compared with other Red Seal celebrities ... our policy will be – so far as he is concerned – to see how much we can make the other fellow pay for him without getting stung again ourselves.[16]

Any advances on Luisa Tetrazzini would not be resisted with much vigour either, as Child thought she was past her best, and it was part of his game plan to 'load the Columbia Company up with a creditable list of has-beens'. This, he thought 'would be the safest way of bringing them to their senses as to prices to be paid artists'. This was as maybe, but Dixon thought Tetrazzini worth continuing to cultivate. 'She came like a bolt from the blue,' he observed. 'The sudden win out was so quick that two continents had their breath taken away and recovered so quickly that they forgot her in three years.'[17] Then the war had intervened to make her star fall still further. She was, however, once such a name that Dixon thought a comeback not impossible, and that it would cost the nominal sum of 35,000 lire to keep her from the competition.

In handling Melba, Dixon counselled that even though she was 'essentially a business woman', she was also 'a snob' and that a 'letter or bit of attention from the head of a concern is more to her than money'. He acknowledged her fading ability, but made it clear that he thought this did not matter to her loyal audiences. 'Melba is an institution. You can't get away from it ... She will hold her sway till the very last farewell concert is given. She will give some. We ought never to let her name go onto a competition catalogue.'[18]

The plan worked. Victor and HMV kept most of their big names and Columbia might as well have burned most of the money that it spent on the artists. Ultimately the US company went into a spiral of decline. By February 1922, it was going for a 'voluntary adjustment of finances'. Chairman Francis Whitten pointed out that 'in common with many other companies, we have been through a period of severe shrinking in the volume of business, accompanied by large depreciation of inventory values and other unfavourable factors ... 1921 sales were approximately $19m against $47m in 1920'.[19] In the same period, the company went from a profit of $7.3m to a loss of $2.3m. Meanwhile, Columbia had racked up a debt of $23m by 1921. Three shareholders responded to this request with an application for receivership on grounds of insolvency. A Delaware judge dismissed this application, but by late 1923, those calling for receivership had got their way. In contrast, over the same period, the British subsidiary had forged ahead, and this shift in the balance of power turned out to have an intriguing result in the mid-1920s.

Because America did not join the Great War until 1917, the US talking machine industry had avoided direct contact with the worst of the problems that faced the European industry in 1914. At the outbreak of hostilities, *Talking Machine World* was as positive about the future as it could be, judging from the following headline: 'BUSINESS AND THE EUROPEAN WARS – The Effect On Our Industries Will Temporarily Be Bad – But Disturbed Conditions May Be Followed by Domestic Activity and Merchant Marine Development to Handle Exports.'[20]

Elsewhere in the same issue, a series of advertisements, aimed at dealers lacking in confidence, showed that the US arm of Columbia – its problems notwithstanding – wasn't in the mood to wait around for developments in exports. It was to be business as normal: 'Don't let the scare-mongers hobble your hopes. Crops are good, money is sound, European cash is coming this way and it looks like the biggest fall and winter in history.'[21]

Meanwhile, US Columbia was, like its UK counterpart, early to spot the potential for patriotic discs, but given the USA's neutrality at this point and the country's diverse ethnic mix, it thought it could please all of the warring factions at once: 'With every German and Russian and Austrian and Servian and Belgian and Frenchman in this country breathing battle and oozing patriotism, the completeness of the Columbia foreign record catalogues is a boon to every dealer who can reach a foreign colony.'[22]

Columbia's problems were largely of its own making, but the close ties between Victor and HMV and the two arms of Columbia meant that there was, inevitably, some indirect, knock-on effect from whatever happened in Britain. The likely extent of this was outlined to Eldridge Johnson at the outset of the war by a J. E. Sterett of Price Waterhouse, whose opinion he had sought:

> The measure in which your business will be curtailed ... rests largely on the duration of the war; it has already lasted a month and it certainly looks as though it would continue for several months to come at least ... I assume your European business will be reduced to a negligible quantity both during the war and probably for some time thereafter, and in this connection, reference may be made to the waning of the dance craze which, from my limited means of observation, is likely to become pronounced. People will be compelled to economize and luxuries of every kind will be cut out to a marked extent ... The Victor goods occupy one point of vantage ... that is the relative cheapness of the Victor as a form of entertainment. People must have some amusement and entertainment and the more expensive forms are likely to be prohibitive ...[23]

Sterett went on to suggest that 'a substantial reduction in profits is perhaps inevitable', but thought it unlikely that Victor would make a loss. Johnson replied that he felt Sterett's 'forecast of the situation is about as good as we can expect'. With uncharacteristic short-sightedness, he expected that 'the actual fighting will be over in less than six months'.[24]

Any decline in the 'dance craze', as mentioned by Sterett, would have hit Victor pretty hard, as it had under contract Vernon and Irene Castle, the husband-and-wife team whose gyrations were largely responsible for the fad. In addition, James Europe, the black bandleader who supplied the Castles with their backing music, was a Victor artist. In the event, music for dancing grew even more popular, particularly in the period immediately after the war, but neither Vernon Castle nor James Europe were around to capitalize on it. An Englishman by birth, Castle enlisted with the Royal Flying Corps, the predecessor of the RAF, and became a First World War air ace. In 1917, he returned to America to become a flying instructor and died in a plane crash at Fort Worth, Texas. Europe also went to war, becoming a lieutenant in the 369th Infantry, the 'Harlem Hellfighters'. Like Castle, he survived battle, dying in 1919 on his comeback tour, when he was stabbed in the neck by a mentally disturbed drummer from his own band.

In Britain, the fad manifested itself in the establishment of dance halls, often named 'Palais de Danse' at odds with their suburban situation. The most famous of all opened in 1919 in the west London district of Hammersmith, but further hamlets like Wimbledon had their own palais. Then there were the smart London hotels, each of which employed a dance band, most notably the Savoy, with its Orpheans, directed by Carroll

Gibbons. After 1922, the British Broadcasting Company was to relay these sessions live from the hotel ballrooms, for the hoofers at home. The need for suitable gramophone records was highlighted by the dance celebrity Victor Silvester (famous for introducing the phrase 'Slow, slow, quick, quick, slow' into the English language), who formed his own recording band to get it just right. It all sounds very chic and glamorous, and for the well-heeled it was. For most, though, it was a case of 'undulating on a floor no larger than a dentist's waiting room ... claim[ing] a vacant square foot of space from their neighbours and avoid[ing] bodily contact with the skill of a Japanese commuter'.[25]

Once America joined the war, though, the effects were more tangible for US businesses. In 1918, the US Fuel Administration curtailed all talking machine production to 70 per cent of 1917 levels. This was later reduced further to 40 per cent. At Victor, production of Victrolas fell to 10 per cent of the normal level, but it made up some of the shortfall and contributed to the war effort by taking on munitions work like its English counterpart. While machine sales were depressed, though, records were, as Benjamin L. Aldridge noted in a company history of Victor written for internal consumption in 1964, 'in extraordinary demand'. Distributors were, he observed, bringing 'great pressure [on the company] for current popular numbers ... [and sending] scouts around the country to buy up anything which would play ... At the end of the war, when production was picking up, distributors had back orders on the company for about 50,000,000 records.'[26] The distributors had over-ordered by ten times, and were grateful for the opportunity to revise their orders when it was offered by the besieged Victor management.

Victor also did its bit with regard to patriotic discs, the best-known of which was Enrico Caruso's 1918 recording of 'Over There'. This piece, written by George M. Cohan, the composer of 'Yankee Doodle Dandy' and 'Give My Regards to Broadway', was a little out of the ordinary for the great tenor, but he and Cohan were good friends and the song appealed to the singer. As well as recording it for Victor, Caruso sung it at Liberty Bond rallies and at his usual venue, the Metropolitan Opera House.

At the end of the war, the Gramophone Company devoted a great deal of time and effort to regaining control of Deutsche Grammophon, now owned by Polyphon, a German label that had been active in the pre-war British market, and with it control of the Nipper trademark in Germany.

Unfortunately for them, these efforts were to no avail. The Gramophone Company did, finally, regain its lost matrices, but not until DG had a thoroughly good war selling records made from these masters. Indeed, this trade continued into the 1920s until litigation from HMV and Victor brought this grey marketeering to an end. Its intellectual property restored, HMV re-entered the German market in 1926 with a new company, Electrola, shortly after Columbia had bought the Lindström business.

Some of the matrices returned to HMV had never been released in the UK before. In September 1923, Clara Butt, who had been an HMV artist but had since moved to Columbia, wrote to the newly-established periodical the *Gramophone* to complain that HMV had issued two 'new' records by her – 'Il segreto' and 'Caro mio ben' – which had in fact been recorded between twelve and sixteen years before. 'I desire the general public and your readers in particular to understand that the above-mentioned records are issued at this time without my consent, and I would ask my public not to judge me by these records'. HMV rebutted Butt's assertions the following month by pointing out that the recordings had been made in Germany before the war and that the matrices had only recently been disgorged by the German authorities.

Peacetime found the record business in good fettle, something that would have startled the record moguls if predicted in 1914. More records were being sold than before the war, but the industry was still a small one compared with what it would later become. HMV sold a total of 5 million units in 1919, but the 1920s brought an era when a single record could sell one-fifth of that. In 1924, 24 million records were sold in the UK, compared with 59 million just six years later.

Happiest of all for the all-British operators, the Germans and their cut-price products had been kicked into touch, but there were warnings that complacency must not set in, or the whole trade would be back to square one. In a 1919 editorial, *Talking Machine News* issued a 'Wake Up!' call:

> The old method of doing business by means of German supplies was comfortable, profitable and saved work. Germany, in fact, did the work and had very nearly taken the business from us ... There are some, we fear, who regret the disappearance of the old order. Let us appeal to them to frankly cast aside hankerings after again doing business with the enemy, and to devote their whole energies to furthering the attainment of all-British business. If

not, we shall leave the door partly open, and Germany will enter the aperture and soon will push it wide. Germany, however disorganized at the present time, cannot have forgotten her old wonderful organization and her old methods, and they were – from her point of view – such complete and successful methods that they could not easily be improved upon.[27]

Later that year, *Talking Machine News* continued its anti-German crusade with a report on 'a recent practice of German traders', which was to bill for goods ordered before the war, and to add on surcharges covering storage and interest.

HMV had done well, but Victor had done better. In 1915, the American company had reported profits of $7.3m. The way that HMV had attempted to tackle the Germans head-on by offering its own lines of cut-price, lower quality goods had long been one of several bones of contention with Eldridge Johnson. He conceded that records had been over-priced, but the answer was not in offering inferior recordings, as he made clear in a colourful February 1916 letter to Clark:

> The first fatal mistake the Gramophone Company made was to try and beat the Germans at the cheap machine trade. Birnbaum started this and he might as well have tried to catch a skunk with his bare hands. The next mistake was in not lowering the price of Gramophone records when the Victor cut from one dollar for a ten inch to sixty cents ... The profit in talking machines lies in the middle and high grades at fair prices ... the Gramophone Company could have done the same as the Victor [in terms of business] if they had followed our example ... Ever since Owen left, the policies of the two companies have been growing wider apart.[28]

In July 1920 came the final answer to Johnson's frustrations. Speaking at the annual banquet of the National Association of Talking Machine Jobbers in Atlantic City, he announced that Victor had injected a large amount of capital into the company's English affiliate, in return for 50 per cent of the HMV stock. HMV became, effectively, a subsidiary of Victor.

Even before the deal was concluded, Johnson estimated that it 'means about five years of extra work for me'.[29] The extent of the work needed became apparent over the summer of 1920, which he spent in England, taking a very close look at his new acquisition. It was not an entirely pleasant stay, as he reported to his old friend and former colleague Leon

Douglass:

> I had a very miserable summer in England. The weather was frightful and I
> suffered from colds and all sorts of discomforts … I find conditions there
> require considerable adjustment, but, as you intimate in your letter, it is wise
> to go slow. Business conditions are not the same as they are in the United
> States, nevertheless their methods of distributing the goods can be
> tremendously improved.[30]

He had the misfortune to be at Hayes while the cabinet factory was on a
month-long strike, which can hardly have presented the best impression to
the new proprietor. 'Fortunately,' he commented to Douglass, 'it was
adjusted the day we sailed.' 'We', in this case, meant not only Johnson and
his family, but also Alfred Clark, fellow HMV director Colin Cooper and
sales manager Albert Lack, who were heading for Camden to see how
Johnson – who had joined the HMV board along with his colleague Walter
Staats – wanted things done.

Far from regarding the Victor deal as a humiliation, HMV bosses seemed
perfectly happy to relinquish ultimate control to the new king across the
water. Some parties on the English side were keen to bring the two
operations even closer together in terms of corporate identity, if only to fox
the Customs officers. Some HMV records did not justify a full release in
Victor's territory and vice versa, although there was a small demand for
them. The solution was to import and sell pressings from the originating
company, but this made them liable for import duty. The problem was
partly solved by over-stickering the trademark on import copies, but HMV
sales manager Sydney Dixon thought that a permanent name change could
settle the matter once and for all:

> It seems to me that the big solution is to re-christen both the Victor and the
> Gramophone companies with a joint and similar name. (I am presuming that
> at some future date an amalgamation is intended.) I understand that if the
> labels were similar, they would pass through the Customs Houses either freely
> or with very little trouble.[31]

Perhaps influenced by Clark, an utter Johnson loyalist because of the
friendly patronage he had received over the years, Dixon saw no point in
trying to maintain HMV's name in the partnership. He suggested that 'the

title for the future companies should be the Victor Victrola Company' and even indicated that '[w]e could well afford to miss the word "gramophone" in these later days of its existence', the term having become generic and debased.

The gentlemen of the Victor Talking Machine Company were, however, against such moves. They cited the goodwill that attached to the two companies' names, and counselled against casting such valuable items aside. In addition, '[t]he name Victor-Victrola Company was thought to be particularly objectionable because of its apparent treatment of the word 'Victrola' in a generic sense, that is as the name of a kind of class of machine rather than its true trademark sense indicating origin'.[32] There was also the anti-trust issue. Clark suggested tearing up the existing Victor/Gramophone agreement, now that the two Nippers were in the same kennel, but Victor vice-president Charles Haddon declared that it would be 'contrary to the terms and spirit of the Sherman anti-trust law', and advised that 'if [the existing contract] is unworkable or unsatisfactory from any point in detail ... it would be far better to amend the contract in a formal, legal way.' Haddon also indicated that Victor did not want to be seen by the owners of the company's other 50 per cent to be pushing its weight around:

> There is no merger between the Victor Company and the Gramophone Company, as the Victor Company does not own the Gramophone Company outright, but merely has a (controlling) stock interest and its interest is not to be to the exclusion of the minority stockholders in the Gramophone Company, whose rights the courts will protect.[33]

Of these motivations, the anti-trust matter seems to have been the main issue, not that the concern for the shareholders wasn't utterly genuine and heartfelt. In 1922, the US Department of Justice began complaining that Johnson was monopolizing the business. He responded by suggesting that he had tried several times to offload the onerous responsibility of owning and running Victor with no success:

> I will explain that on three or four occasions I have gone thru all the preliminaries of selling my interests with the purpose of retiring from business ... the Victor Company is considerably larger than I ever intended it to be. [However,] while my responsibilities are much greater than I relish, I have not the slightest intention of allowing the Department of Justice to put

anything over on me, and if Mr Dougherty does not give us the relief that I feel we are entitled to I wish to bring action aimed to accomplish the purpose that I stated to you. The Victor Company has been made the goat and there is something wrong somewhere.[34]

The deal gave them the leverage they needed to get their records released to their liking in the British Empire territories, but that was enough for the time being, and Johnson went out of his way to stress that the stock purchase amounted to rather less than an outright acquisition of HMV. Meanwhile Victor was quick to pick up on the main musical craze of the time, but HMV was a lot slower off the mark.

5 The Coldstream Guards and all that jazz

The dying days of the First World War had seen the emergence of a new sound on record. That sound was jazz, the improvised music of New Orleans. Between the wars, jazz and its various later developments, such as swing, would account for the bulk of popular music sales to young record buyers. The 'dance craze' referred to by one of Eldridge Johnson's financial advisers at the start of the First World War had helped pave the way, while another of the main influences on the new music was ragtime, which had been tremendously in vogue in the decade before 1920.

It was so popular that music hall and vaudeville comedians made records sending the fad up – a sure sign that something had caught the public's imagination. The great comedian Stanley Lupino's first record, issued in 1916 by Edison-Bell Winner, was called 'Have You Got Any Rag?', while one of Wilkie Bard's best-known recordings was of a song called 'You've Got to Sing in Ragtime'.

One of the originators of jazz was the New Orleans trumpeter Freddie Keppard, who was working with his band in New York at the end of 1915. While in town, he was heard by a scout from Victor and invited to make a recording. What happened next has been the subject of some debate over the years, but what definitely didn't happen was a recording. The legend has it that Keppard turned down the chance to make a record because he didn't want other people stealing his sound. Later, however, it was suggested that there was a more mundane, technical reason for passing up the opportunity. At this point, recording methods hadn't changed much since Eldridge Johnson's first experiments in wax, and certain frequencies did not record well, among them those emitted by a string bass. The audible alternative was to bring in a tuba player, but it seems that Keppard refused to countenance replacing his bassman Bill Johnson with anyone else.

So it was that the honour of making the first jazz record went to the Original Dixieland Jass Band, a collection of white musicians from the Crescent City, led by clarinettist Nick la Rocca. On 25 February 1917, they went into Victor's New York studio and recorded two sides – 'Livery Stable Blues' and 'Dixie Jass Band One-Step'. The results were issued and began selling quickly. Oddly, the Victor session was not the ODJB's first encounter with recording. They had already, on 30 January, waxed two sides for Columbia – 'Darktown Strutters' Ball' and 'Indiana' – but these were deemed to be technically unsatisfactory and were shelved. They were, however, hastily retrieved and pressed in large quantities when Columbia saw the kind of business the rival disc was doing.

Over in the UK, HMV was none too quick in picking up on the phenomenon. It decided not to issue the first Victor disc made by ODJB, but started falling into line from early 1918. However, when the band made its first visit to Britain in the spring of 1919, it was Columbia that bagged their services, recording six sides, followed by a further two when they returned in August, and another nine in January and May 1920. As a result, while the band was packing them in and Columbia was raking it in, HMV had to resort to some fairly desperate measures to capitalize on the trend. An advertisement in the April 1919 issue of *Talking Machine News* listed 'New Records of Dance Music on His Master's Voice – All suitable for JAZZING', which turned out to be mostly one-step selections played by that well-known hot combo the band of the HM Coldstream Guards, directed by Major J. Mackenzie-Rogan.

The new music was viewed with high-minded hostility in some quarters. *Talking Machine News* declared a Winner release by Murray Pilcer and his Jazz Band to be 'an unholy row dominated by a banjo which sends forth the semblance of a melody',[1] before adding in a more charitable, though still sniffy, aside that '[w]e must remember that at one time certain competent critics held a poor estimation of Wagner'.[2] The magazine's US counterpart *Talking Machine World* exclaimed in July 1919: '"JAZZ" MAY START ANOTHER WAR!' and reported that the Paris newspaper *Le Matin* was contesting America's claim to be the birthplace of jazz, the concept having apparently originated in Paris at the time of the Directoire:

> Those who had a great taste for noise went to the concerts of the Cat
> Orchestra. There were twenty cats with their heads in a row on the keyboard
> of a harpsichord. The performers by striking the keys worked a device which
> pulled the cats' tails, causing a caterwauling which gradually took on as much
> volume of sound as the jazz band and was fully as musical and entertaining.
> This so-called American invention is only a recurrence![3]

Such broadsides were easy to dismiss when anything with the word jazz on it was flying out of the shops. However, while Victor and Columbia recorded a lot of jazz in the years that followed, many of the most interesting developments were coming from the smaller, independent record labels that had sprung up over the previous decade or so. As certain key patents expired, the stranglehold that Victor and Columbia had on the industry loosened slightly and allowed breathing space for new entrants. According to Roland Gelatt, the business had grown from three manufacturers – Victor, Columbia and Edison – in 1912, to eight in 1914, with eighteen more joining in 1915, and a total of forty-six by 1916.[4] Because of the strength in depth of the incumbents' catalogues, the interlopers had to look for niches that Victor and Columbia weren't serving, and music aimed squarely at the blue collar and rural markets, be the purchasers black or white, fitted this bill admirably. Among these new companies were OKeh, Gennett and Paramount, all of whom played a part in jazz and recording history that belied their relatively modest size.

Otto Heinemann had come with his brother Adolph to the United States in 1914 on behalf of Carl Lindström AG, but found himself stranded at the outbreak of the First World War. He decided to make the most of his situation and went into business in the new country, forming the Otto Heinemann Phonograph Supply Company. It sold motors and other phonograph parts, for which purpose it took over a factory in Newark, New Jersey. For some reason, though, it fought shy of manufacturing any finished machines. Despite this, Heinemann decided to start a record label, for which he chose the name OKeh. The first vertically cut OKeh discs made their appearance in May 1918, to a largely indifferent response.

In October 1919, the Otto Heinemann Phonograph Supply Company was reorganized into the General Phonograph Corporation, with financial backing and help from Carl Lindström AG, now that the trading barriers had been lifted. Shortly after, the OKeh label moved on to laterally cut discs, which had a greater sales potential, given the number of laterally equipped machines in circulation. This potential was realized by an early release on the label – 'Crazy Blues' by Mamie Smith's Jazz Hounds, recorded on 10 August 1920. This disc is claimed, without much evidence, to have sold a million copies within a few weeks, but what is more certain is that it is the first blues record made by a female singer, something which other labels were quick to pick up on.

With this one release, OKeh went from being just another start-up to a bankable proposition. One figure who was instrumental in keeping the momentum up and signing other jazz and blues artists was Richard M. Jones, a black bandleader and pianist who had become OKeh's talent scout and producer in Chicago. The most important, and ultimately influential, of his discoveries was a trumpeter called Louis Armstrong and his group, the Hot Five.

Armstrong had gained some considerable experience of recording as a member of King Oliver's group, which had recorded for Gennett and OKeh, and with Fletcher Henderson's New York-based outfit, which had made discs for Columbia, Vocalion and Perfect (a company that pressed its discs in light brown shellac), among others.[5] In addition, he had worked as a backing musician on sessions by singers including Ma Rainey and Bessie Smith. His first Hot Five session, on 12 November 1925, was, however, his debut as a bandleader. He didn't need long to get into his stride. One of the numbers recorded at the second Hot Five session in February 1926 was 'Cornet Chop Suey', which rapidly became a jazz standard.

Paramount was another new label and it had been founded as a subsidiary of the Wisconsin Chair Company of Port Washington, the parent company having been established in the 1880s by one Fred Dennett. After the turn of the century, it had supplemented its seating business by making phonograph cabinets for other companies. From there, it was a short step to making talking machines in its own right. Then, in 1917, the Paramount label was established, primarily as a promotional device for the company's machines. A studio was established in Manhattan under the auspices of a subsidiary called the New York Recording Laboratories.

It wasn't until 1922 that Paramount began making the type of records for which it would become famous – its 'race' catalogue.[6] Previously, it had handled pressing for a 'race' label called Black Swan, but when the opportunity to buy Black Swan's masters came up, Paramount took it. The prime mover behind this was a black entrepreneur called J. Mayo Williams, who did not seem terribly bothered by the music he recorded, but had a knack for knowing what would sell. From his office in Chicago, Williams oversaw the building of an artist roster that included blues singers like Ma Rainey, Ida Cox, Blind Lemon Jefferson, Blind Blake, Son House and Skip James. After Williams's departure in 1926, roving talent scout H. C. Speir would add another name to this list, that of Charley Patton, one of the most influential of all blues artists. Although Paramount was always more of a blues label, it did record some jazz, most notably Jelly Roll Morton, who did a session in 1923, and Freddie Keppard, who had finally overcome his objections to recording.

Williams had tried valiantly to clean up some of the material that he was recording, but still some doubtful lyrics got through. Charley Patton's 'Spoonful Blues' was a dirge-like acknowledgement of Patton's massive addiction to cocaine. Either Paramount didn't realize this or chose to keep it quiet, as promotional material for the disc featured a drawing of a smartly dressed Patton sitting in a restaurant, awaiting delivery of some soup. Paramount had created a problem for itself, however. The market for black blues records certainly existed, but with many record dealers then unwilling to take such merchandise, how was Paramount going to sell its products? The answer was mail order, a service particularly appreciated by the more rural of the company's customers.

Gennett was another small label formed by a long-established company looking to diversify, in this case, the Starr Piano Company of Richmond, Indiana, which had been mass-producing musical instruments since 1872. In 1893, a Texan of Italian extraction called Henry Gennett bought into the business and, in time, came to play a vital role in its running. In 1915, Starr moved into records, bringing out a range of vertically cut (hill and dale) discs bearing the Gennett label. Laterally cut discs would have been preferable from a commercial point of view, given the number of suitably equipped machines in use, but Victor held the patent and Gennett was initially nervous of infringement. Then the company decided to press ahead with lateral discs anyway, a move which led to legal action from Victor.

The Victor action was resolved in the independent's favour, and the Gennett record business began in earnest. Henry's son Fred Gennett was deputed to oversee the recording programme, and with the help of the manager of the Starr Piano shop in Chicago, Fred Wiggins, a catalogue of recordings was built up. It was Wiggins who urged Gennett to give jazz a try, having seen the impact of the New Orleans Rhythm Kings (NORK) on the Windy City crowds. Gennett himself had no interest in jazz, but a great interest in things that sold, so in August 1922, NORK pitched up at the Richmond studio to make their first discs.

The studio was a spartan affair, a room in a warehouse that backed onto a heavily used railway line. It was a regular occurrence for sessions to stop while a train rumbled past. The New Orleans Rhythm Kings were followed into that noisy room by Joe 'King' Oliver – featuring the young Louis Armstrong – Hoagy Carmichael (who wrote 'Stardust' as an instrumental then woke up the Gennett recording engineer in the middle of the night so he could record it while it was fresh in his head) and Bix Beiderbecke.

Jazz was, however, only a part of Gennett's activities. To make the business pay, Fred Gennett decided that he would record or press anything, for a price. Chain-store labels such as Sears and Roebuck's Silvertone were bread and butter for Gennett, while speeches by William Jennings Bryan, hotel bands, vaudeville artists and symphony bands all passed through the Richmond works. Interestingly, one regular contract customer was the Ku Klux Klan, which, for a short while in the 1920s, ran its own record label. The selections were usually adapted hymns – 'The Old Rugged Cross' became 'The Bright Fiery Cross', while 'Onward Christian Klansmen' explains itself – and were credited to groups such as 'The Klansmen with all-white chorus'. How did a company who did so much for black music come to accept business from hooded bigots? As far as Gennett was concerned, all money was good money. In the words of Rick Kennedy and Randy McNutt, '[t]hey quietly pressed the discs because the Klan paid cash'.[7]

By 1915, when it entered the talking machine business, the Aeolian Company was already well known as a maker of player pianos and pipe organs, with headquarters in New York and London. Both the London and New York bases were called Aeolian Hall, the London branch being in the former Grosvenor Galleries off Bond Street.[8] Meanwhile, the British factory was at Hayes, close to the HMV works. Its first discs, issued under the Aeolian-Vocalion name, were, like Edison's Diamond Discs, vertically cut, with 150 grooves per inch. However, the Aeolian-Vocalion talking machine was fitted with a 'universal' tone arm, which could be adapted to play either vertical discs or the lateral platters offered by Victor and Columbia. Not surprisingly, it found an enthusiastic audience who preferred not to be tied to one format. By 1918, however, as patent threats receded, Aeolian-Vocalion had transferred to the lateral cut, and shortly after that dropped the Aeolian part of the label name.

Those in charge of the Vocalion label also came to learn the value of the new rhythmic music that was starting to emerge. The ODJB and King Oliver were enlisted for some recordings, while, later, Duke Ellington made some of his earliest discs for Vocalion. In 1925, however, the Aeolian Company's disc operations were taken over by Brunswick, Balke and Collender. In the UK, business continued independently of the new ownership, with the Vocalion company moving into the cheaper end of the market towards the end of the 1920s. Using General Electric's non-royalty electric recording method, it began the Broadcast label in 1927 offering 7-inch and 8-inch discs which were claimed to run for the same length as a conventional 10-inch disc, while retailing for just 1/6. In 1930, these were superseded by the Broadcast Twelve, which was, confusingly, a 10-inch disc, but with the purported playing time of a larger record.

The Vocalion records might have been cheap, but the musicianship on them was always first class, and many of the records stand up well today. The pianist, arranger and director of the Vocalion studio band was Harry Bidgood (who also recorded on accordion as Primo Scala) and the line-up of his 'Broadcasters' invariably included the best session musicians from the name bands, some of whom became famous bandleaders in their own right, such as the trombonists Ted Heath and Paul Fenoulhet. The main Vocalion studio had been at Duncan Avenue, just off the Grays Inn Road, although some location recordings were undertaken, mostly at the Stoll Picture Theatre in Kingsway, where use could be made of the Jardine pipe organ. In 1931, the recording facility moved to Holland Park Avenue for just six months, until the company was taken over by another major player in the cheap market, Crystalate, in mid-1932. From then on, the recordings were made at the Crystalate studios in Broadhurst Gardens, West Hampstead, an imposing building which had once been Hampstead Town Hall (it was not an administrative centre, merely a hall for the Hampstead residents). In addition to its good acoustic, studio one (of two) at Broadhurst Gardens had a permanently installed Wurlitzer theatre organ.

Brunswick, Balke and Collender had been a manufacturer of bowling and pool equipment before its entry into the record business just after the First World War. Part of the mythology of Brunswick's establishment was that the company had been engaged in making phonograph cabinets for Edison, but after a row about manufacturing standards, had been left with a large number of unused cabinets. It then decided to make use of them and give its former customer some competition. Others indicate that the company had a business alliance with Pathé. Both may be true. Whatever the truth of the story, Brunswick began manufacturing phonographs in 1916, and the records followed 1920, with the announcement of the first list of discs – 10-inch at 75c and 12-inch at $1.25 – in that January's *Talking Machine World*.

The first head of the Brunswick record division was William A. Brophy, aided by Walter Haenschen as the head of the popular record department. Another key employee was ex-Edison associate Frank Hofbauer, who came in as head of the studios, which were established in the top two floors of a thirteen-storey building at 16–18 East 36th Street, New York, with some other recording being undertaken in Chicago. With the head office set up at 35 West 32nd Street, two pressing plants were brought on stream, one in Long Island City, New York, the other at Jersey City. By the middle of the decade, these had been supplemented by further production facilities in Los Angeles, Michigan, Knoxville, Rockford, Toronto and, overseas, in Paris. The company had entered the UK market almost concurrently with its US debut, having forged an alliance with the music publishing and retail firm Chappell's. In the UK, the discs were branded initially as Brunswick Cliftophone, incorporating the name of a phonograph marketed by the company.

One of the mainstays of the early catalogue – Carl Fenton's Orchestra – did not truly exist. The band was an assortment of session musicians under the baton of none other than Walter Haenschen, his real name having probably been deemed too Germanic for the record-buying public. In time, however, real stars came to Brunswick. One of the first was the bandleader Isham Jones, who signed up in 1921. The most celebrated of the early signings, though, was a Jewish singer who made his name singing Negro and Negro-influenced songs, adopting blackface for the benefit of the audiences at his live performances. In 1924, Al Jolson joined Brunswick.[9] His fame reached unprecedented levels in 1927, when he starred in *The Jazz Singer*, the first talkie. The film was made by a relatively small outfit called Warner Bros, and it made the reputation of both the company and the film's star, but Brunswick also had two pieces of the action, being responsible both for Jolson's commercial recordings – such as the best-selling 'Sonny Boy' and 'Mammy' – and for the pressing of the 16-inch records that were played in synchronization with the film as part of the cumbersome Vitaphone sound-on-disc system adopted by Warner.

There was, however, more to Brunswick than simply Jolson. The young Duke Ellington made some of his first recordings for the label. It was Jolson, however, who awakened the interest of Jack and Sam Warner in taking over the Brunswick business. They were also interested in the young man who was responsible for these hit discs, one Jack Kapp, who had become Brunswick's recording director in the late 1920s. Kapp's 'thinnish loving-cup face' was prone to be the vehicle for such utterances as 'I know how to keep my pulse on the multitude'.[10] One contemporary description of Kapp was 'a man of no taste, so corny, he's good'[11] – high praise indeed in a business which had rarely overestimated the public taste. In April 1930, impressed by Kapp's success with the multitude, Warner Bros acquired the Brunswick record business for $8m.

Brunswick, Victor and Columbia realized that they needed production facilities on both the east and west coasts. The early 1920s was a boom time for records, and it was difficult for each to meet demand from one factory. Victor announced its intention to build a plant at Oakland near Los Angeles in April 1923, five months before Brunswick showed its hand, although Brunswick managed to get their factory open first. Responding to the news, *Talking Machine World* commented that 'Pacific Coast dealers are handicapped at present by the long distance from the factories which produce the most popular merchandise, especially in the matter of records of popular song hits and dance music'. The situation was so bad that sometimes a hit's 'peak [was] reached before the new records reach the Coast'.[12]

The Oakland plant, which, as well as pressing records would include a recording studio, would address this problem. Operational from 6 May 1924, the first record to be pressed there was 'Oriental Love Dreams' by the Coon-Sanders Nighthawks, which had been recorded in Chicago. The first Oakland recording to make the cut was 'Rip Saw Blues' by Art Landry's Orchestra, which dated from June. While Victor was making a landgrab in Oakland, Columbia was, unfortunately, hamstrung by its recent bankruptcy and was unable to consider any similar expansion. However, by 1926, the company was in better health, and it finally purchased 73,000 square feet of factory space in Oakland.

Nowhere near as many new labels emerged in the UK during the same period, but the smaller British labels were like their American counterparts in their willingness to try out things that, for one reason or another, would make the major firms throw their hands up. Edison-Bell was in third place in the British market, some way behind HMV and Columbia. Its main label, Winner, had been operating since 1912, offering 'a catalogue of brass band music, light orchestral pieces, music-hall celebrities and sentimental songs appealing to the unsophisticated'[13] at roughly 2 shillings a pop. In 1921, however, a new policy was brought into play, as Joe Batten, who had joined Edison-Bell the previous year, recalled:

It was decided to compete with the two 'big fellows', as HMV and Columbia were known, with a new venture called Velvet Face.[14] To me was assigned the onus of building a catalogue of good music. I was in for a fight, one after my own heart, and I was soon giving and receiving some hard knocks. The gramophone world is a small one; whenever I began negotiations with a well-known conductor, singer or instrumentalist, it would at once become known to the other companies ... Sometimes I won, sometimes they did; nevertheless my catalogue became thick with a list of artistes and a selection of titles which began to be my pride.[15]

Among those who went along with Batten were Dr Adrian Boult, who conducted his first session while soaking wet, having cycled from central London to Peckham in driving rain, Hamilton Harty and Eugene Goossens. However, the conductor for Velvet Face's greatest achievement was Batten himself. This was the 1924 recording of Elgar's *Dream of Gerontius*. Despite the composer's close links with HMV, the piece had not yet been recorded, Fred Gaisberg having declared the problems involved to be insuperable:

> I longed to do it [explained Batten]. To record such music would be a labour of love, an act of homage to a great composer. And apart from the aesthetic motives, another voice whispered to me that if it could be done, what a feather it would be in my cap, how Velvet Face could crow over HMV, to accomplish a recording which they had declared to be impossible.[16]

The length limitations of the discs meant that Batten had to abridge the work 'in which every bar seemed indispensable', while the acoustic recording process required a much reduced ensemble than that usually deployed to play the piece. Nine string players took the place of over forty, a choir of eight stood in for sixty to 100 singers, and the sound of the mighty organ was replaced with, of all things, a bass concertina. Despite these abridgements, the results – which retailed either as eight individual double-sided discs at 5/6 each or in a 'handsome, strongly bound Album' containing all of the words at £2 and 5 shillings – were good enough to gain laudatory reviews from all. 'No doubt there are still details which need attention ... But blemishes there must be in an undertaking of this calibre,' wrote the *Gramophone's* pseudonymous reviewer Percy Passage in October 1924, adding that he had 'honestly mentioned such weaknesses as I noticed. But this in no way detracts from the general excellence of the Velvet Face achievement'.[17]

Batten's achievement had also been noticed by his peers in the industry, as had always been the intention. '*Gerontius* certainly made a stir in the dovecotes marked HMV and Columbia, and it opened the way to my appointment with Columbia a few years after,' he asserted thirty years later. Meanwhile, the composer himself was greatly impressed by Batten's resolve. He had been kept informed by a clarinettist friend involved in the recording and '[o]nly his loyalty to HMV prevented him from coming to the studio'.[18]

Velvet Face had, rather more cheekily, set about recording the works of Gilbert and Sullivan, an enterprise hindered by HMV's exclusive contract with the D'Oyly Carte. Fortunately, the ever-resourceful Batten found a way around his lack of access to the relevant scores. He enlisted musicians who were known to be familiar with the work and amended piano copies of the music in red ink.

The gramophone was still viewed by some as not quite respectable, but, doubtless aided by the edifying efforts of Batten and other commercially minded patrons of the arts, the tide was turning. In 1922, the popular novelist Compton Mackenzie announced in the *Daily Telegraph* that he had finally come round to the idea:

> I have only recently discovered the gramophone. Until lately I supposed it to be nothing but a detestable interruption of conversation and country peace, the golf of sound. Gramophony was a noise to me rather more unpleasant than would be the combined sounds of a child running a hoop-stick along a railing, a dentist's drill, a cat trying to get out of a basket in a railway carriage, and a nursemaid humming upon a comb wrapped in tissue paper.[19]

The state of the art, he observed, had progressed considerably since he had first experienced it, both in terms of technique and repertoire:

> I had heard old records of Mischa Elman; but violin records ten years ago were very different from what they are now. In those days the squeak of a bat would have been almost as inaudible. As for the bands and orchestras – but let us forget them, although I regret to add that 'His Master's Voice' still allows currency to some ancient outrages upon music. There is a ghastly record of Brahms's *Hungarian Dance* in D minor played by Joachim which is only fit for a museum, and even there should never be played. However, it is ungrateful to

speak of such when nowadays the same company has given us that first *Hungarian Dance* divinely played by Kreisler and as perfectly rendered.[20]

Mackenzie's conversion had been caused by *force majeure* rather than any sudden shaft of enlightenment. Fond of listening to music while he wrote, Mackenzie had bought, on hire-purchase, a piano roll-operated Aeolian organ, but had become disappointed at the limited repertoire available for the machine. He tried to return it to the manufacturer but was reminded of the binding HP agreement. In its stead, he was offered one of their gramophones and a selection of records, which he accepted reluctantly. However, when the equipment was delivered to his home on Herm in the Channel Islands, he was pleasantly surprised by the sound quality and within two months had spent £400 on a collection of over 1,000 discs.

The response to his *Telegraph* outing was enthusiastic and inspired him and his brother-in-law Christopher Stone to start the *Gramophone*, the first magazine to take a serious view of records and their making from the perspective of the listener. In the first issue, Mackenzie promised, after apologizing to the public 'for inflicting upon it another review' that it would be 'an organ of candid opinion'. He admitted that the editorial policy would be 'largely personal, and as such it will be honest but not infallible'. Nonetheless, the industry undoubtedly gained from the endorsement and enthusiasm of such a well-known figure.

Mackenzie was right. Sound quality had improved, but it was still some way from perfection. Nonetheless, record companies had always been fond of making extravagant claims for the fidelity of their recordings. Even tinfoil was praised for its stunning clarity. The logical extreme was reached by Edison, who promoted his Diamond Discs with a series of demonstrations called 'Tone Tests'. In these, the original artist would be hidden behind a curtain with a Diamond Disc reproducer, and audiences would be invited to guess which sounds were live and which came from the record. To be fair, Edison probably had a point, as his vertically cut discs and the jewelled point of the reproducer used were capable of much higher quality sound than a steel needle rattling about in a lateral groove composed partially of abrasive matter.

The London branch of Columbia had made a considerable advance in the early 1920s with the laminated surface records that it marketed under the 'New Process' name. These discs had a core made of low-grade shellac compound, as used by everyone else, but the difference was that Columbia

– or more precisely the Standar (sic) Chemical Engineering Company, which had developed New Process on the record company's behalf – used a method of bonding a cellulose-based surface to this core, which gave a much higher reproduction quality. To be fair, Edison had been on the case before Columbia. The Blue Amberol cylinders were celluloid, while the Diamond Discs had a paper-based core to which a synthetic surface was laminated. Columbia New Process records, however, were not half an inch thick, which the Edisons were, and could be played on the more common lateral phonographs. Record companies had been advertising 'scratchless' surfaces for years, but for once, the manufacturer's hyperbole was justified. A mint condition New Process disc played back on modern equipment is much less noisy than any other 78s of its era or, indeed, later.

For all of Columbia's advances, however, the method of getting the music into the grooves had been in use, with the odd modification, from the days of tinfoil. Certain instruments recorded badly, while others failed to register at all, with the frequency range limited to around 2,088 cycles per second at the upper end. Moreover, all recording had to be undertaken in the studio, as the diaphragm would struggle to capture any sound at all from a distant stage or podium. How little the recording process had improved by the early 1920s is illustrated by the recollections of Gerald Moore, the legendary accompanist, who made his first, faltering steps in the studio on a 1921 HMV session with the singer Fenee Chemet. He described the room as 'purely utilitarian: no soft lighting, no carpets or curtains', referring disparagingly to the reflective wooden walls as 'fences', as he recalled his voice booming 'as if my head were in the resounding womb of some giant double-bass'. As for the studio piano, he:

> was appalled at the metallic harshness of its tone; it had the brazen splendour of a brass spittoon. This brittle sound was not to be attributed entirely to the acoustics of the chamber, for I found on examination that the piano, by the tuner's art, had been rendered as percussive as possible by the filing down of the felts on the hammers. The anti-upholstery campaign had extended even to my piano.

Just as had happened to Joe Batten twenty years earlier, Moore was instructed, on his Chemet debut, to play *forte*. 'I protested that it was impossible to bang out the notes of a lullaby [the piece being recorded was 'Berceuse']; I should wake the baby. The result, in the test played back to us, was that I was unheard. I did not relish this.' So he complied. Something else Moore did not particularly relish was the lack of eye contact with the singers:

> It must be remembered that the horn was the centre of our world, immovable, and of course the singer had to stand in front of it. Nay, more than this he would have his head halfway down the trumpet ... his buttocks were all I could see of him while my piano would be as far away as the length of a billiards-room. It is vital for the accompanist to hear what the singer is doing and my difficulties under these conditions can be imagined since his sounds were not emanating from the end of him nearest to me.

Proximity to the horn became a hard-fought issue on duets. 'Each wanted to shine, each wanted to hog the trumpet, and the charging and pushing that went on made me marvel that they had any breath left for singing. Victory usually went to *avoirdupois*, a welter being no match for a heavyweight,' Moore observed, later wondering, 'How we ever succeeded in making records and good records at that, remains a mystery to me to this day'.[21]

Unsurprisingly, the record bosses all knew privately that an electrically based system of recording – using microphones and amplifiers, such as those used in radio broadcasting, to drive the cutting stylus with greater efficiency – would be preferable to the prevailing method. As early as 1903, in the very first issue of *Talking Machine News*, the possible uses of electricity in recording were being discussed, although the writer, F. J. Turquand, concentrated on motive power for turntables[22] and amplification of recordings rather than actual recording.

The problem was making an electric recording system work. A rudimentary electrical recording method was developed by Lionel Guest and H. O. Merriman in 1919, and it was used to record the burial ceremony of the Unknown Warrior at Westminster Abbey in 1920. The fruits of this experiment were pressed up by Columbia and given a limited release, but the system was considered unsatisfactory for commercial use.

Nearly all of the major companies were devoting a considerable amount of time to experiments with electrical recording, but none came to fruition. The exception was Victor, which didn't bother because 'electrical recording smacked too much of radio',[23] an area of business into which the company had entered without much enthusiasm.

Eldridge Johnson wrote in a letter to his son in February 1924:

> I do not believe the radio business is going to cut a very large figure in the line
> of amusements, but the trade expect the Victor Co to do as much, in their line,
> as any other company, and will make us a lot of trouble if we do not give them
> a line of our goods in combination with a good receiving set … I do not
> believe, however, that the scheme of broadcasting music will replace talking
> machines, it may, however, slow up our expansion. But there is the feature of
> privacy, selection, repeat and the sense of proprietorship in a talking machine
> that no general broadcasting scheme can hope to substitute.[24]

Perhaps Victor was hoping to benefit from whatever its British affiliate came
up with. In November 1923, a young engineer called Brenchley Mittell had
been appointed by HMV managing director Alfred Clark specifically to
look into electrical recording. However, his chances of success were
hampered greatly by the lack of resources at his disposal. In an interview
given when he retired in 1957, Mittell said that 'there was absolutely nothing
going on in the way of research at Hayes'.[25]

The answer, when it arrived in 1924, came from outside the record
business. It was the work of J. P. Maxfield and H. C. Harrison at Western
Electric's Bell Research Laboratories, and Mittell had been lucky enough to
see them at work. The conditions in which they worked were in stark
contrast to his own experience. For starters, the Bell Laboratories had a
research staff of 1,200, all divided into groups, several of which competed to
produce an electrical recording system. Although his visit to the lab had
been illuminating, there wasn't a lot that Mittell could do about it.

If record companies chose to adopt the Harrison and Maxfield system, the
upper frequency limit of records would be increased, from 2,088 cycles per
second to 6,000 cycles per second. String basses and conventionally
constructed violins could be recorded properly without a tuba or a Stroh
being brought in as a substitute. Musicians could sit in a normal spatial
relationship rather than having to crowd around a single horn, and pianos
could come down from their stilts. It was just what the industry and the
listening public needed. It wasn't quite as simple as buying the gear from
Western Electric and rigging it up, though. The industry was once again
dominated by patents, and this time, the main patent was held by a company
outside the industry, which demanded a royalty on each record sold.

In the beginning, it looked as if Western Electric would license the system exclusively to Victor, but it did not move fast enough. Eldridge Johnson had been ill for some time, primarily with depression, and the Western Electric opportunity came during a particularly bad bout. As a result, a draft contract sat unsigned for a month. There was also the possibility that the company was finding it hard to overcome its earlier lack of enthusiasm for electric recording, despite its obvious superiority. Whatever the reason, Victor's chance for exclusivity disappeared before it could sign anything. Columbia had not been meant to know about the Western Electric success, but word had leaked out and now it was demanding to be let in on the magnificent new development.

Columbia had found out through Frank Capps of Pathé's New York office, an old friend of Louis Sterling. Western Electric had sent its test waxes to Pathé so that they could be pressed into records for evaluation purposes. All of this was done under conditions of great secrecy, but curiosity got the better of Capps and his colleague Russell Hunting, and they played one of the discs surreptitiously. 'What they heard coming from the records took them completely by surprise,' reported Fred Gaisberg. 'For the first time they heard sibilants emerge from the trumpet, loud and hissing!'[26] Capps sent copies to Sterling along with 'a letter worded in the most urgent terms'. Sterling was as astonished as Capps and Hunting had been, and he set sail for America on the *Mauretania* on Boxing Day 1924, having cabled Western Electric telling them to do nothing until he had seen them.

Gaisberg, being affiliated to Victor, had known about the developments since the autumn of 1924, when Hunting visited London:

> He [Hunting] said, 'Fred, we're all out of jobs. Come down here and I'll show you something that will stagger you.' ... He swore me to secrecy before playing the... unauthorized copies of the Western Electric experiments ... I saw that from now on any talking machine company which did not have this electric recording system would be unable to compete with it.[27]

Sterling later told Gaisberg that he had reached the same conclusion himself the moment he heard the illicit pressings.

Sterling's persistence resulted in Columbia being offered a licence on the same terms as Victor, but he then hit an obstacle. Western Electric had stipulated that only American companies and their affiliates could acquire the system. HMV qualified through its ties with Victor, while UK Columbia qualified as a subsidiary of the American company. Unfortunately, the American company was in the process of reconstruction after its 1923 bankruptcy, and was in no position to make major investments. Sterling tried to impress on them the long-term benefits of electrical recording, namely that anyone who didn't adopt it didn't have much of a long-term future. His paymasters were unimpressed. There was no money for anything.

Having been presented with what he knew to be a *sine qua non*, Sterling was not inclined to let the matter pass. The UK company was prospering. It had become a public limited company in 1923, and production was on the up. He felt, quite reasonably, that he had the upper hand. So, he sought the help of the J. P. Morgan banking firm, and in March 1925, the British company bought 60 per cent of its American parent, paying $50 each for the 51,000 shares. As well as the finance from Morgan's, the move was partly funded by a share issue which increased the company's capital from £200,000 to £600,000. Sterling – who became chairman of the American company – chose to explain the decision to *Talking Machine World* on patriotic rather than business grounds:

> In the first place, I am a New Yorker, who has been representing the Columbia Co. in Europe for sixteen years ... The European company has been very successful and is doing the largest record business in Great Britain. The European company's shares on the London Exchange are at four-and-a-half times par and the company is earning about 75 per cent net on its capital issue. We feel confident that eventually the Columbia Phonograph Co., Inc. will be equally successful in the United States.[28]

The factory at Bridgeport, Connecticut had been running far below capacity, and Sterling vowed to build it up gradually, pointing to the fact that the London factory had been running at three-quarters of capacity for all of its twenty-five years. Consequently, William T. Forse, the works manager at Bendon Valley, took over the US plant temporarily, awaiting the arrival of R. H. Gloetzner, who had been poached from Heinemann's General Phonograph Company.

By 1927, UK Columbia owned almost 100 per cent of the American company, and the group had expanded further through acquisitions, including in 1925 the purchase of a large stake in Transoceanic Trading of Amsterdam, the ultimate holding company of Carl Lindström AG. By

November, these overseas holdings had been hived off into Columbia International, with plans to acquire more stock in these companies. Then, in November 1926, Columbia bought the Lindström-affiliated OKeh label. A month earlier, the group had opened its 96,000-square-foot Australian plant at Homebush, near Sydney.

Among other labels, the Lindström acquisition had brought Parlophone – as Parlophon had become – into the Columbia fold. The label's artists and repertoire manager was Oscar Preuss, a Londoner who had joined Odeon in 1904 at the age of fifteen and who soon became a distinguished recording engineer. He had moved into the Parlophone job in 1923, working at the studios in Lindström's City Road premises. However, when electric recording came in, the Parlophone recording operation shifted not to the Columbia studios near Westminster Cathedral, but to a church in Maida Vale.

As exciting a development as electric recording was, the companies were in no hurry to trumpet its arrival. If they did, they feared that sales of acoustically recorded discs would plummet, a dangerous possibility considering that these composed the vast majority of their back catalogues. Columbia did not announce the advent of the system that it called 'Viva-Tonal' until January 1927, by which time it had been in use for over eighteen months. A similar thing happened with Victor and its 'Orthophonic' products.

A casualty of electric recording was the old wood-panelled studios. These were designed to amplify and reflect the sound as much as possible for the sake of the diaphragm, even though little of the natural reverberation made itself heard on the finished records. With the sensitivity of the Westrex microphones and cutters, such harsh room tone was unnecessary and, it was thought, undesirable. For example, the HMV studio at Hayes, which had opened in June 1912 and which sported a moveable ceiling, carried on with electric recordings until mid-1927, when it was converted to office space. Various other premises with more suitable acoustics had been leased, including the Small Queen's Hall in Portland Place for smaller, popular recordings and the Kingsway Hall – a Methodist church – for larger orchestral sessions. Columbia, meanwhile, adapted its studio facilities at Petty France near Victoria station.

Location recording, nigh-on impossible under the old conditions, became feasible. Indeed, one of the most famous early electric recordings was a Columbia disc of 'Adeste Fideles' sung at the Metropolitan Opera House in New York by an 850-strong choir. The fact that the audience was audible and even joined in meant that Columbia was able to advertise the finished product as the work of 4,850 voices. Compare this to Joe Batten's cut-down choirs on *Dream of Gerontius*. HMV ordered a mobile recording van on a Lancia chassis, and this was used on many historic recordings, including choirboy Ernest Lough's 1927 reading of 'O for the Wings of a Dove'.

As grateful as the record companies were that someone had cracked the mystery of electric recording, they felt that they were paying a steep price for the innovation. Western Electric demanded $50,000 up front, and then a royalty on each disc sold. In Columbia's case, the royalty varied from 0.875 of a penny to 1.25d, according to the size of the disc.

There were alternatives, but they did not match up. Some of the cheaper labels, such as Broadcast, used Marconi's non-royalty system. Meanwhile, Brunswick offered its so-called 'Light Ray' system, developed by General Electric, which incorporated a photo-electric cell. Despite claiming to capture all the frequencies audible to the human ear, it turned out to be a disappointment and before long, even they were licensing the Westrex system, although Brunswick's own electrically powered gramophone, the Panatrope, managed to find favour with the public.

Sterling's reverse takeover of the American Columbia company was followed later in the 1920s by another major sale: that of Eldridge R. Johnson's stake in the company he had founded. The rise of radio had hit Victor very hard indeed in 1924 and 1925, as the company had previously been doing so well that it had allowed itself to become complacent. Crucially, it had maintained a resistance to entering the field of wireless manufacture and had been affected accordingly, the decline being alleviated only by the sudden appearance of the Orthophonic Victrola and electrically recorded discs, as well as the belated signing of a business alliance with the Radio Corporation of America.

Johnson had, as we have seen, made several attempts to sell the company, beginning almost at the start with his various coquettish overtures towards the Gramophone Company. If HMV's terms had been agreeable, it is possible that Johnson would have cut and run long before 1926. Then there was the Department of Justice, which continued to view Johnson's business with immense suspicion. The claims that he made about having tried to sell the company were well founded, as, it appears, was his assertion that he was dismayed at the size to which the Victor company had grown.

The primary motivation for Johnson cashing in at the point that he did, however, was his poor health. From 1915 onwards, he was beset by depression and had withdrawn from the active management of the company for several years. In his absence, his trusted lieutenants stewarded the company with a sure hand, but by 1926, most of these long-serving men had resigned or retired – some taking several attempts to make the final break. Vice-president and treasurer Charles Haddon was the first to make a move, tendering his resignation in 1916. 'When a man has to drive himself to perform the daily duties that were formerly a pleasure to him,' he wrote to Johnson, 'it is evident that he is not as efficient as he ought to be in the service of his employers'.[29] In short, he said, he was 'absolutely tired out' by the 'constant pressure' of the industry. Johnson assumed that a major part of Haddon's problem was his tendency to clash with the company's general manager Louis Geissler, but Haddon assured him this had nothing to do with it. In his reply, Johnson had also cited his own indisposition and it would appear to have worked, for Haddon retracted his resignation and carried on in his post as treasurer until 1919 and as vice-president until 1921.

Oddly enough, Geissler was the next to try to get out, in April 1918, when he gave notice of his intention to leave on 1 January 1919, declaring himself 'mentally tired out'.[30] Geissler's resignation as general manager was accepted, but he remained a director for another three years. Later in 1918, however, came the exit of chairman Leon Douglass, a founder member of the company, followed shortly by Albert Middleton, then in 1923 by distribution director Ralph Freeman and a year later by recording laboratory director Calvin Child. Writing to Douglass in July 1924, Johnson bemoaned these departures. 'When you review the list of men who have gone, it is appalling,' he observed. As well as being personally saddening to him, the losses had a distinct financial aspect:

> Besides the loss of the services of these men the company lost a great investment, in a way, because their compensations in the line of salaries, commissions, dividends, special payments, etc. etc. have amounted to approximately ten and a half million dollars and they hold, at present, 55,214 shares, over 15 per cent of the Victor stock … the trouble is that I must reconstruct the organization from men who are not so heavily financially interested and that makes the matter more difficult.[31]

Johnson and his management team had run the company as a benevolent dictatorship. For several years until 1915, each member of staff received a large turkey and a commensurate supply of cranberries at Christmas. This act came to an end only when it emerged that several men from the cabinet works had used their seasonal gifts to enter the poultry trade. The company, however, was changing.

The sale became a serious prospect in 1923, when Johnson returned to J.E. Sterett, his adviser at Price Waterhouse, for his opinion. Sterett observed that any purchaser 'would be doing more than buying a security. He would, in fact, be acquiring the controlling interest in a large and highly technical business.' He went on to inform Johnson that the market for Victor shares was 'limited' and that only small blocks of stock could be disposed of at present. Small blocks sold by conventional means could, he argued, achieve a very gratifying $160 per share. However, a holding the size of Johnson's could only be disposed of through an underwriting syndicate or something similar. 'In these circumstances,' noted Sterett, 'the current market quotations do not represent the fair market value of a large block of the stock.'[32] Sterett suggested that a corporation should be formed, with Johnson transferring his holdings of Victor stock to it, creating a three-tier share structure. This idea came to nothing.

The sale plans were put on hold, but revived after the radio debacle, and this time, Johnson received an offer from two New York banking houses – Speyer and Co, and J. W. Seligman. 'My health will never permit me to work hard again and conditions in the business have changed so that the company will be better off in the hands of large financial interests who are in a better position to make co-operative arrangements with the electrical interests,' he wrote in a cable to Douglass.[33] Reports differ as to the amount he received for his stock. Roland Gelatt reports Johnson's share as $28m, with another $12m being spent on mopping up the holdings of the other directors. However, the official history of Victor – which is presumably drawn from company documents – puts Johnson's windfall at $23m and that of the other directors at $7m. The price had come down from $160 to $115 a share, but after what the company had been through, this was a considerable premium over the current price of Victor stock. Johnson insisted that this offer be extended to his fellow shareholders, who accepted gratefully, and the transaction was completed on 6 January 1927.

Characteristically, Johnson began to wonder if he had done the right thing. 'I do not feel very cheerful and I hate to sell more than anything I ever did,' he wrote to Douglass in that initial cable. On the eve of the deal's consummation, he wrote to Sterett saying that he did not 'know whether I am pleased with the matter of selling my Victor Stock or not ... I am quite satisfied with the profits I have made during my thirty-six years as a business man but I really hate to give up such an interesting enterprise.'[34] One consolation was that all of his old associates were now 'very well fixed indeed'.

Johnson had been reluctant to sell until he found the right buyers. 'I only hold a comfortable majority, and if I parted with that my successors might not be satisfactory,' he wrote to Douglass in July 1924. When Speyer and Seligman came along he viewed them as perfect. As investment bankers, they had the money to see Victor through whatever was to come. He commented to Douglass: 'I could have made it pay me much more but I had an opportunity to put it into fairly good hands without destroying the organization and at the same time give every other stockholder a chance to get out on the same basis, which I thought was too good to let slip'.[35] Unfortunately he had forgotten the principal function of venture capitalists – to invest and then seek a return on their investment, usually by selling up. So it was that within a year of Johnson and associates selling their stocks, the new owners were in talks with David Sarnoff of the Radio Corporation of America – founded in 1919 – with a view to selling the Victor company on. The discussions took the best part of another year, but the deal was concluded on 15 March 1929, with RCA paying a reported $150m for the Victor business.

Business was good during the brief ownership of Victor by the New York bankers. In 1927, net income was $7.3m, with a million Victrolas being manufactured and sales of 37.6 million records. The Speyer and Seligman interlude was not, however, merely a holding operation. Expansions were made during the two years, most notably the full acquisition of the former Berliner Gramophone Company of Canada, in which Victor had held a stake since 1909 and a majority holding since 1923.

Johnson was to regret the sale bitterly for the rest of his life, but in reality, it is hard to see what else he could have done. He was in no fit state to go on running the company himself, and he thought that it might be too much for his son's constitution:

> Of course, I might have continued the company and made Fenimore president, but while he is quite capable, I do not believe that his health would

stand it. He is very strong physically, surprisingly so; his muscles are as hard as iron, but he has the same nervous temperament that I have, and while I feel that the Victor Company can win out and even do better in the future than it did in the past, I also know that there are many troubles ahead which can only be controlled by tremendously hard work on the part of the chief executive. Fenimore remains in the organization but his responsibilities will be limited. At present he is happy and satisfied.[36]

As 1929 wore on, Johnson's move turned out to be a shrewd and timely one.

6 Brother, can you spare 75c for a gramophone record?

Radio's effect on record sales in the 1920s seemed bad enough at the time, but it turned out to be a small-scale rehearsal for the Great Depression and its effects. In America, the 1920s had been a period of great prosperity, as the Federal Reserve set interest rates below market levels and promoted easy borrowing. The result was a massive growth in stock market values. At the end of the year in 1925, the US stock market had been valued at $27bn, by October 1929, this had increased to $87bn. Shares in the American Columbia company, valued originally at 10 shillings, had risen to £15, and US banking firms – led by J. P. Morgan – showed considerable interest in taking back this thriving business from its British owners. At such an inflated price, Louis Sterling was only too happy to sell, and beginning in the spring of 1929, all but 16 per cent of the Columbia company was sold back to US institutions – primarily Morgan's – making Sterling and his London colleagues very wealthy men.

Such growth was all very well if it could be sustained but, in time, the Federal Reserve acknowledged that it could not, and attempted to address the issue with a series of interest rate increases, beginning in July 1928. Although this action had been intended to cool the market down, the prevailing investment patterns continued largely unmodified. By October 1929, then, the market was ready for a correction, a periodic stock market occurrence in which inflated prices find a more realistic level. On the morning of Thursday 24 October 1929, the correction began, with some prices dropping early in the day. However, instead of riding the storm, the money men panicked and sparked a major rush of selling. At the close of trading, the Dow Jones industrial average was down 9 per cent and nearly 13 million shares had changed hands – beating the previous Wall Street record by over 4 million. The record was not set to last long. Despite the banks moving in to buy stocks and shore up the market, and the emollient words of President Herbert Hoover, the selling frenzy continued and over 16 million shares changed hands on 29 October, trumping Black Thursday's figure by some margin. It became clear that this was the start of a long-term decline.

Another factor contributing to the start of the Depression had been the advent of tighter fiscal controls after the Clarence Hatry scandal. Hatry was a colourful character with a history of dubious enterprises. In 1929, he announced his intention to take over the British mineral firm United Steel. However, as his cash reserves were non-existent, he had to formulate a debt package to close the deal. Unfortunately, in doing so, he opted to cook the books, creating balance sheets for his companies that looked far more favourable than they really were. He got his comeuppance when he was discovered forging stock certificates. Humiliated out of the running, Hatry declared bankruptcy on 20 September 1929. The Bank of England had more or less encouraged market speculators, and so the United Steel deal was such a major issue that the revelation of Hatry's fraud caused the Dow Jones to lose 2 per cent on 20 September.

Consumer spending suffered, and so, consequently, did the record industry. Of the principals, the only casualty was Edison's phonographic operations. To the last, Edison had remained loyal to the cylinder, continuing to manufacture Blue Amberols alongside his Diamond Discs. The whole enterprise had become a distant also-ran compared with the activities of Victor and Columbia. With the exception of the odd recording by the likes of innovative jazz bandleader Fletcher Henderson, Edison had failed to attract any star names to his labels. He also did not adopt electric recording until 1927, perhaps because of a conviction that his time-honoured methods continued to be superior. By the time he came round to the concept, the competition had a head start. In late 1929, the unthinkable happened and Edison issued an electrically recorded, laterally cut disc, in concept indistinguishable from the Victor and Columbia records that he had maintained to be inferior. However, on 1 November, before such heresy could take hold as company policy, Edison announced his withdrawal from the phonographic industry, fifty-two years after his initial experiments with tinfoil had begun the whole business.

The Warner Bros ownership of Brunswick also foundered in the harsher new economic climate. The new owners had seemingly done everything right. The music division vice-president Herman Starr took Brunswick under his nominal control, but, despite being an accountant by training and thorough by inclination, he let the hitmaking Kapp do whatever he needed to maintain the winning run. Kapp had repaid the trust by discovering a second star artist to supplement Jolson, the ex-Paul Whiteman vocalist Bing Crosby. Crosby had three massive hits in short order – 'Out of Nowhere', 'Just One More Chance' and 'At Your Command'. Unfortunately, these weren't enough to persuade the Warners to ride out the industry downturn and in December 1931, barely eighteen months after buying Brunswick, Warner Bros took an $8m bath and offloaded the whole record operation.

There were other casualties among the smaller independent labels. The Starr Piano Company struggled on with its Gennett division for a while after the Wall Street Crash, but finally the Electrobeam Gennett label (as it had been known since it adopted electric recording) succumbed in December 1930. The company continued in a limited way, with its Champion subsidiary as an outlet for country releases, but this also closed in 1934. Without sentimentality, or the thought that they might be historically important in the future, all of the masters and copper matrices were scrapped. Paramount also declined rapidly after the Depression kicked in, with the Wisconsin Chair company calling time on its subsidiary in mid-1932. What of Paramount's intellectual property, enshrined on those copper matrices? Some of the masters went to Starr Piano, which had always helped Paramount with contract recording and presumably had some use for some of them as Champion discs. The vast majority, however, went for scrap as well, although employees were allowed to help themselves to whatever they had use for. One Paramount man is reported to have built a chicken coop out of the discarded metalwork.

In the UK, the industry giants – HMV and Columbia – decided to huddle together for warmth and comfort in the sudden coldness of the economic climate. Such a move had been rumoured in more prosperous times, and some talks were entered into around 1929, but they cooled off, largely due to Louis Sterling's lack of enthusiasm. The initial motivation came from the chairman of both RCA and its parent company, General Electric. Columbia was, marginally, the smaller company, and would have been the junior partner in any amalgamation, something Sterling would have found hard to countenance, especially given Columbia's reputation as the more innovative and enterprising of the two. He told the RCA board that the answer was no, unless he was allowed to quit. As Sterling himself was one of Columbia's primary assets, the idea withered.

The press, however, managed to keep the story alive for the next couple of years. 'Negotiations between the two biggest gramophone companies were recently resumed after their collapse last year,' said the *New York Times* in March 1930. 'It is understood the chief points blocking an agreement have now been settled and that a merger is all but completed between the companies with a total capitalization of almost $25,000,000.'[1] The talks were, indeed, back on, largely at the instigation of Columbia's backers J. P. Morgan, which also had interests in Victor/HMV. However, over a month later, instead of reporting the consummation of the deal, all that the *New York Times* could offer was that Morgan's Thomas Cochrane was 'conferring in London' with HMV and Columbia and that news of 'the long-forecast announcements ... is expected hourly'.[2]

All went quiet until March of the following year, when coverage resumed with the news that 'a plan to merge the Columbia Graphophone Co. Ltd, and the Gramophone Co. Ltd, in a new holding company was under negotiations'.[3] To what extent the earlier reports had been wishful journalistic thinking is uncertain, but this time, the *New York Times* was bang on the money. On 19 March 1931, four days after that brief report, the Gramophone Company board met in the boardroom over the HMV shop at 363 Oxford Street and noted that both they and the Columbia board would be recommending the merger to shareholders.

The plan was to create a new company, Electric & Musical Industries Ltd (referred to from the start as EMI), to act as holding company for both the Gramophone Company and the Columbia Graphophone Company, which would retain their separate identities. This was considered important because of the American connections – Victor and Columbia were pitched rivals and might not take kindly to having their UK and European releases siphoned through the same label. Upsetting them was something that was to be avoided at all costs, given the market importance of American repertoire, and the forced divestment of the Victor and Columbia holdings in the British companies meant that the relationship became a simple matter of licensing. Before long, though, it was realized that the companies' cheap labels could be merged into one without causing any unrest, and so in 1933, Regal and Zonophone combined to form Regal Zonophone.

Sterling remained opposed to the deal, but now being only a 1 per cent shareholder in Columbia, he recognized that he no longer had his old power of veto. Added to this, the financial context had changed. Following the stock market crash, both companies were making vastly reduced returns: in 1930–1, the combined operations announced profits of £160,983, compared with £1.42m the previous year. Most worrying was the fact that those emasculated profits came entirely from Columbia, while HMV was losing money. Total record sales for the two companies had dropped from 30 million discs in 1929 to 20 million in 1931. The deal looked attractive to the Columbia investors because their company relied on a range of externally produced components for its machines, whereas the HMV line at Hayes was almost entirely made in-house. Consequently, a merger would result in massive efficiencies.

So it was that the head office and factory for the new operation was to be at the HMV site in Hayes, with Columbia's plant at Bendon Valley, Wandsworth being closed down. One remnant of the old plant made the transfer – as a result of the merger, HMV could now use Columbia's laminating patents to its own advantage.[4] In addition, the first board of the new company was to consist of nine members, five of whom – Alfred Clark, John Broad, His Excellency Marchese Guglielmo Marconi,[5] David Sarnoff and Trevor Williams – came from the HMV side. The balance – Sterling, Michael Herbert, Lord Marks (formerly Sir George Croydon Marks) and financier Edward de Stein – were Columbia men. Although these factors made HMV look like the senior partner in the deal, Columbia's better financial position and Sterling's acknowledged dynamism meant that the reality was rather different. Clark was to be chairman, but the catbird seat, the managing directorship, was to be Sterling's. Looking back from a distance of twenty-six years, Sterling was inclined to observe that he had 'brought with him ... a very active, aggressive, intelligent organization which the Gramophone Company did not possess'.[6]

By the end of June, both sides had near-unanimous acceptances of the offer. In order for the combination to pass muster with the anti-trust authorities, the balance of Columbia's stake in its US parent had to be sold. A buyer for the whole US Columbia business was found in the Grigsby-Grunow company, the manufacturer of the Majestic range of radios. The deal had been announced in December 1931, with Columbia shareholders receiving a $10 a share stock dividend. A controlling stake in the Japanese Nipponophone company, which had been purchased by Sterling in 1927, was passed to the American company, for the sake of territorial neatness.

The EMI merger coincided with the establishment of what was to become the most famous recording studio complex in the world – those at Abbey Road in north-west London's St John's Wood district. For all of Columbia and Sterling's innovation, the idea of setting up a large, purpose-built studio complex was an HMV scheme, promoted mainly by Osmund Williams, Trevor Williams's go-ahead young son, who joined the company as head of the artists' department in 1927. Perhaps surprisingly, Fred Gaisberg was against the scheme, but the plan was approved and efforts turned to finding a site. A Georgian house at 3 Abbey Road came up for sale in 1929, a venue that Williams and his assistant David Bicknell immediately thought had the scope for the development in hand. Plans were drawn up by Wallis, Gilbert and Partners – best known as the architects of the famous Hoover building on the Great West Road – to use the house itself as an administrative block and to build three new studios across the property's garden. On 11 November 1929, the purchase of the freehold of the 22,750-square-foot site for £18,000 was approved by the HMV board, as was £25,000 of expenditure on the buildings.[7]

The first test session in the largest studio, designated number one, took place on 7 October 1931, by which time, commercial recording in the smallest studio, number three, had already begun. The grand opening of number one was to have taken place on 11 November 1931, two years to the day after the acquisition of the site, but the company was informed that it would be impossible to get the press along on Armistice Day. So, the opening took place the following day, beginning with filming for a Pathé newsreel at 9.30, and the main event – a recording session in which Sir Edward Elgar conducted his *Falstaff* suite in front of an audience including the likes of George Bernard Shaw – followed an hour later.

For all of the thought and planning that had gone into the studios, an assessment of the results from number one and three was taken and the outcome was not encouraging. It was noticed that Columbia dance band recordings by Debroy Somers and Jack Payne 'had a brighter and freer tone with possibly more room resonance'[8] than HMV recordings of the same titles by Jack Hylton and Ambrose. Meanwhile, recordings made by Ray Noble with the New Mayfair Orchestra in studio three 'showed promise, yet ... [were] rather under-recorded, [and] ... also lacking in the upper register'. On one set of HMV recordings, the sound was described as 'blanketty' and it had to be re-recorded at Kingsway Hall.

As ground-breaking as the enterprise was, these acoustical problems were a recurring theme for the first few years of Abbey Road's working life. Members of the engineering staff argued that in number three, the acoustical conditions were greatly different from those promised by the acoustical contractors who specified the treatment of the walls. The medium-sized studio two did not open until early 1932, delayed by an eleventh-hour enquiry into the escalating costs of the project. Although there were problems with demand for studio space outstripping supply, this hiatus was a blessing in disguise, as it allowed some of the lessons learned from the first two studios to be put into practice. The EMI engineers argued that number two should have a 'wood block floor', 'brick walls' and a 'solid plaster coffered ceiling with lighting'. This would create conditions 'the exact opposite to those prevailing in studio no. 3, and ... we shall be able to make much more brilliant records with the rigid construction which is undoubtedly required for Dance and Military Band work'.[9] In the event, this was exactly what happened and number two found itself in high demand from the moment of opening. The other two studios were refitted acoustically in the early years of the Second World War, since when they have maintained a good reputation.

As regards equipping the new complex, the old Westrex gear was installed, but it was quickly pensioned off. Both Columbia and HMV had continued their researches in an effort to develop a system freeing them of the onerous Westrex royalties and in 1931, it was the Columbia team that prevailed. The prime mover in this effort had been Alan Dower Blumlein, a 25-year-old engineer who had joined Columbia in March 1929 after several years working for Standard Telephones and Cables, like Western Electric, a subsidiary of Bell Laboratories. His main field of endeavour there had been on the telegraphic side, developing undersea cables, multiplexing systems to allow several messages to be sent and received simultaneously over the same wire. He was also well aware of the efforts of his American colleagues Harrison and Maxfield.

His innovative reputation preceded him and Columbia's head of research Isaac Shoenberg thought him perfect for the electrical recording challenge. Upon his arrival at the studio-cum-laboratory in Petty France, Blumlein found a 'rudimentary' experimental apparatus consisting of 'a capacitative microphone, an amplifier based on a public address system and a moving iron cutter, similar to that which Western Electric were manufacturing', but rather more promisingly he found an enthusiastic team including H. E. Holman and H. A. M. Clark (invariably known as 'Ham' because of his initials and his amateur radio fixation). Over the next year or so, under Blumlein's direction, the team came up with an integrated moving coil system, from microphones to cutters, which managed to avoid every patented aspect of the Western Electric system. On top of which, Blumlein's innovations in electro-mechanical damping had reduced resonance in the cutting head, allowing a cleaner and more vibrant recording than the Westrex apparatus, with a better dynamic range. Columbia applied for patents on the new system, in the names of Blumlein and Holman, on 10 March 1930, and they were granted, becoming patents 350,954 – 'Improvements in Electro-mechanical Sound Recording Devices more especially of the Moving Coil Type' – and 350,998 – 'Improvements in Apparatus for Recording Sounds upon Wax or other Discs or Blanks'.

Continued experimentation was needed to make the system commercially ready, and by the time it was, the merger had happened and Abbey Road was about to open. In December 1931, however, studio manager F. H. Dart had declared himself 'quite satisfied that the Columbia recording machine gives as good results as that of Western Electric...We would suggest that you instruct the Recording department to start using the Columbia machine at once to save any further Western Electric royalties'.[10] This was seized upon gratefully by the accountants at Hayes, who were to see nearly half a million pounds paid out to Western Electric before the system was finally decommissioned in the mid-1930s.[11] Judged against these figures, the expense of Blumlein's custom-built amplifiers – £153 and fourpence each – looked like a good investment.

As part of the merger, the Columbia and HMV research departments were amalgamated into a new building at Hayes to be called Central Research Laboratories, under Shoenberg's overall control. Blumlein's first job had been helping Columbia to catch up with the technology of the day, but his next preoccupation was to be with binaural recording (later known as stereo), a field in which he was truly ahead of his time. Between 1931 and 1933, he laid down the principles of stereo recording on disc, including the 45/45 groove with its vertical/lateral pattern and sum and difference decoding of the signal. These he enshrined in patent number 394,325. In addition, he produced several interesting test recordings at CRL, which have become known as the 'walking and talking' tests. Unfortunately, it was decided that there was little or no commercial potential at that time for a whole new system of recording and reproduction. Stereo discs, when they emerged in the late 1950s, adopted Blumlein's 45/45 system largely unmodified, but by then, the patent had expired. Had it not been for the Depression, the hi-fi boom of the 1950s might have come a lot earlier.

A similar economic resistance to new technology was making itself felt at RCA Victor. In 1931, the company launched a range of 10-inch and 12-inch discs which revolved at $33^{1}/_{3}$ rpm, giving roughly double the playing time of conventional 78 rpm discs. The speed had been chosen because it was the same speed as the sound-on-disc systems used in the early talkies. Duke Ellington recorded some long-form discs, consisting of medleys of his best-known material, and an attempt was made to transfer suitable classical and modern orchestral repertoire to the more expansive medium. Unfortunately, new equipment was required to play the records, and the take-up was pitiful. Edward Wallerstein, newly appointed as general manager of RCA's Victor division in July 1933, thought the idea not without promise, but in the short term, all he could really do was take them off the market. He would, however, return to the concept.

As unaccepted as they were, the Victor long-players were, by adopting a slower speed, a step in the right direction. Edison had, a few years previous, tried to develop a long-playing disc with 450 ultra-fine grooves per inch,[12] which revolved at 80 rpm. The problems with these records were manifold, not least the difficulties that were experienced with pressing such tiny grooves accurately and then keeping the tone arm from skipping.

Of course, there were quite a few shareholders who held stocks on both sides and who had been quietly lobbying for the Columbia/HMV merger. One such was Captain H. G. Bayes, who wrote to David Sarnoff, trying to impress on him the efficiencies that could be gained from an alliance:

> As a shareholder in both the Columbia and HMV Organizations, I write to ask if you cannot possibly bring them together under one head. Here we have two fine organizations competing with one another to the great disadvantage of both, competing in advertising, in the erection of new establishments, and in the wireless field. It appears to myself and many others that it is absolute foolishness, as if brought together in combination with yourselves you could control throughout the world in these particular fields.[13]

Sarnoff forwarded the note to Alfred Clark, indicating that Bayes had directed his note to the wrong person and that Clark could 'say to him whatever you like'. The general's response indicates, perhaps, that talks were already underway by this stage and that he saw no harm in Clark mollifying a shareholder with good news. However, it might also be construed as a little dismissive, a quality that was beginning to mark out RCA's attitude to its new line of business, which had cost a large sum to get into but which went into decline almost immediately the deal was signed. The attitude became so noticeable that there were concerns at Hayes that RCA was planning to abandon the record side altogether. The plant at Camden could be turned over entirely to radio set production and, if the worst came to the worst, sold off as a prime piece of industrial real estate.

This view is backed up by the account of Charles O'Connell, who ran RCA's Red Seal division between 1930 and 1944. In his memoirs, his personal perception was that the 'union of the phonograph industry with the ... young and vigorous radio industry' was a 'shotgun wedding', which RCA didn't enter 'with much enthusiasm'.[14] However, in response, he reported that he had been 'informed by Mr Sarnoff personally that this is not and never has been the case' and that Sarnoff himself had accomplished the merger 'because he believed in the logic and effectiveness of the combination'. O'Connell professes his happiness to stand corrected, but elsewhere in the book, he makes it clear that he was not entirely convinced by Sarnoff's likely revisionism.

For example, his comment on his appointment to the RCA staff was that his 'job really was not so much to develop the record business as to extricate the company from it ... RCA had no faith or interest in recorded music, then at the nadir of its popularity.'[15] He goes on to suggest that RCA might have pulled out of records 'had it not fallen heir to a number of long-term contracts with accompanying obligations'. As evidence, he explains that his first task as musical director was aiding Victor's vice-president Lawrence B. Morris to 'talk certain ... artists out of the financial obligations Victor owed them, because there were insufficient sales to support them'.

In spite of this seeming corporate philistinism, O'Connell somehow managed to maintain high standards during his stewardship of the Red Seal division. The Norwegian soprano Kirsten Flagstad came to Victor, although her first recordings disappointed O'Connell not through any fault of the singer, but 'because at the time we could not afford the use of an adequate orchestra or the rental of a suitable room in which to record'.[15] Things weren't much easier with the singer Lily Pons. Engaging her to record was 'tantamount to gambling a lot of Victor's money, for she had at the time made no appearances in the United States and had no public here'.[17] Even when she had established herself, O'Connell admitted that 'on a purely dollars-and-cents basis her services were never, for us, a good investment'. Her departure to Columbia was, nevertheless, a 'matter of regret' to the RCA man. The main agent behind Pons's defection was the conductor Andre

Kostelanetz,[18] whose services Pons had on occasion tried to force on O'Connell for her sessions. O'Connell was against the idea, not least because Kostelanetz was a Columbia artist, but also because he 'wanted an abler conductor ... he is a first-class workman, but we were doing opera, not the Coca-Cola hour'.

O'Connell was well experienced with 'abler conductors', as the likes of Eugene Ormandy and Arturo Toscanini were both Victor artists at this time. Ormandy came into O'Connell's orbit through a curious transaction that illustrates perfectly Victor's corporate parsimony in the post-Depression era. Arthur Judson, the orchestral manager who had been responsible for the foundation of the Columbia Broadcasting System, alerted O'Connell to the fact that the Minneapolis Orchestra, which was at the time under the Hungarian Ormandy's tutelage, had an archaic American Federation of Musicians-approved contract which required the musicians to work a certain number of hours a week. This time could be filled with anything – primarily rehearsals and concerts, but also, if there was time, recording. As long as this came within the orchestra's normal working hours, no extra remuneration was required. O'Connell realized that this was the proverbial gift horse. The result was 'an enormous group of recordings, made with the most extraordinary skill, sureness, and celerity; and we acquired them virtually for nothing ... The record business gained an infusion of new blood that ultimately resulted in its complete and vigorous recovery'.[19]

For the second set of Minneapolis sessions, O'Connell 'did not have the heart' to exploit the musicians so, and arranged $2,500 from Victor, which was matched by Ormandy from his own pocket. Once again, the recordings were a success, and O'Connell estimated that, by 1948, such an undertaking would have cost nearer $80,000 than $5,000. However, when it came to making a third set of recordings, the AFM had woken up to what was going on and indicated that recordings fell outside the orchestra's normal run of activities. Henceforth, full union rate would have to be paid. With the orchestra's recording reputation established and sales in general in the ascendant, this 'would not have been a hardship for Victor', but Edward Wallerstein nixed the idea.[20] Ormandy – known to his musicians as 'Gene the Jeep' because of his efficiency and robustness as a conductor – remained with Victor, though, having taken over from Leopold Stokowski at Philadelphia, and this alliance provided the label with a great many worthwhile recordings.

As an aside, Victor's curious attitude to paying the Minneapolis men contrasts rather starkly with O'Connell's experience at the hands of John Hammond, a member of the RCA board of directors. The 'cynical, superior, cruelly witty, shrewdly acquisitive'[21] Hammond had installed in his home a large pipe organ and when the French organist Joseph Bonnet visited him, he suggested that O'Connell might like to make some recordings. Unfortunately, O'Connell took the view that Hammond's instrument was 'extraordinary, interesting but quite badly organized'.[22] Nonetheless, in the interest of politics, he acceded. Afterwards, he was surprised to receive a bill from Hammond for the use of the organ. 'The records were made at Mr Hammond's insistence, not on my initiative, and perhaps would not have been made at all except for his prestige as a director,' argued O'Connell, who added that it 'did seem strange that Mr Hammond would levy a charge against his own company for the use of his house in making records that he particularly wanted and the company especially didn't.'[23]

Toscanini was no jeep, but instead the 'dictator of the baton'.[24] He was so powerful that he could even cast David Sarnoff 'into exterior darkness ... when displeased'. Toscanini had debuted in the United States in 1908, taking up residence at the Metropolitan Opera until 1915, after which he returned to his native Italy. He took over the New York Philharmonic in 1926, where he remained for ten years, making a few Victor recordings at the very end of his tenure. Although he told the Philharmonic management that he would never compete with their operation, he was persuaded back to New York by Sarnoff, who wanted him as head of the NBC Symphony Orchestra. By this point, prosperity had begun to return to the entertainment business and as part of the bait, Sarnoff felt able to offer Toscanini his own custom-built studio at NBC headquarters in Rockefeller Plaza.

Although the NBC orchestra was intended purely as a broadcasting venture, presumably to maintain the letter, if not the spirit, of the non-competition agreement, it was not 'very long before the matter of recording developed'.[25] Unfortunately, O'Connell was less impressed with Toscanini's new studio – numbered 8H in the NBC hierarchy – than either the Maestro or Sarnoff and he suggested that Carnegie Hall should be used instead. Studio 8H 'was unquestionably one of the most unsatisfactory music rooms, from an acoustic point of view, I have ever known ... I knew that ... any recordings made in 8H would sound tight, dull, and lifeless'.[26] Nevertheless, the Maestro prevailed and the sessions were sent from 8H down an equalized line to the RCA recording facility on 24th Street.

It was perhaps with the inferiority of 8H in mind that O'Connell deflected the Maestro's congratulations on the first session by making 'little of my part in the work' and suggesting that 'the maestro himself was responsible that the records were good'.[27] Unfortunately, Toscanini either misunderstood, or chose to misunderstand this, as an 'impudent' statement that 'he, not the recording staff, was responsible whether records were good or bad', and this led to a brief period in the outer darkness for O'Connell. However, the recordings from 8H had turned out 'exactly as I said they would be' and, when Toscanini got over being offended, he saw the sense of using the proven acoustic qualities of Carnegie Hall.

Another technically fraught session involved a location recording of Pierre Monteux conducting the San Francisco Symphony Orchestra. The main problem was that there was no portable recording equipment available at the time. Once again an equalized telephone line was pressed into service, this time between San Francisco and the RCA Victor studios in Hollywood. However, just in case, O'Connell had laid on a rig to record the sessions on sound film. That he did was just as well, as when the film recording was transferred to disc, it was found to be superior to the down-the-line recording. As a bonus, had it been necessary, the film would have facilitated editing, but it would be some time before this discipline became of any use to the record industry and by then film had been superseded as a pure sound medium.

His secretary between 1941 and 1944, Adele Freedman (now Siegal), remembers O'Connell as an 'absolutely wonderful' boss:

> He was really so charming. He could charm the hinges off the door, which he needed when dealing with some of the artists. Everybody was in love with him, including me. He was very tall – six feet or more tall – and quite dashing. He used to wear coloured silk shirts that he had made at Saks on Fifth Avenue. Lilac and raspberry, all colours of the rainbow.[28]

Unfortunately, after some years with RCA Victor, he began to wonder whether his charm was being put to the best possible use. In particular, he came to regard his work as 'too little music and too much business'.[29] Especially problematic was the intervention of a 'crackpot sales organiza-tion ... permitted to encroach upon my field and even ... given certain powers relating to the repertoire to be recorded'.[30] The crackpots had decided that the record-buying public needed a recording of Tchaikovsky's B flat minor piano concerto by Vladimir Horowitz, conducted by Toscanini, his father-in-law. All very well on paper, but the company already had a perfectly good recording of the piece by Artur Rubinstein, through its connection with Rubinstein's label HMV. The salesmen got their way and the Horowitz and Toscanini set was issued, but a large number had to be recalled after it was discovered that the wrong master had been used for one of the discs.

He had also 'developed a passionate antipathy toward useless, trivial, misdirected, and unworthy work, and much of mine … could be so described'. In this, he included the molly-coddling he was called upon to demonstrate towards the talent. 'I had played ping-pong most of the night with Jascha Heifetz (a good player and a bad loser); jumped naked and shivering into Albert Spalding's icy pool at 7 a.m.; listened to Toscanini's jokes, comprehensible only in their earthiness'[31] and breakfasted on brandy with 'one of the world's greatest musicians', a movie star and a South American lady who had murdered her husband and pleaded self-defence.

The best efforts of the Edison-Bell company notwithstanding, the new EMI combine might well have had a near-monopoly of the British record market, had it not been for the intervention of an enterprising Welsh-born stockbroker called Edward Lewis. Although the Depression was just about the worst time in the twentieth century to be establishing a record company, one organization made its debut immediately before the Wall Street crash and managed to survive numerous near-disasters to become a major force in the industry for nearly half a century. That company was Decca, which had grown out of Barnett, Samuel, a musical instrument specialist, in business since 1832. In recent years, Decca had supplemented its main activities with a sideline in gramophones – one of which, the Decca portable, became an iconic item through its popularity with troops in the trenches of the First World War. Barnett, Samuel had also been a British agent for the Odeon, Jumbo and Fonotipia combine, but it had never made its own range of discs.

In 1928, the Samuel family decided to float the company on the stock market. At this point, Edward Lewis came on the scene, alerted to the opportunity by Colonel E. D. Basden of Barnett, Samuel's chartered accountants. Lewis had just set up in business on his own and took 'little notice' of Basden's overtures at first, primarily because of Barnett, Samuel's lack of interest in making anything other than the hardware. Lewis remembered remarking:

A company manufacturing gramophones but not records was rather like one making razors but not the consumable blades ... I was not particularly excited at the prospect, for having seen the tremendous activity and great rise in the shares of Columbia Graphophones and the Gramophone Company, based on the boom in records, I felt that whilst the gramophone was a dull affair marketwise, records were like magic on the Stock Exchange.[32]

Lewis changed his mind when he saw Barnett, Samuel's 'excellent profit record' and so his firm were the brokers for the Decca Gramophone Company (as the Barnett, Samuel company had become) offer when it went through in September 1928, with 370,000 10-shilling shares being sold at 24 shillings and ninepence each. The issue was oversubscribed by some twenty times, many of the takers being Decca wholesalers and dealers. Although he was pleased at the way the issue had gone, the lack of a record arm still troubled Lewis, who at this point had no executive involvement with the company. Hearing that Noel Pemberton-Billing's Duophone Unbreakable Record Company was in trouble, Lewis saw an opportunity to buy the Duophone business, complete with its 75,000-square-foot factory, formerly the Rapson Tyre Company's works, at Shannon Corner, New Malden. Lewis tried to impress on the Decca directors, who included Basden as chairman, his belief that 'with the well-known Decca trademark and ... distributing organization ... a Decca record would surely succeed where others were failing'.[33] The Decca directors failed, however, to see Lewis's logic and turned the scheme down flat.

Undeterred, in January 1929, he registered the Malden Holding Company and formed a syndicate to buy the factory in his own right. The cash consideration for the shares was £515,000, which meant that, with the price of the factory, Lewis had to find £660,000 from the new company's share issue. On top of this, the managing director, J. A. Balfour, suggested that the company needed £240,000 of working capital, but Lewis decided to go for £340,000 'because it seemed easier to raise a million than nine hundred thousand'. This decision was to prove fateful to the degree that Lewis observed nearly twenty years later '[I]f it had not been for that decision there would perhaps be no Decca Company today'.[34]

Lewis realized that he needed copper-bottomed names for the board of the new company, and to this end persuaded Sir George Fowler, senior partner of Balfour's solicitors and a director of the Eagle, Star and British

Dominions Insurance Company, to become chairman. One of the directors that Fowler brought on board was one of his best friends, Sir Sigismund Mendl, a director of the National Discount Company. However, his law practice, his insurance interests and Decca were far from being the only concerns that Fowler was involved with at this time, as Hugh Mendl, Sir Sigismund's grandson, recalls:

> My grandfather was a professional City gent. He said to George Fowler: 'I've given up one or two things, and I'm looking for a couple of things to do. Do you have any suggestions?' Fowler said, 'Yes, there's a company we're floating called Smith's Potato Crisps, and there's another company that is in awful difficulties, called the Decca Gramophone Company, and I am looking for somebody to take over a certain amount of responsibility as a member of the board, not necessarily an executive one.' My grandfather went home and told my grandmother, 'George Fowler offered me a couple of jobs today and the one I thought I'd take is Smith's Potato Crisps.' My grandmother said, 'What on earth are they?' 'Well,' he said, 'apparently, you buy packets of potatoes, ready cooked.' My grandmother's knowledge of cooking extended to going into the kitchen every morning, seeing cook and giving the orders. That was all she knew. I think once she boiled a kettle, but didn't like the sound of it much. She said, 'Don't be so silly. Who on earth is going to buy potatoes ready-cooked? Your servants do that sort of thing.' So my grandfather told George Fowler that he'd have a go at the Decca.[35]

The Decca shares were issued on 28 February 1929, the offer being twice oversubscribed. It was suggested by Sir Sigismund Mendl that the company's £300,000 cash reserves should be put on deposit with the National Discount Company, who could offer a good rate of interest. Lewis, however, decided to stick with the company's existing bankers, the National Provincial Bank, which was hardly surprising, as his father, Sir Alfred Lewis, was a senior executive at that very institution. This connection came in very handy when other more independent institutions might have called time on Decca.

However, even before the company could issue its first list of records, a vote of no-confidence was registered by some of the speculative investors, who sold out too hastily and caused a run on the Decca share price. All through the early stages of the company's foundation, Lewis had made it clear that he had no intention of taking an executive role, but the financial problems meant that he found himself getting dragged more and more into the company's day-to-day operation.

The first records appeared in July 1929. Although the company's administrative centre was the old Barnett, Samuel factory in Brixton Road, the studios had been set up in the Chenil Galleries in King's Road, Chelsea. The hall they used had been a popular venue for BBC outside broadcasts, but the *Phono Record* assured its readers in September 1929 that 'Decca have carried out intensive research so as to attain the best acoustic results, and the methods adopted are based on the very latest practices'. The result of this 'intensive research' was to cover the walls in heavy drapes, rendering 'the atmosphere decidedly oppressive'.[36] Unlike HMV and Columbia, which were both experimenting with multiple microphone techniques, the Decca method in these early days relied upon the musicians and singers creating a natural balance to be captured by a single microphone – hidden behind screens depicting 'a pleasing rural aspect', it was said, to avoid distracting or alarming the musicians.

The first artists to make their presence felt in Chelsea were the dance bands of Billy Cotton and Ambrose, along with the Decca Military Band under Julian Clifford. Meanwhile, the Hastings Municipal Orchestra made its debut in the inaugural list with some discs made on location. The records had been previewed with lavish trade press advertisements in June, and these were followed by announcements in the national press in July, which, the company claimed would get 'all record lovers … talking about Decca Records. Everybody with a gramophone will want to hear them – will be going to their music dealers to buy them'.[37]

The effect of the new line was not quite as cataclysmic as the advertisements claimed, but Decca records sold well from the start. The real advances were, however, made when it was decided to use price to pursue market share. The Decca popular series, with magenta labels, had been priced at 3 shillings, as per HMV and Columbia, but in August a supplementary line on blue labels at 2 shillings, sixpence less than Zonophone or Regal, was launched. While other labels had cheap records, Decca was planning to make a virtue of the fact that it was offering all-original recordings by name artists at the lower price, rather than second-raters or old discs that had been cascaded to the cheaper mark.

The growth of the new venture was hampered almost immediately by financial events in New York. As an active stockbroker, Lewis remained at one remove from the company he had created. Indeed, one prospective client of Lewis's was Hatry, who approached him in mid-September 1929 asking him to place some shares. Lewis refused, and Hatry's collapse followed barely a week later. Fowler had become ill and decided to step down from the chairmanship, so Sir Sigismund Mendl took his place. Mendl had never planned to become very involved in Decca, but like Lewis, he found himself increasingly pulled in as the company's difficulties mounted. Hugh Mendl recalls:

> It wasn't intended to be my grandfather's main preoccupation, and he continued in his various other City jobs after that, but Decca was always there – he called it 'the wayward daughter'. Those were rough old days. The telephone was cut off on occasion. I remember once when I was staying with my grandparents, Lewis arrived while I was having breakfast with my grandfather and asked my grandfather if he could come to the City. The reason was that the bank refused to give the firm any more money and the staff had to be paid. This was on a Friday morning and they were paid rather late. My grandfather had sufficient reputation to be able to go with Lewis, not in Lewis's Austro-Daimler, but in my grandfather's more staid Austin. So, they went to the City, and that's how the staff were paid that week.[38]

As matters got worse, Lewis argued for a further price reduction, this time to 1/6, the same price as the cheaper labels in the Vocalion and Crystalate stables, such as Broadcast and Imperial. 'I argued that a record at 1s 6d with the Decca mark would not only eat into the turnover of higher priced records but would surely take a great deal of business away from the lower priced ones'.[39] Reductions were feared from HMV and Columbia, and Lewis believed that by acting now, a march could be stolen. A compromise of 1/9 was suggested, but Lewis dismissed it as a fudge. He got his way with the board only after the HMV/Columbia merger was announced, and the prospect of dealing with a monolith like EMI on the same price basis became too much to contemplate. His intervention was, however, not appreciated by the recently appointed managing director S. C. Newton, and began an distinct enmity between the two men.

There were two main reasons for Lewis's increasing involvement. Firstly, he had persuaded a great many friends to invest in the now-faltering venture, and he felt a personal duty to them. The clincher, however, was a tour of Decca dealers that he undertook in the summer of 1931 in his Austro-Daimler, accompanied by his old friend E. N. 'Teddie' Holstius, former publicity manager for British Celanese. The distribution of Decca records was revealed to be patchy at best, with many record dealers admitting that they didn't sell Decca, instead directing the two men to the cycle shop around the corner. However, far from making him disheartened, Lewis could see only golden opportunities. 'The worse the distribution, the more our hopes rose, for the greater were the potentialities,' he enthused.[40] Upon their return to London, Lewis announced that he was taking over from Newton as managing director and that Holstius was joining the company as advertising and publicity supremo. Newton was shunted off to run a subsidiary, the John Grey musical instrument company, but he left the group altogether when it became clear that there was no prospect of a comeback.

Decca was setting up just as radio stations broadcasting from the continent – such as Radio Paris, Radio Normandie and, most famously, Radio Luxembourg – were beginning to beam powerful signals into Britain and challenge the BBC's hegemony. All provided a more ready outlet for pop records than the staid Corporation, and Decca as the non-establishment record company took the logical step of buying time on one of the stations, Radio Paris, for a sponsored programme. These shows – presented by Christopher Stone, broadcaster and editor of the *Gramophone* – were made on wax at the Chenil Galleries, processed at the New Malden factory and then flown to the studios of the French station from Croydon aerodrome for transmission. Unfortunately for Decca, this gambit was frowned upon, and they were asked to desist by the industry body, the British Phonographic Industry, which they did at the end of the contract.

Times were still hard, and would continue to be for some years, but the company undoubtedly benefited from being run by one man with vision, utter conviction and a vested interest in seeing Decca pull itself out of the mire. He also had an interest in the pop of the day. Some have suggested over the years that Lewis had Van Gogh's ear for music and an interest only in the bottom line, but Hugh Mendl disputes this: 'He didn't like jazz or classical music, but he did like popular music. He had led a fairly harem scarem life, as a result of which he knew all of the dance bands of the day.'[41]

Perhaps Lewis's own tastes were responsible for the largely popular output of Decca in its earliest days. His distrust of jazz is understood to have hardened considerably when some July 1933 recordings by a visiting Duke Ellington failed to sell in any noticeable quantities. Apart from the Hastings discs and an early attempt at William Walton's 'Façade', little attempt was made to build any serious repertoire. Any commercial requirements for such were dealt with by licensing recordings from Deutsche Grammophon and issuing them with an orange label as the 'Decca Polydor Series'.

One of the best known of all the dance bands was that of Jack Hylton and in November 1931, Lewis pulled off the coup of poaching Hylton from HMV. To entice Hylton over from the entrenched company, Lewis had to offer the bandleader and impresario 40,000 ordinary shares in Decca, which were to be held in the name of his City of Panama-registered holding company, Jack Hylton Inc. Then, in March 1932, he became a director of the company, a move that did not meet with universal approval. 'My grandfather was absolutely furious,' Hugh Mendl relates. 'He said, "You don't have that sort of man as a director." Because he was an artist, but also because he wasn't a gentleman, he wasn't actually terribly nice.'[42] Frank Lee, who joined Decca in 1930 as a junior member of the artists and repertoire staff, working with Walter Yeomans, John Gossage and Tawny Neilsen, later remembered Hylton as 'a bit of a martinet' but 'very good value'.[43]

Hylton's unpleasant side and his unorthodox financial arrangements were easy to overlook when his records were selling. His first Decca recording, a Leslie Sarony-written novelty number called 'Rhymes', gave the label its first big hit. Lee recalled that the BBC had raised an objection to some aspect of the lyrics, which required Sarony, who was the main singer on the session, to do some last-minute substitution. Perhaps because of the mild suggestiveness of the number, it sold 300,000 copies, an amazing figure for such straitened times and even more of an achievement when remembering that he had recorded the same title in his last Zonophone session. Decca, however, was first to the market and cheaper, which riled EMI no end. They tried to slap an injunction on Decca releasing Hylton's discs, but to no avail. No doubt their corporate blood pressure was raised even further whenever they received letters from Lewis, as all of his correspondence at this time bore proudly a sticker proclaiming: 'Jack Hylton & his Orchestra now record exclusively for Decca'.

There were other less obvious advantages in having Hylton on the label. His mere presence on the label gave Lewis the leverage to increase his wholesale prices by a halfpenny per disc, bringing in some much-needed extra cash. He could also entice some of his show-business friends to join the fledgling company. One such was the gap-toothed, banjolele-playing, Lancashire comedian George Formby, himself the son of a music-hall star and recording pioneer.

These benefits apart, the chairman was not the only one to have his nose put out of joint by Hylton's arrival. Hylton made sure that he had first dibs on any songs that came in, which put Bert Ambrose, previously Decca's star bandleader, in the unfortunate position of having to take whatever Hylton had rejected. In time, this was sidestepped by issuing Ambrose's discs on the Brunswick label. Decca had acquired the British Brunswick business in 1932 for £15,000. Previously, the records had been handled by the music publisher Chappell's. Although the acquisition forced Decca to increase its overdraft with the National Provincial Bank from £50,000 to £65,000, it brought in quality American repertoire by Bing Crosby and Guy Lombardo, among others, and a couple of employees who were to become increasingly important to Lewis: Harvey Schwarz, who later ran the company's radar business, and Harry Sarton, who took over the artists department.

Brunswick had been acquired from Warner Bros in December 1931 by an outfit called the American Record Corporation, a subsidiary of Herbert Yates's Consolidated Film Industries, which seemed to specialize in gathering flagging companies under one umbrella and trying to make a go of them. Read and Welch refer to it as a 'company of ... lost causes'.[44] ARC had grown out of the Scranton Button Works of Scranton, Pennsylvania, which had geared up for contract pressing work. One of its main customers was the Emerson Phonograph Company, which produced a popular 50c range of discs on the Regal label (not to be confused with UK Columbia's Regal operation). In August 1922, Scranton acquired the Regal label in its entirety from Emerson. The new owners began to develop Regal's repertoire, moving away from masters supplied by Paramount's New York Recording Laboratories towards the output of Independent Record Laboratories, which it took over completely in 1924.

The acquisition of IRL and its studios was followed in November 1924 by the purchase of the entire record business of Emerson, which saw its future primarily in radio. The next major expansion was the forging of an alliance with the British company Crystalate in 1927, which included a reciprocal agreement for the releasing of each other's masters. Over time, the business relationship became much closer, leading almost to merger. In July 1929, the American Record Corporation was formed under the presidency of Louis G. Sylvester, comprising Scranton as the pressing operation, with Cameo and Regal as its labels.

The American Brunswick takeover was Scranton and ARC's first real entry into the high-class record market, its other output frequently being dismissed as 'dime-store' fodder. The quality end of ARC's business was supplemented when its subsidiary, the Sacro Enterprise Company, acquired the US Columbia company from the ailing Grigsby-Grunow company. It is thought that Grigsby-Grunow regarded the record company as a tool to help it compete with RCA. Just over a year after the acquisition, Sterling had tried to reassure B. J. Grigsby of Grigsby-Grunow that things would get easier. 'I am very glad to hear that your relationship with the RCA is becoming more friendly and am sure that conditions in the USA, particularly in the radio industry, are such that it is time for everybody to get together instead of scrapping with one another,' he wrote. Unfortunately, it was not to be. On 16 April 1934, Grigsby-Grunow went into receivership and the record arm was put up for sale.

One suitor for the business would have meant the return of US Columbia to British ownership once again. The Decca company had narrowly escaped the bank foreclosing on it in 1933, and was about to post a £67,000 loss for the year to March 1934, but Lewis was keen to get into the US market. Columbia was on offer for just $75,000, a bargain price, and, with the help of some friendly American investors, the initial cost to Decca would be a mere £7,500. Lewis hoped to spread the cost further by enticing William Paley to come in on the deal, but Paley passed. Lewis paid one immediate visit to New York to set the offer out, and then returned on the *Mauretania* on 29 June to finalize the deal. He was met at the dock with the news that the American Record Corporation had gazumped him.

Lewis, however, did realize his American ambitions, getting a measure of revenge on ARC in the process by poaching one of their key men. The evening that he arrived in New York, he dined with Brunswick's head of Artists and Repertoire, Jack Kapp, who announced that he was in the market for a new venture. 'We decided there and then to form a new record company,' Lewis reported in his memoirs. The timing was not ideal, he freely admitted. 'Most new companies are formed in the last stage of a boom. American Decca was started at the end of an unparalleled slump'.[45]

Kapp had achieved something unheard of in those days. He had succeeded in inserting a clause into the contracts of his star artists stating that if he, Jack Kapp, were to leave Brunswick, the contract would be invalid. In this way, he felt sure that he could bring Guy Lombardo, Bing Crosby, the Boswell Sisters, the Mills Brothers and Glen Gray's Casa Loma Orchestra over from Brunswick to the new company. Furthermore, he thought that

Warners would want to sell their record plant on West 54th Street and the offices and studios at 799 Seventh Avenue.

So it proved on both fronts, and with the $270,000 of finance that Kapp estimated would be sufficient, Decca Records Inc. was established on 1 August 1934, taking offices in New York's famous Flatiron Building. The English company duly assigned its trademark to the new venture for use in North and South America. Lewis was chairman, Kapp was president and Brunswick's treasurer Milton Rackmil came over to fulfil the same role. Kapp, Rackmil and E. F. Stevens Jr, who had come over from Columbia to be sales manager, were rewarded with shares. Meanwhile, freed of the Brunswick responsibility, Hermann Starr – who had negotiated the sale of the pressing plant – felt able to join the new company as a director.

Again Lewis pressed for keen pricing to build up market share. 'Jack Kapp wanted to follow the existing pattern with 75, 35 and 25 cent records,' Lewis explained. 'I could see no hope of success ... to succeed we had to not only capture ... sales but also to increase the total volume'. Lewis believed that offering name artists such as Crosby and Lombardo on a narrowly profitable 35c disc would not only 'take business from competitors' but also 'increase the over-all turnover of the industry when it seemed that it might well have touched bottom'.[46] Lewis's view prevailed and all seemed set for the launch of the label's first catalogue, accompanied by a $25,000 advertising campaign.

Unfortunately, not all was as it seemed. A crucial $100,000 of pledged funding failed to materialize, casting the grand plans into disarray. Worst of all, Lewis realized that 'if the American company went down it would drag the English company with it'.[47] Evasive action was required and Lewis's rescue plan amounted to asking investors in the British company to sell some of their debentures and plough the proceeds into the new US company. Thus was financial disaster narrowly averted. However, there was still a technical disaster to contend with. Rogue shards of metal were being found in the shellac mixture in such consistency as to suggest that someone was trying to sabotage the Decca launch.

Nevertheless, records were making their way out of the factory,[48] and soon the company had its first 100,000-selling hit, with 'The Music Goes Around and Around' by Riley and Farley. Despite such successes, the company was a hand-to-mouth operation for its first couple of years. Cheques written in favour of clients on the west coast were routinely sent by mail in the hope that the time taken for their cross-country transportation by rail would buy Decca some valuable breathing space. When the debts were closer to home, creditors became all too familiar with the 'pleasant enough waiting room'[49] at the Decca offices. Ruthrauff and Ryan, the advertising agency behind Decca's launch campaign, was one such creditor, their treasurer setting up camp in the waiting room and threatening to send in the bailiffs for non-payment of its $25,000 bill. Lewis was due to return to London, but could not, lest the dispute bring the company down. It was with relief that Lewis managed to persuade them that their best chance of getting their money was to let him return to Britain.

Sometimes, the creditors were Decca's own artists, as Hugh Mendl recalls:

> Bing Crosby and his brother Everett were very understanding and wouldn't take the royalties when there weren't any to pay, whereas Guy Lombardo used to send his brother up, looking very Italian and Mafia-like, and sit in the outer office until they got the money.[50]

Back home, Decca continued to expand, despite not being in the best of financial health. The venerable but ailing Edison-Bell company had been absorbed by the Brixton upstart, while EMI and Decca clubbed together to buy the commercial record business of the British Homophone Company, which included the Sterno label.[51] The greatest prize of all, though, came in March 1937, when Decca took over the Crystalate company for £200,000.

In business since 1901, Crystalate had, like Brunswick in the States, begun as a billiard ball maker, but it is thought to have been involved in record manufacture on a third-party basis from very early in its history. In the 1920s, it had achieved some success with the 1/6 a go Imperial label, and had forged close corporate ties with ARC in the US. Towards the end of the decade, it had taken on the UK record-producing arm of Aeolian-Vocalion, inheriting their Hayes factory as part of the amalgamation. By the 1930s, given its ARC affiliation, it was unsurprising that its main focus was on the production of cheap records for chain stores. From 1931 onwards, it had made the Eclipse range exclusively for Woolworths – 8-inch discs that featured popular songs of the day and retailed for 6d. Slightly more upmarket was the 10-inch Rex series of discs, which sold for a shilling each.

It was, however, another Woolworths label – the Crown range – that caused trouble for Crystalate and made it vulnerable to takeover. The discs had been increased from 8-inch to 9-inch, but by early 1937, the retailer wanted a full 10-inch disc while retaining the sixpence retail price. This was, Lewis said, 'an impossible proposition', but he foresaw that the 'Woolworth cheap record seemed in any case doomed'. The 'long-term future of Crystalate as an independent record unit was hazardous' but 'the Rex business would prove of immediate value to Decca', as it would take up spare capacity at the New Malden factory. Lewis made overtures and found the Warnford-Davis brothers, Roy and Darryl, who ran Crystalate, receptive. The pair moved into Brixton Road and continued to run the company more or less as an autonomous unit. Meanwhile, Lewis's predictions for the cheap record seemed well founded. In September, all manufacturers upped their 1/6 discs to 2/-, at which Decca took the opportunity to raise the price of Rex discs from 1/- to 1/6.

Quite apart from utilizing spare capacity at the factory, the acquisition proved to be a very good move on at least one other level. For all of the end product's cheapness, Crystalate had set great store by the quality of its recordings. It had two acoustically good and well-equipped studios in the former Hampstead Town Hall at Broadhurst Gardens, West Hampstead, one of which even had a Wurlitzer theatre organ. In addition, Broadhurst Gardens was home to one of the best engineering teams in the whole industry, headed by chief engineer Arthur Haddy, and including such luminaries as Kenneth 'Wilkie' Wilkinson. In 1933, Decca had vacated the Chelsea studios in favour of a new recording premises in the former City of London Brewery building at 89 Upper Thames Street near St Paul's Cathedral. The first releases from the new complex came out on 1 April 1933, although recording seems to have continued at Chelsea for a year or so after. When Crystalate came into the fold, however, it was no contest. The Upper Thames Street studio was not on the ground floor, so every time a grand piano was needed for a session, it had to be winched in by crane. Broadhurst Gardens was modern and easily accessible.

By the end of 1938, all recording had ceased at Upper Thames Street and the Decca recording staff moved to work under Haddy at West Hampstead. One of these was a young engineer called Arthur Lilley, who had been employed originally to mind the Decca record shop beneath the Chelsea studios. However, when Frank Lee found him playing the studio piano during a lull one day, Lilley found himself being promoted. Decca was recording a great many music-hall artistes, including George Formby whose only free day was Sunday, and Lee was looking for someone to lighten his workload at weekends. Lilley was asked if he wanted to help out at sessions and so began the career of one of Decca's most distinguished recording engineers.

Shortly after the Crystalate takeover, Lewis arranged a reconstruction of the company's financial affairs on both sides of the Atlantic, which put Decca on an even keel for the first time in its history. American Decca was heavily in debt to the English company, but these loans and notes – totalling $699,250 – were converted into ordinary shares with an assumed value of $5 each. Thus the English company became a shareholder in the US company rather than a creditor and 'the balance sheet [was] put into a healthy condition'.[32] In the year to 31 August 1937, the American company posted its first profit – $80,000 – while in the year to 31 March 1938, its English benefactor managed a net profit of £15,000.

When Lewis had offered William Paley a chance to come in on Decca's putative purchase of the US Columbia company, the radio magnate demurred, perhaps because he had seen what had happened with RCA and Victor, and during Grigsby-Grunow's brief stewardship of Columbia. By 1938, however, he was coming round to the idea that the Columbia Broadcasting System should own its own record label. The natural choice was the American Record Corporation, which owned the label that had given the network its name; Columbia having been involved in the network's foundation, but having sold out barely a year later due to heavy losses. In 1927, it had invested $163,000 in United Independent Broadcasters, the radio network founded by orchestral impresario Arthur Judson as a competitor to RCA following a disagreement with David Sarnoff about the airtime available for his musicians. UIB changed its name to the Columbia Phonograph Broadcasting Company. Paley, the son of the proprietor of the La Palina Cigar Company, had been awakened to the possibilities of radio through buying advertising time for the family business. So, in January 1929, he bought the failing Columbia network with its twenty-two affiliated stations for $400,000, renaming it the Columbia Broadcasting System.

In July 1938, an agreement was drawn up between Consolidated Film Industries and CBS giving the broadcaster an option to acquire the American Record Corporation for $635,000, but this option was not exercised. By the time the deal was concluded in December, the price had risen to $700,000, but Paley had secured an asset perhaps more important than any other – the services of Edward Wallerstein, who had left RCA Victor in the summer and relished the possibilities of being allowed to run a company his own way.

Wallerstein was, in the words of George Avakian, who began working for Columbia in 1940, possessed of 'vision with a capital V'.[53] Specifically, his vision involved the development of a long-playing record. He had been involved with Victor's attempts in this field at the start of the 1930s and, despite the project's failure, he had never lost the faith. In the shorter term, Wallerstein directed the reorganization of ARC into a new company called Columbia Recording Corporation, which was achieved by May 1939. The Brunswick and Vocalion labels were sold off to Decca, so that attention could be concentrated on the Columbia label, with OKeh being revived for a range of cheaper, popular discs, majoring in jazz and swing.

The CBS takeover of ARC caused some problems for EMI in England, which dealt with both Columbia and the other ARC companies, but under different contracts. Wallerstein wanted to rearrange matters such that all popular material would be supplied as per ARC's agreement with EMI, while all classical material would come through the long-standing contract between the two Columbias. Unfortunately, the by-now Sir Louis Sterling was not happy with the idea. EMI was able to produce most of the classical recordings it needed for itself, but it needed US pop to keep up with the demands of younger record buyers. The problem lay in the fact that the royalties in the ARC and EMI deal were higher than those in the Columbia contract, and EMI had been hoping for the Columbia contract to become the prevailing agreement. Under Wallerstein's plans, though, the cost of Columbia's pop catalogue to EMI looked set to rocket, and Sterling suggested that EMI might prefer not to renew the ARC contract next time it came up. Wallerstein made it clear that if EMI did not renew, they would receive no popular recordings.

The importance to EMI of Columbia's pop repertoire over classical can be gauged from some of the correspondence that flew between Hayes and New York in the early days of Columbia's new ownership. In March 1939, Columbia's Ronald Wise tried to interest Rex Palmer, head of the EMI international department, in the recordings of the competent but rather anonymous conductor Howard Barlow with the Columbia Broadcasting Symphony Orchestra. Palmer was underwhelmed. The Barlow recordings were 'not of such interest to us as experience has proved during recent years that recordings of standard works, to achieve a market and compete successfully with Toscanini and Bruno Walter, must be made with Artistes of international reputation'.[54]

Conversely, on the pop side, Columbia had vast numbers of internationally renowned acts, particularly in swing and jazz. 'I think that we really have something in Count Basie; that his records will appeal to more than just the hot trade,' wrote John Hammond to EMI Columbia's Hugh Francis in May 1939. 'I don't want to say too much in this letter but by the time you receive it, we will have signed up the number one band of the country [Benny Goodman] as far as records are concerned, which is making us all very happy.'[55]

The debate about the contracts did not reach its conclusion until November 1940, when, after much discussion and the intervention of a world war, Wallerstein agreed to a single contract taking the royalty structure from the Columbia agreement, but including the flat fee from the ARC contract, albeit reduced to $20,000. The person who had originally stood out for harmonization of terms was, however, no longer around. The relationship between Alfred Clark and Sir Louis Sterling had never been an easy one, and following the 1937 Coronation honours, when Sterling had been knighted, jealousy had amplified the chairman's enmity towards the managing director considerably. 'From that moment on there was no peace,' Sterling said in 1957.[56]

As managing director of EMI, Sterling had, ex officio, held the managing directorship of both HMV and Columbia since 1931, without actually having it written into his contract. Now, the envious Clark saw a chance to settle Sterling's hash by suggesting that separate MDs for HMV and Columbia be appointed. Sterling would retain his EMI post, but he knew that this was a non-job. He 'was on the verge of a nervous break-down from overwork' but 'he felt he could not have the post without the work attached'.[57] The death of a director gave Clark the majority he needed.

A sinecure was never going to suit someone as active as Sterling, so he resigned immediately, on 10 May 1939, just a month after Fred Gaisberg's retirement. Not content with ousting the main architect of EMI's success, Clark set about trying to deny Sterling his pension by asserting that there had never been a resolution passed allowing a director to participate in the company scheme. The fact that the EMI pension scheme was substantially the old Columbia programme, set up by Sterling himself in the mid-1920s, was lost on Clark and the board, who voted that directors like themselves were not eligible for a company pension. Sterling's replacement was an outsider, Sir Robert McLean, and Clark's animosity sparked a fifteen-year run of bad management at EMI, which nearly brought the company to its knees.

Even with the contract matter settled, relations between Columbia and EMI were not entirely unstrained. The American company had been thinking of making moves into South America, challenging the dominance that EMI had inherited from Odeon. The idea had not occurred before because of the close ties between the companies. Any objections disappeared when it began to look likely that Columbia would contract its South American pressing to RCA Victor. The Odeon plants had a considerable amount of spare capacity, in particular the factory at Buenos Aires, which had been 'enlarged to a point where it could supply the territory's needs many times over'. If Columbia was going to enter the South American market, why should RCA get the pressing fees?

By September 1940, though, Wallerstein had deferred his plans in Latin America, preferring to concentrate on the home market. EMI and the other UK companies were looking to their home market as well, but for different reasons.

7 Don't you know there's a war on?

Unlike the First World War, the Second World War did not cause a fall in entertainment expenditure. If anything, demand increased. In the UK, food was to be rationed from January 1940, but entertainment was rationed as soon as war broke out. Every theatre and cinema in the country closed the day war was declared (although they soon re-opened when the government realized their morale-boosting value). Meanwhile, the BBC had reduced its two networks, the National and the Regional Programme, into one, the Home Service. In this sudden austerity, it was no wonder that records continued to sell. Indeed, between 1939 and 1945, the value of record sales in the US increased from $44m to $109m,[1] while in the first year of the war, EMI saw its unit sales increase by 1 million.

Moreover, the Second World War differed from its predecessor in that it was rather less unexpected. Almost everyone – with the exception of the *Daily Express*, which declared as late as the end of August 1939 that 'there will be no war' – had seen it coming for most of the late 1930s. It was one of the factors that led Hugh Mendl, grandson of the chairman of Decca, to give up his studies:

> I was up at Oxford and I was convinced there was going to be a war, and everybody else was sitting here plodding away in the hope of getting a good degree and so on, and I thought, this is just bloody silly. My tutor told me that I would probably get a good second, but I certainly wouldn't get a first. I was intended for the Diplomatic Service, which I wasn't looking forward to very much, and I wouldn't get in without a first.[2]

So Mendl decided to enter the music business. Sir Sigismund did not greet with enthusiasm the news that his grandson wanted a proper introduction to the 'wayward daughter'.

> When I told my grandfather, 'I'm sorry, I don't want to go into the Diplomatic

Service, I want to go and work for Decca,' my grandfather was so shocked, rather as though you, how can I put this politely ... if you were the owner of a large chain of brothels in Port Said, and you had a grandson who could, if he had wished, have married Princess Anne, and he said, 'Actually I don't want to, grandpa, I want to marry one of the girls in Port Said.' That was how my grandfather greeted the suggestion that I should go and work for Decca. He sought out de Stein [Sir Edward de Stein, a director of EMI] and told him the sad story. 'Expensive education, decent family, and he wants to go and work for Decca. I want him, if he insists, to go and work somewhere more respectable.' Edward de Stein, whom I never met, but to whom I am eternally grateful, told my grandfather, 'I never do favours for friends, because they always come back to embarrass you.'[3]

The chairman had to admit defeat and so sent Hugh to see Edward Lewis, who in the political uncertainty could offer no more than a six-month try-out in the postroom.

In those days, before widespread graduate training schemes and the like, a postroom job could often be the first rung on the executive ladder. Lewis certainly saw it as a good way of learning the way the company worked. Mendl explains: 'He said, "Unless a letter is addressed personally to somebody fairly senior, open it all. You'll find out what the company's about more or less from that". Quite true, of course. Not long after the war began, Lewis sent for me and said, "Well, you've been here six months now. How are you liking it?" I said, "I love it, sir. It's what I want to do". He said, "Well, you seem to be going along all right. Are you going to be called up?" I was expecting to be called up any time, so I said yes. He said, "Well, you've got a job at Decca until then if you want it."'

Mendl then moved from the postroom into other work around the building, but he met with resistance because of his family ties. 'I was shoved in with the company secretary, a man called Freddie White, [who] didn't like me,' he recalled. 'Everybody in Decca was dead set against me ... Oxford bloody accent and chairman's grandson, expensive clothes, I'm not a bit surprised.' However, he continued to work there until his call-up.

The rise of the National Socialists had impacted on the record industry several times before the outbreak of war. In April 1933, just over two months after Hitler became chancellor, EMI was on the lookout for a new manager for its Electrola subsidiary – German, but not Jewish 'because of the political situation'. A month earlier, Louis Sterling had been informed that 'it is dangerous for the Lindström Company to have a board composed of so many Jews'. His German adviser was 'positive that very soon the government will instruct Lindstroem to make a change and that it was better to pre-empt than wait for orders'.[4]

This was hard for Sterling to take. He was himself proudly Jewish, but he had to go through with it. Matters were further complicated by the fact that any communications between Hayes and Lindström in Berlin were liable to be intercepted and read by the Nazis. Sterling wrote his instructions to an intermediary, who memorized the message, destroyed it and then went to tell Lindström's managing director Max Straus verbally. Despite such deft if egregious political manoeuvres, Lindström quickly fell foul of the new order. In July 1933, Straus and three employees were arrested, following an order from Amsterdam for 250 records 'containing on one side an international selection, and on the other side a Radical Socialist selection, and the company had no right to press that kind of record in Germany'.[5]

Although it is tempting to view Sterling's willingness to populate the Lindström board with gentiles as a craven act, it must be remembered that he was running a business and had a responsibility to the EMI shareholders. In mitigation, when the extent of Hitler's hatred of the Jews made itself apparent, Sterling devoted a great deal of time and effort to removing as many of EMI's Jewish employees as possible from danger at the hands of the Nazis. The most common mechanism for this was to write with a job offer overseas, thus giving the recipient a legitimate reason to leave Germany. In many of these cases, however, Sterling had been unable to find a real job for the refugee, and it had been agreed secretly that the recipients would merely use the letter as a way out and not try to hold the company to its 'offer', an arrangement that was seized gratefully. Whether the Nazis realized what was going on is unknown, but Sterling was a prominent enough Jew to be high on the Nazi hitlist in the event of a British invasion.

The political fallout of the Anschluss in spring 1938 had made it impossible for Bruno Walter to record with the Vienna Philharmonic, which he had conducted on records for many years. His last session with the Vienna musicians had been Mahler's Ninth Symphony at the Musikverein, and the twenty resulting records had been, in artistic terms, 'extraordinarily successful',[6] said Fred Gaisberg, not least because the VPO was 'Mahler's own orchestra' and Walter had given the premiere of the symphony. He moved to work with the orchestra of the Paris Conservatoire, 'an

Thomas Alva Edison with his 'baby', the phonograph.

One of the phonograph's earliest appearances in print, from the *Illustrated London News*, 3 August 1878.

Above Edison's invention anthropomorphized for the sheet music of a topical song, 1878.

Left The phonograph performs for advertising purposes, c. 1900.

The Gramophone Company's first studio in Maiden Lane, London, c. 1898, with Ms Amy Williams at the elevated pianoforte.

Right Fred Gaisberg – the first of the great recording engineers and the man who brought Caruso to the gramophone.

Emile Berliner, inventor of the gramophone, and Charles Sumner Tainter, the tea-addicted Yorkshireman behind the graphophone, c. 1919.

Below An Edison 'Gold Moulded' wax cylinder case from c. 1905.

Above Forced to move into the disc business, Edison came up with the 'Diamond Disc' and claimed that it was indistinguishable from a live performance. Whatever the truth of the claim, even rivals were forced to admit privately that it was a quantum leap in reproduction quality.

Right The Edison-Bell company achieves the 'impossible' and puts HMV's nose out of joint into the bargain.

Left Jack Hylton and his band at the microphone (emphasis on the singular) in the 1920s.

Right November 1931: Edward Elgar opens studio 1 at Abbey Road, witnessed by Paderewski and George Bernard Shaw (on the steps) and EMI chiefs Alfred Clark and Louis Sterling (at the front of the crowd).

Above By 1957, each section of the band had its own microphone.

Right Mike Ross-Trevor in the control room of Levy's Sound Studios, London, 1964. Not many faders on the mixing desk, but they were enough for the Tremeloes, Jimi Hendrix, the Who and many others.

instrument of fine possibilities,' said Gaisberg, but the rapport the conductor had with the VPO was not to be easily replicated. 'You know, it is like a honeymoon, oftentimes things do not go so well,' Walter rationalized after his first attempt with the Paris orchestra.

One of the last British bands to visit Germany was that of Henry Hall, which played a month-long engagement at the Scala in Berlin in February 1939. EMI and Electrola were keen to make as much capital out of the trip as possible, but they were hamstrung by Nazi orthodoxy in the matter of selecting titles for release, just as Hall was in choosing his concert programme. A Columbia executive noted in an August 1938 internal memo that the programme presented some difficulties due to restrictions on non-Aryan music. In the event, Hall's management were unable to finalize an acceptable programme until the week before the beginning of the engagement. Curiously, the 'St Louis Blues' was allowed, despite being very non-Aryan. Its composer, W. C. Handy, was a black man from Alabama.

The war meant that once again EMI was cut off from its European subsidiaries, which were responsible for the best classical repertoire in its catalogues. Meanwhile, Decca lost access to the Deutsche Grammophon classical material that it had been issuing in its Polydor series. In 1941, DG was sold to the German electrical combine Siemens. Despite this, EMI's producers tried to maintain something resembling business as usual at Abbey Road and in the other recording halls used by the company. One such producer was Walter Legge, who had joined the Gramophone Company in 1927 and had made his reputation within the company with the establishment in 1931 of the Hugo Wolf Society. In such straitened times, HMV was understandably wary of recording such marginal repertoire as the songs of the Slovenian-born composer Wolf, but Legge convinced his superiors that such a venture could be made to pay if it were on a subscription basis, sessions proceeding only when sufficient orders had been received, and the finished products being sold only to the subscribers, including a mysterious number of Japanese orders. The Wolf discs were a success and in time were placed in the general catalogue, but Legge's career was never marked by such prudence again. He became a classical producer of note, but equally noteworthy were his extravagance and his utter disregard for efficient use of resources. Certainly, the war was not going to make him pull his horns in.

In September 1943, following praise for some recordings, Legge felt it necessary to point out that the 'records are remarkable not by any accident or chance circumstance, but because adequate time and the greatest care were devoted to their production'.[7] He argued for 'careful rehearsal and intensive work in the studios' despite the obvious cost objections, and took a side-swipe at 'four-sides-a-session' records, that then being the normal expected output.

One of Legge's superiors, C. H. Thomas, was 'inclined to Legge's view ... The nearer we reach perfection in technical recording it follows that the greater the perfection in performance will be demanded of the artiste.'[8] F. B. Duncan, another senior EMI executive, was less impressed, having picked up on Legge's suggestion that the Columbia and HMV 'serious' repertoire should be under unified control, including the overseas operations. It was, he believed, 'an attempt [by Legge] ... to establish some central control over the world listings.' He moved quickly behind the scenes to put Legge in his place:

> We want to make quite clear the proper limitations ... of our Artiste Managers. There seems to be some impression that our Artiste Manager sings the piece, plays the violin, or conducts the orchestra ... The job of the Artiste Manager in the main is to make the necessary arrangements in contacting the artistes ... make sure that they come to the studios ... properly rehearsed.[9]

Legge's perfectionism was reflected in the number of waxes he could get through before achieving his desired result. Unfortunately, wax was in short supply, and alternatives were being investigated, including metal discs coated with cellulose. At one point it was suggested that the metal discs could be run in parallel and used to check on a take. Wax masters were playable only once, which rendered them unusable, so it was not possible to listen back to a performance until test pressings had been made. Legge defended his profligacy with the thinnest veil of concern for efficiency. 'We cannot afford to pay orchestras for listening to their own efforts. Even with Maggie Teyte and [Gerald] Moore this slowed down the pace of the session.'[10] One colleague took Legge's concerns at face value and expressed amazement that he should suddenly have become an enthusiast for economy.

Fortunately, both Decca and EMI were less affected by the European cut-off when it came to popular repertoire. The US remained a source of good material, but in the patriotic and sentimental mood that war brought, home-grown talent was having its day. Decca had inherited from British

Homophone's Sterno label (which it had purchased jointly with EMI in the late 1930s) a young singer from the East End called Vera Lynn, whose string of wartime hits – most notably 'We'll Meet Again' and 'The White Cliffs of Dover' – laid the foundations of a long career. However, the most popular form of music in wartime was undoubtedly swing music and big band jazz, exemplified by the likes of Benny Goodman, Count Basie, Duke Ellington, Artie Shaw and, perhaps most famous of all, the orchestra of Glenn Miller. As the record label of Miller, Shaw and Ellington, RCA Victor (and by definition HMV) was in a good position to capitalize on this popularity, closely followed by Columbia, which had Goodman, Basie and Gene Krupa.

Unfortunately for the American labels, however, their good luck ran out. The entry of the United States into the Second World War, on 7 December 1941, as a result of the Japanese bombing at Pearl Harbor, had made it harder to receive imports from Asia. Shellac, being sourced mainly from India, became a scarce commodity. In April 1942, the War Production Board ordered all non-military use of shellac to be cut by 70 per cent. So, demand for records was high, but supply could not meet it. Similar shortages occurred in the UK, and on both sides of the Atlantic, salvage drives were organized, in which music lovers were encouraged to return any worn and unwanted records for recycling.[11]

As if that didn't make matters hard enough, James Caesar Petrillo, the president of the American Federation of Musicians, had become exercised, on behalf of his members, about unremunerative use of their work, such as in jukeboxes or when played on the radio. At the AFM's convention in Dallas in June 1942, the union resolved to put a recording ban into action. Recordings made exclusively for home enjoyment were exempted, as were those made for the war effort, but as it was almost impossible to prevent records finding their way into jukeboxes and playlists, the ban amounted to a total blackout, effective 1 August 1942. It would be dropped only when the record companies agreed to pay the union a royalty on each record sold to help its members make up some measure of the revenue they had supposedly lost.

As with Decca in 1929, this was not a good time to be establishing a new record label, but March 1942 had seen the first releases from Capitol. The company had been set up as a label for songwriters, and it boasted two of the biggest in the business as its founding partners – Buddy de Sylva (who put up the initial $10,000 capital for Capitol) and Johnny Mercer. The consortium had been assembled by Glenn Wallichs, owner of the famous Wallichs' Music City record store in Hollywood, who had met Mercer in 1935 when he came in to the shop to have a radio installed in his car. Capitol's first issue ('The General Jumped at Dawn'/'I Found a New Baby' by Paul Whiteman's New Yorker Orchestra) sold disappointingly, but it fared better with Mercer's 'Strip Polka' – which, along with its follow-up 'GI Jive', became a forces favourite – and Freddy Slack and Ella Mae Morse's 'Cow Cow Boogie'. Indeed, the company was able to enjoy the fruits of these two successes unmolested as the majors did not have time to make cover versions of either record before the AFM ban kicked in.

The record companies tried to call Petrillo's bluff. The musicians would, soon enough, need the work. In the meantime, they had a backlog of unreleased recordings that would see them through. Petrillo had, however, timed things to perfection. Many of the best session musicians were being called up, leaving a drought of talent. The musicians were in a seller's market. Even Miller joined the Army, forming a new orchestra, the US Army Air Force Band, out of the cream of the dance-band musicians in the services. Sam Donahue did the same for the Navy. Having a stockpile did not help much when it came to the new pop hits that were being minted and broadcast seemingly every day, but vocalists were not included in the AFM orders (neither, through some strange quirk, were harmonica players). As a result, some new recordings were made, but singers who would previously have enjoyed the luxury of instrumental backing found themselves set against choirs.

There were also some ready-made masters available from independent producers, and Capitol bought in some of these to keep the wolf from the soundproofed studio door. One of these masters came from an outfit called the Nat King Cole Trio, beginning an association that would end only with Cole's sadly premature death in 1965. The progressive bandleader Stan Kenton also joined Capitol around this time, as did the husband and wife team of Paul Weston and Jo Stafford. On the executive side, Dave Dexter had come in as publicity, public relations and advertising chief in 1943, while James B. Conkling became head of A&R the following year. Dexter would remain with Capitol into the 1970s, while Conkling would move on to greater heights with other companies.

Knowing the strength of his position, Petrillo's bluff remained uncalled. His resolve is well illustrated by the fact that, when the dispute was referred to the National War Labor Board and they ordered a settlement, he refused to recognize the body's authority. He defied even the personal intervention of President Franklin D. Roosevelt. US Decca, without the depth of catalogue that Columbia or Victor could offer, was the most vulnerable of the three main American record companies. Consequently it was hardly a surprise when they turned out to be the first to accede to Petrillo's demands, signing a royalty arrangement with the AFM in September 1943. The musical *Oklahoma!* had opened to rave reviews since the imposition of the ban. Decca took advantage of its AFM enfranchisement by issuing a full-cast recording. It also made the most of Victor's indisposition by signing the violinist Jascha Heifetz to a short-term contract.

Although Decca's cave-in weakened RCA and Columbia's position, they continued to hold out until they could hold out no more. Edward Wallerstein was the first to bow to the seemingly inevitable, signing the AFM contract on 11 November 1944. Wallerstein outlined his reasoning in a telegram to Judge Vinson of the Office of Economic Stabilization:

> We have waited ... sixteen months [since the dispute was referred to the Board] for action by one or more branches of the government ... eight months since the filing of the Opinion by the panel recommending that the War Labor Board 'exercise its power to terminate the strike' ... two months and a half since the War Labor Board, apparently unable in any other way to enforce its order, certified the question to the President of the United States ... [and] almost another six weeks [since] ... he requested Mr Petrillo by telegram to end the strike ... The economic pressures on us are such that we can wait no longer and must now sign or go out of business.[12]

Out on a limb, RCA had no choice but to sign up. The ban had lasted for twenty-seven months. The terms of the RCA contract, which must be assumed to be typical of all those signed with the AFM at the time, set up a structure of royalties to be paid directly to the union (how much actually reached the musicians has long been a subject for debate), ranging from a quarter of a cent for records retailing at under 35c up to $2^1/_2$c on records retailing at more than $2.

The whole affair resembled the situation between the broadcasting networks and the American Society of Composers, Authors & Publishers (ASCAP), which had, in 1940, presaged Petrillo's ban with similar demands. The broadcasters responded by declaring that as of 1 January 1941, no music by ASCAP-registered composers or musicians would be played on air. They had followed this up by forming their own royalty clearing house, Broadcast Music Incorporated (BMI), and signing up as many non-ASCAP artists as they could, finding a particularly rich seam among black musicians and composers such as Duke Ellington. However, the large number of popular artists and composers who came under the ASCAP banner meant that the broadcasters had to cave in eventually and sign with ASCAP if they were going to offer their listeners the latest sounds.

One of the factors that made settlement imperative had been the relaxation of shellac restrictions, which once again allowed supply to meet demand. However, research was ongoing into synthetic alternatives. Both RCA and EMI had been looking into the possibilities of vinyl as early as 1939, but both had been wary of pursuing the matter too hard for fear that high-quality surfaces would show up the deficiencies of the original matrices. There was another argument for sticking with shellac. One vinyl-based compound developed by RCA, which it called Vitrolac V-142, cost nearly six times more to produce than the high-grade shellac used for Red Seal discs.

A considerable amount of experience with vinyl had been gained from the making of V-Discs, the records made for and shipped to American servicemen and women between 1943 and 1949. Petrillo had allowed these to be made and issued under his 'war effort' clause, but his assent was given under the strict understanding that all matrices and discs were to be destroyed at the end of the war.

V-Discs had their origins in a suggestion made by Captain Howard Bronson, a musical adviser to the US Army Recreation and Welfare Section. He believed that soldiers would appreciate discs of military band music and the like, as a morale-booster. His superiors agreed and a consignment of 16-inch shellac transcription discs was organized to be sent from the Armed Forces Radio Service. The programme did not get under way properly until Lieutenant George Robert Vincent became involved. Vincent, a member of the AFRS technical staff, who had seen service in the First World War and worked for Edison, made the point to Bronson that the G.I.s would appreciate something a little more contemporary than what was being offered. Bronson saw the point, and approved the release of popular material, but told Vincent that there was no budget available for doing so. The financial officer, Howard Haycraft, proved Bronson wrong by apportioning $1m to Vincent's scheme.

Having decided on the name and commissioned a logo from a commercial artist at a cost of $5, Vincent went about building up a staff. In came Private Steve Sholes, who had, in peacetime, been a member of the RCA Victor A&R staff, Morty 'Perfect Pitch' Palitz – ex of Brunswick, Decca and Columbia – and another RCA man, Walt Heebner. Heebner had the job of persuading Petrillo, who agreed at the end of October 1943, albeit with the aforementioned conditions.[13]

Immediately, it became apparent that shellac was not going to hold up to being despatched to theatres of war all around the world. Vinylite, as developed by Union Carbide, was thought to be an ideal substitute, but it was already in heavy demand from the military for other uses, and so its consistent supply could not be guaranteed. As a result, while vinylite became the main material for V-Discs, other fillers were used. In addition to the records, a special spring-wound 'V-Disc' phonograph, with replaceable steel needles, was manufactured. RCA Victor's pressing plant at Camden had enough spare capacity to take on the majority of V-Disc production (Columbia also did some, but chose to stick with shellac). Thirty different discs were to be sent in 'kits' and in the first week of the programme, 1,780 such packages were sent out.

The material on the discs was gathered from a number of sources. The broadcasting networks were only too willing to help, providing feeds from their studios to the V-Disc headquarters in New York, where discs were made. In addition, when the V-Disc organization began its own recording programme, the broadcasters and the record companies made their studios available, whenever practicable. A number of V-Discs were made in CBS Playhouse 3 – formerly Hammerstein's Theater, now the Ed Sullivan Theater – on Broadway. Others were made at Playhouse 4 – which later became the Studio 54 nightclub – while Columbia Records's Liederkranz Hall was a regular V-Disc venue. Toscanini's precious 8H was pressed into service, not least on the V-Discs recorded by the maestro with the NBC Symphony Orchestra. The Hollywood film studios also pitched in with repertoire, line feeds and studio time. To ensure that all of the possible bases were covered, a portable rig was available to record bands wherever they were working, in theatres and dance halls.

The involvement of jazz writer and musician George Simon helped bring in some of the biggest names in swing, including Benny Goodman, Count Basie, Louis Armstrong and Ella Fitzgerald, for various recordings, including some all-star jam sessions which made the most of the six-minute playing time of the 12-inch 78 rpm discs. One of Simon's biggest coups was to assemble the combined orchestras of Jimmy Dorsey and Tommy Dorsey for a session at Liederkranz Hall. The V-Disc programme is also notable for being responsible for Fats Waller's last recordings.

Research being undertaken by Decca in London meant that when the improved fidelity offered by vinyl was viable for mass production, it would be matched by matrices containing the full range of audible sounds. The company had embraced war work enthusiastically, not least as a means of survival in uncertain times. As Edward Lewis told Hugh Mendl in 1939: 'I don't know if there'll be a Decca after the war'.[14] Part of the New Malden factory was converted for use as a chroming plant for Rolls-Royce Merlin aero engines, but the crowning glory of Decca's wartime endeavour was the development of a radio navigator – radar – which was used with great success in the Normandy landings. The inventor of the Decca Navigator, W. J. O'Brien, had been brought into the company by Harvey Schwarz, the American who had come in when Decca bought British Brunswick.

So it was that the new Decca recording technique was created in response to a request from the military. RAF Coastal Command needed to train its men to distinguish the different sounds of Allied submarines and German U-Boats. A record of their noises was thought to be the ideal tool, but the subtle nuances of the various sounds, vital to recognition, was beyond any of the existing recording systems, which were good to, at best, 10,000 cycles per second. At Broadhurst Gardens, with a team of assistants, Arthur Haddy set about increasing the headroom of the wax recording system to 15,000 cycles per second, the limit of human hearing. This was achieved with a new custom-built microphone, the Decca FR-1, and a new moving coil disc-cutter.

The demands of Coastal Command satisfied, Decca was then able to use its new wonder tool on domestic, commercial recordings. The first sessions took place at Kingsway Hall in May and June 1944, with Sidney Beer conducting the National Symphony Orchestra. One of these recordings, Tchaikovsky's Fifth Symphony in E Minor, with Dennis Brain as horn soloist, was the first to be issued, in December 1944. These earliest releases were put out without fanfare or publicity, but Lewis realized that with the right name and the right spin, the improved recording quality could become a potent marketing tool. So it was that Haddy's system became known as 'Full Frequency Range Recording' or 'FFRR'. Decca's advertising and publicity manager Francis Attwood was inspired to suggest a trade-mark consisting of the letters 'FFRR' emanating from a human ear, and this made its debut in July 1945 with an advertisement in the *Gramophone*. Lewis later observed that Attwood's design was 'to become of immense value'.[15] FFRR had, said the inaugural advertisement, 'been in daily use in the Decca recording studios for the past twelve months' and the records made by the process 'demonstrate the unquestionable superiority of Decca full frequency range recording'.[16]

The technology soon filtered over to the pop side, adding lustre to recordings by Mantovani, the pianist Charlie Kunz and Ted Heath and His Music. For a short while, Attwood's logo began to appear at the bottom of the record labels, in the area usually reserved for the music publisher's details. Decca's re-entry into the classical music market, on its red label 'K' series (pop records had blue labels and an 'F' prefix – both bore the bust of Beethoven and the declaration that Decca was 'The Supreme Record', which the label's releases had carried since 1929) allowed the company to make up for the loss of the Deutsche Grammophon and Polydor catalogue. The enterprise was nominally under the control of Harry Sarton, head of the artists' department, but he 'kept a low profile in the classical field',[17] being primarily a popular music man and more used to dealing with artists like Vera Lynn and Mantovani.

Instead, the main figure in Decca's classical flowering was Victor Olof, a string player and orchestral administrator, who became known to all, not entirely affectionately, as 'the Baron' because of his imperious manner. Personally handling all of the largest and most prestigious record dates, Olof was assisted by Christopher Jennings, a young producer who divided his time between the pops and the serious side, and Terrence Gibbs, who took on the smaller sessions. 'He confined himself rather to the, dare I say, camper end of the classical catalogue,'[18] remembers Hugh Mendl of Gibbs. In 1947, the classical music activity was sufficient to justify the appointment of another staff member, John Culshaw, who had been working in Attwood's publicity department.

The studios at Broadhurst Gardens had been judged too small for large orchestral sessions, even the large studio one. So, other halls were tried, including Wembley Town Hall and Kingsway Hall. HMV had been using this venue – a Methodist church – almost since the start of electric recording in 1925, but the demand for it had decreased from sixty-five sessions a year in 1928 to fifteen in 1940. This meant that there was spare capacity enough to accommodate Decca. It had its downside, being situated directly above the Piccadilly line shuttle between Holborn and Aldwych, and thus susceptible to rumble from the tube trains. It was also very shabby – Walter Legge had almost made a sport of complaining about the decaying fabric and decor of the building. That could be forgiven, though, when its world-class acoustic was taken into account, along with the presence of a very fine organ. By 1953, EMI and Decca had entered into a formal agreement for the exclusive use of the hall as a recording venue. By the 1960s, the annual cost of hiring Kingsway Hall was £12,775, compared with £600 at the time of HMV's first contract in 1928.

Olof had some considerable success in wooing big names to Decca, despite its status as a relatively unknown quantity. Among them was the conductor Wilhelm Furtwangler, but his transition to the label was not without its problems. Chief engineer Kenneth 'Wilkie' Wilkinson had developed various microphone placement techniques that brought out the best in the FFRR system. However, when recording Brahms's Second Symphony at Kingsway Hall, the ageing Furtwangler became 'excessively nervous and edgy', which he eventually put down to the fact that the engineers were using more than one microphone. He stipulated that one microphone should be hung over the orchestra and all of the others disconnected. When the results came out, 'the critics were bewildered by the change in the famous Decca sound', Furtwangler's Brahms being 'diffuse and muddy' compared with 'the usual combination of warmth and clarity ... the pity of it all was that the performance ... was remarkable'.[19]

Before long, Decca's classical work was moving further afield than Wembley and Kingsway, into the newly liberated continent. The main impetus came from Decca's Swiss agent, an orthodox Jew called Moses Aron Rosengarten, better known as Maurice. Rosengarten was, in the words of Culshaw, 'tiny, reserved and as sharp as a cut-throat razor'.[20] Immediately after the war, he suggested to Lewis that the company should begin recording European orchestras on their home turf. Lewis, however, was wary of making too great a commitment to the Continent. Before the war, Decca had directly operated subsidiaries throughout Europe, which it had been forced to close when times were tight.

Given Rosengarten's acknowledged shrewdness, it probably wasn't altruism that motivated the offer that he then made to Lewis. He would fund all of the sessions personally, in exchange for a royalty. Lewis, knowing the quality of the continental orchestras, could not refuse. Olof took on the European sessions, with Culshaw deputizing back in London. In time, Rosengarten would take Decca back into Germany through Teldec, a joint venture with Telefunken, as well as signing conductors like Ernest Ansermet (who had, briefly, recorded for Decca in the company's very earliest days) and George Szell. One of his greatest coups, though, came when HMV unaccountably failed to renew its contract with the pianist Wilhelm Backhaus after forty years. Rosengarten swooped and Backhaus spent the rest of his career with Decca.

EMI was watching Decca's advances with great interest. When the first FFRR ad appeared in the *Observer* in June 1945, F. B. Duncan asked research head Isaac Shoenberg whether it was possible that Decca had managed to register the four letters as a trademark. Shoenberg replied that he saw 'no reason why Decca should not be able to register as a trademark the device [the ear logo] in question as a whole, though I think they would be required to disdain exclusivity of the letters'.[21] It is probable that Alan Dower Blumlein would have been on the case independently, but he had been killed in a plane crash in June 1942, while testing the H2S radar system. Before long, EMI developed a rival system called Extended Range, but Decca had the edge.

The leap in recording quality gave Decca a chance to establish itself in the US market. The company had sold the majority of its stake in US Decca during the war, the funds having come in useful to pay for the radar and recording research, while also shoring up the company's balance sheet. 'All overseas investments were supposed to be sold, except you were allowed to keep a nominal holding, to help the war effort,' explains Hugh Mendl. Although the sellout was forced by circumstances, it was a source of relief for Lewis, who had not been able to impose the kind of control over US Decca that he would have liked. Kapp, as others in the industry observed, was running the company as though he owned it, and consequently Lewis felt that the English company was not getting enough of its masters released in America. Mendl recalled:

> The trouble really began when the American company was sold. We could not get them to release our records, any more than EMI could with RCA Victor and Columbia. They didn't want to know about British records. American Decca issued the token Ambrose, because he was American in a way, wasn't he? There was an awful battle, as we had begun to do well with all our records during the war.[22]

Free of Kapp, Lewis decided to start a new American company, but was unable to use the Decca name. So it was that the FFRR records made their entry into the US market through Decca's newly established subsidiary London Records. The records were accompanied by a range of suitable record players, from the serviceable but fairly humble Deccalian, retailing at £35/4/1 to the magnificent over-engineering of the Decola, with its walnut casing, eight-record changer and triple-loudspeaker system (advertised as 'What a Ming vase is to the connoisseur'), which went out at a startling £173/5. Decca had sent samples of one combination radio and record player – the Piccadilly – to America with a view to finding a wireless manufacturer willing to provide a tuner suitable for American wavelengths, so that the machine could be sold in the US market. Although it was a comparatively modest instrument, those who heard it were startled by the fidelity of reproduction and came to the conclusion that it was some way better than most of what was currently available. However, the plans foundered when no radio manufacturers came forward. Read and Welch suggest that it was a conspiracy by the complacent American manufacturers, eager to avoid competition.

While Decca was developing FFRR, research was ongoing at Columbia into long-playing discs. Edward Wallerstein had kept the faith since Victor's abortive 1930s experiment. He felt sure that if the product and the timing were right, the long player could take off. With this in mind, Columbia had, at Wallerstein's instigation, been recording all sessions since 1939 on 16.5-inch lacquers that revolved at $33^1/_3$ rpm. George Avakian, a young producer who had worked on jazz reissues before the war, but who had returned as a junior member of the A&R staff, recalls: 'His instructions were "We must preserve all of these, because one day, if we want to produce a long-playing record, it'll be much easier to work from these discs than from the metal parts of finished production masters."'[23]

Traditionally, credit for the long-playing disc is given to Peter C. Goldmark, the head of the CBS radio research laboratories. Occasionally, contributions to the work from an engineer called William S. Bachman, who had previously worked for General Electric, where he developed the variable-reluctance cartridge, are acknowledged. Avakian, who in 1947 became head of Columbia's popular album department, remembers it differently:

Goldmark was the first person to work on the long-playing record for many years, but he failed completely to make it work. There was a race between RCA and CBS to develop colour television. The CBS system, which was developed by Goldmark, involved a colour disc, with three primary colours rapidly revolving. The quality was quite good, I thought, but NBC had a plain box, which was much more practical, so the industry opted for the NBC system. This was devastating to William Paley.

He was also upset because his man Goldmark had failed to produce a workable long-playing record. So, he decided to shut the research programme down completely. Wallerstein told Paley, 'Look, let me work with my engineers on the project, because I still have belief in it', and so the deal was struck between him and Paley that it would be the responsibility of Columbia Records to pay for the development under Bill Bachman, who was hired by Wallerstein from General Electric specifically to develop long-playing records, if possible. Bachman built upon what had been done so far unsuccessfully, but he went off into new directions which finally pulled the whole thing off, so that in less than two years, we had 200 LPs on the market. Part of it was the compound, which was developed so that it would stand up under the pressure of the slow-speed movement underneath the pickup. Part of it was also that his playback equipment was improved to such a degree that there was less distortion and less surface noise than ever before. Mr Paley was very glad to see this happen, because it meant that his company was really doing something.[24]

Paley's approval, however, had its limits, as Avakian discovered when he was asked to speak about the LP achievement on a radio programme: 'Before the afternoon was out there was a call from Paley's office saying, "Avakian cannot do this broadcast, and nobody at Columbia Records is to talk to anybody about the long-playing record, except through my office."' Paley was so upset by Goldmark's double failure on colour television and LP that he was unable to countenance admitting that someone else, even someone within his own company, had, within two years, made a workable LP system. So he organized a cover-up:

From then on, the CBS radio laboratory and Peter Goldmark were credited as the developers of the LP. There are a few photographs and a few articles in which Bachman is mentioned, and Bachman is seen standing on one side of a photograph in which Goldmark is playing an LP, but it's always a secondary role, with no explanation. Bachman is in there, but no one is ever aware of how important he was.[25]

The new discs finally made good use of ex-RCA engineer Jim Hunter's vinyl expertise, for he had joined Columbia as production director. Having settled on the material for the discs, it was then decided to use a 1-mil (one-thousandth of an inch) groove, less than half the width of a 78 groove. Initial experiments resulted in a disc with a playing time of seven or eight minutes a side, but Wallerstein argued that this did not constitute a long-playing record. Looking at the timing of a number of classical pieces, he worked out that a playing time of seventeen minutes a side would allow the majority of the classical repertory to fit on two sides of a disc, and directed the engineers to work on this basis. This was achieved in autumn 1947, with a 12-inch disc.

The first Columbia LPs were launched at the Waldorf-Astoria in New York on 20 June 1948. Wallerstein was accompanied on the day by Goldmark and Goddard Lieberson, head of the Columbia Masterworks division. He took the podium next to a stack of 78s that were 8 feet in height. Next to them were the same recordings on LP, a pile just 15 inches high. To excite interest in the system, Columbia had reverted to one of its old gambits – produce a cheap player and sell it at a low price, with the hope of making its real money on the discs themselves. A manufacturing alliance with Philco was arranged and a machine which attached to the household radio set was offered for $9.95 – its cost to Columbia. The company offered the attachments for a year, by which time LP was on the way to being established. Columbia's first LP hit was the cast recording of *South Pacific*, featuring Ezio Pinza and Mary Martin.

At the time of the launch, the American music industry was in the middle of another AFM recording ban. The 1947 Taft-Hartley Act, which concerned labour relations, had made it illegal 'to cause or attempt to cause an employer to pay or deliver or agree to pay or deliver any money or other thing of value, in the nature of an exaction, for services which are not performed or not to be performed'. The royalties paid by the record companies to the union came under this heading. Petrillo, unsurprisingly, took this very badly and declared a cessation of all recording from 1 January 1948. However, this time the record companies knew that he was perfectly capable of bringing the musicians out on strike, and so went into stockpiling overdrive in the last months of 1947. For Columbia, with its new format, the need to do so was particularly acute. Thus the 'diskeries', as

Billboard was wont to call them, were far more comfortably situated than they had been in 1942, and the ban lasted less than a year this time, being settled once a mutually acceptable trustee was found to administer the royalty fund. While it was in force, however, some surprise hits came out of the stockpile. George Avakian takes up the story:

> We had to record Sinatra with a vocal group behind him, and it sounded pretty bad, but the AFM ban helped me get credit for at least two million seller singles including one by Frankie Yankovic and his Yanks, which was a polka band out of Cleveland. Mr Wallerstein came to me and said, 'George, you know the ice box pretty well' (the ice box was the unreleased material we had), 'can you find something that we've never released that might have some commercial value?' I started investigating and the one that hit was an instrumental by Les Brown which had never been released because it didn't have a vocal; a beautiful dance band arrangement of 'I've Got My Love to Keep Me Warm'. I just listened to unreleased material, thought it was a possibility, put it out with no expectation and – BANG! – it was a smash hit because it had no competition. It was unique and it came out at the right time.[26]

Paley had invited RCA's General David Sarnoff to see the new development and offered to license the LP to RCA, but Sarnoff had demurred. Paley had not realized, or perhaps chose to ignore, the fact that the LP was not patentable and thus not licensable. The only aspect that could be copyrighted was the term 'LP', which Wallerstein trademarked immediately. He also set about offering Columbia know-how to any companies that wanted it, on the basis that this would increase the market for all. RCA remained silent on the issue until February 1949, when it emerged with its own microgroove disc – a 7-inch platter rotating at 45 rpm. It was no long-player, but it proved to be a hi-fi replacement for the 78. The result was that the two major record companies were offering two completely incompatible products. The RCA 45s had a large spindle hole, whereas the Columbia LPs had gone with the standard small spindle. New machines were generally equipped with either 33⅓ or 45, but not both. The so-called 'battle of the speeds' was a fraught time for the industry, with many hesitating to make a commitment until either 33⅓ or 45 had established itself. However, equipment manufacturers soon began to offer multi-speed machines, and the two formats found popularity for different purposes.

That the LP and the 45 were marvellous achievements is beyond doubt. That they improved immeasurably the sound quality available to consumers is equally unquestionable. Similarly, the amount of research and development work put in by Bill Bachman, Vin Liebler and their RCA counterparts. The fact remains, however, that most of the components had been available for many years. The jewelled stylus had first been put into commercial use by Edison at the start of the century, giving far better fidelity than a one-shot steel needle. Electrical amplification had been a goer since the 1920s. And yet many gramophones, until the advent of microgroove, were unamplified and almost all continued to use steel needles. Vinyl was first used for records in the 1930s, but even without changing from shellac, the Columbia New Process surfaces had shown what was possible. The absence of abrasive fillers, designed to wear the steel needles into the shape of the groove, would have all but eliminated the frying bacon sound associated with 78s, but this practice persisted until the last 78s were manufactured in the early 1960s. Why did an obviously unsatisfactory technology last so long?

Good marketing at the start had given Victor and Columbia's lateral discs a sales lead. The depression had killed the desire to upgrade or buy new reproduction equipment. Up to the end of the 78, the companies made discs that could be played on their very earliest machines. It could be argued that this showed commitment to all of their customers, but it is equally possible to argue that they were working on the 'if it ain't broke, don't fix it' principle to the detriment of sound quality. It would not be the last time the business resisted a revolutionary idea.

Despite, or perhaps because of, its affiliations to both Columbia and RCA, EMI was not the first on the UK market with a microgroove disc. The company was right in the middle of what even EMI's official historian Peter Martland is duty bound to call 'fifteen years of mediocre management'.[27] Sir Louis Sterling's successor Sir Robert McLean had not stayed in post very long, and there are suggestions that many people at the company did not take to his patrician manner. Added to this, the set-up was that McLean ran the administrative side of the business, while Alfred Clark continued running the commercial side. After a while, McLean decided that he was ready to take on the running of the business as a whole and tried to make Clark stick to his contracted one day a week. Never one to take things lying down, Clark presented the board with an ultimatum – either him or me. Naturally, the board sided with the chairman.

McLean's replacement, who joined in 1946, was Sir Ernest Fisk, who had enjoyed a distinguished career with Marconi's Australian subsidiary Amalgamated Wireless. He had been a pioneer in radio broadcasting down under, and had received the first direct messages from England in 1918. His was the first human voice heard by radio between England and Australia in 1924. He had also chaired various government committees. All of that was very well, but did it qualify him to run Britain's largest record company at a time of critical transition? Unfortunately not.

Fisk attempted to rescue the company by dividing its operations into subsidiary companies, an act that caused only more bureaucracy and confusion. His worst decision, however, was to stick with shellac, holding off on the new-fangled microgrooves for the time being. If Alfred Clark had still been around, it is possible that he would have pressed the issue harder, at least on the 45 rpm front. He had been such a Victor loyalist over the years, it would be hard to imagine anything coming out of Camden that didn't have his wholehearted approval. It was exactly this loyalty that had caused him to resign. The film company Metro-Goldwyn-Mayer had decided to enter the record business, bringing with it a wealth of movie stars and soundtrack material. EMI, in an effort to spread its risks, decided to take on the MGM contract for the UK. This was, Clark argued, a foolish move, likely to upset both RCA and Columbia, particularly the former. In December 1945, he announced his intention to resign and followed through in March 1946.

If Fisk had intended to avoid upsetting either RCA or Columbia by not favouring one format over the other, he had succeeded only in offending both. The decision cost EMI a lot of goodwill with its long-standing American partners and lost the company ground in its home market. The first EMI LPs and 45s reached the market in October 1952, by which time Decca had already been offering microgroove records for over two years. Wallerstein had shown the technology to Edward Lewis and an EMI executive – probably studio head Brenchley Mittell – at roughly the same time, and while both liked what they saw, only Lewis did anything about it. Wallerstein offered Lewis full co-operation in the hope of making EMI budge. The new format found an enthusiastic proponent in Arthur Haddy, who saw its potential as a medium for FFRR recordings. The ability to run through classical pieces without a break every five minutes also swayed him. Brian Masters, who joined Decca's engineering staff in 1968 and became a friend of Haddy's, remembers him enquiring, 'I ask you, did Beethoven write the Eroica for symphony orchestra and ruddy autochanger?'[28]

Decca brought out its first LPs in June 1950, and the launch was accompanied by another stroke of genius on the part of Francis Attwood. Placing a series of striking advertisements in the *Gramophone*, he used the opportunity to pull EMI's nose in a vaguely coded manner for failing to pick up on the wonder of the age. The most blatant of the advertisements mentioned 'the doubting Thomases', a clear reference to C. H. 'Harry' Thomas, although a later promotion could be construed as even more of a dig. It carried the strapline 'Striding ahead' and showed a soldier's leg on the march. Under his boot, seemingly about to be crushed, was the word 'Hayes'. When pressed, Attwood merely said that this was the name of the artist, and that it was not a reference to EMI. That the message was hitting home became clear after an advertisement depicting those who resisted LP as ostriches with their heads in the sand. The following month, the Johnson Talking Machine Co. Ltd – a dormant subsidiary of EMI – took a full page to tell the story of 'Dickie and the Ostrich', in which a small boy called Dickie was informed that an 'ostrich does not put its head in the sand but can run very fast'.

When LP was being developed, the plan was to copy from the session onto a master disc, assembling the required track order as one went along. However, direct disc recording required almost superhuman concentration on the part of the musicians, particularly on long classical pieces. Fortunately, by the time the new format had reached commercial maturity, magnetic tape had emerged as a recording medium. Columbia ordered its first tape machines in 1947, and had soon abandoned direct cutting.

Magnetic recording had been a theoretical possibility since Vladimir Poulsen's invention of the Telegraphone wire recorder in 1898. Unfortunately, the sound quality of the wire recordings was too low for critical musical uses, but the principle had been established. Experiments in the field continued. In 1929, Ludwig Blattner unveiled the Blattnerphone, which used 21lb reels of 6mm steel tape passing a recording head at 5 feet per second, giving a running time of twenty minutes a reel. While the BBC was impressed enough to order some machines, the system was far from perfect. It was possible to cut and edit the tape, but the only method of joining the ends was to weld them, the results passing over the playback heads with an audible clunk. Later on, the idea of bonding ferric particles to waxed paper tape had been tried with some success, but the paper did not have the required robustness for repeated use.

The answer came with the improved polymers that were developed in the 1930s. Once a stable plastic base had been formulated, magnetic tape came on in leaps and bounds, particularly in Germany. On 19 November 1936, Sir Thomas Beecham and the London Philharmonic Orchestra had assembled in the concert hall at the BASF works in Ludwigshafen to record a selection of pieces by Mozart, Rimsky-Korsakov and Dvořák among others on the BASF company's new magnetic tape. BASF's advance was not picked up by the likes of EMI or Decca before the war.

Magnetic tape was used extensively by the Germans once the war was under way. Some broadcasts by Adolf Hitler and William Joyce – Lord Haw-Haw – were pre-recorded and then played out when needed. 'Eric Maschwitz[29] once told me that when he was in the Army, he had marched into the Radio Luxembourg studios to arrest Lord Haw-Haw,' reports Hugh Mendl. 'He knew he was there, because he could hear him on the radio. So he marched in there, and there was a tape going round. Nobody on our side had seen a tape at that time.'[30] Others, who were no less surprised than Maschwitz at what they found, were more able to understand the principles of what was happening. In 1943, John T. Mullin, an American serviceman stationed in Britain, found himself listening to late-night classical music broadcasts from Germany. Maintaining a live orchestra for such continuous broadcasting would, he worked out, be a prohibitively expensive under-taking. So it followed that the programmes were recorded, but there was an absence of the usual clicks, pops and surface noise present on records. How were they doing it? Mullin found out when he was posted to Germany at the end of the war, where he came across the AEG Tonschreiber tape machine. He applied to bring examples back to America, where he worked on improving the electronics. A tape of quarter-inch width was settled on, as was a recording speed of 30 inches per second.

Mullin's work came to the attention of the singer Bing Crosby, who had been looking for a way to pre-record his popular radio show. The machines were put into use for this purpose with great success. Unfortunately, none of the major audio equipment manufacturers of the time picked up on the advance, and the job of developing a commercial tape recorder fell to Alexander M. Poniatoff and his small company based in Redwood City, California – Ampex. The hardware axis of Ampex was complemented by the decision of 3M to manufacture Scotch brand audio tape.

Over in the UK at Hayes, EMI's Central Research Laboratories were working on their own machine, having also acquired samples of the AEG bounty. The fruits of this work was the EMI BTR-1 (the initials stood for British Tape Recorder), the first of which was installed at the Abbey Road studios in the summer of 1948, with six more joining it later in the year. Although the machines were expensive, it was worked out that the use of tape would provide an annual saving of £3,750 over the use of wax blanks. The economies were aided by the fact that EMI had also thrown itself headlong into the tape-making business, with its Emitape brand.

Columbia acquired examples of both the Ampex and EMI machines, but settled on the American machine, sending the BTRs back to their manufacturer. This slight was compensated for by the fact that the BTR-1 and its successor the BTR-2 became the British industry standard, finding use at almost every independent studio, with the BBC and even with the company's main rival – Decca had a BTR-1 on hand for all sessions by the autumn of 1949. Jimmy Lock, who joined the London independent studio IBC in 1958, and later went on to become one of Decca's star classical engineers, remembers the EMI recorders with great fondness: 'The BTR-2 was a marvellous machine. Solid as a rock, as it were. They hardly ever went wrong. They had great transports and the wow and flutter were extremely good on them. They weighed half a ton, or at least it seemed like they did.'[31]

One of the great benefits of magnetic tape was that it allowed editing. There had, in the past, been a few brave souls who had attempted to edit by dubbing the required portions of a recording to a new disc in real time, but success in this endeavour depended on split-second timing and awesome concentration. With the precious few available tape machines in demand for studio sessions, long-players of archive material had to be compiled in precisely this manner. George Avakian remembers the troubles his colleague Howard Scott went to. 'He was given the terrible assignment of transferring all of these 78s and discs onto master discs, no tape, you see. You can imagine how hard it was to do this. Getting the sound to match from the interior of a disc that is distorting. It was a nightmare, he said.'[32]

Decca producer John Culshaw, who was doing much the same over in London, concurred:

> The only way ... to make an LP from existing 78 rpm records was to try to join the end of one side to the start of the next, while the result was simultaneously recorded (or 'cut') on a lacquer, revolving at $33\frac{1}{3}$ rpm. It was a nightmare. Studio Two at West Hampstead had been converted for the

operation, with a row of turn-tables along one wall ... I stood there with a score and began a countdown during the last thirty seconds of a side and then shouted 'Drop!', at which point one engineer would fade out the side that had just ended while another, with luck, would lower the pick-up on the beginning of the next side. If anything went even slightly wrong there was nothing to do but go back to the beginning, and as every LP had to be cut at least twice in case of an accident during processing at the factory it was a tedious and frustrating business.[33]

Culshaw was so affected by the whole experience that to the end of his life, if he heard certain pieces of music in concert, he had to restrain himself from jumping to his feet and shouting 'Drop!' at what would have been the end of each side.

8 Picking up the pieces

At the end of the Second World War, the British political scene received a shake-up. With rationing still in force and conscription set to continue for almost another twenty years, the electorate turned to the Labour Party to reconstruct the country. Over in the US, Harry Truman was the surprise winner of the presidential elections. By the turn of the 1950s, though, the Tories were back in power at Westminster, and about to preside over a decade in which prosperity grew so much that Prime Minister Harold Macmillan was able to announce that the populace had never had it so good. Despite all of these upheavals, the record industry looked much the same as it had in 1939. The US business consisted of RCA Victor, Columbia and Decca, with the upstart Capitol making some inroads. In Britain, the pattern was replicated almost exactly by HMV, Columbia and Decca. This was recognizably the same structure that had prevailed since the birth of the industry, with the exception of Decca, but as it had entered the market just as Edison was leaving it, the number of players remained the same.

In the intervening years, independent labels had come and gone. Some innovated in the field of technology, some in repertoire, some in both. Others chose not to innovate at all, preferring to mirror the status quo in search of a quick pound note. All of those who were remotely successful had been subsumed into the major companies, a process that continues to the present day. The majors had enjoyed fifty years of unmolested empire building. All of that was to change over the next twenty years with a massive change in the worldwide business, which saw ancient alliances coming to an end, new partnerships being forged and a whole new spirit of independence manifesting itself for the first time since the Wall Street Crash. Through it all, the old stagers would keep going, but they were never to have it so cosy again.

One newcomer was Chess, the Chicago-based label set up in 1950 by a pair of Polish immigrant brothers, Leonard and Phil Cryz. They had arrived in the US in 1928, ten years after their father had gone to the New World to make his fortune in scrap metal. Leonard set up a liquor store in one of the rougher districts of the city, before moving on to running his own bars. The next step was to open a club, which he did in 1945 with the Mocambo Lounge. Visiting performers would sometimes make recordings at the club, which awakened the brothers' interest in the idea of setting up a record label, particularly one serving the race market. Their first venture into the record business came in 1947 with the Aristocrat label, a partnership with an associate called Art Sheridan. The first Aristocrat artist was blues singer Muddy Waters.

Then came the Chess label, which took their anglicized name, and was later supplemented by subsidiary labels like Checker and Argo. Muddy Waters moved over to the new label as well, with Chuck Berry, Howlin' Wolf, Bo Diddley and John Lee Hooker joining in later years. Despite this wealth of talent, the brothers did not feel inclined to give their artists the star treatment. Infamously, Waters was once found to be earning his keep through the extra-musical pursuit of painting the studio. Multi-tasking was evidently a big thing at Chess, as rival label boss Ahmet Ertegun of Atlantic remembers:

> The first time I went to Chicago, I went to visit Chess, to see what the place looked like. There was one girl at the entrance, who was like a receptionist – she had a typewriter and answered the phone. Then Leonard showed me around the offices and so forth. I said, 'Where's the accounting department?' He looked at me and laughed. 'Well, that girl there, she's an accountant.' I said, 'She's an accountant, she's a receptionist, she's a secretary and she answers the phone. Does she make up the royalty statements?' He said, 'Yeah, she makes up the royalty statements.' All of these guys had trucks and they went around with new releases, a whole bunch of records on the truck, going round the countryside, selling them for cash. Not only that, but calling on every radio station along the way and dropping a little money here and there. That's what we had to compete with.[1]

Leonard's son Marshall had become involved in the company as a young boy, learning the business from the ground up. 'I was in the shipping room. I loaded trucks. One time I asked my father what my job was. He got pissed at me and said, "Your job is watching me".[2] So, when Leonard died in 1969 at the age of fifty-two, it was natural that his son should take high office, but in the aftermath of Leonard's death, the label was sold to the tape manufacturer GRT, which changed the dynamic slightly. 'I stayed on as president of Chess under the GRT Corporation, but I hated it,' Chess explained. 'GRT had no understanding of black music or a family-owned business.' Marshall quit his job and went off to work for the Rolling Stones, who had been heavily influenced by most of the artists on the Chess roster.

Over in Cincinnati, Ohio, another small independent was making a name for itself with 'race' music, and country and western. King was set up in 1943 by Syd Nathan, a former speakeasy drummer, pawnbroker and jukebox salesman, every inch the cigar-chomping record man of the aged cliché. The first record to come out on King was 'The Steppin' Out Kind'/ 'You'll Be Lonesome Too' by the Shepherd Brothers, a *nom de disque* for Merle Travis and 'Grandpa' Jones. Jones would go on to become a mainstay of the King label, despite Nathan's miserly offer of $5/_8$ of a cent per side released.

By the end of the 1940s, King had taken up residence in a former ice factory on Cincinnati's Brewster Avenue, into which the shrewd Nathan packed a studio and a pressing plant as well as the offices. The studio was 'austere' with soundproofing tiles on grim concrete walls, but still it had a 'clear and funky sound ... with depth and presence'.[3] In there, producers such as Henry Glover, Ray Pennington, Louis Innis, Gene Redd and Ralph Bass did their work with artists like Little Willie John – the originator of the song 'Fever' – the Royals, who later became Hank Ballard and the Midniters – the band behind the risqué 'Work with Me, Annie' – and the Delmore Brothers, who were enjoying a revival on King after their earlier career successes on RCA's cut-price Bluebird pop label. It was not until the mid-1950s, though, that King's biggest star joined the label. This was the man who would later glory in a plethora of titles, each underlining his extreme grooviness, including 'the Godfather of Soul', 'Soul Brother number one' and, rather superbly, 'the Minister of the new new superheavy funk'. Enter James Brown.

Nathan, being a middle-aged Jew, was not all that enamoured of Brown's music. On occasion he would try to veto releases, without avail – most memorably 'Papa's Got a Brand New Bag', which went on to become one of Brown's best-known hits. On another occasion, when Brown decided that he wanted to record a live album at the famous Apollo in Harlem, Nathan refused to fund the project, forcing Brown to bankroll it himself. Despite the differences, though, Brown's records sold like crazy, and when that happened, it was music to Nathan's ears.

Nathan was joined in 1958 by Hal Neely, who brought a previously unheard-of degree of organization to King. For example, master tapes and discs were at last kept in a temperature-controlled vault. Neely also promoted the acquisition of other catalogues, most notably that of the New York jazz label Bethlehem in 1961, a purchase that brought in recordings by Duke Ellington and Mel Torme among others. Despite these innovations, King was too closely linked to its founder and when his health began to fail, so did that of the label. Seymour Stein, who was later to co-found Sire Records, was in the frame to succeed Nathan, but couldn't take to Cincinnati life:

> Syd Nathan took to me in a big way. He adopted me almost as a son. His own son was retarded. He'd take me out to Cincinnati during the school holidays and I really learned the record business. He had everything there. I learned to press records. I was terrified. I was afraid I'd get my hands cut. I remember it was a Nina Simone Bethlehem LP with 'I Loves You, Porgy' on it, which contains the line 'Don't let him handle me with his hot hands'. I wondered if it wasn't prophetic. Syd offered me a full-time job in 1961, and I stayed there for three years. If I'd stayed there, I probably could have taken over the company, but I got homesick for New York. King was self-contained. It had great country acts and great R&B acts, but there wasn't the action on the street.[4]

As a result, King effectively died when Nathan succumbed to heart disease in March 1968, aged sixty-three, having racked up 10,000 recordings in a quarter of a century. Neely, who had moved on to the Starday label, returned to buy King for $1.75m, and merged it with his current company. The Starday-King combination was then sold on to the Lin Broadcasting Corporation. In 1971, Neely bought the business back for $3.5m, and after selling the Brown catalogue to Polydor for $1m, he set about running King with the help of music publisher Freddie Bienstock and songwriters Jerry Leiber and Mike Stoller. Unfortunately, clashes occurred, the dream team broke up and in 1973, the King operation was dispersed to various buyers.

The Duke-Peacock operation, established by Don Robey in Houston in 1949, is notable for being one of the first successful labels to be owned and run by a black businessman. It grew out of Robey's Bronze Peacock Dinner Club at 2809 Erastus Street in the Texas town, after Clarence 'Gatemouth' Brown, an artist managed by Robey, had experienced disappointing record sales through Eddie Mesner's Aladdin label. Robey rationalized that he could do better himself and so detailed one of his staff to find out what was involved in running a record company.

Once informed, the Peacock label brought out its first release, Brown's single 'Didn't Reach My Goal'/'Atomic Energy', in late 1949. Other artists soon joined Peacock from the fields of both gospel and R&B. From the gospel side, Robey had considerable success with the Original Five Blind Boys, although he obviously believed in spreading his bets, at one time having 100 similar groups under contract. In R&B he had Big Mama Thornton, who recorded the original version of Leiber and Stoller's 'Hound Dog' in 1953. Also signed to the label was the ill-starred Johnny Ace, who died in a game of Russian roulette in 1954. A tragedy, to be sure, but one that provided Ace with the crossover hit – 'Pledging My Love' – that had eluded him in life.

Richard Penniman, better known as Little Richard, and with a foot in both the gospel and R&B camps, also recorded for Peacock. At this stage of his career, though, he was nowhere near as successful as he was to become later with Art Rupe's Specialty label. His stint with Peacock is notable mostly for his allegations that Robey had used violence to make him sign a contract, just one of many intimations that the burly Robey was not the respectable businessman he made himself out to be.

In the mid-1950s, Robey's empire expanded with the acquisition of the Memphis-based Duke label. Around the same time, Duke-Peacock began to hit big with Bobby 'Blue' Bland. The company did not, however, get its first national hit until 1965, when its Back Beat subsidiary released 'Treat Her Right' by Roy Head and the Traits, a white group from Houston. So convincing was the black sound of the record that Robey successfully prevented Head from appearing on television in order to maintain the illusion. By the early 1970s, such successes were a thing of the past and Robey decided to cash in, selling the Duke-Peacock business to ABC-Dunhill in 1973. Robey died just two years later at the age of seventy-one.

Viewed from the perspective of the twenty-first century, the most important of the independent labels that sprung up after the Second World War is Atlantic. Although it is now part of the Time Warner behemoth, not only does it survive as a recognizable entity, but one of its founders is still involved, nearly six decades on from its first release. That co-founder is Ahmet Ertegun, younger son of a Turkish diplomat. When his father was stationed in Britain, he and his elder brother Nesuhi came to love jazz, catching the orchestras of Cab Calloway and Duke Ellington when they played the London Palladium in 1932.

Two years later, the Ertegun family had moved to America, where Munir Ertegun had become Kemal Ataturk's ambassador to Washington. Once ensconced in the capital city, the brothers Ertegun were able to feed their jazz obsession with visits to Waxie Maxie Silverman's Quality Music Shop. 'My brother and I were serious collectors, and we started in the thirties, collecting the cutouts from the twenties. We were collecting the Hot Fives, Bessie Smith, Jelly Roll Morton, King Oliver and all of that. In addition, we were going to jazz clubs all of the time.'[5]

Indeed they were. The holy grail for Ertegun and his brother was Harlem. On one occasion, young Ahmet cadged a trip to New York with the commander of the Turkish air force and went AWOL in the sainted district, having given his guardian the slip by asking to go to the cinema. Instructing a cab driver to 'take me to Harlem', he ended up at the Plantation Club. 'Even with his Turkish complexion, Ahmet Ertegun was the whitest cat in the place,' Ertegun's friend and colleague Stan Cornyn later observed.[6] He was having such a good time, both there and later at an after-hours drinker, that he did not show up at the Turkish consulate until 8 a.m., by which time he was the subject of a massive search.

If it became harder for Ertegun to get to the source, his father's position and influence made it relatively easy to entice jazzmen to the embassy for impromptu sessions and socializing. From there, it was a logical progression for the brothers to start promoting their own jazz concerts, which they did between 1939 and 1941. Unfortunately, in 1944, their father died, and their mother and sister moved back to Turkey. The boys, however, decided to stay on, in Ahmet's case, ostensibly to write a thesis on St Thomas Aquinas.

The reality was rather different, though. Far from throwing himself into his studies, Ertegun was instead immersing himself in a record venture that he had persuaded Waxie Maxie to underpin. There were to be two labels. Quality – after Silverman's shop – would handle jazz and what was beginning to be known as rhythm and blues, while Jubilee would major in gospel. Contrary to Ertegun's expectations, the first releases failed to catch fire and the business foundered. An attempt to release some recordings that he had made of Boyd Raeburn's progressive jazz orchestra went the same way when no distributor could be found.

Undeterred, Ertegun decided to have another go. This time, he enlisted Herb Abramson, a dental student who had been working for National

Records, a label owned by a paint manufacturer called Al Green (no relation to the soul singer). Abramson put $2,500 of his savings into Ertegun's new venture, while Ertegun himself had to persuade another dentist, Dr Vadhi Sabir, the family's practitioner in Washington, to put up another $10,000 to get the idea off the ground. In response to Richard Bock's Los Angeles-based label Pacific Jazz, Ertegun and Abramson called the new venture Atlantic. It opened for business in October 1947, using a $65-a-week suite at New York's Hotel Jefferson as both an office and a home for Ertegun and his cousin, the poet Sadi Koylan.

Friends and relatives in Turkey were kept in the dark about the Erteguns' entrepreneurial activities. Ahmet recalls: 'Our mother would be embarrassed to say, "They're in the record business", so she would say, "They're doing research in African-American music." If my father had been alive, my brother and I couldn't have gone into any business. He wouldn't have allowed us to.'[7]

The timing of the decision could have been better. Atlantic's first recording session was on 21 November 1947 and the second Petrillo ban was due to start on New Year's Day 1948. In the time they had available, Ertegun and Abramson laid down sixty-five sides, only half of which were of releasable quality, the others being 'learning experiences'.[8] As the ban wore on, however, Ertegun discovered that there was a nefarious way around the AFM. Other labels were recording in Europe, which 'turned out to be New Jersey'.[9] Petrillo appeared to be acting in musicians' best interests, yet many of them were so desperate for work that they approached Ertegun and offered to work surreptitiously for half the union scale.

Although Nesuhi Ertegun was not yet involved, Abramson had brought his wife Miriam in to help out. Stan Cornyn described her main contribution as being 'bright, caustic and impatient with dumb guys'.[10] Ahmet Ertegun expands:

> Our whole thing was day-to-day survival, and Miriam kept us on a very strict schedule. She was a very ethical, hardworking business manager. We wanted to make sure that we had enough money to make recording sessions, to pay our rent and survive. I had a very good partner in Herb. I knew about music, but I didn't know about the business. Herb knew who was a good music business lawyer, where he would get inexpensive pressings, how to get them shipped. How you send samples to radio stations, how you get records played. Everything.[11]

The close attentions of Dr Sabir also helped keep Atlantic on the right track:

> He had invested what for him was a lot of money and so he came every week
> to look at the books. What we had done, how much we had spent. He was a
> great friend of mine, and he would come up once every week or couple of
> weeks, we'd go out for dinner. We had nothing to hide, and we paid our
> royalties. We were probably the only ones that did that. We ran our company
> very differently to any other independents.
>
> We're the only one of all of those labels still in business, and there's still
> somebody from that time, namely me. I'm accused of every trespass that's
> been done against black people and artists in the rhythm and blues world. It
> all falls on me. Which is a joke. Motown! I mean, Motown would not let the
> RIAA look at its books so Motown could never give a platinum or gold record.
> There were no gold records at Motown, even though they sold millions,
> because they would not allow anybody to look at their books. That's a fact. I'm
> not saying they were worse than anybody. They were probably better. They
> probably treated their artists better than other labels. Look, I'm not the one to
> judge. I don't know who did what. I know that Herman Lubinsky used to take
> photographs giving Wynonie Harris a Cadillac [worth much less than the
> royalties Harris was really owed]. That kind of thing.[12]

Atlantic was run rather differently from the majors too, if an early
experience is anything to go by:

> They paid Bing Crosby, they paid Louis Armstrong, but they didn't pay
> Bumble Bee Slim, you follow what I'm saying? When we'd been in business a
> year or two, and we'd had some chart activity, two gentlemen came to see us
> from Columbia Records. They offered to take over our label and distribute it
> for us. I said, 'Really? What would you give us for that?' They said, 'Five per
> cent royalty.' I said, 'What about the artists?' He said, 'You're not giving niggers
> royalties, are you?' I said, 'Yes we are'. He said, 'Well, you're going to spoil the
> whole business for everybody.'[13]

The first glimmerings of the chart activity that Ertegun mentioned came
with the release of 'Drinking Wine Spo-Dee-O-Dee' by Stick McGhee.
McGhee had originally recorded the number for an outfit called Harlem
Records, but when this version sold out and Atlantic's New Orleans
distributor found itself with a strong demand for the disc, Atlantic stepped
in with a speedy cover version. The initial approach went to Brownie

McGhee, but when he explained that his brother – the original artist – was staying with him, the pair were brought into the studio. The instrumentation was beefed up from the sparse Harlem version and McGhee received a royalty in contrast to the flat fee he got for his earlier recording, which became significant when the record went on to sell beyond Ertegun's wildest expectations. Accounts vary. Stan Cornyn says 40,000. Justine Picardie and Dorothy Wade, in their book *Atlantic and the Godfathers of Rock and Roll*, say 400,000. Ahmet himself says 700,000. Whichever is closest to the true figure, it was more copies of one record than Atlantic had ever sold before.

Another early smash for the label was 'Chains of Love' by the great blues shouter Big Joe Turner, which lodged in the charts for the entire second half of 1951. The number was written for Turner by one 'A. Nugetre' (try reading it backwards), and, because of the singer's illiteracy, the composer had to stand next to him whispering the next line immediately before he sang it – perfectly. 'Nugetre' was unable to read music, so he took to singing his compositions in coin-operated record booths, the results of which were then transcribed by arrangers.

The Hotel Jefferson had to be vacated when the building was condemned, and the company moved to 301 West 54th Street, before decamping in 1952 to 234 West 56th Street, a wooden-framed brownstone occupied on the ground floor by Patsy's restaurant, a favourite haunt of Frank Sinatra, among others. These premises doubled as an office and a recording studio. At the end of the working day, all of the desks were piled up and microphones were laid out. The man responsible for the evening work was engineer and producer Tom Dowd. Another change occurred shortly afterwards, in 1953, when Abramson was drafted into the US Army and posted to Germany. To fill his shoes, in came Jerry Wexler, who, as a *Billboard* writer, had been responsible for renaming the 'race' charts as a 'rhythm and blues' listing. Whether through shrewdness, faith in the label or a combination of the two, Wexler insisted on becoming a partner. For $2,063.25, he became owner of 15 per cent of Atlantic (later raised to 30 per cent), paying $1,000 of it by turning his pickup truck over to the company as an asset. In return, Atlantic got good value. 'From that first morning I walked through the office door at 234 West 56th Street,' he said, 'Atlantic Records claimed my heart and soul'.[14]

The post-war growth of the new wave of independents gave the majors a run for their money, but one label launch of the era was in another category altogether. The entry of the Dutch electrical giant Philips into the record market had been expected and feared for some time. The company made record players, and, as Edward Lewis had rationalized twenty years earlier, it seemed silly for them not to make the consumables as well.

The suggestion that Philips should produce software as well as hardware came from a member of the board, Hendrik Hartong. To this end, the company that represented Decca in Holland was acquired and Philips entered the record business in September 1950. The small company had been renamed Philips Phonografische Industrie and the new enterprise set up offices and a factory at Baarn in the Netherlands. The reach of the new company was boosted further with the acquisition of Polydor's French operation from Siemens.

Britain followed: the first office was a room in Century House, Philips Electrical's head office on London's Shaftesbury Avenue, occupied by two ex-EMI men – Norman Newell and Len Smith – and their secretaries. From this base, Newell and Smith set about building a local repertoire very vigorously, offering the likes of Flanagan and Allen, Gracie Fields and Geraldo's Concert Orchestra.

The first English Philips releases came out in January 1953, billed as 'The Records of the Century'. The fourth disc on the label was a glorious curio, featuring the character actress Hermione Gingold with the gruff television personality Gilbert Harding ploughing their way through 'It Takes Two to Tango' and 'Oh Grandma'. Unfortunately, it was met with precious little enthusiasm. They 'strive hard to be funny,' wrote Oliver King (aka the great discographer Brian Rust) in the *Gramophone*, but 'Gilbert Harding sounds dreadfully embarrassed'.[15]

Another early signing was the comic actress June Whitfield, and when 'Gentlemen Prefer Blondes' hit British screens in late 1953, she was called in by Newell to record a version of the hit song 'Diamonds Are a Girl's Best Friend'. It was not, however, an exact cover. 'For some unknown reason, I approached it more like Ethel Merman than Marilyn Monroe,' Whitfield admitted gamely years later. 'A reviewer in the *Evening Standard* said, "This girl obviously does not know the difference between diamonds and glass."'[16]

A number of musical directors were involved in those early British Philips sides, including Geoff Love and Peter Yorke, but one name came to predominate over all others over the years. Already busy at the BBC with orchestrations for the Goon Show, Wally Stott (or Angela Morley, as she is now known) remembers that the call 'came out of the blue' from a session fixer:

> It was a man called Harry Benson, who called me one day and said, 'If you were to get the job of musical director for a new international recording company based in London, would you use me to book the musicians?' So of course I said yes. If I'd said no, I might never have heard anything about it again, but I said yes. Nothing happened for a week, then I was asked to do an arrangement of 'Ecstasy' for Geraldo's Concert Orchestra, to be recorded at Conway Hall, and I didn't realize that that was for Philips. That might have been my audition, or the thing that swayed the decision, but after that, I was asked to do sessions conducting on my own. I came in whenever they wanted to to a recording. I'd talk to Norman Newell and the artist and we'd fix keys and routine the numbers.[17]

Conway Hall was the venue for the larger Philips sessions, but smaller dates were done at IBC, a studio set up in the 1930s by Captain Leonard Plugge to serve his Radio Normandie station. 'I used to love working in Conway Hall with strings,' said Morley, 'because it has a beautiful acoustic, but I used to hate doing anything in IBC because it was absolutely dead as a doornail and in those days, they didn't know how to use echo.' In 1956, when the record company had moved to offices at Stanhope Place in Bayswater, a studio with an eight-channel mono desk was installed on-site, but this, from Morley's point of view, was no better than IBC:

> I always hated that studio. It was covered with acoustic tiles. There are two ways of looking at recording: there's the musician's way and the engineer's way. Musicians love to hear a natural resonance in the studio, which you get from wood panelling, a wood floor and a high ceiling. Engineers love it to be absolutely dead, so that there's no resonance at all, and then they replace the resonance with reverberation. That's OK for him, but for artists and particularly singers, when you sing and you can't hear anything come out, it just makes everybody demoralized.[18]

From the outside, it seemed as though Philips had it made in global terms. In most major territories worldwide, the company already had a distribution infrastructure and staff on the ground. Thus it would make sense for the new record operation to plug into that network. When Philips set up shop as a record company in Britain, it followed the model perfectly. It piggy-backed on the company's existing presence. It wasn't always as simple as it might have appeared, though. 'My task was to try and get the other Philips companies around the world interested in this business,' explains Coen Solleveld, who had joined Philips in 1942, and had spent the post-war years working for the company in Indonesia. 'Philips might have been luckier than most other companies to have these subsidiaries worldwide, but it was not so easy to convince them to enter a business that they didn't know the first thing about.'[19]

In many territories, Philips got around this by allying itself with an existing record distribution company. One such territory was South Africa, where Philips joined up with a small independent called Trutone. 'Philips decided they were coming to South Africa. In those days, big corporations were rather casual about it,' recalls David Fine, who had joined Trutone in 1951:

> We've got an office in Johannesburg, we've got accounting machines, we've got trucks, we're going into the record business. What they knew about the South African record business was zero. So I heard on the grapevine that Philips were coming and I went to see if we could get their manufacturing business for our factory, which eventually we did. Philips sent a man from Holland to interview me about what we knew about manufacturing, which wasn't very much. Then they invited me over to Holland to show me the latest techniques. This was about 1956–7. I was very impressed with what I saw, compared with how we did things. Whatever they did, they did well. There is no question – Philips records were well made, but it was an expensive process and we had to get up to their standard to get the licence, which fed through into our own output.[20]

While much of the rest of the world was pushing ahead with 33⅓ and 45, South Africa continued to rely on much more primitive technology:

> In those days, it was no good having a record for the black market that you didn't have a wind-up gramophone for. We used to measure it in the sale of gold and steel needles. That was our barometer. We sold millions of them, and you could graph it, as they declined... We were pioneers of introducing the transistorized, battery-operated record player. It wasn't state of the art, but it did its job and was fairly well accepted. It gave better reproduction certainly than the wind-up gramophone.[21]

Although South Africa was segregated socially and politically, there were no such restrictions when it came to trade. 'The government never impeded doing business with the blacks and black Africa,' Fine reveals. 'That was all encouraged. It was an economic entity and the country had to exist. That's not to say that a more liberated black population wouldn't have been a bigger buying market, that's for sure.'[22]

Once established in South Africa, Philips was able to entrench itself firmly by recording local repertoire. But shortly after it entered the record business, Philips gained an excellent source of international repertoire, even though Solleveld stresses that it was only ever seen as 'temporary'. This was the American Columbia catalogue.

The problems between American Columbia and its long-standing British affiliate had begun some time before the LP became an issue, although EMI's decision to hold off on introducing vinyl microgroove discs is unlikely to have helped relations. In October 1945, Edward Wallerstein had, on a visit to London, pronounced himself unhappy with the bias that he perceived in EMI's corporate command toward the HMV/RCA Victor axis. As an example, he cited one issue of the *Gramophone*, in which HMV had three advertisements, and Decca had two, but Columbia had only one. He also felt that Columbia's US classical catalogue was not getting a fair crack of the whip with EMI, which was understandable from the British company's side, as it already had much the same repertoire, recorded by Walter Legge and David Bicknell with Europe's finest orchestras. He wanted also to remove various trading restrictions embodied in the companies' 1932 agreement.

Relations were strained further in 1949 by the devaluation of sterling under the Labour chancellor of the exchequer Sir Stafford Cripps. This move, while undoubtedly necessary for the British economy, meant that Columbia was suddenly receiving 70 per cent less from EMI than it had been before. By this point, Wallerstein had stepped down from the presidency of Columbia, to become chairman and CEO. His successor in the presidency was Frank K. White, CBS treasurer since 1937, but merely an interim manager, and at the start of 1951, he was succeeded by James B. Conkling, previously the head of A&R at Capitol. Conkling was a worthy successor to Wallerstein. In George Avakian's view, Conkling was another visionary, the pair being:

by far the two best record company presidents of all time. Wallerstein strove for seventeen years to get a long-playing record on the market, and Conkling recognized that it was the most important record medium at a time when the trade publications and the industry in general was still concentrating on the three-minute single. William Paley hired Conkling to come in for five years and those five years [...] really set Columbia up for all time.[23]

Conkling had been born in 1915 in East Orange, New Jersey, not too far from the Edison plant. He had studied at Dartmouth College in New Haven, and played trumpet in various dance bands there. After graduation, he had married into show business; his wife Donna was one of the King Sisters, who were to become a big act in the 1940s. During the Second World War, he served in the Navy, but was discharged following a serious injury. Looking for work, he turned to his college friend Paul Weston, who was involved with Capitol Records, and began producing sessions for artists like bandleader Stan Kenton before progressing to the position of head of A&R.

At Capitol, he had been responsible for signing the guitar genius Les Paul, reputedly with a contract written on the back of an envelope. He also founded the company's two music publishing operations, Ardmore Music for ASCAP composers, and Blackwood Music for those affiliated to the rival BMI. While he was undoubtedly a shrewd operator, this co-existed with a gentle manner and a sense of fairness to those who worked with him. Stan Cornyn describes him as 'a Spencer Tracy type, a reassuring guy... with an attentive smile.'[24]

The arrival of Conkling had coincided with Columbia giving EMI the required two years' notice of the termination of its contract. Obviously disappointed, Sir Ernest Fisk pronounced himself hopeful that a new contract could be negotiated. For Columbia, though, the point of no return had been reached. In November 1951, Columbia signed with Philips in Europe, effective January 1953. Even though the decision had been taken and the contracts had been signed, EMI still harboured hopes of winning Columbia back. Brenchley Mittell, ever the loyal servant of the EMI board, tried to persuade Lieberson that the large sums that Philips had promised Columbia for the promotion of its records would ultimately burnish the Philips name rather than Columbia's, which EMI still owned. Columbia's response was, perhaps unsurprisingly, to offer to buy the world rights to the name, but when Fisk set a price of £2m, interest cooled.

The reasons for Columbia's move were outlined by Conkling in a letter to the EMI board. Quite simply, he believed it to be 'unfortunate' that in some parts of the world, Columbia records were handled by the same company that distributed the company's 'keenest competitor' – RCA. The set-up brought 'certain basic problems ... since we know that in this country it requires all of our energy and a singleness of purpose to maintain our competitive standing vis-à-vis RCA Victor ... It is therefore difficult for us to believe that such highly competitive activity could satisfactorily exist where one parent company, in effect, controlled the activities of both.'[25]

Conkling caused further consternation at EMI when he announced his intention to take Columbia into South America in its own right from 1 January 1953; it was currently distributed by the various Odeon companies there. A major problem with the move was that most of Columbia's existing capital in South America had been frozen, and could not be spent anywhere other than South America. As a way out of the impasse, Conkling suggested that the immoveable funds be used to buy one of Odeon's subsidiaries from EMI, but this met with firm resistance from Industrias Electricas y Musicales Odeon in Buenos Aires.

One of the questions posed by the end of American Columbia's association with EMI concerned what would happen to the classical material recorded by the English Columbia label and its European associates, now that it no longer had an outlet. The solution was for EMI to form its own US label, which it did in 1952.

There was no chance that the new EMI operation could use the Nipper trademark, as RCA had the rights for America and its other traditional territories. Instead, they looked back to the company's first trademark, Theodore Birnbaum's Recording Angel of 1898, and consequently the new American label was named Angel. The matter of who was going to run the show was solved when EMI bought Cetra-Soria, an American company affiliated to the Italian label Cetra. Under Dario Soria's guidance, the first Angel releases came out in September 1953.

One of the label's earliest issues was Walter Legge's recording of *Tosca*, made at La Scala in Milan with Maria Callas, Tito Gobbi, de Salata and di Stefano. Such was Legge's regard for the recording that he suggested Angel should not release a note of opera until it was ready. 'I beg you in your own interests to hold up the other Italian operas until *Tosca* is published. If we start with *Tosca* we shall probably sell the rest on the reputation we make with it.'[26] Another selling point for the new Angel discs was that they came factory-sealed, a state of affairs that led Legge to suggest jokingly the advertising line 'Every Angel a virgin'.

At Capitol, Conkling's job as head of A&R had been unusual in that it amounted to much more than just dealing with artists and repertoire, thus equipping him for the wider demands of the Columbia job. 'Conkling, as head of A&R in a company which had nothing but pop artists and repertoire, was effectively the executive vice-president of the company,' explains Avakian. As such, he had a major say in administrative matters but his ultimate goal had eluded him and the company's sales manager Hal Cook. At that time, independent distribution was the norm, with the distributors dividing up the various labels between them, but as Avakian observes:

> Jim and Hal got the idea that they needed company-owned distributors, with complete control over certain territories … By about 1958, Columbia had its own distributor in every part of the company except a part of Texas and Oklahoma. That's an extraordinary thing. That was possible not only because of the vision that Cook and Conkling had, but also the power of the product that we had developed in that time.[27]

The LP programme had, in a very short time, gone from strength to strength. The two-LP set of Benny Goodman's 1938 concert at Carnegie Hall sold well 'and continues to do so today', but Columbia's first huge long-playing success is perhaps less well remembered. Arthur Godfrey was a major name in mid-twentieth-century American entertainment. His Thursday night television variety show was a ratings topper, as were his daily radio programmes. In British terms, the closest thing to his style and appeal was Billy Cotton, with his *Band Show*. He scored, says Avakian, by featuring 'a cast of regulars who represented the demographic breakdown of his audience. A young girl singing for the teenage boys. A young boy – Julius LaRosa – singing for the teenage girls. Mama and Papa listened to Frank Parker and Marion Marlow and so on.'

In 1953, Godfrey's writers assembled a TV spectacular for this cast, with twelve songs, one representing each month of the year:

> The morning after that broadcast, my merchandising manager, Stan Caven, bolted into my office and said, 'Hey did you see the Godfrey show last night? We should make an album of what he did.' I hadn't seen the programme, but

after he'd described it, I picked up the phone and called Arthur. I said to him, 'That show you did last night is a natural for a record album, twelve songs and so forth. Can you book some time? I'll get the studio and all that.' Within two weeks we'd recorded it, and within two weeks we had it on the market, and it went off like a skyrocket.[28]

Part of the fuel for Godfrey's skyward progress came from a shrewd pricing stratagem. Columbia had got the idea that LP sales would explode if the retail price of the discs could be pushed below $4. Studies undertaken by the company's financial man Bill Wilkins showed that even the most optimistic costings could not get below the magic figure. Then, inspiration struck Conkling. 'Jim came through with the idea that broke the ice,' Avakian recalls:

He said, 'There's one variable we haven't thought of, and that's the copyright royalty. Ninety per cent of what you record is standard material, and it's all published by these old-time publishers. If we go to them and say, 'Look, give us a rate for 1 year of $1\frac{1}{2}$ cents, instead of 2 cents' (which was the standard in those days). 'We believe that we can lower the price and sell many more copies than ever before. You will make far more money than you are making now at 2 cents.' Plus, Bill Wilkins' studies had shown that if you could build the volume up to a certain point, the cost per LP would drop so much that you could get under $4. Cardboard and paper were so cheap that you could afford to manufacture say 10,000 packages/sleeves at a time and throw away 5,000 if you didn't sell them, or just put them in a corner and keep them there just in case. Also, we decided that after the first exposure we would only manufacture as many records as were necessary, based on the orders that came in.[29]

The publishers went for the reduced royalty and were rewarded handsomely when the sales went berserk. The other record companies, however, had not caught on to Columbia's ruse:

The funny part about it was that I would often go and have lunch at Lindy's, where all the showbiz people and record people would gather for lunch. I'd walk in and the other guys from other companies would start laughing at me and yelling, 'Hey, George, we know what you're doing. We know the numbers. How long can you keep on losing money? You've got to give up' because they were all still selling at four dollars-something. They didn't know about it. The publishers weren't telling them, because they wanted 2 cents from everybody else. So, the answer I always gave was a twist on an old joke – 'Oh well, we make it up on the volume.' But it was true. We did make it up on the volume and that's what made it possible. Eventually word got out and everybody else went down to $3.98, and the publishers, we had to give 2 cents to them eventually, but we could afford it because the volume of business had grown dramatically.[30]

As the head of both Columbia's popular albums department and its international division, George Avakian found himself working very closely with Philips, but he approached them with a little trepidation:

At first I thought 'How do we get them off the ground?', but they were eager and ready to go, unlike their British counterparts in EMI. We were a bit leery, since they had no pop records at all, and they had no classical music that was of any interest to anybody, except the greatest orchestra of all, which was the Concertgebouw. That was exactly why they were interested in us, but we quickly realized, 'Hey, this is not a handicap, this is a great thing. They need us desperately, and so they're going to bust their balls to make a huge success of the Columbia catalogue, especially on the pop side.' What sold me so completely was their pointing out something that I had never really thought about, and that is that we had two of the biggest movie stars in the world singing for us – Doris Day and Frank Sinatra – which meant that everybody in the world had seen them on the screen and heard them sing. So, even if they didn't buy records, they knew that they were singers and now we had a company that was going to go push, push, push, and that's exactly what happened. They were wonderful people, very receptive to ideas and quite imaginative, as well as being awfully nice. Philips had enthusiastic young people and they were eager to take risks. They were ready to set up concerts for artists and things like that.[31]

Although Avakian's work covered everything from Arthur Godfrey to Edith Piaf, it is for his jazz productions that he is best known to record buyers: 'Jazz has represented perhaps 15 per cent of my work, but because I wrote signed annotations of such albums at a time when producers were not credited, I acquired the much narrower reputation.' Of all the jazz artists produced by Avakian, pianist Erroll Garner – a great improviser – was probably the most prolific. Each session with Garner resulted in a vast number of highly usable masters. 'Oh, he was beyond belief,' Avakian recollects fondly. 'Talk about consistency! I wrote on the back of one of his later albums that he made sixty-eight takes in a row, and only one of them was a repeat. The extra take was about a chorus and a half where he stopped himself and said, "Keep it going, I'm going to start again".'

Other recordings required more work. Avakian re-signed Duke Ellington to Columbia in 1956, after a few years with various other labels, including Capitol. With orchestras like his in the doldrums commercially speaking, he needed to come back to Columbia with a bang. Avakian suggested that Duke should record a live LP at the Newport Jazz Festival and that he should write a suite for the occasion to maximize press interest. 'Duke got it ready, but the band had not rehearsed it conscientiously. As the musicians were about to go onstage, Duke told them, "I know we're all worried about the new suite, but let's do our best, and then cut loose with one of our old ones."'[32]

The 'old one' turned out to be an explosive performance of 'Diminuendo in Blue' and 'Crescendo in Blue', featuring Paul Gonsalves, although Gonsalves got confused and blew into the microphone set up by the Voice of America, who were recording the concert for a broadcast, instead of the designated Columbia Records microphone alongside it. The suite went down wonderfully at the show, but an obviously worried Ellington came off the stage and his first words to Avakian were, 'How did it go?' Avakian replied: 'We've got a great performance in "Diminuendo" but we have a sound problem.' Avakian recalls: 'He said, "Yeah, I saw it. Gonsalves wouldn't get up to the right microphone." I said, "Duke, I thought the suite came off very well, and don't worry about those cracked notes by Hodges and Cat Anderson, because we can fix that in the studio easily. So, I think we're home free." His words to me were, "George, you've heard it once. I know that work. There's a lot of work to be done." I said, "Well, we'll get it fixed."'

Fortunately, the day before, Ellington had arranged a contingency plan:

He had called me at Newport and said, 'George, this long work isn't really ready, but it has got to succeed. I can't have it played badly, and I can't have it be cancelled. Can we get into the studio on Monday? Book the entire day, and in the morning, I'll come to the studio with [Billy] Strayhorn [Ellington's long-time musical collaborator] and the score, we'll listen to the tape and decide what has to be done. The musicians can stand by at the hotel and then come in at 1 o'clock.' That's exactly what we did. He came in about 10.30 with Strayhorn, reviewed everything and decided that with the suite, they'd just do the whole thing over and decide afterwards what they were going to put in.[33]

The results were edited together according to Ellington and Strayhorn's instructions, and the unrepeatable Gonsalves performance was re-equalized painstakingly in short segments, in order to bring his tone out as much as possible. Acetates were then sent to Ellington. 'After a very, very nervous twenty-four hours or so, Duke called and said, "George, I have two things to tell you about that. One of them is that it's perfect. Don't change a thing. The second is thank you."' For the rest of his life, Ellington would announce that he was 'born in 1956 at the Newport Jazz Festival'.[34]

Then there was Miles Davis. Miles had been with Bob Weinstock's specialist Prestige label but the trumpeter, well aware of the better resources and distribution at Columbia, had been pursuing Avakian for years. With Prestige, Miles was a jazz star. With Columbia, he became a star, period. Avakian decided to put Miles with larger groups after his involvement with Gunther Schuller's *Music for Brass* recording:

> That gave me the idea that what I had to do with Miles was expand the nine-piece [*Birth of the Cool*] orchestra to maybe fourteen or fifteen. I proposed this to Miles and said, 'There are only two people who can do this properly. One is Gunther, of course, the other is Gil Evans', who had been the force behind the original nonet. I said, 'Take your choice', and I knew he'd say Gil.
>
> The plan developed rather quickly into the nineteen-piece orchestra, which we all know about. The only instruction I gave them was 'Give me one composition which I can call *Miles Ahead*, because that's going to be the name of the album.' That's exactly what happened, and that was how we were able to shift Miles away from just the small market for the quintet, into something which, to my great surprise, became extremely commercial, sold a million copies and made him a big name in Europe.[35]

Jim Conkling's initial contract with Bill Paley had been for five years. It came to an end in 1956, and, satisfied that he had got the company into good shape, he wanted to retire. He had done well from his share options, so he was able to do just that. His successor as president of the record company was Goddard Lieberson, previously executive vice-president. Although he appeared to be every inch the urbane New Yorker, Lieberson was, in fact, an Englishman by birth, having emerged in the Staffordshire town of Hanley in 1911. He had joined Columbia in September 1939 as assistant to the head of the Masterworks division, and he soon stepped up to head the department himself.

Lieberson was undoubtedly talented, but George Avakian argues that he would not have been able to shine as much as he did without the solid foundations put in by his predecessors:

> Goddard coasted on their groundwork, and he broadened the concept of a catalogue that had every possible kind of recording for every possible customer. Although he did not produce the first original-cast show album – that was Decca, with *Oklahoma!* – he established Broadway musicals as a solid record category. We got along splendidly because his forte was knowing when to leave the best people in the company alone.[36]

Others fell under his spell totally. 'He really was a magical kind of person,' remembers Bruce Lundvall, who began his distinguished record business career in Columbia's marketing department in July 1960:

> One of my early jobs was as a product manager for Broadway shows and Goddard of course was the dean of that. I would come in on Sunday morning and watch Goddard produce all of these great Broadway show albums. First of all, he was a musician, so he understood exactly ... he was really very hands on. But he also had this wonderful sense of humour, this wonderful personality and charisma. He was on a first-name basis with all of these Broadway stars.
>
> We would just sit there on Sunday, all day long. The show would open a week before and on Sunday they'd make the record, because that was the only day they were off. Goddard would pull this whole thing together, probably going on long into the night. He would always work with an engineer called Fred Plaut, who was a wonderful guy who was also a great photographer. I usually left about five or six and it was still going on. He would do all the choral numbers together, then all the individual standout performers separately, and it was all very well organized. He was able to charm these people in such a way that he always got great performances from them. He was always on the floor. I don't remember him in the control room so much.

It was really Camelot for me. Goddard was the president, and in every area of the company they had really gifted people. Mitch Miller was the head of A&R and there were people like Irving Townsend, Teo Macero and John Hammond on the A&R staff. It was really quite magical. Mitch was in charge of pop, but then he made this big transition to 'Sing Along with Mitch'. So he was producing records, but mainly he was a recording artist and television star.[37]

George Avakian also worked with Fred Plaut, remembering him for technical skills both in the studio and with a camera (the cover shot on Michel Legrand's *I Love Paris* LP is one of his), as well as for his more idiosyncratic behaviour:

Fred was one of the great engineers. He knew his equipment, and he had great taste. He was classically oriented, but I used him on a lot of pop sessions. I was doing a Johnny Mathis session and I wanted more volume on a climactic bit of the brass, in between the vocal sections. Fred said, 'I can't give it to you. It'll distort.' I said, 'Come on, Fred, I need it.' He did, and when I listened to it later on, it was slightly distorted, so Fred was right. Fred was Alsatian, he had an unusual accent, and he was very fluent in French and German of course. We had great fun fooling around with the German language. Fred spattered his conversation with things like *scheisskopf* and so on. It was always fun working with him.[38]

And there was the added bonus of a first-rate studio:

That was 205 East 30th Street, which was an old Armenian church, which became a Greek church and then was bought by CBS to replace that terrific Liederkranz studio, over on East 58th Street, which was turned, unfortunately, into two TV studios. Luckily, Vin Liebler, the head of the engineering department, was scouting all the time finding a place and he came up with this church, which turned out to be in some ways I think even superior to Liederkranz. And then that went down because the owner of the building – we weren't able to buy it – the owner of the building got an offer to tear down the whole building and put up a big apartment complex, which, of course, was far more profitable. We organized a committee to save it and get it landmarked. It didn't work.[39]

The post-war era found RCA in something of a lull, at least on the pop front. Swing bands, a staple of the RCA roster before and during the war, were not selling as well as they had. Meanwhile, in other areas, RCA had to settle for second-rate artists. 'Publicizing the pop side depends on the artists on the roster,' argues Alan Kayes, who began his RCA career in 1945 as publicity manager for the record division, before rising to become commercial manager of the classical operations and then, in 1950, the head of Red Seal A&R. 'If you don't have the top artists, it doesn't figure. We had Perry Como and Eddy Arnold, who were both popular, but as far as female singers were concerned, none of those that we had were of the calibre of Dinah Shore.'[40]

RCA and Columbia had maintained their entrenched positions with regard to each other's microgroove formats for some time. Eventually, however, it became obvious that both systems had their uses – LPs for extended works and collections, the 45 as a replacement for the 78 rpm single – and that each company would have to drop their objections and begin making both formats. 'I remember on one occasion that Bill Paley came into the office and David Sarnoff demonstrated the 45 rpm system to him,' Kayes remembers. 'Subsequent to that, we went into LP and Columbia went into 45s. The history of the record business had always been that the instrument dictates the methodology.'[41] RCA's entry into the LP market was, however, undertaken on distinctly its own terms. The engineers at Camden had made improvements to the format, such that Columbia's head of production Jim Hunter realized that it might be necessary to re-cut some of the earlier Columbia LP issues.

Hunter had been with RCA before he joined Columbia, and Alan Kayes suggests that there was a certain amount of to-ing and fro-ing between the companies as far as staffing went. However, one of the key RCA appointments of the post-war era actually came from outside the record industry, in 1949. George Marek had been an advertising executive, as well as writing about music, mainly for *Good Housekeeping* magazine. In doing so, he had acquired considerable influence, and when he formulated a plan for RCA's record division, Sarnoff took it very seriously indeed. 'He presented his plan, Sarnoff was impressed and so he invited him into RCA as director of Red Seal,' recalls Adele Siegal, who became Marek's secretary.[42]

Whereas O'Connell had been the epitome of charm and a musician to boot, Marek was 'quite authoritarian,' says Alan Kayes, a quality that some found hard to accept, including Kayes himself. 'I had known George over the years, but I found him difficult to work with. It was a clash of personalities. I always thought of myself as a team player. George was not, he was very much a solo figure.'

Solo or otherwise, Marek dominated RCA from 1949 well into the 1970s.

9 Pop goes the weasel

The loss of the American Columbia repertoire had been a considerable blow to EMI. In the 1950s, and particularly in the first half of the decade, the British pop scene was dominated by American acts. Some of the biggest were Frank Sinatra, the 'Nabob of Sob' Johnnie Ray and Guy Mitchell. Columbia had them all under contract. Even the producer responsible for many of their hits, Mitch Miller, was becoming a recording star in his own right with his sing-along LPs. Something had to be done to make up the shortfall created by the US label's defection to Philips.

The first step that EMI took was to beef up its pop A&R staff complement. Into Columbia came Ray Martin and Norrie Paramor, with Walter J. Ridley joining HMV at around the same time. Meanwhile, Oscar Preuss – the head of EMI's smallest label, Parlophone – was heading towards retirement and so set about appointing an assistant who, it was expected, would succeed him when he left. In 1950, he employed a young man fresh out of the Fleet Air Arm called George Martin. All four men were experienced musicians. George Martin had played piano for dance bands and as a classical soloist, Ray Martin was a bandleader, Paramor had been the pianist in Harry Gold's Pieces of Eight, and Ridley had worked in music publishing, where his skills as an accompanist were often put to use. The fact that they 'had not been directly connected with the record business, but understood it'[1] gave them a fresh perspective on everything, but more important was the fact that if something needed re-scoring on the spot at a session, each of them could handle it. In 1954, the management of the record division moved from Hayes to offices at 8–11 Great Castle Street, over a dress shop and the A&R men divided their time between the new premises and Abbey Road studios. However, while the office move marked the beginning of a consolidation for EMI's record interests, there were two separate entrances. One for the HMV, which was still sold through a network of approved dealers, the other for the 'factored marks', such as Columbia and Parlophone, which were sold by conventional wholesale methods.

As far as the American problem went, there was nothing to stop Paramor, Ridley or Martin from copying the chart from a US pressing, drafting in a singer and recording a cover version, and quite often they did. However, when the original had been made by one of EMI's American affiliates, this usually led to ructions. For example, one of UK Columbia's biggest selling artists in the mid-1950s was Eddie Calvert, 'The Man with the Golden Trumpet', who had four weeks at number one in 1955 with 'Cherry Pink and Apple Blossom White'. All very well, only the top spot had been vacated two weeks before by Perez Prado's original, recorded for RCA and so released on HMV. This was one of the reasons why Conkling had terminated the Columbia contract – how could he be sure that EMI would put all of its efforts behind selling his recordings if similar offerings came from RCA or from EMI's own producers?

The Calvert example was unusual, as it was the original US recording that sold best. So it became obvious that EMI had to find another American label to represent and, if possible, buy outright, to avoid the risk of losing the catalogue in the future. That label turned out to be Capitol. From a faltering start in 1942 just as the first AFM recording ban was getting under way, the Hollywood-based Capitol had become a force to be reckoned with. Stars like co-founder Johnny Mercer, Nat 'King' Cole, Les Paul, Jo Stafford (the wife of Paul Weston), Peggy Lee and Kay Starr had helped build Capitol up considerably. The simple ruse of typing personalized labels for DJ copies of records also helped, by appealing to the disc jockeys' vanity and gaining the fledgling operation more airplay than it had any right to expect. The company's sales in 1942 had been $192,000. In 1948, they were $18m. Capitol had turned the so-called 'Big Three' – RCA, Columbia, Decca – into a big four. In 1949, Capitol became the first label anywhere to offer discs at all three speeds – LPs at 33 $\frac{1}{3}$ rpm, and singles on both 45 rpm and 78 rpm.

Having come this far in just twelve years and with plans for a striking new headquarters building in Hollywood approved – the now-famous Capitol Tower – it was no wonder that EMI should have looked to Capitol as the answer to its transatlantic troubles. The move was aided by the fact that EMI had finally started to climb out of its stretch of managerial moribundity, which had begun in 1939 with the exit of Sir Louis Sterling. The turning point was the appointment in 1954 of Joseph Lockwood to the board, an engineer by trade who had spent most of his career in milling. He joined initially as vice-chairman and then, shortly afterwards, rose to succeed Sir Alexander Aikman – a City gent who had replaced the apoplectic Alfred Clark in 1946 – as chairman.

At the same time as he stepped up to the chair, he also took on the role of chief executive officer of EMI and set about whittling down the confusing structure set up by Fisk. He also curtailed the activities of various unprofitable divisions, which included the manufacture of radios, televisions and record players. 'His ruthless reconstruction of the business in the 1950s undoubtedly saved EMI from bankruptcy,' argues EMI's official historian Dr Peter Martland.

Although Lockwood brought sound business sensibilities to the company, he was a success on two other levels. He was just fifty at the time of his appointment; his predecessor was already sixty when he took the job in 1946. He also took an interest in EMI's creative talent, a marked contrast to Sterling's replacement, Sir Robert McLean, who had, Sterling suggested, treated staff as though they were building the colonial railways that he had overseen before joining EMI. Thus revitalized by new blood, on 13 January 1955, it was announced that EMI had bought a controlling interest in Capitol for $8.5m. At the time, there was a rumour that the disgruntled Decca had ordered all of the Capitol metal matrices to be loaded into vans and dumped on the doorstep at Hayes, the rough treatment rendering them useless, and forcing EMI to remake them at great expense. Happily, this seems to have been an apocryphal tale. 'Sir Edward Lewis's attitude was exemplary. He understood the position and made no difficulties about terminating the licensing deal, which he could have held us to,' recalled EMI executive L. G. Wood in a 1984 interview.[2]

There was two casualties of the sale of Capitol to EMI. One was a mooted pressing plant in Germany, the other the European classical division. At the same time, the management of EMI had feared that they might also lose the RCA Victor contract, thus bringing to an end the alliance that had brought the gramophone to the British Isles in 1898. The contract was due for renewal, and while Brenchley Mittell had succeeded in his negotiations in 1952, all parties concerned knew that the next renewal round would be a tricky and potentially painful business.

The EMI board realized that the Capitol purchase might upset RCA, but decided to press on anyway. The logic seemed to be that RCA would move away some time, and that with Capitol on board, EMI was far better equipped to cope with the loss. In addition, plans were laid to extend the domestic recording programme. David Bicknell, head of the artists' department, estimated that, in 1954, around half of EMI's output had been sourced from RCA. Consequently, he argued for a 50 per cent increase in recording to anticipate the effects of the loss of Victor. At such a rate, he reckoned, the shortfall could be made good in two years. The plan was agreed, although, at the same time, the decision was taken to retain both the HMV and Columbia identities.

Walter Legge was none too enthusiastic about the idea of becoming divorced from RCA. He pointed out that the company that gained the RCA contract for Europe 'would have a collection of great names of considerable propaganda value'. Bicknell's belief that an increase in recording would make up for the loss had, Legge argued, skated over one important variable: the name recognition of the artists involved. '[W]e left out of our calculations the fact that the people who want records by Toscanini, Rubinstein, Horowitz, Heifetz etc. will buy them from whichever company sells them.'[3] On the other hand, Glenn Wallichs was all for the divorce, being keen to have all of the EMI catalogues under his wing in America.

Negotiations for the new contract, effective from 1957, began in October 1955. A group of RCA executives – Manie Sachs, Alan Kayes, Al Watters, Pat Kennedy, Howard Letts and Ed Stanley – came to the UK and set up camp at Claridges. While in town, they would be visiting both EMI at Hayes and the various Decca premises.

Watters was prepared to discuss a further five-year deal with EMI, but on the proviso that RCA could send a team of its own merchandising and marketing people to work with EMI's own teams. In November, the talks moved to the more exotic climes of Bermuda. Despite the surroundings, the discussions did not go well. RCA wanted access to all of the HMV repertoire, while EMI wanted to offer RCA only a part of it. RCA wanted its own label in the UK, but was unwilling to offer a reciprocal arrangement in the US. To cap things off, one member of the EMI team noted that none of the RCA negotiators had the slightest knowledge about the origin of the Nipper trademark or the relations that had existed between the two companies.

Relations worsened further over RCA's plans to record *La Bohème* with Sir Thomas Beecham conducting and the soprano Victoria de los Angeles – both of them contracted EMI artistes. In years gone by, this would have been acceptable, as the recording would have been available to HMV through its agreement with RCA. However, the prospect of granting RCA the use of de los Angeles for a recording that might soon be a rival's property in the UK was not acceptable. RCA merely presented the plan as a fait accompli, which prompted howls of pain at EMI head office.

To be fair, EMI had been responsible for a similar manoeuvre in 1954, when it transferred its planned recording of *Norma* with Maria Callas from HMV to Columbia in the UK and Angel in the US. RCA would have had access to an HMV recording, but if it were issued on Angel, it would be a direct competitor, and the American company regarded this as 'a violation of the spirit of the agreement' between the two. EMI defended its decision by indicating that the piece came under a contract with La Scala in Milan and that RCA had been unwilling to contribute to the heavier royalties and costs incurred in recording there, plans to record *Madam Butterfly* having been scuppered by RCA on cost grounds. Added to this, George Marek had been less than positive in his praise of Callas following a visit to La Scala in June 1953, suggesting that she lacked 'top'.

Talks broke down after the Bermuda round, and in January 1956, EMI asked RCA if there was any chance of them restarting in the near future. Indirectly, in March 1956, came the answer. As of May 1957, RCA Victor would no longer be represented in the UK and the Commonwealth by the Gramophone Company. In April 1956, RCA Photophone Ltd, the company responsible for marketing RCA's film sound system, became RCA Great Britain Ltd, in preparation for taking on the group's record business as well. The pressing and distribution were to be handled by EMI's only major rival, Decca. Leonard Brown cabled Edward Lewis, who was in New York, with the terse message: 'Congratulations to you'.[4] The *Daily Express* reported the new alliance with the evocative headline: 'DECCA GRABS EARTHA KITT'.

Some have suggested that the worsening relationship between the two companies had made a renewal impossible. However, there is a wealth of evidence to suggest otherwise. EMI managing director Leonard Brown had been reassured in 1954 by RCA vice-president Meade Brunet that the Capitol acquisition would make no difference to relations between the two companies. Furthermore, it is apparent from all records of the discussions that RCA were perfectly happy to renew, but on their own terms, which EMI found unacceptable. Alan Kayes suggests that there was another factor in the decision to switch representation:

> I had a very good relationship with my opposite numbers at HMV. I got on very well with David Bicknell in particular, he was a splendid fellow. I suspect that our relationship with HMV could have lasted longer were it not for the

legal considerations. One of our corporate attorneys had suggested that we should seek alternative representation, because of the anti-trust laws.[5]

In any divorce, the division of the record collection is said to be one of the hardest parts. The rows about who owned what were greatly magnified in the HMV and RCA break-up. David Bicknell argued in favour of keeping all pre-1949 RCA matrices, as RCA had seemingly reissued all that it could from this era, whereas EMI had not begun to market much of this vintage material. He believed that there was still a good market for the likes of Caruso, Kreisler and Paderewski. RCA's lawyer John Hill put paid to this idea, though, ordering all pre-1949 matrices to be destroyed. Hill was the sole objector, as RCA's sales department were so preoccupied with new product that they did not wish for Decca to reissue any vintage material for quite some time.

The sole exception to Hill's order was the agreed retention of fifty Victor 78 rpm sides – including some by John McCormack and Alma Gluck – for a further five years, in exchange for fifty HMV sides – comprising five Beethoven concertos and the Eroica Variations played by pianist Artur Schnabel with the London Symphony Orchestra – that were being used on anthologies. Surreptitiously, EMI also decided to retain some matrices in anticipation of their copyright lapsing at the end of the statutory fifty-year period. As a result, the EMI archives were known to contain RCA matrices as late as 1968.

Decca had the great good fortune to gain the RCA catalogue at a time when its pop division was undergoing a renaissance, all thanks to the efforts of one man – a former trucker from Memphis called Elvis Presley. Sam Phillips had set up his Memphis Recording Services at 706 Union Avenue, Memphis, in January 1950, having come from a career in radio. In 1952, having licensed a couple of masters to labels such as Chess, he decided to launch his own label, which he called Sun. When Elvis Presley walked in one Saturday in the summer of 1953, he was just another customer wanting to make a private recording on an acetate disc, a service that Phillips offered for $3.98 plus tax.[6] Phillips's operation of his own label was a draw for the young man, though. While he waited for his turn in the studio, he asked Phillips's business partner Marion Keisker if she knew of anyone who needed a singer. She asked who he sounded like. He replied, 'I don't sound like nobody.' That much became apparent when he ran through a pair of old hits – 'My Happiness' and 'That's When Your Heartaches Begin'. Here was a white boy who sounded black. Phillips thought he was 'interesting' and asked Keisker to keep his details on file, which she did with the note: 'Good ballad singer. Hold.'

Despite Presley persisting with his visits to 706 Union Avenue, Phillips was unable to find any use for him until May 1954, when he returned from recording the Prisonaires in Nashville with a song that he thought would suit the young singer. As it transpired, the song did not work out, despite a few attempts, but Phillips decided to enlist guitarist Scotty Moore and bassist Bill Black from the Starlite Wranglers and see what Presley could do. At the first session, abortive attempts were made at recording an old Bing Crosby hit, 'Harbor Lights', and then 'I Love You Because', but none came up to scratch. Thoughts turned to packing up, going home and trying again the following evening, but at the last minute, Presley suggested trying 'That's All Right', a blues number written and originally recorded by Arthur 'Big Boy' Crudup. Phillips knew it well and decided it was worth a try. They had a go. This was it.

That session took place on Monday 5 July 1954. The three were recording again on the following two nights, but on Wednesday, Phillips decided to finish early, so he could visit influential local DJ Dewey Phillips of WHBQ. Dewey Phillips reacted immediately by asking for two acetates, which Sam Phillips delivered the following day. That night on his show, Dewey Phillips placed one copy on each of his turntables and played the number continuously for an hour. At the end of it, an avalanche of telephone calls and telegrams had come in. Phillips had a ready-made market for the disc, but there was a small problem. None of the other sessions had come up with a suitable B-side. So Presley, Moore and Black returned to 706 and laid down a hyped-up version of Bill Monroe's bluegrass hit 'Blue Moon of Kentucky'. The result was issued on Sun and it took off in the label's territories.

By mid-1955, Presley was a major celebrity in and around Tennessee, and a name on the country and western scene, having appeared on the Louisiana Hayride and Grand Ole Opry radio shows. However, a former pet cemetery owner of German extraction called 'Colonel' Tom Parker was, by this time, in the process of insinuating himself into the position of Presley's manager, and he indicated that the singer had gone as far as he could with Sun. Oddly enough, the idea of a contract buy-out also appealed to Sam Phillips. Contrary to popular perception, a small record company's problems are not over the moment the hits start happening. Quite often, they get far, far worse. Distributors – who were more concerned with large labels that could guarantee a regular throughput of material – would refuse to pay small labels on time and the result was that the independents would have to wait for a long time before they saw a financial return on their hits. During this time, they still had to find the money to record and some labels succumbed to their cash flow problems, despite being profitable on paper. So it was not too surprising that Phillips was finding the cost of keeping up with the demand for Presley's records almost too much. Unfortunately, this did not cut any ice with some of Phillips's backers, including his own brother Jud. All they saw was that Presley discs were selling fast and they wanted their pound of flesh. If the price was right, the sale of Presley's contract would enable Phillips to pay off the backers and invest in his remaining artists, who included Carl Perkins – just about to have a massive hit with 'Blue Suede Shoes' – and Johnny Cash.

Word got out that Presley's recording contract might be on the market and, before long, the likes of Capitol, Mercury, Chess, Dot and Atlantic had shown their hand. Parker, however, as the manager of RCA artists Hank Snow and Eddy Arnold, was keen on placing his new protégé with the label that he knew best. Luckily, RCA's country and western promotion manager had heard Presley and was trying to persuade RCA's head of speciality singles, Steve Sholes – the V-Disc veteran – to give Elvis a try.

The price set by Phillips was $35,000 with an additional commitment to take on the $5,000 of back royalties that he owed Presley.[7] RCA felt unable to meet this figure, with William W. Bullock, the head of the singles division, offering only $25,000. Phillips gave Parker a deadline of 15 November, after which the offer to sell would be withdrawn. Bullock held out until the last possible moment and then, presumably fearful that the price could only get higher, agreed to all of Phillips's conditions. According to Jerry Wexler, Atlantic had been willing to go up to $30,000, but he was slightly 'relieved that the final price was over our heads. If Elvis had accepted our offer, we would have struggled to come up with the thirty grand.' Like everyone else, Wexler could have had no idea about what was going to happen with Presley. He had no 'inkling that he'd emerge as the Jesus of rock. I simply dug his voice.'[8]

The deal, underpinned by a publishing contract from Gene Aberbach of Hill and Range, was signed at 706 Union Avenue on 21 November 1955. The contract included the transfer of all Presley's Sun masters to his new label, and gave the singer a royalty of 5 cents a record, 2 cents more than he was getting from Sun. His first RCA session followed on 10 January 1956 in the company's Nashville studio, situated in the same building as the Methodist TV, Radio and Film Commission. There Sholes had assembled Presley's Sun band, augmented with drummer D. J. Fontana, pianist Floyd Cramer and on second guitar, Scotty Moore's hero Chet Atkins. The lead title that day was 'Heartbreak Hotel', written by Mae Boren Axton, an associate of the 'Colonel'. When all was wrapped up, Sholes found that his bosses did not like Axton's downbeat song and ordered a fresh session with new material. Sholes's response was that, while a further session was arranged for the near future in New York, the company needed to have a new Presley record on the market quickly, and so 'Heartbreak Hotel' should be released immediately.

RCA's pessimism was unjustified. Backed by RCA's national promotional clout, which came out in full force to justify the outlay on Presley's contract, it was a hit. The New York sessions, which, with the Nashville tapes, resulted in Presley's first LP, included his own recording of Carl Perkins's 'Blue Suede Shoes'.

In the UK, the job of releasing Presley's RCA debut fell to HMV. Sholes had sent the results of the session to Wally Ridley 'with a note saying that I probably wouldn't understand a word and wouldn't know what on earth the records were all about but that I should release them as the singer was going to be an absolute giant.' Sholes was partly right. 'We got the worst press we had ever got for an HMV release … it was a disgusting record – and we got no broadcasts on [Radio Luxembourg]. Then nine months later the whole Presley thing suddenly broke over here.'[9] By which time, of course, HMV no longer had RCA.

Phillips's decision to sell out Presley's contract for $35,000 has been retrospectively painted as the proverbial mess of potage, but the fact is that it was a very good deal for a relatively untried singer at the time. Added to this, he invested the money shrewdly, first in Sun and then in a fledgling hotel chain called Holiday Inn.

Capitol had not been Decca's only source of US repertoire in the first half of the 1950s. American Decca remained a contributor of masters, which came out either on the Brunswick or the Vogue-Coral label (Vogue being a French label that Decca had ties with and Coral being a subsidiary imprint for the American company). This was the route by which, later in the decade, the company got access to Bill Haley and the Comets and Buddy Holly. The loss of Capitol, though, left a large dent in Decca's revenue and remedial measures were needed to make up the lost income. So Decca turned to the great many independent labels that were springing up in America and, taking the name of its US subsidiary, introduced a new label, London American. 'It was because of losing Capitol that Lewis gave the green light to London to pick up all the masters,' recalls Hugh Mendl. 'For several years, that was the backbone of our business. I don't think it would have happened if he hadn't needed something to make up for the hole left by Capitol.'[10]

At the UK end of London American, releases were overseen by Geoff Milne, but a large proportion of the label's impetus came from America, where it came under the auspices of the head of foreign distribution and publishing Mimi Trepel. 'Our job was to get the material,' explains Diana Weller, her assistant from 1958 onwards. 'It involved contacting smaller American record labels that had no distribution overseas, and then shipping their records to Decca House. If they liked them, we would then make the deal, either for an individual master or for a label's catalogue. It was also our responsibility to let the foreign affiliates know what was being released and to supply them with artwork and publicity material.'[11]

Trepel and Weller found some impressive material for Milne to work with. London American was, for some years, the UK outlet for Atlantic, as well as labels like Dot, Imperial, Monument, Hi and, indeed, Sun. The relationship went even further with labels like Monument in Nashville and Hi in Memphis, in both of which Decca invested. Although by the mid-1950s it was best known for the boy-next-door crooner Pat Boone and his sanitized versions of rock and roll numbers, Dot had been in business since 1951, having grown out of Randy Wood's record shop in Gallatin, Tennessee. Then there was Cadence, founded in 1953 by Arthur Godfrey's musical director Archie Bleyer primarily as a vehicle for Godfrey's young male singer Julius LaRosa, who had been let down by Columbia. In the later 1950s, Bleyer and Cadence had struck gold with a pair of harmonizing brothers called Don and Phil Everly.

Another label picked up by London was Specialty, which had been founded in 1946 by Art Rupe. Picking up on the fact that US Decca was the only major serving the R&B market, Rupe set about plugging the gaps with boogie-woogie artist Joe 'the Honey Dripper' Liggins, Percy Mayfield, Guitar Slim, Sam Cooke and Lloyd Price, although Specialty really took off when Little Richard joined. Rupe had initially rejected his demo tape, but after eighteen months of badgering, he and his production associate

Richard 'Bumps' Blackwell gave in. The result of his test session in New Orleans was good enough to release as a single, and 'Tutti Frutti' gave Little Richard his first hit as well as giving the world a new word – 'Awopbopaloopbopawopbamboom'. More smashes followed – 'Long Tall Sally', 'Ready Teddy' and 'Rip It Up' among them – before Little Richard got some of that old-time religion and renounced pop in 1959.

With catalogues like these to draw upon, London American, from being born out of dire financial necessity, had become a pretty hip label. In return, the American company was doing a reasonable trade in British Decca masters by the likes of Mantovani. The two operations were run very differently, though. To all intents and purposes, Lewis *was* Decca and his influence pervaded much of the company's activity. In New York, London was run very much independently by a combination of American executives and British ex-pats. One of the key figures at this stage was Leon 'Lee' Hartstone, an American, supported by Dudley Toller-Bond, an Englishman who had been involved in the radar programme.

The difference between the two companies was clearly marked by changes in Lewis's personality. 'In London, he exuded formality,' says Diana Weller. 'He even had his own private elevator. When he came to the US, however, he was different. At that time he was not yet Sir, and our office was structurally very different. It was just two floors, nothing fancy at all. We didn't have an elevator, so he had to walk up the steps.'[12] Hugh Mendl concurs. 'Lewis always referred to everybody by their surname. I was always Mendl. But when I saw Lewis in New York, I was always Hugh. In New York, he'd take me out to lunch, we would get drunk together and he'd sing Bing Crosby songs. He was two different people.'[13]

Decca had also had some considerable success during the 1950s with its domestic pop recordings. Before the decade was very old, though, the company had to cope with the loss of artists' department head Harry Sarton, who dropped dead of a heart attack on 1 April 1951. Hugh Mendl had returned to Decca after the war as a plugger, promoting the company's records to radio stations:

> Lewis said, 'In America, you know, they have people who persuade the radio stations to play their records.' They weren't known as pluggers then. He said, 'I'd like you to do the same. And, of course, the factory is having difficulties. We can't get the shellac yet.' They were terribly short of stock. 'I want you to look after the BBC record library and see that they always have supplies of our

records, because they pay for them. I would like you to start persuading some of these people to play them.'

That was a job I did with varying success for a few years. I was sent for by the British Phonographic Industry [trade body] and reprimanded for trying to persuade the BBC to play records. I seemed to have forgotten that we didn't want them to play records. 'We can't stop them buying records, but we aren't very interested, because if people can hear them on the wireless, they won't buy them, will they?' This was the British Phonographic Industry. I went to see Lewis and said, 'I've been told to stop.' He said, 'Who told you that?' I said, 'Gray', who was the export manager of Decca and was head of the BPI at the time. Lewis said, 'Well I should have thought you would have realized that Gray's a fool. He's always been a fool. I don't know why I keep him. Don't pay any attention to what he says – idiot!' So I didn't.[14]

After Sarton's death, though, Mendl found himself producing records. The bandleader Jack Jackson had tipped Decca off about a pianist called Winifred Atwell, and so Sarton's assistant had rushed up the road to catch her act at the Brixton Empress. The assistant approved and so Sarton dictated a letter inviting Atwell to record, his last act before going home and dying that evening. Mendl recalls:

The poor man had been grossly overworked. He died in his early forties. There was no one in charge of the artists department. The letter had been dictated by him and so I was allowed to record Winifred Atwell. She didn't know what to record, and I didn't know what to record, so we did a cover job of a song called 'Jezebel' – [originally recorded by] Frankie Laine. And that gave me a taste for making records. I went into the studio and I didn't have a clue what I was doing.[15]

Sarton's replacement was Frank Lee, who had worked at Decca in the 1930s before leaving to join Radio Luxembourg.

Despite his Atwell experience and a previous session with a singer called Reggie Goff, Mendl did not immediately become a producer. 'Frank Lee told me I could be the label manager for Brunswick, which was no great excitement,' Mendl observes, more interested in making records than repackaging US catalogue. At the same time, a label manager was appointed for Capitol, by the name of Dick Rowe. Over the next decade, Rowe and Mendl would become the company's main pop producers.

Atwell was the first in a run of best-selling artists for the label. For the first time, there was a reasonably well-regarded way of gauging the popularity of a disc, with the introduction in November 1952 of the *New Musical Express* top twelve. Atwell managed three in the top ten in the year before defecting to Philips in December 1953. David Whitfield, 'the Singing Bricklayer', notched up eleven top ten hits, including two number ones, between October 1953 and January 1957. Jimmy Young, in his pre-Radio 2 days, was another Decca star, with two number ones and three further top ten placings between August 1953 and September 1956. There were also blockbusters from the various light orchestras contracted to the company. Mantovani had four top tenners between December 1952 and November 1953, including a number one with the 'Moulin Rouge' theme. The bulk of his considerable sales, though, were on LP, particularly in America. In addition, Frank Chacksfield got both 'Limelight' and 'Ebb Tide' into the top ten in 1953–4.

Then there were the unexpected hits, such as 'Rock Island Line' by Lonnie Donegan, the record that kicked off the skiffle movement and inspired a generation to take up the guitar. Trombonist Chris Barber's band had been formed from the musicians sacked by Ken Colyer. Having recorded Colyer and been impressed, Mendl wanted to record Barber:

Frank Lee said, 'You can make a record with these people. Pay them £35, no royalty, and pass the publishing to Burlington', which was Decca's company. They were very very good, but the only problem was that their repertoire at the time wasn't quite enough for an LP. So they went to the Railway Hotel next door for a pint or two of Merrydown cider, and after some discussion, Barber and Donegan said, 'Would you like us to do a bit with the skiffle group?' Anyway, Arthur Lilley [the engineer] and I went out and had a cup of tea, and when we came back, Barber's bass player – called Jim Bray – had walked out in a huff ... Washboard was Beryl Bryden, Barber on bass. I said, 'Chris, I don't want to be unkind, but you're a trombone player.' He said, 'I've had three lessons from a classical bass player and I think I can get by.'[16]

The result spent sixteen weeks in the *New Musical Express* chart, peaking at number eight, and launched Donegan's solo career. Although Decca was the first company to record the likes of Chris Barber and Lonnie Donegan, the job soon passed to broadcaster, entrepreneur and jazz fan Denis Preston. He had set himself up as an independent producer, under the business name of Record

Supervision, following an altercation with Frank Lee. As Mendl remembers:

> Denis said, 'somebody ought to sign Chris Barber and all of those people, you know, I'm sure they're going to sell records. They're more than just a lot of old jazzers from the 100 Club.' So I set up a lunch between Frank Lee and Denis Preston, with the idea that we should have something a little more permanent, and that Denis should have a piece somehow. The lunch was the biggest disaster I have ever known. It started fine – they were discussing motor cars, because they were both car fans. And then Denis Preston, who did drink quite a bit, started to talk dirty and say things about ladies' genital organs and things of that sort. Frank Lee as you may know was not terribly interested in ladies' genital organs and the hatred on both sides mounted, so Denis went out and started up on his own.[17]

The chance to make a lot of money from the skiffle craze and the traditional jazz boom passed to Pye Nixa, a relative newcomer to the business which licensed Preston's productions. Nixa Records had been founded in 1950 by New Zealander Hilton Nixon, who had noticed the classical LPs that were being issued by small American independents such as Westminster and Concert Hall, and spotted a niche for them in the British market. As well as organizing full-scale classical recordings in London, it also offered a line of popular singles from various sources, including the Pacific label in France. In the February 1951 issue of the *Gramophone*, it was advertising its 'Stars from the Continent', who included Josephine Baker, Claude Luter, the French female singer Dany Dauberson and Graeme Bell's Jazz Band – who, despite recording in France, were Australian.

In 1953, 51 per cent of Nixon's company was bought by Pye, a Cambridge-based company that had started in 1896 as a maker of scientific instruments and diversified into radio, making components such as valves as well as full receiving sets. The company was acquired in 1928 by Charles Orr 'C. O.' Stanley, who was to control its destiny for the next thirty years, in which time it moved into television – making cameras, transmission equipment and receiving sets – and, ultimately, the record business. In 1955, Pye acquired the Polygon label, which had been set up by Alan A. Freeman in 1949 and had become best known for the recordings of the child star Petula Clark. Polygon was folded into the Nixa operation and the whole became known as Pye Nixa.

In 1959, half of Pye Records was sold to ATV, the ITV company that served the Midlands during the week and London at the weekends. This was a prelude to ATV's eventual acquisition of the whole Pye Records business. Pye had been part of the ATV consortium from the start, supplying equipment to the new company and supplying C. O. Stanley to the ATV board. At the head of ATV was Lew Grade, a Charleston dancer-turned-impresario, whose company the Grade Organisation was the agent responsible for booking most of the major British actors and show-business figures. As a result, the Pye record operation had access to a wealth of talent and, before long, a symbiotic link between Pye Records and ATV had sprung up. As an example, Bruce Forsyth presented ATV's flagship show *Sunday Night at the London Palladium*. He also recorded for Pye.

As well as building up its domestic catalogue, Pye continued to develop the licensed repertoire that had been its foundation. In the mid-1950s, it took on the distribution of Irving Green's Chicago-based Mercury label (which it lost to EMI in 1958), as well as representing Vanguard. Later, the Pye International label was launched for the licensed American repertoire, like London American at Decca.

Pye achieved a notable first by beating its rivals to the market with stereophonic records. By the late 1950s, a quarter of a century after the initial experiments undertaken by Alan Blumlein in the UK and Bell Laboratories in the US, the world was judged to be ready for binaural, or stereophonic, as they had now become known, recordings. Pre-recorded stereo audio tapes had been available since 1956, when they were introduced by RCA, but their retail prices were far higher than those of the equivalent record, reflecting the then-labour-intensive production methods involved.[18]

Blumlein had developed and patented a workable stereo disc system, using a single groove with the modulations for each channel carried on one side at 45 degrees to the perpendicular. The patents had lapsed in the interim, meaning that Blumlein's system was available to all who wanted to use it, but research continued into alternatives. Westrex promoted one method, closely based on the Blumlein 45/45 principle, while Decca's research team, under the supervision of Schwarz and Haddy, tested several systems, including one where two channels were eked out of a single groove by a sum-and-difference-type decoding process. Just to confuse matters further, Columbia came up with a third system.

Fortunately, the lesson of the battle of the speeds – arguably the last vestige of the old-style patent rows – had been learned by the record companies. The major European and American labels decided, at Edward Lewis's urging, to discuss the merits of the various offerings and decide on a common system once and for all. The winner was the Westrex system, and thus by definition, Blumlein. This decision was ratified on 25 March 1958 and the race was on to get the first stereo LPs to the marketplace. A small US label called Audio Fidelity had jumped the gun rather and issued a Westrex system LP before there were any cartridges available to play it.

Pye issued its first stereophonic LPs in August 1958. Decca and EMI were not far behind – the latter now being much more receptive to innovation. The former had kicked its stereo programme off with a sampler LP, assembled by Frank Lee, but with contributions from nearly all of the staff producers. Haddy went out and recorded railway sounds at West Drayton station. Hugh Mendl indulged a personal passion and pitched in with the sound of a Formula 1 race. John Culshaw contributed the sounds of Ernest Ansermet rehearsing. The whole production was held together with a commentary by BBC announcer Geoffrey Sumner, whose opening line 'This is a journey into sound' has since been borrowed countless times for other recordings.

Meanwhile, some of the hits from the monaural days were being remade in stereo, the new format sometimes demanding infinite pains, for example, the stereo version of Frank Chacksfield's 'Ebb Tide' that Raymond Horricks was detailed to produce:

> I went down to Hastings beach and recorded the gulls and the sea in stereo, and put it on the record. I had to bribe the lifeguard down there to let me buy some electricity for the equipment. I also had to go down there with boxes of old fish to bring the gulls in. I discovered it was the only beach on the south coast with pebbles where you could get the sound of the sea against it. I'd never dealt with seagulls before. I could deal with musicians. We got the microphones up, then I brought out this big box of fish guts, took it down onto the beach. The problem is that the gulls make a different sound when they're gobbling and eating on the fish guts, and it wasn't the kind of sound we wanted. We had to wait an hour or so until they'd been fed and then when they were disappearing we caught the sound. There are some things that you have to do in the record industry… [19]

Other companies were slower to catch on, among them the British arm of Philips. When Angela Morley was asked to make an LP of London-inspired music for the American market in 1958, she resisted all of Philips's attempts to make her use the standard facilities:

That was requested by Nat Shapiro of Columbia in America. Johnny Franz [Philips's head of A&R] said, 'We'll do it in Stanhope Place.' I said, 'No, I won't do it in Stanhope Place. First of all, Stanhope Place doesn't yet have stereo.' He said, 'Well, not everybody has stereo.' I said, 'Well yes, but this is a recording for the United States, where everything now is offered either stereo or mono. There is the choice. In any case, with the orchestra that I'm going to use, it's not big enough.' So I really took a stand on that and we ended up in Walthamstow Town Hall with stereo recording equipment.[20]

Horricks had transferred from Attwood's sleeve note department to the Decca artists and repertoire department. Frank Lee offered him the job after he had compiled a successful LP of Spike Hughes's 1930s New York jazz sessions. Immediately, however, he found himself exposed to Decca company politics:

I think Ted Lewis had a great communications problem. Why I criticize him, with the benefit of hindsight, is that he believed in 'divide and rule'. Instead of making the sales manager S. A. Beecher-Stevens, the artists manager Frank Lee and the publicity manager [Francis] Attwood work together, he seemed to revel in making them daggers drawn.[21]

A good example of this was Horricks's own divisional move. 'Attwood was furious. Prior to this, he had never revealed any special interest in my work … but now he made up his mind that I was "indispensible". Since he […] refused to speak directly with Frank Lee, the matter therefore went "upstairs".'[22] Lewis, though, declined to intervene, with the result that Horricks had to resign from the company, giving a fortnight's notice, and rejoin it, as a producer, the Monday after finishing work in the sleeve department.

Attwood's oddness was not merely limited to his attitude to his colleagues in other departments. He was 'a very strange being indeed. As publicity manager, it was his wont to be as reclusive as possible'. Horricks's interview with him took place 'after hours' in a darkened office and with his face in retreat behind a large green lampshade'. He delighted in informing the young interviewee that, as a young boy, he had disobeyed doctor's orders not to read or eat late at night by smuggling novels and bags of apples under the bedclothes. When he emerged into the light, from beneath 'a thin veneer of slicked-down hair and behind the huge beak of a nose, his complexion had the whiteness of a man plagued by stomach ulcers'. Added to his pebble glasses, this led Horricks to think 'so much for disregarding the advice of one's medical practitioners'. Later, Attwood offered Horricks some other more personal advice:

> Initialling and passing back to me some artwork and written copy, quite out of the blue he said, 'If you ever need a woman, try the prostitutes in Maddox Street. They're cheaper than elsewhere in the West End. And they're reliably clean.' I thanked him politely, but added that I had every intention of marrying soon.[23]

Frank Lee would have been equally uninterested in the shady ladies of Maddox Street, but not because of any imminent nuptials. Lee was gay, something that might have been at least partially responsible for Attwood's campaign against him. Although he was relatively discreet about his predelictions in the pre-Wolfenden era, he was still obvious enough to be known as 'the Queen of Decca'. 'He liked to surround himself with desirable young men, most of whom were quite straight and quite impervious to any suggestions, so nothing ever happened,' recalls Hugh Mendl. Lee was also prone to mild narcolepsy. 'There were memorable moments when he used to doze off on the sessions,' remembers producer Mike Smith. 'He'd wake up and stop the session. You'd think, "We had a bloody good take, and he's just ruined it".'[24]

To begin with, as a junior producer, Horricks was relatively immune from sniping, but once he'd notched up his first big success – Ted Heath and His Music's recording of 'Swinging Shepherd Blues', which got to number three in the charts in 1958 – it was a different matter:

> Of course, it did me an enormous amount of good in the record industry ... Inside Decca, on the other hand, it meant that my real troubles had begun ... I came to be regarded with a mixture of envy and apprehension ... The first thing I would ask the secretary I shared with Hugh Mendl upon returning [from the studios] was 'Who's been gunning for me this time?'

The troublemakers did not include Lee, Rowe or Mendl, the last being, in Horricks's view, 'far too clever for the Decca politics which he genuinely disdained'.[25]

Mendl agrees that this was the case: 'Well I tried not to get involved, because I saw no particular point. However, there were people with whom I was careful not to pick quarrels because I knew they could cause trouble.'[26]

Similarly divided were the pop and classical departments, despite the departments being nominally under the management of Frank Lee. Occasionally, there was friction. Horricks recalls:

> John Culshaw and I never particularly got on, from the moment when he was trying to record Kirsten Flagstad in Decca number one, and I had to get Lita Roza down from the control room, where she'd been listening to a playback. We had to walk through and Kirsten Flagstad must have said to John 'Who are these people?' I, as a very junior producer, got reported to Frank Lee. How else could I get Lita out, except down the fire escape? I don't think I ever really spoke to John after that because I knew that instead of speaking to me, he'd gone to Frank Lee who was my boss and his boss. He should have spoken to me directly. Eventually, the classical department was hived off.[27]

Horricks was able to make the crossing to the classical side once, though, thanks to the RCA connection. Knowing that producer Michael Williamson was in need of extra help on the recording of Handel's *Messiah* that he was planning to make at Walthamstow Town Hall with Sir Thomas Beecham conducting, Horricks volunteered. What he witnessed was eventful to say the least. Joan Sutherland had been the original soprano on the session, but a clash between her and the conductor was very much in evidence almost from the off, due largely to Sutherland's embellishment of her part. Beecham called a break and took Sutherland into a dressing room 'to instruct this singer in the elements of Handelian singing'.[28] The impromptu lesson turned into a stand-up row, out of which Beecham emerged announcing that Sutherland 'is no longer a part of this recording. If she ever was!'[29] Beecham called the powers-that-be at RCA, explained his actions and within forty-eight hours the sessions resumed with Jennifer Vyvyan in Sutherland's place. 'After that, it all went very well,' Horricks comments:

> Tommy was in a relaxed mood at the end, and said, 'Some years ago I was approached by the management of the New York Philharmonic. The orchestra's fortunes were very low and they wanted me to recommend someone good for bringing up standard of playing and good at box office. My

American tour had ended, and I was just about to get on the boat for England, but they took me to lunch. I made various recommendations, all very good, gifted rising conductors. And then I got on the boat, got into England on the Sunday morning, opened the papers and who do you think they'd picked? That bloody old charlatan Toscanini.[30]

In the late 1940s on a business visit to Abbey Road, George Avakian had also witnessed Beecham's mischief first-hand:

Leonard Smith, who was in charge of the classical department, invited me to meet him at the Abbey Road studios and he said, 'I've got to finish up something with Sir Thomas.' Beecham was there listening to some takes that he had recorded. So he said, 'He's a very pleasant guy, he won't mind, you just come and sit and listen. You'll enjoy his comments.' Which I did. He was approving one of the sides of a symphony, on 78 of course in those days, and he couldn't make up his mind. He said, 'Let's play those two over again.' So we played them, and he turned to me and said, 'It's so hard to judge. We'll decide on the basis of what you like, sir.' Jesus Christ! And he called me sir. So, I tried to get out of it and he said, 'Not at all, not at all. You're a member of the public, and the public should decide what is best, not just me alone.' I was appalled. I finally expressed my judgement and later I said to Leonard, 'I hope he's not paying attention to me because he knows, I'm sure, what he wants.' Leonard said, 'Of course he does, but he's just playing a game which he enjoys so much. He wanted to hear it again and just thought he would have some fun.' He was a delightful person, like a hummingbird, always in motion.[31]

The 1950s at Decca also saw the ascendancy of W. W. 'Bill' Townsley, Lewis's loyal factotum. He had, effectively, come with the furniture, having joined Barnett, Samuel in October 1926. His initial posting with Decca had been at the New Malden factory, where he became works manager. However, he fell foul of the company's transatlantic expansion, as Hugh Mendl explains:

When London began to get a reputation, Townsley fell down on deliveries. Lewis was in America, so dear Harvey Schwarz was in charge and he fired Townsley. Townsley went home, waited until Lewis returned, pitched up at Brixton Road and sat outside Lewis's office. And Lewis liked playing one off against the other, so to spite Schwarz, he said, 'You can come and help me, I suppose, Townsley', and so Townsley sat in the next-door office and his job was to write up the daily pressing figures and fetch things from Lewis's car and things like that.[32]

To this, Ray Horricks adds the observation: 'In the days when Sir Edward smoked, Bill was there with the lighter'.[33]

From this apparent sinecure, Townsley became the company's general manager, in which role he was not renowned for his open-mindedness or innovation. 'I called him Dr No,' relates Tony Hall, who joined the Decca promotion department in 1954. One of Hall's ideas that Decca said yes to was the expansion of its Tempo label into modern jazz. So, between 1955 and 1960, Hall moonlighted at the West Hampstead studios, making LPs with the likes of multi-instrumentalist Tubby Hayes, vibraphonist Victor Feldman and Jamaican trumpeter Dizzy Reece, all of which are now highly prized collectors' items. Decca's motivation for giving Hall his head was, however, not likely to have been any great desire to offer the best of the British jazz scene. 'I think they allowed me to produce these records mainly just to keep me quiet and to make sure that I did my proper day job,' Hall theorizes.[34]

Townsley was so clueless about the way the creative side worked that when Benjamin Britten's *War Requiem* became a great success, he asked John Culshaw if Britten could write another. Then there were his crude interventions in delicate negotiations, as Mendl relates:

> I was talking to the manager of a rock and roll band on the telephone. They were talking to Polydor and us, and they were talking about serious money. Townsley came into my office. He had no idea. I could have been speaking to God for all he knew, and I was talking the technicalities of so on and so forth. Townsley shouted out, 'Dunno who you've got there, but offer 'im two grand. Two thaasand paahnds' ... I'm sure the poor man heard it.[35]

One of the most prolific engineers working in Decca's studios at that time was Arthur Lilley, who had begun in the Decca shop back in the 1930s, and had never quite overcome the snobbery of his superiors. But the artists and the producers loved him to bits because of his musicality and his unobtrusive ability to enhance whatever ideas they had. Arranger Johnny Keating remembers an exchange with him during the making of an album with the singer Caterina Valente. Keating wondered aloud why the sound they were getting was not as good as the sound Capitol was getting on its

Frank Sinatra and Nat 'King' Cole records:

> There followed a pregnant pause, followed by another long drag on the fag. Then Arthur looked at me and half barked these immortal words: 'If they'll play quieter I'll give you the bloody Capitol Records Sound'... I went straight back into the studio. Spoke to the musicians ... We made one more take and after listening to it the deep secret of good sound ... was no longer a secret. We had just discovered Utopia.[36]

Lilley was also respected greatly by the younger engineers, such as Jimmy Lock, who joined Decca in 1963:

> He was a lovely engineer and a lovely man. Arthur was, I think, one of the most instinctive balance engineers I've ever met in my life. He could just lay his hands on a mixer, when all seemed chaos, and get a balance like I've never seen. I worked with him on a couple of recordings – one of them was the *Porgy and Bess* with Maazel, and the other one was a *Salome* for EMI. I let Arthur have the orchestra on that, so that I could concentrate on the voices. He would never ever crush a climax, that's what I loved about Arthur. Even though it would peak over the top. He would just hold it. He could build a balance so superbly. I've never known anyone like him. He liked doing what he did do, the pop music, but he was a little bit wasted, in my opinion, and I think he was somehow suppressed from classics because he was that good.[37]

On the pop LP side, Mendl had set about assembling a catalogue of cast recordings from the West End shows, as Lieberson did for Columbia and Broadway. Back in the pre-vinyl days, he had witnessed a 'disastrous' recording of Noël Coward's *Pacific 1860* with the composer, Mary Martin and Mantovani, after which Decca's interest in the shows had died out. With the rise of Joan Littlewood's workshop at the Theatre Royal, Stratford, and Lionel Bart, though, Mendl thought it was worth another try. 'I'd always had an interest in the musical theatre. I had actually met Cole Porter and emerged unscathed. I was very fascinated.' The first project was the Mermaid Theatre production of *Lock Up Your Daughters*, with lyrics by Bart and music by Laurie Johnson of *Avengers* theme fame, followed by the Stratford production of *Fings Ain't Wot They Used t'Be* and later *Oliver!* and *Maggie May*, the last of which Ray Horricks describes as 'the hardest job I've ever done in my life', due to the drunkenness of the show's star, Rachel Roberts:

I had a row over the telephone with Rex Harrison, whom I never met. He said, 'What are you doing to my wife?' I said, 'She's wrecking my recording.' He got off the phone, and he must have said something to her because she came back. It was awful. I did seventeen edits in the three minutes of her ballad.[38]

One of Decca's other Lionel Bart projects – an LP of music-hall songs with the singer Georgia Brown – caused Mendl as many headaches as Roberts had for Horricks, but ended on a pleasingly absurd note:

Frank Lee had missed out on the whole Larry Parnes and Lionel Bart thing and he was very upset that I was recording Paddy Roberts.[39] I don't know why, Paddy was a nice enough chap. He wouldn't obstruct it, he just wasn't very keen, and he was terribly proud of the fact that he had brought Tom Lehrer to Decca. He suddenly decided that Lionel Bart could be used to make funny records just like Paddy Roberts. It was a bit of a disaster, I'm afraid, but because of this Lionel was duly flattered of course and he went to Frank with the idea of doing these cockney belters with Georgia Brown. Frank said, 'I think you ought to do it with Ted Heath' – he was quite close to Ted. Ted Heath said, 'Yes, you can use my arranger Johnny Keating.'

I have to tell you, they were not very happy sessions. Poor old Ted was deaf as a post, Keating and Bart were not very much in sympathy with each other, Georgia Brown was wavering and in the end, Lionel walked out and then we finished off the album. I thought she did it very well. When the artwork came around, I was rather surprised to see that the album had been 'produced by Lionel Bart', so I duly blew my top, as one does. I, five foot four or whatever, stood looking at Frank Lee, six foot four or whatever, and said, 'I produced the record. Lionel Bart quarrelled with everybody and walked out. He didn't contribute a damned thing. He didn't write the songs, I don't think he even chose the songs. I don't mind Lionel getting billing, because he is, after all, the draw, but I think there should be acknowledgement of the producer.' Instead of the usual little thing, the sleeve department must have been tipped off by somebody, and this large credit appeared.[40]

In addition to promoting the renaissance in the British musical theatre, there was, in Mendl's view, another motivation for the exercise: 'It was one way of making EMI's life as hard as possible. My contempt for them was immense. I think we all prefer the underdog, and EMI had all of the arrogance of the BBC without any of the education.'

As Decca approached the end of the 1960s, it had come a long way from being a company that had to worry about having its telephones cut off. In the year to March 1959, the group – including its radar business and the manufacture of radios, televisions and record players – recorded sales of £21.8m, up £850,000 on the previous year, with a net profit of £1.03m, up £100,221 on 1958. Meanwhile, the company was challenging EMI in terms of its market share for discs. In 1960, when manufacturer sales of records in the UK were estimated to be worth £15m, EMI had 38.4 per cent of the total market, with Decca just 1.4 per cent behind.

The exit of RCA meant that the need for EMI to maintain two separate chains of command had disappeared. As a result, in 1957, the two constituent elements of the group's record business – the Gramophone Company and the Columbia Graphophone Company – became EMI Records Ltd, under the management of C. H. Thomas. For all of its arrogance, EMI had the good sense to follow the pattern set by Decca as regards licensed repertoire. Of that 38.4 per cent market share in 1960, 4.4 per cent came from miscellaneous American labels released in the UK by EMI. This activity was driven largely by Leonard G. Wood, known universally as L. G., who became managing director of EMI Records in 1959, when C. H. Thomas went over to the international side of the business. Born in 1910 and brought up near Hayes at Harlington, Wood had joined his largest local employer in the 1930s, first in the order department, then as a salesman, in the days when EMI instructed its reps to carry a bowler hat even if they never planned to wear it, and to carry cigarettes, even if, like Wood, they didn't smoke, so that they could offer one to a client at critical moments.

'Len was great – very old-school English,' recalls Derek Everett, who joined EMI at Great Castle Street in 1954 as the man who printed the labels for the promotional copies, but who soon moved over to the A&R side. 'He was always Mr Wood and it was always "Everett, old chap" and "Pop up, old chap".'[41] Although Wood was indeed old school and had been coming up through the ranks during the bad, blinkered era of Clark's dotage and Fisk's Luddism, he was open-minded and thus well suited to the Lockwood regime.

The open-mindedness showed through in some of the labels that he bagged for EMI. He negotiated a catalogue deal with Syd Nathan at King in

Cincinnati, whose country and soul output was hardly natural territory for an English gent. One King artist was indirectly responsible for Derek Everett getting his first job at EMI:

> We were just talking about things and he [Wood] said, 'Are you interested in music?' I said, 'Oh yes.' 'Final question old chap. Have you ever heard of Bonnie Lou?' I said, 'Yes, she's number twenty-nine in the charts this week with whatever it was' [probably 'Tennessee Wig Walk']. He said, 'Really? That's quite correct. How did you know that?' I said, 'Well, while I was waiting, I picked up the magazine in the office outside, looked at the chart and it happened to say that she was at number twenty-nine, otherwise I'd never have heard of her.' He said, 'That's wonderful, old chap. You've got the job. Start Monday.' And that's how I got into the music business.[42]

Wood also brought in the ABC-Paramount label, which brought in number one hits like 'Diana' by Paul Anka and 'I Can't Stop Loving You' by Ray Charles. Everett says:

> He was hard, but fair, I always thought. 'We'd just lost Columbia and we were about to lose RCA, so we were trying to get American labels. Capitol was set up as a separate department. We weren't supposed to speak to them. They were down the road, and they were special. We were still trying desperately to get American hits. 'Diana' was the first big one they picked up, which came from ABC Paramount. That was all growing. I was in the right place at the right time, and grew with it.[43]

Then there was the Roulette label, run by the Mafia-friendly Morris Levy, who was about as far from gentlemanly as it was possible to get. The founder of the New York jazz club Birdland, Levy had been hauled up by the authorities for not having a public performance licence. When he learned how the business of copyright worked, he registered himself with ASCAP and BMI, appointed himself publisher of the original numbers that were being performed every night at the club and began coining it in. The move into records followed in 1956 when he founded Roulette. The first connections with EMI came up two years later, and resulted in records like 'Why Do Fools Fall in Love' by Frankie Lymon and the Teenagers becoming massive British hits. The following year, EMI licensed the whole Roulette catalogue, but it proved to be less successful than expected.

Levy's attitude to the talent was robust: 'Artists are pains in the asses ... a lot of them are just imbeciles and they are ignorant. They say, "Look what big thieves Atlantic and Roulette were, they paid four cents a record, and they took advantage of the artists" Bullshit. There is no need to apologise ... If anyone was abused, it was the record companies.'[44] He was even reputed to have told an artist enquiring about royalties that he should try Buckingham Palace.

One who stood up to him was the British jazzman John Dankworth, who had signed to Roulette after several years with Parlophone. Upon arriving in New York for the 1959 Newport Jazz Festival, he was alarmed to discover that Roulette had lined up another of their artists, a female singer, to perform with the Dankworth band. Realizing that this was a try-on by the label, Dankworth 'strode up to the man in charge with fire in my eyes' and made the point that only one singer performed with his band, his wife Cleo Laine. 'I surprised myself with my own belligerence,' Dankworth recalled in his memoirs, 'but it worked like a dream ... the record men disappeared as if by magic.'[45]

Levy was also knee-deep with Alan Freed, the disc-jockey who popularized rock and roll. Freed had joined New York's WINS station in 1954, shortly after which he enlisted Levy as his manager. When Levy set up Roulette, he gave Freed 25 per cent of the company's stock, but when Freed sold it off to people who were too shady even for Levy, he forced Freed to retrieve the shares.

Freed's popularity meant that a play on one of his shows guaranteed an instant hit. He was quick to capitalize on this, and record labels soon came to realize that money had to change hands if they stood a chance of getting their record on the Freed show. Jerry Wexler learned this the hard way, when Atlantic had a major cash flow problem and the partners were taking no salary. Up until this point, Atlantic had been paying $600 a week:

> to keep Alan happy. It was a purely defensive move. The baksheesh didn't guarantee play for any particular record; we were only buying access ... When hard times set in for us, I felt sure Alan would be sympathetic ... 'I'd love to, Wex, but I can't do it,' he answered. 'That's taking the bread out of my children's mouths.' With that memorable declaration, he took us off the radio.[46]

There was nothing new to the idea. Music publishers had, for years, showered bandleaders with blandishments when they deigned to record one of their songs. Nor was Freed alone. Apart from the biggest stars, DJs in the deregulated US radio market were not necessarily well paid, and the extra cash offered by the record labels was always welcome. At the end of the 1950s, though, Congress decided that that the practice of bribing DJs – which, by this time, had gained the snappy name of payola – needed to be stopped. Perhaps the final straw had been the disc jockey convention held at Miami Beach's Americana Hotel in 1959. Roulette had spent over $15,000 on an all-night party, with Count Basie's band, a limitless supply of bourbon and breakfast laid on for the survivors. It had been billed as 'bar, barbecue and breakfast'. The *Miami News* called it 'babes, booze and bribes'.

Congress classified payola as a misdemeanour, and set a maximum tariff of a $10,000 fine and a one-year jail sentence. Freed emerged from the hearings in 1960 with a tiny fine and no imprisonment, but his career was over. His success had been a high-profile affair, and so was his downfall. Others who were called to account fared better. One was a Boston DJ called Joe Smith, who had actually declared his 'gifts' as taxable income. A Congressional Representative quipped that as gifts were not income per se, the government probably owed Smith some money. Another was Dick Clark, the apparently squeaky-clean host of ABC's *American Bandstand* show. Clark, it emerged, had more conflicts of interest than Freed had probably ever thought of. He owned stakes in record labels, pressing plants and music publishers. Grateful label bosses had assigned him copyrights in exchange for exposure. Meanwhile, his wife had benefited from the odd fur-coat-shaped token of esteem. Despite all of this, Congress decided that Clark was a 'fine young man', slapped him on the wrist very faintly and allowed him to get away with it on condition that he divested himself of his various interests. So much for the show trials. It was unsurprising that payola continued, albeit better disguised, and, indeed, it was to return.

Following EMI's disappointment, the Roulette contract was picked up in the UK by Top Rank, the record arm of the bakeries-to-cinemas combine the Rank Organisation, established in 1958. To run the show, Rank had poached Dick Rowe from Decca, bought its own wholesaling firm and taken on a lot of American catalogue, including Roulette and with it the Dankworth band's discs. The combine soon got cold feet about records, though, and offloaded the business to EMI. Derek Everett was sent to make sense of the new acquisition:

I was fiddling about doing bits and pieces on different labels, but then I was summoned into the office by Len [Wood] – 'Everett, old chap, there's something for you to do. We've just taken over Top Rank. Their offices are at the top end of Oxford Street. Go over there and see what you can find, would you?' Thursday afternoon they all had jobs, Friday morning at 11 o'clock, no one had a job. The offices were in North Row. The only one there was a doorman. I said, 'I'm from EMI Records.' He said, 'Oh yeah, I'm expecting someone. It's all in there, mate.' And there were these offices that had been totally gutted. Anything that moved had been taken. Files on the floor, boxes, empty filing cabinets. I assume that everybody thought, 'Sod it, we've lost our jobs, we'll take what we want.' All the equipment had gone. So I had to round it all up, all the files, all the bits and pieces, try to work out what deals they had.[47]

The outlook was improving for the domestic catalogue. For Columbia, Norrie Paramor and Ray Martin had built up a roster that included singers Ray Burns and Michael Holliday, as well as the aforementioned Eddie Calvert, who managed two number ones and two top tenners in the 1950s. Meanwhile, Martin had, himself, contributed two top ten hits to the Columbia catalogue as a bandleader. Over at HMV, Walter Ridley had brought in Malcolm Vaughan, who got into the top ten four times despite being so rhythmically deficient that Ridley had to mouth the lines to him in the studio as he sang them. More proficient were Ronnie Hilton and Alma Cogan, who had three top ten singles and a number one between March 1954 and December 1955, with a great number of Cogan's singles figuring lower in the charts up to 1961. It was by no means a doddle, said Ridley. The competition saw to that. 'We were always looking for talent. It wasn't easy. Decca and Philips were all chasing it too, looking for talent that could be moulded. You went anywhere you thought you could find it.'[48]

The opposition was not merely external, either. Although the corporate structure had, to some degree, been unified, the heads of the various EMI labels remained keenly competitive, particularly as several labels were coming out with their own versions of the same song. How did this happen? The 1950s were the last hurrah of Denmark Street or Tin Pan Alley, where most of the music publishers resided. They controlled all of the new material and promoted it vigorously. Sales of sheet music were still a money-spinner, so they had more interest in getting a song heard as widely as possible than in giving one company an exclusive monster hit. If the publishers offered a song to all of the labels and the broadcasting bandleaders, this form of spread-betting maximized their chances of good business. The labels, however, would frequently see their promotional efforts benefiting a rival label, if their version happened to be unavailable or if, as was sometimes known, the retailer had a bias towards one particular recording organization. As Hugh Mendl says:

> It was always the song. We had to cover other people's things. Once a month, publishers would come down and play you a bit of a song and you would then say, 'Who else has done this?' and they'd say, 'I'll give you an exclusive if you'll give me someone like Vera Lynn or Anne Shelton' and sometimes they did. It was very much the publishers who decided. It was the publishers who decided what to plug.[49]

Derek Everett backs this up:

> In that particular era, the music publisher was king. It wasn't the record company, it was the music publisher, and they used to play games. There were two or three of them that I used to battle with. You'd fix a release date on a title ... one of the worst, bless him, because he was very good to me in later years, was the sore with the bare head at Leeds Music, Cyril Simons. He was a bugger at that, he was an absolute sod. He'd fix a date – 'Derek, we've got a definite date, son, May 3, definite date, no problem.' At about three o'clock on 2 May, you'd get a call from him: 'Derek, you know that song? It's coming out tomorrow and Cliff's done it.' Thanks. He used to do it all the time.

But the publishers made it worth Everett's while in other ways:

> The music publishers were fairly heavy drinkers and heavy lunchers. I think my whole life, between probably 1960-something and when the music publishing started to die was fuelled on good lunches from the publishers. There was no reason at all most of the time ... Keith Prowse were the best, the Phillips brothers, Jimmy and Bill. Two or three of them had permanent tables at Wheeler's the fish restaurant, as it was, in Frith Street. The whole place was full of music business people ... Jimmy Phillips lived in Brighton. He used to get in at eleven, then it was over the pub, then to the restaurant, back at three-thirty, ready to catch the four o'clock train to Brighton. I used to think I was in the wrong business. Now it's just like a licence to print money because

music publishers do absolutely nothing except send out statements, collect money from MCPS, PRS and buy catalogues. They don't actually plug records or songs any more.[50]

Ray Horricks remembers the social dimension of Denmark Street only too clearly, particularly Elton Box of Box and Cox:

Both Dick Rowe and Hugh Mendl steered well clear of Boxie. Not out of any personal dislike but because beside his publishing office he also owned the Street's 'Club': where serious drinking began at an uncomfortably early hour and Michael Carr and other songwriters held pragmatic court. Still, as the long-term copyright owner of 'Galway Bay' and most recently Bill Haley's 'Alligator Rock', he had to be visited periodically; so as the junior of Decca's production team I was detailed off.

With his sleek centre parting and thin gigolo moustache, at our first meeting I came upon Boxie cracking open and devouring an enormous pile of walnuts. He offered me some; as well as a seat. I accepted the seat. Whereupon my backside promptly struck the floor: all the springs had gone in his old cowhide settee.

Boxie himself took no part in the discussion about songs which followed. He just carried on munching walnuts. For he had at that time as his assistant Ben Nisbet (later of Feldman Music), to whom he left the day-to-day running of affairs ... his one other contribution came at the end of an hour, when I arose off the floor to leave. 'Pop in and see us again, Horricks old boy', he said. 'Even if it's only to stick your head round the door and say, "*Sod ya!*"' Primed by Dick and Hugh, I resisted his invitation to proceed into the Club and join him for a gin mixed with Newcastle Brown.[51]

By the end of the 1950s, this set-up was changing. It was the era of rock and roll, and Tin Pan Alley was far from well geared to serving the demand for the new music. Almost every US label decided that it had to have a rock and roll element to its catalogue. RCA had Elvis, obviously, while American Decca had both Bill Haley with his Comets and Buddy Holly with his Crickets. The company, always alive to harsh economic realities, might have been expected to jump at the chance to sign such a talented singer and songwriter as Holly, but A&R man Bob Thiele met with major resistance when he played colleagues the demo of 'That'll Be The Day' sent to him by New Mexico-based independent producer Norman Petty. In the end, sense prevailed and the label released the demo as it stood. As befitted a high-class organization, Columbia alone resisted the charms of rock and roll, sticking to what it knew best – crooners like Johnnie Ray and, later, Tony Bennett, Mitch Miller's singalongs, leading-edge jazz and blockbusting cast LPs.

In the UK it was perhaps natural that there should be a similar movement. Most of the British rock and rollers were under the management of Larry Parnes, the former owner of a string of ladies' fashion shops. Parnes's success in the music business at this time was such that he became known as 'Mr Parnes, Shillings and Pence', and his charges were instantly recognizable by their unlikely-sounding stage names, the forename deliberately friendly and homely, the surname chosen to sound hard and aggressive. Decca had been in on the craze early doors with the Bermondsey-born, Parnes-managed Tommy Steele (born Thomas Hicks) and his debut disc 'Rock with the Caveman'.

Before long, though, the label had started moving Steele into the category of 'all-round entertainer' and a string of family-pleasing discs ensued. Rawer material came to Decca later on when they managed to sign Billy Fury (born Ronald Wycherley) from under the nose of Jack Baverstock at the Philips subsidiary Fontana. Fury went on to have eleven records in the top ten between 1960 and 1965. Meanwhile, Columbia's English affiliate Philips was proving less sniffy than its US counterpart, and had signed Parnes's protégé Marty Wilde (or Reg Smith, as he was christened), and was to get a creditable run of six top ten hits out of him between 1958 and 1961, the highpoint being 'A Teenager in Love', which scored a number two in June 1959.

Perhaps the best of the lot, however, came from outside the Parnes stable. Television was starting to become a showcase for pop music, due largely to the work of producer Jack Good. Having joined the BBC's graduate training scheme after studying at Oxford, Good devised a series called *Six-Five Special* beginning in February 1957. This was the first show on British television to present live rock and roll, taking the lead from *American Bandstand* over the Atlantic. Consequently, it was also the first show to feature a rock and roller called Cliff Richard (or Harry Webb, as he was worse known).

Webb had been born in India, but raised in Cheshunt, Hertfordshire, where he met a guitarist called Ian Samwell, with whom he formed a band, the Drifters. The group made a demo recording in the studio at the HMV shop in Oxford Street, and although both EMI producer Norman Newell and Decca man Hugh Mendl were Cheshunt residents, the demo was submitted, instead, to Norrie Paramor at Columbia. Impressed by what he heard, he signed the singer, who had been renamed Cliff Richard by his then-manager John Foster, and his motley backing band.

For their debut record, Paramor lined up a cover of an American hit, Bobby Helms's 'Schoolboy Crush'. Richard, however, had other ideas, ideas that marked the beginning of the end of the reliance on Tin Pan Alley and professional songwriters. While travelling on a Green Line bus, Samwell had written a number that Richard thought superior to the Helms song. Paramor disagreed, but took Samwell's song for the B-side. A recording session was arranged for 24 July 1958 in the number two studio at Abbey Road, the bulk of which was given over to recording 'Schoolboy Crush'. Samwell was relegated to second guitar, while session man Ernie Shear was drafted in to play lead, joined by cigarette-holder-toting double bass player Frank Clarke. Only the Drifters' drummer Terry Smart was allowed to do what he normally did.

When the A-side was done, the senior engineer on the session vacated the panel and let his young assistant Malcolm Addey take over for the 'throwaway' B-side, which was called 'Move It'. The result was a revelation – the first proper British-originated rock and roll song, made all the better by an engineer who understood precisely what was needed, as a result of being the right age. Samwell's hurt pride was alleviated slightly by the fact that Shear and Clarke got the feel of the thing so well: 'At the time I felt that ... Ernie was playing Bill Haley licks, but in retrospect he did a heck of a good job. Also we felt that ... a stand-up bass ... wasn't real rock and roll any more ... but [Frank Clarke] was a terrific guy and he played beautifully with great energy,' he said nearly forty years after the event.[52] Paramor was still not convinced, but he came round to the merits of Samwell's song after he played an acetate for his teenage daughters, who indicated the superiority of 'Move It' in no uncertain terms. Flipped over, the single came out at the end of August 1958, stayed on the charts for seventeen weeks, reaching number two and beginning a recording career that still shows no signs of flagging, although, despite everything, Cliff has never been able to break America. The meteoric rise was aided no doubt by Richard's regular appearances on Good's new ITV programme *Oh Boy*.

Samwell and Smart soon left the band, being replaced by four young musicians who, like Richard, frequented the 2 Is coffee bar in Soho – guitarists Hank B. Marvin and Bruce Welch, bass player Jet Harris and

217

drummer Tony Meehan. At Richard's suggestion, Paramor thought that the new model Drifters might be worth a punt as recording artists in their own right. Their audition for the contract took place in the producer's Great Castle Street office, the band having set up their guitars, amplifiers and drums in front of his desk. Paramor took them on in February 1959, with a penny royalty per disc sold, to be split four ways. (Lucky old Cliff got a penny all to himself, rising to 1¹/₂d after the first year of his contract.) Unfortunately, their first few releases, such as 'Feelin' Fine' and 'Saturday Dance', flopped. In June 1960, though, by which time they had changed their name to the Shadows, following legal representations from Atlantic's vocal group also called the Drifters, they recorded 'Apache', an instrumental that gave them their first number one. Again, Paramor had his own ideas about the A-side, preferring a rocked-up version of the old traditional number 'Quartermaster's Stores', retitled 'Quatermasster's Stores' as a nod to Nigel Kneale's science-fiction character Quatermass, then the subject of a popular BBC series. Fortunately, Paramor once again deferred to youthful judgement and switched the sides, but not before he had, not a little corruptly, arranged for his brother Alan's company, Lorna Music, to publish the new arrangement of the B-side, arrangements of traditional tunes being regarded as original compositions. Although 'Apache' had been written by someone else, namely singer Jerry Lordan, and the B-side had been in the public domain, Welch and Marvin would soon become accomplished songwriters, supplying themselves, Richard and later other artists with hit songs.

If Cliff and the Shadows represented a quantum leap in British pop, with their relative self-sufficiency when it came to material and the ensuing success, there was an even bigger advance on the way. And it was going to come from the unlikeliest of all EMI's divisions.

10 Paris, Liverpool and British West Hampstead

'George Martin really is one of the nicest people in the business – a lovely man,' says Hugh Mendl. There was a time, though, in the late 1950s and early 1960s, when Martin's then-employers EMI did not necessarily hold him in the same high regard:

> George, I believe, was in terrible trouble at EMI because Norrie Paramor, Ray Martin and all of them were coming up with hits – mostly covers. The Johnny Dankworth and Peter Sellers records that he made were lovely, but they weren't enough. George was very gentlemanly and had a good musical background, but he was in danger of losing his job. So Dick Rowe and I tried to get George, but Frank Lee wouldn't have him, and that's when Ray Horricks joined us. Frank Lee didn't fancy him, I think. He said, 'No, I don't like him.' End of discussion.[1]

So, when the Beatles signed to Martin's Parlophone label in June 1962, both sides were all too conscious that this was perhaps their last chance. Mark Lewisohn, in his exhaustive book *The Complete Beatles Recording Sessions*, quotes Martin's attitude to signing them as being 'I've nothing to lose'.[2] The band, meanwhile, had been refused by Columbia and HMV in December 1961, after their manager Brian Epstein sent to the EMI sales department a copy of a record that they had made for Polydor in Hamburg with the singer Tony Sheridan. More infamous, however, was their rejection by Decca, following an audition on New Year's Day 1962. Epstein had arranged for them to be seen by Mike Smith, Dick Rowe's assistant. Also auditioning that day were Brian Poole and the Tremeloes, a Dagenham-based group. Epstein had dictated the repertoire that the Beatles were to use to impress Decca, and in so doing, all but ignored the songwriting ability of John Lennon and Paul McCartney:

> I wanted both [says Smith], but Dick [Rowe] said, 'You can have one, you can't have the other', so I took the band that was better in the studio. I still believe

that. And of course, Brian Epstein had this thing about what they should record for the audition being what he considered to be possible singles. So they wound up doing very few of their own songs, and doing things like 'Sheik of Araby' and 'Three Cool Cats'. It's not the best performance you'll ever hear. And of course it didn't have the input of Mr Starr. Pete Best was the drummer and I think Pete was a lot better than Ringo. Had I have gone for it, I think it would have been very different, because I'm a totally different person to George. At the same time, I think I'd have got far more involved than he ever did, so the chances of me still being alive are remote. I also think there would have been major ructions, certainly between Lennon and I, seeing the path of light together. At one point I was scratching like mad and the Beatles were selling millions and millions and millions of records, and I thought 'Ooh, wrong!' but again, to be realistic, I think I'd be dead.

Smith joined Decca in 1958, having previously worked as an engineer at the BBC. One of his colleagues had moved and joined the mobile crews that recorded classical music all over the world. Smith followed, but his dreams of mind-broadening travel were soon shattered. 'I went to Decca and spent the next two years as classical editing engineer in British West Hampstead. Terrible place.' His transfer to the pop side of things came about in a faintly surreal manner, following his involvement in the creation of a private joke recording entitled 'Frank Lee – Iron Man of Commerce'.

That was started by another engineer, who bottled out. He said 'I'm going to get fired if he hears this.' I played it, and it was in very rough form, but it wasn't that rude. So I added a few bits to it. 'When war broke out, Frank went to work for Radio Luxembourg, because they were neutral.' All manner of things about his homosexuality. It was amazing. The thing that went through it all the time were these girls singing 'Mr Lee, Mr Lee, Mr Lee, Hup! Mr Lee, Mr Lee, Mr Lee, Hup!'

Studio boss Arthur Haddy, mischievously, had the record pressed and a copy reached Lee. Smith was summoned to Decca House for what he expected to be a carpeting. In fact, Lee had taken it rather well (there are doubts as to whether he understood it all), and Smith was promoted. 'Extraordinarily, I came out of it, having been an eleven-pound-a-week engineer, a thirteen-pound-a-week producer.'[3]

According to Hugh Mendl, once the Beatles became successful, Dick

Rowe decided that it was unfair to make Smith carry the can and shouldered the blame himself:

> [Rowe] never heard them. He hadn't seen them. After the Beatles had been turned down, Dick told me the story and he said, 'I don't think we should ever mention Mike Smith's name about this. We owe it to him.' I said, 'Why?' and he replied that Mike had come in saying, 'I heard two bloody good bands yesterday' … Dick asked him if he was absolutely sure, Mike replied that they were both marvellous, and so Dick asked which he would have if he could only have one. Mike replied, 'Oh, Brian Poole and the Tremeloes. They're professionals.' Dick Rowe's decision was the right one, because he got the acetate – and I heard the acetate – and well, it was awful.[4]

Smith, however, has a different, if not entirely incompatible recollection: 'After the problem with the Beatles, he [Rowe] put his head in the office and said, "I've just been with the chairman. I didn't tell Sir Edward Lewis it was you that turned the Beatles down." Oh, thanks very much. Quite a frightening time, but there you go.'[5]

Mendl adds that Epstein had previously tried to use his influence as the proprietor of Liverpool's largest record shop to get his boys accepted by Decca:

> First of all he saw our sales manager Beecher-Stevens, and said, 'I want to record a group I've got, and I think they're very good.' Beecher-Stevens said, 'No, I can't do a thing like that. I can talk to somebody for you.' Epstein said, 'I'll tell you what. I'll take 2,000 records off you if you take them.' Beecher-Stevens didn't ever do anything about it, because he thought you don't do business like that.[6]

It has long been a subject of conjecture as to whether Epstein did exactly this with EMI. It is far from implausible. If EMI wanted to keep such an important customer sweet, but not put too much at risk, where better than Parlophone? If it failed, it would bury itself, if it succeeded, then Parlophone would receive a much-needed boost. A win-win situation.

The official version, however, is that Epstein took the Decca audition tape to the HMV shop on Oxford Street to get it cut onto a disc. The engineer responsible liked the sound of the music and suggested that Epstein take it upstairs to Sid Coleman in the offices of Ardmore and Beechwood, EMI's music publishing subsidiary. Coleman in turn suggested that Epstein give George Martin a try. According to Martin himself, Epstein 'groaned inwardly and realized he'd hit rock bottom'.[7]

Nonetheless, the band trooped into the Abbey Road studios on 6 June 1962, for a test session in which they recorded three originals, 'Love Me Do', 'Ask Me Why' and 'PS I Love You', as well as an old chestnut, 'Besame Mucho'. Martin was so unbothered by the prospect that he greeted them, then went for a cup of tea, leaving the session in the hands of his assistant Ron Richards. After they had recorded 'Love Me Do', though, Richards called his boss and suggested that he return to the studio. It was a promising sort of sound, but not enough to convince Martin to sign them on the spot. What did convince him was their sense of humour. When he asked if there was anything about the session they didn't like, George Harrison replied, 'Yeah, I don't like your tie.' So it was that the Beatles became Parlophone artists, with the contract backdated to 4 June, thus allowing EMI to keep ownership of the 6 June session tape.

However, the first recording session proper did not take place until 4 September, by which time original drummer Pete Best had been replaced by Ringo Starr, following Martin's reservations about Best's timekeeping. Like Paramor, Martin had a ready-made song for the band, in this case 'How Do You Do It', written by Mitch Murray. After a desultory run-through, the band persuaded Martin to let them try 'Love Me Do'. Still not happy with the rhythm, Martin arranged another session for the following week, calling in a session drummer called Andy White. 'Love Me Do' was finally issued as a single on 5 October 1962. It entered the charts the following week, staying in for eighteen weeks and peaking at seventeen. EMI had given one of its largest customers what he wanted and gained a modest hit for themselves. It was the follow-up, though, that propelled the Beatles into a different league. As soon as instruments had been downed on 26 November 1962 at the end of recording 'Please Please Me', Martin informed the Fabs that they had just made their first number one, which, if you believe the *NME*, *Melody Maker* and *Disc* charts, they had indeed done.[8] The rest is history, geography and every other subject on the school syllabus.

Except, that is, in America. Capitol had been offered the hot new signings as a matter of course, but Dave Dexter – who had been assigned by Capitol president Alan Livingston to review all externally created product offered to the label – passed on the opportunity. Like Mike Smith and Dick Rowe, he has been pilloried for this decision since, but at the time, all were merely working on the best information available to them. Derek Everett says:

> You weren't going to get them all. That was the argument, and a perfectly fair
> argument really, that Capitol had about the English invasion of America. They
> couldn't have had them all. You should have had this, you should have had that.
> No way. We met with them and talked with them, and there was no way a
> company could have accommodated all that product and made it successful. It
> wouldn't have worked. In 1963, the Beatles were just another group striving for
> success.[9]

Through the work of Wood, Everett and others, EMI had good contacts with
some of the small US labels, and it was these that benefited from Capitol's
short-term short-sightedness. One such was the black Chicago-based label
VeeJay, but sadly it soon hit financial trouble and EMI's American lawyer Paul
Marshall terminated the agreement. Wood tried Dexter again, but found him
willing to take only the Australian yodeller Frank Ifield, and so a licensing deal
was arranged with another small independent, Swan. Dexter finally gave way
in December 1963 with the release of 'I Want to Hold Your Hand'.

In return, while solvent, VeeJay had been able to help EMI out with
various gaps in its catalogue. 'I loved all that they did,' says Everett:

> We had hits out of it, and they got us out of a hole with the blues thing when
> Pye had success with the Chess catalogue. VeeJay used to be put up at the
> selection meetings every Friday and turned down. We don't want all that, old
> chap, it doesn't sell. So that was fine. And then when Pye began to have success
> with Chess, Chuck Berry and all that, and the blues boom started happening,
> LG said to me, 'Everett, don't we have any of this music?' I said, 'Yes, we have
> a great label called VeeJay.' He said, 'Put it all out, old chap, put it all out.' So
> that's when we had hits with John Lee Hooker and Jimmy Reed. Top ten
> records, and everybody had been turning them down every week saying, 'No
> market for that, old chap.' EMI was a cautious company, but you can't put
> everything out. The timing was right, someone else had opened the market up
> and we came through on the back of it. We had some marvellous stuff there.[10]

As well as their own material, the Beatles were covering a lot of R&B sounds
from the US. Their second album, *With the Beatles*, featured three stormers:
'Money' by Barrett Strong, 'You Really Got a Hold on Me' by the Miracles

and the Marvelettes' 'Please Mister Postman'. All three had been originated by the Tamla-Motown organization in Detroit, the creation of an ex-boxer, saucepan salesman and car assembly line worker called Berry Gordy Jr.

Having turned his hand to songwriting and had considerable success with his compositions for Jackie Wilson, such as 'Reet Petite', Gordy was disturbed to find that the credits and thus the royalties for the B-sides of these hits were being given to relatives of Wilson's manager Nat Tarnopol. As a B-side earns the same as the A-side, this meant that they were getting a lot of money for vastly inferior work, even if it were really theirs, which is questionable. Gordy argued that he should be allowed to write and claim the credit for the flip sides, but Tarnopol was having none of it. Gordy walked out.

The only way to get fair treatment, Gordy decided, was to start his own label. His sister Gwen had reached a similar conclusion and opted to set up Anna Records (named after another Gordy sibling), with the help of Chess's distribution network. Instead of joining up with his sister, Berry Gordy wanted to stand or fall on his own merits. To do so, however, required money, something he didn't have. Fortunately, there was a trust fund into which each member of the family paid regularly. Loans could be drawn from it, but only with a very good reason and the unanimous support of the other fund members. After grilling Berry Jr good and proper, the family lent him $800 in January 1959, using future royalties as security.

Gordy's label was originally to be called Tammy, after a Debbie Reynolds hit, but when this was found to be registered already, he modified it to Tamla. His run-in with the unscrupulous Tarnopol had also stressed on Gordy the importance of publishing, so he set up a company called Jobete, taking the first two letters of each of his children's names. With this in mind, it is perhaps unsurprising that Tamla was a family business from the off. When a house was acquired at 2648 West Grand Boulevard as the company's offices and studios, Gordy's father and one of his brothers were responsible for the soundproofing, while sister Loucye set up office upstairs as head of the manufacturing department. When he was interrogated by his family over the loan, Gordy had particularly resented the minute detail demanded by sister Esther. Now, though, he saw that she was just the sort of person he needed to keep a tight rein on things, so, with her husband, George Edwards, she took over the accounting.

The first couple of releases achieved some mild success, but Tamla was hamstrung by its lack of national distribution. Gordy got around this by licensing some of the company's recordings, variously to United Artists and Chess, but Gordy knew that this meant that other people were continuing to get too large a share of his money, something that he cared enough about to write it a love song. Tamla's first national release under its own steam came in the summer of 1960 with 'Way Over There' by the Miracles, led by Gordy's friend and protégé William 'Smokey' Robinson. It did the job. Gordy celebrated the success by starting a second label – Motown, a corruption of 'Motortown' as Detroit was known – ostensibly to release the group records, while Tamla majored in the solo artists.

In these early years, everything at Motown – save for pressing – was done in-house. The songwriters, who included Gordy himself and Robinson, worked at the company, the studio was on-site, and the backing came from a house band assembled by Gordy's A&R chief William 'Mickey' Stevenson – which generally included the rock-solid rhythm team of James Jamerson on bass and 'Benny' Benjamin on drums. Both were heavy drinkers, but on the studio floor, this became irrelevant. 'Sometimes … Mickey would have to find him, root him out of some dive … But once Benny had those sticks in his hands, drunk or sober, he was the best,' said Gordy.[11] Also brought in-house was the selling. Gordy's maxim for the company was 'Create, Sell, Collect', and in late 1960, he appointed Barney Ales, a white salesman whom he had known from one of his independent distributors.

The company's output found its way overseas almost immediately. In the UK, Philips were the first to pick up on the Detroit sound, releasing the Marvelettes' recording of 'Please Mister Postman' in 1961. The catalogue soon passed to Oriole, a relatively small independent operation, but the 'Motown wasn't accepted by the BBC, because they had this big thing about black music being too black, so British artists covered the songs,' explains Eddie Levy, the son of Oriole's founder Morris Levy (no relation to the Morris Levy behind Roulette), and himself now a successful music publisher:

> Brian Poole did 'Do You Love Me'. There were some great great records. My father said, 'We've just got to make it a little more commercial to make it work with the British public and get it played.' But when the renewal came up, they wanted a huge amount of money, and we couldn't renew. So, they went to Stateside/EMI and then they had 'My Guy' by Mary Wells, which was very commercial.[12]

Gordy had taken on what Levy had said, but Levy was not the one to be benefiting from it.

EMI's Stateside label had been created in 1962 to provide a home for the company's various licensed US labels, and for the spoils of the Top Rank acquisition. Derek Everett was in charge of the new operation and he found that, the new commercial outlook notwithstanding, it was still hard to find acceptance for the Detroit sound: 'The general consensus from the radio and the reviewers was that they were all the same record. I used to get this all the time."It's the same record, old son. This Marvin Gaye? It's the same as Smokey Robinson".' If the business of selling Motown to the British was hard, his dealings with the Detroit executives brought some relatively light relief:

> Barney Ales and Phil Jones called themselves the ugly Americans. They were funny. Most people thought they were terrible, but I thought they were great. They were hard guys. We'd sit and argue, thrash things out heatedly, but once it was over, it was ... down the pub or off to the restaurant or whatever. You could have some wonderful social evenings, then ten o'clock next morning, you'd be back shouting and screaming at each other. 'You're not promoting this' – 'Yes, we are.'[13]

By 1964, acceptance had been gained and the Tamla-Motown imprimatur was so potent that EMI made an exception to its entrenched policy of never allowing licensees their own label identity, conscious that they might be building up a name that could pass to a rival at the time of the next contract renewal. It had also done this with Liberty, which had been founded in California in 1955 by Al Bennett, Sy Waronker and Ted Keep. Initially, its UK ties were with London American, who enjoyed hits with Liberty artists like Eddie Cochran and the Chipmunks, but the representation moved to EMI in 1961. L. G. Wood was summoned to the Savoy Hotel by Bennett to discuss the deal, 'acceptable to me except for one detail, which was that he wanted to launch his records on his own label here in the UK,' Wood remembered in 1984:

> None of us thought it was very wise to set up American labels here. I wanted the repertoire. I thought fast and said we had a deal. I went back to Manchester Square to get the contract drawn up, and also to see Sir Joseph [Lockwood]. I said, 'I've got a confession to make, I've broken the rules.' He said, 'That's OK. You know what you're doing, I'll leave it to you.' Within half an hour, Ted Lewis was on the phone to Lockwood. It was a good job I'd told

him. We did very well out of that Liberty deal, and I'm sure I made the right decision. The only thing you can say is that it probably opened the door for American companies to ask for the same thing.[14]

Later in the 1960s, Liberty built up its empire by taking over the Pacific Jazz and Blue Note labels, before being itself subsumed into United Artists.

The licensed repertoire issued by the majors was not merely limited to material sourced from overseas labels. In the UK, there was a growing supply of independent producers. Denis Preston had been the first, and he was still a major operator, although he had now switched his outlet from Pye to EMI's Columbia label. 'Denis was a good music man, and he made great records,' says Derek Everett, whose memories of Preston are not solely musical:

> His meetings were to be savoured. He drank all day, every day, but you would never know he'd ever had a drink. He was as sharp as a tack. You'd watch the bottle of brandy disappear, but the glass was always full. I don't drink at all now, but I drank a bit then, although I was never a heavy drinker. The bottle was slowly emptying, but ... you'd never see where it went in that triangle between the bottle, the glass and his mouth. Ten o'clock in the morning, it would be, 'Right lads, what are you drinking?' And you'd go, 'No, Denis, no, wait until a bit later.' 'Coffee, lads? Put something in it.' Stoned by half-past ten and you had the rest of the day to get through. But he made some great stuff.[15]

Some of the new independents, like John and Rik Gunnell, were managers and promoters who moved into production so that they could keep a tighter control over the recording activities and earnings of their artists, who included Georgie Fame. Others were musicians who had crossed over to the other side, like Mickie Most, who had been half of an act called the Most Brothers.[16] One of Most's biggest early successes was 'House of the Rising Sun' by the Animals, reputedly recorded for just £8. As a traditional number, it was in the public domain, but only organist Alan Price knew that if he put his name down as the arranger he would get the compositional royalties. This caused ructions in the band (drummer John Steel argued, memorably, that Price hadn't arranged his drum part), and hastened his departure for a solo career.

At this stage, though, the biggest of the independent producers was a Gloucester-born former TV repairman called Robert George Meek, better known as Joe. He had begun his recording career in 1954 when he joined the IBC studios in Portland Place as a balance engineer. After a period working on location recordings for Radio Luxembourg, Meek moved into the studio proper and was soon in high demand because of his open-minded approach to the process. When the sound of marching was required for Anne Shelton's 1956 number one 'Lay Down Your Arms', Meek (or rather his assistant, Adrian Kerridge) supplied the effect convincingly by shaking a box of gravel. One aspect of this troubled him, though. IBC was used to a greater or lesser degree by all of the major companies – particularly when EMI and Decca shut down for their fortnight's holiday, as was then the way – and these were the days when a song was liable to be covered by the opposition. So, Meek sometimes found himself engineering both the original and the cover, and being forced to give away the secret ingredient he had concocted for the original. One that he didn't give away was the secret behind Humphrey Lyttelton's driving 'Bad Penny Blues', which was to place a microphone very close to the snare drum and also to bring up the volume of Johnny Parker's piano part. The result was a number nineteen hit on Parlophone, not at all bad for a jazz record.

Meek's unorthodox attitude got him into trouble with IBC's manager Allen Stagg, so when Denis Preston – a regular IBC customer – asked if Meek wanted to come with him and help set up a new studio, he jumped at the chance. The new venture, Lansdowne Studios, situated in the basement of a residential block in Holland Park, opened in early 1959, but Meek did not last the year out. He had started to have mild success as a songwriter, and he kept badgering Preston to use his songs. When he did so on a stressful session with a large orchestra, and was slapped down, he stormed out of the building, leaving Adrian Kerridge to finish the job. He was told not to bother coming in the following day.

From an apparent disaster, Meek soon decided that this was a great opportunity to set up his own studio, and bolder still, his own label. One of IBC's clients had been an independent label called Saga, which had carved a market for itself by offering decent original recordings of the classics, as well as some pop and jazz, at a low price. Jimmy Lock, who had worked with Meek at IBC, became Saga's chief engineer:

Saga was the first recording company to make new recordings and sell them at budget price. This, of course, captivated the attention of the press. How could it be done? We went away to do recordings like the Brandenburg Concertos in Germany with Harry Newston, and then I used to go to France for the disc-cutting at the Pathé Marconi studios. The performances weren't bad, and were extremely well received.[17]

Lock had left IBC because he feared for the longevity of pop. 'I loved IBC, but it seemed to me an ideal opportunity, because I wanted to go into classics. I liked doing pops, but I could see quite clearly that a pop engineer aged very quickly.' By 1959, though, Saga wanted to expand its pop reach and the company's managing director William Barrington-Coupe thought Meek was the man to do it. A joint venture called Triumph Records was set up and Meek moved his operation into the toy warehouse in Holloway Road where Saga had its offices and Lock kept his location recording equipment and editing facilities. The first Triumph discs were issued in February 1960, with the advertising slogan 'Triumph – Records made for the Hit Parade' and the promotional push of a sponsored show on Radio Luxembourg, 'It's a Triumph'[18].

Among the label's earliest releases were 'Green Jeans' by the Fabulous Flee-Rekkers – a high-speed rock and roll rejig of 'Greensleeves' with double-tracked saxophone well to the fore – which peaked at number twenty-three, and 'Chick A'Roo' by singer Ricky Wayne backed by the Flee-Rekkers (who were obviously not fabulous when they were backing someone else). Triumph's greatest triumph came in May, when 'Angela Jones' by Michael Cox was released. A sickeningly sweet love song, it nonetheless had a highly memorable 'hook', and it climbed to number seven in the charts. The success was not a cause for jubilation, though. The tiny label struggled to keep up with demand for the disc, and Meek was disturbed to find vast numbers of unfulfilled orders at the warehouse, which could have sent the record even higher. Equally perturbing was the large number of records that had been despatched for which the company had not yet been paid. Worst of all, though, was the withdrawal of Saga's largest customer, Great Universal Stores, which left the company unable to fulfil any of its grand plans.

Meek extricated himself from the mess of Triumph and threw himself into a new venture funded by the owner of Saga's parent company, Saga Films, Major Wilfred Banks. The new company was to be called RGM Sound, and the idea was to create masters that could then be licensed to the majors. Meek found himself a three-storey flat over a leather goods shop at

304 Holloway Road, in which he set about building a studio, using cast-off equipment from Saga and whatever came to hand. The main tape machine was a Danish-made Lyrec, which Jimmy Lock[19] had acquired for the classical side of things. 'That was a great machine – a TR16. Twin track, and you could edit on it – it had a beautiful editing block,' recalls Lock.[20] Because of the building's layout, musicians were often not in the same room as their colleagues. Sometimes, the bathroom was used for vocal tracks because of its natural reverberation. Some musicians looked upon Meek's set-up with derision at first, but this soon dissipated when they heard the sound he was getting. Arranger Ivor Raymonde remembered one occasion when he was trying to speak to Meek, but finding it difficult because of the sound of drummer Kenny Clare coming over the speakers:

> The drum mikes were open … A choir mike was open … there'd be a string mike open … two trumpets and a trombone: that's six microphones were open … Joe turned off Kenny Clare's drum mikes and not a sound … came out of the string mike or the trombone mike or the brass mike or the choir mike, which technically is almost unbelievable in this tiny room … How he did it, I don't know…[21]

The major labels were less impressed, as Meek's enthusiasm for overdubbing, using two tape recorders to layer the sound, was introducing distortion into the masters, but the material was strong enough for them to overlook this point more often than not. Dick Rowe, who had moved from Decca to Top Rank, was all set to be an enthusiastic customer, until the collapse of Top Rank and the sale to EMI. Fortunately he resurfaced at Decca and took on quite a few RGM masters, as did Pye. Obsessed with the late Buddy Holly, Meek wrote 'A Tribute to Buddy Holly' for Mike Berry and the Outlaws, which was released on HMV. However, Meek's first big independent success came in July 1961 with 'Johnny Remember Me' by John Leyton, which hit number one for Top Rank, aided by Leyton's appearances in the TV drama *Harpers West One*. The ethereal sound of the record excited some controversy in the music press about the use of recording gimmicks, but Meek countered this with the argument that 'Even Frank Sinatra has echo effects. Pop records today must be as exciting as possible'.[22] Even more effect-laden was the record that was to prove Meek's crowning glory, an instrumental that he had written in honour of the Telstar communications satellite, and recorded with Billy Fury's backing band, the Tornados. Released on Decca, it went to number one in August 1962.

RGM productions continued to hit the charts over the next few years, including 'Have I the Right' by the Honeycombs, which was a number one in 1964, and 'Just Like Eddie' by Tornados bass player Heinz Burt, which reached number five. By 1966, though, Meek's star was on the wane. He had also become intensely paranoid, convinced that the studios were bugged by EMI and Decca, who were trying to steal his secrets, which had come a long way technically from shaking trays of gravel. Consequently, orders would be given in scribbled form rather than verbally. Meek was a promiscuous homosexual, and his mental state was not aided by his arrest for cottaging in 1963. There was also a protracted court case brought by a French composer who claimed that 'Telstar' had been plagiarized from him, during which Meek had built up £150,000 in royalties, none of which he could touch until a verdict was reached.

By 1967, he was in a bad way. 'I met Joe Meek for the first and only time a matter of weeks before his death,' recalled Decca engineer Brian Masters:

> He had been invited to some kind of industry gala – highly unusual, given the fact that he was supposedly one of 'yesterday's men' – and he turned up looking totally bedraggled and complaining that he didn't want to go in the first place. While talking to Wally Ridley, he claimed to be about to start a new record and film enterprise with [songwriter and long-time collaborator] Geoff Goddard, bizarrely adding that he had ordered a gross of red light bulbs and several gallons of fixing fluid for his bathroom. Nobody could ever take him seriously, but I suppose that had he claimed to be able to record number one singles on his stairs, nobody would have believed it without the evidence of the records he made.[23]

Even at this point, it looked as if EMI, at the behest of Sir Joseph Lockwood, might be interested in signing Meek to an exclusive contract. Tragically, though, on 3 February, following an altercation with his landlady Violet Shenton, he shot her dead then turned the gun on himself. The date was eight years to the day after the death of Buddy Holly.

The increased reliance on independents was the beginning of the end for the traditional A&R man, who signed the artists and supervised the sessions. Instead, after the signing, the A&R man might drop into the studio to see how things were going, but that was it. Mike Smith and Dick Rowe were both of the old school and the decision to pass on the Beatles had not affected either too much. Rowe had rescued things by picking up on the Rolling Stones. Hugh Mendl recalls:

> Dick Rowe was judging an amateur talent contest in, I think, the Isle of Man. He didn't know who was on with him, but next to him was George Harrison. Dick was a very nice bloke and said to George, 'I'm sorry. I feel so embarrassed.' George said, 'We were terrible, weren't we?' Dick said, 'Well, I've only heard the acetate, but yes.' George replied, 'I know we were. We hadn't had any sleep, we hadn't had anything, we'd driven down overnight. We were awful. I don't blame you.' Then he leant over and said, 'I'm sorry you had all this trouble in the press about it. Do you want to do yourself a bit of good? There's a band called the Rolling Stones and they appear at the Station Hotel, Richmond.' Dick said he couldn't wait to get back to London and the very day, he found out where they were and went out and heard them.[24]

Meanwhile, Mike Smith had gone on to build his reputation as a producer with records by Brian Poole and the Tremeloes, the Applejacks and Dave Berry. However, his progress was impeded by the dreaded Decca politics:

> Dick Rowe was able to make sure that he was the man, as far as Lewis was concerned, and that was the reason I left. I'd had the success with Brian Poole and the Tremeloes, but then I'd discovered that I was earning less than the Tremeloes' van driver. I had three records in the top ten, so I said, 'Right Dick, I want a raise.' He said, 'You can't have one.' 'Right,' I said, 'I want a royalty'. He said, 'You can't have one.' I said, 'Right, I'll go then.' He said, 'Ta ta.' So I walked out. What he hadn't realized was that Brian and the Tremeloes' contract was up, so I took them to CBS.[25]

When Philips had gained the Columbia contract in 1951, Coen Solleveld knew that the arrangement was 'temporary', and that the American company's long-term goal was to have its own wholly-owned subsidiaries in each territory. Philips countered this by expanding in its own right and striking an important new business association with the German company Siemens, owners of the Deutsche Grammophon/Polydor operation. In 1962, the two groups entered into a joint venture called the Grammophon-Philips Group.

DG had been predominantly concerned with German domestic output before the Second World War, but it had ended up bankrupt, in which state it was scooped up by Telefunken, who sold it on to Siemens in 1941. Post-war, the Hanover factory was found to be 'remarkably well preserved'[26] and the new owners set about rebuilding the classical repertoire and looking to foreign markets. The breakthrough was the Archiv Produktion series, assembled under the leadership of Dr Fred Hamel, which attempted to create a representative set of recordings covering everything from the Gregorian period to the eighteenth century. This began in 1947 with recordings of Johann Sebastian Bach's organ works, as well as a stab at his cantatas. The label was introduced into the UK in 1954. The Polydor label concentrated on pop material. In the 1960s, following the alliance with Philips, Roland Rennie was brought over from EMI and together with Horst Schmolzi, he spearheaded a concentrated effort to establish the name in the UK, both with imported material such as Bert Kaempfert and local repertoire. By the end of the 1960s, Polydor had the Atlantic catalogue in the UK and a range of artists from the Who to Cream.

This integration could not necessarily be taken for granted – one company was German, the other Dutch, and memories of what the Germans had done to Holland less than twenty years earlier were still pretty fresh. Added to this, both companies were predominantly hardware-based and the record business required a different mindset. Fortunately, the presence of musically minded men in both parent companies aided the assimilation in the early years. 'Major investments had to be approved by the shareholders in the Shareholders' Delegation Meetings which were held a few times a year,' Coen Solleveld explains. These meetings consisted of representatives from both boards and Hartong, Frits Philips and Dr Ernst von Siemens 'were all very favourably disposed towards the music business.' However:

> The assisting staff of our shareholders ... was used to thinking in terms of bricks and mortar, machines, tools, tangible assets, having and retaining a certain calculable value. For them it was difficult to appreciate the fact that in our business, one actually buys intangible assets ... The element of 'goodwill' we tended to purchase and calculate was unusual for them and somewhat frivolous to their standards.[27]

CBS began to establish itself around the world in May 1962 with the launch of CBS in Great Britain and the Republic of Ireland. In a *Billboard* advertisement placed shortly after the campaign for world domination had begun, CBS announced that while it had 'achieved pre-eminence in domestic [American] consumer sales, the company's establishment of CBS Records reflected a desire to broaden the international markets for domestic repertoire as well as to contribute to the development of local produce within key areas of the world'.[28]

As far as the British operation was concerned, Philips was still involved as manufacturer and distributor, but the label had its own identity, as opposed to having its product released on the Philips or Fontana labels. This marked a change in industry policy, for companies like EMI and Decca had traditionally been dead set against allowing foreign affiliates their own label identity. There had been isolated exceptions to this. EMI had released American Columbia material in South Africa on the CBS label since the mid-1950s. As EMI still owned the Columbia name in the UK and Europe, the CBS name was a useful fallback for the US company.

Similar arrangements followed in Japan and South-east Asia. Although Columbia took great pains to set up a local recording programme in each territory, the South-east Asian market went mad for soundtracks such as *My Fair Lady, Camelot, The Sound of Music* and *West Side Story*, an outcome that surprised New York considerably. Next, in August 1962, Columbia opened three wholly-owned subsidiaries in South America, then Greece, Spain, Holland, Denmark, Norway, Sweden, Finland, Italy, France and Germany.

Despite the grand claims for the importance of locally recorded material elsewhere, the English CBS operation, run by John Humphries, remained primarily an outlet for the American Columbia repertoire. That, however, changed in March 1965 when CBS did what it had done in France and Germany and took over an eligible independent with its own studio. At first, there were suggestions that CBS was in serious discussions with Jeffrey Kruger's Ember organization, but, if so, these turned out to be fruitless.

The company that CBS bought was Oriole, which had been in operation since the 1930s. It was run by the Levy brothers, Morris (not to be confused with his unsavoury US-based namesake) and Jacques, whose father was the proprietor of Levy's Record Shop at Whitechapel in the East End of London. 'It became a very very famous shop,' explains Eddie Levy, Morris's son. 'They imported the first jazz records, they had a little record label called Levaphone and they also hired out bicycles at the same time. A lot of famous British jazz musicians came to the shop to listen to the early jazz records in the 1920s and 1930s.'[29]

The retail business was followed by the establishment of Levy's Sound Studios at 73 New Bond Street, London, primarily as a private recording facility, run by Jacques. Chappell's, situated nearby, was a regular customer for its discs of library (or 'mood') music, used by broadcasters and film makers. Meanwhile, Levaphone had developed into the Oriole label, which was run by Morris from separate premises at 104 New Bond Street.

In the 1950s, producers like former dance band pianist Jack Baverstock set about building up a roster of home-grown talent for the Oriole label that included singer Russ Hamilton, who reached number two in 1957 with 'We Will Make Love', and skiffle expert Chas McDevitt, who got to number five in the same year with 'Freight Train'. Then, in the early 1960s, the chart presence was maintained by the singer Maureen Evans, who reached number three in 1962 with 'Like I Do'. Tamla-Motown apart, Oriole had also licensed several important American labels. 'They had Mercury at one time,' says Eddie Levy:

> The story was that we needed new presses at the factory, so Mercury put them in and in turn got a partnership with Oriole. Due to certain problems, my father eventually split with them, but through the Mercury period, there was 'Earth Angel' by the Platters, 'Mad About the Boy', Dinah Washington, a lot of famous records. Russ Hamilton was one of the rare records, of which one side was number one in America and the other side was number one here. Jack Baverstock walked off with Russ Hamilton when he went to America and signed him to MGM, but he disappeared down the drain.[30]

The main money-spinner for Oriole, though, came through following the lead set out much earlier on by the likes of Vocalion and Crystalate and allying itself with Woolworths to produce a cheap range of discs, under the name Embassy. The material generally consisted of cover versions of current pop hits, and Mike Ross-Trevor, who joined Levy's Sound Studios as an engineer in 1963, remembers that the standard of the recordings was creditably high:

> Some of them were really good. Embassy was their main source of revenue. It was massive. Every Monday morning, in a three-hour session, we used to record four records that had hit the top ten the previous week. Quite often, if it involved an orchestra of session musicians, it would be the same musicians who had played on the original ... There were singers who sounded vaguely

like the originals, but of course it wasn't an exact impersonation. It was good, though. Some of them really worked.[31]

Unusually for a relatively small label, Oriole had its own factory, situated at Aston Clinton in Buckinghamshire. Mike Ross-Trevor suggests that this was the main attraction for CBS:

> They didn't really want Oriole records, but what they did have was a state-of-the-art pressing plant and distribution network. The building's still there as the Sony distribution centre, although it's been enlarged greatly since those days. They weren't interested in the studio, either, but they suddenly found that they had one. It was one room, one control room and a little reception area. People literally walked in off the street and saw me. We had a little EMI console, custom-built. It was fourteen channels in, three channels out, straight into the three-track Ampex.
>
> It was an old ballroom and it used to be a dancing school in the twenties. It had a huge domed ceiling and it still had the spindle for the glitterball. When I first went there, they had a false ceiling across the studio, to stop sound going up into the dome and bouncing back down again and everything was very dry, because that was the sound of the day. Very controlled. A lot of screens, a lot of curtains. As the studio progressed, we took the ceiling down, because everything became more open. Once we took that ceiling down, the sound improved 100 per cent and I think it put the studio on the map. From the point that we took the ceiling down, we started getting really good work.[32]

Eddie Levy suggests that CBS was always interested in the whole package:

> I think CBS were looking for a full set-up in the UK, and the perfect buy was Oriole, because it had a factory, a studio and its own distribution. The offer was tempting for those days. Quite a lot of money, a six-figure sum, although I don't remember exactly. There was all the usual nonsense that Oriole would continue as a label, but that lasted five seconds.

The acquisition – described at the time by Goddard Lieberson as 'the world's worst kept secret'[33] – was finalized in September 1964. The first releases under the new arrangement were to hit the shops in March the following year. In the meantime, the company also had to break off its renewed ties with EMI, which had been representing the subsidiary Epic catalogue since 1962.

Morris Levy continued as managing director of the renamed CBS Records. Lieberson had said at the September 1964 press party that he wasn't planning to draft in any American staff to run the show. 'The way things are going, I think we could do with importing some British staff,' he quipped, flattering the Oriole employees.[34] In time, however, CBS did send over a couple of Americans to take care of the day-to-day running, one was Maurice Oberstein, who moved into marketing, the other was Ken Glancy, who had replaced Mitch Miller as head of A&R at Columbia, and who became managing director of the UK CBS operation, while Levy became vice-chairman. While opinions are divided on Oberstein, or Obie, as he was generally known, all agree that Ken Glancy was one of the good guys.

One of Glancy's appointments was Rodney Burbeck, who came in from a career in journalism to become press officer. In his view, the Oriole purchase was primarily to guarantee a UK outlet for American material. 'You did feel very much a small part of the company and I remember reading the annual report for CBS and the UK was part of "offshore" operations,' he observes. 'We weren't terribly high on their list of priorities, so we had to make our presence felt, but on the other hand we had this great catalogue of artists which helped enormously as a leverage.'[35]

The UK company's attempts to make its creative presence felt were not, initially, as successful as had been hoped. The head of A&R was Reg Warburton, who had occupied the same role in the Oriole days. Warburton – David Whitfield's former pianist – was a talented musician and a good producer, but with beat groups in the ascendant, his experience was almost from another age. The hits started to happen when Mike Smith came over from Decca, bringing Brian Poole and the Tremeloes with him:

CBS really didn't want the Tremeloes. They wanted Brian Poole as a solo artist, so I spent a lot of money recording him, and it did absolutely nothing. Fortunately, I was able to get a minimum deal for the Tremeloes – a very, very bad deal.

The first record was done at Regent Sound on Denmark Street – 'Here Comes My Baby'. It wasn't really happening on the session so I went down the Gioconda, the coffee bar, and said, 'Anybody play piano?' This massive bloke stood up and said, 'Yeah, I play piano.' I said, 'All right, come in.' I think we agreed ten pounds. He came in and said, 'Where's the part?' I said, 'We haven't got a part.' 'Where's the chord sheet?' 'We haven't got a chord sheet.' So I had to sit there and write it out. That was Big John Goodison. He sat at the piano, played and the hair stood up on the back of my neck. It was just wonderful, and it all went on from there.[36]

'Here Comes My Baby' reached number four in February 1967, but the follow-up did even better, as Rodney Burbeck remembers:

> We put 'Silence is Golden' out by the back door with no promotion, and yet it was a number one mega-selling record. One of those quirks of the business. You don't always hear it when you're sitting in an A&R meeting, but when I heard it played on the radio while I was in my car, I thought, 'Hold on, that's great – is that one of ours?' I remember punching the air outside the car.[37]

By 1967, CBS had moved its offices from New Bond Street to Theobalds Road and Reg Warburton had been shifted sideways to become studio manager. His replacement was Derek Everett, over from EMI, where he had risen to become head of the licensed repertoire division:

> On top of the Trems, we had Mike's association with Keith Mansfield, the Love Affair, Christie, Georgie Fame, obviously. The hits just kept coming. We were fortunate, we turned it around. The story of Georgie Fame is lovely. After I ... went to CBS, I was at a function, on the steps of the place, and I was either going in or coming out. Rik [Gunnell] was going in the opposite direction. He grabbed my arm and said, 'Del, do you want Georgie?' I said, 'Yes'. He said, 'Right, he's yours. Talk to you tomorrow.' 'Let's work out a deal?' 'No, he wants to be with you.' That's how the deal came about, one of those strange things.[38]

Smith produced Fame's third number one hit, 'The Ballad of Bonnie and Clyde', the gestation of which had been highly problematic:

> After the session, I took the four-track back to the office and said to my secretary, 'Look, whatever you do, guard that with your life, I'll pick it up later on tonight.' She put it on the desk and put the phone on top of it. Of course, phones have magnets in. So when we got to the studio to do the remix, there's clicks all the way through the rhythm track. Fortunately only the rhythm track. I got a band together that night – Georgie was very fussy about his rhythm section. Certainly [pianist and arranger] Arthur Greenslade was there. We relaid the rhythm track to the voice and the front line, and got away with it. It's got a mistake in it. He should sing about putting all the money into a 'burlap bag', but in fact he says 'dulap bag'. I never noticed it until one day years afterwards.[39]

The same record caused trouble for the publicity department. Rodney Burbeck tells the tale of attracting the attention of the boys in blue after setting up a photo opportunity involving an actor and an imitation machine gun. 'Somebody from a nearby office rang up the police and said there's a raid going on, there's a man with a machine gun, and the flashing blue lights arrived.'[40]

Another of Smith's number one hit productions, 'Everlasting Love' by Love Affair, courted controversy when it emerged that the only member of the actual band on the record was sixteen-year-old singer Steve Ellis. 'Love Affair was a total joke, that was all session guys. It would have been [ex-Tornados drummer] Clem Cattini, [bassist] Russ Stapleford [keyboardist], Alan Hawkshaw and [percussionist] Denis Lopez. Denis was a lunatic. It was nothing unusual to see Denis Lopez come flying off the false ceiling halfway through the session.'[41]

The quality of the musicianship helped make the records successful, but this was also the age of the wacky publicity stunt. Burbeck's department, undeterred by their brush with the law, was up there with the best of them:

I helped to invent flower power. When 'San Francisco (Be Sure to Wear Flowers in Your Hair)' by Scott McKenzie came out, I had this idea of sending lots of bimbos, scantily dressed, to Bank Underground station in the morning, with bunches of flowers. I just told them to hand out flowers to men in bowler hats and tipped off Fleet Street we were doing this. We got lots of pictures in the press of bowler-hatted businessmen looking embarrassed because they were being given flowers. The bimbos were told if they were asked why, they were just to say, 'Wear some flowers in your hair.'[42]

Meanwhile, the company was also taking an unorthodox attitude to pushing the classics. 'I was cheek by jowl with the classical department, and there was a great lady called Quita Chavez, who was head of classical A&R,' says Burbeck:

She had a great way of enthusing the sales team, who were only interested in the latest pop record. I can remember one sales conference where she was presenting a record by the organist E. Power Biggs, I think, and she said, 'Here's a great record by Biggsy, let's hear it for Biggsy' and all the reps went, 'Yeah, Biggsy.' She wound up the volume and it sounded great. We had Leonard Bernstein too, that was a bit of a purple patch for him. She suggested

I might like to come with her to the airport to meet him at Heathrow to help her do the glad hand – I wasn't aware at the time why I was a male being taken to meet Mr Bernstein – it later became clear.[43]

The new company was lucky. It had the clout of its American parent when it needed it, but in other aspects it was a start-up, able to work from a blank sheet. 'It was just incredible,' says Everett.

I still say it was the best five years of my life. Incredibly hard work, but it was wonderful. We had lots of misses, but when we had the budget meetings each year, luckily, the A&R budgets worked. Richard Robinson was the financial man. Every year we'd have the same argument: 'Derek, you're putting out too many records.' 'Yes, probably.' 'You're spending too much money.' We used to have this famous saying: 'Only issue the hits.' Every year, we used to have this and I'd say, 'If I could only do that, first of all, I wouldn't come in. I'd sit on a yacht in the South of France, phone in once a month and tell you what to put out. Why would I even bother if I knew 100 per cent what was going to be a hit? It doesn't work like that, sorry.' 'Yes, but you must know.' 'I don't. You do your best, you make your decisions, you work with everything that goes together to make these things, and a little luck comes into it.' Anyway, the budgets used to work.[44]

While all of this had been going on in Britain, the parent company in New York had also undergone some changes. In 1965, Columbia president Goddard Lieberson had appointed a new administrative vice-president to oversee the record division, a young lawyer called Clive Davis. Davis had joined the company in November 1960 as one of the company's two corporate lawyers. The other was Harvey Schein, and when he went off to run Columbia's international operation, Davis stepped up to become the company's senior lawyer. In this position he oversaw contract negotiations, and found himself becoming more friendly with the artists and their managers than had previously been a Columbia lawyer's lot. He also saw the company through a complex suit that the Federal Trade Commission had brought against its mail-order discount record club. The club had begun in 1955, and after initial loud protests at the unfairness of it all, RCA and Capitol bowed to the inevitable and, in 1958, started their own record clubs. The Columbia club remained distinct, though, in that it had arranged deals with other labels to offer more than just Columbia repertoire. RCA and

Capitol thought this was illegal, the retailers agreed and so, unfortunately, did the FTC. Davis arranged a defence based on the fact that the labels who were licensing their product to Columbia could not afford to develop their own clubs and that the whole operation was expanding the market rather than cannibalizing existing business. The licensees backed him up fully, as did some artists and music publishers. The case was thrown out.

Bruce Lundvall, who also joined Columbia in 1960, could see that Davis was being groomed for high office. 'We had won the suit and obviously everyone had their eye on Mr Davis, the brilliant young attorney. I remember going into his office and seeing papers all over the floor. It was a very different Clive Davis, you know. With his button-down shirt, and his tie undone.'[45]

However, the speed with which Davis scaled the corporate ladder surprised even himself. 'Lieberson had gotten some idea of my skills when we travelled together; but I wasn't thinking *that* big ... I was still a newcomer to the business and – most important of all – a man without any background in marketing or music,' he wrote in 1974.[46] His first battle in the top job was to exert some kind of control over the company's A&R. A Harvard report had suggested that the function be merged with marketing, an idea that displeased Goddard Lieberson. He complied with the report by making marketing vice-presidents Bill Gallagher and Len Levy responsible for A&R, but only if they reported to him on this matter rather than to their actual manager, executive vice-president Norman Adler. Adler was miffed at this slight, and when Lieberson offered him the chance to move sideways and take over the musical instrument division, which included Fender guitars, he took it. He then offered Clive Davis the position of administrative vice-president, which amounted to much the same as Adler's old job but with the responsibility for A&R added.

Why did Lieberson, described by Davis himself as 'truly a master politician',[47] refuse to give the comparatively experienced Adler – another lawyer made good – the job that he eventually gave the greenhorn Davis? Presumably he hoped that Davis would be more pliable than Adler. If so, Lieberson had misjudged his man. Davis was never going to be a cipher. Lieberson soon realized that Davis was no mean politician himself and began to feel that his authority was being usurped by his own appointment.

Davis almost immediately came to the conclusion that Gallagher and Levy were ill-qualified to sign artists, and he made his feelings quite clear. Initially they felt able to ignore him, arguing that the orders he issued to them were beyond his authority. Eventually, he issued them with an ultimatum. Appoint an A&R chief for each of their departments or leave. When Lieberson made him executive vice-president and general manager, their defence crumbled. In 1967, Gallagher and Levy left Columbia.

Clive had no such qualms about his own ability to spot talent. Even though Davis was the first to acknowledge that the company had a great many talented producers, he decided to take a hands-on approach to signings. The anti-rock bias so enthusiastically promoted by Mitch Miller was not where the company needed to be in the late 1960s, he thought. Columbia had to embrace the new sounds. His suspicion that the company could not stick to crooners and showtunes was backed up when the Broadway cast albums of *Mame* and *Cabaret* sold a fraction of the figures achieved by the likes of *My Fair Lady*.

In his autobiography *Clive: Inside the Record Business* he refers frequently to 'my' signings, and many who worked with him at the time have suggested that these efforts were more collective than he liked to admit. This is a fair point, but Davis later suggested to Fredric Dannen that the issue was really one of where the buck stopped. Producers might come to him with acts they thought Columbia should sign, but only Davis had the authority to sanction the signings. Whatever the exact truth of his role in the label's various acquisitions, his heavy involvement in all aspects of operation is undeniable, as this reminiscence from Bruce Lundvall illustrates:

> I was essentially his head of merchandising and then his head of marketing. He was very hands on, a very challenging guy to work for. From what I've heard he hasn't changed at all. People don't. We would do a trade ad in *Billboard*, and he'd want to rewrite the copy. We'd have to go up to his office and sit there with the art director. He was that hands on. I got on very well with him, but if you wanted to disagree with him, you had to do that privately, not in front of other people. He wouldn't tolerate that. He was really somebody who was very success-oriented ... Very often, I would call him at night from home, and say, 'Clive, I have a different opinion on this, I want to talk to you about it.' He would always listen and every once in a while, I'd win a small point. Not often.[48]

Davis also claimed credit for the rationalization of the inventory issues associated with producing both mono and stereo LPs. Assured by Bill Bachman that stereo records would play on mono machines, he removed the $1 price differential between mono and stereo, bringing both to $4.79. He assumed 'this would eventually lead to a phase-out of monaural records, but gradually. It eliminated monaural records practically overnight.' When this assertion appeared in Davis's memoirs, Lieberson said that the decision had been taken years before Davis's rise to prominence.

So to Davis's rock crusade. The label already had Simon and Garfunkel and Bob Dylan. The latter had been signed by John Hammond as an out-and-out folkie, but by the time of Davis's ascension, he was heading towards rock, much to the temporary chagrin of his fans. The first of Davis's own signings, then, was Donovan, who had been styled as the 'English Dylan' (despite being Scottish). This was followed by a catalogue deal with Lou Adler's Ode label, which brought in the aforementioned Scott McKenzie hit. Then came Chicago Transit Authority (later streamlined to plain old Chicago under which name they sold in huge quantities), Laura Nyro and Blood, Sweat and Tears. The most famous of Davis's signings, though, at least in terms of the anecdotes that it generated, was Columbia's 1968 contract with Big Brother and the Holding Company, an outfit with a lead singer called Janis Joplin. Davis had been after them since seeing them at the 1967 Monterey festival.

Some of the old-style Columbia acts, however, remained sacrosanct, even when their contract demands were large enough to endanger the company's financial stability. A year after his elevation to administrative VP, Davis found himself with a major headache. Three major contracts – Bob Dylan, Barbra Streisand and Andy Williams – were all due to expire at the same time, and the managers of all three were happy to talk to other companies. To make matters worse, both Streisand and Williams wanted more than $1m apiece for a five-year contract, which at a time when Columbia's pre-tax profits were around $5m a year was a major deal. $500,000 or lower was the norm back then. In exchange for giving in on the money, Davis exacted a commitment from Williams and Streisand to record three albums a year for the duration of the contract.

In contrast, the financial demands made by the Philadelphia Symphony Orchestra under Eugene Ormandy were kicked firmly into touch. The orchestra wanted a $2m guarantee, but Davis argued that classical recordings failed to recoup on far less. When it emerged that RCA had made an offer close to the demanded sum, CBS chairman William Paley and president Frank Stanton gave Davis the answer he wanted: no. The chance to give RCA a bloody nose while saving a couple of million was too good to miss. The nose was to be made even bloodier by the systematic release of the backlog of Philadelphia recordings that Columbia had built up.

The American innovations were viewed with approval by the British subsidiary. 'The American stuff was world-beating,' Derek Everett asserts. 'Dylan, Simon and Garfunkel. They were album sales, and what we did were singles.' Other employees were relatively immune to New York's far-reaching influence, though – for example, John Goodison, the piano player that Mike Smith had plucked from a Denmark Street coffee bar, and who had become Smith's assistant. Smith recalls:

> He wasn't the most diplomatic person. We had one occasion when we were getting pressure from the big kids from the States, and Clive Davis was over. We were in my office in Theobald's Road, and Clive's really giving me a bad time. John just happens to wander in, and he's a big man, and he's listening to this.' Suddenly, he says, 'Mike, shall I hit him?' I laughed nervously and said, 'No, John.' He didn't know who it was, but even if he did, he wouldn't have cared.[49]

The main competition for Davis's repositioned Columbia came not from RCA, EMI or Decca but from a relatively new entrant into the market, albeit one with a long history in other fields of entertainment and a bit of previous in the record game. In 1958, twenty-six years after it baled out of Brunswick, Warner Bros had re-entered the record business. Jack Warner had recently explained to his brothers that he was going to sell his stake in the business to bankers, headed by one Serge Semenenko, and that they should do the same, when in reality he had no intention of doing so. The result was some very upset siblings and Jack Warner in unopposed charge of the family business. His big idea was to establish a record label. Soundtracks – from both film and TV – were big money, so it made sense to keep them under the same umbrella.

An early option surveyed by Warner was to buy into an existing business, and a dialogue was established with Lew Chudd's Imperial label. When this came to nothing, though, a fresh start looked like the only way. One person who was not too keen on the idea was Herman Starr, who ran the Warner music publishing business, and who remembered all too clearly the Brunswick debacle. He argued forcefully that if such folly was to go ahead, there was only one man he'd consider to run the new venture, and that was Jim Conkling. Conkling had retired two years earlier, but couldn't help responding to a challenge. He worked out a plan showing that the Warner Bros label would need capital of $2m before it moved into profit. To Warner, who had lost $8m on Brunswick a quarter of a century earlier, $2m was bearable – less than the cost of one flop movie.[50]

The plan was approved, so the next step was to build up a management team. Unsurprisingly, Conkling went after the men he knew and trusted best. As sales vice-president, in came Hal Cook, who had worked closely with Conkling at Capitol and Columbia. From the Columbia era, he brought in engineer Lowell Frank and, as soon as he could get hold of him, A&R man George Avakian. Avakian's desire to leave Columbia had been fuelled by the inverse proportion between the amount of profit he was making for the company and the appreciation he was receiving for it:

I was exhausted and actually rather depressed by the realization that I had made millions of dollars in profit for the company and I couldn't get any royalties. The company's policy was to allow salary increases on a regulated schedule. I got a raise every single year, and I got bonuses almost every year. I was running two departments – popular albums and international – which suddenly had become by far the two most profitable parts of the company. Originally they were nothing. It wasn't just me who created the profit. I had the support of an entire company, the advertising people, the sales people and so on. But if anything went wrong with a product that I was in charge of creating, the first person to get it in the neck would be me. So I took the position that I was what has since been known in the industry as a 'key man', but I couldn't get any 'key man' money. I had always thought of myself always as a company man, and it took me a long time to realize that I was a cog and considered replaceable, except that they wouldn't have known who to find to replace me.

I had seen the confidential reports that were made for the industry by the Graduate School of Business at New York University and *Billboard* magazine. They surveyed record sales of all the major companies and the information was distributed only to those who subscribed to the scheme. By the second quarter of 1957, the report showed in its various breakdowns that the Columbia Records popular album department brought in 82c of every dollar spent in that quarter and, within the industry, Columbia pop albums accounted for 26c of every dollar spent in the United States on all kinds of records. Now, that's a shocking figure, but there it was. That helped put me in kind of a spin. I realized that I'd just been working myself to a fare-thee-well,

and I developed a combination of mononucleosis and hepatitis simultaneously, which I'm told is almost impossible. I began to feel 'I've got to quit,
as much as I love the work, or I'll make myself seriously ill.'[51]

A brief period in partnership with Dick Bock of the small specialist label
Pacific Jazz followed, during which Conkling asked him to help out with
some productions for the new label, including singles and an LP with the
actor Tab Hunter. However, when Bock almost fell victim to the cash flow
hell caused by the distributors' cavalier treatment of small labels, he
suggested that Avakian take the permanent job that Conkling was offering:

> As a result, I was the producer of the first chart record in the history of Warner
> Brothers Records, before I had even joined. The plan there was to have an
> across-the-board album company, as well as everything else, because Jim had
> seen what had happened with albums at Columbia. Now he had the two key
> guys for this purpose, Hal Cook and myself. However, we ran into the severe
> problem of not having any stars. The immediate solution was to tie into the
> Warner television shows.[52]

The most successful of these was *77 Sunset Strip*. The series starred Efrem
Zimbalist Jr, a Yale classmate of Avakian's and a son of the famous classical
violinist, but unfortunately he had inherited little of his father's musical
ability. So the actors who were heard on hit singles and an LP were Ed
Byrnes (who played the character of Gerald Lloyd Kookson III, aka
'Kookie') and Connie Stevens (who sang 'Kookie, Kookie, Lend Me Your
Comb' to him). As Byrnes was unable to carry a tune, with or without the
aid of a bucket, his contribution was entirely spoken.

The Warner Bros label was launched in March 1958, with the news that
the first releases would be available from September. The focus was on
albums, all in stereo, and in this regard the absence of stars became critical.
There were some big names there, but they had to record under
pseudonyms because they were contracted to other labels. Pedal steel
guitarist Alvino Rey (one of Conkling's brothers-in-law) was there, as Ira
Ironstrings, with an LP called *Ira Ironstrings Plays Music for People with
$3.98, Plus Tax, If Any*. This was followed by *Ira Ironstrings Plays with
Matches, Ira Ironstrings Plays Santa Claus (Christmas Music for Those
Who've Heard Everything)* and *Ira Ironstrings Destroys the Great Bands*, but
the jokey name meant little to the buying public, although now the records

are regarded as easy listening classics.

When the label turned out not to be the hoped-for success, there was talk of closing the whole operation down, but Conkling felt sure that they could trade their way out of the abyss. Starr agreed to let Conkling carry on, but with very tight controls on what could be spent, and a reduction in the number of staff from 130 to twenty-nine. As at their previous companies, Conkling and Cook had gone for dedicated distribution facilities, but these went in the retrenchment as well.

The label's big break almost never happened, because of the spending controls that were in place. The Everly Brothers, who had brought in a number of huge hits for the independent label Cadence, were on the market. George Avakian explains:

> Cadence was started by Archie Bleyer, who was the musical director for Arthur Godfrey and an old friend, so that's how that tie-in came in. Archie started the record company in a kind of left-handed way. I don't know what happened, but I think Mitch Miller wasn't interested in really pushing Julius LaRosa as a singer. I never thought of him as a possibility, beyond being part of the Arthur Godfrey cast, but Archie saw him as a potential pop singer, because he did appeal to young girls. So, Archie started a record company called Cadence, and for some reason, Arthur got angry about it. Arthur fired Julius LaRosa, on the grounds that he was being faithless. He didn't fire Archie, which was good because he couldn't have replaced him.
>
> So then Archie signed the Everlys to a three-year contract. They became so popular that Archie was quite frank in saying, 'I can't possibly renew. They're asking for a lot of money and they deserve it.' I was constantly being invited to previews of films that had music scores. I went to one, and I happened to sit right behind Archie. I said to him, 'Archie, I want you to know that I'm not going to try and sign the Everly Brothers. You can keep them.' He said, 'Yeah, but I can't do anything with them anyway.' So that was the turning point in worrying about whether Archie's feelings would be hurt.[53]

After some discussion, Starr okayed the Everlys deal, which was an expensive one for its time:

> The contract was something that Jim Conkling dreamed up, and we were able to advertise it as a $1m contract, the biggest contract in the history of the industry – even bigger than anything that Frank Sinatra had been able to get.

And the way it was less painful to Warners was that it was spread over ten years. Jim's contract idea worked beautifully and we started recording the Everlys and had a wonderful time. 'Cathy's Clown' [the Everlys' first big hit on WB] was probably on the first session. We recorded in Nashville, because we needed the musicians there. I went down there and spent about three or four days there each time, and we sat around, and I didn't contribute very much. I just listened to what they were doing, rehearsing. It was a very wonderful relaxed atmosphere, and completely unlike New York.[54]

The vindication was completed when Avakian recorded a virtually unknown comedian called Bob Newhart, but neither he nor Conkling were around to see the label fully into its turnaround period. Avakian had been enticed to RCA by George Marek, and Conkling was coming to the end of his contracted two years. His situation was made problematic by his decision to cash in his Warner Bros share options, with what Warner and Starr regarded as indecent haste. Charged with choosing his own replacement, he went for Mike Maitland, who had previously run the sales department at Capitol, but left when he was passed over for the label presidency. One of his masterstrokes at Capitol had come about in response to Frank Sinatra's decision to leave and start his own label, Reprise. Maitland repackaged the back catalogue and offered it in a two-for-one deal, all but crushing the start-up.

Ensconced at Warner Bros in beautiful downtown Burbank, Maitland brought in Joe Smith, the former Boston DJ fresh from the payola hearings, as head of national promotion, and set about increasing the label's penetration. The signing of the folk act Peter, Paul and Mary aided matters greatly. Just as the label's fortunes were beginning to pick up, though, Maitland's past came back to haunt him. Following the success of the film *Ocean's Eleven*, Warner Bros wanted Sinatra to sign a movie contract. Reprise, with a roster containing nearly all of Sinatra's pals, like Sammy Davis Jr and Dean Martin, hadn't caught fire as quickly as Sinatra had hoped, and with the help of his lawyer Mickey Rudin, a Warner Bros purchase of Reprise became an integral part of his new movie deal. All of this had been negotiated without Maitland's knowledge and presented to him as a fait accompli. He remained in post, but Sinatra never spoke to him in all of the time that they were to be professionally associated.

Reprise was run by Mo Ostin, a former accountant who had won his record business spurs with Norman Granz's Verve label. It had been feared, not least by Ostin himself, that he would be a casualty of the merger when the deal became final in September 1963. However, the way that he set about bringing the artist roster down to manageable proportions and modifying the company for its new situation had appealed to Maitland, who decided to keep the two labels going separately, with Joe Smith being promoted to run the WB division.

In the UK, Warner Bros had been distributed by Decca, while Reprise went through Pye. Following the merger, WB switched to Pye. Walter Woyda, who joined Pye in 1970 to head up its pre-recorded tape division, believes that Warners favoured Pye because of its lack of bureaucracy:

> Pye wasn't the big Decca or the big EMI where everything had to go through powerhouses. I was in direct contact God knows how many times a day with Louis Benjamin [the managing director put in by Lew Grade], and when things were decided, we went hell for leather with them. There was that personal contact between people. Nobody in Pye at the top level was not available. People liked the contact and the speed with which they dealt with things.[55]

Ray Horricks had left Decca in 1962 to start Pye's new Piccadilly pop label, and he reached a similar conclusion:

> I had been lured away at larger salary after the Newley hits, but one of the great things about Louis Benjamin was that, unlike Sir Edward Lewis at Decca, I didn't have the problem of access. Although he was a hard driving man, Louis Benjamin was very accessible. It was explained that Alan Freeman and Tony Hatch had the Pye label, but that this was the new label Piccadilly, and I had the artists on it.[56]

As well as having hits with Joe Brown and Johnny Keating, Horricks was enlisted to work on records made by visiting Reprise stars. First came a Sinatra LP with arranger Robert Farnon, with Horricks overseeing the subsidiary stereo recording, and then Sammy Davis Jr's tribute LP to the stars of the London Palladium, which Horricks produced himself[57] at the newly opened studios in the ATV and Pye head offices. The LP[58] was recorded while Davis was appearing at the Palladium, and so sessions had to begin at midnight, after he had come off-stage. Perhaps inevitably, he would bring his army of celebrity well-wishers from the theatre with him, and so Horricks had to seat them 'two-deep around the studio walls' to keep the control room clear. Then, on the last night, come the musicians' union-stipulated tea break, Davis went out one door as an army of waiters from the Berkeley Hotel came in another with trolleys full of chicken salad, strawberries and cream, wine and coffee, arranged as a 'thank you' from the singer to the orchestra and the technical staff. In this twenty minutes, Davis had disappeared to another studio nearby to record a jingle for Shell. As Horricks says, 'What a man!'

The Pye, WB and Reprise contract was not merely one-way traffic, it was reciprocal. Pye artists such as singer Petula Clark and the Kinks were released in the US on Reprise. The rockier end of the scale was to become increasingly valuable in the years to come, although things were to get a lot weirder than Muswell Hill's finest. Joe Smith was instrumental in signing the Grateful Dead to WB, while Reprise got the likes of Captain Beefheart and the Magic Band. Other less way-out signings included Joni Mitchell, Beach Boy Brian Wilson's former collaborator Van Dyke Parks and songwriter-turned-singer Randy Newman. From being a sleeve-note writer (albeit a double Grammy-winning one), Stan Cornyn became vice-president of Creative Services and presided over many highly memorable, literate and amusing advertising campaigns.

Rock was emphatically not Mo Ostin's bag. He had begun his career at the jazz label Verve. Reprise in the pre-WB era had not been cutting edge but somehow he managed to build what Jerry Wexler called 'possibly the most tasteful and commercial record label of its day', bringing in some of the best new rock acts in the process. How did he do it? Stan Cornyn has a few ideas, which he outlined in the programme copy he wrote for Ostin's 2003 induction into the Rock and Roll Hall of Fame. First, the cons:

Mo's ears...have never been called Golden. Mo Ostin never fixed a single's hook. Facing a keyboard, he never could do an E Flat diminished. He never claimed to know how a take might catch more fire. He attended few record sessions, and even when he did, never leaned over the engineer's shoulder to suggest a thing. He never partied 'til four. He took no drugs. He didn't dance, couldn't even hop well. He didn't know better than his employees. He was unlike record execs who came before ...

Now the pros:

With a growing appetite for individuality, Mo began stunning us with side-of-the-ditchers like the Fugs, Tiny Tim, Zappa, the Kinks, Hendrix, what *is* this stuff, Mo?...Mo's signings took on the courage of a believer, often like Galileo in Rome, when no one could understand it. Mo sought the dedicated, non-usual artist. Not only that, he stuck with the ones he signed ... Mo's Warner/Reprise became a Field of Dreams, whose motto read 'If you let them play their music, the people will come...'

The combination of dangerous signings plus flip and determined marketing, attracted singer-songwriters and then, as LSD began outselling Pepsi, acid-drenched amp bangers ... He employed record nuts like Lenny [Waronker], Andy [Wickham], Teddy, and – oh, I knew I shouldn't have started this list, because there were just dozens of us – men and women Mo adopted as his own ears. [We] grew beards, bought ankhs, wore Nehru shirts, because we believed in this revolution. We indulged the revolution's stars. For the Grand Guignol rock act Alice Cooper, it was arranged that, instead of a normal inner sleeve on 'School's Out', Alice'd have a paper inner sleeve of pink ladies' panties. 'Of course.' Mo was number one in Coddling.

Other record companies didn't catch on. They thought this odd music was noise. Mo knew better. If he could not understand what he heard, he'd listen more, and ask more people.[59]

While all of this increased grooviness was getting under way, in 1967 Warner Bros had been acquired by Seven Arts, a company best known for its TV syndication business, for which it had previously acquired a large chunk of the WB film archive. The deal saw Jack Warner receiving $20 a share for his one-third of the business, with everyone else receiving just $5 per share. Still in acquisitive mood, the head of the renamed Warner-Seven Arts, Elliott Hyman went after Atlantic. His timing was perfect. By this stage of the game, most of Atlantic's rivals and contemporaries had been taken over or had gone under. In the 1950s, they had gone big with Ray Charles and Bobby Darin, maintaining the momentum nicely in the 1960s. Meanwhile, the company had switched its European representation. 'We really established ourselves in England as a label after we left Decca,' explains Ahmet Ertegun. 'We had a deal with Polydor, and Robert Stigwood was our A&R chief. Then I began signing a lot of English artists – Cream, Blind Faith, Led Zeppelin, Emerson Lake and Palmer, Yes, King Crimson and Mott the Hoople'.[60]

Jerry Wexler and Nesuhi Ertegun, however, were unsure of how long it could all go on and were in favour of cashing in while still riding high. Ahmet Ertegun was against the idea, but the votes of his two other partners

251

over-ruled him, and a deal was agreed to sell Atlantic for $17.5m. This had seemed like a lot of money to Wexler and the Ertegun brothers, but their euphoria was diminished somewhat by the fact that Atlantic's cash reserves meant that Warner-Seven Arts was, in effect, getting the company for just $10m. Moreover, after twenty years of successful independence, corporate life and becoming a salaried employee, albeit one with a large shareholding in the new group, did not sit well with the Atlantic men. Ahmet Ertegun says:

> By far the worst business decision I ever made was agreeing to sell Atlantic to Warner-Seven Arts. To begin with it was foisted on me. By that time, Miriam had left the company. Jerry Wexler and my brother both were a bit older than me, and they wanted to sell. They didn't want the hassle and running the risk of losing everything. It seemed like a safe road and they more or less talked me into it, but I really did not want to. I fought them off until the very end. Once in, though, I became much more a part of the group than they did. I decided, well I'll make the best of it.[61]

In the event, Seven Arts's ownership of Warner was a brief and, for the record men, not particularly enjoyable interlude. In 1969, Hyman decided to sell out, following a heart attack. At this point, the Erteguns and Jerry Wexler made a bid to buy their label back for $40m. Hyman said no. Instead, the vastly expanded group – valued at $400m – was sold on as a job lot to Kinney Services, a diverse company to say the least. It had begun as a funeral operator, before making the move into car parks and office cleaning. Then, in 1967, with the purchase of Ted Ashley's Ashley Famous talent agency, the group moved into the show business. The man behind the expansion was a sharp entrepreneur called Steve Ross, who was also rumoured to be friendly with the Mob.

Ertegun was unimpressed by the arrival of Kinney. 'When we sold it, we had short contracts, and by the time Steve Ross came in, I had decided to leave and I think so had my brother,' he reveals. He was not, however, prepared for Ross's charm offensive. 'I told him we were leaving. He did everything in the world to make us stay. My brother wanted to have a soccer team, so that's how we started the Cosmos soccer club. That was one of many bonuses he gave us to stay on.' Most famously, Ross, who had no idea about rock music, had boned up on the subject to impress Ertegun. Although Ertegun was still intent on leaving, he had dinner with Ross, and

A 1924 advertisement for the Decca portable gramophone – a favourite in the trenches but, in peace time, just the thing for garden parties and punting trips.

Left Sir Edward Lewis, the buccaneering stockbroker who took Decca into the record business and kept competition alive in the British music industry.

Right Decca calls a halt to its war of advertising against EMI, 1953.

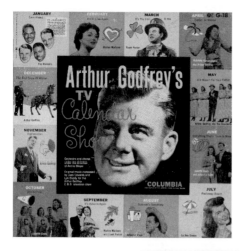

Arthur Godfrey's TV Calendar Show – released in 1953 and one of the first big hits of the long-playing era.

Columbia in the ascendant: Goddard Lieberson (a.k.a. 'God'), Broadway composer Jerry Herman and a young Clive Davis present Angela Lansbury with some wall ornaments, July 1967.

Meanwhile in Decca studio 3… (left to right) producer Ray Horricks, engineer Arthur Lilley (resting chin on hand), composer/arranger Johnny Keating, pianist Reg Guest and producer Tony d'Amato search for the Capitol Records sound on a Caterina Valente session, July 1964.

Above right & left HMV and Columbia advertise their wares in the programme from the 1928 show *So This Is Love*. HMV might have the 'jolliest songs', but Columbia has the 'original theatre artists', a competitive advantage the company maintained for many years.

Right Nipper's French cousin, c. 1935.

Left The *Minneapolis Journal*'s take on the recording debuts of Taft and Bryan, 1908.

Right Bruce Lundvall, ex-Columbia and Elektra, now head of Blue Note and benefactor of Ms Norah Jones.

Far right Doug Morris, ex-Atlantic and now chairman, CEO and general head of absolutely everything at the frighteningly vast Universal Music.

Above EMI chairman Sir Joseph Lockwood and the Beatles celebrate their mutual good fortune.

Right A 1984 trade ad for Dire Straits on CD. Their next album – *Brothers in Arms* – would establish both the band and the format as major forces.

happened to mention his latest signing, the group Blind Faith. Ross now had his chance. A friend's son had given him all of the information about the new group, so he was able to answer with 'You mean the one with Stevie Winwood on the organ plus the old Cream, and you haven't got a record but you've sold out Madison Square Garden?'[62] Ertegun decided to give him a second chance.

For all of his dubious associations, Ross turned out to be a good overlord for the seemingly disparate Warner-Reprise-Atlantic grouping, leaving Ostin, Smith, Ertegun and Wexler largely to their own devices. 'He thought the music business must be easy, because we seemed to be bringing in a lot of cash, no problem. As a result, he would put anybody in to be the general head of it. So every company would be running itself, but they would have to report to somebody who would be the nominal head of music.' This was bearable, as long as Ross's appointee could be ignored, which was generally what happened. 'The previous environment had not been that bad, it was just that Warner-Seven Arts was run by a bunch of idiots,' observes Ertegun. 'Steve Ross was a kind of salesman/conman type, but he was very, very generous, open, good-hearted and I got along with him fine. Everything was great.'[63]

In 1970, the group was supplemented by the acquisition, for $10m, of the Elektra label. The company had begun twenty years earlier, founded by Jacob 'Jac' Holzman, a hi-fi nut '[a]s nerd as has ever been born',[64] and his college friend Paul Rickolt. Elektra had begun as the result of a bet between the two that they could make a better LP than the major labels – a bold pronouncement considering that LP had only just been launched. With each putting in $300, they began recording. The first Elektra release was a recording of a suite of German and Japanese poems set to music by the composer John Gruen. The company's mode of recording was cheap. One microphone, one tape recorder, all recorded on location wherever the music happened to be. Folk music, which suited this mode of working, became a staple of the Elektra catalogue.

From its highbrow start, Elektra had found by the mid-1950s that collections of bawdy songs sold better and began a run of LPs with titles like *When Dalliance Was in Flower and Young Maidens Lost Their Heads*, which proved popular with servicemen. Holzman had bought Rickolt out for $1,000 when he was drafted into the Army. In his place, came Leonard Ripley, who put in $10,000 and took on some of the recording responsibilities. In 1958, however, Ripley – prompted by his wife Alexandra, who took umbrage at the fact that her husband had invested more than Holzman, but only had a minority stake – sued Holzman. With financial help from his father and record retailer Sam Goody, whom Holzman had stood up for four years earlier when he went bankrupt, Holzman bought Ripley out for $25,000.

The Elektra that Kinney was so keen to buy was very different from the company that had made the smut LPs. In 1965, the company had employed Paul Rothchild, who took Elektra into rock music, with the Paul Butterfield Blues Band and the Doors. Then there was Judy Collins, maintaining Elektra's links with folk music. Holzman had, in the meantime, seen the future mapped out for him. Returning from what Stan Cornyn calls a 'Journey of Discovery' to Hawaii, he decided to sell the company and retire to the island. He achieved the first part, but not quite the second, as he continued to be heavily involved in Elektra for several more years.

The arrival of Kinney brought an end to one aspect of the old order, though. The existing overseas affiliations were replaced by wholly owned subsidiaries. In London, Pye was abandoned in favour of a new company called the Kinney Record Group, run by former ex-Pye executive Ian Ralfini with the help of the Beatles's former PR man Derek Taylor. All of these new operations reported to a new company – WEA International – and it was natural that Ross should choose the son of an ambassador to represent his record group overseas, Nesuhi Ertegun.

Another US operation was pulling away from the old licensing model. In June 1962, the Music Corporation of America, the country's largest and most powerful talent agency, had bought an 80 per cent controlling interest in Decca Records. The timing of the move was inflammatory, coming in the middle of a Justice Department investigation into MCA's stranglehold on the entertainment business. Not content with representing the talent, the company had built a very profitable television production arm, responsible for such hits as *The Phil Silvers Show*. MCA's main motivation for buying Decca was to gain the Universal film operation that Milton Rackmil had bought eleven years earlier. There were links already. MCA owned the Universal lot, which it then rented to Rackmil's ailing production company, which had sold off its valuable pre-1948 archive and not really grasped the potential of television production.

Before the Justice Department could order MCA to do anything, it announced that it would voluntarily sell off its agency business to concentrate on television, film and records. When it emerged that the proposed management buy-out of the agency was to be funded by a loan from MCA's founder, Jules Stein, the government cried foul and gave MCA twenty-four hours to close the agency, which it did. President Lew Wasserman sent a terse letter to all clients stating that MCA was 'no longer engaged in the representation of talent in the entertainment industry and you may seek representation by anyone you desire.'[65]

Towards the end of the 1960s, the MCA-owned US Decca labels finally broke free of the English operation that had created them in the 1930s. A British subsidiary was set up at the MCA building on Piccadilly under Brian Brolly, but the new management was not as sure-footed as their Kinney counterparts had been, if Derek Everett's experience was anything to go by:

> Well, they went out on their own and got into a terrible state. Brian Brolly was managing director, bless him. He used to keep calling me at CBS. 'Derek, do you know about so and so?' 'Yeah.' 'Er, what do I do?' 'Well, Brian…' 'Oh thanks, Derek. Must have lunch'. And you'd think, 'Who's running this outfit?' A lovely man, but he didn't seem to know what he was doing at that point.[66]

Added to this, the UK side of things was definitely a susbidiary, says Roger Watson, who had begun his career working for Tony Hall at Decca, and who came in as head of promotion. 'The UK company was in the pockets of the American company. We were very much a branch office.' Even so, it was possible to have some indigenous successes, one of which was the original London concept recording of *Jesus Christ Superstar*:

> We had Mike d'Abo [from Manfred Mann], Ian Gillan [from Deep Purple] and the Trinidad singers on that session, which we did at Olympic in Barnes. The band was the Grease Band. Everyone was offered a session fee or a royalty. Ian Gillan, who didn't need the money, took a royalty. So did the Trinidad singers. Mike d'Abo took a session fee. It then went on to sell 7 million double albums. It was huge. That was great to be involved with. I was getting a bit browned off with promotion. I wanted to go into production and so I really got a feel for being in the studio.[67]

Having supplied so much advice to Brolly, it was perhaps unsurprising

255

that Everett should get the call when Brolly left:

I don't quite know how the MCA thing came about. I was getting a bit tired at
CBS, it was doing very well. I always remember a lunch one day with Glancy,
and I thought I'd set the wheels in motion. You get that feeling after five years
and, I don't know. I said, 'Look, I might come to you one of these fine days and
say I want to leave.' He said, 'Why?' 'Well, I think that we've achieved all that we
can achieve. We can only level off or go down.' He said, 'Do you really think
that? I wish I had your faith.' I said, 'It's running, it's only going to do what it
does now. Nothing else can be done. You've got to keep stoking it now or get
the kicks in the backside for it going down.' Anyway, he said, 'You don't have a
problem. Any time you want to go, let me know.' But that didn't work out.

We had a sales conference coming up and I had to do a presentation, so I'd
done all this, I'd done all that. Again, I got a phone call one evening, about six
o'clock. I was in the office. 'Derek, you still there? Come up, I've got a couple
of people here.' So I go upstairs and inside is Oberstein, Robinson and the
company secretary, George Shestopol ... So we're just sitting there. 'All right
for the sales conference?' 'Yeah.' 'Speech ready?' 'Yeah.' 'Music ready?' 'Yeah.'
'Well, I've got you all here to tell you that I've left,' says Glancy. I'm
dumbfounded. I know nothing. I was close to him. The other three looked at
me and said, 'You knew.' I'd been approached by MCA and I was going to go
to him the following week and say I want to leave. So my mind's gone blank.
I'm thinking, 'Oh my God, what am I going to do? Who do I go to now? It's
sales conference week.'[68]

Everett eventually got his freedom, but not before having some fun at the
expense of Oberstein (of which more later). One of the star artists on
MCA in this period was Neil Diamond, but he was slow to take off in the
UK:

He had three albums out in the UK catalogue and they'd all sold about 3,000
copies, if that. He was nothing. Suddenly, he came up with 'Sweet Caroline', he
came over, promoted it and, whoosh, the career takes off, and you're a hero
and it's wonderful. Until you fall out with him, but that's another story. These
guys are lovely. When he first came over, he hadn't had a hit and he was
wonderful. He'd do anything anywhere. The next time, he was a little bit
difficult. He wanted a party. I said, 'Let me try an idea. I'd like to repeat
something that we did with Andy Williams at CBS. We did a wonderful after-

show party after the Albert Hall. We did it at a nice venue, we got the people over from the Albert Hall, all the invited guests, you come round, shake a few hands and we give them dinner. It worked a treat. It was wonderful.' And it was. The thing we did for Andy was marvellous. 'I ain't doing that,' he said. 'Fine', I said, 'if you don't want to do it, don't do it.'

The next time Diamond came to the UK, he had come round to the idea, but wanted to organize it himself, which he did in a friend's penthouse flat off Piccadilly. 'It was the biggest fiasco I'd ever seen in my life,' recounts Everett, still shuddering at the memory:

It was just a penthouse flat, but it had a little balcony at the back over which somebody had put a tarpaulin. By the time I got there, you couldn't get in. Richard Harris was in there, apparently, on a bit of a bender, complaining that he was hot and that he was going to rip the tarpaulin off the roof and do all sorts of maniacal things. I thought, 'I'll go in, make sure I'm seen and then get the hell out of here.' So I did that, made sure a few people saw me, saw someone with a camera, got them to take a picture of me, thank you very much. When he [Diamond] gets there, he refuses to go in. 'I'm not going in there. It's too many people.' I said, 'I don't believe this. First of all you don't do one when it's properly organized, this time you want to do it, now you won't go in.' He said, 'I'm not going in there.' I said, 'There's hundreds of people in there who can't move, the perspiration's running down their faces, they can't get to the bar, I don't think you're very popular.' It disintegrated a bit after that, our relationship.

The next time he came in – we used to pick him up with the chauffeur and arrange all that – he wouldn't tell me where he was staying. He rented a house and said, 'I don't want Everett to know where I am.' Fine, but the fact that we booked the chauffeur to take him there doesn't appear to have entered his head.[69]

At the threshold of the 1970s, everything had changed. Former associates were now pitched rivals, out to get as much of the global market as they could, and new operators had come in to divide the spoils further – one being a powerhouse of former independents all still being run in a largely autonomous manner. Meanwhile, more competition was on its way.

11 The spirit of independence

Musically, the late 1960s and the early 1970s were a wonderfully fertile time. In the US, Warners and Columbia had made the counterculture pay. Meanwhile, in the UK, progressive rock bands such as Yes, Genesis, Pink Floyd, Emerson, Lake and Palmer, and lesser lights like Van de Graaf Generator, were stretching out and using long-playing records to accommodate longer songs and themed compositions. Unfortunately, as the 1970s wore on, such expansiveness coincided with a grave crisis in raw materials. The precious and all-important vinyl was derived from oil, for which both the US and Britain were reliant on Middle Eastern countries, which had banded together in 1960 to form the Organization of Petroleum Exporting Countries.

Call it a cartel or just good old-fashioned collective bargaining, but in October 1973, against the backcloth of the Yom Kippur war, the OPEC members decided that they weren't being paid enough for their oil. The result was an embargo on supplies to the US and a 70 per cent price rise on supplies to its allies. This was bad news for an industry that was just getting into double albums and triple gatefold sleeves. When West Coast funk band Tower of Power recorded a song 'Only So Much Oil in the Ground' ('We can't cut loose without that juice,' they told us over a righteous groove) on their 1974 Warner Bros album *Urban Renewal*, the sentiments might as well have come straight from WB high command in beautiful downtown Burbank.

When the oil situation was coupled with a strike by the British coal miners, the UK was plunged into an energy crisis that forced Edward Heath's Tory government to declare a three-day working week, with frequent power cuts in the evening. So, with the wax itself at a premium and the electricity to run the turntables equally scarce, business in the record industry was far from buoyant. After such slumps, it had been traditional to pull out some marvellous new innovation to re-enthuse the purchasing public. This time the big idea was quadraphonic sound. Decca was in the forefront of the experimentation, as it had been with stereo. Engineer Brian Masters remembers:

> Some time around 1970, we started recording tests in quadraphonic sound. Using studio downtime and specially booked time, we would record everything from violin solos to speech recitations to full orchestras. Union restrictions at the time meant that we couldn't set up a second set of microphones on legitimate existing sessions and record a special feed in a separate room, as this would classify as 'double recording', and would require a special fee. I'm sure Decca would have paid the fee – they were, after all, shelling out for the musicians a second time around anyway – but it was banned. At least with specially booked musicians, we could stop and start them at will and nobody minded people coming in and moving microphones. The musicians very much entered into the spirit of things as an exciting experiment, and I only recall one dissenter who, when asked if he'd mind joining a conga around Studio One, darkly muttered, 'Piss off. I'm a percussionist, not a fucking party act.'[1]

Sadly, with equipment expensive and several incompatible systems on offer, quad did not catch on, and surround sound's day was delayed a little longer.

A large part of the musical expansion that took place in the late 1960s and early 1970s was due to a new wave of independent labels, all carving out healthy reputations for themselves at the expense of the majors. Once again, many of them sprung from the need to serve niches that the established labels were ignoring.

One such label was Island, founded in 1962 by Chris Blackwell, the son of a white Jamaican plantation owner, to give the music of his home island, particularly reggae, an outlet. The company's initial entry into the British market came through a licensing deal with Philips – Blackwell's Island produced the masters and they were then released on either Philips or Fontana. The biggest hits of the label's early years had been 'My Boy Lollipop' by the fifteen-year-old Jamaican singer Millie Small – which reached number two in 1964 – and a brace of number ones from Birmingham's own Spencer Davis Group – 'Keep on Running' and 'Somebody Help Me'. Their bass player, Muff Winwood,[2] recalls:

> I don't know how many years he [Blackwell] had been over here. Not that

long, but he was releasing lots of Jamaican records which sold well to the Jamaican population. He had come to Birmingham while Millie was on tour, and somebody told him that we were the best band in Birmingham. He came to see us and that led to him managing us. Then, as we became more successful, also his own Jamaican labels became more successful, and he decided to have an indie label. At that time, my brother [Steve Winwood] and I were both a little disillusioned with the band that we were in, and my brother said to me that he was going to form this group called Traffic. I thought it was an ideal moment to get out myself, and Blackwell said to me, 'You're an ideal person to work in a record company, will you come and work in this fledgling Island?' I wasn't given an A&R job. It was like any independent that you get today, three or four blokes in a room, running around, doing everything. That would be in about 1968, I suppose.'

By the start of the 1970s, with the help of Traffic's massive success, Island had built up its own distinct label identity, and was on the verge of breaking free of Philips. Based initially in Oxford Street, the company moved to Notting Hill in 1970, where it had established its own studio in a former church in Basing Street. From this base, the company grew massively. Winwood expands:

We went from four blokes in a room to forty people. The record industry, really, had exploded in the late 1960s on a worldwide basis and continued to do so right through the 1970s. Island was a hot, happening little label and it grew along with the rest of the industry, really. We had lots of interesting acts that led the way. I plugged at Radio 1, I also phoned up booking gigs for the acts at universities and things like that. We managed the bands, we did everything. I don't think you can do that now. We also published them, agented them and marketed them. We did everything for them. To be fair, Chris was the final arbiter of taste. We all pitched in with things and ideas, but at the end of the day, he very much had the final say.'

The acts that took Island into its next stage included Cat Stevens, Jimmy Cliff, Fairport Convention and Free. Meanwhile the label also gave shelter to acts who were influential and important beyond their sales figures, such as Nick Drake and John Martyn. Later, in the mid-1970s, came more smash artists, such as Bob Marley and the Wailers, and the Sparks. The latter represented Winwood's first step into production, which was to become the main part of his career. 'I couldn't get anybody to produce them. So I said to Chris, "I know what's supposed to happen with this thing. I'll produce them. I know music." I'd never bothered to do this before. So I produced them and we had a big hit. I started to get people phoning in, asking me to produce things.'

Winwood brought the subject up with Blackwell and asked him how he wanted to play it. The answer that came would still have been unthinkable in a corporate environment like EMI or Decca, where staff were staff and freelancers remained utterly separate, and shows how different Blackwell and his ilk were to their predecessors in the industry. In short, he gave Winwood the go-ahead to moonlight:

> He suggested that I should run the studios. By then we'd moved out of Basing Street and into Hammersmith, but we kept the studios. He said, 'I need someone to run that, so why don't you run it and do production? If you want to produce anybody outside, you can do, you can make your own deal, get any money you earn, you can do what you like as long as you run the studios. This was fantastic, so I then went off and did that in the mid-seventies.[5]

All along, Blackwell was a 'hands-on' label boss, as Richard Elen, who joined Island Studios as an assistant engineer in 1971, remembers:

> He would be involved in a lot of sessions, either actually producing in the case of his special friends who were signed to the label, notably the Wailers and Traffic in my period, or sitting in. He had a special rapport with the reggae bands, having been brought up in the Caribbean. He would speak to you in cultured English about some aspect of the recording and then turn to the band and switch into Jamaican patois, very impressive. We used to do a lot of reggae. Not just the Wailers, but all kinds of Jamaican etc artists, and they were great fun to work with. It's a joke now, but I am sure that on one of those sessions, a guy in the band during the mix said he wanted 'Full boost at all frequency, man.'[6]

Elen also remembers Blackwell as a risk-taker, something that marked out most of the new independent label bosses:

> I suspect he did a lot of things on whim or suggestion or what felt good to him at the time, and not from any good business reason. He would never have signed Mott the Hoople, for example, if his girlfriend at the time hadn't said she liked them. But his genius was also seeing the potential of Jamaican music in the UK. He would bring the original eight-tracks over from the Jamaica studios, overdub on them at Basing Street and mix. In those days record companies were up for taking chances – probably the reason why the music scene was so lively and exciting in those days, unlike today – and he certainly did.[7]

Like Virgin later, Chrysalis – the label name being inspired by the names of its founders Chris Wright and Terry Ellis – was tied up with Island in its earliest days. 'Terry Ellis was the manager of Jethro Tull, and they joined Island. Then he and Chris brought Roxy Music in. We eventually gave them their own label, Chrysalis, and that was when Chrysalis crystallized,' Muff Winwood explains.

Roger Watson joined Chrysalis's music publishing arm just as its record label was coming into being: 'Chris Blackwell said he'd give them a label if "Thick as a Brick" [by Jethro Tull] made top ten. It did, so he did.' In 1975, Watson was despatched overseas to expand the business:

> I'd hit twenty runs off Chris when he was living in Wokingham. We were in the elevator at Bird Street next morning. He said, 'Well done Roger, come up, I've got a proposition for you.' I thought he was going to ask me to captain the cricket team, but Terry wanted me to go to America. They gave me an hour to think about it, I had my leaving party on Friday and I was on the plane on Sunday.
>
> Terry had hair down to his belt, so he was nicknamed Doris. You always thought you could shoot the shit with him, because he looked like a dude with the hair, but he was serious.[8]

Over in the States, Chrysalis tied up with Warner Bros and got to work. As well as the Tull and Procol Harum, there was a young English singer called Leo Sayer to work on, and later Billy Idol, Pat Benatar and Blondie. 'It was a great time,' Watson states. 'English music was hot. I used to drive over to Burbank once a month with our new releases and play them to [Ed] Rosenblatt, [Stan] Cornyn and [Mo] Ostin. However, the plan was to go independent as soon as we could. We went for independent distribution and we hired a guy who knew the independents well.'

While Island was getting under way in the UK, the USA saw the foundation of A&M Records by musician Herb Alpert and promotion man Jerry Moss. However, while the company undoubtedly satisfied the niche occupied by the infuriatingly catchy records made by Alpert with his Tijuana Brass, the main motivation for the two partners was to exercise more control over their work. 'Herb and I had both separately produced records before we got together and we'd leased the masters to the major companies,' explained Jerry Moss in a 1973 interview with *Music Week* magazine. 'We felt that was unsatisfactory because we didn't have any say in the product once it had been leased ... We never got the feeling they gave the records everything they had.'[9]

Starting with each partner contributing a master and $100, the company took its first steps in the summer of 1962, initially as Carnival Records, a division of Moss's Irving Music publishing business. The first release was 'Tell It to the Birds', which featured Alpert as the lead vocalist, but was released under the name of his son, Dore Alpert. It sold almost 15,000 copies in Los Angeles, where the pair were based, but did less well elsewhere, so they licensed it to Randy Wood's Dot label. The second release, Moss's contribution 'Love Is Back in Style' by Charlie Robinson, 'didn't do anything',[10] but with the profits from 'Tell It to the Birds' plus $750 from Dot, they were well under way.

Between that and the next release, it had been discovered that another label was already trading as Carnival, and so Alpert and Moss renamed the company after their initials. The first A&M release was 'The Lonely Bull (El Solo Toro)' by Alpert, this time using his own name. 'That record we didn't sell to Dot,' reflected Moss. 'We kept it and we eventually sold 700,000 records nationally ... [which] brought in over 100,000 dollars.'[11] The label had been a part-time pursuit for both, but with this success, they moved into Alpert's garage and went full-time.

The following year, A&M moved to offices on Hollywood's Sunset Boulevard. Although the LP of the 'The Lonely Bull' was a top ten hit, the label didn't have another major success until 1965, when Alpert's recording of 'A Taste of Honey' reached number one in the *Cash Box* charts.[12] By the end of the year, Alpert's group had brought in the label's first two gold records, and the company had grossed nearly $6m. The drought had been partially due to increased competition from the majors: Moss pointed out to *Music Week* that CBS had countered with a soundalike act called the Arena Brass. Despite these incursions, the Alpert output had sold steadily, at one point accounting for nearly 80 per cent of the label's income. Also, A&M was building a catalogue with the likes of Sergio Mendes and Brasil '66, and the Baja Marimba Band.

At EMI in London, Derek Everett was trying his best to help Alpert and Moss, but was meeting with some resistance from the bean-counters:

> We'd picked up some singles from A&M – a couple of Tijuana Brass things – and I wanted to try and get a deal for the catalogue. While I was away on holiday, a guy called Frank Chalmers – I think he was in the international business – met with either the lawyer or one of Herb Alpert or Jerry Moss and came up with the classic line to them when they said they'd like to make it a catalogue deal. He said, 'You don't have a catalogue, old chap', meaning they'd only got half a dozen records or something. I came back and I said, 'I can't believe you said that to somebody'. He said, 'Well they haven't, old chap. They've only got six records. A catalogue's 500 records.' All that nonsense. I thought I'd better talk to LG [Wood] about it and I said, 'He's turned that thing down.' 'Yes,' he said, 'there's not much I can do about it. He's done it. What's done is done.' So that was that.
>
> Fairly hot on the heels of it, I think, Larry Utall of Bell Records was looking for a deal. We had a couple of records from him and I said we should turn it into a catalogue deal. Chalmers, again, said, 'No, not worth it', and they'd just signed Del Shannon. I said we should have it. So, I remember this meeting, the three of us, Chalmers, myself and LG, and it's going back and forth … and eventually LG said, 'What do you think, Everett?' I said, 'We should definitely do it. They've got Del Shannon' and whatever other artists they had. He said, 'All right, we'll go with it. On your head be it, young man.' It was one of those deals and it was a very successful deal as it happens. We had the hits. We had all of these battles to take care of all the way through.[13]

In November 1966, A&M moved into the place it was to call home for the rest of its existence – Charlie Chaplin's old film studios on North La Brea

Avenue in Hollywood – at the same time as it opened an East Coast office in Philadelphia. As well as the offices, the Hollywood complex was to house A&M's four in-house recording studios. In 1967, A&M began distributing Creed Taylor's CTI jazz label, whose artists included guitarist Wes Montgomery, a massive seller in jazz terms. At the same time, a connection with Denny Cordell and David Platz of Essex Music in London brought in the Move, Procol Harum and Joe Cocker. Then, in 1969, the same year as A&M began a close association with Island in the UK, came the act who were to bankroll A&M through the 1970s, the Carpenters. In 1970, after Lou Adler had fallen out with Clive Davis, Alpert and Moss began distributing Adler's Ode label. This move brought in the mammoth success of Carole King's *Tapestry* LP, which spent fifteen weeks at number one on the *Billboard* pop album chart in 1971.

The hits just kept on coming. Captain and Tennille. Humble Pie. Paul Williams. Peter Frampton. Squeeze. Joe Jackson. Then, in March 1978, the group who were to dominate proceedings for the next few years until the three protagonists decided that they couldn't stand each other – the Police.[14] A major rock act like this was just what A&M needed at the end of the 1970s. A global recession was under way, and it served to scupper A&M's plans to build its own distribution network. By the end of the decade, the company had abandoned its independent distributors and pressing plants and had signed with RCA for both functions in the US.

Unlike Island and A&M, who were born in an earlier era, and came of age in the 1970s, Virgin was a precocious child of that decade. Its equally precocious founder was Richard Branson, a Stowe-educated entrepreneur who, before he was even in his twenties, had established a national magazine called *Student* and begun the Virgin record retail business. In 1971, the retail arm had a nasty run-in with the inspectors from HM Customs and Excise when it was discovered that Branson had been obtaining export licences for records that he was buying for the major labels, without actually exporting them. Instead, the discs were going straight into the Virgin shops, avoiding the tedious encumbrance of purchase tax. Saddled with a £60,000 fine for the subterfuge, Branson rationalized that the best way to get out of a hole was to trade out of it. So the company set about expanding rapidly, opening new branches all over the country and, at the suggestion of Branson's South African-born cousin Simon Draper, a record label.

Virgin had already moved into the creative side of the industry when Branson had bought a manor house in Shipton-on-Cherwell, Oxfordshire, with a view to turning it into a state-of-the-art residential recording studio, allowing artists to 'get their heads together in the country' as was then popular. To buy the Manor (as it became known), he had borrowed from banks and members of his family, setting a pattern for the way that Virgin would expand in the future. In this regard, he was not so dissimilar to Edward Lewis forty years earlier.

The logic behind the Virgin label was that the company's 'three businesses [studio, label and shops] were mutually compatible and would benefit the bands we signed, since we could reduce prices at the Manor, the manufacturing end, and increase promotion at the shops, the retail end, while still making our own profit'.[15] Like Island and A&M, Virgin also realized the value of having its own music publishing division from the off, keeping all of its copyrights in the family.

The first artist to join the label was Mike Oldfield, an introspective type with a background in folk music, whose contract gave him a 5 per cent royalty on 90 per cent of wholesale (the 10 per cent deduction was for breakages, as was traditional across all royalty-based contracts throughout the history of the business, although the practice of making the artist bear this cost is highly questionable), potentially a great improvement on the old penny per single that Cliff, the Shadows and the Beatles all got when they started out. Oldfield was allowed to use the Manor when it wasn't being used by other artists, and over the winter of 1972 and the spring of 1973, in this piecemeal fashion, he assembled a record called *Tubular Bells*.

Oldfield's LP hit the shops on 25 May 1973, part of Virgin's four-album launch release. The others were *Flying Teapot* by Gong, *The Faust Tapes* by the German band Faust and *Manor Live*, a jam session featuring the singer Elkie Brooks. To get things rolling, the heavy-going Faust record was offered for the price of a single, which, Branson reflects, 'won attention for the new Virgin Music label, although probably more on the grounds of fool-hardiness than judgement'.[16] At the rock-bottom price of 48p, the disc shifted 100,000 copies in a month.

In the long term, though, it was *Tubular Bells* that made the running, and at full price, too. Sales were disappointing initially, but they went stellar after forward-thinking Radio 1 DJ John Peel got behind the record, raving over it on his show. It went on to sell 13 million copies (and counting), a fact that sits amusingly with the fact that Branson initially queried the £20 cost of hiring a set of tubular bells for Oldfield, announcing that he hoped they were worth it.

It was decided to approach Island and ask if they were willing to undertake a pressing and distribution deal for the new label. The answer came back that Island was interested in Virgin, but only if they were licensing the label, as they had Tony Stratton-Smith's Charisma. The terms of the licensing deal were very favourable, but while the risks to Virgin would have been greatly reduced, so would the potential rewards. The maths spoke for itself. With Island, Branson and Draper estimated, a million copies sold would bring in £285,000 for Virgin. On their own, 600,000 copies would bring in £920,000. Threatening to take their business to CBS, Virgin got their own way. 'Our gamble that we could promote it [*Tubular Bells*] ourselves made us our first fortune,' said Branson.[17] To serve the US, a deal was set up with Ahmet Ertegun at Atlantic.

After a couple of years, though, it became obvious that Virgin was subsisting almost entirely on income from Mike Oldfield's releases. With the help of Ken Berry, who had started out in the company's Notting Hill shop, the roster was expanded. Then, in 1977 came the chance for the free-and-easy Virgin to show its mettle and succeed where other more orthodox companies simply had to fail. In October 1976, EMI had signed the Sex Pistols, after punk-friendly staff producer Mike Thorne had taken his boss, A&R man Nick Mobbs, to see the band playing in Doncaster and sold him on the idea. Their first single, 'Anarchy in the UK', came out in early November, around the same time as their infamous appearance on Thames Television's magazine programme *Today* in which presenter Bill Grundy hit on one of the group's hangers-on[18] before goading the band into swearing profusely.

With the resulting media furore, the group came to the attention of EMI chairman Sir John Read. The band went off on tour and as the headlines got more and more lurid when the band were banned in several of the scheduled stops, Read and the board decided that they were not suitable for a respectable organization such as EMI (which also owned a large chunk of Thames). As Mike Thorne says:

> The tour staggered through a few more gigs, not good for business on the road but terrific for record sales. The outrage started to percolate even further through, to 'them above'. And then up to the chairman's office. EMI was a pillar of the establishment at that time, and the biggest chiefs might reasonably expect an eventual mention in the New Year Honours list and

letters to add to the end of their name. But here were these noisy children causing outrage and singing sarcastic songs about our nice Queen in the year before her Silver Jubilee.[19]

Mobbs was summoned to a meeting with Read, in which the situation was laid out. The Pistols were to be dropped by EMI, who forfeited the £50,000 they had given the band on signing.

Next stop: A&M, for whom they signed in a staged ceremony directly outside Buckingham Palace in March 1977, price £75,000. They proved to be too much even for the laid-back A&M, although the signs were clear enough after the signing when Sid Vicious threw up all over the desk of managing director Derek Green. After two months, during which the label released nothing by their new signings, the Pistols were again dropped. Simon Draper had turned them down before their signing to EMI and had watched the circus with regret. Now, Virgin got a second chance, winning the UK rights to the band's first LP for £15,000 with £50,000 to follow for the rest of the world. Immediately, the group's manager Malcolm McLaren set about trying to get the band sacked again, so that he could take the money and run to another label, but to his 'horror and bemusement we refused to be outraged'.[20] The LP *Never Mind the Bollocks* – including 'EMI (Unlimited Edition)', a scathing attack by the band on their old label – was the hoped-for controversial success, with the authorities swooping on the Nottingham Virgin store because of the rude word in the title. Virgin won the ensuing obscenity case after James Kingsley, a linguistics professor at the city's university, was cross-examined by the counsel for the defence, the barrister and novelist John Mortimer. Kingsley explained that 'bollocks' was an ancient word for priests and that the term had come to mean 'rubbish' – 'due to priests' sermons being full of it'.[21] Kingsley's testimony was lent further veracity by the fact that he turned out to be a vicar himself. The case won Virgin a lot of kudos, and wiped out its by-now embarrassing hippie image. Over the next few years, it would become home to the Sparks, XTC, Human League and Phil Collins.

Meanwhile, other labels were doing their bit to push back the boundaries of taste. Warners became involved in a two-and-a-half-year fight with the pressure group Women Against Violence Against Women regarding 'sexually violent images in record advertising'. WAVAW had proposed a boycott of all WEA product following a Rolling Stones billboard ad for *Black and Blue* (the exact nature of the ad is unknown). Warners parried the coverage with some unintentionally funny statistics that it thought showed the company and the industry in a favourable light. Wrote *Billboard:* 'Bob Rolontz, WCI information director, estimates that perhaps 50 out of 5,000 album covers might be considered "violent" and that few acts intentionally aim for a violent album cover.'[22] Readers familiar with Spinal Tap and the *Smell the Glove* controversy will recognize the situation.

There was no such licence at EMI, but prudishness was not the only one of chairman Sir John Read's failings. He also presided over the group's diversification into other non-musical areas. Its military links had been kept up and it had also developed a sideline building medical equipment, including the revolutionary computerized tomography (CAT) scanner. Revolutionary it might have been, but it also created massive financial problems for EMI, which, rather than licensing the machine to General Electric, had set up its own factory. Miffed, GE created an alternative and marketed it vigorously. EMI's American factory ran at a massive loss for its short life.

There was also the expansion into film production and exhibition, theatre ownership, pubs, restaurants and hotels, but the company did not excel in any of these areas. Musically, Capitol had recovered from an $8m loss at the start of the 1970s, under the leadership of Bhaskar Menon, who had come over from HMV's Indian company. Meanwhile, the UK outlook was good, despite the Beatles' split at the start of the decade, with artists like Pink Floyd, Steve Harley and the evergreen Cliff all signed to the label. Despite this, EMI's muddled portfolio, coupled to the deepening recession, had brought the company perilously close to bankruptcy by 1979. The only way to avoid such a fate was to find new investors, perhaps even a new owner. The first stop was the US film group Paramount, owned by the Gulf & Western conglomerate, which seemed likely to buy 50 per cent of EMI in July 1979. Talks fell apart over the construction of the board – Paramount wanted a majority, something EMI wasn't prepared to countenance. However, before discussions ceased, Decca was able to have some fun at its annual sales conference, handing out badges declaring it to be 'The Great British Record Company'. The solution finally came later in the year, when EMI was bought by the British-owned Thorn Electrical Industries, to form Thorn-EMI.

CBS had gone through its own upheavals. When Ken Glancy left for RCA in 1970, there were the predictable rumours about the succession. Knowing that he was headed for MCA whatever happened, Derek Everett decided to have some fun:

We're going down the stairs, [Maurice] Oberstein grabs me and says, 'Right, it's you or me.' I said, 'What's you or me?' He said, 'The next one. Take Ken's place.' I said, 'Oh, Obie, it's you. Go away.' But I got home and I thought, 'No, this is stupid, I'm not just going to do this. I'm going to play a few games now. I'll go in tomorrow morning, call Obie and tell him I've had a rethink. You or me.' So, I did. Now I've never seen a man change so much, personality wise, in such a short space of time, as he did in the next few weeks. Everyone was his friend, he was bouncing around. I thought, 'Here's the start of the political campaign.'

I was trying to work out how to get out and eventually, I went to Peter de Rougemont, who headed up Europe, at the sales conference, and said, 'Look, Peter, I have a problem. Ken's gone, and I was about to hand in my notice, because I want to be released. I've been offered the job at MCA.' 'Ah, very bad timing,' he said. 'Look, can we reach a compromise? Will you stay for a few weeks and say nothing?' So that was the three weeks or so I had planned playing games with Obie and vying for the presidency, which neither of us would have got. After all that nonsense, he didn't get it.[23]

That someone else was Richard Robinson, the wheelchair-bound accountant who had asked Everett for more hits each year. Mike Smith recalls:

The first time I went over to New York for CBS was with Richard. He was very much an accountant, a grey man. An extraordinary success with the ladies, despite being in a wheelchair, and it was a bit embarrassing on the plane, because he had to use a bottle. I remember on one trip, I went off to the gents to empty his bottle and we hit an air pocket.

He was so impressed with Clive, because he knew the numbers. We came back to London, and were having a meeting. Richard was talking about a young lady singer that we had at the time, and the American trip was still very much with him. He said, 'Well, I've got to say, that young lady really has got her shit together' and all of these heads went [swivel] 'What did he say?' It was wonderful the way he came out with it.[24]

Before contracting polio, recounts Smith, Robinson had harboured dreams of becoming a professional golfer.

> He probably would have been very good. There was one occasion when we had a CBS conference in Ireland, I think in Limerick. We'd all flown over, but it was very difficult for him to fly because of his chair, so Lloyd, his chauffeur, had driven him over on the ferry, then drove down to where we were. When he arrived, we were all waiting on the steps of the hotel. Richard, bless his heart, said, 'Very nice, I'm very pleased to see my young executives waiting for me.' Lloyd went round the back of the Jag, opened it up, we got all our golf clubs out and we pissed off.

It was under Robinson's watch, and with Reg Warburton in charge of studios, that CBS UK vacated the old ballroom in New Bond Street and took up residence in a purpose-built complex in Whitfield Street, much closer to the Theobalds Road offices. 'I started seeing the rest of the company again,' jokes Mike Ross-Trevor, who had been largely left to his own devices at the old place:

> New Bond Street was not considered by the American guys to be a serious studio. The fact that we were churning out loads of hits was by the way. It wasn't considered a great orchestral room. So a lot of the American producers who came over and wanted to do orchestral projects would go to Olympic in Barnes, Abbey Road and CTS. CBS suddenly realized they were spending an awful lot of money in these studios for their visiting artists. People like Tony Bennett and Barbra Streisand would come over and they were recording in all of these other studios. So they decided they needed a decent big orchestral room with all the facilities, so they built this place.
>
> They cleared the site in 1970, and we opened in June 1972. It was designed by a Dutch guy called van Kleven, who also designed A&M studios in Los Angeles. Back then we had several people from the States come in and say, 'My God, it's A&M' ... It's very versatile; you can literally record anything in

this room. You can record a classical chamber group, an orchestral film session, you can do a pop band, a big band.[25]

Mike Smith was less concerned with the building's acoustic versatility, though: 'It's built next door to a pub, and I wanted a hatch through.'[26] Mike Ross-Trevor recalls that planning permission was requested from the local authority, who said no. The hatch wouldn't have seen much use, though, had it been built. Shortly after the studio opened, Smith left the company to go independent.

The same year as Whitfield Street opened, Robinson was succeeded by Dick Asher, one of CBS's seemingly limitless supply of lawyers, sent over from New York, who lasted until 1975, when he went back to run the record division's international arm. Only then did Obie get a look-in. Muff Winwood, who joined CBS in 1978, remembers some of his idiosyncrasies:

Oh, he was an extraordinary character. He always wore weird hats everywhere. His antics were bizarre ... you'd be called up to a meeting in his room, the secretary would say, 'He's in,' and you'd walk in, look around the room, and you couldn't find him. You'd call 'Obie?' and he'd say [gruff voice], 'I'm here.' And then he'd be sitting in the corner, next to the radiator, on his backside, on the floor behind the desk. You wouldn't have even seen him. He'd say, 'Come and sit here,' and you'd have to go and sit next to him. He always had this red terrier, Charlie, and Charlie would be sitting at the desk, and Obie would be eating sandwiches. He'd be saying, 'I'm going to fucking do this' and 'I'm going to fucking do that' and then take a piece of the sandwich, give it to Charlie, then he'd carry on eating, give a piece to Charlie, all while the meeting was going on. He'd always do weird things like that. Despite all that, he knew how to motivate people. He was a great motivator when it came to standing up, making speeches and driving the company.[27]

Under Clive Davis's management, Columbia in the US had maintained its lead and continued to invest in rock, overcoming the death of Janis Joplin and the split of Simon and Garfunkel with the growth of Santana and Chicago, as well as the $4m acquisition of Neil Diamond from MCA. Despite all of this, on 29 May 1973, Davis was summoned to the office of Arthur Taylor (who had become CBS president after Frank Stanton had been upped to vice-chairman) and fired. The ostensible reason for the sacking was the matter of some $94,000 in expense account irregularities, including an estimated $18,000 spent on a barmitzvah party for Davis's son, Fred, and $53,000 on improvements to Davis's home.

Davis claimed, in his memoirs, to be astounded. 'Taylor and CBS's attorneys had known the complete facts behind each of the specific allegations in the complaint for a month and a half before my firing. Indeed, I had *volunteered* many of the facts,' he argued. The problem was that the facts, as Taylor viewed them, were rather different to those presented by Davis, based upon documents found in the office of David Wynshaw, the company's former head of artist relations. Wynshaw, it appeared, had been responsible for creating the fake invoices for Davis's disputed claims. For example, Fred Davis's barmitzvah had been charged to the company as a non-existent party for Liza Minnelli. Davis's supporters argued that his personal and professional lives were so closely intertwined that the party amounted to a Columbia gathering. Or as the British trade journal *Music Week* put it: 'Many mystified executives regard Clive Davis's alleged "misdemeanours" as being normal perks in American record business at presidential level.'[28]

Taylor had some sympathy with this view and suggested that, had Davis been honest and indicated that the bash was a goodwill gesture to friends and associates, the company would have been happy to foot at least some of the bill. Davis instead claimed that Wynshaw had acted without his knowledge or authority, which Taylor found hard to believe. 'It had never occurred to me that Wynshaw was anything but a selfless person totally dedicated to making my life free to handle the business of the company,' said Davis in his autobiography, a curious statement for a man who prided himself on his close involvement with all aspects of his company's running. The credibility gap made Davis's position very shaky indeed. Worse still, Wynshaw was closely associated with Pasquale Falconio, aka Patsy Falcone, a high-ranking member of the Genovese family. Falcone had been indicted on drugs charges, and the mere possibility that Davis himself could have been associated with Falcone removed any last vestiges of doubt. Davis had to go.

The irregularities had been found in an audit prompted by Project Sound, another government-led payola investigation. Davis had, in 1971, arranged a pressing and distribution deal with Kenny Gamble and Leon Huff, the independent producers behind The Sound of Philadelphia. Davis let Gamble and Huff arrange their own promotion, and, as it transpired, they were not averse to bribing disc jockeys. Whether Davis knew of this and condoned it has never been satisfactorily established. After his arrest, Wynshaw made all manner of claims about CBS operating a hidden payola slush fund, but he could well have just been trying to give the investigators what they wanted to hear in exchange for leniency. Whatever the truth, Wynshaw's claims resulted in the whole of Columbia being under investigation. Two years after his arrest, Wynshaw was sentenced to a year in jail for defrauding CBS. In 1976, Davis pleaded guilty to one charge of tax evasion, pertaining to $8,800 of vacation expenses. The mountain laboured and brought forth a mouse. Bruce Lundvall says:

> Clive's departure was a very unpleasant one. It was a very difficult time. We went in front of a grand jury for a year and a half, as you know, all of us, because of what happened there. I don't know that Clive did anything incorrectly. There was the barmitzvah of his son and having the apartment redecorated, and that kind of stuff, which has been a matter of public record. I wasn't privy to who paid for what. I was one of the first people who was called in front of the general counsel of the company to find out what I knew, and I didn't really know anything. I said, 'Yes, I went to the barmitzvah' and 'Yes, I worked for Clive', but I wasn't aware of any wrongdoing. I suppose it was really minor malfeasance than any major crime. What really happened to everybody was that the whole company was put under a microscope … It was a tremendous over-reaction and of course the government was involved here too. It was during the Nixon administration, CBS News was not kind to Nixon, the pressure was down on media companies, particularly CBS. Who knows what the real story was? We were all accused of being guilty until proven innocent unfortunately. We just worked there. It was a very, very traumatic year for many people. We had attorneys going through our files, pulling out memos, all that kind of stuff. All of us were assigned criminal attorneys.[29]

As all of the record division was under investigation, none of them could be promoted to replace Davis, so to fill the breach, CBS sent an executive from the television division called Irwin Segelstein, while Goddard Lieberson resumed involvement in the record company's day-to-day running. Lieberson put on a brave face and explained that the reason for his return was his ambition 'to produce a rock 'n' roll hit'.[30] Naturally, there was suspicion about Segelstein, as Lundvall says:

> Goddard was brought back, I'm sure, much more for credibility, and Irwin was thought of as kind of a spy, but he turned out to be one of the greatest men I've ever worked for. He ended up being totally supportive of all the people that worked in the records division. He went native. He got to love the people in the records division. He was from television, he really did not know the record world, but he certainly knew how to deal with people.[31]

Davis's conviction did not bother his new employers. After abortive discussions with Chris Blackwell about the set-up of an American subsidiary for Island, Davis had, in 1974, accepted a call from Columbia Pictures to run their record division. Davis took the company's ailing Bell label and renamed it Arista. With the help of artists like Barry Manilow, and a link-up with Tony Stratton-Smith's Charisma label, after only eight months of operation it was the number eight label in the US, both for single and album sales, as well as making 'substantial profits as against a loss' in the previous year.

Quite apart from having to cope with an internal investigation and the loss of its high-profile chief, Columbia, in the immediate aftermath of Davis's exit, had to deal with the loss of a major artist – Bob Dylan. Dylan had agreed to a two-album deal with Asylum, sold partially on the fact that the label's founder, David Geffen, was also promoting his upcoming run of concerts. Unfortunately for both parties, the first album of the contract, *Planet Waves*, was a rush job, recorded in three days. The 500,000 seats for the concerts were oversubscribed ten times, but the LP sold only 700,000 copies, respectable enough, but short of the million that Geffen had promised to shift. Geffen was then perturbed to be informed by Dylan that the second part of the deal had been agreed only on a handshake, and that the next disc would not be given to Asylum. In the event, *Before the Flood* was released on Asylum, but Dylan returned to Columbia immediately afterwards, much to his and their relief.

Geffen had begun his career in the postroom at the William Morris Agency, a position that aided him in intercepting a letter from UCLA, indicating that it had no knowledge of him, contrary to the claim that he had made on his job application that he had attended the university. Even by the bearpit standards of the William Morris Agency at the time, Geffen was ruthlessly ambitious and he quickly climbed the ladder. He moved into management in the late 1960s, looking after the career of singer Laura Nyro. The fact that Nyro was a CBS artist brought him into contact with Clive Davis.

Davis became Geffen's mentor, but this relationship was upended when Geffen moved into the orbit of Ahmet Ertegun at Atlantic as a result of the formation of Crosby, Stills and Nash. The initial plan was to ask for Stephen Stills to be released from his Atlantic contract so that Geffen could take the supergroup to Davis at Columbia. Jerry Wexler blew up at the suggestion, but Ertegun was more pragmatic. Instead, he suggested that Geffen get a release for Graham Nash from Columbia and bring CS&N to Atlantic. Davis regarded it initially as a betrayal, but eventually agreed to the deal, in exchange for Atlantic's contract with Poco. Retrospectively, Atlantic got the better end of the deal.

Ertegun took over as Geffen's mentor, but was not inclined to take on board everything that his protégé offered, and one of his refusals resulted in the foundation of Asylum. Geffen had tried to interest him in Jackson Browne, suggesting that he would 'make a lot of money'.[32] Ertegun replied that he already had a lot of money, and that Geffen could make a lot of money if he had his own record company. Moreover, if he wanted to do so, Atlantic would come in as a 50 per cent partner. Geffen almost tore Ertegun's arm off in accepting. The idea was unleashed on the world in the summer of 1971. Browne was a charter member of the new label, soon joined by the Eagles and Joni Mitchell. An attempt to entice Laura Nyro over to the new venture failed.

Barely a year after the foundation of Asylum, Steve Ross offered to buy the 50 per cent of the label that Warner Communications didn't already own, and told Geffen to name his price. Geffen opted for $7m, an astronomical sum for such a new label, but Ross's instant acceptance gave him pause to wonder if he could have asked for more. Geffen felt worse when the value of Warner shares began to fall rapidly, as he had accepted part-payment in stock. After much grousing, in August 1973 Ross gave Geffen overall responsibility for Elektra as well as Asylum. Later in the decade, Geffen made an inauspicious entry into the film business, but in 1977 was diagnosed with cancer and began to re-evaluate his life. He relinquished all executive responsibilities and took things easier. He undertook a little lecturing at UCLA, whence he had claimed to have graduated at the start of his career.

*

Even before the Clive Davis incident had engulfed the American record industry, the UK had its own scandal to contend with. The UK and the lofty BBC, it seemed, was not immune to payola. Being British, though, the whole affair was equal parts saucy seaside postcard, Whitehall farce and Monty Python, rather than a matter for the Mob. On St Valentine's Day 1971, the front page of the ever-reliable *News of the World* (aka the 'News of the Screws') alleged 'cash payments to obtain plugs for records ... the use of call-girls to entertain well-known BBC personalities ... rigging of the 'top twenty' record charts ... [and] girl "record pluggers" working on a bed-for-plugs basis'.[33]

This affair centred on one Janie Jones, who, when she wasn't running her terrible web of corruption, was a recording artist for President Records, a small label allied to Ed Kassner's eponymous music publishing firm. A central plank of the Screws' proof was that a plugger had claimed to have the popular BBC request show *Two-Way Family Favourites* 'sewn up'. This was obligingly illustrated when a record was dedicated, on air, to a list of names that turned out to belong to sundry *News of the World* hacks and the assistant editor's dog. When exposed, one DJ Tony Brandon explained his presence at one of Jones's orgies by saying that he was 'always on the look-out for new songs', and Jones's husband happened to be a songwriter.

By May 1973, nine individuals, including Jones (real name: Marion Mitchell), her now ex-husband John Christian-Dee and the singer Dorothy Squires had been charged 'with offences connected with the alleged bribery of BBC men to "push" certain records'.[34] Five others were wanted, including Kassner. As the trial wore on, various juicy details emerged, including the fact that Jones's home had a two-way mirror in front of which sexual acts were performed for the benefit of voyeurs, that a young woman had been paid to dress 'as a twelve-year-old girl with flat shoes'[35] and that the girls in Jones's employ had been threatened with 'heavies' employed by the singer, songwriter and comedian Kenny Lynch. Furthermore, Jones was accused of trying to drug Christian-Dee 'to endanger his life or cause grievous bodily harm'.[36] After all of these gamey revelations, Jack Dabbs, the BBC producer at the centre of the *News of the World* allegations, was acquitted, but Jones got seven years for procuring.[37]

To avoid any future laundering of soiled linen, the BBC introduced a set of guidelines to ensure that its men remained incorruptible. Absurdly, a half-bottle of champagne was allowed, being classed as a gift, whereas a full bottle was regarded as a bribe. This was discovered and publicized gleefully by indie label Dart Records, when it tried to promote 'Time is Tight' by Simon Park's 52nd Precinct. Dart director Tim Satchell was advised by Radio 1 controller Derek Chinnery that 'they had been given things like doughnuts and T-shirts recently but a bottle of whisky would not be acceptable. A half-bottle of champagne however would be acceptable. I didn't ask about half-bottles of whisky.'[38]

'We thought it was all rather funny,' says Clive Stanhope, one of the partners in Dart. 'So did everyone else, and that's why it got so much publicity, but the BBC didn't like us for doing it.'[39]

As an independent label, Dart was never quite in the same league as Island or Virgin. 'We had bands who used to be big, like the Swinging Blue Jeans,' recounts Satchell thirty years on. 'We also had a hypnotist called Romark – Ronald Markham – who made records on how to stop smoking and live longer. Unfortunately, he had a heart attack and died.'[40] Dart also had on its books a witch doctor. Even after Chinnery's diktat, Satchell tried his best to make a favourable impression with the Radio 1 types, 'pouring drink down their throats at the BBC Club and sweet-talking the secretaries who typed the playlists'.[41]

Another, arguably greater, scandal may well have gone undetected, its perpetrator maintaining a reputation as an honest broker and an industry ambassador right up to his death, as Derek Everett reveals:

There are all sorts of stories about what Obie got up to at CBS. I think there were a few bits of money exchanging hands somewhere along the line for deletions. Over-production. He was in charge of the production and also the deletions. Now, if you put those two together ... one of the big things that Obie and I used to fall out over all the time was deletions. He was the deletion king and I was the 'leave it in the catalogue' king. We used to have these meetings, but he always had the final say, so it never really made any difference. But he also did the production quantities and overstocks. Put that together, and it's a very lethal combination, really. It could all be rumour, but you're in total control, no one questions you about how many, when you take it out, whether you put too many in, and a lot of big artists would be well over-produced. Simon and Garfunkel, you'd suddenly have 50,000 more than you needed, and you'd think, 'Why, where are they going?' And the next time you looked, there'd only be 10,000 more than you needed. 'Where have they gone?'[42]

*

Meanwhile, RCA had been losing ground since the 1960s, having strengthened its reputation for conservatism just as the rest of the world was going the other way. As the decline wore on, the company lost direction. The company had gone out on its own in the UK in June 1969, and the following October, it had enticed Ken Glancy from CBS to run the show. Quite a few of his old mates from CBS got the call to come and join him, including publicity man Rodney Burbeck and A&R chief Derek Everett. 'He always used to say to me, over the years, "Whatever you do, Derek, don't go to RCA,"' Everett observes. 'So, I said to him, "But you always told me" … He said, "I know what I've always said, but there's the offer that you can't refuse, and I've just had it."' Unfortunately, Glancy's original instinct had proved to be correct. The RCA job was very much a poisoned chalice. He impressed the corporate overlords enough to be offered the position of president and CEO of the whole RCA Records group in the US, which he took up in January 1974. Within three years, however, he was back in the UK, demoted to run the British subsidiary.

Glancy's demotion had not been any reflection on his management skills, merely a reflection of RCA's corporate mentality, or, rather, its lack of a coherent mentality of any description. 'Glancy lost the battle over there, because he backed the wrong horse in some political battle,' Everett elucidates. 'The one he backed lost, but the guy who won was fired about a month later anyway.' Soon after accepting Glancy's invitation, Everett had seen the RCA political machine at first hand:

> He had a wonderful thing, Glancy. He'd never bother you at the weekend. In all the time I worked with him, I think I had two phone calls at the weekend, ever. However, once, when I hadn't been there long, he said, 'What are you doing at the weekend, kid? I've been lumbered with one of these management course things and I want someone to come with me. It'll probably be a pain in the arse.' I said I'd go with him. So we went to this country mansion, all the usual nonsense, Americans and guys from other divisions.
>
> We're sitting there, having a drink in the evening, and this guy comes over and says, 'Excuse me, do you mind if I take Ken away for a moment?' 'No, be my guest' – whoever you are, probably some president of something or other. So, off they go. He comes back after a little while and says, 'Sorry about that.' 'What was it?' 'Oh, it was all to do with America and basically they've just found out that they made a mistake. They shouldn't have kicked me out, but it's too late.'

The whole thing was mad. Our division reported to an international division in New York, and they changed people like I change socks. Every week there was a new person. 'Hello, I'm so and so from international, I run so and so.' Three weeks later, 'Hello, I'm from international...' Various Americans kept coming. The ones I never used to like were what I called the General Brigade, because I think most of them were ex-Army or -Air Force generals. They all had these shaven haircuts and bullet heads. They used to come into meetings and you'd always get the same thing: 'My daughter likes so and so. Do we have anyone like that?'[43]

Despite the generals' vicarious curiosity about the latest developments, the US company had done little from the 1960s onwards to keep its roster up to date, apart from healthy activity on the country and western front, including the opening of a new studio complex in Nashville in 1964. In 1977, its most successful cash cow passed over to the other side. Elvis had left the building. Rodney Burbeck remembers the occasion all too clearly:

It is true that RCA at that time made a lot of money out of dead recording artists – not least Glenn Miller, Jim Reeves and then Elvis Presley. I was at home when the phone rang, nine o'clock-ish, and it was one of the radio stations and they said, 'Elvis has died.' My immediate corporate PR response was, 'Oh shit.' I said, 'Can I get back to you?' So I rang my opposite number in New York at RCA, and they said, 'Yeah it's true, don't say anything.' I explained that I couldn't deny it, if he's dead he's dead – it was out on the wires. New York just said, 'We'll get back to you, but in the meantime don't say anything until we get a statement'. The guy rang back and said, 'All we're going to say is RCA Records is deeply distressed to hear of the death of Elvis Presley' and that's it and I said that they couldn't just say that. You have to say what a great guy he was, what great records he produced and how pleased we are for all the records we sold. And he said, 'No, you can't say that.' They didn't want to upset [Colonel Tom] Parker.

Anyway, the phone at my flat in Kensington didn't stop ringing. The radio station rang me and I said, 'Yeah, he had a great commitment to rock and roll, he started it all and the whole industry has a great debt to pay to him.' Apparently this was recorded and then sold on to a radio station in the States and my phone rang about 4 a.m. and my opposite number in America said, 'Hey, what have you been saying? You're being broadcast over here, saying what a great guy he was.' Anyway, I was up all night and got to the office about 7 a.m. and the phone rang all the next day and thereafter ... People were queuing in record shops to buy anything by Elvis Presley. It was this quirk of human nature, somebody famous dies, they want to buy their books, records and want to see their films and watch their TV programmes. So naturally we pressed all the buttons at the factory in Washington, County Durham, and everything we had available was being rushed out to the shops. I got a call from the London *Evening News* asking, 'How dare you capitalize on the death of somebody?' 'Well, hold on a minute,' I said. 'We don't go out and grab people in the street and push them into record shops and make them hand over money to buy their records and, apart from that, how many extra newspapers have you sold?'[44]

There had been some successes from the UK end, though. In the glam rock era, RCA had the Sweet and, more enduringly, David Bowie. Previously what the record company said would have been the last word, but Bowie's management flexed its considerable muscle and PR supremo Burbeck didn't get much of a look-in on the Thin White Duke's career:

I wasn't too much involved in that because the main man Tony DeFries [Bowie's manager] decreed that he wanted to do it all himself. I clearly remember going into a meeting with Ken Glancy and being introduced to Mr DeFries. I put forward my publicity plan and he just shook his head and said, 'No, we're not doing any of that, we're not doing *Melody Maker*, we're not doing this' and I said, 'Oh, why is that?' The interpretation was, not that it was said to me in so many words, he was doing a Colonel Parker. The word was DeFries had learnt from that – keep the man difficult to get to and you will then create a myth and a persona and you will then create a demand even though the demand wasn't actually there in the first place. But by saying you can't have him, then Fleet Street would want him. It was very frustrating as a PR not to be able to. However, as much as he was not liked, one has to hand it to DeFries that he did create this great persona, and Bowie did the business on stage.[45]

Later in the 1970s, punk was rearing its ugly head, but Everett found it as hard to understand as any old-school record executive:

> The General Brigade had started asking, 'What is this punk?' We did a couple of deals and I thought, 'I think I'm doing the wrong thing here.' That punk thing was very strange. It was all pre-business, you went and pre-sold a number, pick a number, 100,000 records. The act would pre-sell 100,000 records and it would never sell another copy. It would go into the charts at anything between ten to one for one week, then descend. It was very weird. I never got to grips with it at all.

Everett found Europop easier to understand, even if his colleagues didn't:

> We had the two girls from Spain, Baccara. That was a smash. We presented it at the meeting – a smash all over Europe, the summer hit. It wasn't guaranteed, but almost. The promotion man – a Scottish guy – refused to promote it. He said, 'I'm no' taking this around anywhere. It's crap.' 'So what?' 'I'll get thrown out of every office I visit.' In the end, he was persuaded to take it round. He came back next week: 'I told you I'd get thrown out, I'm the laughing stock of the business, I'm no' promoting this record.' While this is going on, it's starting to sell, of course. The bloody thing went to number one.[46]

The grouping established by Philips and Siemens in 1962 had gone from strength to strength globally, despite the natural tensions between the two owners. The main driver in most territories had been the company's focus on local repertoire. In the UK, the two sides had maintained very distinct identities, which was seen to be a good thing, and utterly separate support systems, which was deemed to be less so. In 1979, having worked with him in South Africa for many years, Coen Solleveld persuaded David Fine to run PolyGram UK, and he set about reducing the duplication:

> I made some management changes and I rationalized the operation. It was part of the PolyGram ethos to be competitive between Polydor and Phonogram – silly competitive. We'd bid for the same artists, we had separate sales forces, and never the twain shall meet. The first thing I did was combine the sales forces, which made for more efficiency. They even had separate accounts departments, which I centralized. We slashed the costs and started to

make money. My good friends in Hanover and Baarn hadn't thought it was ever going to be possible. They thought that Britain was inherently inefficient, but that they had to be here because of repertoire. Instead of which, we turned the tables and became one of the most profitable parts.[47]

The picture for PolyGram US was more complicated. Solleveld had moved from Holland to the US in 1978, just as the company was in a massive American expansion drive. This had begun in 1963 with the purchase of Chicago independent label Mercury, and the momentum had been slow to increase, but by 1978, PolyGram had grown to become the first record label to reach more than $1bn in turnover. A major contributor to this landmark figure had been the soundtrack albums contributed by the Robert Stigwood Organization for *Saturday Night Fever* and *Grease*. Unfortunately, PolyGram had trouble following these successes up. The soundtrack to RSO's *Sergeant Pepper* movie sold gold, but returned platinum. Harvey Schein came over from Warners, where he had pitched up briefly after leaving Sony, to run the US company, but didn't last long.

Particularly calamitous was PolyGram's investment in Neil Bogart's label Casablanca – a 50 per cent stake in 1977 and the rest of the company in 1980. Casablanca's main emphasis was on disco music, although it also had the heavy rock band Kiss on its books. Bogart had started his career in Philadelphia with Cameo-Parkway, and later moved to Buddah before striking out with Casablanca in 1973. Initially, the label went through Warners, but a bust-up between Bogart and Mo Ostin ended that arrangement in late 1974. Enter PolyGram. Bogart's motto was 'Whatever it takes' and in his case it took top-of-the range Mercedes cars for all the executives and a large supply of all kinds of drugs. PolyGram ended up footing the bill for this excess, and coupled with the soundtrack misses, the company turned into a massive lossmaker, losing $220m before it returned to profitability in 1985.

David Fine believes that PolyGram's US push was doomed to failure because of the clash of cultures. 'It was a typical example of a non-American company trying to break into a market which they were ill-equipped to do, and that's always a disaster. They sold quite a lot of product, but they never quite got on top of the American cost structure. In later years, it wasn't a failure, but compared to the effort involved ... ' The man who had to deal with the mess was Dick Asher, who had joined PolyGram in October 1985, following twenty years with CBS. 'Dick Asher tidied it up. He was a very tough disciplinarian, so the losses went, but we never really broke through there.'[48]

Other companies were even worse off. Decca had, in the first instance, been largely the creation of one man: Edward Lewis. In a way, then, it was oddly fitting that the company should, to all intents and purposes, die with him, although the name would live on in the classical field under its new ownership. In the 1960s, the company had promoted a wealth of new initiatives. When the introduction of stereo proved too subtle an innovation for most record buyers, Decca had been the first of the British record companies to head into the gimmicky 'ping-pong' stereo field, with its Phase 4 Stereo line. Instead of trying to give listeners the impression that they were sitting dead centre in front of a concert stage, Phase 4 batted sounds between the speakers just so that listeners could really hear the difference between stereo and mono, and rest assured that they were getting real value for money.

The impetus for the programme came from the American arm, Hugh Mendl recalls: 'Lee Hartstone of London Records in New York asked for "ping-pong" stereo, because a man called Enoch Light was doing rather well with these records.' As a result, an American producer, Tony d'Amato, was sent over to run the new operation. The name came not from any technical advances, but from the fact that Frank Lee had a Phase 2 Sunbeam Alpine. The launch coincided with the opening of the cavernous new number three studio at West Hampstead:

> Number three was always being used by Tony d'Amato for Phase 4, and it suited the rest of us very well because we could then go wherever we wanted outside of Decca. But some marvellous recordings came out of number one too – that was where Mantovani recorded in the days before number three opened. I did a lot of Mantovani recordings, and I must say that it always worked for me easier in number one than in number three. It had also a permanent stage, whereas if you wanted a stage in number three you had to build one. You needed a stage for big musicals, Gilbert and Sullivan and things like that.[49]

The Phase 4 output was resolutely middle of the road. Apart from Mantovani, the label took on Ted Heath and His Music, and Ronnie Aldrich and His Two Pianos. 'Lee Hartstone had heard Butch Bannister,[50] the engineer, and Ronnie Aldrich mixing a piano and strings thing. He said, "That's what I want", says Mendl. As gimmicky as the early Phase 4 discs were, they sold well. Later on, they settled down and the gimmickry was soft-pedalled in favour of music. Ted Heath's band could get back to playing big band jazz rather than sound effects.

Phase 4 snared Leopold Stokowski, but the bulk of Decca's classical recordings in this era were made in conventional stereo, and very fine they were too. Arguably the high watermark of the label's output was the complete recording of Wagner's *Ring* cycle made by Georg Solti with the Vienna Philharmonic, under the watchful eye of John Culshaw. The process had begun with *Das Rheingold* in 1958, and concluded with *Götterdammerung* in 1964.

Added to this, the pop side maintained a considerable momentum. In 1967, the company had established a progressive offshoot called Deram, which became home to bands like the Moody Blues, whose *Days of Future Passed* – executive producer Hugh Mendl – became one of the best-selling albums of its time. The wheels didn't start to fall off the cart until the early 1970s, but Mendl had seen it coming a little earlier. Due to Decca politics, though, he found himself unable to do anything about it:

At one stage in the late 1960s, I said to Lewis, 'Can I write you a report? I'm dead worried and you know how I feel about Decca.' He asked me if I could do it over the weekend as he was going to New York on Monday and it would give him something to read on the plane. I worked night and day and did all the obvious things, you know – more independent producers, moving A&R and promotion together to the West End, having each label with its promotion man, and basically to keep Townsley off our backs.

Lewis went to New York, did whatever he had to do in New York and he came back and said, 'Oh, I read your report. Very interesting. Very interesting. I read it twice on the plane going over. Full of very revolutionary ideas.' Well, he thought that they were because he was comparing it with the old, but there was nothing very revolutionary about it – it wasn't any great work of genius on my part. You could have asked an office girl how it should be and she would have said, 'We don't like Miss Bruce saying, "Girls will not wear trousers to the office".' You know, all that sort of thing.[51]

A measure of the company's old-fashioned outlook can be gained from the fact that Frank Lee had been pensioned off, Mendl says, largely because of his increasing lack of discretion about his sexual preferences:

> His proclivities had become extremely embarrassing to some of the people at the top. It didn't worry us, of course, but he had become a very great liability. We used to have classical meetings in Switzerland, with Maurice Rosengarten, and Frank took his little friend off to the meeting and he stayed in the hotel, and Rosengarten wouldn't have that. The venomous Townsley had it in for Frank Lee for years, and he thought he'd done a good day's work when he'd got rid of somebody. He didn't think of the future, ever.[52]

There had been attempts to inject new blood into the organization, but these had not worked out as planned. In October 1974, Ken East, who had been running EMI's Australian operation, came in as MD. He stayed only a year. 'I thought, "Oh well, this is going to save us", says Mendl:

> He got great support from a lot of people in Decca, but he didn't really know how to handle Lewis. If he had been sufficiently dedicated and if Lewis had been sufficiently open with him, he could have saved Decca. The trouble was that Lewis lost his fire, that Townsley was there and that neither of them was capable of changing. I was by their standards young, but I was in my fifties. Not that my age mattered. I really believed, and I still do, that if you are a proper record man, you change with the taste.[53]

In 1978, Mike Smith was appointed as A&R head, but unfortunately, it turned out to be the wrong Mike Smith – a London Weekend Television producer rather than the old Decca/CBS hand, and a man whose breath reputedly smelled of Kit-Kats.[54] The original Smith maintains to this day that the job had been intended for him:

> Suddenly Decca were advertising for an A&R manager and all the guys are saying, 'Why don't you apply?' I said, 'There's no point.' And then, the press comes out, new A&R manager at Decca – Mike Smith. So I'm getting phone calls saying, 'Nice one.' I say, 'It's not me.' They said, 'Well, it's got to be you.'

He was married to Sally James of *Tiswas* fame. I went to Decca a few times to sell masters, and every time I went there, he wasn't there. He'd gone out. The security guys that were there were the ones that I knew when I was at Decca and they're going, 'Why did they get him? He's a fucking cunt. He's done this, he's done that, he's spent £40,000 on having the office redecorated – £40,000. Nonsense.'

Then I got the story from [songwriter] Bill Martin that one day Sir Edward is walking down the corridor with Bill Townsley and Mike Smith comes towards them. Bill Townsley says, 'I don't think you've met our A&R manager, Mike Smith.' Sir Edward said, 'That's not Mike Smith. Mike Smith used to work for us. I know Mike Smith.' Apparently ... they asked around in the business about Mike Smith, got the story back on me and not the story back on the other one. It was a joke. They hired him on my reputation. I met with one of his secretaries – *one* of his secretaries – at one point, and she said, 'Well, we've got the Mike Smith that had all of the hit records.' He'd never had a hit record in his life. She said, 'What about so and so?' I said, 'That was mine.'[55]

In 1969, Decca had 22.8 per cent of the British LP market, second only to EMI, which had 26.5 per cent. In singles terms, it was fifth, behind EMI (with 37.2 per cent), CBS, Polydor and RCA, with 5.3 per cent. In 1979, it could command only 3.6 per cent of the LP market and 1.3 per cent of the singles market. As a group, Decca was still highly profitable, bringing in a net profit of £4.1m in 1978, on turnover of £186,300, but the bulk of this was coming from the non-record activities, such as the Navigator division. As early as 1968, L. G. Wood had suggested to Lewis that EMI should buy Decca. He stressed the strengths of a combined classical catalogue, and added that it would be the company's only chance to stay in British hands, as well as creating a sizeable bulwark against the incursions being made by the newly liberated American companies. Lewis passed up on the offer, but in 1976, Peter Andry, the head of EMI's classical division, renewed the offensive. Both had recognized that Lewis was Decca and that no real plan of succession had been instituted.

Added to which was Lewis's weakness in the face of organized labour. 'He was very afraid of the unions and he always gave into them,' observes Mendl:

We had trouble in the factory and it was a case where, to be honest, the union were on very weak ground indeed, and I didn't think they were going to get away with it. Other unions, such as the Musicians' Union, didn't think that the factory workers would get away with it. Lewis caved in. He just said to Townsley, 'We've got to agree. We need to get those records off to America. It's only a bloody few thousand. What's that?' He was by nature the conservative. He told people that they should vote Conservative. When I did the Churchill records [a collection of his wartime speeches], he was absolutely enchanted that I wasn't a Bolshevik.[56]

Almost to the last, suggestions that Decca was for sale were hotly denied, primarily because Lewis genuinely had no intention of selling, despite being gravely ill with leukaemia. In May 1979, he was looking at various independent labels with a view to purchasing, but was disturbed to find that the most attractive ones had all been bankrolled by rival majors – PolyGram had large stakes in Ensign and Charisma, while WEA was backing Radar, Jake Riviera's follow-up to the punk and new wave powerhouse that was Stiff. Apart from the stakes held by Lewis and his family, the ownership of Decca shares was vested in a small number of large stockholders, among them Sarah Diemenstein, daughter of Maurice Rosengarten, and her husband Jack. Jack Diemenstein took great delight in pointing this out to L. G. Wood, along with the fact that he and his wife owned a sizeable tranche of EMI stock, as well as giving the impression that he would throw his lot in with Nesuhi Ertegun and WEA, for whom he was full of praise.[57]

When a sale became inevitable, it was PolyGram who emerged victorious, which Coen Solleveld traces back to an earlier piece of wishful thinking:

I had known Sir Edward Lewis since Philips took over Decca's company in Holland, and I had always asked him, if he ever wanted to sell, to think of us. About fifteen or twenty years later, I received a call from his male secretary, Bill Townsley, who said, 'The chairman would like to talk to you.' He asked if I was still interested. I said I was. I came over, and it took us an hour to make the deal. It was not a difficult decision.[58]

The deal became final in January 1980 after several months of negotiation. The nominal purchase price was to be £9.5m, but this was dependent on future performance. Should the company do worse than had been promised, the price could go as low as £5.5m, do well and it could go as high as £15.5m. The redundancy costs were estimated at £2.5m, but the record division's assets, such as the pressing plant at New Malden and the West Hampstead studios, were valued at £11.5m. As PolyGram had a modern plant at Walthamstow, New Malden was surplus to requirements and closed on 29 February 1980.[59] Staff with more than thirty years' service were presented with silver discs, but one employee smashed his at the presentation, in front of Bill Townsley and Lady Lewis. The pop side of the label was wound down, but the classical side carried on, run by Culshaw's successor Ray Minshull. The studios closed in late 1981 when the new Decca Recording Centre – a depot for mobile rigs and an editing facility rather than a studio – opened at Kilburn.

Lewis was not around to enjoy the windfall. He died on 29 January 1980, 'as if unable to witness any longer the piecemeal selling-off, like so much scrap, of his beloved company', in the words of *Music Week*. The same editorial mused that Lewis had planned to spend only a short while in the record business, putting the company on the right track, before returning to stockbroking. That he hadn't, and had not arranged a succession, 'was probably the worst mistake of his career'. However, it is likely that Lewis never realized he was getting out of touch. In 1957, he had told the *Spectator* that the reason behind his success in records was 'because I have the mind of a teenager'.[60]

The decline of the company almost proved too much for Hugh Mendl as well, as he suffered a heart attack just as the PolyGram deal was being settled:

> It was the stress of working for a dying company, which had been your life for forty-odd years, and it happened at the BPI annual Christmas get-together at Warners, where all the titans of the industry were sitting around, from Len Wood down. I was taken away in an ambulance to the Middlesex Hospital, and the larger the record company, the less interest they showed in the fact that I was at death's door ...
>
> I was told to go home and rest, but I became very, very bored. Bill Hanmer, the personnel man at Decca, said, 'Why don't you come in and see us?' so I would go into Decca House and read the trade papers, go upstairs to the famous senior executive staff luncheon club and then go down, and

Townsley would come and bore me about something that had been going on, then I'd go for another little walk and get a cab home. As a result of which, in spite of the fact that the specialist had told me that I was never to work at any executive job again, the man who was responsible for pensions at Decca said I had not left through ill-health, which I had, but I had left through being made redundant, therefore they could not make my pension up to the full amount, and I never won the battle. That's life.[61]

Despite the dispute, Mendl helped Philips handle the handover and acted as unofficial ombudsman for those being made redundant:

I just sat there, people came and told me their troubles and I wrote rude letters to people about the way the staff were being treated, not being told what their rights were, not being given advice on future employment, all that sort of stuff. Reinhard Klaasen was there for Philips, and he asked me things like, 'How do we get rid of Ronnie Aldrich?' and 'Do you think we should keep Gilbert and Sullivan/D'Oyly Carte?' And on going-home day, I walked out and got a taxi home. I'd left some things in my office, including my diaries. There was a girl who was remaining whom I kept in touch with and I asked if she could go into my old office where, in my filing cabinet, she would see two sets of diaries. The ones in which I wrote down sessions and lunch appointments, and the one in which I wrote down thoughts, grievances, pleasures and things. She rang me up later and said, 'I have to tell you that I went into your office, and it's all been stripped bare. There's nothing there, but I'll try and find out where they've gone.' I never heard another thing, so that was that.[62]

The decline of Pye was less readily explained. Always more of a singles operation than an album company, its market share in the former category had grown from 4.8 per cent in 1969 to 6.8 per cent in 1979, while its portion of the LP market had remained around the 3 per cent mark for the whole of the decade. So the company was doing good business, and it was expanding into new fields. In the mid-1970s, it established an offshoot called Pye Disco Demand to handle all of the dancefloor releases that it had, and in the late 1970s, it went further by developing the Calibre R&B label. Meanwhile, through its licensing relationship with the New York label Sugarhill, Pye was responsible for the first rap hit to reach the British charts – 'Rapper's Delight' by the Sugarhill Gang, which reached number three in December 1979.

In the 1980s, however, the business withered away to nothing. The first step in the fall seems to have been the loss of the Pye name. The electronics business and, along with it, the Pye trademark, had been bought by Philips. A concession had been granted to ATV allowing them to trade as Pye Records until 1980, after which a new settlement would need to be negotiated. 'When that came up and we negotiated with Philips, they wanted the earth of a royalty on every record,' explains Walter Woyda, by now the managing director of the company:

> It was a ridiculous idea. I think a lot of us knew that if we lost the name of Pye Records, it would be a really uphill struggle to keep it going, even though we had great artists. So they formed a company called PRT – Precision Records and Tapes. But the name really didn't mean anything to consumers at all.[63]

Pye's well-being was not aided by upheavals at its parent company, Lord Grade's Associated Communications Corporation (Grade had been elevated to the peerage in Harold Wilson's infamous 'Lavender' list of 1976). Since 1968, ATV had held the ITV franchise for the Midlands, but the majority of its networked programmes were produced outside the region at its Elstree studios. ATV Centre at Birmingham produced regional shows, local news and *Crossroads*. In 1980, during the franchise renewal round, the Independent Broadcasting Authority had forced ATV to concentrate more on its regional commitments. ACC's stake in the franchise was reduced to 51 per cent with the arrival of new, local investors such as the East Midlands Electricity Board. The name was changed to Central Independent Television on 1 January 1982, and production at Elstree was wound down in favour of a new complex at Nottingham.

Grade was also heavily involved in film production, but had taken a massive bath on *Raise the Titanic*, in which ACC had a 45 per cent stake. The film took about $8m in the US, of which $3.6m went to ACC, but Grade's company had already spent $8m on printing and advertising. This shortfall made the company vulnerable to a takeover, and Australian businessman Robert Holmes à'Court began buying up blocks of non-voting stock in ACC. The decisive moment for Grade's control over the company he founded came with a shareholders' revolt, led by Lord Matthews[64] of Trafalgar House – owners of the *Daily Express*.[65] Walter Woyda recalls:

> Victor Matthews caused the big bust-up, and made Lord Grade do a deal which I'm sure he regretted for the rest of his life. I remember going at night from my office to the car park at Cumberland Place with stacks of reporters walking along with me, saying, 'What's happening?' So I decided at sixty to take early retirement. I didn't get on with the Australians at all. They really had no interest in it. They didn't buy ATV. Lew Grade thought they were buying ATV to really build it up, but they didn't have any interest. They were asset strippers.
>
> He was an astounding man, Lew Grade. I used to go into the office before I flew off to, say, Los Angeles – six o'clock in the morning, half past five. He was always there. And I used to have breakfast with him. I can truly say I loved Lew Grade. If you went to him with something and said, 'Look, I've got a sneaking suspicion that if we have this, we have a chance of being a hit,' he'd say, 'Well, if you think so, go ahead with it. How much is it going to cost?' He was a great entrepreneur. But that wasn't the theory thereafter. When Holmes à'Court came in, he was only interested in one thing – the bottom line. He always used to say – I'll remember it to this day – It's no good being number three or four company, I'm only interested in number one companies. Well, we knew that we would never be EMI.[66]

PRT soldiered on until the late 1980s. By early 1989, the pressing and distribution arm had been closed and the catalogue had been sold to Castle Communications. Pye Records had disappeared and left barely a trace after nearly forty years in business.

12 You can spread jam on them

At the start of the 1980s, the bulk of the record industry's business was still based on a product the fundamentals of which had been laid down 100 years earlier. The coming of vinyl, microgroove and stereo notwithstanding, an undulating surface was still being dragged around under a sharp object. It was primitive, but it worked and, most importantly, it continued to sell. In the long term, however, its fortunes were in decline. In the UK in 1977, 81.7 million vinyl LPs had been delivered into the trade, with a wholesale value of £131.2m.[1] Pre-recorded cassettes then accounted for only 18.5 million units or £35.1m of the whole, while eight-track cartridges – a short-lived format aimed mainly at in-car use – represented 1.1 million units or £2.2m. By 1982, the cartridge was dead and LP sales had dropped to 57.8 million (at a value of £139.2m), while cassette had forged ahead to sell 31.5 million units, worth £71m.

Audiophiles, however, felt that both vinyl and cassette left a lot to be desired. Vinyl left them battling with clicks, pops, assorted surface noise and rumble from the turntable motor. Cassettes, which crammed four audio tracks (two sides in stereo) onto a tape one-eighth of an inch wide, played at $1^7/_8$ inches per second, some way short of the 15 and 30 i.p.s. offered by professional tape recorders. Despite the restrictions, improvements in equipment – not least the development of the Dolby noise reduction system – and tape composition had made ever-increasing levels of fidelity possible. Unfortunately, this was less obvious on commercially bought recordings, which had been transferred from the master tapes to cassette several times faster than their playing speed, providing efficiency at the cost of sound quality.

The answer was to go digital. Digital recording technology had been available to recording studios since the late 1970s, converting sound waves to binary code and eliminating the hiss inherent in analogue tape. EMI and Decca had both developed their own proprietary systems. The latter was built to a particularly high specification, capable of recording in 20-bit resolution. It was based upon an open-reel video recorder using 1-inch tape and sprung from the company's abortive research into the creation of a digital video disc. However, when digital recording systems were developed commercially by 3M, Sony and Mitsubishi, it was these that became the industry standards.

The next step was to develop a digital carrier for use in the home. Once again, the benefits of standardization had been realized, and in September 1977, twenty-nine manufacturers grouped together to form the Digital Audio Disc conference to work towards this end. Three systems were shown by the DAD grouping at Salzburg in June 1980, an electro-static method developed by JVC, a mechanical system created by Telefunken and an optical disc jointly developed by Philips and Sony. Although the DAD conference endorsed both the JVC and the Philips/Sony systems, it was the latter that found favour with equipment manufacturers.

Philips had been working on a laser-read video disc system since the early 1970s, and it was always planned to apply the technology to sound as well. By this point, under the guidance of the technical director of Philips's audio division Lou Ottens, thoughts had moved towards a small disc, read by laser. Within a further two years, a working prototype had been developed and, in March 1979, a press conference was held at Philips HQ in Eindhoven to demonstrate the new system, which had been named 'compact disc'. Ottens then led a delegation to Japan to show the system to that country's electronics manufacturers, with a view to forging a partnership with one of them. The initial focus had been on Matsushita, the owners of JVC, Technics and Panasonic, but in the end, Philips went with Sony.

This was partly because Sony had already been undertaking its own researches and a lot of the work it was doing was complementary to Philips's development. As a result, one Sony engineer observed that the combined forces of the two companies had achieved three years' work in the ten months from August 1979 to the announcement of the 'Red Book' CD standard in June 1980. Sony had begun by developing a prototype digital audio disc the same size as a conventional LP, but this resulted in a playing time of over thirteen hours, which was thought to be overkill. When Philips showed up with an 11.5-centimetre disc, the answer was at hand. Philips had already done the groundwork, but Sony made three important contributions to the finished product. Philips's research had been based upon a 14-bit system, but Sony insisted that the CD should be 16-bit, giving a better performance in terms of fidelity and lack of noise.

Sony had also developed an error correction process on playback that was superior to Philips's own system, and so it was adopted. Most famously, though, Sony argued for a 75-minute playing time. Philips had been working on the basis of an hour's duration for each disc, but Sony's executive deputy president, Norio Ohga, a conservatoire-educated classical music enthusiast, took Beethoven's Ninth as an example of a piece that ran for longer than an hour. The longest recording, a 1951 reading by Wilhelm Furtwangler, was found to be seventy-four minutes long, and so this became the preferred length for the new disc. To accommodate this, the diameter of the disc was increased to 12 centimetres and Ohga was satisfied. The basics were in place, but it was still a squeeze to get the machines and the first discs out in time for Ohga's immoveable Japanese launch date of October 1982. The European launch was set for March 1983. Nonetheless, both launches happened on schedule. Sony came out with its CDP 101, Philips with its CD 100.

On top of this tight schedule, Sony and Philips had to contend with resistance from some of the major record labels. At a *Billboard*-sponsored conference in Athens in April 1981, many record men indicated very strongly that they disapproved of the CD. It wasn't a case of simple Luddism. The technological advance offered by CD was fully acknowledged. Indeed, that was the root of the problem. Jerry Moss of A&M argued that if, as claimed, the disc offered a perfect replica of the original master, this would make piracy considerably easier. The whole affair then became far less seemly. 'At some point, executives stood up and began to chant a slogan that sounded like a Madison Avenue nightmare,' reported John Nathan in his history of Sony, '"The truth is in the groove! The truth is in the groove!"'[2]

David Fine, who was CEO of PolyGram UK at the time, had some sympathy with the likes of Moss, but knew that progress was inevitable.

> These early days were quite difficult. Even people who we knew well like Jerry Moss were asking, 'What do we need it for?' I can see why. They were a creative company. Jerry and Herb did wonderful stuff. They didn't do any manufacturing, they had a perfectly good carrier called the LP and they didn't need their lives disrupted. They didn't have the long-term technical commitment or adventurous spirit. They just accepted whatever came along. They certainly weren't going to be the frontrunners of change.[3]

Fortunately, both Philips and Sony had access to record companies of their own to get the ball rolling. Philips had PolyGram, while Sony had a close relationship with Columbia in the US, its main manifestation being the two companies' joint venture in Japan, CBS-Sony Records, which had been operating since 1968. This had come about after Columbia's failed attempt to buy back into its former subsidiary and long-time Japanese partner Nippon Columbia. When talks faltered, the chief of Columbia's international division, Harvey Schein, was introduced to Sony's Akio Morita and CBS-Sony was established. There had been some haggling on whose name came first, and Schein was happy that Columbia prevailed. He was less chuffed when Norio Ohga said no to his proposed scheme by which Columbia would be paid more for its masters than they had cost.[4] Nonetheless, the CBS-Sony relationship had worked well, and when Sony wanted to set up a CD plant in America, Columbia was a natural partner.

The job of convincing the rest of the industry and the outside world of the value of CD fell to Jan Timmer, who had stepped across from Philips's consumer electronics division to become president of PolyGram upon Coen Solleveld's retirement in 1982. 'Jan's a star,' says Fine, unequivocally:

> He was the father figure behind the CD. If you hadn't had a father figure like Jan with total absolute commitment, it could have fizzled out like any other product. You hear about Sony's involvement, but Sony, certainly at the time it was launched, brought nothing to the table marketing-wise. PolyGram had always been wonderful at marketing records, but to put the system across, Timmer had this unbelievable conviction in the digital carrier. He loved anything that was digital. He was an evangelist.[5]

The complicated process involved in producing the lens that focused the laser made sure that the players were expensive items, and so the first machines were aimed at the audiophile market. Sales of the discs were correspondingly small. In the first nine months of CD's availability in the UK, 300,000 discs were sold, with a retail value of just £2.6m. The economies of scale afforded by mass production soon enabled the price to come down, bringing the machines and the discs into the mass market. In 1985, 3.1 million CDs were delivered into the UK trade, with a retail value of £33.5m. That year was also the first when sales of cassettes outstripped vinyl LPs, shifting 55.4 million units in the UK at a retail price of £243.3m compared with 52.9 million at £250.9m.

This format shift was growing the overall market at a considerable rate. Between 1976 and 1985, spending on records and tapes in the UK increased from £254m to £665m, although this actually amounted to a smaller share of consumer spending, from 0.335 per cent to 0.317 per cent, the level having peaked in 1978 at 0.356%. The progress continued. In 1986, cassette forged ahead further to 69.6 million units, which brought in £277.9m compared with £239.5m garnered in the retail market by LPs. Cassette's supremacy was, however, to be short lived. In 1992, its position as the leading sound carrier had been usurped by CD, which sold 70.5 million units compared with cassette's 56.4 million units, at retail values of £345.7m and £685.2m respectively. Vinyl, by this point, had been reduced to a rump of 6.2 million units at retail values of £39.7m.[6]

One artist that did very well out of the growth of CD was the English band Dire Straits. In the mid-1980s, the available repertoire was still relatively limited. In 1986, there were only 10,200 titles available. To many, it seemed as though the band's *Brothers in Arms* offering was the only pop album available in the new format, and the way it was being pushed was no accident. Their manager Ed Bicknell had worked out a deal with Philips where the band became poster boys for CD:

In 1982, Mark [Knopfler, Dire Straits's leader] and I had been invited to go to Phonogram studios in the bowels of New Bond Street to listen to a new audio carrier. We didn't know what it was; nobody called it CD. It was one of the first two or three prototype machines, and a man in a white coat played us 'Private Investigations'. Mark said, 'This is fantastic, I can hear myself breathing behind the acoustic guitar passages.' Philips wanted to use this recording as a demonstration disc for the format, because it had this particular sound and ambience.

When the band were recording what became *Brothers in Arms*, I knew we were going to do a big tour, but there was one market we were not sure of and that was the US. Our success in America had been erratic. The first album was huge, the second not so huge, the third album did 900,000 without a hit single, which was pretty good. The last album in America had five tracks, one fifteen minutes long, no hit single, but that had managed to do 800,000. We were going to try doing arenas in America for the first time, rather than 3,000 to 4,000-seater theatres. We were doing arenas everywhere else. So I thought about looking for a sponsor, but I was nervous about sponsorship. It didn't sit well with my romantic view of it all, but I had to be pragmatic. We were probably looking at quite a big financial loss on the tour.

One day, a guy calls up from an ad agency, saying that they acted for Sony, and wondering if Mark would appear in a trade ad for Sony CD players with a couple of other people. I remember that Cliff Richard was one of the others. Being a good manager, I asked what was in it for us. He said, 'We can give you free CD players,' but we'd already got them – the first Philips machines. I put the phone down, and found myself sitting at my desk in silence for ten minutes, staring at the wall. Then I had kind of a cosmic moment, and I thought, 'Fuck, of course.' I rang up Ramon Lopez, then chairman of PolyGram [who had joined the company after running EMI], a wonderful record man, a fantastic guy and very bright intellectually. One of things I tell young managers is never to be afraid of telling huge lies. I rang Ramon and asked, 'How would your parent company feel if the biggest act on the label sponsored their rival company's new carrier?', which was not what had been mentioned at all. This guy wanted Mark for a print ad. The CD had been jointly developed, but they were still rivals. Ramon, in his beautiful slow Spanish way, said, 'Ed, what are you saying to me?' I replied that we'd had an offer of a worldwide sponsorship deal with Sony for their CD players, which was a complete and utter lie. 'Let me see what I can do,' Ramon said.

The very next day, a couple of guys arrived from Eindhoven, with no appointment, and we hammered out a deal. We got £150,000 plus another £25,000 to Mark for the rights to use the music in the ads. Plus, we got fifty free CDs each, which took longer to get than any other part of the exercise. In the end, they couldn't get them from within the company so had to send people out to shops to buy them. This is so typical of corporations. Not least because everyone had picked Deutsche Grammophon classics. No pop. We were all musical snobs. Crosby, Stills and Nash? Fuck 'em.

People might look at it now and say it wasn't a very good deal. However, the most important part was not the money they gave to us, but the money they could spend promoting the product in conjunction with us. I knew I could get into record shops with advertising, posters and displays, I knew we'd have adverts in the music press, but I wanted to get into the shops selling the hardware. So we were in every hi-fi store and every Philips ad. Philips had much greater spending power than PolyGram. They indicated that they were going to spend £3m on the campaign. I thought, 'Fucking hell, that's big wonga, if we can get that, do it right, manipulate them,' and I mean that in a friendly way, and 'supply them with the elements they need, which was a big record, I could promote my band on back of a new format.' There was another advantage. This was the only product that the band members really felt comfortable endorsing. When Knopfler had heard the demo he thought it was fantastic. It was a product directly associated with what we did, but also, we had no one else who wanted to sponsor the group. We were not a Pepsi or Coke kind of act and we weren't the sort of band who would have done tobacco or alcohol.[7]

The alliance coincided with and contributed to the mass acceptance of the new format, something that Bicknell hadn't foreseen:

I'd love to say, 'Yes, I'm a genius, it was all planned' but I can't. We had just signed up to sponsor the most important product launch ever by the parent company of our record company. The trickle-down effect on the record companies was as if some nuclear device had been positioned above the head of each managing director. It made them think, 'We'd better do some more for Dire Straits.' In return, we were able to deliver a phenomenally successful record and tour, and it was one of the rare occasions where this much-bandied word 'synergy' actually worked. It all came together … [8]

Compared with the ever-shrinking cost of the hardware, which came really low when methods were developed to press the all-important lenses out of plastic rather than grinding them in optical glass, the discs themselves remained a premium-priced product. BPI statistics suggested that there was no other way. Even assuming a retail price of £10.99 for a CD against £5.99 for a vinyl LP, the record company was making just 30p profit on each unit in either format. The BPI said that CDs, at £2.40 each, cost four times as much as LPs to manufacture and package, and the real money was being made by the retailers, who were getting £2.91 per CD, rather than £1.26 on a vinyl LP. The somewhat nebulous heading of 'royalties, marketing and other costs' accounted for £3.95 of a CD's price and £3.05 of a vinyl LP.

For all of the hay he and his artists were able to make, Bicknell was uncertain of the record companies' costings, a factor that led to his involvement in Gerald Kaufman's House of Commons Committee into CD pricing in 1992:

> I had seen a BPI yearbook, in which a pie chart appeared saying that artists received an average of £1.32 per CD. This was in about 1992. I, like everyone else, looked at this in total disbelief, and rang up half a dozen managers I knew. I rang Roger Forrester [Eric Clapton's manager], Steve O'Rourke [manager of Pink Floyd] and Tony Smith [manager of Genesis]. I said, 'Don't tell me the figure, but are you being paid more than a pound?' And they all went, 'No, don't be ridiculous.' If this was the average, it suggested some were getting far higher, but I couldn't find anybody. We were looking at this pie chart and thinking, 'This is bollocks. Other A&R costs? What's that?'[9]

Bicknell was summoned to address the committee in a letter that hinted heavily that if he didn't come voluntarily he would be subpoenaed. His mathematical studies, however, meant that he didn't take too much persuading.

> I went along and delivered my evidence, as I believed to be the case. One thing I said, I knew would be quoted as soon as it had come out of my mouth. I said that the record companies had discovered North Sea oil. They were selling people the same stuff twice and getting more money second time around. As a piece of capitalism, it's totally brilliant. But in doing so, I said, they were basically screwing artists and consumers, and the figures they were using to justify it were complete rubbish.
>
> Later, I learned a lot more about the issue of pricing and I did shift my position slightly. What the politicians were doing was oversimplifying it to a point that was silly. There was another point of view from the people in classical music and the small independents. I had been thinking of it in a one-dimensional way, concentrating on the five big majors. It got its day in the press, Rob Dickins [then Warner UK chairman], who's a friend, memorably refused to appear with me on *Newsnight*. Yawn. Once the politicians got their pound of flesh out of it, it petered out. I don't know if it's attributable to that, but the price of records from the consumers' point of view came down, generally speaking. It was driven by market considerations, primarily by arrivals of supermarkets and Woolworths, and

the massive discounting that was, is and will go on from the major record companies to the major retail chains. I still think they're too highly priced, though.[10]

Price notwithstanding, CD sales continued to rise astonishingly into the 1990s. The format did not just replace LP and cassette, it created a vast number of new sales. In 1977, the UK industry had shifted 101.3 million units, the bulk of which – 81.7 million – were LPs. In 1998, total unit sales were more than doubled – 210.3 million – at a retail value of £1.86bn – with CD representing 175.7 million of these units and £1.47bn of the value. Although a lot of this growth was driven by the new material available, part of this will have come from the desirability of the object itself, and a large part from the repackaging of old catalogue – effectively selling people what they already had again.

With figures like these, it was no wonder that Sony became keen to get in on the 'software' side as well as the hardware axis. Just as Edward Lewis rationalized in the late 1920s, making the equipment but not the records was like making razors but not the blades. Luckily, by the mid-1980s, their long-standing American musical partner was vulnerable to takeover. Lawrence Tisch, the owner of the Loew's cinema chain, had bought into CBS, but had little interest in the record side of the business. In 1986, it was proposed to sell Columbia's music business to Nelson Peltz, chairman and CEO of Triangle Industries, an outfit known for making packaging products, copper wire and coin-handling products, but no experience of records.

Understandably, Walter Yetnikoff, president of Columbia's record division since Irwin Segelstein returned to television in 1975, was aghast, and when Yetnikoff became aghast at something, everyone knew it. He was prone to smashing inanimate objects and shouting down the telephone in Yiddish when things weren't going his way. He was also heavily into substances of all kinds. It had once been so different. Like Harvey Schein and Clive Davis, Yetnikoff joined the company as a lawyer, and in 1961, had become Schein's deputy at the international division, succeeding Schein when he went to Sony in 1971. Back then, he was a quiet, courteous, proper sort. 'I first knew Walter when he was a young lawyer, drawing up contracts with the Gallo group, because we had the CBS relationship. Even on a Sunday, he'd be in a tie,' recalls David Fine.[11] After his promotion to the presidency, however, Yetnikoff changed dramatically. 'I think he was living in the aura of artists, trying to be an older groupie,' Fine observes. Certainly many of the artists enjoyed having a larger-than-life record company boss with a rock star lifestyle of his own.

Bruce Lundvall, who had become president of Columbia in the US under Yetnikoff, remembers the metamorphosis well:

> Walter's personality completely changed. I've never seen someone have a personality change like he did. When he was running the international division, he was rather shy, he would never make speeches. He had a real tough time at our conventions getting up in front of an audience. He was very ill at ease. And suddenly he became a powerbroker, very outspoken, very dynamic, and very, very aggressive. I liked him very, very much. He was terrific. We had a great relationship for quite some time. He had a great sense of humour.[12]

Most of Yetnikoff's aggression was aimed at WEA, in particular, Mo Ostin. Banners were made for the Columbia sales conference bearing two words: 'FUCK WARNER'. 'I remember him saying to me, "Screw Mo Ostin, he's a short little Jew",' says Lundvall, recalling one outburst:

> I said to him, 'But you're a taller Jew than he is, what kind of talk is this? For Christ's sake, Mo Ostin is a very fine man, a lovely man, you know. How can you talk this way?' He said, 'We're going to bury those people, we're going to have the leading market share.' He went on a crusade at one point to sign people away from Warner Bros specifically. James Taylor – I ended up taking the credit for signing James, because I spent the time with him. Walter paid the money. We had a terrific act: good guy, bad guy. That's how we lost Paul Simon, because he had a fight with him, and I thought I had saved the deal. Walter insulted him in some meeting and that was the end of that.[13]

This then was the kind of firepower that Larry Tisch faced over the Nelson Peltz issue. Tisch made Yetnikoff an offer, albeit one so steep he probably never thought he could take it up. If Yetnikoff could match Peltz's $1.25bn offer in cash, he could buy the record division. His years in international had brought him close to Norio Ohga at Sony. Sony undoubtedly had the money, and they were interested, but no sooner had they put their marker down than Tisch came back with the news that William Paley was against the sale. The idea was off the menu for a few months, before Tisch indicated that he thought he could swing Paley.

There was only one problem. The price had now increased to $2bn. Sony co-founder Akio Morita swallowed hard and agreed the price. Even when the stock market crashed on Black Monday, 19 October 1987, and the price remained the same, Sony remained committed. So committed that it let Tisch keep $40m that had been overpaid into the pension fund. So committed that when Tisch slapped down Yetnikoff's assertion that, as the deal would be closing in late November, Sony should be entitled to the November and December revenue, Sony let the matter pass and let Tisch keep the fruits of the busiest two months of the year.

The deal was finalized in February 1988, ninety-nine years after Columbia had been established. Nine months later, in a *Billboard* supplement celebrating the company's centenary, Yetnikoff – who had been elevated to the position of president and CEO of CBS Records Inc., with Tommy Mottola (not only a former artist manager but also former artist, under the name T. D. Valentine) taking over in his old position – said of the new owners that it was 'nice to be wanted again', a dig at the company's former parent, CBS Inc. He added that Sony was 'a great company to be associated with ... [they're] familiar with how a record company works', that they were 'very sensitive to the artists: any artist who's come back from Japan, Cyndi Lauper or whoever, has been ecstatic about the way they've been treated', and that they were 'not afraid to invest in the future'. He also observed, amusingly, that the record industry was 'the most people-intensive business there is, next to prostitution' and that 'the attitudes and the enthusiasm of the people here are much more positive than a year ago. It all bodes well.'[14]

Sony might well have been unafraid to invest in the future, but in time it became harder for them to see Yetnikoff as a part of that future. He was instrumental in the group's 1989 acquisition of Columbia Pictures for $5bn and the disastrous and expensive wooing of Peter Guber and Jon Peters to run the show. Added to which, his erratic behaviour as a result of his prodigious intake had done him no favours, and he spent various periods in rehab. His relations with Michael Jackson, one of the Columbia group's biggest acts, were strained. He fell out with Bruce Springsteen when he asked New Jersey's finest not to take part in an Amnesty International benefit, because he viewed the organization as anti-Israel. Worst of all,

Columbia was slipping into second place in the market, behind the dreaded Warner.

On 1 September 1990, a week after it had printed suggestions of a rift between Springsteen and Yetnikoff, *Billboard* printed an interview with Yetnikoff in which he denied that he was to leave the company. He had signed a new three-year contract, effective from April 1991, and he declared that it was Ohga's 'desire to have me remain as long as I wish to remain'. This was, on the surface, true enough and Sony had issued a press statement to this effect. However, *Billboard* also printed a statement from Springsteen's manager Jon Landau indicating that 'neither Bruce nor I have had a significant conversation with him in nearly two years'.

A fortnight after the appearance of the interview, three-year contract or no three-year contract, Yetnikoff was out. The departure was tickled up initially as a sabbatical, after which Yetnikoff would collaborate with Ohga on 'long-term projects affecting the future growth of Sony'. No such collaborations occurred. Yetnikoff had been unceremoniously sacked. Mottola took over completely, and by October 1993, he had been elevated from president of Sony Music US to president and chief operating officer of Sony Music Entertainment worldwide.

By the time of Yetnikoff's departure, the American industry was embroiled in another round of payola controversies. Barred by a largely ineffectual law from bunging DJs directly, the major record companies had resorted to paying independent promotion men several million dollars a year to do the job for them. By the 1980s, several major players, led by Joe Isgro on the west coast and Fred DiSipio on the east, had carved up the market between them. Collectively, they were known as 'the Network'. The majors had tried to break the Network's stranglehold on promotion several times, but each time, the pluggers had proven conclusively that they could make or break a record, and the record companies fell back into line. If one company dropped out, the others would just regard it as a competitive advantage and carry on. The pull-out had to be unanimous.

The Network's activities were brought to greater prominence by the attentions of Marvin Rudnick, a Los Angeles prosecutor who had been introduced to their strange world while investigating some considerable unpleasantness at MCA. It had emerged that a convicted fraudster called Sal Pisello had insinuated his way into the company and organized the sale of 5 million of MCA's cut-outs to John LaMonte, a Philadelphia wholesaler, via the perennially savoury Morris Levy. LaMonte had been promised star names in his consignment, but when he found that the good stuff had been skimmed off, he refused to pay. In return, Levy's partner, Gaetano 'the Big Guy' Vastola, rearranged LaMonte's face. Plenty there for an organized crime expert to be chewing on, and when some MCA-friendly cops alerted Rudnick to the Network, he wondered if he wasn't being thrown a decoy. He looked into Isgro anyway.

NBC News investigator Brian Ross got in on the act as well, obtaining footage that purportedly showed Isgro and DiSipio meeting with infamous hood John Gotti, and alleging that the pluggers were in the pay of the Mafia as well as the record companies. The attorney general weighed in, as did Tennessee senator Al Gore, and the record companies, led by the RIAA, finally acted as one. No more independent promotion. Stan Cornyn's epitaph was best: 'It was the end of an era of amazing grease.'[15]

The Sony-CBS deal is usually seen as the start of the merger mania that struck the record industry in the 1980s and 1990s, but it had been pre-dated by the German publishing group Bertelsmann's takeover of RCA in December 1986. Bertelsmann had entered the record business in 1958, when it started Ariola Schallplatten. It moved into the US market in 1979 with the purchase of Clive Davis's Arista operation from Columbia Pictures. Then, in July 1984, it had entered into a joint venture with RCA, called RCA-Ariola, with the troubled American company holding 75 per cent of the stock. However, in December 1985, RCA itself was bought by General Electric and some businesses were sold off, including the record division, which became Bertelsmann Music Group, while retaining the RCA trademark.

Unsurprisingly, given Davis's dynamism and RCA's moribundity, Arista was the powerhouse for the new BMG operation. Roger Watson recalls Clive revelling in the nickname given to him by the senior Bertelsmann executives – 'The Jew in the Crown'. Watson had returned to the UK after more than ten years in the US with Chrysalis. Following a brief stint with Island working on film soundtracks, he moved to run the British side of Arista: 'It was an interesting time. I came from the relative obscurity of special projects to the frontline with Clive, and all the benefits and stresses that entailed. It was a steep learning curve. I suddenly had thirty people working for me, and I also had to get used to kow-towing to Clive, and him ringing you all of the time.'

As with his experience at MCA in the late 1960s and early 1970s, Watson was conscious of being very much a colonial outpost. 'He [Davis] used the

UK office as his marketing operation. He was always on. He knew everybody, everybody knew him, but the day-to-day running of the office was a nightmare. We could never get anything away from the UK.'[16]

There was one exception to the one-way traffic between New York and London. Arista UK under Watson was able to offer Davis the singer Lisa Stansfield, in whom Davis immediately saw the potential. 'We played Clive "All Around the World" and he said, "This isn't just a hit, this is a number one"'. Another singer who benefited from Davis's patronage was Whitney Houston. Brought into Arista by one of his A&R men, Davis took over all aspects of Houston's career, resulting in an album that became the best-selling debut ever by a female singer. In contrast to these achievements, RCA just muddled along.

The various mergers happened for different reasons. Sony and Matsushita – which bought MCA in 1990 – were hardware manufacturers buying into software. Bertelsmann was a media company expanding its reach into new areas. Others, however, saw the majors spreading their bets by buying up the most prominent of the independent labels. As will have been seen in earlier chapters, there was nothing new about consolidation, but this time, the earlier mergers happened against a background of apparent economic prosperity rather than as a reaction to hard times.

As the world slipped into recession in the early 1990s, the mergers continued, but apart from the usual harrumphing protests about the awfulness of prevailing conditions, the business was nowhere near as badly affected as it had been in the late 1970s. In the UK, there was a mild dip in music retail sales in 1990, down from £1.21bn to £1.18bn. In 1991, there was a recovery to £1.21bn, then another dip in 1992, but between then and 2001, sales increased year on year. In addition, CD sales remained unaffected throughout, the falls coming from dwindling LP and cassette revenues.

PolyGram – which by this point was 90 per cent owned by Philips, following Siemens's decision to divest and a subsequent share issue – was the first of the majors to make a move, snapping up Island and A&M within two months of each other in 1989. The Island acquisition, which was finalized in August, included the record label, Island Music Publishing and Island Visual Arts, but not Chris Blackwell's Blue Mountain publishing operation, and cost PolyGram somewhere north of $300m. The company's global contracts with WEA were left to run out, and then folded into the new owner's network. Then, in mid-October, came the announcement that PolyGram had bought A&M for $500m.

In both cases, the plan was to let the companies continue as they were with complete autonomy. 'We intend to leave Island as it is,' PolyGram president David Fine said at the time of the Island deal. 'It will continue to be run by Chris Blackwell, and he will have the benefit of our worldwide resources ... We have not bought the company to strip it down.'[17] On the A&M matter, Fine had said that 'We regard the individuals as a crucial part of the deal.' The reality worked out rather differently, something that Fine was at least half expecting.

'You can't really retain your founder executives,' he now rationalizes. 'That wasn't a shock. It would have been nicer had one found a way to accommodate them but they're too used to doing things their own way, sometimes efficiently, sometimes inefficiently.' The corporate life represented a learning experience for Blackwell, but one that, while initially illuminating, soon palled. 'Chris was never that interested in the money and budgeting side, and in the very early part of the acquisition we were able to show him how Island was performing ... I think he found that interesting, [but] I think he found it too restricting.'

The loss of Blackwell, Alpert and Moss, while regrettable, was salved by the value the acquisitions brought in other areas:

> I don't think PolyGram had cause to regret, because of the catalogue values that they got. We had the licence for A&M in quite a lot of markets and so we were able to prove what we could do with A&M, in terms of compilations and things, that they couldn't do for themselves. We had a marketing muscle more than the independent ever had. With PolyGram's experience, we really knew how to market catalogue. Look at the *Now* series that we did with EMI. They sell a million of each record. It's a given. It's amazing what you can do if the marketing muscle is there. That's why those catalogues were hugely important. Of course it brought in great artists – Sting and artists like that.[18]

MCA had been in acquisitive mood in 1988 when it joined with the venture capitalists Boston Ventures to buy Motown – which it already distributed – for the bargain price of $61m. MCA took 20 per cent with Boston Ventures owning the balance of the company. MCA had first offered to buy the company from Berry Gordy in 1986, and they had all but reached the altar when Gordy had second thoughts about selling his heritage. Two years on, though, Motown was in trouble. 'We had too much overhead and had to gross $40m a year just to break even. Selling wasn't just the right thing to do, it was the only thing to do,' argued Gordy in his memoirs.[19] Shrewdly, Gordy kept his publishing company Jobete out of the deal, and was able to sell 50 per cent of it to EMI in 1996 for $132m.

Boston Ventures had been called in 'because a decision was made at MCA that Motown was not worth $61 million,' said Irving Azoff, who was boss of MCA's record division at the time and the main proponent of the deal, primarily because he wanted to keep the Motown distribution business. These words came a year later when Azoff had left the company, and he estimated that 'if Motown were purchased today, it would fetch three times that'.[20] In the event, the MCA/Motown deal ended acrimoniously in the courts and in 1993, Boston Ventures sold the company to PolyGram – which had taken on the label's distribution in 1991 – for £325m.

MCA had never quite reached the top table of all the record labels. Azoff, the former manager of the Eagles and another industry wild man, although in a subtler way than Yetnikoff,[21] had made great strides, but the company still only accounted for 4 per cent of the market share. The 1979 acquisition of ABC-Dunhill had helped matters a bit, but the label's image took a knock with the Sal Pisello affair. MCA's musical reach had been improved by the arrival of David Geffen and his labels. In 1980, upon returning from his health-related exile, Geffen had climbed back into bed with Steve Ross at Warner, who bankrolled another label for the former agent, this time called simply Geffen Records. One of the label's first signings was John Lennon – emerging from an exile of his own after five years as a house-husband bringing up his son Sean – and his wife Yoko Ono. Their comeback album, *Double Fantasy*, failed to set the charts alight until it gained a gruesome publicity boost with Lennon's murder on 8 December 1980. The first single from *Double Fantasy*, '(Just Like) Starting Over', had been on the UK charts since 8 November, but didn't make it to number one until 20 December. This was not enough, though. Other superstars who had joined the label, such as Elton John and Donna Summer, were all disappointing in sales terms.

The first signs of a rift with Warners occurred when WEA offered Geffen a $3m, three-year contract for foreign rights to the label. Lawyer Allen Grubman thought he could get between $15m and $17m a year for Geffen, and, shrewdly, targeted Yetnikoff at CBS, who was ever delighted to stuff Warners in any way he could, from poaching James Taylor to snaffling whole labels. In such matters, all financial sense departed him and he agreed to take on Geffen overseas at $15m a year. Some at Warners felt betrayed. Not Mo Ostin. He saw the bright side, which was that CBS would end up paying the start-up costs for a Warner label.

The label continued to underperform, making Yetnikoff wonder whether his Warner-baiting hadn't come at a very high price indeed. Four years after it was established, it still hadn't shown a profit. Neil Young's sojourn at the label descended into recriminations when Young delivered albums like the futuristic *Trans* while Geffen demanded some rock and roll. Young soon returned to Warners. One of the label's successes, the platinum-selling Sammy Hagar, was approached to join Van Halen, a Warner Bros act. Geffen used the poaching to pick a fight with Mo Ostin, which he thought would help simplify his upcoming renegotiation with Steve Ross, by declaring Ostin unfit to take part in discussions due to personal enmity. Geffen made the seemingly unreasonable demand of a $5m, five-year deal. When Ross rejected that, Geffen said he'd sign if Ross would give him the half of Geffen Records that Warners owned. Having sunk millions into the project for little return, Ross agreed.

Ostin told Ross that he had made a mistake: 'Now is the time to buy Geffen Records. It's not the time to give it up for nothing.'[22] Ostin was right. Over the rest of the 1980s, Geffen gained momentum. Heavy metal group Guns 'n' Roses became huge, and former Eagle Don Henley's solo career hit stride. By 1989, Geffen Records – with sales of $225m and a host of gold and platinum discs – was being pursued by Thorn-EMI, MCA, Paramount and, perhaps surprisingly, Ross. However, saddled with debt following the Time Warner merger, Ross was unable to make an offer that pleased Geffen and fell out of the running. Thorn-EMI offered $350m in cash and stock in the new combined group. In March 1990, reports started appearing that EMI was set to buy Geffen's company for $750m, a surprising announcement considering Geffen's well-publicized low opinion of EMI's business acumen, following EMI's incompetent handling of the Asylum catalogue in the early 1970s. MCA's bid, on the other hand, while lower, was stock-based, insulating Geffen against paying tax on his windfall. Geffen was to receive 980,000 shares in new preferred stock, worth $535m, making Geffen MCA's largest shareholder. Geffen went with MCA.

For years, the MCA group had been rumoured to be on the brink of merging with Paramount, but nothing came to fruition. Over in Japan, though, the American market was being watched carefully by the electronics company Matsushita, following the Sony purchases of CBS and Columbia Pictures. Sony's Betamax video system had lost the war against JVC's VHS format (incidentally, JVC had early links with the record industry, the letters of its name standing for 'Japan Victor Company'), partially because of the relative wealth of pre-recorded material that was available for VHS. Sony was never going to be caught without a ready supply of software again and Matsushita felt it needed to follow suit. A meeting between Lew Wasserman and the leaders of Matsushita was engineered by Hollywood agent Michael Ovitz and in 1990, it was announced that the Japanese company was to buy MCA Universal for $6.13bn in cash. Geffen took his $540m share in cash. Wasserman, MCA's guiding light since the 1940s, took his in Matsushita stock.

The Japanese ownership was not, however, a happy one. On the film side, the budget for the Kevin Costner movie *Waterworld* was increasing daily at a rate that alarmed the new paymasters. In the fourth quarter of 1994, group profits had increased fourfold, but MCA's profit growth was a mere 5 per cent. Matsushita decided to sell up at a loss rather than continue to throw money at MCA. In March 1995, the Canadian drinks group Seagram bought MCA for $5.7bn.

Not to be outdone, EMI joined in the consolidation rush. In 1989, it bought a 50 per cent stake in Chrysalis in 1989, acquiring the balance of the company two years later. It also ramped up its presence in music publishing. During the 1980s, it had bought the Robert Mellin, Sydney Bron and Lawrence Wright publishing firms and in 1989, it bought SBK Entertainment World for $295m. Its highest-profile purchase, though, was that of the Virgin Music Group – including both the record label and the music publishing business – in March 1992 for £510m in cash and £50m of assumed debt. Just a month before, Bertelsmann had been the hot favourites to purchase Virgin, but EMI managed to outbid them. The label had been doing particularly well with the likes of Phil Collins, Janet Jackson and Bryan Ferry, and had just landed the Rolling Stones contract, including the band's lucrative post-Decca back catalogue.

Again, the outward appearance was that the new owners wanted continuity. Richard Branson – who received 60 per cent of the purchase price, and needed it desperately to keep his airline going through its ongoing battles with British Airways – was to be chairman for life, and his lieutenants Simon Draper and Ken Berry – who got 10 per cent and 5 per cent respectively of EMI's cash[23] – were to run the company as EMI employees. Draper soon withdrew, but Berry stuck around to become a power in the land with EMI. While financially rewarding, the sale was emotionally a bit much for Branson. 'For the first time in my life, I had enough money to fulfil my wildest dreams,' he wrote in his autobiography, but he earlier admitted that he had left the staff briefing about the sale and 'set off at a sprint down Ladbroke Grove, tears streaming down my face' all the while passing newspaper hoardings advertising a windfall that 'should have dried the eyes of most grown men'.[24]

Branson had done well. With other independents, there was almost nothing to sell. A case in point is Stiff. It had been formed in 1976 just as punk was taking hold. Over the next decade, it had a remarkable run of hits from the likes of Nick Lowe, the Damned, Elvis Costello, Jona Lewie, Ian Dury and the Blockheads, and Madness. By 1986, though, the label had collapsed, and the catalogue was dispersed piecemeal to various purchasers including Virgin, which took Madness.

Acquisitions such as the Virgin and CBS deals might have been good news for the new owners, but they didn't necessarily go down terribly well with the talent. Sony had to deal with a major grievance from George Michael. Michael had followed up the best-selling album *Faith* with *Listen Without Prejudice Volume I*, which sold to a far more selective audience. Relations between Michael and the label worsened to the point in October 1993 when he started legal proceedings against the company to get out of his contract. He felt that its relative failure had been down to the lack of enthusiasm with which it had been promoted. Michael alluded to the massive campaign that Sony had undertaken for Mariah Carey (who was later to marry label boss Tommy Mottola), but Sony responded that such campaigns were used to break new acts. Whatever the truth of the situation, the figures made it look as though Sony wasn't really bothering:

> [Columbia vice-president Fred] Ehrlich was asked by [Michael's counsel Mark] Cran about the promotional costs for *Listen Without Prejudice*. He admitted that the company spent only $23,000 on its promotion during the first quarter of 1991, and that the total television and print budget had been less than the $650,000 spent to advertise the *Faith* album.
>
> Cran asked why sales of *Listen Without Prejudice* were 'less than a quarter of the sales that *Faith* had in the US, while its worldwide sales were roughly

half of the previous album.' Ehrlich replied, 'The eight million units that *Faith* sold were an extraordinary amount ... it wasn't a typical record. It went eight times platinum, and there are not many artists who do that, and can do it consistently.'

Cran also cross-examined Ehrlich about the $180,000 budget for advertising the album on MTV and for test-marketing it in the San Francisco area, claiming, 'That's not much for an album where you expect to sell a million copies ... it was a derisory sum to spend on this album for its launch.'[25]

At stake was artistic freedom. Michael felt he should be allowed to make whatever record he wanted to make, and the record company should get behind it no matter what. Burial through lack of promotion was a form of censorship, or so ran Michael's logic. The case was not settled until July 1995, but it came out in Michael's favour. Sony continued to receive a royalty from his future recordings, and gained a greatest hits compilation with some new material, but Michael was free to take his music wherever he wanted. Initially that was to Virgin in the UK and the newly established Dreamworks SKG, but since then he has done the unthinkable and returned to Sony.

Meanwhile, Virgin saw one of its longest-serving bands, XTC, go on strike. Many years before, the band had been in litigation with a former manager, their £400,000 costs being paid by the record company in advance of royalties. The result was that Virgin was making a lot of money from the band's records, while the band itself was seeing none of it. They demanded a renegotiation of their contract, a frankly pitiful affair that had remained largely unchanged from their first days as an untried new wave outfit. When this was refused, XTC downed tools. The fact that Virgin had been sold to an organization that made missiles – Thorn-EMI – didn't dispose them too kindly to their record company either. The strike lasted six years – XTC were finally released and set up their own label.

Despite these disruptions, the Virgin purchase was to prove a good one for EMI, continuing to contribute a profitability 'just short of EMI's'.[26] After the near-disaster of the late 1970s, though, the group had not been untroubled in the 1980s. Turnover of staff – particularly at the senior executive level – was high until Rupert Perry was summoned back from the States by Bhaskar Menon ('a useless manager, but a charming dinner companion' says one former colleague, while others regard Menon as the best thing to happen to EMI since Louis Sterling) in April 1986 to run EMI Records UK. His predecessor, Peter Jamieson, had lasted three years, as had Jamieson's predecessor, Cliff Busby. This turnover had resulted in too many situations where the people who had initiated a project were no longer with the company when it came to fruition. Their successors, meanwhile, were preoccupied with their own pet schemes. Perry set about trying to establish continuity and stability, in which he largely succeeded. Parlophone, one of the individual label identities that had disappeared in 1973 when then-MD Gerry Oord adopted an overall EMI label brand, returned.

The company was still capable of the odd inspired decision, one of which was hiring Bruce Lundvall in 1984. Lundvall had left Columbia in 1982, having been approached by Joe Smith about coming to WEA to run Elektra's East Coast office. As a sweetener, he offered Lundvall – a jazz fan who had delighted in indulging his passion at Columbia – his own jazz label, Elektra Musician. 'I told Walter a year before I left that I was going to leave the company, because I was no longer happy there,' Lundvall indicates. 'I said, "It's gotten very bureaucratic, it's gotten very politicized. I'm no longer happy, because I'm not involved with artists the way I used to be".' The company had become very big indeed, and so Lundvall had lost touch with the main point of the business, which, as far as he was concerned, was music. Instead, he had found himself undertaking tasks which were both utterly unsuited to him, not to say mind-numbing. One was liaising with Bill Paley about the establishment of a new cassette plant in Georgia:

> I was never going home at night. I was doing all the convention speeches, which were now twice a year, you know, and refereeing politics between people. It was no longer fun. I said, 'I want to go and do something small, and do things that interest me. I want to sign artists, I want to do marketing and those are the areas that I do well. Joe finally convinced me that I ought to come and do creative work in a smaller environment. My wife was thrilled because she assumed I would be home more at night, which I certainly wasn't, but I thought I might be.[27]

Sadly, the Elektra job panned out a little differently than billed, in other ways than the working hours. Lundvall liked the atmosphere that Steve Ross had built up, but was less enamoured of the narrowness of the musical outlook:

Steve Ross was running Warner Communications and it was as though each of the record companies was individually owned by these guys, whether it was Ahmet, Joe Smith, or Mo Ostin and so on. It was that kind of attitude. I liked it. I thought it was very entrepreneurial, very progressive, very creative. However, there was really a built-in creative bias, which I didn't expect. I was used to working with every type of artist, from Johnny Mathis to Bruce Springsteen to Dylan. There was a built-in musical snobbery there that said you had to be involved only with very fashionable, current, hip music, whatever that meant. Early on at Elektra, I brought in Rupert Holmes [of 'Pina Colada Song' fame] and everyone laughed at me. He was not a hip artist, but I didn't understand what that was. I was used to Columbia Records where we had Neil Diamond, Barbra Streisand and Johnny Mathis, and all the rock and roll artists and all the most adventurous jazz artists all under one roof. It was really a rock and roll mentality at that time at Warner ...

I had a problem in the jazz area, because this was a very unpopular area of music, and it wasn't representing an upside that would be significant. But I did have a couple of artists who did well, like Bobby McFerrin. Jac Holzman loved the idea that I was bringing jazz into the company, which it had not really had an involvement with, but Jac was really now a consultant at that point, and Joe Smith was running Elektra. Joe was a jazz fan, so he was very supportive ... [But] frankly, after a period of time at Elektra, I think he got a little bored with it.[28]

The answer to Lundvall's problems came when Bhaskar Menon invited him to dinner after an RIAA board meeting, and asked if he wanted to run Blue Note Records. It had come into EMI's ownership in 1979 as part of the United Artists-Liberty record group. The label had been established in 1939 by German émigré Alfred Lion, with a double-header session by the boogie-woogie pianists Albert Ammons and Meade 'Lux' Lewis. Lion was soon joined by another German fleeing the Nazis, photographer Francis Wolff, and the pair were given a lot of help in distribution by Milt Gabler of the Commodore record shop and label. Unfortunately, the company was hit in its infancy by the AFM ban, and became one of the first companies to reach terms with the union in 1943. However, even with this head start on the others, it was not until after the war, when bebop was on the rise, that the label truly established itself. Through the 1950s, it recorded the likes of

Thelonious Monk, Art Blakey, Hank Mobley and, briefly, Miles Davis, and then in the 1960s it kept up the momentum with Herbie Hancock, Lee Morgan and Horace Silver. After the sell-off to Liberty in 1965, though, Blue Note lost its way. Alfred Lion withdrew from active involvement in 1967, as a result of ill-health. By the time EMI bought it, it was moribund, concerned only with reissues. Efforts had been made by reissue producer Michael Cuscuna to revive the label as an outlet for new material, but nothing happened until Lundvall was lured by Menon. Blue Note was, however, only part of the job:

[Menon] said, 'We have two companies on the west coast, Capitol and EMI America, but we don't have a label on the east coast, so I'd love to start a pop label.' I said to myself I have to do this, because I still had one foot in pop music and one in jazz, so that was it. I said, 'Absolutely, yes, if I can get out of my contract.' Of course ... I knew Krasnow would be thrilled to get rid of me. Which he was. I walked into his office the next day and said, 'Look, Bob, I have an opportunity to do something that I really want to do. We've put this company back on target, we're making money now. You don't really need to have two of us now.' He said, 'Hey man, this is the best thing in the world for you', shook my hand, and the next day I was out. And I was thrilled. And I've been with EMI ever since.[29]

Initially, the Blue Note side was dominant. 'We had the jazz catalogue and we had a full staff of people, we kept it small and we built it as we grew, but essentially, the Blue Note reissues kind of supported our overhead at the beginning,' Lundvall points out. There were some critically acclaimed new signings on the Blue Note side, including the virtuoso guitarist Stanley Jordan and the vocalist Bobby McFerrin, both of whom achieved massive sales in jazz terms. However, the pop label Manhattan soon began paying its way. 'Richard Marx became our biggest success, and then Natalie Cole ... Robbie Nevil was one of our first signings, who eventually had a gold album. We made a small deal with Gamble and Huff, we had a gold album with the O'Jays and got close to that with Phyllis Hyman. It was a start-up label, but we did pretty well for a new label.'

Although order and stability had taken over at the record group, Thorn-EMI as a corporate entity proved less easy to steer. By 1995, a demerger of the music operations from the rest of the business would be the 'best way of unlocking shareholder value'.[30] Unlocking shareholder value was a polite way of saying that the group was broke and that the only chance it had of survival was as two separate parts, a reversal of the situation that had prevailed in 1979. 'That's what it takes to get the shares up from £11 to £18,'[31] said Thorn-EMI chairman Sir Colin Southgate of the demerger, which was passed by the group's desperate shareholders in August 1996.

WEA's participation in the merger merry-go-round, with the 1989 combination of Warner Communications and Time-Life, was intended to guarantee the group's future stability. It almost ended up having the opposite effect. In the early 1980s, there had been an abortive attempt to combine with PolyGram, but by the end of the decade, the desire to merge was driven by imperatives other than growth. Steve Ross had been ill with cancer of the pancreas and although it had been beaten into remission once, he was keen to realize his assets while putting the company on a safe footing after his death. Time-Life, run by Gerald Levin, was found to be interested, and a straightforward debt-free merger was on the cards until Martin Davis of Paramount showed his hand with a bid for Time-Life. Consequently, the bloodless merger became a purchase, with Warner shareholders receiving 465 new shares in the new Time-Warner for each old Warner share they owned. Ross, personally, made $193m from the deal. The downside was that the buy-out left the new company with a debt pile of $16bn.

The situation brought some harsh new economic realities into the Warner operation. Like Motown before it, a phenomenal amount of business had to be done just to keep on an even keel. 'We no longer had the pleasure of making gobs of money to smooth our days and nights,' explained Stan Cornyn. 'Now we needed to make gobs.'[32] As Ahmet Ertegun observed, Ross had traditionally put in 'anybody to be the general head' of the music operations. Once it had been David Horowitz, then Elliott Goldman, both of whom took care of business while largely deferring to the label heads. However, in the new, cash-strapped Time-Warner, the 'anybody' of the day, a former politician called Robert J. Morgado, began to stamp his authority, such as it was, on the record side of the business. Morgado had made his name in the company with a round of downsizing following the group's disastrous investment in the Atari video games company in the early 1980s.

His first move was on the WEA international business, which he felt was run in a very lax manner by Nesuhi Ertegun. He brought Ramon Lopez in, ostensibly to co-run the business – now renamed Warner Music International – with Ertegun. Lopez had joined the company a little earlier, having been enticed from PolyGram by Ostin. Ertegun knew what was up and retired to return to producing jazz albums, before becoming involved with the IFPI's anti-piracy campaign. Morgado might well have had a point about Ertegun's style of management being an anachronism in the modern industry. 'The truth was that Nesuhi always grew WEA International slowly, laissez-faire in his own, autocratic way,' admitted Stan Cornyn.[33]

Far less understandable, though, was the way that Morgado handled Mo Ostin, who had been, more than anyone else, responsible for the record group's successful growth. In 1970, he had risen from running Reprise to become president of Warner Bros Records, covering both the WB and Reprise labels. The empire-building of the previous holder of the position, Mike Maitland, had been scuppered by Ahmet Ertegun, who had suggested to Steve Ross and Ted Ashley that Ostin and Joe Smith were far more vital to the company than Maitland, but that their achievements were not as well trumpeted. Result: Maitland out, Ostin promoted, Ertegun and Smith in as executive vice-presidents.

Fast forward to the early 1990s. Although Morgado was nominally his boss, Ostin still reported to Steve Ross. After Ross's death in December 1992, though, the scene was set for a change in the lines of command. Ostin now reported directly to Gerald Levin, but 'Morgado was determined to end the final music baronies that Ross had nurtured,' in the words of Cornyn.[34] Ultimately, when it came to renewing Ostin's contract, Levin informed Mo that he would have to report to Morgado in future. A plan of succession was also drawn up: Ostin to continue as chairman and CEO for the first half of the three-year contract, then just as chairman, with Lenny Waronker, who had been with the label since the 1960s, stepping up to the CEO's position. Ostin decided to sleep on it and stuck the unsigned contract in his desk. The final straw came when Morgado elevated Atlantic's co-chairman and CEO Doug Morris to the presidency of a new umbrella company for all of the labels. In effect, Ostin would be reporting to Morris. On 15 August 1994, Ostin told Levin that he was leaving. Two months later, Waronker did the same. At a dinner to mark Ostin's exit in December, Charles Koppelman of EMI surveyed the guest list, which included all of Morgado's oustees, such as Waronker, Nesuhi Ertegun, Bob Krasnow and distribution chief Henry Droz. His comment on the man-management catastrophe? 'They broke up the Yankees.'[35]

Having dealt with the old guard, the Morgado steamroller moved on to the new faces. He tried to move the newly elevated Doug Morris back to Atlantic and bring Warner UK's chairman Rob Dickins over to replace him. When the Morris loyalists, such as Atlantic's Danny Goldberg and Elektra's Sylvia Rhone, heard of the plan, they went ballistic and threatened a revolt. Dickins, who had been Concorded over to discuss the succession, was sent back to London, fuming. Morris returned to his exalted post and shortly afterwards Levin fired Morgado, with a $60m parachute, all the while trying to entice Mo Ostin back into the fold. Morgado's successor was Michael Fuchs, who had been with Time-Life for more than twenty years, running the HBO cable channel. Morris, flushed with success, made a move on Lopez's international division, but this proved to be his downfall. Fearful of future insurrections, in June 1995 Fuchs fired Morris. By November, when Morris pitched up at MCA, replacing Alvin Teller, Levin had fired Fuchs.

How did a once-proud company come to this mass of hirings, firings and general blood-letting? Ahmet Ertegun, perhaps mindful of the fact that the sign over the door still says Time-Warner, blames the departed Morgado squarely:

> Morgado was some sort of megalomaniac who knew nothing about music. He was a political kind of guy, he'd worked for the governor of New York State. He came in and totally screwed up our record division. He did everything wrong. He fought with Mo Ostin. He had ideas to do all sorts of things. He was probably one of the most arrogant, stupid men I've ever met. It was all brought on by Steve Ross, and after that, whoever was running the company, nobody cared much about the music division and they kept putting up people to run it who were non-music people. Michael Fuchs, [Bob] Daly and [Terry] Semel, who were movie people. They would never take somebody from the cable divison and tell them to run the motion picture division, but they would take anybody and let them run the music. With Doug, you see, what they did was to force people into political games within the corporation. There was no leadership from the top. It was everybody fighting everybody else.[36]

The last – to date – of the great mergers was the biggest of all. In June 1998, Seagram, the owner of MCA, clinched a deal to acquire the 75 per cent of PolyGram that Philips owned for a total of $10.4bn. This coincided with the

Bronfmans' decision to get out of the liquor business, and there had been talk of them buying EMI, but this came to nothing. The Philips group was having a hard time of it in the late 1990s, making a 268-million-euro loss in 1996. With Jan Timmer having retired as president of Philips, much of the company's attachment to its record subsidiary had gone. In the 1998 Annual Report, Timmer's successor Cor Boonstra wrote: 'We decided to sell PolyGram because we believe that PolyGram will add more shareholder value together with Seagram's Universal music and film operations than as a separate subsidiary of Philips.' He added that there was an apparently irreconcilable difference in culture between the two. '[T]he competences required to run this business are quite unlike those needed elsewhere in the company, and the very different nature of the business means its contribution to strengthening the Philips brand was marginal at best.'[37]

No doubt the price being offered by Seagram was a huge factor in deciding Boonstra's mind, but David Fine, who had retired from PolyGram in 1990, is unsure that it was the right decision: 'I don't know if it was a good idea. The price was enormous, but on the other hand, PolyGram's profit contribution to the group was also very big.' At the same time, Fine wondered if Siemens regretted selling out when they had. 'Philips bought out Siemens's share and this was minuscule money compared to what they eventually got for it. We're talking $50m–$100m, when eventually Philips got $10bn, half of which could have been Siemens's.'[38]

Universal took ownership of PolyGram in December 1998. Naturally there were casualties of the merger. In January, the A&M artist roster was cut from sixty-five to twenty and the label's own offices were closed and sold. Alpert and Moss had left five years before and were involved in a lawsuit against PolyGram for earnings that they alleged had not been paid. Alain Levy, who had been Fine's successor as president and CEO, was out of a job, as Doug Morris emerged at the top of the company. In terms of heritage and global branding, however, there was an upside. For the first time since the Second World War, the Decca name – previously controlled in the UK and Europe by PolyGram and by MCA in the US – was owned globally by one company, and could once again be used without restrictions.

Not all independents were vulnerable to a full takeover by the majors. Some were instead offered pressing and distribution deals in exchange for a stake, such as PolyGram's alliance with Andy Macdonald's Go Discs, home to Billy Bragg, Paul Weller and the Beautiful South. The major bought 49 per cent of the label in 1987, but when, in 1996, it decided to exercise its right to buy the rest of the equity, it found itself without a label to speak of. Bragg had already gone, having given his shares to a trust for the label's staff, who were to share in the proceeds of any sale, Weller was all set to leave and join Macdonald at his new Independiente label. Go Discs disappeared from view in early 1997, with the artists that PolyGram wanted to keep being farmed out to its other labels.

Of a similar nature was Sony's decision to buy 49 per cent of Alan McGee's Creation label in 1992. Over the next seven years, the outfit went from being a piddling indie label to representing the vanguard of British guitar pop, including Teenage Fanclub and Primal Scream, and most successfully of all, Oasis. McGee now calls the Sony deal a bad move. The label's lesser lights, who would have been indulged under the old order, were being left to fall by the wayside. Even though McGee had retained a marginal majority, Sony demanded results: 'It was always just gonna be one-way traffic.' In 1999, Sony bought the portion of Creation it didn't already own, and, as with Go Discs, it imploded.

Other joint ventures had been more successful, notably those on the black music side. Motown had been the first black-owned label to make a major impact on the global industry in its own right. Others had been influential musically, but Motown was taken seriously as a business, and Berry Gordy's example provided inspiration for later black entrepreneurs. One of these was Marion 'Suge' (pronounced 'Shoog', short for 'Sugar'), owner of the rap label Death Row, which would become, he proclaimed, the 'Motown of the nineties'. Some were only in it for the music, others were reformed gangsters. A few remained utterly unreformed, and it appears that Knight, closely allied to the Bloods, a notorious LA gang, fell into this category.

A former LA Ram footballer and drug dealer, Knight's entrée into the music business came through his friend Mario Lavelle Johnson, a DJ who worked under the pseudonym Chocolate. Johnson said that he had been involved in the writing and production of 'Ice, Ice Baby' by the white rapper Vanilla Ice (aka Robert van Winkle), but not paid. Knight sorted the matter out by negotiating with van Winkle on the balcony of a hotel room fifteen storeys up. Funky Enough Records, Knight's first attempt at starting a label, foundered, but in November 1992, he began discussions with Jimmy Iovine, whose label Interscope was a quasi-independent venture bankrolled by Warners. Having enlisted Dr Dre, the producer behind the popular NWA

(Niggaz With Attitude), Knight's label idea was very bankable, and Iovine said yes.

The label became known as Death Row, and as its CEO, Knight appeared to have maintained his unconventional approach to negotiation. Knight also managed artists and he is reputed to have re-negotiated Jodeci's contract with Andre Harrell of Uptown Records – later to run Motown – in a gents' lavatory. Accounts differ on Knight's choice of technique. One suggests a gun was held to Harrell's head. Another has Harrell's head being forced down a toilet bowl. Yet another has Knight threatening to violate Harrell unless his terms are agreed. The office set-up was unorthodox, too, with Knight's gang member friends using the premises as open house and sponging off the employees.

Whatever the backroom controversies, Death Row had a startling run of hits beginning with Dre's album *The Chronic* and continuing with Snoop Doggy Dogg and Ice-T's heavy metal outfit Body Count. The label also inherited Tupac Shakur from Interscope. Shakur had initially resisted the move. It was obvious that Iovine wanted to put a bit of clear blue water between him and the rapper for the sake of his relations with Warner. Even if the window-dressing had succeeded, it would have probably been to no avail. Although by 1995 Time Warner owned 50 per cent of Interscope, it had become 'an utter embarrassment ... Snoop Doggy Dogg had been accused of murder. 2Pac had been convicted of sexual abuse. Dr. Dre was a drunk driver'.[39]

Despite support from Quincy Jones, the TW board wanted out. In September, Iovine and his business partner Ted Field bought Warner's 50 per cent of the company for $115m. The following April, it sold the same stake to MCA for $200m. In the interim, as Stan Cornyn observed, 'Tupac became the first artist to debut at number one on the charts while serving a jail sentence for sexual assault.' Jail also beckoned for Knight. He was already on probation following an assault prosecution in 1992, and he had been missing appointments for statutorily required drug tests.

Over on the east coast, Death Row's rival was Sean 'Puffy' Combs, who, if he had ever been running with the gangs, had cleaned up his act mightily. After an apprenticeship with Andre Harrell at Uptown, he started his own company Bad Boy Entertainment, and signed a deal with Arista to distribute the label's output. One of the stars on the label was Biggie Smalls, aka the Notorious B.I.G., aka Christopher Wallace, but he had to play second fiddle to Bad Boy's boss, who contrived to make guest appearances on everything the label put out, which led Knight to comment from the podium at an awards ceremony that artists who didn't want the 'owner of your label on your album, or in your video or on your tour' should 'come to Death Row', an obvious dig at Combs. This was the first open indication of bad blood between the two companies and the depths to which that ran have never been satisfactorily explained. On 7 September 1996, returning with Knight from watching a Mike Tyson fight in Las Vegas, Tupac Shakur was shot by persons unknown. A week later, he was dead from his injuries. Six months later, Biggie Smalls was shot dead in Los Angeles. There were suggestions that the West Coast rap big wigs had been involved in sanctioning Smalls's killing, which happened after Knight had spent five months in jail for breaking his parole by failing to turn up for drug tests. Following a colourful trial, in which the DA Lawrence Longo was asked to step down, having benefited from Knight's hospitality and being the father of a Death Row recording artist, Knight was sentenced in February 1997 to eight years in prison.

As the record industry approached the twenty-first century, the big boys were bigger than ever. Once again they were the only game in town and seemingly impregnable. In 1911, annual European record sales were estimated to be 35 million units, worth between £5M and £6m. At 2002 prices, that inflates to around £314m. In 2001, the UK market alone registered retail sales of £2.11bn, with a total of 225.9 million albums delivered into the trade that year across all formats. The business had, indeed, come a long way from Nipper's first listening session.

The industry had become an effective lobby, happy to confer with whoever was in power. In 1989, the Tory Education Secretary Kenneth Baker was booed at the Brit Awards as he announced plans for the Brit School for Performing Arts and Technology. Cliff Richard took the rebellious audience to task for this act of ingratitude, voicing the opinion of numerous industry grandees present. In 1997, when a new Labour government replaced the Tory administration after eighteen years, it tried to link itself to the music industry, and the industry – led by Alan McGee of Creation – let it. Labour was down with the kids. Labour was the party that backed the 'Cool Britannia' of Britpop – exemplified by Blur and Oasis.

McGee was a true believer, but the expediency of many who schmoozed Mr Tony can be gleaned from an experience recorded by KLF member and all-round cultural terrorist Bill Drummond at the 1998 Labour Party Conference. Attending a fringe session entitled 'Lights, Camera, Action –

the New Creative Economy', the 'last face I was expecting to see' was that of Warner chairman Rob Dickins, 'one of the most charming men on the planet', with whom Drummond had dealt when he managed Echo and the Bunnymen. Dickins made it clear that he was equally surprised to see Drummond:

> Of course, Dickins wants to know why I am here. As I don't know myself, I am unable to give him any sort of satisfactory answer. He tells me he came down with Mick Hucknall, how they watched Big Tone do his thing together. How Big Tone had total class, like a great pop performer who knew how to communicate to a mob-filled arena but still make it all ring true. Rob throws in a revelatory anecdote: the last time he saw Tony Blair was when he took him to a Simply Red concert. They sat together admiring Mick Hucknall's voice, stage presence and professionalism, and chatted about all-time great singers and the great prospects for New Britain. I ask Rob if he came to last year's Labour Party Conference. He gives me a look as if to say, 'Don't be stupid.'[40]

Unfortunately for them, no amount of lobbying could change what happened next. In 1999, global music sales grew by 1.5 per cent in value to $38.5bn, while CD sales increased by 3 per cent to 2.4 billion units. In 2002, though, global music sales fell by 7 per cent in value and by 8 per cent in volume, following a 5 per cent drop in value and a 6.5 per cent fall in unit sales the previous year. What went wrong?

13 Caught Napstering

The blame for the record industry's slip into reverse gear is laid firmly at the feet of Internet users and owners of CD burners, most of them average citizens, law-abiding in every way other than their attitude to copyright. In the old days, radio play apart, there were three ways a person could get hold of the music they wanted to hear: 1) buy the commercially available record; 2) buy a pirated copy, usually on cassette, with a fuzzy photocopied inlay card; 3) get a friend to tape it for you. Option two required a fair bit of capital investment on the part of the pirate, in terms of the equipment needed for mass production. Thus it was that pirate record, tape and CD factories sprung up in areas of the world where copyright laws were observed with laxity or not at all. After the fall of the Berlin Wall, the former Soviet Union was a natural breeding ground for such enterprises, as it had been for Norbert Rodkinson and the nefarious Finkelstein back in the early years of the twentieth century.

Now, however, technology makes everything much easier. The first CD recorders that appeared at the start of the 1990s cost over £10,000 and each blank disc went out at £30 or more. Nowadays, CD burners that fit into a home computer can be bought in the high street for £50, while a pack of 100 blank discs can often cost less than £20. Result: anyone can make a CD, and many do, although few go to the bother of originating the music that goes on the discs. Home taping, for years the industry's bugbear, has become burning: faster and with much better sound quality, indistinguishable to most ears from a factory-made disc. The tipping point, with regard to price, was around 1999–2000, just when the sales figures went into reverse. Coincidence? Jay Berman, chairman and CEO of the International Federation of the Phonographic Industry (IFPI), doesn't think so:

> There's a difference between what we would call piracy and what we would describe as home copying. The difference is that one takes place in the person's home and it's very difficult to deal with, even in cases where it might be illegal.

The other is a large-scale commercial activity that goes on in the market place. Are there degrees of seriousness? They're both serious.

Up to a year ago [the interview took place in September 2002], piracy manifested itself mainly in large-scale commercial plant operations. With the advent of CD-R, it's become much more of a cottage industry, and much more difficult as an investigative issue, to find out where this is … You know, it looks very much like cassette piracy. Finding the garage with sixty burners hooked to each other is a lot different to finding the plant in the Ukraine. That is a serious problem today as CD-R has increasingly become the medium of choice for the pirates.

The IFPI is adamant that music piracy is more than just selling hooky CDs – quite often it is linked to other, less savoury forms of organized crime. 'I think it's more so today than ever before,' says Berman. 'I think it's linked to drugs, I think it's linked to terror, I think it's linked to a lot of things. It's a cash generator and it makes a lot of other things possible.'[1]

Then there is the Internet. Until recently, the distribution of music over the worldwide web has been hamstrung by the prevalence of slow dial-up connections and the gargantuan sound files required. A minute of uncompressed, CD-quality stereo audio in WAV format takes up roughly 10 megabytes of memory. The answer had been developed in the early 1990s by the Fraunhofer Institute in Germany – MP3 (or MPEG-1 Layer 3 compression, to give its full name). It took until the development of Winamp, a freely distributed decoder and player, in 1997 for MP3 to achieve mass acceptance, but when it did, it speeded up the distribution process. At 256 kilobits per second, the sound was almost indistinguishable from CD, and the files were five times smaller. Even at 128 kbps, the sound was reasonably acceptable, and this time, the data was compressed to eleven times smaller than its original size.

So far so good, but MP3 distribution needed what the IT chaps call a 'killer app', of the kind that Winamp had been to the MP3 listening experience. In 1998 it came, in the form of Napster, a file-sharing network developed by a teenage computer student from Massachusetts called Shawn Fanning. The idea had come about in response to his room-mate's complaints that Internet music sites were often out of date, with dodgy links. Fanning worked on creating a piece of software that would allow friends with Internet-connected computers to share MP3 files between them. Fanning gave a test version to thirty or so friends and asked them not to pass it on. They passed it on. The response told Fanning he was on to something, so he consulted his uncle, John Fanning. In May 1999, Fanning the elder set about establishing a company and looking for investors. By October, Napster had over $2m of capital.

Unfortunately, it had also aroused the interest of Jay Berman's successor as chairman and CEO of the Recording Industry Association of America, Hilary Rosen. In December 1999, the RIAA sued Napster for copyright infringement, alleging that 'Napster has created, and is operating, a haven for music piracy on an unprecedented scale ... a giant online pirate bazaar'.[2] In June 2000, the RIAA followed up with a request for an injunction to shut Napster down. The judge agreed and awarded a temporary injunction, but the decision was overturned by the appeal court. Napster had gained an immeasurable amount of publicity and notoriety, and membership shot through the roof. Meanwhile, the major record labels were mounting their own legal challenges.

The heavy rock band Metallica was in the front line of the anti-Napster acts, but not all artists followed the RIAA line on file-sharing. Dave Stewart of the Eurythmics told an Internet conference in London that '[a]nything anarchistic like Napster is good – it makes artists ask why they are not in control of what they are doing ... Artists of any worth or strength will rise up and take control of the situation'.[3] Take control away from the record companies, that is. Meanwhile, Prince, who had spent the mid-1990s fighting to extricate himself from Warner Bros for similar reasons to George Michael's battle with Sony, weighed in on Napster's side, perhaps unsurprisingly and with barely concealed glee. 'From the point of view of the music lover, what's going on can only be viewed as an exciting new development in the history of music,' he argued. 'And fortunately there does not seem to be anything the old record companies can do about preventing this evolution from happening.'[4]

Despite such ringing endorsements and Napster offering the record companies a reputed $200m a year in licensing fees, the service was on a hiding to nothing, and gave in to the legal onslaught in July 2001. Only one major company, Bertelsmann, had reacted to Napster in anything like a positive manner. It took a stake in Napster in October 2000, with a view to using the service as a platform to launch a legal, subscription-based download service. In July 2001, after the closedown, it sent one of its executives, Konrad Hilbers, to see the transition through. Finally, in May 2002, it bought Napster out. However, instead of joining with Bertelsmann in turning Napster over to their own uses, the rival companies turned on Bertelsmann. It was funding Napster, ergo it was a pirate. No mention of the fact that Napster was inert, pending its migration to fully paid legal status, something they could all have benefited from. In November 2002, the CD burner and software manufacturer Roxio made a $5m offer for Napster – which had descended into Chapter 11 bankruptcy. It was accepted.

At last, in November 2003, after nearly two years in abeyance, Napster was relaunched as a subscription service. At the time of the launch, it offered a catalogue of 500,000 titles, each of which could be downloaded for 99 cents. Unfortunately for Napster, the interregnum had seen competitors popping up, the most notable of which was Apple's iTunes online store. Apple has the immense advantage of also offering the must-have gadget of the day, the iPod MP3 player. The 40 gigabyte model can hold 10,000 songs. The iPod was selling at the rate of two a minute in the last quarter of 2003, and many such customers, who have made a major investment in Apple, will stick with Apple for the software as well. In the first week of its relaunch, Napster claimed to have sold 300,000 downloads. Apple claimed 1.5 million.

It's obvious that the old Napster's ascendancy had an impact on the cosy little world of the record industry as it stood, but should it bear the main responsibility for the trade's current malaise? Not really. Stock markets readjust to reflect changing values every so often, sending companies to the wall, the Wall Street Crash being perhaps the most extreme example. CD grew the recorded music market to unprecedented levels. In 1955, a total of 59.9 million records – 33, 45 and 78 rpm – were manufactured in the UK. Two years later, once rock and roll had taken hold, this had grown to 78.3 million units. In 2001, the UK pumped out 225.9 million albums, across LP, cassette, CD and minidisc. It's still early days yet, and it might just be that the CD boom was a freak occurrence, and that the current drops in sales are merely the market settling back into a more sustainable pattern of growth.

Equally likely, though, is that these technological advances and their enthusiastic take-up have merely exposed the fact that record companies have been overcharging their customers for years and underpaying their artists. This is a neat trick when you consider that the record companies are the only really superfluous part of the chain. People will always want to create music. Others will always want to listen to it. But will there always be a need for companies that prepare artist royalty statements, raking off several times what the artist earns for the privilege?[5]

These are weaknesses that the record companies have had time and resources enough to address, but ultimately they flunked them in favour of maintaining the status quo. Part of the problem is cultural. A large chunk of the listening public has got used to getting its music for free over the Internet. If record companies had themselves embraced MP3 early enough and sold access to the sound files, the idea of free distribution wouldn't have gained such currency. If the industry had bought up the Napster network and added digital rights management into the mix, it would have gained a global distribution network that used its customers' hard drive space and Internet connections. How's that for low overheads? Instead, they chose to fight it all the way, just as EMI fought vinyl in the 1950s and Jerry Moss fought CD in the 1980s.

Napster was the tallest poppy, and was dealt with decisively, but once the principle had been established, there was very little to stop others creating their own software. In its place as a provider of free MP3s, we have Gnutella, WinMX, Kazaa, SoulSeek and a host of other peer-to-peer networks to choose from. Kazaa is particularly interesting. If a file is in heavy demand, users with a high 'participation level' rating get it first. Those with a 'Supreme Being' participation level are 'really doing your bit', as if it were a bring and buy sale. Unfortunately, intrusive advertisements make it clear that Kazaa is no altruistic exercise.

In many ways, Napster's worst mistake was to set itself up as a conventional business, because it gave the record industry something to sue. When it declared copyright ownership in its software, the record companies found this very rich indeed. The network afforded by Napster's software was utterly decentralized, existing only in the computers of the members who were online at a given time. With an estimated 58 million users by the time it closed in 2001, it would have been interesting to see the RIAA try to chase all of them.

Believe it or not, in June 2003, that was precisely what the RIAA claimed it was going to do. With Rosen on the way out, seemingly to become a daytime TV presenter, it fell to president Cary Sherman to announce that the Recording Industry Association of America would be pursuing individual computer users who share files via peer-to-peer networks, and imposing fines of up to $150,000 per song. 'The law is clear and the message to those who are distributing substantial quantities of music online should be equally clear – this activity is illegal, you are not anonymous when you do it, and engaging in it can have real consequences,' said Sherman, in a press release. 'We'd much rather spend time making music then dealing with legal issues in courtrooms. But we cannot stand by while piracy takes a devastating toll on artists, musicians, songwriters, retailers and everyone in the music industry.'[6]

If the RIAA were seriously planning to bring legal action against every file-sharing citizen, the only sane and rational response would be 'Wake us up when you're finished.' The reality, of course, is that the RIAA has neither the stomach nor the resources for any such thing. Instead, it is hoping that a few headline-grabbing show trials will scare the public into compliance. When, in September 2003, the RIAA announced that it had begun proceedings against the first 261 naughty downloaders, the two who got all the coverage were Brianna LaHara, a twelve-year-old girl from New York, and Durwood Pickle, a 71-year-old grandfather from Texas. LaHara is reported to have said, 'Out of all the people, why did they pick on me?' The answer is simple. Picking on a young, innocent girl was guaranteed to maximize the coverage. The same goes for Mr Pickle, who claims never to have downloaded any music, but to have let his grandchildren have a free run on his computer. White-haired old grandfather, instantly memorable name, the media will love it and send the RIAA's message loud and clear: It could be you, it's naughty, so don't do it. LaHara's mother, fearful of the potential penalties, settled with the RIAA for $2,000. However, it could well take just one headstrong downloader and a liberal lawyer willing to pick holes in the RIAA's case to bring the whole modernized pillory down. In the meantime, while the campaign will have the desired effect on some, a great many others will weigh up the statistical risks – small numbers are being singled out, apparently at random – and continue to download.

In the extreme, the RIAA's campaign amounts to taking action against most of the computer users in the world. Not only is this impossible, it is also stinkingly bad customer relations. At an Oxford Union debate on file-sharing, Hilary Rosen asked the filesharers present to raise their hands. She then asked them to keep their hands in the air if they still bought records, and was reported to be visibly crestfallen when the vast majority of mitts remained aloft.

One fundamental flaw in the record companies and the IFPI's argument is to assume that every download equals a lost sale. Of course, some will be downloading with no intention of spending anything ever. Others, though, will have spent as much of their disposable income as they can on records and will be downloading to supplement that. There's no way they can afford to spend more on music, so no sales have been lost, but the music is being heard. Maybe the downloaders will buy the next album, or want to upgrade the sound quality. Best of all, however, downloading has kyboshed one of the record companies' oldest tricks: selling an album on the basis of a hit single, regardless of whether the rest of the album is any good or not. Take a trip to Kazaa and download the album, and you might find that the single was the only bit worth buying.

This heavy-handedness also tends to rebound hideously. Madonna made an MP3 of herself saying, 'What the fuck do you think you're doing?' then disguised it as a track from her new album and set it loose on the P2P world. Once downloaded, it really made people think. Indeed, it made some think how lucky they were to have a clean sample of Madge swearing, which they then incorporated into new tracks of their own. The results can be found at the Madonna Remix Project website (http://www.irixx.org/madonna/madonnaremix.html). There is even talk of the material girl trying to license some of the remixes back in a belated piece of face-saving.

Of course, there has been no shortage of politicos eager to help the becalmed industry. Howard Berman, the Democrat representative for California, promoted a bill in 2002 that aimed, he said, to help 'copyright owners ... use reasonable, limited self-help measures to thwart rampant, notorious P2P piracy'.[7] It all sounds reasonable enough, but what he really means is that he wants to make it legal for the RIAA to hack into the computers of US citizens and stop them from accessing files that might or might not be illegally acquired MP3s. The data protection and privacy implications of this 'reasonable' proposal are obvious and very unreasonable.

Berman is adamant that technologies exist to 'only impair the piracy of a copyrighted work on a P2P network', leaving all other functions unharmed. Other US politicians go further. Utah Senator Orrin Hatch, who fell out of the running for the Republican presidential nomination at the Iowa caucuses in January 2000, announced in June 2003 that he was 'all for' remotely ruining personal computers as a last resort in the fight against online piracy. 'If we can find some way to do this without destroying their machines, we'd be interested in hearing about that,' he said, but added, 'If that's the only way, then I'm all for destroying their machines.'[8] Can't you just hear the lawyers rubbing their hands at the thought of the suits for loss of personal and business data?

Why are Berman and Hatch showing such an interest? Well, Hatch claims to be a musician of some kind, although his wild, technically inept pronouncements savour more of blowing his own trumpet than any more elevated instrumental skill. Could it have anything to do with the fact that between 1997 and 2002, Hatch received $24,000 in campaign contributions from AOL Time Warner, while Berman collected $30,050 from AOL, $27,341 from Vivendi Universal, $11,000 from Steven Spielberg, Jeffrey Katzenberg and David Geffen's Dreamworks SKG and $7,000 from Sony? Cary Sherman has described Berman as 'a true friend of the creative community' – he seems to be far more intimate with the capitalists running the business than with the creatives themselves.

The statements made in support of Napster by Dave Stewart and Prince seem less perverse when the kinds of deals offered by record companies are taken into consideration. Robbie Williams added to the support in January 2003 when he said that he thought that music piracy was 'a great idea' and that he had heard only 'a lot of hot air'[9] from the industry about what they were doing to keep it in check. This is probably the sound of a young man winding up his record company – EMI – because he's just relieved them of £80m, and they need him more than he needs them. Such victories for the artist are rare, Ed Bicknell, former manager of Dire Straits, admits:

I don't know where this is going to go. On one hand, I feel not a sense of satisfaction, but a sense of bizarre justice about what's happening. The record industry, particularly the monoliths and their predecessors, has, since the 1950s, fucked the talent completely. Even the successful talent has been fucked. It's all done in this backslapping 'Isn't it great, guys? We're all at number one' manner. There is a total inequality of bargaining power all the way along the line, unless you happen to be in the unusual and lucky circumstance of being out of contract when you're a superstar, for example Robbie Williams.

When that happened with the Straits in 1991, I absolutely took the line that having been fucked, I was going to fuck them as hard as I could. I'm not proud of that and it made me feel about myself as a person differently to how I would like to feel. I'm not trying to sound like I'm on some high moral thing here, but in business, you sometimes do things that you wouldn't do to a mate. I had no compunction at all in screwing a corporation. If I ever am in that position again, which I hope not to be, I would still have no compunction in stuffing them. In the twenty-five years I worked with Phonogram, I got through sixteen or seventeen managing directors. It made me feel that it was a farcical way of running a business. I think they're incredibly inefficient and absolutely hopeless to deal with. You can find yourself spending hours arguing with someone about a print ad that costs £80. They will have spent £500 in time and resources arguing with you.[10]

That's the manager of one of the biggest-selling acts ever talking, and he thinks they were stiffed. Others feel the same way. Take a look at the Blair-friendly Simply Red. In 2000, after fifteen years with WEA, they rode off into the sunset, leaving an unrenewed contract behind them. Over that fifteen years, Mick Hucknall was estimated by his management to have made £20m in royalties. Nice work if you can get it, but even nicer was the £192m that WEA was estimated to have made from Simply Red in the same period. In 2003, Hucknall released a new album on his own label, sold through the band's website for just £8.50 (or through conventional retailers for a little more). It was estimated that the band needed to sell 1 million copies to break even, not really a problem for a major act, and especially not at around two-thirds of the price of a major label CD. Everything after that comes straight back to the artist. No middle man.

Ahmet Ertegun admits that artists might have got the rough end of the deal once, but suggests that matters have improved greatly:

In the days of Bessie Smith and Ma Rainey in the twenties, they never expected to get any money from their records. They recorded in order to become famous, tour and make money. So that's the general background of all of this. Today we've got to a point where the big black artists make two or three times what the record company makes. The big hip-hop artists and the rap artists dictate their terms. I read somewhere that Dr Dre got $50m just to continue making records. Time changes everything. Dr Dre's production of Eminem sells 20 million albums. That's the biggest artist in the world right now.[11]

It seems strange that just as technology made it easier for smaller operations to succeed in this strange and wonderful business, the majors reacted by getting even bigger, but this is precisely what happened. In 2000, Universal merged with the French utilities company Vivendi. Then, in November 2003, it added Dreamworks Records to its corporate portfolio. Dreamworks' principal executive Mo Ostin said of the deal: 'Universal is acquiring a wonderful asset and the sale will assure the strongest possible future for our artists.'[12] Universal Music is run by Doug Morris, who, as an old Warner Bros hand, presumably realizes that the greatest asset of all in the new acquisition is Mo Ostin himself.

At the same time as Universal was linking up with the sanitation-to-transport megalith Vivendi, Time Warner threw its lot in with the Internet service provider AOL, becoming AOL Time Warner. Meanwhile, EMI looked at a merger with Bertelsmann and then got all the way to the altar with AOL Time Warner before being rebuffed on anti-trust grounds. 'I think it was very serious and it was the Commission that said no,' Bruce Lundvall outlined in December 2002. 'They didn't want to see the whole record industry in the hands of four conglomerates. We remain an independent company, which I hope we'll stay. One never knows, but I would certainly hope so.'[13]

By 2003, though, AOL Time Warner was in deep trouble, saddled with $19bn of debt and, in the underperforming AOL division, a brand name of questionable value. By September 2003, the corporate name reverted to Time Warner. It had also become clear that several of the group's divisions were available, at the right price, in an attempt to reduce the debt. The book publishing arm endured several uncertain months before it became clear that no suitors were interested in paying as much as the parent company wanted. More interest was shown in the record division. Bertelsmann looked at a joint venture, but talks proved abortive. The reason for the Germans' loss of interest became apparent in November 2003 when it was announced that Bertelsmann was merging its music operations with those of Sony in a 50/50 joint venture. The big five is now down to four.

Even with all of this consolidation, the industry seems unable to commit to a unified direction. At one point, EMI and Vivendi Universal were preparing to sue Bertelsmann for its involvement in Napster, at the same time as EMI was preparing, along with Sony, to sell content to Roxio for the relaunched, legitimized Napster. Meanwhile, Sony and Universal sold their Pressplay online service to Roxio. Also, Sony makes CD burners and the blank discs, while AOL is one of the main portals through which downloaders get their online jollies.

Does this tangled mess resemble a strategy in any way, shape or form? Ed Bicknell doesn't think so:

> I can't help but reflect that a large part of the predicament is of the record companies' own making, or their parent companies' making. Back in the 1980s, Sony and Philips were making double-deck tape machines. Now, who

is making blank CD-Rs? Sony and Philips. They're undermining the business. AOL is a vast access point for people who want to download. These companies don't think as one, that's for sure. Alain Levy said to me when he left PolyGram, one of the problems he had was that the Philips board did not understand the business. That's true of Sony, AOL and Bertelsmann.[14]

EMI can perhaps be excused for its uncertainty. Even before the industry as a whole went into panic mode, EMI was having one of its periodic fits of the jitters. In January 1998, the company posted its first profits warning in a decade, blaming problems in the Far East. Shares had been performing poorly enough following the demerger from Thorn-EMI, but on this announcement, they plummeted 48.75p to 430p, begging questions of when a suitor would show their hand. Seagram, before it plumped for PolyGram, looked like a goer, while Bertelsmann also sniffed Nipper's hindquarters enthusiastically. Why, an EMI-Bertelsmann merger would even have brought the alert old terrier under one global ownership once again. (This would no longer apply – EMI has sold its right in the trademark to the HMV retail chain for a figure, it is rumoured, far less than BMG would have paid.)

Far East aside, there were problems closer to home. With Sir Colin Southgate relinquishing the executive part of his chairmanship to move to the Royal Opera House, president of recorded music Jim Fifield wanted desperately to become CEO of the whole EMI Group, but the board were less enthusiastic about the idea. In April, Fifield resigned, taking a £12m payoff. In the year to May 1999, this settlement and disappointing performance from the Spice Girls contributed to an £80m fall in profits to £227m.

Fifield's replacement was Ken Berry, who was to receive a pay deal worth up to £3m a year in salary, with a further £1.5m in performance bonuses and stock, less than the £6.9m Fifield got in his last year with EMI, but still a lot of wedge. It was also a lot less than the £17m per album that he pledged in 2001 to Mariah Carey, newly free from her contract with Sony and her marriage to Sony chief Tommy Mottola. On her past record this seemed like a safe bet, but two factors had not been taken into account. She was a star in decline, having peaked in 1993 with the album *Music Box*, which sold 20 million copies. Additionally, she was, to put it politely, showing signs of stress, having suffered an 'emotional breakdown' and spent much of early 2001 in a clinic. The first album of her EMI–Virgin deal, *Glitter*, sold just 2 million copies.

Berry was fired in October 2001, with another bonanza compensation package, this time £5m. His estranged wife, Nancy Berry, who also worked for the company and had been romantically linked with quite a few of its artists, followed a week later. In came Alain Levy, three years after he had been ditched by PolyGram following the Seagram takeover, on a basic salary of £700,000 a year, topped up with generous share options. This relative modesty was only right and proper seeing as Levy's first task was a 'slash and burn' round of job cuts – shedding 1,800 of a total 9,000 staff.

Levy denied strenuously that it was all Mariah's fault. 'With or without Mariah Carey this would have happened,' he told the *Daily Telegraph*. 'The company was not the right dimension for the market we are now in. For instance, our Virgin record label organization was a complete duplication of our other EMI record labels in several countries.'[15] Mariah got her cards as well, albeit with a £38m payoff, buying out the rest of her contract. Does this deal make sense? Only if EMI is absolutely certain that it could do nothing more with her. Two more albums like *Glitter* and the company could easily double its losses on the deal, through marketing and overproduction. Since then, however, Carey has pitched up at Universal, who seem to have no complaints. So much for investing in artists.

Another part of preparing EMI for the 'right dimension' was to close the Swindon CD factory that had opened in 1987, and concentrate production at the company's Uden plant in the Netherlands, a possible sign that the company was starting to review its attachment to shiny discs and conventional distribution. There are a host of new improved formats currently being offered – DVD-A, HDCD, SACD – but it is uncertain whether any of them offer anything to entice anyone but the keenest audiophile. In any case, the confusion of different formats contrasts with the consensus that allowed CD to sweep all in its path. Traditionally, each company has maintained its own factories, largely because they didn't feel they could trust anyone else to handle their business. With a massive over-capacity in optical disc production, holding to this view is folly.

As a result of these cuts, EMI seems healthier than it has done for years, although that's, admittedly, not saying much. For all of Sir Joseph Lockwood's good work, the EMI of recent years still owed more to the hidebound HMV of old than it did to the adaptable, vigorous Columbia half of the 1931 partnership or the entrepreneurial Virgin. This is a legacy that dates back to Alfred Clark's ousting of Sir Louis Sterling in 1939. Moreover, the current relatively rosy picture may be only a semblance of health. Operating profits in the year to March 2003 were up from £190.9m to £254m, but turnover was down from £2.45bn to £2.18bn. You can only make a fifth of the workforce redundant so many times before there's no one left.

Consolidation being where it's at, further savings would have been possible if EMI had taken over the Warner record business, a deal that it spent much of the second half of 2003 trying to tie up. In November, the British company confirmed that it had made an offer, worth a reported £920m. This was a neat reversal of three years earlier, when EMI desperately wanted to be taken over by Time Warner. Unfortunately for EMI, theirs was not the only hat in the ring. A consortium headed by former Seagram boss Edgar Bronfman, the mastermind behind the Universal takeover of PolyGram and the subsequent sale of the consolidated group, had expressed an interest in taking over the whole Warner Music business – both records and publishing. By the end of the month, the Bronfman group had prevailed and Time-Warner's debt was $2.6bn lower.

Bronfman's victory left EMI with a slightly uncertain future. The share price dropped to 163.84p – still some way off the twelve-month low of 88p, but far below the 750p mark, where EMI shares hovered in January 2000 when the original Warner merger was on the cards. By missing out on Warner this time, EMI was suddenly vulnerable to a venture capital takeover.

Undeniably, EMI can still attract the talent. On the face of it, the Robbie Williams deal might seem as big a gamble as the Mariah Carey one was, but it breaks new ground by including a cut of his touring and merchandising revenue as a hedge against relying on record sales. Then there are Kylie Minogue, Coldplay and Norah Jones. The latter is a particularly salutary tale, showing what can happen when an old-school record man is allowed to operate free of corporate control and proving that Morgado-style stupidity on the human resources front is alive and well in the corporate high command at Time Warner. Norah, daughter of Ravi Shankar, and one of the hottest acts in the world right now, was discovered by white-bearded, jazz-loving Bruce Lundvall:

This year [2002–3], with Norah Jones, we're going to have the best year in our history. I had a vision to do something beyond jazz, and that was to create a whole division of adult music for adult listeners, so we started the Manhattan label again. I brought in Arif Mardin and Ian Ralfini, who were giants in the business. I hadn't seen Ian for many years, but I ran into him at a Dianne

Reeves concert at the Lincoln Center about two years ago. We had lunch later in the week and Ian was telling me how they were going through this really depressing time at Atlantic, because as part of the AOL Time Warner group policy everyone over fifty-five was being retired, including himself and Arif. I said, 'My God, Arif has had more hit records than anyone. All he wants is an office. He's been with Atlantic for forty-three years and now they're making him retire. He's utterly depressed.'

I said, 'Wait, wait, wait. Manhattan no longer exists, but we still own the name. Suppose we could start Manhattan again as a boutique label, not fully-staffed, nothing like that.' In this business climate, you can't suddenly hire a hundred people. He said, 'Are you serious?' I said, 'If you guys aren't going to kill me with your salary requests, I'll see if we can do this.' Ian said, 'Arif and I just want to work. We don't want to retire.' I said, 'We'll build some wheelchair access here for the three of us and we'll teach these young kids how it's done.' For me, this was a miracle. Ken Berry said, 'You mean to tell me you can get Arif and Ian here?' I said, 'Of course. They're relatively well-heeled financially, so it's not about money. They just want to work.' I had already signed Norah, but she needed a producer, so I brought Arif into the situation.[16]

The result won eight Grammies. Lundvall's wheelchair joke now seems less Victor Meldrew than *Victor Ludorum.*

The Norah Jones model seems simple enough to emulate – look for the talent and market it. The flip side, though, is that not everyone has the conviction that comes from forty-odd years in the business and the benefit of tuition from Goddard Lieberson. One other who does is Clive Davis and he was the victim of ageist idiocy in 2000, when Bertelsmann forced him to retire as Arista chief. The fact that he had revived Carlos Santana's career probably counted against him rather than for – Santana was a reheated oldie. Ever the politician, Davis chose not to denigrate his bosses (well, apart from referring to one of them as an 'up-and-coming man'), all the while lobbying hard against the move.

'The issue at the end of my Arista contract was really one of equity,' he told the Retail Music Expo in Chicago in June 2001:

It was coupled with the fact that at Bertelsmann in Germany once you hit sixty if they want to stay with you they ask you to move to a consultant's role. But they clearly never wanted to separate from me; in fact they offered me an important corporate chairmanship that was a very big step for them. Earlier in my career Warner Bros chairman Steve Ross had come to me, after my years at Columbia, and asked if I would become chairman of the Warner Music Group. It was flattering, but the answer was no, because what I do is at a musical level. I don't want to be a corporate chairman. I don't want to attend branch openings and manufacturing plant meetings. I want the opportunity to work with music at the creative level and at the label level. Plus I wanted to continue with my major equity position.

Shrewdly, after a quarter-century of unbroken success, he knew he could dictate his severance terms, so he asked for upwards of $150m towards a new label – owned 50/50 by Davis and BMG – to be called J Records. Then he was allowed his pick of his old company's staff. 'My heads of legal and business affairs, finance and most of my A&R staff were given the opportunity to get out of their Arista contracts and come join me. It was an incredible offer and we're in the enviable position to be the "instant major" that I wanted and dreamed about.'[17] The label was more a vanity exercise than an 'instant major' and lost money all along, but one signing – Alicia Keys – was enough to show that Davis still had the old magic. By the end of 2002, Bertelsmann had rethought its position, bought Davis's 50 per cent of J back for more than $50m and asked him back into the corporate fold, this time as chairman of the entire RCA record division. In the meantime, his replacement at Arista, rap producer Antonio 'LA' Reid, had failed to distinguish himself and so his position was looking rather shaky.

However, even the likes of Davis and Lundvall are likely to founder if the companies they work for cling to the old business models. Traditionally, the record business has been slow to adapt to new systems. It's always easier to stick with the old, and usually it has done until the last possible moment. Now, that's not an option. Even among the most ardent anti-piracy advocates, there has been a steady realization that the marketplace has changed and nothing will turn the clock back completely. 'Part of the problem is that in the world up to now, we were always in the business and the pirates were trying to get into our business. Now we're trying to get into the business that the pirates are in,' says Jay Berman. 'I honestly believe that more people listen to more music than ever before. It's a question of how you reconfigure the business to take advantage of those circumstances.'[18]

There have been some reconfigurations. Record companies are taking more seriously than ever the licensing of recordings for use in films, television and advertising – known as 'synchronization' rights. Moreover, when it was revealed that the mobile phone ring-tones market was worth half the value of the CD single market, some companies were quick to spot the opportunity. Universal was the leader – now all newly released Universal CDs contain an insert, advertising the officially sanctioned ring-tones for that artist. Even jazz wunderkind Jamie Cullum (or rather the composers of his repertoire, such as George Gershwin, Cole Porter and Dave Frishberg) has made it into the ring-tone business.

Back with the core business, though, the record industry as a whole has new competitors. Millions of them, in fact. And it needs to start competing. These new players may have an unfair advantage over the oldies in that they don't have to pay for the product they're distributing, but record companies should be finding a way to sell in the new market instead of trying to enforce the unenforceable and issuing press releases about the menace. Almost any other business would welcome a zero-overhead distribution system with open arms. To compete, record companies would simply have to issue good music, sell it at a fair price and give a fair proportion of that price to the artists and composers. I can't believe for one minute that there wouldn't be a profit margin of some sort in that. The record companies might be on for a smaller margin, something that they seem unable to accept, but if the price was right, they could stand a decent chance of making back the difference on volume. In the meantime, downloaders may well be flouting the law, but chances are that if the record companies had acted earlier they could have contained the digital situation and turned it to their advantage.

So is the record industry responding to the crisis by promoting good music? Some bits of it are. Sadly, other elements (naming no BMG UKs – home of Simon Cowell's *Pop Idol* stable) are going for a quick turnover fix. The classical canon has largely been recorded in unmatchable performances, so further recordings of the same repertoire do not make economic sense. 'Frankly, it's lovely to open your books at the start of the year knowing that just about half of your turnover is guaranteed from repertoire you already own, both popular and classical,' admits David Fine. 'That gave you strength. The Philips and Deutsche Grammophon relationship built the most important classical catalogue in the world. PolyGram, to the end of my time, had half the world classical market.'[19] There were certain exceptions who were allowed to record whatever they liked:

There was a time when you really allowed artists every possible indulgence. If they wanted to make a record, if they were one of your artists, you allowed them. If von Karajan wanted to make a symphony that you had five of already, you let him do so, because he was von Karajan, and you didn't want to disturb the relationship. Today you would say no, because it's not affordable. He was a giant. He also had an extraordinary arrogance and he was going to leave his footprint everywhere.[20]

The packaging of classical repertoire in a similar manner to pop music has created a crossover market while, to some degree, ghettoizing the legitimate concert scene. Nigel Kennedy's massive promotion in the 1980s might have contributed to EMI's bottom line, but it also contributed to Kennedy's nervous breakdown. Then it was the Three Tenors; now we have the Opera Babes. We're back where we were in 1902: Arias in bite-size chunks shorn of context and marketed. In their rush for mass-market money, the majors have left several musical niches unserved, in which independent labels like Hyperion have thrived. 'We don't do a lot for Sony here in the big room,' admits Mike Ross-Trevor, who was chief engineer at Sony Music Studios in London until it closed in September 2003. 'Sony's very much pop-oriented. We got involved in a Sony project last year, the Opera Babes, and that's about the only thing I can think of. All of the interesting classical sessions are third-party work for independent labels'.[21]

Similar cannibalizations are ongoing in pop – especially the *Pop Idol* TV tie-ins such as Gareth Gates and Will Young, a pair of glorified karaoke singers trotting out lame cover versions of threadbare old songs. That is probably bad for the business in the long term, suggests music publisher Eddie Levy:

> We're in the plastic toy market at the moment with these manufactured groups and artists, who are doing a lot of damage. They give a few people some instant turnover, but it's not creating proper acts, and it's not creating international acts. With the technical input of the studios now, you're going to make my dog be able to sing, but you're not having any impact on the US market. And it's not really doing anybody any good. Obviously I'd be delighted if they recorded a song that I administer, but it's not real talent coming through.[22]

Back catalogue should be a more stable source of quick, pain-free turnover, but too many opportunities are being missed. In 1998, PolyGram put out *Song Review*, a one-CD collection of Stevie Wonder's hits. In 2002,

Universal put out *The Definitive Collection,* a two-CD set covering
the same ground. While the labels seem happy to repackage the same
stuff *ad infinitum,* there is a wealth of deleted material that could be earning
money rather than mouldering in a vault. In many cases, absurd second-
hand values will make latent demand for a certain record abundantly clear,
but in the past, a CD reissue with a full production run might not have been
justifiable. Now, however, CD-R makes it possible to produce one-off on-
demand copies. Alternatively, the archives could be digitized and offered as
digital downloads, at a price. It's happening already in book publishing with
digital printing. There's even a precedent in the record industry. Until the
1950s, EMI offered a custom pressing service: for £4 10 shillings, it was
possible to order three copies of any deleted 78rpm record in the company's
collection.

All too often, though, record companies don't really realize what they
have. George Avakian helped Columbia with its jazz reissues for many years.
After all, his entrée to the record business before the Second World War had
been archive research, and as the main producer for much of the 1950s, he
remembered who did what and when, giving the label an invaluable head
start. When, however, he found himself being squeezed out due to office
politics in the late 1990s, the company's advantage was lost. His
replacement, Phil Schaap, managed to waste hundreds of thousands of
Columbia dollars buying up spurious, dubbed acetates of the Benny
Goodman Carnegie Hall Concert in preparation for a CD reissue. Avakian,
on the other hand, knew where the originals were and could have told
Columbia at the start (Goodman had given them to Howard Scott, the
classical producer who had created the original LPs). A lot of pride had to
be swallowed before they asked him. Not content with displaying such
ineptitude, Schaap then took every opportunity to denigrate Avakian's
work. Meanwhile, complaints about errors and other flaws in various
Schaap reissues at Columbia kept mounting, and he was finally dismissed.
When the time came to reissue the Tempo jazz LPs produced in the 1950s by
Tony Hall, they had to be dubbed from disc, because the master tapes were
untraceable. 'Yes, nobody knows where they are and they don't seem to give
a shit,' remarks Hall, ruefully.[23] Even EMI, which has an exhaustive and
meticulously maintained archive, regularly releases CD reissues with no
documentation other than a bare tracklisting.

If they want to survive, record companies will have to work harder to
endear and justify themselves to artists. The hoary old prog-rockers

g direct to their loyal fanbase over the Internet and
disc than they ever did when they were with EMI.
nbtastic 1980s pop-funk combo Level 42 was asked by
2002 if selling individually autographed discs over the
own from his days as a platinum-plated unit shifter. His
: 'Instead of making 10p on each copy I sell, I make £10'.
You   to be well established for it to work out, either. One
unknown ba... Clear (www.clearweb.org), formed a limited company and
sold shares in themselves at gigs.

Messages of endearment and justification should also go out to the fans.
Much of the anti-piracy discussion and the methods used to prevent
copying, such as CDs that won't play in computers, are merely alienating the
new consumers. The earliest copy protection systems could be defeated by
blacking out the rim of the disc (where the protection data resided) with a
marker pen. Now some companies (EMI being the worst culprits) are using
a system in which the disc is designed to play normally on standard hi-fi
equipment, but which substitutes painfully low-resolution MP3s when the
disc is listened to using a computer. Quite rightly, many consumers want
CD-quality sound from their CDs no matter what equipment they use to
play them, and some are boycotting the companies that use this copy
protection system. Whatever happened to the customer always being right?
Charles Kennedy of Invisible Hands, a small London-based indie,
distributed by Universal, states unequivocally, 'I'll never put any anti-piracy
device on our CDs. You mustn't treat your customers as criminals.'[24] What's
more, as far as he's concerned, 'If the industry spent what it's spending on
fighting piracy on developing artists, it wouldn't be in trouble. Business is
great, it couldn't be better.' Warner Bros in the 1960s and 1970s endeared
itself to music fans by appearing to be, if not necessarily as one with the
counterculture, at least not hostile towards it. The enthusiasm for
downloads is also a generational thing. Some teenagers wouldn't know what
to do if abandoned in a record shop with a wallet full of tenners. Record
companies should be doing some good PR work to win over these young
downloaders. Trying to criminalize them will only increase the rebellious
cachet of the act.

The moment the game stopped being entirely about manufacturing and
shifting units, the record companies were in trouble. They were the best at
it. Indeed, they were just about the only ones at it, the barriers to entry being
so high and a century's worth of competitive advantage having been traded

on comprehensively. Now every personal computer is capable of becoming a multi-track recording studio, mastering operation and a global distribution network. The only thing stopping me making another *Sergeant Pepper* is my lack of talent.[25]

Suddenly, a large portion of the music industry's output became intangible. Almost overnight, the industry went from overwhelming, quite awesome and deeply smug certainty to being very frightened indeed. With the factory rationalizations, the record industry is becoming less of an industry. Music is in rude health, and something called the music business will be with us for a long time to come, but the only survivors will be those who have the will and the wit to adapt. Some are hiding behind the anti-piracy veil.

Some veterans, like Ahmet Ertegun, believe it's simply a matter of keeping one's (in his case considerable) cool:

> The basic motivation is always the same. It all comes down to one thing. It's all a matter of finding songs, finding artists, putting them together and, if you can, making hit records. If you can't find the people to make hit records, then it's not a good business to be in. The dark times we're going through aren't going to leave us soon, because I think there are many pressures on the record companies. The costs are getting higher, the artists are unhappy even though they're getting more than they've ever gotten. They would like to get more. The record companies feel cheated because they very often spend a lot of money and can't make their money back. The artists become big stars, make films and personal appearances, and the record companies don't participate. So we're in for a lot of controversy, but basically, as far as I'm concerned, I would just be happy to be left alone to make as good records as we can, with whatever artists we can find, and we will try to make them happy.[26]

Others admit they're all at sea, such as Sony's Muff Winwood:

> Audio CDs aren't sexy any more. We've had twenty years of this, and it's been wonderful. I often explain it a bit like the demise of the miners. We rant and rave and say we've done great for the country, why should things be so bad for us, the record industry has always been a great flagwaver for this country. Frankly, the record industry is like it is because people don't care about records any more. They can download them, but most importantly I don't think they necessarily have the time to listen to them. When you and I were

younger, you could buy a new record and have an hour spare to listen. You find the hour now. Any kid. They're either on the Internet, texting each other on their telephones, playing games or they're watching music on the interminable number of digital channels, let alone the interminable number of radios. So where do you even have the time to stop and listen to a CD?

The delivery method is there, but we'll have to work out how to make money from it. From now on, record companies will become music banks. Contracts will be more like the EMI deal with Robbie Williams – taking a piece of everything that the artist earns. As record labels, we only take our profits from the sales of their records. They make money on selling T-shirts themselves, their publishing is often with someone else, all their other activities, ticket sales, are all theirs. We will have to have a piece of those in the future, to be able to invest. The outlook for CDs is poor. For music, it's fine. There will always be music.[27]

AFTERWORD

The hardback edition of this book took the story of the record industry up to November 2003, a time when many top executives were moaning very loudly about the unfairness of their various predicaments. What has happened since then? Well, they're still moaning, despite an apparent stabilization in fortunes. In the first half of 2004, global sales of recorded music grew in volume by 1.7 per cent, according to figures collected by the International Federation of the Phonographic Industry. The strongest growth was in the US, which managed to increase volume by 5 per cent, while the UK saw a more modest 0.6 per cent rise. The value of these sales fell from US$14.1 billion to US$13.9 billion, but the IFPI admits that the figures 'reflect a slowing of the rate of decline ... of the past four years', declaring it 'the best first half-year result achieved since 2000'.[1]

The stabilization could be the result of a number of factors. With audio sales continuing to drop, albeit by less than in previous years, the IFPI attributes a large part of the improvement to a 26.2 per cent increase in DVD music video sales. In addition, the fact that volume sales have increased while their value has declined slightly may mean that the industry is starting to get to grips with the issue of pricing and value for money. If so, this is long overdue. If not, why not?

In Germany, Bertelsmann Music Group is trying out one new approach to value by launching cheaper 'no-frills' versions of CDs, without artwork but with the title plainly printed on the disc. The idea was explained to *Der Spiegel* by Maarten Steinkamp, head of BMG Germany, in July 2004: 'The cheap version [which is expected to cost £9.99] will look the same as one burned at home ... That is our anti-piracy CD.'[2] Unfortunately for Steinkamp, I suspect that many will figure that if a CD that costs seven pounds looks like a home-burned CD-R, they might as well get someone to burn them a CD-R for free. If record companies could guarantee a fully-specified product selling for £7 or £8, then they could probably win back a lot of trade. Nonetheless, Steinkamp's move is an indication that someone in a position of power is actually trying to adapt to the new circumstances in which the industry finds itself – a significant advance on the record business complacency that informed consumers have come to know and hate.

He seems also to have realized that the imperious attitude taken by some record executives in recent years has done nothing to endear them to their customers, actual or potential. Rather than putting stern, patronizing, alienating anti-piracy stickers on all CDs sold, he has suggested that 'It would be better for us to write, "Thanks a lot for buying something from us."' What a nice man. He's right, too, just as he is when he declares, 'The music industry has sat motionless on its backside for far too long.' Here's hoping that others in the business begin to exhibit similar levels of enlightenment and candour.

Steinkamp now works for a much larger company than he did in November 2003. In July 2004 the European Commission approved finally the merger between Sony Music and BMG. The Commission decided that the concerns raised by competitors were minor, as was a threatened round of approximately three thousand redundancies, or about 25 per cent of the combined workforce. Furthermore, the Commission came to the conclusion that allegations of price-fixing among the major record companies were groundless, although regular record buyers might choose to differ. Is the merger a good idea? For Clive Davis, the answer is yes, because it means that he can do a lap of honour around the offices of the company that sacked him in 1973. Longer term, the benefits are less certain. There are questions as to how well the two different corporate cultures will integrate and, more fundamentally, there is the question of whether the major record companies should be getting bigger when the greater flexibility of smaller organizations might be more useful.

Not that such considerations will dissuade EMI and Warner Music Group from shacking up if the conditions are right. If the rumours are to be believed, the longest, coyest courtship in the history of the industry since HMV tried to buy Victor, and vice versa, is back on, just as soon as Warner Music completes its projected public flotation. The Sony-BMG merger puts the new company slightly behind the vast Universal Music Group in terms of market share, with EMI and Warner now trailing some way behind the two monsters. By merging, EMI and Warner could achieve heavy cost savings to add to those that the individual companies have been making. In April 2004, EMI announced a further 1500 redundancies as it sold off its factory in Holland, closed its US plant altogether, and instituted a 20 per cent cut in the number of its artists, just as Warner was undertaking a similar spring clean. EMI's decision to move out of physical manufacturing may prove to be a very shrewd move as downloads start to play more of a part in sales, but one wonders how much spare flesh is really left on the company.

These four companies represent the bulk of the industry, and the trade bodies that represent them collectively have continued with their various schemes and ruses designed to restore the industry to its former glory. In particular, the RIAA's campaign to take every broadband-enabled American computer owner to court continues to wend its painfully slow way. The fact that it is the sort of idea that makes sense only after an all-day session in the pub ('Look, we should just go after everyone who's downloaded anything ever … Oi, did you spill my pint? Outside, now. You're my besht mate, you are …') has not deterred the British Phonographic Industry from trying a similar stunt in the UK.

In October 2004, the BPI announced that it was instituting legal proceedings against twenty-eight – count 'em – people who had consistently made their music collections available online. Yes, they're coming for you. Just not, in all probability, any time soon. Once again, the main beneficiaries will be the lawyers. If the industry didn't spend so much on pointless legal activity, it might be able to reduce prices to a compelling level.

Speaking at the 2004 In the City conference in Manchester, former PolyGram boss John Kennedy – who had just been announced as Jay Berman's successor at the IFPI – said that he is firmly behind the RIAA and BPI policy of pursuing individuals through the courts. 'It will make the biggest impact when you know of someone that's been sued,' he declared. 'When the parents of so-and-so down the street have had to put their hands in their pockets for 2000 euros.'[3] Elsewhere at the same conference, US technology journalist Andrew Orlowski told delegates that they were 'sitting on a gold mine … most people in technology wish they had the problems of the record industry'. He added, 'It's unrealistic to think that this tap can be turned off.' The question here is, who to believe or trust? – an informed observer of the industry like Orlowski, or a lawyer like Kennedy who freely admits that 'if there's money involved I'll do absolutely anything.'[4]

The record industry has presented the downloading issue as one of the lawless trying to get something for nothing. While some downloaders undoubtedly are of that persuasion, the evidence seems to suggest that many others are using their access to free music to supplement and inform their purchasing. The industry's standpoint is at best a grotesque oversimplification of the real state of affairs and at worst a sickening piece of moral blackmail. Informed consumers are a dangerous variable to an industry largely based on bullshit, and so they obviously need to be stamped out. Meanwhile, bleating about illegality seems rather hypocritical when at least one label head has been threatened with prosecution for criminal damage, as a result of his company's predilection for promoting its releases via the medium of illegal fly-posting.

The impossible dream of running every last downloader out of town is not the only big idea currently being propounded by the BPI and the IFPI. They are also at the forefront of a campaign to extend the fifty-year copyright period that currently applies to sound recordings in the UK. BPI chairman Peter Jamieson likes to claim that this is all about protecting the artists and ensuring future revenue for investment in new talent. The British record business, he says, 'has less time to earn from its work than other UK creative industries – recording copyright suffers from unfair discrimination at the hands of copyright law'. A simple retort to this would be the suggestion that record companies try and maximize their earnings from a recording during the fifty-year period, but that would obviously be too much like hard work.

For reasons of spin, the industry is presenting the fifty-year term as though this is a shocking new menace, when in fact it has lived quite happily with the fifty-year term ever since the passing of the 1911 Copyright Act. If record companies were so bothered about the length of the copyright period, they had an opportunity to do something about it in 1996 when copyright in written works (including musical compositions) was standardized throughout the European Union at seventy years after the creator's death (compared with the previous UK term of death plus fifty years). Back then, the hottest discs passing into the public domain were by Frankie Laine, Spike Jones and His City Slickers, Perry Como, Bing Crosby and Felix Weingartner, and no one seemed particularly bothered about protecting their rights.

Anyone with an ounce of sense could have seen that recordings by ongoing cash cows like Elvis Presley, the Beatles and Herbert von Karajan would in time fall into the public domain. The fact that no one did so highlights the short-termism of the record industry. Meanwhile, the idea that it desperately needs the money from sales of early rock and roll in order to guarantee its investment in new artists is deeply depressing and shows how complacent and hidebound the business currently is. When RCA Victor signed Elvis, it wasn't relying on recordings from 1905 to fund the deal.

If the desired extension of copyright is all about keeping the artists in bunce, what of the lesser-known talents whose deleted recordings languish in company archives with no prospect of reissue? An extension of the copyright period would grant major record companies a licence to carry on doing nothing, at the same time putting smaller specialist labels out of business and reducing the amount of choice available to music lovers. Labels specializing in public domain recordings have been the saviour of more obscure items that would otherwise have remained unavailable. Artists receive no royalties from the release of public domain material unless they also wrote or arranged it, but then they receive no royalties at all if the recordings in question remain in copyright but are unavailable.

Artists who favour the extension seem to do so largely because they believe what their record companies tell them. Obviously, the record bosses aren't going to tell them that, once their recordings enter the public domain, they can reclaim their back catalogue for free and release it themselves. If the artist in question is popular, other labels will be competing; but if added value means extra sales, who can add value to a package better than the artist who made the original recording? Artists arguing for the copyright extension are arguing for further enslavement to a corporate monolith that has already given them a bum deal. Happily, outgoing arts minister Estelle Morris is not, at the time of writing, rolling over and doing the record industry's bidding. She told *Music Week* that if the extension were to be granted, 'all relevant government interests, as well as our EU partners and the European Commission, would need to be convinced that this is justified'.[5]

The presence of public domain material in the market does not stop the record companies that originated the recordings from competing or benefiting. Sony/Columbia has done very well with its remastered and extensively-annotated boxed set of the Louis Armstrong Hot Five and Hot Seven recordings, despite the presence of a number of good independent releases carrying the same material. Perhaps the record companies might have a case for the extension if they were to commit themselves to making their archives of deleted recordings available in some form or other. If not, the industry should consider taking the lead of the book-publishing business, where contracts routinely provide for the reversion of rights to the writer/creator if the publisher lets a book go out of print.

What else has been going on? Congressman and friend of the RIAA Howard Berman's original bill, which would have allowed copyright holders to hack into the computers of file sharers, did not make it onto the US statute book. However, his subsequent brainwave – the Piracy Deterrence and Education Act of 2003, introduced by Berman and his colleagues Lamar Smith and John Conyers – did, being passed by the House of Representatives in September 2004. This sets a potential tariff of three years in jail for file swappers caught for the first time, with six-year sentences for repeat offenders. The overwhelming impression is of using a sledgehammer to crack a nut, underlined by Berman and Co.'s determination to distract the FBI from its important involvement in the wars on terror and drugs in order to locate the nuts who download. Even Michael Jackson, not noted in recent years for his sanity, thinks that this legislation is going a bit too far.

There has also been a subtle reclamation of the word 'download' by the record industry. In November 2003 all downloading was wrong, or so the record companies would have had us believe. However, now that iTunes, the legalized Napster and other paid-for services have finally got their feet under the table, we are being asked to distinguish between legal downloads and illegal downloads. All very well, but if the record companies had embraced downloading in 1998 or 1999, it is likely that illegal downloading might not have taken off in quite the way it did. The advent of an official download chart, as happened in the UK in August 2004, is indicative of the industry's belated change of heart; but perhaps the executives should be keeping an equally close eye on what is being downloaded illegally, so that they know what deleted gems are worthy of reissue.

The industry persists in its belief that one illegal download equals one lost sale, which is a fallacy: people will download things on which they would never dream of spending their hard-earned cash. Felix Oberholzer-Gee, of Harvard Business School, and Koleman Strumpf, of the University of North Carolina, examined the logs of downloads kept by file-sharing networks, tracking songs from the 680 best-selling albums of the period. They found that there was no correlation between the number of times a song was downloaded and the sales of the CD that included it. Oberholzer-Gee estimated that, at best, it took five thousand downloads to equal one lost CD sale.

On the human resources front, Arista head Antonio 'LA' Reid was given his cards by Bertelsmann in February 2004, to no one's great surprise, after several years of mounting losses. Within a month, he had pitched up at Universal to run the Island Def Jam operation. He is reported to be on a much more modest salary than he had become used to, but with extensive bonuses if success is achieved. Meanwhile, Sony's decision to close its London recording studios in September 2003 has been proven to be the lunacy it seemed at the time, following the facility's reopening in spring 2004 as the independent Whitfield Street Studios. Sade's former producer Robin Millar now runs the show, Mike Ross-Trevor continues to lay an educated hand or two on the giant Neve mixing desk in studio 1, and the venture seems to be thriving.

The record industry may not be thriving in quite the same way, but there is a prospect of genuine recovery if the companies really want it. Over the last year, some within the industry have shown a laudable willingness to adapt, to think radical thoughts and to get on with competing effectively in a marketplace where the old certainties have disappeared, rather than wasting valuable man-hours crying over their disappearance. Admittedly, others have proved themselves to be as complacent and idiotic as ever; but it's a start. However, if the record industry wants to guarantee its future existence it will have to rethink its attitudes and its business models far more than it has done, and to go on rethinking them on an almost daily basis. Unless it does so, the return of the good times is unlikely.

NOTES

Chapter I

1   Lampblack is a very finely powdered kind of soot.
2   Translation taken from *The Fabulous Phonograph* by Roland Gelatt (Appleton-Century, New York, 1965), p.23.
3   Ibid., p.24.
4   He also lodged an estimated 600 unsuccessful or abandoned patents. Of course, as will become apparent, Edison – like many other inventors – left some of his more ingenious creations unpatented, so that the opposition would not discover how it was done.
5   From autobiographical notes written by Edison in 1908–9, included in *Thomas Edison and Modern America: A Brief History with Documents* by Theresa M. Collins and Lisa Gitelman (Bedford/St Martins, Boston and New York, 2002), p.46.
6   Ibid., p.66.
7   *Scientific American*, 22 December 1877.
8   Quite possibly taken from the elephant that was killed by electrocution when Edison was trying to demonstrate the danger of the rival Westinghouse alternating current system compared with his own direct current system. It was as an offshoot of this smear campaign that the electric chair was invented, by Edison's protégé Harold P. Brown.
9   From a draft letter to one of Edison's potential backers, included in *Thomas Edison and Modern America: A Brief History with Documents* by Theresa M. Collins and Lisa Gitelman (Bedford/St Martins, Boston and New York, 2002), p.51.
10 The story of how Edison later tried to develop a talking doll is a sorry one. Using a miniaturized wax cylinder and replay device that was prone to malfunction, vast numbers had to be recalled. However, before the shortcomings became apparent, dolls were presented to such well-connected sprogs as Archduchess Elizabeth of Austria.
11 From US patent number 200,521, entitled 'Improvement in phonograph or speaking machines'.
12 Quoted in the *Illustrated London News*, 3 August 1878, p.114.
13 *The Speaking Telephone, Talking Phonograph and Other Novelties* by George B. Prescott (D. Appleton & Company, New York, 1878), p.306.
14 Ibid., p.307.
15 Ibid., p.305.
16 'Edisoniana', *Punch*, 18 January 1879.
17 From British patent number 1,644, entitled 'Edison's Improvements in Recording and Reproducing Sounds'.
18 'Edisoniana', *Punch*, 18 January 1879.
19 'The Song of Mr Phonograph' (G Schirmer, New York, 1878), reproduced in *From Tinfoil to Stereo* by Oliver Read and Walter L. Welch (Howard W. Sams/Bobbs-Merrill, Indianapolis/New York, 1959), pp.479–81.
20 Much the same was said for Errol Flynn's party trick of playing the piano with his penis.
21 *New York Times*, 25 March 1878, quoted in *Thomas Edison and Modern America: A Brief History with Documents* by Theresa M. Collins and Lisa Gitelman (Bedford/St Martins,

Boston and New York, 2002), p.67.

22 From the *Burlington Hawkeye*. Reprinted as 'Echoes from the Phonograph: What Mrs. Barstinglow Heard After Three Days' Absence from Home', *The Sun*, 21 April 1878 (omits final paragraph); and as 'The Phonograph: An Evening with the Machine in a Western Town', *Evening Post*, 16 April 1878. Archived at http://www27.brinkster.com/phonozoic/a0132.htm.

23 *Illustrated London News*, 3 August 1878, p.114.

24 Letter from Alexander Graham Bell to Gardiner G. Hubbard, 18 March 1878, held in the Bell Papers at the manuscript division of the Library of Congress. Also quoted in *A Business History of the Gramophone Company 1897–1918* by Peter Martland (Corpus Christi College, Cambridge, 1992).

25 Curiously, as the Volta Laboratory Associates were deserting the telephone in favour of the phonograph, Edison was heading in the other direction, gaining twenty-five telephonic patents after 1880.

26 *Music on Record* by Fred Gaisberg (Robert Hale, London, 1946), also quoted in *Sound Revolutions* by Jerrold Northrop Moore (Sanctuary, London, 1999), p.9.

27 The box was opened at the behest of the Dictaphone Corporation in 1937, and the cylinder was played.

28 Quoted in *The Fabulous Phonograph* by Roland Gelatt (Appleton-Century, New York, 1965), p.36.

29 Ibid.

30 *Spectator*, 30 June 1888.

31 Ibid.

32 An MP3 of it can be downloaded at http://www.nps.gov/edis.

33 Edison had told Gouraud that he wanted him to record the prime minister by sending him a cylinder ending with the lines: 'Gouraud, agent of my choice/Bid my balance sheets rejoice/Send me Mr Gladstone's voice.'

34 *Pitman's Common Commodities and Industries: Talking Machines* by Ogilvie Mitchell, (Sir Isaac Pitman and Sons, London, 1922), p.29.

35 Ibid.

36 *Talking Machine News*, January 1904. In a laboured pun on one of the phonograph's components, the journal added: 'If an old phonograph man does not know anything about governors; who should, anyway?'

37 From an interview in *Talking Machine News*, June 1903.

38 Spencer's father was famous throughout America for having developed a particular style of copperplate handwriting, then popularly taught in schools.

39 From *Music on Record* by Fred Gaisberg (Robert Hale, London, 1946), p.45.

40 *Edison Phonograph Monthly*, January 1904 – the recording can be heard at http://tinfoil.com/cm-9910.htm.

41 'The Career of "Casey" (Mr Russell Hunting) – a man of many records', *Talking Machine News*, July 1903.

42 Ibid.

43 I can vouch for this. I made a tinfoil recording at the Edison National Historical Site, and I had to bellow to make any impression.

44 Theoretically, two cylinders of the same performance, recorded by this method, could be synchronized to create stereo, assuming a sufficient gap between the two recording horns.

Chapter 2

1 There is a question over the efficacy of Berliner's microphone. In 1887, he admitted that, in use, 'a person heard sounds, but could not generally make out the words I spoke'. Perhaps Bell bought Berliner's device knowing it was a duffer, but hoping that ownership of his patent would allow them to copy Edison's more effective version covertly.

2   Even the best 180 gram audiophile pressings suffer from side-end distortion to some degree. In the 1920s, a brave attempt to combat this came in the form of Noel Pemberton-Billing's 'World Record', which utilized a special mechanical attachment to maintain a constant speed under the stylus of 20 inches per second. This involved starting at 33^1/$_3$ rpm and speeding up gradually as the spiral of the groove becomes smaller. It never caught on.

3   *Music on Record* by Fred Gaisberg (Robert Hale, London, 1946), p.15. This quote also appears in Jerrold Northrop Moore's excellent biography of Gaisberg – *Sound Revolutions* (Sanctuary, London, 1999).

4   Ibid., p.16.

5   The cylinder machines all had feed screws to guide the stylus across, and this was one of the most jealously defended aspects of their patents. Berliner's feed screw-free system was presaged by Cros, the Frenchman having predicted a groove 'capable of guiding a moving body'.

6   *The Fabulous Phonograph* by Roland Gelatt (Appleton-Century, New York, 1965), pp.146–7.

7   From a trade notice issued by the American Graphophone Company, 15 October 1896.

8   The date of this event is generally agreed to be some time in 1896, although Gaisberg claimed it was 1895.

9   Quoted in *His Master's Voice was Eldridge R. Johnson* by E. R. Fenimore Johnson (Dover, Delaware, 1974), p.36.

10 Extract of letter from Eldridge Johnson to Elsie Fenimore Cooper, 2 January 1895 – held in EMI Archives.

11 *Music on Record* by Fred Gaisberg (Robert Hale, London, 1946), pp.28–9.

12 The headquarters were situated in the rear portion of the Cockburn Hotel, which had its main entrance on Henrietta Street.

13 'How I Sing to Make Records' by W. H. Berry, *Talking Machine News*, May 1903.

14 *Joe Batten's Book* by Joe Batten (Rockliff, London, 1956), p.33.

15 Ibid.

16 Darby was a school friend of Gaisberg's younger brother William. When William Gaisberg was offered a job with Berliner, his father advised him to pass, fearing the consequences of two sons in such a precarious business. He recommended Darby for the post. Will eventually joined the company, in 1901, presumably when his father had been satisfied of its longevity.

17 *Music on Record* by Fred Gaisberg (Robert Hale, London, 1946).

18 Ibid., p.61.

19 For the rest of his life, Barraud was called upon frequently by the Gramophone Company to produce official replicas of the Nipper painting. Some, including one for the Victor Talking Machine Company boardroom in Camden, were exact replicas, to the point that Barraud painted first a phonograph, before painting the gramophone over this.

20 Letter from William Barry Owen to Eldridge Johnson, 1 July 1901.

21 It is more likely to have been added later by a senior colleague of Owen's, acting with the benefit of hindsight, than it is to have been a contemporary comment by Owen's secretary on her bitter experience with it.

22 *Talking Machine News*, July 1903.

23 Edison and the others used thin French glass. Bettini favoured mica.

24 Quoted in *From Tinfoil to Stereo* by Oliver Read and Walter L. Welch (Howard W. Sams/Bobbs-Merrill, Indianapolis/New York, 1959), p.77.

25 As it turned out, Johnson's lieutenants were notable, over the years, for their loyalty, whether this was due to ERJ's inspiring example, his choice of subordinates or a combination of the two. Not everyone present in the lab at this time, however, felt an allegiance to Johnson, as we will discover later.

26 Letter from Eldridge Johnson to William Barry Owen, 24 January 1901 – EMI Archive.

27 Letter from Eldridge R. Johnson to William Barry Owen, 12 March 1901 – EMI Archive.

Chapter 3

1 'Coster singers' were variety artists who sang and spoke in a cockney dialect. The accent was associated with 'costermongers', as market traders who sold fruit and vegetables were known. Popular artists in the genre included Albert Chevalier and Gus Elen.
2 Letter from Eldridge Johnson to William Barry Owen, 18 November 1901 – EMI Archive.
3 *Talking Machine News*, November 1903.
4 Letter from Eldridge Johnson to the gentlemen of the Gramophone Company, 25 June 1901 – EMI Archive.
5 This was the first of the twenty-four officially sanctioned replicas that he was to produce in the coming years.
6 The prices were on a sliding scale, informed by the number of singers involved and their celebrity. Caruso's 12-inch discs were $3, while the 1907 Victor recording of the quartet from *Rigoletto* went out at $6 to cover the cost of the four singers – Caruso, Antonio Scotti, Bessie Abbott and Louise Homer.
7 Cable from Eldridge Johnson to the gentlemen of the Gramophone & Typewriter Co., Ltd, 26 April 1904 – EMI Archive.
8 Letter from Cal Child to William Barry Owen, 9 May 1904 – EMI Archive.
9 *Talking Machine News*, May 1903.
10 Circular issued by the Columbia Graphophone Company in the US, 1898.
11 *Talking Machine News*, October 1903.
12 *From Tinfoil to Stereo* by Oliver Read and Walter L. Welch (Howard W. Sams/The Bobbs-Merrill, Indianapolis/New York, 1959), p.52.
13 From National Phonograph Company promotional literature, quoted in *Thomas Edison and Modern America: A Brief History With Documents* by Theresa M. Collins and Lisa Gitelman (Bedford/St Martin's, Boston/New York, 2002), p.138.
14 Statement issued by the Edison-Bell Consolidated Phonograph Company, quoted in *Pitman's Common Commodities and Industries: Talking Machines* by Ogilvie Mitchell (Sir Isaac Pitman and Sons, London, 1922), p.40.
15 Bulletin to dealers from the Columbia Phonograph General Company, 30 April 1909.
16 Letter from Eldridge Johnson to Alfred Clark, 3 February 1913 – EMI Archive.
17 As a performer, he continued to record for other companies throughout his involvement with Sterling.
18 *The Fabulous Phonograph* by Roland Gelatt (Appleton-Century, New York, 1965), p.123.
19 From Gaisberg's diaries, quoted in *Sound Revolutions* by Jerrold Northrop Moore (Sanctuary, London, 1999), p.66.
20 From Fred Gaisberg's diaries, quoted in *Sound Revolutions* by Jerrold Northrop Moore, (Sanctuary, London, 1999), p.73.
21 *Castrati* were, as their name suggests, male singers who had been castrated. The testicles were removed before the onset of puberty and the breaking of the voice, preserving a soprano tone for the rest of their lives. The popularity and earning power of such singers in eighteenth-century Italy had made the operation particularly common among large, poor families, who felt that as long as the eldest son could carry on the line, the manhood of some or all of his younger siblings could be sacrificed for the financial good of the family.
22 The surviving *castrati* were not cast out immediately, however. Moreschi remained in the choir until 1913, and with his departure passed the last of his kind in active service. He died in 1922, at the age of sixty-four.
23 *The World of the Castrati* by Patrick Barbier, trans. Margaret Crosland (Souvenir Press, London, 1996), p.239.
24 *Enrico Caruso: His Life and Death* by Dorothy Caruso (Simon & Schuster, New York,

1945), p.140.
25 *Music on Record* by Fred Gaisberg (Robert Hale, London, 1946), pp.50–1.
26 Ibid., pp.41–2.
27 Now home, believe it or not, to a call centre, possibly the grandest location for such anywhere in the world.
28 *Variations on a Personal Theme* by Landon Ronald, p.104, quoted in Moore, ibid., p.134.
29 *Music on Record* by Fred Gaisberg (Robert Hale, London, 1946), p.30. For some reason, probably connected with avoiding embarrassment to Rodkinson's family, Gaisberg changed his name to 'Max Rubinsky'. Similarly, Raphoff became 'Rappaport'.
30 From Fred Gaisberg's diaries, quoted in Moore, p.75.
31 Letter from Alfred Clark to Eldridge Johnson, 27 July 1908 – EMI Archive.
32 Letter from Eldridge Johnson to Alfred Clark, 10 May 1908 – EMI Archive.

Chapter 4

1 *Joe Batten's Book* by Joseph Batten (Rockliff, London, 1956), p.62.
2 *Music on Record* by Fred Gaisberg (Robert Hale, London, 1946).
3 Advertisement in *Talking Machine News*, September 1914.
4 Quoted in *Since Records Began* by Peter Martland (BT Batsford, London, 1997), p.73.
5 Letter from Alfred Clark to Eldridge Johnson, 1 August 1914 – EMI Archive.
6 Letter from Alfred Clark to Eldridge Johnson, 10 August 1914 – EMI Archive.
7 *Talking Machine News*, September 1914.
8 'Sir Louis Sterling – A Pioneer of a Great Industry' by W.S. Meadmore, the *Gramophone*, June 1937, p.5.
9 The Alhambra was on the site now occupied by the Odeon cinema.
10 This name was used by HMV for many years on recordings made by its in-house orchestra, composed of session men.
11 Letter from Alfred Clark to Eldridge Johnson, 27 May 1915 – EMI Archive.
12 *Talking Machine News*, May 1918.
13 Ibid.
14 Letter from Calvin Child to Sydney Dixon, 12 May 1919 – EMI Archive.
15 Ibid.
16 Ibid.
17 Letter from Sydney Dixon to Eldridge Johnson and Alfred Clark, 22 October 1919 – EMI Archive.
18 Ibid.
19 *New York Times*, 4 February 1922.
20 *Talking Machine World*, 15 August 1914.
21 Columbia advertisement in *Talking Machine World*, 15 August 1914.
22 Ibid.
23 Letter from J. E. Sterett of Price Waterhouse, 29 August 1914 – EMI Archive.
24 Eldridge Johnson's reply to J.E. Sterett, 5 September 1914 – EMI Archive.
25 *And the Bands Played On* by Sid Colin (Elm Tree Books, London, 1977), p.13.
26 *The Victor Talking Machine Company* by Benjamin L. Aldridge (RCA Sales Corporation, Camden, NJ, 1964). Reproduced in *The Encyclopedic Discography of Victor Recordings* by Ted Fagan and William R. Moran (Greenwood Press, Westport, 1982), pp.80–1.
27 *Talking Machine News*, February 1919.
28 Letter from Eldridge Johnson to Alfred Clark, 23 February 1916 – EMI Archive.
29 Letter from Eldridge Johnson to Leon Douglass, 24 June 1920 – EMI Archive.
30 Letter from Eldridge Johnson to Leon Douglass, 27 October 1920 – EMI Archive.
31 Letter from Sydney Dixon to Alfred Clark, 5 January 1921 – EMI Archive.
32 Letter from Charles Haddon, vice-president of Victor, to Alfred Clark, 24 January 1921 – EMI Archive.

33 Ibid.
34 Letter from Eldridge Johnson to Maurice Bower Saul of law firm Saul, Ewing, Romich and Saul, 28 September 1922 – EMI Archive.

Chapter 5

1   *Talking Machine News*, April 1919.
2   It would appear that *Talking Machine News* chose an unrepresentative example of the new sound. In *Jazz Records 1897–1942*, Brian Rust observed that 'Despite the name, this is not a jazz band in the accepted sense.'
3   *Talking Machine World*, 15 July 1919.
4   *The Fabulous Phonograph* by Roland Gelatt (Appleton-Century, New York, 1965), p.190.
5   Henderson's band had made some Diamond Discs for Edison, but these were before Armstrong joined.
6   Nowadays, it's probably easiest to use the term 'music of black origin'.
7   *Little Labels, Big Sound* by Rick Kennedy and Randy McNutt (Indiana University Press, Bloomington and Indianapolis, 1999), p.5. In Britain in the 1930s, the British Union of Fascists had a similar 'no questions asked' deal with Decca.
8   This would later become the home of the BBC radio light entertainment department, before reverting to the name Grosvenor Gallery when it was bought by the auction house Sotheby's.
9   Although he was a bona fide star while Haenschen was obscure then and is nearly forgotten now, Jolson did have something in common with the erstwhile Carl Fenton. His real name was Asa Yoelson, but he had been prevailed upon to adopt a less ethnic stage name.
10 *Exploding* by Stan Cornyn with Paul Scanlon (HarperCollins Entertainment, New York, 2002), p.8.
11 Ibid. Unattributed quote.
12 *Talking Machine News*, 15 April 1923. Quoted in 'Victor in the West: The Oakland Pressing Plant' by William J. Nicolson – http://www.garlic.com/~tgracyk/oakland.htm.
13 *Joe Batten's Book* by Joe Batten (Rockliff, London, 1956), p.56.
14 Velvet Face had, in fact, predated Winner, first appearing in 1910, but it had disappeared shortly afterwards, remaining dormant until the 1921 revival.
15 *Joe Batten's Book* by Joe Batten (Rockliff, London, 1956), pp.56–7.
16 Ibid., p.58.
17 *Gramophone*, October 1924.
18 *Joe Batten's Book* by Joe Batten (Rockliff, London, 1956), p.58.
19 'Music of the Day' by Compton Mackenzie, *Daily Telegraph*, 2 September 1922, quoted in *Gramophone: The First 75 Years* (Gramophone Publications, Kenton, 1997), p.15.
20 Ibid. *Gramophone* corrects Mackenzie on the matter of the Brahms piece, suggesting it was the fifth dance, not the first.
21 *Am I Too Loud?* by Gerald Moore (Hamish Hamilton, London, 1962), pp.59–61.
22 Many users of the various electric recording systems did not trust the mains as a means of motive power, due to fluctuations in the supply. So, while the cutting heads were electric, the lathes remained driven by gravity-operated motors, in many cases until the 1950s.
23 *The Fabulous Phonograph* by Roland Gelatt (Appleton-Century, New York, 1965), p.224.
24 Letter from Eldridge Johnson to E. R. Fenimore Johnson, 5 February 1924 – EMI Archive.
25 Typescript of interview with B. E. G. Mittell, 24 September 1957 – EMI Archive.
26 *Music on Record* by Fred Gaisberg (Robert Hale, London, 1946), p.81.
27 Ibid., p.82.
28 *Talking Machine World*, 15 March 1925.
29 Letter from Charles Haddon to Eldridge Johnson, 21 August 1916 – EMI Archive.

30 Letter from Louis Geissler to Eldridge Johnson, 9 April 1918 – EMI Archive.
31 Letter from Eldridge Johnson to Leon Douglass, 15 July 1924 – EMI Archive.
32 Letter from J. E. Sterett to Eldridge Johnson, 21 June 1923 – EMI Archive.
33 Cable from Eldridge Johnson to Leon Douglass, 6 December 1926 – EMI Archive.
34 Letter from Eldridge Johnson to J. E. Sterett, 5 January 1927 – EMI Archive.
35 Letter from Eldridge Johnson to Leon Douglass, 21 December 1926 – EMI Archive.
36 Ibid.

Chapter 6

1   *New York Times*, 8 March 1930.
2   Ibid., 26 April 1930.
3   Ibid., 15 March 1931.
4   Unfortunately, within a couple of years, the economic situation had worsened to such a degree that both HMV and Columbia ditched the laminated discs and reverted to standard rough shellac with abrasive filler, a state that remained until the demise of 78s in the 1950s. Such is progress.
5   HMV had acquired the faltering Marconi business in 1929.
6   Notes from interview with Sir Louis Sterling, 12 November 1957 – EMI Archive.
7   In the event, this had to be raised to £32,500, while adjacent properties were bought, primarily for the expansion space afforded by their gardens.
8   Minutes from conference on recording, 7 December 1931 – EMI Archive.
9   Internal memo from F. H. Dart to W. M. Brown, 15 December 1931 – EMI Archive.
10 Memo from F. H. Dart, 9 December 1931 – EMI Archive.
11 Abbey Road made the switch immediately, but some foreign outposts continued with the Western Electric system for a couple more years.
12 Compared with 150 grooves per inch for conventional 78s and 250 for later LPs.
13 Letter from Captain H. G. Bayes to David Sarnoff, 12 November 1930 – EMI Archive.
14 *The Other Side of the Record* by Charles O'Connell (Alfred A. Knopf, New York, 1947), pp.128–9. O'Connell's book is an especially interesting document. It takes the form of a series of pen portraits of classical music stars, based on O'Connell's experiences of working with them. For its time, it was amazingly frank and even now, some of O'Connell's brutally honest observations about the goings-on of people very used to getting their own way can cause a sharp intake of breath. The author observed that writing the book had 'eliminated' him 'from the recording business'. So it proved, and several of those mentioned in the book sent him to Coventry. Their loss, history's gain. Charles O'Connell died on 1 September 1962, aged only sixty-two.
15 Ibid., p.65.
16 Ibid., p.149.
17 Ibid., p.21.
18 Kostelanetz is best known in the UK for his recording of 'With a Song in My Heart', which used to herald each edition of 'Two Way Family Favourites'.
19 *The Other Side of the Record* by Charles O'Connell (Alfred A. Knopf, New York, 1947), p.66.
20 Lest Wallerstein, who is generally held to be one of the good guys, should appear in a less than favourable light on this issue, O'Connell is scrupulous in suggesting that Wallerstein was acting on instructions from the tightwads in Victor's high command. 'When he later resigned to organize the Columbia Company, where he had complete authority and a free hand, he immediately made a contract with Minneapolis' (O'Connell, p.67).
21 Ibid., p.319.
22 Ibid.
23 Ibid., p.322.
24 Ibid., p.101.

25 Ibid., p.115.
26 Ibid., p.116.
27 Ibid., p.103.
28 Author's interview with Adele Siegal.
29 *The Other Side of the Record* by Charles O'Connell (Alfred A. Knopf, New York, 1947), p.ix.
30 Ibid., p.239.
31 Ibid., p.vii.
32 *No CIC* by E. R. Lewis (Universal Royalties, London, 1956), pp.10–11.
33 Ibid., p.15.
34 Ibid, p.18.
35 Author's interview with Hugh Mendl.
36 'The Decca Record Factory', *Phono Record*, September 1929.
37 Advertisement in the *Gramophone and Talking Machine News*, June 1929.
38 Author's interview with Hugh Mendl.
39 *No CIC* by E. R. Lewis (Universal Royalties, London, 1956), pp.25–6.
40 Ibid., p.28.
41 Author's interview with Hugh Mendl.
42 Ibid.
43 From a 1984 interview with Frank Lee held in the British Library Sound Archive.
44 *From Tinfoil to Stereo* by Oliver Read and Walter L. Welch (Howard W. Sams/Bobbs-Merrill, Indianapolis/New York, 1959), p.405.
45 *No CIC* by E. R. Lewis (Universal Royalties, London, 1956), p.54.
46 Ibid., p.53.
47 Ibid., p.60.
48 US Decca was renowned for its shoddy pressings for some years after the launch – Decca records could be relied upon to wear out and become grey very quickly.
49 *No CIC* by E. R. Lewis (Universal Royalties, London, 1965), p.63.
50 Author's interview with Hugh Mendl.
51 The artistic spoils were divided between the two companies. Decca, most notably, got the American pianist Charlie Kunz. British Homophone remained in business as a custom pressing company.
52 *No CIC* by E. R. Lewis (Universal Royalties, London, 1965), p.75.
53 Author's interview with George Avakian.
54 Letter from Rex Palmer to Ronald Wise, 10 March 1939 – EMI Archive.
55 Letter from John Hammond, Associate Recording Director, ARC, to Hugh Francis, 11 May 1939 – EMI Archive.
56 Notes from interview with Sir Louis Sterling, 12 November 1957 – EMI Archive.
57 Ibid.

Chapter 7

1 Figures from *An International History of the Recording Industry* by Pekka Gronow and Ilpo Saunio, trans. by Christopher Moseley (Cassell, London, 1998), p.38.
2 Author's interview with Hugh Mendl.
3 Ibid.
4 Letter from Louis Sterling to a Mr Goldstein, 22 March 1933 – EMI Archives.
5 Document in EMI Archive, dated 20 July 1933.
6 *Music on Record* by Fred Gaisberg (Robert Hale, London, 1946), p.150.
7 Memo from Walter Legge to C. H. Thomas and F. B. Duncan, 28 September 1943 – EMI Archive.
8 Memo from C. H. Thomas to F. B. Duncan, 6 October 1943 – EMI Archive.
9 Memo from F. B. Duncan to C. H. Thomas, 2 October 1943 – EMI Archive.

10 Memo from Walter Legge to C. H. Thomas, 21 July 1944 – EMI Archive.
11 Heaven knows how many rare recordings from the acoustic era became even rarer at this time.
12 Telegram from Columbia president Edward Wallerstein to Judge Vinson, 11 November 1944 – quoted in *From Tinfoil to Stereo* by Oliver Read and Walter L. Welch (Howard W. Sams/Bobbs-Merrill, Indianapolis/New York, 1959), pp. 334–5.
13 Mercifully, Petrillo's wishes were ignored, and a complete set of V-Discs resides in the Library of Congress. Nevertheless, post-war ownership of V-Discs was at one point so illicit that one man served time in jail simply for having a large collection of the records.
14 Author's interview with Hugh Mendl.
15 *No CIC* by E. R. Lewis (Universal Royalties, London, 1956), p.89.
16 Advertisement, *Gramophone*, July 1945.
17 *Putting the Record Straight* by John Culshaw (Secker and Warburg, London, 1981), p.109.
18 Author's interview with Hugh Mendl.
19 *Putting the Record Straight* by John Culshaw (Secker and Warburg, London, 1981), p.69.
20 Ibid., p.90.
21 Memo from Isaac Shoenberg to F. B. Duncan, 20 June 1945 – EMI Archive.
22 Author's interview with Hugh Mendl.
23 Author's interview with George Avakian.
24 Ibid.
25 Ibid.
26 Ibid.
27 *Since Records Began: EMI: The First 100 Years* by Peter Martland (BT Batsford, London, 1997), p.148.
28 Author's correspondence with Brian Masters.
29 Songwriter responsible for 'A Nightingale Sang in Berkeley Square', one time head of light entertainment at the BBC, and husband of Hermione Gingold.
30 Author's interview with Hugh Mendl.
31 Author's interview with Jimmy Lock.
32 Author's interview with George Avakian.
33 *Putting the Record Straight* by John Culshaw (Secker and Warburg, London, 1981), p.83.

Chapter 8

1 Author's interview with Ahmet Ertegun.
2 *Off the Record: An Oral History of Popular Music* by Joe Smith (Warner Books, New York, 1988), p.114.
3 *Little Labels, Big Sound* by Rick Kennedy and Randy McNutt (Indiana University Press, Bloomington and Indianapolis, 1999), p.66.
4 Author's interview with Seymour Stein.
5 Author's interview with Ahmet Ertegun.
6 *Exploding* by Stan Cornyn (HarperCollins Entertainment, New York, 2002), p.85.
7 Author's interview with Ahmet Ertegun.
8 *Exploding* by Stan Cornyn (HarperCollins Entertainment, New York, 2002), p.82.
9 *What'd I Say*, Ahmet Ertegun et al. (Orion, London, 2001), p.36.
10 *Exploding* by Stan Cornyn (HarperCollins Entertainment, New York, 2002), p.82.
11 Author's interview with Ahmet Ertegun.
12 Ibid.
13 Ibid.
14 *Rhythm and the Blues* by Jerry Wexler with David Ritz (Jonathan Cape, London, 1994), p.74.
15 *Gramophone*, February 1953.
16 Author's conversation with June Whitfield c. 2001.

17 Author's interview with Angela Morley.
18 Ibid.
19 Author's interview with Coen Solleveld.
20 Author's interview with David Fine.
21 Ibid.
22 Ibid.
23 Author's interview with George Avakian.
24 *Exploding* by Stan Cornyn (HarperCollins Entertainment, New York, 2002), p.17.
25 Letter from Jim Conkling to the EMI board, 14 December 1951 – EMI Archive.
26 Letter from Walter Legge to Dario Soria, 11 September 1953, quoted in *On and Off the Record: A Memoir of Walter Legge* by Elisabeth Schwarzkopf (Faber and Faber, London, 1982), p.309.
27 Author's interview with George Avakian.
28 Ibid.
29 Ibid.
30 Ibid.
31 Ibid.
32 Ibid.
33 Ibid.
34 *A Portrait of Duke Ellington: Reminiscing in Tempo* by Stuart Nicholson (Sidgwick and Jackson, London, 1999), p.309.
35 Author's interview with George Avakian.
36 Ibid.
37 Author's interview with Bruce Lundvall – incidentally, Townsend and Macero were both given their jobs by Avakian.
38 Author's interview with George Avakian.
39 Ibid.
40 Author's interview with Alan Kayes.
41 Ibid.
41 Author's interview with Adele Siegal.

Chapter 9

1   National Sound Archive interview with L. G. Wood, 1984.
2   Ibid.
3   Memo from Walter Legge to Brenchley Mittell, 16 May 1955 – EMI Archive.
4   Telegram from L. J. Brown to E. R. Lewis, 8 March 1956 – EMI Archive.
5   Author's interview with Alan Kayes.
6   A tape copy was $1 extra.
7   Peter Guralnick, in his excellent biography of the young Presley, *Last Train to Memphis*, points out that the figure demanded by Phillips was $10,000 more than Columbia had paid Mercury for the far better established Frankie Laine in 1951.
8   *Rhythm and Blues* by Jerry Wexler with David Ritz (Jonathan Cape, London, 1994), p.125.
9   *Abbey Road* by Brian Southall (Patrick Stephens Ltd, Wellingborough, 1982), p.55.
10 Author's interview with Hugh Mendl.
11 Author's interview with Diana Weller.
12 Ibid.
13 Author's interview with Hugh Mendl.
14 Ibid.
15 Ibid.
16 Ibid.
17 Ibid.
18 In those days, the tapes had to be copied in real time. Later on, methods were developed

where the tapes were dubbed at high speed.

19 Author's interview with Raymond Horricks.

20 Author's interview with Angela Morley.

21 Author's interview with Raymond Horricks.

22 From *An Eye for an Eye or Stéphane Grappelli: A Case of Libel* by Raymond Horricks (unpublished MS).

23 Ibid.

24 Author's interview with Mike Smith.

25 From *An Eye for an Eye or Stéphane Grappelli: A Case of Libel* by Raymond Horricks (unpublished MS).

26 Author's interview with Hugh Mendl.

27 Author's interview with Raymond Horricks.

28 *The Music Goes Round and Round: A Cool Look at the Music Industry*, edited by Peter Gammond and Raymond Horricks (Quartet, London, 1980), p.95.

29 Ibid., p.96.

30 Author's interview with Raymond Horricks.

31 Author's interview with George Avakian.

32 Author's interview with Hugh Mendl.

33 Author's interview with Raymond Horricks.

34 Author's interview with Tony Hall.

35 Author's interview with Hugh Mendl.

36 *From Holyrood to Hollywood: The Johnny Keating Story* by Johnny Keating (JKM Music, London, 2002), p.65.

37 Author's interview with Jimmy Lock.

38 Author's interview with Raymond Horricks.

39 Roberts was a South African-born Tin Pan Alley songwriter who found fame in his own right as a singer of humorous, mildly bawdy ditties. His rhymes were in the Noël Coward class and his Mendl-produced LP *Strictly for Grown-Ups* is a delight.

40 Author's interview with Hugh Mendl.

41 Author's interview with Derek Everett.

42 Ibid.

43 Ibid.

44 *Atlantic and the Godfathers of Rock and Roll* by Justine Picardie and Dorothy Wade (Fourth Estate, London, 1992), p.45.

45 *Jazz in Revolution* by John Dankworth (Constable, London, 1998), p.126.

46 *Rhythm and the Blues* by Jerry Wexler with David Ritz (Jonathan Cape, London, 1994), p.129–30.

47 Author's interview with Derek Everett.

48 National Sound Archive interview with Walter Ridley.

49 Author's interview with Hugh Mendl.

50 Author's interview with Derek Everett.

51 From *An Eye for an Eye or Stéphane Grappelli: A Case of Libel* by Raymond Horricks (unpublished MS).

52 *Seventeen Watts: The First Twenty Years of British Rock Guitar, the Musicians and Their Heroes* by Mo Foster (Sanctuary, London, 1997), p.135.

Chapter 10

1 Author's interview with Hugh Mendl.

2 *The Complete Beatles Recording Sessions* by Mark Lewisohn (Hamlyn, London, 1988), p.17.

3 Author's interview with Mike Smith.

4 Author's interview with Hugh Mendl.

5   Author's interview with Mike Smith.

6   Author's interview with Hugh Mendl.

7   *The Brian Epstein Story* by Debbie Geller (Faber and Faber, London, 2000), p.46.

8   The *Record Retailer* chart insisted that Cliff Richard's double A-side 'The Next Time'/'Bachelor Boy' had pipped the newcomers.

9   Author's interview with Derek Everett.

10 Ibid.

11 *To Be Loved* by Berry Gordy (Headline, London, 1994), p.126.

12 Author's interview with Eddie Levy.

13 Author's interview with Derek Everett.

14 National Sound Archive interview with L. G. Wood, 1984.

15 Author's interview with Derek Everett.

16 Most's real name was Michael Hayes, and his 'brother' Alex Wharton, under the name Alex Murray, became a Decca staff producer.

17 Author's interview with Jimmy Lock.

18 At this time, each of the major labels had its own show on Fab 208. Most famously, Decca had its 'Teen and Twenty Disc Club', through the membership of which it amassed a huge and highly valuable database of record buyers' names and addresses.

19 Saga had arranged to have Lock's National Service deferred, but when the company went down the tubes, the exemption no longer applied and he had to go into the forces for his statutory two years. Upon demob in 1963, he joined his former IBC colleague Jack Clegg at Decca in Broadhurst Gardens, West Hampstead.

20 Author's interview with Jimmy Lock.

21 *The Legendary Joe Meek: The Telstar Man* by John Repsch (Cherry Red Books, London, 2001), p.140.

22 *Melody Maker*, c. January 1962, quoted in *The Legendary Joe Meek: The Telstar Man* by John Repsch (Cherry Red Books, London, 2001), p.130.

23 Author's correspondence with Brian Masters.

24 Author's interview with Hugh Mendl.

25 Author's interview with Mike Smith.

26 Speech by Dr Ernst von Siemens, 24 October 1972, reported in *Gramophone: The First 75 Years* (Gramophone Publications, Kenton, 1997), p.98.

27 Letter from Coen Solleveld to author, 26 May 2003.

28 *Billboard*, 16 March 1963.

29 Author's interview with Eddie Levy.

30 Ibid.

31 Author's interview with Mike Ross-Trevor.

32 Ibid.

33 'It's Official: CBS–Oriole Deal' – *Billboard*, 3 October 1964.

34 Ibid.

35 Author's interview with Rodney Burbeck.

36 Author's interview with Mike Smith.

37 Author's interview with Rodney Burbeck.

38 Author's interview with Derek Everett.

39 Author's interview with Mike Smith.

40 Author's interview with Rodney Burbeck.

41 Author's interview with Mike Smith.

42 Author's interview with Rodney Burbeck.

43 Ibid.

44 Author's interview with Derek Everett.

45 Author's interview with Bruce Lundvall.

46 *Clive: Inside the Record Business* by Clive Davis with James Willwerth (Ballantine Books, New York, 1974), p.21.

47 Ibid, p.332.

48 Author's interview with Bruce Lundvall.

49 Author's interview with Mike Smith.

50 The previous year, *The Spirit of St Louis*, the Billy Wilder-directed, James Stewart-starring biopic of Charles Lindbergh, had lost $6m.

51 Author's interview with George Avakian.

52 Ibid.

53 Ibid.

54 Ibid.

55 Author's interview with Walter Woyda.

56 Author's interview with Raymond Horricks.

57 The record sleeve bears a joint credit for Horricks and Alan A. Freeman, but Freeman's involvement in the studio was minimal.

58 Which is, incidentally, a superb piece of work, particularly Johnny Keating's arrangement of Charlie Chaplin's 'Smile', which borrows very heavily from 'Desafinado', the then-current hit by Antonio Carlos Jobim, and to great effect.

59 Quoted from Stan Cornyn's original draft for his programme copy on the occasion of Mo Ostin's Rock and Roll Hall of Fame induction, which he very helpfully and generously sent to me when I asked him a question about Ostin.

60 Author's interview with Ahmet Ertegun.

61 Author's interview with Ahmet Ertegun.

62 Quoted in *Exploding* by Stan Cornyn (HarperCollins Entertainment, New York, 2002), p.134.

63 Author's interview with Ahmet Ertegun.

64 *Exploding* by Stan Cornyn (HarperCollins Entertainment, New York, 2002), p.149.

65 Telegram from Lew Wasserman, quoted in *The Last Mogul: Lew Wasserman, MCA and the Hidden History of Hollywood* by Dennis McDougal (DaCapo Press, New York, 2001), p.301.

66 Author's interview with Derek Everett.

67 Author's interview with Roger Watson.

68 Author's interview with Derek Everett.

69 Ibid.

Chapter 11

1 Author's correspondence with Brian Masters.

2 Christened Mervyn.

3 Author's interview with Muff Winwood.

4 Ibid.

5 Ibid.

6 Author's correspondence with Richard Elen.

7 Ibid.

8 Author's interview with Roger Watson.

9 'Jerry Moss – Past, present and future': Interview with Rob Partridge and Brian Mulligan, *Music Week*, 17 February 1973.

10 Ibid.

11 Ibid.

12 At the same time, A&M also had the number two – 'You Were on My Mind' by We Five.

13 Author's interview with Derek Everett.

14 Stories of the band members' enmity are legion. One involves Sting playing a gig with several broken ribs after a dressing-room punch-up with drummer Stewart Copeland. Unsurprising, when you consider that Copeland had a word written on each of his four tom-toms – 'FUCK', 'OFF', 'YOU' and 'CUNT' – thought to be directed at Sting.

15 *Losing My Virginity* by Richard Branson with Edward Whitley (Virgin Publishing, London, 1998), p.112.

16 Ibid., p.122.

17 Ibid., p.131.

18 The hanger-on in question would later become known as Siouxsie of 'and the Banshees' fame.

19 'The making of the Sex Pistols' "Anarchy in the UK" single' by Mike Thorne, www.stereosociety.com.

20 *Losing My Virginity*, by Richard Branson with Edward Whitley (Virgin Publishing, London, 1998), p.159.

21 Ibid, p.163.

22 *Billboard*, 17 November 1979

23 Author's interview with Derek Everett.

24 Author's interview with Mike Smith.

25 Author's interview with Mike Ross-Trevor. The studio was all that Mike said and more. Sadly, Sony closed it in September 2003. Mike is now much in demand as a freelance engineer.

26 Author's interview with Mike Smith.

27 Author's interview with Muff Winwood.

28 Tom Dooley (diary column), *Music Week*, 9 June 1973

29 Author's interview with Bruce Lundvall.

30 *Billboard*, 23 June 1973.

31 Author's interview with Bruce Lundvall.

32 Quoted in *The Operator: David Geffen Builds, Buys and Sells the New Hollywood* by Tom King (Broadway Books, New York, 2001), p.141.

33 *News of the World*, 14 February 1971.

34 *The Times*, 18 May 1973.

35 Ibid., 11 July 1973.

36 Ibid., 17 July 1973.

37 Upon her release in 1977, Jones was taken up by punk band the Clash and immortalized in song.

38 *Billboard*, 27 October 1973.

39 Author's interview with Clive Stanhope.

40 Author's interview with Tim Satchell.

41 Ibid. Despite two chart placings – one at 43 and another at 52 – Dart quietly disappeared in the late 1970s. Satchell returned to his previous career of journalism, while Stanhope became the proprietor of a successful reggae label, and then a pioneer in the field of audio books.

42 Author's interview with Derek Everett.

43 Ibid.

44 Author's interview with Rodney Burbeck.

45 Ibid.

46 Author's interview with Derek Everett.

47 Author's interview with David Fine.

48 Ibid.

49 Author's interview with Hugh Mendl.

50 As Arthur Bannister was affectionately known to his colleagues. To be a Decca engineer, it seems to have helped if you were called Arthur.

51 Author's interview with Hugh Mendl.

52 Ibid.

53 Ibid.

54 I am indebted to the late Brian Masters for this intelligence.

55 Author's interview with Mike Smith.

56 Author's interview with Hugh Mendl.

57 In time, WEA would indeed acquire Teldec, which was controlled by Diemenstein.

58 Author's interview with Coen Solleveld.

59 A fifth of the 500 staff were able to transfer to the radar division, which was sold separately to Racal Electronics.

60 'Terrible Ted' by Robert Hancock, *Spectator*, 20 September 1957.
61 Author's interview with Hugh Mendl.
62 Ibid.
63 Author's interview with Walter Woyda. IBA restrictions meant that the ATV name – itself a very potent brand – could not have been used to replace the Pye name.
64 Matthews became known in Auberon Waugh's Diary in *Private Eye* as 'Lord Whelks', due to his humble origins.
65 In the earliest days of ITV, Grade had persuaded the two largest newspaper groups – Beaverbrook Newspapers and the Mirror Group – to invest in his company, for which each got a seat on the board.
66 Author's interview with Walter Woyda.

Chapter 12

1   UK statistics compiled by the BPI.
2   *Sony: The Private Life* by John Nathan (HarperCollins Business, London, 1999), p.143.
3   Author's interview with David Fine.
4   Schein later spent a few years in the 1970s running Sony America, before leaving to join Warners briefly then moving to PolyGram.
5   Author's interview with David Fine.
6   I was still an enthusiastic contributor to this rump. I only received my first CD player as a Christmas present in 1991.
7   Author's interview with Ed Bicknell.
8   Ibid.
9   Ibid.
10 Ibid.
11 Author's interview with David Fine.
12 Author's interview with Bruce Lundvall.
13 Ibid.
14 *Billboard*, 19 November 1988.
15 *Exploding* by Stan Cornyn (HarperCollins Entertainment, New York, 2002), p.323.
16 Author's interview with Roger Watson.
17 *Billboard*, 12 August 1989.
18 Author's interview with David Fine.
19 *To Be Loved* by Berry Gordy (Headline, London, 1994), p.5.
20 'Not Amy Irving – An Exclusive Interview with Irving Azoff' by David Adelson, *Hits* magazine, 18 December 1989.
21 Such as sending a boa constrictor to a former friend as a wedding present.
22 Quoted in *The Operator: David Geffen Builds, Buys and Sells the New Hollywood* by Tom King, (Broadway Books, New York, 2001) p.391.
23 The remaining 25 per cent went to the Japanese company, which had paid $150 million for a quarter of Virgin Music Group in 1989. It also owned 50 per cent of Virgin in Japan.
24 *Losing My Virginity* by Richard Branson (Virgin Books, London, 1998), pp.454, 452.
25 *Billboard*, 27 November 1993.
26 *Since Records Began: EMI: The First 100 Years* by Peter Martland (BT Batsford, London, 1997), p.263.
27 Author's interview with Bruce Lundvall.
28 Ibid.
29 Ibid.
30 *Daily Telegraph*, 17 August 1996.
31 Ibid.
32 *Exploding* by Stan Cornyn (HarperCollins Entertainment, New York, 2002), p.349.
33 Ibid., p.322.
34 Ibid., p.388.

35 Quoted in ibid., p.410.
36 Author's interview with Ahmet Ertegun.
37 Philips Annual Report 1998, p.4.
38 Author's interview with David Fine.
39 *Exploding* by Stan Cornyn (HarperCollins Entertainment, New York, 2002), p.418.
40 *45* by Bill Drummond (Abacus, London, 2001), pp.264–5.

Chapter 13

1   Author's interview with Jay Berman.
2   'Recording Industry Sues Napster for Copyright Infringement', RIAA press release, 7 December 1999.
3   BBC News Online, 11 October 2000.
4   From Prince's website – http://www.npgonlineltd.com – quoted in BBC News Online, 10 August 2000.
5   For the lowdown on contracts and how artists get bilked, I recommend *Confessions of a Record Producer* by Moses Avalon (Backbeat Books, London, 2002).
6   'Recording Industry To Begin Collecting Evidence And Preparing Lawsuits Against File "Sharers" Who Illegally Offer Music Online', RIAA Press Release, 25 June 2003.
7   Statement of Rep. Howard L. Berman, 'For the House Judiciary Subcommittee on Courts, the Internet, and Intellectual Property Hearing on "Piracy of Intellectual Property on Peer-to-Peer Networks", 26 September 2002.
8   'Destroy "pirate" Pcs, says politician' BBC News Online, 18 June 2003.
9   'Music piracy "great", says Robbie', BBC News Online, 19 January 2003.
10 Author's interview with Ed Bicknell.
11 Author's interview with Ahmet Ertegun.
12 Dreamworks/Universal press release, 11 November 2003.
13 Author's interview with Bruce Lundvall.
14 Author's interview with Ed Bicknell.
15 'EMI Goes Pop', *Daily Telegraph*, 24 March 2002.
16 Author's interview with Bruce Lundvall.
17 Clive Davis's speech to the Retail Music Expo, Chicago, 3 June 2001.
18 Author's interview with Jay Berman.
19 Author's interview with David Fine.
20 Ibid.
21 Author's interview with Mike Ross-Trevor.
22 Author's interview with Eddie Levy.
23 Author's interview with Tony Hall.
24 Author's interview with Charles Kennedy.
25 Although I must admit to knocking off a couple of very passable Lonnie Donegan cover versions all by myself – drums, bass, guitar and vocals.
26 Author's interview with Ahmet Ertegun.
27 Author's interview with Muff Winwood.

Afterword

1   IFPI press release, 30 September 2004.
2   As reported in the *Daily Mail* and *Daily Telegraph*, 6 July 2004.
3   Reported in music industry journal *The Hit Sheet*, 8 October 2004 – I was at In the City but was prevented from attending Kennedy's oration and making my own notes by the fact that I was partaking in a rather sparsely-attended panel next door.
4   Quoted in *Music Week*'s online coverage of In the City.
5   *Music Week*, 25 September 2004.

FURTHER READING

I hope that the general reader will find enough detail in this book to satisfy their curiosity about the history of the record industry. I hope too that those who already had some knowledge on the subject have finished the book knowing a few things that they didn't know before.

Some, though, may well want to know more about particular facets of the business, perhaps running the risk of ending up as obsessed as I am. Fortunately, some of these aspects are covered in detail by other books, many of which I have consulted. For even more information on the labyrinthine early history of the business, readers are directed to *The Fabulous Phonograph* by Roland Gelatt and *From Tinfoil to Stereo* by Oliver Read and Walter L. Welch. The latter can be fairly hard going. However, it contains some information that is available nowhere else. If you need to know more about the recording and studios, *Good Vibrations* by Mark Cunningham is the book to have. Other items of further reading can be located in the endnotes.

Apart from the books listed below, I drew extensively upon historical newspapers and back issues of various industry periodicals, such as: *Talking Machine News*, *Talking Machine World*, *Billboard*, *Cash Box*, *Music Week*, *Melody Maker* and *New Musical Express*. In addition, some excellent material was found on websites maintained by record enthusiasts. One of the very best and longest-established is Tim Gracyk's site http://www.garlic.com/~tgracyk/ which contains a wealth of material on the early history of records and recording. As for the others, website addresses are liable to frequent change, so it is perhaps safest to say that a list of currently available links can be found at http://www.louisbarfe.com.

Aldridge, Benjamin L., *The Victor Talking Machine Company* (RCA Sales Corporation, Camden, NJ, 1964)

Alexander, Robert Charles, *The Life and Works of Alan Dower Blumlein* (Focal Press, Oxford, 1999)

Avalon, Moses, *Confessions of a Record Producer* (Backbeat Books, London, 2002 – second edition)

Bailey, Paul, *Three Queer Lives* (Hamish Hamilton, London 2001)

Barbier, Patrick (trans. Margaret Crosland), *The World of the Castrati: The History of an Extraordinary Operatic Phenomenon* (Souvenir Press, London, 1996)

Batten, Joe, *Joe Batten's Book: The Story of Sound Recording* (Rockliff, London, 1956)

Beishuizen, Piet (ed.), *The Industry of Human Happiness* (International Federation of the Phonographic Industry, London, 1959)

Birch, Will, *No Sleep Till Canvey Island: The Great Pub Rock Revolution* (Virgin,

London, 2000)

Borwick, John (ed.), *The First Fifty Years: Celebrating the Fiftieth Anniversary of IFPI* (IFPI Secretariat, London, 1983)

Branson, Richard with Edward Whitley, *Losing My Virginity* (Virgin, London, 1998)

Caruso, Dorothy, *Enrico Caruso: His Life and Death* (Simon and Schuster, New York, 1945)

Colin, Sid, *And the Bands Played On* (Elm Tree Books, London, 1977)

Collins, Theresa M. and Lisa Gitelman, *Thomas Edison and Modern America: A Brief History With Documents* (Bedford/St Martin's, Boston, 2002)

Cook, Richard, *Blue Note Records: The Biography* (Secker and Warburg, London, 2001)

Copeland, Peter, *Sound Recordings* (British Library, London, 1991)

Cornyn, Stan with Paul Scanlon, *Exploding: The Highs, Hits, Hype, Heroes and Hustlers of the Warner Music Group* (HarperCollins Entertainment, New York, 2002)

Culshaw, John, *Putting the Record Straight* (Secker and Warburg, London, 1981)

Cunningham, Mark, *Good Vibrations: A History of Record Production* (Penguin, London, 1996)

Dankworth, John, *Jazz in Revolution* (Constable, London, 1998)

Dannen, Fredric, *Hit Men: Power Brokers and Fast Money Inside the Music Business* (Times Books, New York, 1990)

Davis, Clive with James Willwerth, *Clive: Inside the Record Business* (Ballantine Books, New York, 1974)

Day, Timothy, *A Century of Recorded Music: Listening to Musical History* (Yale University Press, New Haven and London, 2000)

Drummond, Bill, *45* (Abacus, London, 2001)

Dyer, Frank Lewis and Thomas Commerford Martin, *Edison: His Life and Inventions* (Harper Brothers, New York, 1929)

Ertegun, Ahmet, et al., *What'd I Say: The Atlantic Story* (Orion, London, 2001)

Fagan, Ted and William R. Moran, *The Encyclopedic Discography of Victor Recordings* (Greenwood Press, Westport, 1982)

Foster, Mo, *Seventeen Watts: The First Twenty Years of British Rock Guitar, the Musicians and Their Heroes* (Sanctuary, London, 1997)

Gaisberg, Fred, *Music on Record* (Robert Hale, London, 1946)

Gammond, Peter and Raymond Horricks, *The Music Goes Round and Round: A Cool Look at the Music Industry* (Quartet, London, 1980)

Gelatt, Roland, *The Fabulous Phonograph: From Edison to Stereo* (Appleton-Century, New York, 1965)

Geller, Debbie, *The Brian Epstein Story* (Faber and Faber, London, 2000)

Gillett, Charlie, *The Sound of the City: The Rise of Rock & Roll* (Souvenir Press, London 1996 – third edition)

Gold, Harry, *Gold, Doubloons and Pieces of Eight: The Autobiography of Harry Gold* (Northway Publications, London, 2000)

Goodman, Fred, *The Mansion on the Hill: Dylan, Young, Geffen, Springsteen, and the Head-on Collision of Rock and Commerce* (Vintage, New York, 1998)

Gordy, Berry, *To Be Loved* (Headline, London, 1994)

Grade, Lew, *Still Dancing: My Story* (Fontana, London, 1988)

Gronow, Pekka and Ilpo Saunio (trans. Christopher Mosley), *An International History of the Recording Industry* (Cassell, London, 1998)

Guralnick, Peter, *Last Train to Memphis: The Rise of Elvis Presley* (Little, Brown, London, 1994)

Heath, Ted, *Listen to My Music: The Fabulous Success Story of the Famous Band Leader* (Frederick Muller, London, 1957)

Horricks, Raymond, *An Eye for an Eye or Stéphane Grappelli: A Case of Libel* (unpublished MS)

Johnson, E. R. Fenimore, *His Master's Voice Was Eldridge R. Johnson* (Dover, Delaware, 1974)

Jones, Max and John Chilton, *Louis: The Louis Armstrong Story 1900–1971* (Mayflower Books, St Albans, 1975)

Keating, Johnny, *From Holyrood to Hollywood: The Johnny Keating Story* (JKM Music, London, 2002)

Kennedy, Rick and Randy McNutt, *Little Labels, Big Sound* (Indiana University Press, Bloomington and Indianapolis, 1999)

King, Tom, *The Operator: David Geffen Builds, Buys and Sells the New Hollywood* (Broadway Books, New York, 2001)

Lewis, E. R., *No CIC* (Universal Royalties, London, 1956)

Lewisohn, Mark, *The Complete Beatles Recording Sessions* (Hamlyn, London, 1988)

McDougal, Dennis, *The Last Mogul: Lew Wasserman, MCA and the Hidden History of Hollywood* (DaCapo Press, New York, 2001)

Martland, Peter, *A Business History of the Gramophone Company 1897–1918* (doctoral dissertation – Corpus Christi College, Cambridge, 1992)

Martland, Peter, *Since Records Began: EMI: The First 100 Years* (BT Batsford, London, 1997)

Merriden, Trevor, *Irresistible Forces: The Business Legacy of Napster and the Birth of the Underground Internet* (Capstone, Oxford, 2001)

Mitchell, Ogilvie, *Pitman's Common Commodities and Industries: The Talking Machine Industry* (Sir Isaac Pitman and Sons, London, 1922)

Moore, Gerald, *Am I Too Loud?* (Hamish Hamilton, London, 1962)

Moore, Jerrold Northrop, *Sound Revolutions: A Biography of Fred Gaisberg, Founding Father of Commercial Sound Recording* (Sanctuary, London, 1999)

Napier-Bell, Simon, *Black Vinyl, White Powder* (Ebury Press, London, 2002)

Nicholson, Stuart, *A Portrait of Duke Ellington: Reminiscing in Tempo* (Sidgwick and Jackson, London, 1999)

Nathan, John, *Sony: the Private Life* (HarperCollins Business, London, 1999)

O' Connell, Charles, *The Other Side of the Record* (Alfred A. Knopf, New York, 1947)

Picardie, Justine and Dorothy Wade, *Atlantic and the Godfathers of Rock and Roll* (Fourth Estate, London, 1992)

Pollard, Anthony, *Gramophone: The First 75 Years* (Gramophone Publications, Kenton, 1998)

Read, Oliver and Walter L. Welch, *From Tinfoil to Stereo: Evolution of the Phonograph*

(Howard W. Sams/Bobbs-Merrill, Indianapolis/New York, 1959)

Repsch, John, *The Legendary Joe Meek: The Telstar Man* (Cherry Red Books, London, 2001)

Ro, Ronin, *Have Gun, Will Travel: The Spectacular Rise and Violent Fall of Death Row Records* (Quartet, London, 1998)

Rogan, Johnny, *Starmakers and Svengalis* (Futura, London, 1989)

Rust, Brian, *Jazz Records 1897–1942* (Storyville Publications, Chigwell, 1982: two volumes – A-Lym and Lym-Z)

Schwarzkopf, Elisabeth, *On and Off the Record: A Memoir of Walter Legge* (Faber and Faber, London, 1982)

Smith, Joe, *Off the Record: An Oral History of Popular Music* (Warner Books, New York, 1988)

Southall, Brian, *Abbey Road* (Patrick Stephens Ltd, Wellingborough, 1982)

Southall, Brian, *The A–Z of Record Labels* (Sanctuary, London, 2000)

Taylor, Don, *The English 78 Picture Book* (Artemis Publishing Consultants, Hobart, Tasmania, 1999)

Welch, Bruce with Howard Elson, *Rock 'n' Roll: I Gave You the Best Years of My Life* (Viking, London, 1989)

Wexler, Jerry with David Ritz, *Rhythm and the Blues* (Jonathan Cape, London, 1994)

INDEX

2Pac, 321
3M, 159, 294
77 Sunset Strip, 246

A&M Records, 263–5, 266, 295; sign and
    drop Sex Pistols, 268; studios, 271;
    acquired by PolyGram, 306–7
ABC-Dunhill, 166, 308
ABC-Paramount label
Aberbach, Gene, 193
Abramson, Herb, 167–8, 170
Abramson, Miriam, 168, 252
accordion, 32
Ace, Johnny, 166
acoustic recording, xiv, 95
Addey, Malcolm, 217
Addis, Thomas, 34
Adler, Lou, 243, 265
Adler, Norman, 241
AEG Tonschreiber tape machine, 159
Aeolian company, 91
Aeolian-Vocalion label, 91, 132
Africa, xvii, 44, 66
Aikman, Sir Alexander, 188
Aladdin label, 165
Aldrich, Ronnie, 284–5, 290
Aldridge, Benjamin L., 80
Ales, Barney, 225, 226
Alice Cooper, 251
'Alligator Rock', 215
Alpert, Dore, 263
Alpert, Herb, 263–5, 295, 307, 319
Amalgamated Wireless, 157
Amberol wax cylinder, 51–2
Ambrose, Bert, 114, 125, 129, 151
America, *see* USA
American Bandstand, 212, 216
American Federation of Musicians, 119;
    recording bans, 143–5, 154–5, 168, 187,
    314

American Graphophone Company, 14, 15,
    28
American Graphophone Corporation, 19
American Record Corporation (ARC),
    129–30, 132, 134–5, 136
Ammons, Albert, 314
Amnesty International, 303
Ampex, 159–60
Andry, Peter, 287
Angel label, 176–7, 190
Anglo-Italian Commerce Company, 37, 56,
    57, 58
Animals, 227
Anka, Paul, 210
Anna Records, 224
Anschluss, 140
Ansermet, Ernest, 151, 201
anti-trust laws, 84, 113, 191, 333
AOL, 331, 333–4; lack of understanding of
    record business, 334
AOL Time-Warner, xvii, 166, 318, 331, 333,
    337
Apple, 327
Applejacks, 232
Appleton's Magazine, 27
Ardmore and Beechwood, 221
Ardmore Music, 175
Arena Brass, 264
Argentina, 68
Argo label, 163
Ariola Schallplatten, 305
Arista label, 275, 305–6, 321, 337–8
Aristocrat label, 163
Armed Forces Radio Service, 146
Armstrong, Louis, 89, 91, 147, 169
Arnold, Eddy, 184, 193
Art Landry's Orchestra, 94
ASCAP, 175, 210; broadcasting ban, 145–6
Asher, Dick, 272, 283–4
Ashley, Ted, 252, 317

Asia, xvii, 35, 44, 143, 234
Associated Communications Corporation, 291
Aston Clinton, 236
Asylum label, 275–6, 309
Atari video games, 316
Athens, 295
Atkins, Chet, 194
Atlantic, xvii, 163, 166, 168–70, 193, 195, 233, 317–18, 337; cash flow problems, 211; royalties, 169–70, 211; bought by Warner-Seven Arts, 251–2; European distribution, 251; deal with Virgin, 267; Geffen deal, 276
Attwood, Francis, 149, 158, 202, 203
ATV, 199–200, 249, 291, 292
Atwell, Winifred, 197–8
Audio Fidelity label, 201
Australasia, *see* Oceania
Australia, 103, 157
Austria, 71
Austro-Hungarian Empire, 68
Avakian, George, 135, 152–3, 155, 160, 174, 177–83, 205, 341; joins Warner Bros, 245–8; joins RCA, 248
Avengers, 207
Axton, Mae Boren, 194
Azoff, Irving, 308

Baarn, 171, 283
Baccara, 282
Bach, J. S.: Brandenburg Concertos, 229; Cantatas, 233
Bachman, William S., 152–4, 156, 242–3
Back Beat label, 166
back catalogues, 339–41
Backhaus, Wilhelm, 151
Bad Boy Entertainment, 321–2
Baja Marimba Band, 264
Baker, Josephine, 199
Baker, Kenneth, 322
Balfour, J. A., 123
Ballard, Hank, 164
Banks, Major Wilfred, 229
Bannister, Butch, 285
Barber, Chris, 198–9
Barbier, Patrick, 58
Barcelona, 58
Bard, Wilkie, 86
Barlow, Howard, 135

Barnes, 255, 271
Barnett, Samuel company, 73, 122–3, 125, 205
Barraud, Francis, xvii, 35, 41, 44–5, 64
Barrington-Coupe, William, 229
Bart, Lionel, 207–8
Basden, Colonel E. D., 122–3
BASF, 159
Basie, Count, 136, 143, 147, 212
bass concertina, 95
Bass, Ralph, 164
Batchelor, Charles, 4
Batten, Joe, 33–4, 56, 66, 69, 98, 104; launches Velvet Face label, 94–6
Baverstock, Jack, 216, 235
Bayes, Captain H. G., 117
BBC, xiv, 80, 125, 127, 128, 138, 171, 196–7, 209, 216, 220; and black music, 225; payola scandal, 277–8; record library, 196; tape recording, 158, 160
Beatles, xx, 219–24, 231, 254, 266; split, 269
Beautiful South, 319
bebop, 314
Beecham, Sir Thomas, 159, 189, 204–5
Beecher-Stevens, S. A., 202, 221
Beer, Sidney, 148
Beethoven, Ludwig van, 149, 157, 191; Ninth Symphony, 295
Beka label, 68, 70
Belgium, 34
Bell, Alexander Graham, xvi, xvii, 4, 12–15, 17, 24
Bell, Chichester A., xvi, 12–15, 17
Bell, Graeme, 199
Bell label, 275
Bell Laboratories, xviii, 100, 115, 200
Bell Records, 264
Bell Telephone Company, 24
Benatar, Pat, 262
Benjamin, 'Benny', 225
Benjamin, Louis, 249
Bennett, Al, 226
Bennett, Tony, 216, 271
Benson, Harry, 172
Benz, Karl, 42
Berlin, 34, 56, 61, 65, 140, 141
Berlin, Irving, 24
Berliner, Emile, xvi, xvii, xix, 24–7, 29–31, 35, 38–40, 44, 46, 53
Berliner Gramophone Company, 27, 44, 107

Berman, Howard, 330, 331
Berman, Jay, 324–5, 326, 338
Bermuda, 189, 190
Bernhardt, Sarah, 37
Bernstein, Leonard, 240
Berry, Chuck, 163, 223
Berry, Dave, 232
Berry, Ken, 267, 310–11, 334, 337
Berry, Mike, 230
Berry, Nancy, 335
Berry, W. H., 32–3
Bertelsmann Music Group (BMG), xvi, 310, 333–4, 338; takeover of RCA, 305, 306; approach to Napster, 326–7, 333; lack of understanding of record business, 334; ageism, 337
Best, Pete, 220, 222
Bethlehem label, 165
Bettini, Lieutenant Gianni, 37–8
Bicknell, David, 114, 174, 188–9, 190, 191
Bicknell, Ed, 297, 299–300, 331; on state of the industry, 333–4
Bidgood, Harry, 92
Biederbecke, Bix, 91
Bienstock, Freddie, 165
Big Brother and the Holding Company, 243
Biggs, E. Power, 239
Bill Haley and the Comets, 194, 215
Billboard, 155, 170, 233, 242, 245, 265, 268, 295, 303, 304
Birmingham, 259, 260, 291
Birnbaum, Theodore B., 30, 34, 56, 62–3, 82; Recording Angel trademark, 35, 45, 64, 176
Black, Bill, 192
Black Monday, 303
Black Swan label, 89
Blackwell, Chris, 259–62, 275, 306–7
Blackwell, Richard 'Bumps', 196
Blackwood Music, 175
Blair, Tony, 322–3, 332
Blakey, Art, 315
Bland, Bobby 'Blue', 166
Blattner, Ludwig, 158
Blattnerphone, 158
Bleyer, Archie, 195, 247
Blind Blake, 89
Blind Faith, 251, 253
Blondie, 262
Blood, Sweat and Tears, 243

Blow, Jellings, 36
Blue Amberol record, 52, 98, 110
Blue Mountain publishing, 306
Blue Note label, 227, 314–15
Bluebird label, 164
blues, 88–90, 223
Blumenfeld (Russian retailer), 57
Blumlein, Alan Dower, xviii, 115–16, 151, 200–1; 'walking and talking' tests, 116
Blur, 322
BMI, 175, 210
Boam, Joseph, 48–9
Bob Marley and the Wailers, 261
Bock, Richard, 168, 246
Body Count, 321
Boer War, 22, 72
Bogart, Neil, 283
Bonnet, Joseph, 120
Boone, Pat, 195
Boonstra, Cor, 319
Booth, Edwin, 22
Borwell, Montague, 33–4
Bose, Hemendra, 44
Boston Ventures, 306–7
Boswell Sisters, 130
Boult, Adrian, 95
Bowie, David, 281
Box, Elton, 215
Box and Cox, 215
Bragg, Billy, 319, 320
Brahms, Johannes, 96–7, 150
Brain, Dennis, 148
Brandon, Tony, 277
Branson, Richard, 265–6, 267; sale of Virgin, 310–11
Bray, Jim, 198
Brazil, 68
Brian Poole and the Tremeloes, 219, 221, 232, 237
Brit School for Performing Arts and Technology, 322
Britain (UK), 10–11, 65, 166, 188, 283; coal strike, 258; dance craze, 79; devaluation of sterling, 174; payola scandal, 277; record industry, 16–18, 44, 64, 68, 69–74, 78, 81–2, 87, 94–5, 111, 122, 156, 160, 162, 209, 287, 296–7, 306, 322, 327; wartime record sales, 138
British Celanese, 127
British Empire, 44, 85

British Homophone Company, 132, 142–3
British Phonographic Industry (BPI), 127, 197, 189, 299–300
Britpop, 320, 322
Britten, Benjamin, 206
Broad, John, 113
Broadcast label, 92, 104, 126
Broadcast Music Incorporated, 146
broadcasting networks, 145–6, 147
Broadway musicals, 182, 207, 242
Brolly, Brian, 255–6
Bron, Sydney, 310
Bronfman, Edgar, 319, 336
Bronson, Captain Howard, 146
Brooks, Elkie, 266
Brophy, William A., 92
Brown, Clarence 'Gatemouth', 165–6
Brown, Georgia, 208
Brown, James, 164, 165
Brown, Joe, 249
Brown, Leonard, 190
Brown, Les, 155
Browne, Jackson, 276
Browning, Robert, 17
Brunet, Meade, 190
Brunswick, Balke and Collender, 91–2
Brunswick label, 93–4, 104, 130–2, 147, 194, 197; Warner Bros' ownership, 94, 110–11, 244–5; acquired by Decca, 129, 135, 148
Brussels, 60
Bryan, William Jennings, 50–1, 91
Bryden, Beryl, 198
Budapest, 34, 58
Buddah label, 283
Buddy Holly and the Crickets, 215
Buenos Aires, 66, 137, 176
Bullock, William W., 193
Bumb and König, 68
Bumble Bee Slim, 169
Burbeck, Rodney, 237, 238, 239, 279–80, 281
Burns, Ray, 213
Burt, Heinz, 231
Busby, Cliff, 313
Butt, Clara, 81
Butterfield, Paul, 254
Byrnes, Ed, 246

Cadence label, 195, 247
Calcutta, 34–5
Calibre label, 290

Callas, Maria, 176, 190
Calloway, Cab, 167
Calve, Emma, 30, 37, 76
Calvert, Eddie, 187, 213
Cameo label, 129
Cameo-Parkway label, 283
Canada, 44, 107
Capitol, 143–4, 162, 174, 175, 177, 180, 193, 245, 248, 315; EMI acquires controlling interest, 187–8, 190, 210; relationship with Decca, 188, 194–5, 197; sales, 187; sound quality, 206–7; rejects Beatles, 222–3; record club, 240–1; financial recovery, 269
Capps, Frank, 101
Captain and Tennille, 265
Captain Beefheart and the Magic Band, 250
Carey, Mariah, 311, 334–5, 336
Carl Fenton's Orchestra, 93
Carl Lindström AG, xviii, 67–70, 75, 81, 88, 102–3, 140
Carmichael, Hoagy, 91
Carnival Records, 263
Carpenters, 265
Carr, Michael, 215
Carte, D'Oyly, 96, 290
Caruso, Dorothy, 58
Caruso, Enrico, xviii, xix, 37, 56–7, 58–9, 60, 63, 68, 69, 76, 191
Casablanca label, 283
Cash, Johnny, 193
Cash Box, 263
cassettes, 293, 296–7, 301, 306
Castle, Vernon and Irene, 79
Castle Communications, 292
castrati, 57–8
CAT scanner, 269
Cattini, Clem, 239
Caven, Stan, 177
CBS (Columbia Broadcasting System), 119, 134–5, 152–3, 174, 183, 272, 301, 303; relationship with EMI, 135–7; colour television, 153; payola investigation, 273–4
CBS News, 274
CBS Records, 232, 255–7, 267, 278, 279, 284; launched, 233–4; relationship with Philips, 234; buys Oriole, 234, 236–7; break with EMI, 236; repertoire, 238–40; upheavals, 269–72; sales, 287; *see also* CBS

Records Inc.; Columbia Graphophone Company; Columbia Records

CBS Records Inc., 303, 305, 308–9, 310, 311

CBS-Sony Records, 296

CD: burners, 324; consensus, 335; development, xiv, xv, 294–6; outlook, 344; players, 298; prices, 299–301, 332; 'Red Book' standard, 294; reissues, 341; sales, 296–7, 301, 323, 327

CD-R, xiv, 325

Cederstrom, Baron, 60

celluloid, 50, 52, 53, 98

Central Independent Television, 291

Cetra label, 176

Cetra-Soria company, 176

Ch. & J. Ullmann Frères, 56, 65

Chacksfield, Frank, 198, 201

Chaliapin, Fyodor, 57, 62

Chalmers, Frank, 264

Champion label, 111

Channing, William F., 7

Chaplin, Charlie, 264

Chappell's, 93, 129, 235

Charisma label, 267, 275, 288

Charles, Ray, 210, 251

Chavez, Quita, 239

Checker label, 163

Chemet, Renée, 98

Chess, Marshall, 163–4

Chess label, 163–64, 191, 193, 223–5

Chicago, 89, 90, 163, 200, 223, 283, 337

Chicago (band), 243, 272

Child, Calvin G., 20–1, 46, 47, 76–7, 105

Chile, 68

China, 66

Chinnery, Derek, 278

Chipmunks, 226

Christian-Dee, John, 277

Chrysalis label, 262, 305, 310

Chudd, Lew, 244

Churchill, Winston, 288

Cinch label, 75

Cincinatti, 164–5

cinema, 12, 37, 138

Clapton, Eric, 300

Clare, Kenny, 230

Clark, Alfred, 27, 29, 30, 34, 62–3, 100, 117; directs HMV during war, 70–2, 74; and Victor acquisition of HMV, 82, 83–4; chairman of EMI, 113, 136, 156–7, 188, 209, 335

Clark, Dick, 212

Clark, H. A. M., 115

Clark, Petula, 199, 250

Clarke, Frank, 217

Clear, 342

Cliff, Jimmy, 260

Cliff Richard and the Shadows, 218

Clifford, Julian, 125

Cliftophone, 93

cocaine, 90

Cochran, C. B., 74

Cochran, Eddie, 226

Cochrane, Thomas, 112

Cocker, Joe, 265

Cogan, Alma, 213

Cohan, George M., 80

Coldplay, 336

Coldstream Guards, 87

Cole, Nat 'King', 144, 187, 207

Cole, Natalie, 315

Coleman, Sid, 221–2

Collins, Judy, 254

Collins, Phil, 268, 310

Columbia Broadcasting Symphony Orchestra, 135

Columbia Graphophone Company, 20, 23, 25–6, 32–3, 38–9, 41–6, 65, 68, 110, 118–19, 131; Grand Opera range, 46, 59; graphophone sales, 48–9; Columbia Indestructible Record, 52–3; abandons cylinder production, 53; Columbia-Rena brand, 55; first double-sided discs, 66; financial difficulties, 69, 76–8, 102; acquires Lindström matrices, 70, 75, 81; impact of First World War, 72–4, 78; fire at Wandsworth plant, 75; jazz recordings, 87–8, 89; lateral-cut discs, 91, 156; expands production facilities, 94; position in UK market, 94–5, 96, 102; 'New Process', 97–8, 156; adoption of electric recording, 99, 101–4, 115; acquired by UK Columbia, 102, 104; share value and sale to US institutions, 109, 123; acquired by Grigsby-Grunow, 113, 134; acquired by Sacro Enterprise Company, 130; reorganization, 135; *see also* Columbia Records; Phoenix label; Regal label

Columbia Graphophone Company Ltd, xvi, 76, 101–3, 136, 227; buys American

parent company, 102, 104; merger with
HMV, 111–16, 117, 126; multiple
microphone techniques, 125; impact of
Second World War, 141; classical
repertoire, 142, 176; problems with US
Columbia, 174; in EMI consolidation,
xviii, 186, 187, 189, 190, 335; restructured
into EMI Records Ltd, 209; roster, 213;
signs Cliff Richard, 217; rejects Beatles,
219
Columbia International, 103
Columbia Phonograph Broadcasting
Company, 134
Columbia Pictures, 275, 303, 305, 310
Columbia Recording Corporation, 135
Columbia Records, xv, xvi, xvii 135, 162, 187,
195, 202, 237, 301–2, 313–14; relationship
with EMI, 135–7, 151, 156–7, 174–6, 186,
187, 210, 234; impact of Second World
War, 143, 147; impact of recording ban,
145; development of long-playing
records, 152–4, 174, 184; Masterworks
division, 154, 182; adopts tape recording,
158, 160; royalties, 169; relationship with
Philips, 174–5, 179, 186, 232; problems
with UK Columbia, 174; enters South
American market, 176; increasing LP
sales, 177–9; signs Duke Ellington and
Miles Davis, 180–1; Lieberson joins,
181–2; records Broadway shows, 182, 207,
216, 234, 242; stereo system, 200;
resistance to rock and roll, 216; issued by
CBS, 234; under Clive Davis, 240–3,
272–4, 276, 338; record club investigation,
240–1; rationalization of mono and
stereo, 242–3; rock signings, 243, 258;
rejects Philadelphia Symphony
Orchestra's demands, 243–4; sales, 245–6;
signs Everly Brothers, 247–8; under
government investigation, 273–4; loss of
Bob Dylan, 275; relationship with Sony,
296, 301, 302–4, 305; rivalry with Warner
Bros, 302, 304; jazz reissues, 341; *see also*
CBS Records
Colyer, Ken, 198
Combs, Sean 'Puffy', 321–2
Commodore label, 314
Como, Perry, 184
Compagnie Américaine du Phonographe
Edison, 36
Compagnie Française du Grammophone, 34
Concert Hall label, 199
Concertgebouw Orchestra, 179
concertina, 32
Conkling, Donna, 175
Conkling, James B., 144, 174–8, 181, 187;
joins Warner Bros, 245–8
Consolidated Film Industries, 129, 134
Consolidated Talking Machine Company,
40–1, 44
Consolidated Talking Machine Company of
America, 39
contracts, xiii, 68–9, 73–4, 76
Cook, Hal, 177, 245, 246, 247
Cooke, Sam, 195
Coon-Sanders Nighthawks, 94
Cooper, Colin, 83
copy protection systems, 342
copyright, 191, 210, 212, 324, 326, 328, 330
Cordell, Denny, 165
Cornyn, Stan, 167–8, 170, 175, 250, 254, 263,
305, 316–17, 321
Costello, Elvis, 311
coster singers, 43
Costner, Kevin, 310
Cotton, Billy, 125; *Band Show*, 177
Cottone, Maestro, 59
country and western, 164, 192
Coward, Noël, 207
Cowell, Simon, 339
Cox, Ida, 89
Cox, Michael, 229
Cramer, Floyd, 194
Cran, Mark, 311–12
Cream, 233, 251, 253
Creation label, 320, 322
Cripps, Sir Stafford, 174
Cros, Charles, 1–2, 5, 6, 8
Crosby, Bing, 111, 129–32, 159, 169, 192, 196
Crosby, Everett, 132
Crosby, Stills and Nash, 276, 298
Crossley, Ada, 47
crossover market, 340
Crown label, 132
Crudge, Arthur, 74
Crudup, Arthur 'Big Boy', 192
Crumb, Robert, xvii
Crystalate company, 92, 126, 129, 132–3, 134,
235
Cryz (Chess), Leonard, 162–3

Cryz, Phil, 162
CTI label, 265
Culshaw, John, 149–51, 160–1, 201, 204, 206, 285, 289
Cuscuna, Michael, 315
cycle shops, 48, 49, 69, 127
cylinders, xvi, xix, 4, 13, 23, 25, 39; decline, 49–55; mass-production, 49; politicians' recordings, 50–1; prices, 37, 52, 55; recording session described, 33–4; repertoire constraints, 50

d'Abo, Mike, 255
d'Amato, Tony, 284
Dabbs, Jack, 277
Daily Express, 138, 190, 292
Daily Mail, 72
Daily Telegraph, 96, 97, 335
Daly, Bob, 318
Damned, 311
dance craze, 79, 86
Dankworth, John, 211, 212, 219
Dannen, Fredric, 242
Darby, William Sinkler, 34, 57
Darin, Bobby, 251
Dart Records, 278
Dart, F. H., 116
data protection, 330
Dauberson, Dany, 199
Davis, Clive, 240–3, 244, 265, 270, 276, 301, 337–8; downfall at Columbia, 272–5, 277; Arista operation, 305–6, 337
Davis, Fred, 273
Davis, Martin, 316
Davis, Miles, 181, 315
Davis, Sammy, Jr., 248, 249–50
Day, Doris, 179
de Courville, Albert, 73, 74
de los Angeles, Victoria, 189
de Reszke, Edouard, 46
de Sabata, Victor, 176
de Sylva, Buddy, 143
Death Row label, 320–2
Decca Gramophone Company, xvii, 122–3, 138–9, 143, 171, 187, 189, 212, 231, 244, 269; record prices, 125–6, 133; Polydor Series, 128, 141, 149; acquires Brunswick, 129, 148; radar business, 129, 148, 209; absorbs Edison-Bell, 132; acquires Crystalate, 132–3, 134; profits, 134;

impact of Second World War, 141–3, 148; first original-cast show album (*Oklahoma*), 145, 182; research into vinyl, 148; FFRR system, 148–51, 152, 157; advertising, 149, 158, 174; 'K' series, 149; classical repertoire, 149–50; use of Kingsway Hall, 149–50; sells stake in US Decca, 151–2; launches record players, 152; adopts microgroove and launches LPs, 157–8; adoption of tape recording, 159–60; relationship with Capitol, 188, 194–5, 197; relationship with RCA Victor, 190–1, 204; expansion in US, 194–6; run of best-selling artists, 197–8; Burlington music publishing, 198; launches stereo LPs, 201, 259; company politics, 202–7, 232, 285; sound quality, 206–7 records musicals, 207–8; competition with EMI, 208–9, 213; sales, 209, 287; rock and roll recordings, 216; rejects Beatles, 219–21; holiday break, 228; acquires RGM masters, 230; Tremeloes leave, 232, 237; policy on foreign affiliates, 234; relationship with Warner Bros, 249; Atlantic leaves distribution deal, 251; US Decca breaks away, 255 quadrophonic sound experiments, 258–9; introduces Phase 4 Stereo, 284–5; decline and Edward Lewis's death, 284–9; bought by PolyGram, 288–90; digital recording system, 293; name preserved, 319; *see also* Deram label; London American label
Decca Military Band, 125
Decca Navigator, 148, 287
Decca portable gramophone, 73, 122
Decca Recording Centre, 289
Decca Records Inc., xvii, 130–2, 134–5, 147, 151, 162, 194–5; record prices, 131; profits, 134; impact of recording ban, 145; rock and roll signings, 215; MCA buys controlling interest, 254–5; breaks away from UK Decca, 255
Deccalian record player, 152
Decola record player, 152
Deep Purple, 255
DeFries, Tony, 281
Denmark, 234
Dennett, Fred, 89
Denza, Luigi, 31
Depression, xiv, xvi, xviii, 41, 109–11, 116,

122, 156
Deram label, 285
Detroit, 224, 225–6
Deutsche Grammophon, xvii, xviii, 31, 34, 61, 75, 80–1, 128, 149, 298; sold to Siemens, 141, 232; alliance with Philips, 232–3; Archiv Produktion series, 233; back catalogue, 339; *see also* Polydor
Devine, Andrew, 14
Dexter, Dave, 144, 222, 223
DiSipio, Fred, 304, 305
di Stefano, Giuseppe, 176
Diamond, Neil, 256–7, 272, 314
Dickins, Rob, 300, 318, 323
dictaphone, 20, 26
Diddley, Bo, 163
Diemenstein, Jack, 288
Diemenstein, Sarah, 288
digital recording, 293–4
Dillnutt, George, 35
Dire Straits, 297, 299, 331
Disc, 222
discs, xix, 24–6, 29, 31–2, 39, 43; double-sided, 65–6; first million-sellers, 69–70, 88; increasing popularity, 43, 49; labels, 40, 46; lateral-cut, 53, 90, 91, 110, 156; metal, 142; prices, 45, 46–7, 55, 68, 76, 92, 94, 95, 125–6, 131–3, 178–9, 266; 'scratchless', 67, 98; *see also* records
Dixon, Sydney, 59–60, 62, 76, 77, 83
Dolby noise reduction system, 293
Donahue, Sam, 144
Doncaster, 267
Donegan, Lonnie, 198
Donovan, 243
Doors, 254
Dorian, Frank, 20, 45, 69
Dorsey, Jimmy, 148
Dorsey, Tommy, 148
Dot label, 193, 195, 263
Douglass, Leon, 39, 46, 82–3, 105–7
Dowd, Tom, 170
Dr Dre, 321, 322
Drake, Nick, 261
Draper, Simon, 265, 267, 268, 310–11
Dreamworks Records, 332
Dreamworks SKG, 312, 331
Drifters, 216–17, 218
Droz, Henry, 317
Drummond, Bill, 322–3

Dublin, 34
Duke label, 166
Duke-Peacock business, 165–6
Duncan, F. B., 142, 151
Duophone Unbreakable Record Company, 123
DuPont family, 76
Dury, Ian, 311
Dutch West Indies, 66
DVD-A, 335
Dvořák, Antonín, 159
Dylan, Bob, 243, 244, 275, 314

Eagle, Star and British Dominions Insurance Company, 123–4
Eagles, 276, 308, 309
East, Ken, 286
East Midlands Electricity Board, 291
Easton, Edward D., 20, 76
Echo and the Bunnymen, 323
Eclipse label, 132
'Ecstasy', 172
Edison, Charles, 51
Edison, Thomas Alva, xvi, xix, xx, 16, 22, 23, 38; invention of phonograph, 1–2, 4–10; talent for publicity, 1, 2; early career, 2–4; business acumen, 3, 8; 'muckers', 4; work on electric light, 10–12; interest in cinema, 12, 37; revived interest in phonograph, 14–15; squeezed out of phonograph business, 19; returns to phonograph business, 19–20, 25, 28; experiments with discs, 24; debts, 28; success of 'home phonograph', 28; commitment to cylinders, 49–53, 110; musical preferences, 50; politics, 51; use of name, 52; launches discs, 53–4; introduces jewelled stylus, 53–4, 156; 'Tone Tests', 97; adopts electric recording, 110; withdrawal from phonographic industry, 110; see also Amberol wax cylinder; Blue Amberol record; Edison Diamond Disc
Edison Diamond Disc, 53–4, 91, 97, 98, 110
Edison Electric Light Company, 10
Edison General Electric Company, 11
Edison gold moulded record, 50
Edison Kinetoscope company, 28
Edison National Historical Site, 4
Edison Phonograph Company, 16

Edison Phonograph Monthly, 21, 51

Edison Speaking Phonograph Company, 8, 14

Edison United Phonograph Company, 17–18, 19, 28

Edison-Bell Consolidated Phonograph Company, 28–9, 33, 35, 41, 44, 54, 92; sales, 47; expansion, 47–8; use of Edison name, 52; competes in UK, 94–5, 122; absorbed by Decca, 132, 162; *see also* Velvet Face label; Winner label

Edison-Bell Phonograph Corporation, 17–18, 22

editing, 121, 158, 160–1

Edwards, George, 224

Egypt, 66

Ehrlich, Fred, 311–12

Eindhoven, 294, 298

electric light, 10–12, 16

electric recording, xiv–xv, 7, 92, 99–104, 110; Light Ray system, 104; Orthophonic system, 103, 104; Viva-Tonal system, 103; Westrex system, 104, 115; integrated moving coil system, 115–16

Electrobeam Gennett label, 111

Electrola, 81, 139, 141

Elektra label, xvii, 253–4, 276, 313–14, 318

Elektra Musician label, 313

Elen, Gus, 32

Elen, Richard, 261–2

Elgar, Edward, 95–6, 114

Ellington, Duke, 93, 117, 127, 143, 146, 165, 167; relaunched at Newport Jazz Festival, 180–1

Ellis, Steve, 239

Ellis, Terry, 262

Elman, Mischa, 96

Elstree studios, 291

Embassy label, 235

Ember organization, 234

Emerson, Lake and Palmer, 251, 258

Emerson Phonograph Company, 129

EMI (Electric & Musical Industries Ltd), xvi, xviii, 122, 126, 128, 132, 200, 207; formation, 112–13; Abbey Road studios established, 113–16; relationship with Columbia, 135–7, 151, 156–7, 174–6, 186, 187, 234; bad management, 136–7, 156–7, 187, 209; impact of Second World War, 139–41, 142–3; classical repertoire, 141–2;

adoption of vinyl, 146, 174, 179, 328; use of Kingsway Hall, 150; Extended Range system, 151; relationship with RCA Victor, 151, 156–7, 174, 176, 188–91, 209; takes on MGM contract, 157; butt of Decca advertising, 158; adoption of tape recording, 159–60; forms US label, 176; consolidation, 186; acquires controlling interest in Capitol, 187–8, 190; under Lockwood, 187–8, 209; launch stereo LPs, 201; competition with Decca, 208–9; sales, 209; restructured into EMI Records Ltd, 209; diversification and Thorn purchase, 269; Australian operation, 286; stock ownership, 288; digital recording system, 293; demerger and consolidation, 315–16, 333–6; profits, 335–6; custom pressing service, 341; *see also* Angel label; EMI Records Ltd; Gramophone Company; HMV; Parlophone label; Thorn-EMI

EMI America, 315

EMI BTR-1 tape recorder, 160; BTR-2, 160

EMI Records Ltd, 209–10, 218, 231, 233, 240, 244, 264, 298, 308, 317, 319, 340, 342; relationship with Roulette, 210; takes over Top Rank business, 212–13, 226, 230; internal competition, 213; sign Beatles, 219, 221–2; relationship with VeeJay, 223; creates Stateside, 226; holiday break, 228; policy on foreign affiliates, 234; ownership of Columbia name in Europe, 234; break with CBS, 236; signs and drops Sex Pistols, 267–8; sales, 287; *Now* series, 307 buys stake in Chrysalis, 310; buys Virgin, 310–11, 312, 335; recovery under Rupert Perry, 312–13; buys Blue Note, 314–15; Robbie Williams contract, 331, 336, 344; archive, 341; *see also* Stateside label

EMI Records UK, 313

Eminem, 332

Emitape, 160

Ensign label, 288

Epic label, 236

Epstein, Brian, 219, 221–2

Ertegun, Ahmet, 163, 166–70, 251–3, 267, 276, 314, 316–18; on state of the industry, 332, 343

Ertegun, Munir, 167

Ertegun, Nesuhi, 166, 168, 251–2, 254, 288, 316–17
Essex Music, 265
Europe, 71, 181, 189, 282; impact of Second World War, 141–2; as pseudonym, 168; record industry, 31, 34, 36–7, 56, 67–70, 74–5, 78–81, 150–1, 322
Europe, James, 79
Europop, 282
Eurythmics, 326
Evans, Gil, 181
Evans, Maureen, 235
Evening News, 281
Evening Standard, 171
Everett, Derek, 209–10, 212–14, 223, 226–7, 238, 240–1, 244, 255, 264, 278–9; joins MCA, 256–7, 270; difficulty with punk, 282
Everly, Don and Phil, 195, 247–8

Fabulous Flee-Rakkers, 229
Fairport Convention, 260
Falcone, Patsy, 273
Fame, Georgie, 227, 238
Fanning, John, 326
Fanning, Shawn, 325–6
Faraday, Michael, 11
Farnon, Robert, 249
Farrar, Geraldine, 76
Faust, 266
Fedora, 58
fees, 46, 59, 68, 76; *see also* royalties
Feldman, Victor, 206
Feldman Music, 215
Fender guitars, 241
Fenoulhet, Paul, 92
Fenton, Carl, 93
Ferry, Bryan, 310
'Fever', 164
Field, Ted, 321
Fields, Gracie, 69, 171
Fifield, Jim, 334
Fine, David, 173–4, 282–3, 295–6, 301–2, 307, 319, 339
Finkelstein, (Russian dealer), 62, 324
Finland, 234
First World War, xiv, xvii, xviii, 70, 73, 78–9, 86, 88, 92, 122, 138, 146
Fisk, Sir Ernest, 157, 175, 188, 209
Fitzgerald, Ella, 147

Flagstad, Kirsten, 118, 204
Flanagan and Allen, 171
Florodora, 59
folk music, 253, 254
Fonotipia label, 55, 67, 122
Fontana, D. J., 194
Fontana label, 216, 234, 259
Formby, George, 67, 69, 128, 133
Forrester, Roger, 300
Forse, William T., 102
Forsyth, Bruce, 200
Foster, John, 217
Fowler, Sir George, 123–4, 126
Frampton, Peter, 265
France, 34, 36, 38, 53, 56, 71, 199, 229, 234
Francis, Hugh, 136
Frank, Lowell, 245
Frankie Lymon and the Teenagers, 210
Frankie Yankovic and His Yanks, 155
Franz, Johnny, 202
Fraunhofer Institute, 325
Free, 260
Freed, Alan, 211–12
Freedman, Adele, 121
Freeman, Alan A., 199, 249
Freeman, Ralph, 105
Frishberg, Dave, 339
Fuchs, Michael, 318
Fugs, 251
Funky Enough Records, 320
Furtwängler, Wilhelm, 150, 295
Fury, Billy, 216, 231

Gabler, Milt, 314
Gaisberg, Fred, 13–14, 20–1, 23, 25–7, 29–32, 46, 60, 66, 140–1; recording tours, 34–5, 57–8; Caruso recordings, 57, 58–9; work in Russia, 57, 61–2; autobiography, 70; and recording techniques, 95, 101; opposed to Abbey Road development, 114; retires, 136
Gaisberg, Will, 60
Gallagher, Bill, 241, 242
Gallo group, 301
'Galway Bay', 215
Gamble, Kenny, 273–4, 315
Garner, Erroll, 179–80
Gates, Gareth, 340
Gaye, Marvin, 226
Gee, A. H., 33–4

Geffen, David, 275–6, 308–10, 331
Geffen Records, 308–9
Geissler, Louis, 105
Gelatt, Roland, 2, 14, 27, 106
General Electric Company, 12, 92, 111,
    152–3, 269; buys RCA, 305
General Phonograph Corporation, 67, 88,
    102
Genesis, 258, 300
Gennett, Fred, 90–1
Gennett, Henry, 90
Gennett label, 88, 89, 90–1, 111
Gentlemen Prefer Blondes, 171
George, Lowell, xiii
Geraldo's Concert Orchestra, 171, 172
Germany, 65, 67–8, 71, 80–2, 140–1, 151,
    170, 188, 229, 234; development of
    magnetic tape recording, 159
Gershwin, George, 339
Giannini, Ferruccio, 26
Gibbons, Carroll, 79–80
Gibbs, Terence, 149
Gilbert and Sullivan, 96, 284, 290
Gillan, Ian, 255
Gingold, Hermione, 171
Gladstone, William Ewart, 16, 17, 18
glam rock, 282
Glancy, Ken, 237, 256, 269–70, 279, 281
Glen Gray's Casa Loma Orchestra, 130
Gloetzner, R. H., 102
Glover, Henry, 164
Gluck, Alma, 191
Glucksmann, Max, 66
Gnutella, 328
Go Discs, 319–20
Gobbi, Tito, 176
Goddard, Geoff, 231
Godfrey, Arthur, 177–8, 179, 195, 247
Goff, Reggie, 197
Gold, Harry, 186
Goldberg, Danny, 318
Golden, Billy, 21, 25, 26
Goldman, Elliott, 316
Goldmark, Peter C., 152–3, 154
Gong, 266
Gonsalves, Paul, 180–1
Good, Jack, 216, 217
Goodison, John, 238, 244
Goodman, Benny, 136, 143, 147, 177, 341
Goody, Sam, 254

Goon Show, 171
Goossens, Eugene, 95
Gordy, Berry, Jr., 224–5, 307–8, 320
Gordy, Esther, 224
Gordy, Gwen, 224
Gordy, Loucye, 224
Gore, Al, 305
Gorgoza, Emilio de, 46
gospel, 167
Gossage, John, 128
Gotti, John, 305
Gould, Jay, 4
Gouraud, Colonel George E., 16, 17, 18
Grade, Lew, 200, 249, 291–2
Grade Organisation, 200
Graeme Bell's Jazz Band, 199
Grammophon-Philips Group, 232
Grammy awards, 250, 337
gramophone, xvi, xix, 173, 188;
    amplification, 156; early stars, 57–61;
    foreign sales, xviii; as generic term, 63, 84;
    increasing respectability, 96–7;
    international spread, 34–5; invention and
    commercial development, 24–31; patent
    battles, 38–41, 42–6; *see also* discs; Decca
    portable gramophone; Panatrope;
    Victrola; Zon-o-phone
Gramophone, The, 72, 95, 127, 149, 158, 171,
    174, 199; founded, 97
Gramophone & Typewriter Co. Ltd, 36, 44,
    46, 49, 54; trademark, 45; acquires
    Zonophone, 56, 65; expansion, 55–6;
    profits, 55–6; payments to artists, 59–60;
    efforts in Russia, 61–2; agreement with
    Victor, 63; name changes to Gramophone
    Company, 63
Gramophone Company, xvi, xvii, xviii, 30–1,
    41, 63, 65, 141; incorporated, 34;
    international sales, 34–5; trademark, 35,
    45, 63–4; operations in Russia, 57;
    launches HMV brand name, 63; first
    double-sided discs, 66; impact of First
    World War, 70; attempts to regain control
    of Deutsche Grammophon, 80–1;
    relationship with Victor, 82, 84, 104, 190;
    HMV/Columbia merger, 112, 113; share
    price, 123; restructured into EMI Records
    Ltd, 209; *see also* EMI Records Ltd; HMV;
    Zonophone label
Grand Ole Opry radio show, 192

Granz, Norman, 249
graphophone, 13–16, 19, 20, 23, 25, 28, 37;
    cylinder length, 52; discs, 45; early
    recordings, 21–2; prices, 28, 49; sales,
    48–9; *see also* phonograph
Grateful Dead, 250
Gray, Glen, 130
Grease Band, 255
Great Universal Stores, 229
Great War, *see* First World War
Greece, 234
Green, Al, 168
Green, Derek, 268
Green, Irving, 200
Greenslade, Arthur, 238
'Greensleeves', 229
Grigsby, B. J., 130
Grigsby Grunow company, 113, 130, 134
GRT, 164
Grubman, Allen, 308
Gruen, John, 253
Grundy, Bill, 267
Guber, Peter, 303
Guest, Lionel, 99
Guilbert, Yvette, 37
Guitar Slim, 195
Gulf & Western, 269
Gunnell, John, 227
Gunnell, Rik, 227, 238
Guns 'n' Roses, 309

Haddon, Charles, 84, 105
Haddy, Arthur, 133, 148, 157, 200, 220;
    records railway sounds, 201
Haenschen, Walter, 93
Hagar, Sammy, 309
Haley, Bill, 194, 215, 217
Hall, Henry, 141
Hall, Tony, 206, 255, 341
Hamburg, 219
Hamel, Dr Fred, 233
Hamilton, Russ, 235
Hammond, John, 120, 136, 183, 243
Hancock, Herbie, 315
Handel, George Frideric, 17, 204
Handy, W. C., 141
Hank Ballard and the Midniters, 164
Hanmer, Bill, 289
Hanover, 31, 34, 233, 283
Harding, Gilbert, 171

Harlem 167; Apollo, 164; Plantation Club,
    167
Harlem Records, 169, 170
Harley, Steve, 269
Harpers West One, 230
Harrell, André, 321
Harris, Jet, 217
Harris, Richard, 257
Harris, Wynonie, 169
Harrison, George, 222, 232
Harrison, H. C., 100, 115
Harrison, Rex, 208
Harry Gold's Pieces of Eight, 186
Hartong, Hendrik, 171, 233
Hartstone, Leon 'Lee', 196, 284–5
Harty, Hamilton, 95
Harvard University, 241
Hastings, 201
Hastings Municipal Orchestra, 125, 127
Hatch, Orrin, 330, 331
Hatch, Tony, 249
Hatry, Clarence, 110, 126
Hawaii, 254
Hawkshaw, Alan, 239
Haycraft, Howard, 146
Hayes, 70, 74, 83, 91, 100, 103, 113, 118, 132,
    158, 186, 188, 189, 209; Central Research
    Laboratories, 116, 159
Hayes, Tubby, 206
HBO cable channel, 318
HDCD, 335
Head, Roy, 166
Heath, Edward, 258
Heath, Ted, 92, 149, 203, 208, 284–5
Heebner, Walt, 147
Heifetz, Jascha, 122, 145, 189
Heinemann, Adolph, 88
Heinemann, Otto, 67–8, 88, 102
Helms, Bobby, 217
Henderson, Fletcher, 89, 110
Hendrix, Jimi, 250
Henley, Don, 309
Herbert, Michael, 113
Hertford, 70, 75
Hi label, 195
Higgins, Harry Vincent, 67
Hilbers, Konrad, 326
Hill, John, 191
Hill and Range, 193
Hilton, Ronnie, 213

His Master's Voice, see Barraud, Francis
Hitler, Adolf, 139–40, 159
HM Customs and Excise, 265
HMV, xviii, 63, 66, 68–9, 72, 136, 141, 151, 230; acquires *Talking Machine News*, 72; impact of First World War, 70, 72–5, 78; sales, 74, 81; competition with Columbia, 76, 77; litigation with Deutsche Grammophon, 81; relationship with Victor, 82–5, 104, 112, 122; slow to enter jazz market, 87; position in UK market, 94–5, 96; adoption of electric recording, 100, 101, 104, 115; merger with Columbia, 111–16, 117, 126; multiple microphone techniques, 125; Jack Hylton leaves, 128; classical repertoire, 141–2; impact of Second World War, 143; use of Kingsway Hall, 149–50; advertising, 174; in EMI consolidation, 186, 187, 189, 190, 191, 335; releases Elvis Presley in UK, 194; hit singles, 213; rejects Beatles, 219; *see also* Gramophone Company
HMV record shops, xvii, 112, 216, 221, 334
Hofbauer, Frank, 93
Holiday Inn, 194
Holland, 234, 288
Holliday, Michael, 213
Holly, Buddy, 194, 215, 230, 231
Hollywood, 121, 144, 147, 265; Capitol Tower, 187; Sunset Boulevard, 263
Holman, H. E., 115–16
Holmes, Rupert, 314
Holmes à Court, Robert, 291, 292
Holstius, E. N. 'Teddie', 126–7
Holzman, Jacob 'Jac', 253–4, 314
home taping, 324
Homer, Louise, 76
Honeycombs, 231
Hooker, John Lee, 163, 223
Horowitz, David, 316
Horowitz, Vladimir, 121–2, 189
Horricks, Raymond, 201–4, 206–8, 215, 219, 249–50
Hot Five, 89, 167
Hough, James E., 28, 47–8, 52
House of Commons Committee on CD pricing, 300
Houston, 165, 166; Bronze Peacock Dinner Club, 165
Houston, Whitney, 306

'How Do You Do It', 222
Howlin' Wolf, 163
Hubbard, Gardiner G., 8, 12, 14
Hucknall, Mick, 323, 332
Huff, Leon, 273–4, 315
Hughes, Spike, 202
Hugo Wolf Society, 141
Human League, 268
human voice, 32
Humble Pie, 265
Humphries, John, 234
Humphries, Second Lieutenant S., 73
Hunter, Jim, 154
Hunter, Tab, 246
Hunting, Russell, 21–3, 26–7, 31, 50, 54–5, 72, 101
Hylton, Jack, 114, 128–9
Hyman, Elliott, 251, 252
Hyman, Phyllis, 315
Hyperion label, 340

Ian Dury and the Blockheads, 311
Ice-T, 321
Idol, Billy, 262
Ifield, Frank, 223
Illustrated London News, 6–7, 10
Imperial label, 126, 132, 195, 244
Independent Broadcasting Authority, 291
independent labels, 259, 262, 300, 306–7, 311, 319–20, 340
independent producers, 227–8, 231, 285
independent promoters, 304–5
Independent Record Laboratories, 129
Independiente label, 320
India, xvii, 34, 44, 66, 68, 143, 216
Indonesia, 173
Industrias Electricas y Musicales Odeon, 176
Innis, Louis, 164
International Federation of the Phonographic Industry (IFPI), 317, 324–5, 329
International Graphophone Company, 16
International Talking Machine Company, 65–6, 68
International Zonophone Company, 56, 65
Internet, xiv, 324–5, 326, 328, 342
Interscope label, 320, 321
Invisible Hands label, 342
Iovine, Jimmy, 320–1
iPod MP3 player, 327

Ireland, 271
Ironstrings, Ira, *see* Rey, Alvino
Irving, Henry, 17
Irving Music, 263
Isgro, Joe, 304, 305
Island label, 259–63, 265–7, 275, 278, 305;
    acquired by PolyGram, 306–7
Island Music Publishing, 306
Island Visual Arts, 306
Italy, 37, 56, 57, 68, 234
iTunes, 327

J Records, 338
J. P. Morgan, 102, 109, 112
J. W. Seligman, 106–7
Jackson, Jack, 197
Jackson, Janet, 310
Jackson, Joe, 265
Jackson, Michael, 303
Jamaican music, 259–60, 261–2
Jamerson, James, 225
James, Dick, xx
James, Sally, 287
James, Skip, 89
Jamieson, Peter, 313
Japan, 35, 234, 294, 296, 303, 309
Java, 66
jazz, 86–91, 127, 135–6, 143, 167, 179, 216,
    234, 313–15; modern, 206; traditional,
    199
Jazz Singer, The, 93
Jefferson, Blind Lemon, 89
Jennings, Christopher, 149
Jethro Tull, 262
Jews, 139–40
Joachim, Joseph, 96
Jobete publishing, 224, 308
Jodeci, 321
John Grey company, 127
John, Elton, 308
John, Little Willie, 164
Johnson, Bill, 86
Johnson, Eldridge Reeves, xix, 29–31, 36,
    39–41, 42–7, 53, 56, 62–3, 86; 'improved
    Johnson process of recording', 40; Clark's
    letters to, 71, 75; assessment of war, 78–9;
    HMV acquisition, 82–5; underestimates
    radio, 100; depression, 101, 105; sells stake
    in Victor, 104–8
Johnson, Elsie Fenimore, 30

Johnson, George W., 21, 23
Johnson, Laurie, 207
Johnson, Mario Lavelle, 320
Johnson Sound Recording Company, 40
Johnson Talking Machine Co. Ltd, 158
Johnson-Clark Improved Soundbox, 29
Jolson, Al, 24, 93, 111
Jones, 'Grandpa', 164
Jones, Isham, 93
Jones, Janie, 277
Jones, Joseph W., 42–3, 45, 53
Jones, Norah, 336, 337
Jones, Phil, 226
Jones, Quincy, 321
Jones, Richard M., 89
Joplin, Janis, 243, 272
Jordan, Stanley, 315
Joyce, William (Lord Haw-Haw), 159
Jubilee label, 167
Judson, Arthur, 119, 134
jukeboxes, 143
Jumbo label, 67, 122
JVC, 294; VHS system, 310

Kaempfert, Bert, 233
Kapp, Jack, 93–4, 110, 130–1, 151–2
von Karajan, Herbert, 340
Karns, B. F., 27
Kassner, Ed, 277
Katzenberg, Jeffrey, 331
Kaufman, Gerald, 300
Kayes, Alan, 184, 189, 190
Kazaa, 328, 330
Keating, Johnny, 206, 208, 249
Keep, Ted, 226
Keisker, Marion, 191–2
Keith Prowse, 214
Kennedy, Charles, 342
Kennedy, Nigel, 340
Kennedy, Pat, 189
Kennedy, Rick, 91
Kenton, Stan, 144, 175
Keppard, Freddie, 86, 90
Kerridge, Adrian, 228
Keys, Alicia, 338
King, Carole, 265
King, Mark, 342
King Crimson, 251
King label, 164–5, 209–10
King Sisters, 175

Kingsley, James, 268
Kinks, 250, 251
Kinney Record Group, 254, 255
Kirkby, Stanley, 68–9, 72
Kiss, 283
Kitt, Eartha, 190
Klaasen, Reinhard, 290
KLF, 322
Kneale, Nigel, 218
Knight, Marion 'Suge', 320–2
Knopfler, Mark, 297–8, 299
Koppelman, Charles, 317
Kostelanetz, André, 118–19
Koylan, Sadi, 168
Krasnow, Bob, 315, 317
Kreisler, Fritz, 97, 191
Kruesi, John, 4
Kruger, Jeffrey, 234
Krupa, Gene, 143
Ku Klux Klan, 91
Kunz, Charlie, 149

la Dow, Orville, 39
La Palina Cigar Company, 134
la Rocca, Nick, 86
LaRosa, Julius, 177, 195, 247
Labour Party, 162; Conference, 322–3
Lack, Albert, 62, 83
LaHara, Brianna, 329
Laine, Cleo, 211
Laine, Frankie, 197
Lambert, Thomas A., 50, 52
Lambert typewriter, 36, 55
LaMonte, John, 304–5
Lamonte, Syria, 31
Landau, Jon, 304
Landry, Art, 94
Langtry, Lillie, 37
Lauper, Cyndi, 303
Le Matin, 87
Lebel (Russian retailer), 57
Led Zeppelin, 251
Lee, Frank, 128, 133, 197–9, 201–4, 208, 219, 284, 286; 'the Queen of Decca', 203; joke record, 220
Lee, Peggy, 187
Leeds Music, 214
Legge, Walter, 141–2, 150, 174, 176–7, 189
Legrand, Michel, 183
Lehmann, Lilli, 66

Lehrer, Tom, 208
Leiber, Jerry, 165, 166
Leipzig, 34, 68
Lennon, John, 219, 220, 308
Leno, Dan, 32
Lenoir, Abbé, 5
Leo XIII, Pope, 38, 57
Letts, Howard, 189
Levaphone label, 234–5
Level 42, 342
Levin, Gerald, 316–17, 318
Levy, Alain, 319, 334, 335
Levy, Eddie, 225, 234, 235, 236, 340
Levy, Jacques, 234, 235
Levy, Len, 241, 242
Levy, Morris (Oriole label), 225, 234–5, 237
Levy, Morris (Roulette label), 210–11, 304–5
Lewie, Jona, 311
Lewis, Edward, 122–34, 139, 148–52, 157, 171, 188, 190, 196–7, 205–6, 221, 227, 232, 249, 301; musical tastes, 127, 149; personality, 196; promotes stereo agreement, 200; management style, 202; comparison with Branson, 266; death, 284, 289; decline of Decca, 285–9; afraid of unions, 287–8; out of touch, 289
Lewis, Lady, 289
Lewis, Meade 'Lux', 314
Lewisohn, Mark, 219
Leyton, John, 230
Liberty label, 226–7, 315
Lieberson, Goddard, 154, 175, 181–3, 207, 236–7, 240–3, 274–5, 337
Liebler, Vin, 156, 183
Liggins, Joe 'the Honey Dripper', 195
Light, Enoch, 284
Lilley, Arthur, 133–4, 198, 206–7
Lin Broadcasting Corporation, 165
Lind, Jenny, xviii
Lindström, Carl, 67
Lindstrom group, *see* Carl Lindström AG
Lion, Alfred, 314–15
Lioret, M., 50
Lippincott, Jesse H., 15, 17, 19, 25, 28
Little Feat, xiii
Little Richard (Richard Penniman), 166, 195–6
Littlewood, Joan, 207
Liverpool, 221
Livingston, Alan, 222

Lloyd Webber, Andrew, 255
location recording, 103–4
Lock, Jimmy, 160, 207, 228–9, 230
Lockwood, Joseph Flawith, 187–8, 209,
  226–7, 231, 335
Loew's cinema chain, 301
Lombard, Thomas, 15
Lombardo, Guy, 129–32
London, 29, 30–1, 37, 101; cylinder
  recording companies, 33; 2 Is coffee bar,
  217; 100 Club, 199; Abbey Road studios,
  113–16, 141, 160, 186, 205, 217, 222, 271;
  Aeolian Hall, 91; Albert Hall, 257;
  Alhambra, Leicester Square, 73; Bank
  Underground station, 239; Buckingham
  Palace, 268; Century House, 171; Chenil
  Galleries, Chelsea, 125, 127; Claridges,
  189; Clerkenwell Road, 52, 72, 73;
  Conway Hall, 172; Covent Garden, 59, 60,
  67; Crystal Palace, 10–11, 17; CTS, 271;
  Denmark Street (Tin Pan Alley), 213, 215,
  237, 244; Great Castle Street, 218;
  Hammersmith Palais, 79; Hippodrome,
  73; IBC studios, 172, 228–9; Kingsway
  Hall, 103, 114, 148, 149–50; Ladbroke
  Grove, 311; Lansdowne Studios, 228;
  Levy's Sound Studios, 235; Lyric Theatre,
  59; Maddox Street, 203; Maida Vale, 103;
  Maiden Lane, 31–2, 33, 35, 44, 55;
  Mermaid Theatre, 207; Middlesex
  Hospital, 289; Oxford Street, 213, 216,
  221; Palladium, 167, 249; Petty France,
  103, 115; Piccadilly, 255; Queen's Hall,
  103; Royal Opera House, 334; Savoy
  Hotel, 79, 226; Stanhope Place, 172, 202;
  Theatre Royal, Stratford, 207;
  Westminster Abbey, 99; Wheeler's fish
  restaurant, 214; Whitfield Street, 271, 272
London American label, 195–6, 200, 226
London Hippodrome Orchestra, 74
London Philharmonic Orchestra, 159
London Records, 152, 284
London Symphony Orchestra, 191
Lopez, Denis, 239
Lopez, Ramon, 298, 316–17, 318
Loraine, Violet, 73
Lordan, Jerry, 218
Lorna Music, 218
Los Angeles, 168, 263, 322
Lou, Bonnie, 210

Lough, Ernest, 104
Louisiana Hayride radio show, 192
Love Affair, 238, 239
Love, Geoff, 171
Lowe, Nick, 311
Lubinsky, Herman, 169
Lucas, E. V., 73
Ludwigshafen, 159
Lundvall, Bruce, 182, 241–2, 274–5, 302,
  313–15, 333, 336, 338
Lupino, Stanley, 86
Luter, Claude, 199
Lymon, Frankie, 210
Lynch, Kenny, 277
Lynn, Vera, 143, 149, 214
Lyrec TR16 tape recorder, 230
Lyttelton, Humphrey, 228

Maazel, Lorin, 207
McCartney, Paul, 219
McCormack, John, 66, 191
McDevitt, Chas, 235
Macdonald, Andy, 319–20
Macdonald, Thomas Hood, 20
Macero, Teo, 183
McFerrin, Bobby, 314, 315
McGee, Alan, 320, 322
McGhee, Brownie, 169–70
McGhee, Stick, 169–70
Mackenzie, Compton, 96–7
McKenzie, Scott, 239, 243
Mackenzie-Rogan, Major J., 87
McLaren, Malcolm, 268
McLean, Robert, 136, 156–7, 188
Macmillan, Harold, 162
McNutt, Randy, 91
Madonna, 330
magnetic tape recording, 158–60
Mahler, Gustav, 140
mail order, 90
Maitland, Mike, 248, 249, 317
Majestic radios, 113
Malden Holding company, 123
Mamie Smith's Jazz Hounds, 88
Manfred Mann, 255
Manhattan label, 315, 336–7
Manilow, Barry, 275
Manning, Cardinal, 17
Manor, the, 266
Mansfield, Keith, 238

Mantovani, 149, 196, 198, 207, 284
Marconi, Guglielmo, 104, 113
Mardin, Arif, 336–7
Marek, George, 184–5, 190, 248
Marillion, 342
Markham, Ronald, 278
Marks, George Croydon, 52
Marks, Lord, 113
Marley, Bob, 261
Marlow, Marion, 177
Marshall, Paul, 223
Martin, Bill, 287
Martin, Dean, 248
Martin, George, 186, 219–20, 222
Martin, Mary, 154, 207
Martin, Ray, 186, 187, 213, 219
Martinville, Edouard-Leon Scott de, 1
Martland, Peter, 156, 188
Martyn, John, 261
Marvelettes, 224, 225
Marvin, Hank B., 217–18
Marx, Richard, 315
Maschwitz, Eric, 159
Masters, Brian, 157, 231, 259
Mathis, Johnny, 183, 314
Matsushita, 294, 306, 310
Matthews, Lord, 292
Mauro, Philip, 38–9, 45, 51
Maxfield, J. P., 100, 115
Mayfair Orchestra, 74
Mayfield, Percy, 195
MCA (Music Corporation of America), xvi, 254–6, 270, 272, 304–6, 309, 318; Motown deal, 307–8; buys Death Row, 321
MCA Universal, 310
MCPS, 215
Meadmore, W. S., 72, 73
Meehan, Tony, 218
Meek, Robert George, 227, 228, 229–31
Melba, Dame Nellie, 30, 37, 59–60, 68, 76, 77
Mellin, Robert, 310
melodeon, 32
Melody Maker, 222, 281
Memphis, 166, 191, 195
Memphis Recording Services, 191
Mendes, Sergio, 264
Mendl, Hugh, 124, 126–8, 132, 148–9, 151, 159, 196, 198–9, 205–6, 214–15, 217, 219, 232; joins Decca, 138–9; as record producer, 197, 207–8; records Formula 1 race, 201; and Decca politics, 203–4; contempt for EMI, 208–9; on Decca's rejection of the Beatles, 220–1; and decline of Decca, 284–7, 289–90
Mendl, Sir Sigismund, 124, 126, 138
Menon, Bhaskar, 269, 312, 314–15
Mercer, Johnny, 143–4, 187
Mercury label, 193, 200, 235, 283
Merriman, H. O., 99
Mesner, Eddie, 165
Metallica, 326
Metro-Goldwyn-Mayer (MGM), 157, 235
Metropolitan Opera, 46, 60, 63, 76, 120
Mexico City, 38
Miami News, 212
Michael, George, 311–12, 326
Michaelis, Alfred, 34, 59
Michaelis, William, 34
microphones, 4, 24, 103, 125, 148, 150
micro-phonograph, 37–8
Middleton, Albert, 105
Mike Berry and the Outlaws, 230
Milan, 34, 37, 59; La Scala, 58, 60, 176, 190; Teatro Lirico, 58
Miller, Glenn, 143, 144, 280
Miller, Mitch, 183, 186, 216, 237, 242, 247
Millie, *see* Small, Millie
Mills Brothers, 130
Milne, Geoff, 195
Minneapolis Orchestra, 119
Minnelli, Liza, 273
Minogue, Kylie, 336
Minshull, Ray, 289
Miracles, 223, 225
Mitchell, Guy, 186
Mitchell, Joni, 250, 276
Mitsubishi, 294
Mittell, Brenchley, 100, 157, 175, 188
Mobbs, Nick, 267–8
mobile recording, 104
Mobley, Hank, 315
Monk, Thelonious, 315
Monroe, Bill, 192
Monte Carlo, 59
Monterey festival, 243
Monteux, Pierre, 121
Montgomery, Wes, 265
Monument label, 195
Moody Blues, 285
Moore, Gerald, 98–9, 142

Moore, Scotty, 192, 194
Moreschi, Alessandro, 57–8
Morgado, Robert J., 316–17, 318, 336
Morgan, John Pierpont, 11, 27
Morgan, Lee, 315
Moriarty, Stephen, 16, 17, 18–19, 28, 47
Morita, Akio, 296, 303
Morley, Angela, 171–2, 201
Morris, Doug, 317–18, 319, 332
Morris, Lawrence B., 118
Morrison, Van, xiii
Morse, Ella Mae, 144
Mortimer, John, 268
Morton, Jelly Roll, 90, 167
Moss, Jerry, 263–5, 307, 319; opposition to CD, 295, 328
Most, Mickie, 227
Motown label, 225–6, 316, 320, 321; gold records, 169; MCA deal, 307–8; bought by PolyGram, 308
Mott the Hoople, 251, 262
Mottola, Tommy, 303, 304, 311, 334
Move, 265
Mozart, George, 32
Mozart, Wolfgang Amadeus, 159
MP3, xiv, xv, 325, 327, 328, 330, 342
'Mrs Barstinglow's Phonograph' (short story), 9–10
MTV, 312
Muddy Waters, 163
Mullin, John T., 159
Murray Pilcer and His Jazz Band, 87
Murray, Mitch, 222
music publishers, xix–xx, 175, 178–9, 210, 211–12, 213–15, 310
music shops, 48–9
Music Week, 263, 264, 273, 289
musicals, 73–4; *see also* Broadway musicals
Musicians' Union, 288
Musiphone Company, 33, 56, 66
Muswell Hill, 250

Naples, 34; Teatro Nuovo, 58
Napster, 325–8, 331, 333
Nash, Graham, 276
Nashville, 192, 194, 195, 248, 280
Nat King Cole Trio, 144
Nathan, John, 295
Nathan, Syd, 164–5, 209
National Association of Talking Machine

Jobbers, 82
National Discount Company, 124
National Gramophone Company, 28, 30, 38, 56
National Gramophone Corporation, 39
National Phonograph Association, 15, 19
National Phonograph Company, 20, 52
National Provincial Bank, 124, 129
National Records, 167–8
National Symphony Orchestra, 148
National War Labor Board, 144–5
Nazis, 139–41
NBC, 153
NBC News, 305
NBC Symphony Orchestra, 120, 147
Neely, Hal, 164–5
Negro songs, 21, 93
Neilsen, Tawny, 128
Nesbitt, Ben, 215
Network, the, 304–5
Nevil, Robbie, 315
New Jersey, 168
New Mayfair Orchestra, 114
New Musical Express, 198, 222
New Orleans, 86, 169, 196
New Orleans Rhythm Kings, 90
New York, 86, 89, 125, 194, 196, 202, 211, 280; Aeolian Hall, 91; Birdland jazz club, 210; Carnegie Hall, 47, 120, 121, 177; CBS Playhouses, 147; Flatiron Building, 131; Hotel Jefferson, 168, 170; Liederkranz Hall, 147, 148, 183; Lincoln Center, 337; Lyceum theatre, 21; Madison Square Garden, 253; Metropolitan Opera, 58, 80, 103–4; Rockefeller Plaza, 120; Sherwood Studios, 37; Studio 8H, 120–1, 147; Waldorf-Astoria, 154; WINS radio station, 211; *see also* Harlem
New York Philharmonic Orchestra, 120, 204
New York Recording Laboratories, 89, 129
New York Times, 9, 16, 112
New York University, 245
Newell, Norman, 171–2, 216
Newhart, Bob, 248
Newman, Randy, 250
Newport Jazz Festival, 180, 181, 211
News of the World, 277
Newsnight, 300
Newston, Harry, 229
Newton, S. C., 126–7

Nicole Frères, 56
Nightingale, Florence, 17
Nipper, xvii, xviii, 35, 51, 64, 75, 80, 176, 189, 322, 334
Nippon Columbia, 296
Nipponophone company, 113
Nixa records, 199
Nixon, Hilton, 199
Nixon, Richard M., 274
Noble, Ray, 114
North American Phonograph Company, 15, 19, 27, 28
North American Review, 5
Norway, 234
Nottingham, 48, 268, 291
Novello, Ivor, 72
NWA (Niggaz With Attitude), 321
Nyro, Laura, 243, 276

Oasis, 320, 322
Oberstein, Maurice, 237, 256, 270, 272, 278
O'Brien, W. J., 148
Observer, 151
Ocean's Eleven, 248
Oceania (Australasia), xvii, 44
O'Connell, Charles, 118–21, 184
Ode label, 243, 265
Odeon label, xviii, 55, 65–6, 67, 103, 122, 137, 176
Office of Economic Stabilization, 145
Oh Boy, 217
Ohga, Noria, 295, 296, 302, 304
oil crisis, 258
O'Jays, 315
Okeh label, 88–9, 103, 135
Oklahoma, 145
Oldfield, Mike, 266–7
Oliver, Joe 'King', 89, 91, 167
Olof, Victor, 149–51
Olympic Studios, 255, 271
Ono, Yoko, 308
Oord, Gerry, 313
opera, 67
Opera Babes, 340
Organization of Petroleum Exporting Countries (OPEC), 258
organized crime, xiv, 304–5, 325
organs, 35, 92, 95, 97, 120, 133, 150
Original Dixieland Jazz Band, 86–7, 91
Original Five Blind Boys, 166

Oriole label, 225, 234–7
Ormandy, Eugene, 119, 243
O'Rourke, Steve, 300
Ostin, Mo, 248–51, 253, 263, 283, 302, 309, 314, 317–18, 332–3
Ottens, Lou, 294
Otto Heinemann Phonograph Supply Company, 88
Ovitz, Michael, 310
Owen, William Barry, 30–1, 34–6, 40–1, 43, 47, 55–6, 63, 82
Oxford Union debate on file-sharing, 329

Pacific Jazz label, 168, 227, 246
Pacific label, 199
Paderewski, Ignacy Jan, 191
Pagliacci (Leoncavallo), 69
Paley, William, 130, 134, 153, 155, 175, 181, 184, 243, 303, 313
Palitz, Morty 'Perfect Pitch', 147
Palmer, Rex, 135
Panasonic, 294
Panatrope, 104
Paramor, Alan, 218
Paramor, Norrie, 186, 187, 213, 217, 218, 219, 222
Paramount, 129, 269, 309, 316
Paramount label, 88, 89–90, 111
pareographe, 2
Paris, 34, 36–7, 60, 71, 87; Conservatoire, 140–1; Odéon theatre, 65
Park, Simon, 278
Parker, 'Colonel' Tom, 192, 193, 194, 280, 281
Parker, Frank, 177
Parker, Johnny, 228
Parks, Van Dyke, 250
Parlophon label, 68, 103
Parlophone label, xx, 103, 186, 211, 228; signs Beatles, 219, 221–2; revived, 313
Parnes, Larry, 208, 216
patents, xvii, xix, 3, 4, 43–4, 69, 88, 200; cylinder, 49–50; discs, 40–1, 42–3, 45–6, 90, 91, 113; electric recording, 100, 115–16; gramophone, 26, 38–9; phonograph and graphophone, 2, 5–6, 7, 8, 13–14, 15, 18, 19, 26, 28–9, 38, 52; stereo recording, 116, 200
Pathé Frères, 22, 36–7, 44, 53, 55, 92, 101; newsreels, 114
Pathé Marconi, 229

patriotic discs, 72, 78, 80
Patti, Adelina, 37, 59, 60–1
Patton, Charley, 89–90
Paul Butterfield Blues Band, 254
Paul Whiteman's New Yorker Orchestra, 144
Paul, Les, 175, 187
Payne, Colonel, 19
Payne, Jack, 114
payola, 212, 248, 273–4, 304; in Britain, 277
Peacock label, 166
Pearl Harbor, 143
Peel, John, 266
Peers, Donald, 69
Peltz, Nelson, 301, 302
Pemberton-Billing, Noel, 123
Penniman, Richard, *see* Little Richard
Pennington, Ray, 164
Perfect label, 89
Perkins, Carl, 193, 194
Perry, Rupert, 312–13
Peter, Paul and Mary, 248
Peters, Jon, 303
Petrillo, James Caesar, 143–7, 154, 168
Petty, Norman, 215
Phil Silvers Show, The, 254
Philadelphia, 27, 29, 265, 283, 304; Franklin
    Institute, 24
Philadelphia Symphony Orchestra, 119,
    243–4
Philco, 154
Philips Phonografische Industrie, 171
Philips, xv, xvii, 171–4, 198, 213, 216, 288,
    306; relationship with Columbia/CBS,
    174–5, 179, 186, 232, 234; slowness to
    adopt stereo, 201–2; releases Motown
    records, 225; alliance with Deutsche
    Grammophon, 232–3, 282, 339; deal with
    Island, 259–60; purchase of Decca, 290;
    buys Pye company, 291; CD development,
    294–6, 298–9; PolyGram sale, 318–19;
    double-deck tape machines, 333–4; lack
    of understanding of record business, 334;
    see also Fontana label; PolyGram
Philips, Frits, 233
Phillips, Dewey, 192
Phillips, Jimmy and Bill, 214
Phillips, Jud, 193
Phillips, Sam, 191–3, 194
Phoenix label, 75
phonautograph, 1

Phono Record, 125
Phonogram, 282, 331; studios, 297
phonograph, xvi, 25, 26; commercialisation,
    15–23, 36–7; earliest recordings, 17;
    'home', 28; invention and development,
    1–2, 4–15; prices, 18, 28, 48; V-disc, 147;
    see also Cliftophone; graphophone;
    micro-phonograph
Phonoscope, 54
Piaf, Edith, 179
pianos, 33, 100, 133
Picardie, Justine, 170
Piccadilly label, 249
Piccadilly radio and record player, 152
Pickle, Durwood, 329
Pilcer, Murray, 87
Pink Floyd, 258, 269, 300
Pinza, Ezio, 154
piracy, xiv, 295, 317, 324–6, 329–31, 338, 342;
    in Russia, 62, 324
Pisello, Sal, 304, 308
Plancon, Pol, 59
Platters, 235
Platz, David, 165
Plaut, Fred, 182–3
Plugge, Captain Leonard, 172
Poco, 276
Police, 265
Polydor, 165, 171, 206, 219, 233, 251, 282;
    sales, 287
Polygon label, 199
PolyGram, xv, xvi, xvii, 283, 288, 296, 298–9,
    316–17, 320, 334, 340; buys Decca, 288–9;
    acquisitions, 306–8; *Now* series, 307;
    acquired by Seagram, 318–19, 335, 336;
    classical repertoire, 339
PolyGram UK, 282, 295
PolyGram US, 283
Polyphon Musicwerke, 68, 80
Poniatoff, Alexnader M., 159
Pons, Lily, 118
Poole, Brian, 219, 221, 225, 232, 237
Pop Idol, 339, 340
Porter, Cole, 207, 339
Portugal, 34
Poulsen, Vladimir, 158
Prado, Perez, 187
Prescott, Frederick M., 39, 41, 56, 65, 66
Prescott, George B., 7
President Records, 277

Presley, Elvis, 191–4, 215; death, 280–1
Prestige label, 181
Preston, Denis, 198–9, 227, 228
Preuss, Oscar, 103, 186
Price, Alan, 227
Price, Lloyd, 195
Primal Scream, 320
Prince, 326, 331
Prisonaires, 192
privacy, 330
Procol Harum, 262, 265
producers, xiii–xiv
Project Sound, 273
Prowse, Keith, 214
PRS, 215
PRT, 291
Pryor, Arthur, 31, 50
Punch, 8, 9
punk, 282, 311
Pye company, 199; bought by Philips, 291
Pye Disco Demand, 290
Pye International label, 200
Pye Nixa, 199
Pye Records, 200, 201, 223, 227, 230, 254; distributes Reprise, 249–50; decline, 290–2

Q magazine, 342
quadraphonic sound, 258–9
Quality label, 167
Quinn, Dan, 26

race records, 89, 164, 170
Rackmil, Milton, 131, 254
radar, 129, 148, 151, 196, 209
Radar label, 288
radio, xiv, xviii, 99–100, 104, 106, 129–30, 134, 143, 157, 199; and payola system, 211–12
Radio 1, 260, 266, 278
Radio Luxembourg, 127, 159, 194, 197, 220, 228, 229
Radio Normandie, 127, 172
Radio Paris, 127
radio sets, 118
radio stations, 127, 163, 168, 196
Raeburn, Boyd, 167
ragtime, 86
Rainey, Ma, 89, 332
Raise the Titanic, 291

Ralfini, Ian, 254, 336–7
Rank Organisation, 212
rap, 291
Raphoff (Russian retailer), 57
Ray, Johnnie, xv, 186, 216
Raymonde, Ivor, 230
RCA (Radio Corporation of America), 104, 107, 111, 130, 134; attitude towards record industry, 117–18; colour television, 153; bought by General Electric, 305; *see also* RCA Victor
RCA Great Britain Ltd, 190; sales, 287
RCA Photophone Ltd, 190
RCA Records, 279, 305–6, 338
RCA Victor, xvi, 116–21, 134–5, 137, 147, 151, 162, 187, 270; Red Seal discs, 118, 146, 184; impact of Second World War, 143, 147; impact of recording ban, 145; research into vinyl, 146; relationship with EMI, 151, 156–7, 174, 176, 188–91, 209, 210; develops 45 rpm disc, 155–6, 157, 184; post-war lull, 183–4; under Marek, 184–5; relationship with Decca, 190–1, 204; matrices destroyed, 191; signs Elvis Presley, 193–4, 215; stereo tapes, 200; record club, 240–1; signs Philadelphia Symphony Orchestra, 243–4; deal with A&M, 265; conservatism, 279–81; *see also* Bluebird label; RCA Records
RCA-Ariola, 305
Read, Oliver, 14, 129, 152
Read, Sir John, 267–8, 269
record clubs, 240–1
record industry: ownership, xvi–xvii, xviii; in 1890s, 23; up to 1920s, 41; 1902–3 growth, 47–8; increased competition, 64; post-First World War, 81; new entrants, 88; 1920s boom, 94, 123; Depression era, 109; post-Depression recovery, 119; post-war, 162; problems facing small companies, 192–3; hit by oil crisis, 258; in early 1980s, 293; advent of CD, 300–1; Yetnikoff's description, 303; mergers, 305–6, 316, 318, 332–3; end of twentieth century, 322; decline, xiii–xiv, xx, 323, 324; market corrections, 327; weaknesses, 327–8; lost sales, 329–30; boards' lack of understanding, 334; business model, xiii, xviii, 338; becoming less of an industry, 343; *see also* Britain, record industry;

Europe record industry
record players, 152, 171, 172, 188, 209
record shops, 48–9
Record Supervision, 199
recording: history, xix; techniques, 32, 33–4,
    98–9; technology advances, xiv–xv, 156;
    see also acoustic recording; digital
    recording; electric recording; location
    recording; magnetic tape recording;
    mobile recording; recording bans;
    recording experts; stereo recording; tinfoil
    recording; wax recording; zinc recording
Recording Angel trademark, 35, 45, 64, 176
recording bans, 143–5, 154–5, 168, 187, 314
recording experts, xvii, 23, 34, 57
Recording Industry Association of America
    (RIAA), 169, 305, 314, 326, 328–30
records: 7-inch, 155; 12-inch, 154; 33⅓ rpm,
    xv, 117, 152, 173, 187; 45 rpm, xv, 155–6,
    157, 173, 184, 187; 'battle of the speeds',
    155, 200; cut-price, 68–9, 81, 82; first
    stereo, 201; long-playing, xix, 117, 135,
    152–3, 155–6, 158, 160–1, 174–5, 177–8,
    184; microgroove, xiv, 154–6, 174, 184,
    293; *see also* cylinders, discs; stereo
    recording
Redd, Gene, 164
Reece, Dizzy, 206
Reed, Jimmy, 223
Reeves, Dianne, 336–7
Reeves, Jim, 280
Regal label, 75, 112, 125
Regal label (US), 129
Regal Zonophone label, 112
reggae, 259, 261
Reid, Antonio 'LA', 338
Rena manufacturing Co. Ltd, 55, 62, 66
Rennie, Roland, 233
Reprise label, 248–50, 251, 317
revues, 73–4
Rex label, 132–3
Rey, Alvino, 246
Reynolds, Debbie, 224
RGM Sound, 229–31
Rhone, Sylvia, 318
rhythm and blues, 167, 169, 170, 195
Rice, Tim, 255
Richard, Cliff, 216–18, 266, 269, 298, 322
Richards, Ron, 222
Rickolt, Paul, 253

Ricordi, Tito, 67
Ridley, Walter J., 186, 187, 194, 213, 231
Riga, 75
Rigoletto, 26, 59, 60
Riley and Farley, 131
Rimsky-Korsakov, Nikolay, 159
Ripley, Alexandra, 254
Ripley, Leonard, 253–4
Riviera, Jake, 288
Robert Stigwood Organisation, 283
Roberts, Paddy, 208
Roberts, Rachel, 207–8
Robey, Don, 165–6
Robey, George, 73
Robinson, Charlie, 263
Robinson, Richard, 240, 256, 270–1, 272
Robinson, William 'Smokey', 225, 226
rock and roll, 215–17, 314, 327
Rock and Roll Hall of Fame, 250
Rockefeller, Nelson, 27
Rodkinson, Norbert, 61–3, 324
Rolling Stones, 164, 232, 268, 310
Rolontz, Bob, 269
Rome, 58
Ronald, Landon, 59, 60–1
Roosevelt, Franklin D., 145
Roosevelt, Hilbourne L., 8
Rosen, Hilary, 326, 328, 329
Rosenblatt, Ed, 263
Rosengarten, Moses Aron (Maurice), 150–1,
    286, 288
Ross, Brian, 305
Ross, Steve, 252–3, 254, 276, 308–9, 313–14,
    316–18, 338
Ross-Trevor, Mike, 235–6, 271–2, 340
Rothchild, Paul, 254
Rougemont, Peter de, 270
Roulette label, 210–12
Rowe, Dick, 203, 212, 215, 219–22, 230–2
Roxio, 327, 333
Roxy Music, 262
Roy Head and the Traits, 166
Royal, Belford, 31
Royals, 164
royalties, xiv, xix, 26, 60, 69, 143, 145–6,
    154–5, 169–70, 211, 218, 224, 231, 299,
    312; copyright, 178–9; electric recording,
    100, 104, 115–16; Elvis Presley's, 193–4;
    Mike Oldfield's, 266; Simply Red's, 332;
    see also fees

Roza, Lita, 204
Rubinstein, Artur, 122, 189
Rudin, Mickey, 248
Rudnick, Marvin, 304–5
Ruffo, Titta, 76–7
Ruhl, Otto, 68
Rundgren, Todd, 54
Rupe, Art, 166, 195
Russell Hunting Co. Ltd, 54–5
Russia, xvii, 34, 57, 61–2, 68, 71; Revolution, 62, 74
Rust, Brian, 171
Ruthrauff and Ryan, 132

Sabir, Dr Vadhi, 168, 169
SACD, 335
Sachs, Manie, 189
Sacro Enterprise Company, 130
Saga Films, 229
Saga label, 228–9, 230
'St Louis Blues', 141
Saint-Saëns, Camille, 59–60
Salzburg, 294
Samwell, Ian, 216–17
San Francisco, 312
San Francisco Symphony Orchestra, 121
Sanders, Edwin, 74
Sanders, Joseph, 26, 31
Santana, 272, 337
Sarnoff, David, 107, 113, 118, 120, 134, 155, 184
Sarony, Leslie, 128
Sarton, Harry, 129, 149, 196–7
Satchell, Tim, 278
Savoy Orpheans, 79
Sayer, Leo, 262
SBK Entertainment World, 310
Scala, Primo, 92
Scala label, 68, 72
Schaap, Phil, 341
Schein, Harvey, 240, 283, 296, 301
Schmolzi, Horst, 233
Schnabel, Artur, 191
Schoenberg, Isaac, 115, 116, 151
Schuller, Gunther, 181
Schumann-Heink, Ernestine, 76
Schwarz, Harvey, 129, 148, 200, 205
Scientific American, 5
Scopes, John, 51
Scott, Howard, 160, 341

Scotti, Antonio, 76
Scranton Button Works, 129
Scull, Captain Andrew, 29
Seagram, 318–19, 334–6
Seaman, Frank, 28, 30, 38–41, 42–3, 56
Sears and Roebuck, 91
Second World War, xviii, 38, 115, 136, 138, 143, 162, 166, 175, 233, 319, 341
Segelstein, Irwin, 274–5, 301
Seligman, Theodore, 16
Sellers, Peter, 219
Sembrich, Marcella, 46, 47, 76
Semel, Terry, 318
Semenenko, Serge, 244
Sergio Mendes and Brasil '66, 264
Servia, 71
Seven Arts, 251, 252
Sex Pistols, 267–8
Shadows, 218, 266
Shakespeare, William, 17
Shakur, Tupac, 321, 322
Shankar, Ravi, 336
Shannon, Del, 264
Shapiro, Nat, 202
Shaw, Artie, 143
Shaw, George Bernard, 114
Shear, Ernie, 217
sheet music, xix, 213
shellac, 27, 67, 89, 97, 131, 156, 157, 196; demise, 143, 146, 147
Shelton, Anne, 214, 228
Shenton, Violet, 231
Shepard, Bert, 31–2
Shepherd Brothers, 164
Sheridan, Art, 163
Sheridan, Tony, 219
Sherman, Cary, 328, 331
Shestopol, George, 256
Shipton-on-Cherwell, 266
Sholes, Steve, 147, 193–4
Shore, Dinah, 184
Siegal, Adele, 184
Siemens, 141, 171, 232, 282, 306, 319
Silver, Horace, 315
Silverman, Waxie Maxie, 167
Silvertone label, 91
Silvester, Victor, 80
Simon, George, 147–8
Simon, Paul, xiii, 302
Simon and Garfunkel, 243, 244, 272, 278

Simon Park's 52nd Precinct, 278
Simone, Nina, 165
Simons, Cyril, 214
Simply Red, 323, 332
Sinatra, Frank, 155, 170, 179, 186, 206–7,
    230, 248, 249
Singapore, 66
Sire Records, 165
Six-Five Special, 216
skiffle, 198, 199
Slack, Freddy, 144
Small, Millie, 259–60
Smalls, Biggie, 321–2
Smart, Terry, 217
Smith, Bessie, 89, 167, 332
Smith, Joe, 212, 248–50, 253, 313–14, 317
Smith, Len, 171
Smith, Leonard, 205
Smith, Mamie, 88
Smith, Mike, 203, 219–22, 231–2, 237–8, 240,
    244, 270–2; wrong Mike Smith appointed
    to Decca, 286–7
Smith, Tony, 300
Smithsonian Institution, 12, 13, 14
Smoot, Dan, 33–4, 56, 66
Snoop Doggy Dogg, 321
Snow, Hank, 193
Societa Italiana di Fonotipia, 67
Société des Micro-Phonographes Bettini, 38
Solleveld, Coen, 173–4, 232, 233, 282, 296
Solti, Georg, 285
Somers, Debroy, 114
Son House, 89
'Song of Mr. Phonograph, The', 9
Sony, xv, xvi, 283, 306, 320, 333, 334, 343;
    distribution centre, 236; CD
    development, 294–6, 298; relationship
    with Columbia/CBS, 296, 301, 302–4, 305,
    310, 311; Betamax system, 310; George
    Michael lawsuit, 311–12, 326; political
    contributions, 331; double-deck tape
    machines, 333–4; lack of understanding
    of record business, 334; Music Studios,
    340
Sony Music Entertainment, 304
Sony Music US, 304
Soria, Dario, 176
SoulSeek, 328
Sousa, John Philip, 21, 27, 31
South Africa, 173–4, 234, 282

South America, xvii, xviii, 66, 137, 176, 234
Southgate, Sir Colin, 316, 334
Soviet Union, 324
Spain, 34, 68, 234
Spalding, Albert, 122
Sparks, 261, 268
Specialty label, 166, 195
Spectator, 16, 289
Speir, H. C., 89
Spencer, Len, 21, 26
Spencer Davis Group, 259
Speyer and Co., 106–7
Spice Girls, 334
Spielberg, Steven, 331
Spinal Tap, 269
Springsteen, Bruce, 303–4, 314
Squeeze, 265
Squires, Dorothy, 277
Staats, Walter, 83
Stabat Mater (Rossini), 58
Stafford, Jo, 144, 187
Stagg, Allen, 228
Standar Chemical Engineering Company, 98
Stanhope, Clive, 278
Stanley, C. O., 200
Stanley, Ed, 189
Stansfield, Lisa, 306
Stanton, Frank, 243, 272
Stapleford, Russ, 239
Starday label, 165
Starlite Wranglers, 192
Starr, Hermann, 110, 131, 244, 247, 248
Starr, Kay, 187
Starr, Ringo, 220, 222
Starr Piano Company, 90, 111
Stateside label, 225–6
Steel, John, 227
Steele, Tommy, 216
Stein, Edward de, 113, 139
Stein, Jules, 255
Stein, Seymour, 165
stereo recording, xiv, xv, xviii, 116, 200–1,
    242–3, 259, 293; 'ping-pong', 284
Sterett, J. E., 78–9, 106, 107
Sterling, Louis Saul, 54–5, 62, 66, 72–3, 76,
    130; adopts electric recording and takes
    over American Columbia, 101–2, 104;
    sells Columbia shares, 109; and
    HMV/Columbia merger, 111–13;
    managing director of EMI, 113, 135–6,

140, 156, 187, 188, 313, 335
Sterling & Hunting Ltd, 55
Sterling Company Ltd, 54
Sterling Moulded Records, 55
Sterling Record Company, 54
Sterno label, 132, 143
Stevens, Cat, 260
Stevens, Connie, 247
Stevens, E. F., Jr., 131
Stevenson, William 'Mickey', 225
Stewart, Dave, 326, 331
Stiff label, 288, 311
Stigwood, Robert, 251; *see also* Robert
    Stigwood Organisation
Stills, Stephen, 276
Sting, 307
Stokowski, Leopold, 119, 285
Stoller, Mike, 165, 166
Stone, Christopher, 97, 127
Strakosch, Maurice, 60
Stratton, Eugene, 32
Stratton-Smith, Tony, 267, 275
Straus, Max, 67–8, 140
Strayhorn, Billy, 180–1
Streisand, Barbra, 243, 271, 314
string bass, 32, 86, 100
Stroh, Charles, 54
Stroh violin, 32, 100
Strong, Barrett, 223
stylus, jewelled, 53–4, 156
Sugarhill Gang, 291
Sugarhill label, 290
Summer, Donna, 308
Sumner, Geoffrey, 201
Sun label, 191–2, 193–4, 195
Sunday Night at the London Palladium, 200
Supremes, 225
surround sound, 259
Sutherland, Joan, 204
Swan, Joseph, 11
Swan label, 223
Sweden, 234
Sweet, 281
Swindon, 335
swing, 86, 135–6, 143, 183
Swinging Blue Jeans, 278
Switzerland, 34, 286
Sylvester, Louis G., 129
synchronisation rights, 338
Syracuse, NY, 38

Szell, George, 151

Taft, William Howard, 51
Taft-Hartley Act, 154
Tainter, Charles Sumner, xvi, 12–15, 17, 24
Talking Machine News, 18, 20, 22, 32, 43, 48,
    70, 71, 75, 81–2, 87, 99; acquired by HMV,
    72
Talking Machine World, 69, 78, 87, 92, 94,
    102
talking machines, 25; sales, 48–9; *see also*
    gramophone; phonograph
Tamla label, 224–5
Tamla-Motown, 224, 226, 235
tango, xviii, 66
tape recorders, 158–60, 230; *see also*
    magnetic tape recording
Tarnopol, Nat, 224
Tate, Alfred O., 14
Tate, Harry, 42, 73
Taylor, Arthur, 272–3
Taylor, Creed, 265
Taylor, Derek, 254
Taylor, James, 302, 308
Tchaikovsky, Pyotr Ilyich, 121—2
Technics, 294
Ted Heath and His Music, 149, 203, 284
Teenage Fanclub, 320
Teldec, 151
Telefunken, 151, 233, 294
telegraph, 4, 16
Telegraphone wire recorder, 158
telephone, 4, 12, 15, 16, 17, 24
television, 199, 216; colour, 153
Teller, Alvin, 318
Telstar satellite, 230–1
Tempo label, 206, 341
Tennessee, 192
Tennyson, Alfred, Lord, 16, 17
Tetrazzini, Luisa, 76, 77
theatre, 138; *see also* cinema
Thiele, Bob, 215
Thomas, C. H. 'Harry', 142, 158, 209
Thorn Electrical Industries, 269; *see also*
    Thorn-EMI
Thorne, Ambrose, 73
Thorne, Mike, 267
Thorn-EMI, 269, 309, 312; demerger,
    315–16, 334
Thornton, Big Mama, 166

Three Tenors, 340
Tijuana Brass, 263, 264
Time Warner merger, 309; *see also* Time-Warner
Time-Life, 316, 318
Time-Warner, 316, 318, 321, 333, 336
Timmer, Jan, 296, 319
Tin Pan Alley (Denmark Street), 213, 215, 217
tinfoil recording, 4, 13, 28, 97, 98
Tiny Tim, 251
Tisch, Lawrence, 301, 302–3
Tiswas, 287
Today, 267
Toller-Bond, Dudley, 196
Top Rank, 212, 213, 226, 230
Torme, Mel, 165
Tornados, 231
Toscanini, Arturo, 119, 120–2, 135, 147, 189, 205
Tower of Power, xiii, 258
Townsend, Irving, 183
Townsley, W. W., 'Bill', 205–6, 285–90
trade unions, 287–8
Trafalgar House, 292
Traffic, 260, 261
Transoceanic Trading, 102
transportation, 42
Travis, Merle, 164
Tremeloes, 219, 221, 232, 237–8
Trepel, Mimi, 195
Triangle Industries, 301
Trinidad Singers, 255
Triumph Records, 229
Truman, Harry S., 162
trumpet, 101
Trutone label, 173
tuba, 32, 86, 100
Turner, Big Joe, 170
Turquand, F. J., 99
Twain, Mark, 37
Twin Record Co. Ltd, 66
Two-Way Family Favourites, 277

UCLA, 275, 276
Uden, 335
UK, *see* Britain
Umbria (liner), 31
Union Carbide, 147
United Artists, 225, 227

United Artists-Liberty group, 314
United Independent Broadcasters, 134
Universal, xvi, 319, 332–3, 335, 336, 339, 340, 342; films, 254, 319
Universal Talking Machine Company, 39, 56
Universal Talking Machine Manufacturing Company, 56
Unknown Warrior, 99
Uptown Records, 321
US Army-Air Force Band, 144
US Gramophone Company, 26
US Marine Band, 21
USA, 142, 152, 297; birth of jazz, 87; economy, 65, 109; First World War, 78, 80; government investigations into record industry, 212, 273, 240–1, 254; growth in independent labels, 195; post-war record industry, 162; radio industry, 130; record production facilities, 94; Second World War, 143; wartime record sales, 138
Utall, Larry, 264

Valabhdas Runchordas company, 44, 68
Valente, Caterina, 206
Van de Graaf Generator, 258
Van Halen, 309
Vanguard label, 200
Vanilla Ice, 320
Vastola, Gaetano, 305
Vaughan, Malcolm, 213
V-discs, 146–9, 193
Veejay label, 223
Velvet Face label, 95–6
Verve label, 249, 250
Vicious, Sid, 268
Victor Talking Machine Company, xv, xvii, xix, 41, 43–7, 56, 65, 69, 110, 152; profits, 46, 82; repertoire, 46–7, 66; Red Seal series, 46–7, 65–6, 69, 76–7; fire at Camden plant, 47; agreement with Gramophone and Typewriter Company, 63; introduces Victrola, 63; competition with Columbia, 76–7; impact of First World War, 78–9, 80; litigation with Deutsche Grammophon, 81; relationship with HMV, 82–5, 112, 122; jazz recordings, 86–8; lateral-cut discs, 90, 91, 156; expands production facilities, 94; adoption of electric recording, 99–100, 101, 103; Johnson sells stake, 104–8;

acquired by RCA, 107, 134; *see also* RCA Victor
Victrola, 63, 80, 104, 107
Vienna, 34; Musikverein, 140
Vienna Philharmonic Orchestra, 140–1, 285
Vincent, J. A., 43
Vincent, Lieutenant George Robert, 146–7
Vinson, Judge, 145
vinyl, 146, 148, 154, 156, 174, 258, 293, 328
vinylite, 147
Virgin label, 262, 265–7, 278; deals with Island and Atlantic, 267; signs Sex Pistols, 268; EMI deal, 310–11, 312, 335
Virgin Music Group, 310–11
Vitaphone sound-on-disc system, 93
Vitrolac V-142 vinyl compound, 146
Vivendi Universal, 331, 332–3
Vocalion label, 89, 91–2, 126, 235
Vogue-Coral label, 194
Voice, The, 73
Voice of America, 180
Volta Gramophone Company, xvi
Volta Graphophone Company, 14
Volta Laboratory Associates, 12, 14
vulcanite, 26, 27
Vyvyan, Jennifer, 204

Wade, Dorothy, 170
Wagner, Richard, 87, 285
Wailers, 261
Wall Street Crash, 111, 122, 162, 327
Waller, Fats, 148
Wallerstein, Edward, 117, 119, 134–7, 145, 152–5, 157, 174–5
Wallichs, Glenn, 144, 189
Wallis, Gilbert and Partners, 114
Wally Stott, *see* Morley, Angela
Walter, Bruno, 135, 140–1
Walthamstow Town Hall, 202, 204
Walton, William, 127
Warburton, Reg, 237, 238, 271
Warner, Jack, 93, 244, 245, 248, 251
Warner, Sam, 93
Warner Bros, xiii, xvii, 93, 283, 321, 323, 326, 333, 336, 338, 342; ownership of Brunswick, 94, 110–11, 129, 131, 244–5; establishes record label, 244–8; buys Reprise, 248–50, 251; signings, 250–1; acquired by Seven Arts, 251–2; tie-up with Chrysalis, 262; WAVAW protest, 268;

rivalry with Columbia, 302, 304, 308–9; Geffen deal, 308–9; mentality, 314; *see also* WEA
Warner Bros Records, 317
Warner Communications, 276, 314, 316
Warner Music Group, 336, 338
Warner Music International, 317
Warner UK, 300, 318
Warner-Reprise-Atlantic, 253; acquires Elektra, 253–4
Warner-Seven Arts, 251, 252, 253; buys Atlantic, 251–2
Warnford-Davis, Darryl, 133
Warnford-Davis, Roy, 133
Waronker, Lenny, 251, 317
Waronker, Sy, 226
Washington, Dinah, 235
Washington, County Durham, 281
Washington, DC., 167, 168
Wasserman, Lew, 255, 310
Waterworld, 310
Watson, Roger, 255, 262–3, 305–6
Watters, Al, 189
wax recording, 13, 26, 28, 40, 42–3, 45, 50, 86, 142, 148, 160
Wayne, Ricky, 229
WEA, xvii, 268, 288, 306, 308, 313, 316, 332
WEA International, 254, 316–71
Weinstock, Bob, 181
Welch, Bruce, 217–18
Welch, Walter L., 14, 129, 152
Weller, Diana, 195, 196
Weller, Paul, 319, 320
Wembley Town Hall, 149, 150
West Drayton station, 201
West End shows, 207
Western Electric, xv, 100–1, 104, 115–16
Western Union Telegraph Company, 3, 4, 12, 24
Westminster label, 199
Weston, Paul, 144, 175, 187
Westrex stereo system, 200–1
Wexler, Jerry, 170, 193, 211, 250, 251–2, 253, 276
White, Andy, 222
White, Frank K., 174
White, Freddie, 139
Whiteman, Paul, 111, 144
Whitfield, David, 198
Whitfield, June, 171

Whitten, Francis, 77
Who, 233
Wickham, Andy, 251
Wiggins, Fred, 90
Wilde, Marty, 216
Wilkins, Bill, 178
Wilkinson, Kenneth 'Wilkie', 133, 150
William Morris Agency, 275–6
Williams, Andy, 243, 257
Williams, J. Mayo, 89–90
Williams, Osmund, 114
Williams, Paul, 265
Williams, Robbie, 331, 336, 344
Williams, Trevor, 30–1, 113, 114
Williamson, Michael, 204
Willis, Percy, 18
Wilson, Brian, 250
Wilson, Harold, 291
Wilson, Jackie, 224
Winamp, 325
WinMX, 328
Winner label, 68, 72, 86, 87, 94
Winwood, Muff, 259–60, 261, 262, 272; on
    state of the industry, 343–4
Winwood, Steve, 253
Wisconsin Chair Company, 89, 111
Wise, Ronald, 135
Wolf, Hugo, 141
Wolff, Francis, 314
Women Against Violence Against Women,
    268
Wonder, Stevie, 340–1
Wood, Leo, xv
Wood, Leonard G., 188, 209–10, 213, 223,
    226, 264, 287–9
Wood, Randy, 195, 263
Woolworths, 132–3, 235, 301
Woyda, Walter, 249, 291–2
Wright, Chris, 262
Wright, Lawrence, 310
Wright Brothers, 42
Wynshaw, David, 273–4

XTC, 268, 312

Yankovic, Frankie, 155
Yates, Herbert, 129
Yeomans, Walter, 128
Yes, 251, 258
Yetnikoff, Walter, 301–4, 308–9, 313

Yom Kippur war, 258
Yorke, Peter, 171
Young, Jimmy, 198
Young, Neil, 309
Young, Will, 340

Zappa, Frank, 251
Zimbalist, Efrem, Jr., 246
zinc recording, 25, 32, 40, 42; *see also* wax
    recording
Zon-o-phone, 39, 40, 42, 43
Zonophone label, 66, 69, 75, 112, 125, 128
Zuntz, Heinrich, 67–8

Index of recordings

'A Taste of Honey' (Herb Alpert), 263
'A Teenager in Love' (Marty Wilde), 216
'A Tribute to Buddy Holly' (Mike Berry and
    the Outlaws), 230
'Adeste Fideles', 103
'All Around the World' (Lisa Stansfield), 306
'Anarchy in the UK' (Sex Pistols), 267
'Angela Jones' (Michael Cox), 229
'Apache' (Shadows), 218
'Ask Me Why' (Beatles), 222
'At Your Command' (Bing Crosby), 111

'Bad Penny Blues' (Humphrey Lyttelton),
    228
Beethoven: Eroica Variations, 191
Before the Flood (Bob Dylan), 275
Bellini: *Norma*, 190
'Berceuse' (Renee Chemet), 98
'Besame Mucho' (Beatles), 222
Black and Blue (Rolling Stones), 268
'Blue Moon of Kentucky' (Elvis Presley), 192
'Blue Suede Shoes' (Carl Perkins), 193; (Elvis
    Presley), 194
Box o' Tricks, 74
Brahms: *Hungarian Dance*, 96–7; Second
    Symphony, 150
Britten: *War Requiem*, 206
Business as Usual, 73

Cabaret, 242
'Caro mio ben' (Clara Butt), 81
'Casey as Book Agent' (Russell Hunting), 31

'Casey as Doctor' (Russell Hunting), 31
'Casey at Living Pictures' (Russell Hunting), 31
'Casey's First Experience as Judge' (Russell Hunting), 27
'Cathy's Clown' (Everly Brothers), 248
'Chains of Love' (Big Joe Turner), 170
'Cherry Pink and Apple Blossom White' (Eddie Calvert), 187
'Chick A'Roo' (Ricky Wayne), 229
'Clancy's Prize Waltz Contest' (Len Spencer), 21
'Come Into the Garden, Maud', 33
'Come On, You Boys of London Town' (Violet Loraine), 73
'Cornet Chop Suey' (Louis Armstrong and the Hot Five), 89
'Cow Cow Boogie' (Freddy Slack and Ella Mae Morse), 144
Coward: *Pacific 1860*, 207
'Crazy Blues' (Mamie Smith's Jazz Hounds'), 88
'Crescendo in Blue' (Duke Ellington), 180
'Cujus animam' (Enrico Caruso), 58

'Darktown Strutters Ball', (Original Dixieland Jazz Band), 87
Days of Future Passed (Moody Blues), 285
'Departure of a Troopship' (Russell Hunting), 22, 72–3
'Diamonds Are a Girl's Best Friend' (June Whitfield), 171
'Diana' (Paul Anka), 210
'Didn't Reach My Goal'/'Atomic Energy' (Clarence 'Gatemouth' Brown), 166
'Dimuendo in Blue' (Duke Ellington), 180
'Dixie Jass Band One-Step', (Original Dixieland Jazz Band), 87
'Do You Love Me' (Brian Poole), 225
Double Fantasy (John Lennon and Yoko Ono), 308
'Drinking Wine Spo-Dee-O-Dee' (Stick McGhee), 169–70

'Earth Angel' (Platters), 235
'Ebb Tide' (Frank Chacksfield), 198
Elgar, *Dream of Gerontius*, 95–6, 104
'EMI (Unlimited Edition)' (Sex Pistols), 268
'Everlasting Love' (Love Affair), 239
'Façade' (Walton), 127

Faith (George Michael), 311, 312
'Feelin' Fine' (Shadows), 218
Fings Ain't Wot They Used To Be, 207
Flying Teapot (Gong), 266
'Fortifying the Home' (Harry Tate), 73; (Violet Loraine), 73
'Freight Train' (Chas McDevitt), 235
'Funiculi Funicula', 31

Gershwin: *Porgy and Bess*, 207
'GI Jive' (Johnny Mercer), 144
Glitter (Mariah Carey), 334, 335
Grease, 283
'Green Jeans' (Fabulous Flee-Rakkers), 229
'Guaranty of Bank Deposits'(William Jennings Bryan), 51

'Half a Pint of Ale' (Gus Elen), 32
Handel: *Israel in Egypt*, 17; *Messiah*, 204
'Harbor Lights' (Elvis Presley), 192
'Have I the Right' (Honeycombs), 231
'Have you Got Any Rag?' (Stanley Lupino), 86
'Heartbreak Hotel' (Elvis Presley), 194
'Here Comes My Baby' (Tremeloes), 237–8
'Hound Dog' (Big Mama Thornton), 166
'House of the Rising Sun' (Animals), 227

'I Can't Stop Loving You' (Ray Charles), 210
'I Love You Because' (Elvis Presley), 192
'I Loves You, Porgy' (Nina Simone), 165
'I Want to Hold Your Hand' (Beatles), 223
'I've Got My Love to Keep Me Warm' (Les Brown), 155
'If It Wasn't for the 'Ouses In-Between' (Gus Elen), 32
'If You Were the Only Boy in the World' (Violet Loraine), 73
'Il segreto' (Clara Butt), 81
'Immortality' (William Jennings Bryan), 51
'Indiana', (Original Dixieland Jazz Band), 87
Ira Ironstrings Destroys the Great Bands, 246
Ira Ironstrings Plays Music for People with $3.98, Plus Tax, If Any, 246
Ira Ironstrings Plays Santa Claus, 246
Ira Ironstrings Plays with Matches, 246
'Irish Humour' (William Howard Taft), 51
'It Takes Two to Tango' (Hermione Gingold and Gilbert Harding), 171
'It's a Long Way to Tipperary', 72

Jesus Christ Superstar, 255
'Jezebel' (Winifred Atwell), 197
'Johnny Remember Me' (John Leyton), 230
'Just Like Eddie' (Heinz Burt), 231
'(Just Like) Starting Over' (John Lennon and Yoko Ono), 308
'Just One More Chance' (Bing Crosby), 111

'Keep on Running' (Spencer Davis Group), 259
'Kookie, Kookie, Lend Me Your Comb' (Connie Stevens), 246

'La donna è mobile' (Ferruccio Giannini), 26
'Lay Down Your Arms' (Anne Shelton), 228
'Like I Do' (Maureen Evans), 235
'Lily of Laguna' (Eugene Stratton), 32
'Limelight' (Frank Chacksfield), 198, 201
Listen Without Prejudice Volume I (George Michael), 311
'Livery Stable Blues' (Original Dixieland Jazz Band), 87
Lock Up Your Daughters, 207
'Long Tall Sally' (Little Richard), 196
'Love Is Back in Style' (Charlie Robinson), 263
'Love Me Do' (Beatles), 222

'Mad About the Boy' (Dinah Washington), 235
Maggie May, 207
Mame, 242
'Mammy' (Al Jolson), 93
Manor Live, 266
'Money' (Beatles), 223
'Motoring' (Harry Tate), 42
'Moulin Rouge' theme (Mantovani), 198
'Move It' (Cliff Richard), 217
Music Box (Mariah Carey), 334
Music for Brass, 181
'My Boy Lollipop' (Millie Small), 259
My Fair Lady, 234, 242
'My Guy' (Supremes), 225

Never Mind the Bollocks (Sex Pistols), 268

'O For the Wings of a Dove', 104
'Oh Grandma' (Hermione Gingold and Gilbert Harding), 171
Oklahoma!, 145, 182

Oliver, 207
'Only So Much Oil in the Ground' (Tower of Power), 258
'Onward Christian Klansmen', 91
'Oriental Love Dreams' (Coon-Sanders Nighthawks), 94
'Out of Nowhere' (Bing Crosby), 111
'Over There' (Enrico Caruso), 80

'Papa's Got a Brand New Bag' (James Brown), 164
'Pina Colada Song' (Rupert Holmes), 314
Planet Waves (Bob Dylan), 275
'Please Mister Postman' (Beatles), 224
'Please Mister Postman' (Marvelettes), 225
'Please Please Me', 222
'Pledging My Love' (Johnny Ace), 166
'PS I Love You' (Beatles), 222
Puccini: *La Bohème*, 189; *Madam Butterfly*, 190; *Tosca*, 176

'Quatermasster's Stores' (Shadows), 218
'Questa o Quella' (Enrico Caruso), 59; (Ferruccio Giannini), 26

'Rapper's Delight' (Sugarhill Gang), 291
'Ready Teddy' (Little Richard), 196
'Reet Petite' (Jackie Wilson), 224
'Rhymes' (Jack Hylton), 128
'Rip It Up' (Little Richard), 196
'Rip Saw Blues' (Art Landry's Orchestra), 94
'Rock Island Line' (Lonnie Donegan), 198
'Rock with the Caveman' (Tommy Steele), 216

'San Francisco (Be Sure to Wear Flowers in Your Hair)' (Scott McKenzie), 239
'Saturday Dance' (Shadows), 218
Saturday Night Fever, 283
'School's Out' (Alice Cooper), 251
'Schoolboy Crush' (Cliff Richard), 217
Sergeant Pepper movie soundtrack, 283
Shakespeare, *Richard III*, 17
'Silence Is Golden' (Tremeloes), 238
'Somebody Help Me' (Spencer Davis Group), 259
'Somebody Stole My Gal' (Leo Wood), xv
Song Review (Stevie Wonder), 340
'Sonny Boy' (Al Jolson), 93
South Pacific, 154

'Spoonful Blues' (Charley Patton), 90
'Star of Twilight' (Syria Lamonte), 31
'Stardust' (Hoagy Carmichael), 91
Strauss: *Salome*, 207
'Strip Polka' (Johnny Mercer), 144
'Sweet Caroline' (Neil Diamond), 256
'Swinging Shepherd Blues' (Ted Heath and His Music), 203

Tapestry (Carole King), 265
Tchaikovsky: B flat minor piano concerto, 121–2; Fifth Symphony in E Minor, 148
'Tell It to the Birds' (Dore Alpert), 263
'Telstar' (Tornados), 231
'Tennessee Wig Walk' (Bonnie Lou), 210
Thanks I'll Eat It Here (Lowell George), xiii
'That'll Be the Day' (Buddy Holly), 215
'That's All Right' (Elvis Presley), 192
'That's How I Diddle 'Em' (W. H. Berry), 32
'The Ballad of Bonnie and Clyde' (Georgie Fame), 238–9
The Bing Boys Are Here, 73
'The Bright Fiery Cross', 91
The Chronic (Dr Dre), 321
The Definitive Collection (Stevie Wonder), 341
'The Diver', 33
The Faust Tapes (Faust), 266
'The General Jumped at Dawn'/'I Found a New Baby' (Paul Whiteman's New Yorker Orchestra), 144
'The Laughing Song' (George W. Johnson), 21
'The Lonely Bull (El Solo Toro)' (Herb Alpert), 263
'The Music Goes Around and Around' (Riley and Farley), 131
'The Railroad Question' (William Jennings Bryan), 51
'The Soldiers of the Queen', 33
The Sound of Music, 234
The Sound of Philadelphia, 273
'The Steppin' Out Kind'/'You'll Be Lonesome Too', 164
'The Trust Question' (William Jennings Bryan), 51
'The Whistling Coon' (George W. Johnson), 21
'The White Cliffs of Dover' (Vera Lynn), 143
'Thick as a Brick (Jethro Tull), 262

'Three Cheers for Little Belgium' (Violet Loraine), 73
'Till the Boys Come Home' ('Keep the Home Fires Burning'), 72
'Time Is Tight' (Simon Park's 52nd Precinct), 278
'Treat Her Right' (Roy Head and the Traits), 166
Tubular Bells (Mike Oldfield), 266–7
'Turkey in de Straw' (Billy Golden), 25
'Tutti Frutti' (Little Richard), 196

'Vesti la Giubba' (Enrico Caruso), 69

Wagner: *Ring Cycle*, 285
'Way Over There' (Miracles), 225
'We Will Make Love' (Russ Hamilton), 235
'We'll Meet Again' (Vera Lynn), 143
West Side Story, 234
'We've Been Married Just One Year' (Violet Loraine), 73
'What I Have I'll Hold' (W. H. Berry), 32
When Dalliance Was in Flower, and Young Maidens Lost Their Heads, 253
'When We've Wound Up the Watch on the Rhine' (Violet Loraine), 73
'Why Do Fools Fall in Love' (Frankie Lymon and the Teenagers), 210
'Work with Me, Annie' (Hank Ballard and the Midniters), 164

'Yo Ho! Little Girls! Yo Ho!' (W. H. Berry), 32
'You Really Got a Hold on Me' (Beatles), 223
'You've Got to Sing in Ragtime' (Wilkie Bard), 86